Washington State Fishing Guide

Seventh Edition
Stan Jones, Editor/Publisher

EDITOR AND PUBLISHER: Washington State Fishing Guide is edited and published by Stanley N, Jones, Stan Jones Publishing, Inc. Business office is 3421 E. Mercer St., Seattle, WA 98112-4341. Phone 206-323-3970. FAX 206-323-5820.

ASSOCIATE PUBLISHER: Julie Jones Weiss.

STAN JONES PUBLISHING, INC. is publisher of WASHINGTON STATE FISHING GUIDE (7th Ed. $16.45 pp), PACIFIC NORTHWEST SEAFOOD COOKERY, ($9.45 pp), OREGON SALTWATER FISHING GUIDE ($10.45 pp).

PRODUCTION: Charles B. Summers, Pacific Publication Services, P. O. Box H, 607 West First, South Bend, WA 98586. Phone: 360-875-6091, Fax: 360-875-6071

Printed in the United States of America.

ISBN 0-939936-04-6

Acknowledgements

The seventh edition of WASHINGTON STATE FISHING GUIDE is the result of well over a year's research and re-writing. Every county and park lake and stream listing has been checked and re-checked. Hundreds of new listings are included. Through the cooperation of state agencies, National Forest and Park personnel and many fellow fisherman, fish species in listings have been updated to 1995.

Despite extensive review of the text in this seventh edition right up to press time, there will be omissions and errors. In dealing with the state's thousands of fishing waters, this is inevitable. Moonlight, illegal plants of fish, poisoning of lakes by the state F&W Department to create trout only waters, logging roads replacing trails, more gated access across private property, all contribute to changes.

It has been gratifying that so many fellow sportsmen have contributed valuable information to make this book, hopefully, a substantial help in fishing the state's waters.

With sincere thanks to the following contributors to the 7th Edition, Washington State Fishing Guide: Les Pickersgill, Bob Heirman, Carol Crusan, Wendell Oliver, Harry F.H. Senn, Joe Foster, Dennis Clay, Dave Shorett, Charlie Powell, Karen Perry, Lenny "G" Frasure, Chuck Summers, Gary Christenson, Karl Petterson, Fred L. Peterson, John Truex, Fred C. Peterson II, Scott Steckler, Ben Crusan, Joe Freet, Harold Swaup, Terry Rudnick, Bill Akerlund, Jack Hoyt, Harold E. Dexter, Mark Kimbel, Terry Jackson, Ted Stubblefield, Nancy Stromsen, Del Groat, Bruce Crawford, Penny Falknor, Jack Ayerst, Fred Brandau, Mike Donald, Rick McConnell, Jim Jacoby, Jim Spotts, Jim Cummings, Jim Clapp, Vence Malernee.

Good fishing,

Stan Jones

Cover Photo Credit

Quinault River steelhead being released by Ron Meek. Photographed by Steve Probasco.

Dedication

Frederick Lars Peterson
1925—1995

Fred L. Peterson died Feb. 21, 1995. A close personal friend and colleague for nearly 40 years, Fred was an outstanding outdoor writer for over 47 years. He published his own, respected weekly newspaper, The Outdoor Press for 29 years.

Few, if any, fishing and hunting writers approached Fred in his depth of knowledge and skill in covering the outdoors in Eastern and Central Washington. I am indebted to him for his generous sharing of information on his "beat" for this and prior editions of Washington State Fishing Guide.

And, most of all, I will always be indebted to him for his valued friendship.

Stan Jones

Table Of Contents

Counties of Washington

Trout

There are six species of "trout" in Washington state. Rainbow, cutthroat and browns are true trout, with Dolly Varden, brook and mackinaw actually chars. Most anglers refer to all as trout. They are found in the same type of water, and many of their spawning characteristics are similar. Whitefish are widespread in Washington, but grayling are rare.

With the exception of mackinaw or lake trout, all the trout usually seek small tributaries as spawning grounds, with steelhead, also main river spawners. Some times spawning is done over spring areas in lakes. The females prepare the nests, called "redds," in gravel and males fertilize eggs as they are deposited. Then the eggs are covered and hatching occurs in 6 to 8 weeks.

The young of all species except mackinaw stay in the gravel for 2 to 4 weeks and are fed by the yolk sack which remains attached to the belly of the fish. After the yolk has been absorbed the young fish, or fry, wiggle through the gravel and start to feed on microscopic plant and animal organisms. As they grow larger they eat more aquatic and land insects. Bigger fish feed on fresh water shrimp, smaller fish, crayfish and snails.

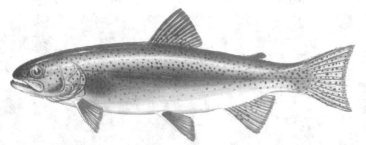

RAINBOW TROUT. (Oncorhynus mykiss). Native to Washington, rainbow are the most important fresh water fish in the state. Sea-run rainbow are called steelhead. Golden trout are the most colorful of all rainbow strains. Environment influences color of fish, but in general rainbow are bluish-green on the back with silver sides and belly. There are black spots along the back and on the dorsal, adipose and caudal fins. A red band sometimes extends along both sides. Rainbow have short heads. The lip bone on the upper jaw rarely extends past the hind margin of the eye. They do not have teeth on the back of the tongue. Rays on fins: Dorsal, 10 to 12; anal, 8 to 12, Gill rakers in first gill arch, 17 to 21. Scales in 115 to 161 oblique rows. Sea-run rainbow (steelhead) have been taken to 36 pounds from Kispiox river in British Columbia. Lake varieties to 42 pounds have been recorded. A 10-12 inch female produces 800 to 1000 eggs. A rainbow over 24 inches may produce from 5000 to 9000 eggs. Most rainbow spawn in the spring.

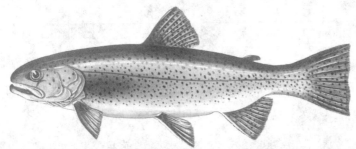

CUTTHROAT TROUT. (O. clarki). Another native, the cutthroat also may migrate to salt-water. It gets its name from red slash marks on both sides of the under jaw. Fish fresh from saltwater may not have these marks, but all have teeth at back of the tongue. Usual color for cutthroat is dark green backs with olive sides and silver belly. Numerous black spots are found on the back and sides, and on the caudal, adipose and dorsal fins. Eastern Washington or mountain cutthroat are more brilliantly colored. Montana black spots are a strain of inland cutthroat. Rays on fins: Dorsal, 8 to 11; anal, 8 to 12. Scales in 120 to 180 oblique rows. Gill rakers in first gill arch, 15 to 22. One of largest cutthroat taken was a 41 pounder from a lake. Sea-run cutthroat are usually 1 to 3 pounds, with an occasional fish 4 pounds. The inland variety in streams is usually smaller. Cutthroat are spring spawners, spawning in headwaters of small creeks.

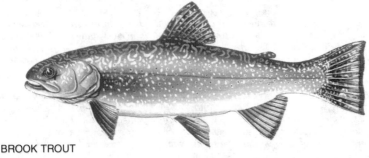

BROOK TROUT

BROOK TROUT. (Salvelinus fontinalis). Brook trout, actually a char, were introduced from the E. coast and have done well in Washington, particularly in alpine lakes and streams and in beaver ponds. Their general color is olive-green, darker on the back and lighter on sides. They have dark wavy markings on back and on dorsal fin. Small green spots appear on the sides, some with red centers bordered with blue. Lower fins often are edged with white along front portion. Rays on fish: Dorsal, 8 to 10; anal, 7 to 9. Gill rakers, 16 to 22. Scales in 197 to 236 oblique rows. A brook of 14.5 pounds has been recorded, but a 3 pounder is large for Washington waters. Spawning is in the fall in spring-fed tributaries or over patches of gravel in lakes. A female may deposit from 500 to 2500 eggs.

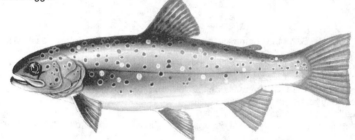

BROWN TROUT. (Salmo trutta Linnaeus). Also called German brown and Loch Leven trout, the browns were introduced from Europe and are found in fair numbers in Washington, principally in central and eastern portions. They have been known to migrate to saltwater. General color is golden brown, with large dark-brown or black spots. A distinguishing characteristic is the light halos around the large dark spots. Rays on fins: Dorsal, 10 to 11; anal, 9 to 12. Gill rakers, 16 to 19. Scales in 116 to 136 oblique rows. Brown trout of 41 pounds have been reported. In Washington a brown of 5 pounds is a heavy fish. Spawning is ordinarily in the fall from October to January. The browns can adapt to warm and sluggish water, but prefer cold tributary streams for spawning.

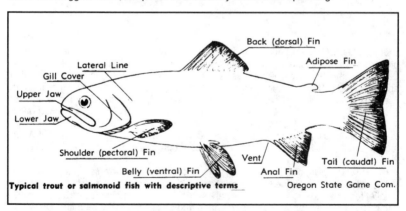

Typical trout or salmonoid fish with descriptive terms   Oregon State Game Com.

GRAYLING. (Thymallus arcticus). Only one lake in Washington, Big Granite in Skagit County, is reported to successfully carry these arctic fish, although there have been limited plants in other waters in recent years. They are easily distinguished by their greatly developed and colored dorsal fin. Grayling are very susceptible to pollution or other changes in their environment, and it is unlikely that their numbers will greatly increase in Washington. In arctic waters they sometimes reach 24 inches, but 12 to 15 inches is more common. Grayling spawn during May and June in streams. They do not construct nests. Chief food is aquatic and terrestrial forms of insects. The fish are spectacular when they rise to dry flies. Rays on fins: Dorsal, 16 to 24 rays; anal, 10 to 12. Scales in 82 to 95 rows. Fresh grayling are delicious eating. The flesh has the taste of thyme, and the scientific name, "thymallus," refers to the odor of this seasoning.

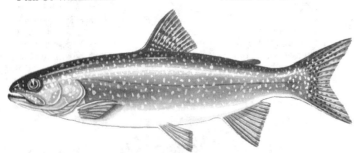

LAKE TROUT. (Salvelinus namaycush). Another char which was introduced into Washington waters. Lake trout, or mackinaw, came originally from the N. portion of N. America. In general the lakers are colored greenish, brownish or grayish, with numerous grey or white irregular spots on back and sides. There are dark and light markings on dorsal, adipose and caudal fins. The tail is deeply forked. Rays on fins: Dorsal and anal, both with 8 to 10 branched rays. Gill rakers in first arch, 10 to 23. Scales in 175 to 228 oblique rows. Lake trout of 60 pounds have been caught. Most are in the 5 to 25 pound range. The fish prefer deep, cold water lakes. Spawning is in fall months, ordinarily over reefs in lakes.

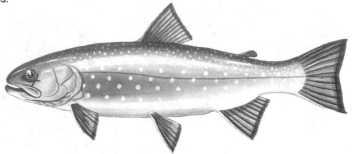

DOLLY VARDEN. (Salvelinus malma). Although native to Washington waters, the complete story on these char is not known. Some fish migrate to saltwater, while others are found in alpine streams. Their general color is olive-green, with numerous round, light spots. The spots close to the lateral line are usually red or orange and larger than the rest. Pectoral, pelvic and anal fins are often bordered with white. Sea-run dollies are silvery and the spots are pale. Rays on fins: Dorsal, 10 to 11; anal, usually 9. Gill rakers in first arch, 14 to 22. Scales in 186 to 254 oblique rows. A 32 pound Dolly Varden was taken from Pend Oreille lake in Idaho. Fish to 10 to 15 pounds are not unusual in Washington waters, but 1 to 3 pounders are more common. Spawning is in streams in the fall.

WHITEFISH. (Prosopium williamsoni). The Rocky Mountain whitefish is found in many Washington streams These fish are related to the salmonoids, differing in that they have smaller mouths and larger scales. They are silvery in color, sometimes with a dark-bronze back. There are few if any spots on the head and adipose fins. Rays on fins: Dorsal, 11 to 14 rays; anal, 10 to 13 rays. Gill rakers, short and thick, 20 to 26. Scales in 74 to 90 oblique rows. Mouth is small with no teeth. Most whitefish are under 12 inches, with an occasional fish to 18 inches. They are found chiefly in cold and swift streams where they feed on the bottom on aquatic insect larvae. Whitefish are good eating, will take a fly and are generally under-rated by fishermen. Spawning takes place in the fall.

Spiny Rays

Although not native to Washington, the spiny ray or warm water group of fish are now widespread in the state and provide year-around fishing in many waters.

Spiny rays have one or more sharp spines or bones in the rays of the dorsal and anal fins, in contrast to the soft rays of salmon or trout. They reproduce so rapidly that they can crowd out trout or other species and stunt their own species. Three families of spiny rays are present in Washington: Perch, Sunfish, and Catfish

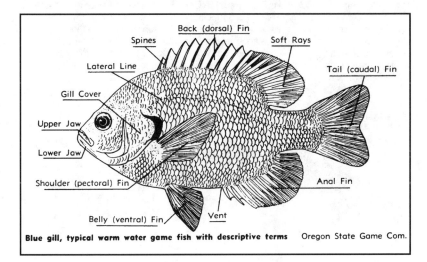

Blue gill, typical warm water game fish with descriptive terms   Oregon State Game Com.

Perch

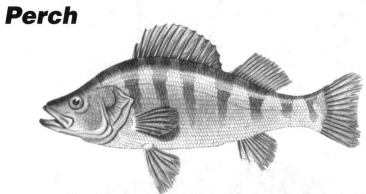

YELLOW PERCH. (Perca flavescens). The yellow perch is shaped somewhat like a trout, and is brassy-green or yellow in color. The first dorsal fin has 13 to 15 spines, and the second dorsal usually has 1 spine and 13 to 15 soft rays. Anal fin has 2 spines and 7 rays. The pelvic fins nearly touch. Scales in 74 to 88 rows. Yellow perch spawn in late winter or early spring, with females depositing flat, ribbon-like bands over weeds or sticks on sandy bottoms. A female may produce 10,000 to 40,000 eggs. Most yellow perch are under 12 inches. Some over 1 pound are taken in Washington waters. Perch eat insects, small fish and crustaceans, and often feed in schools.

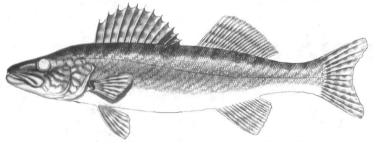

WALLEYE. (Stizostedion vitreum). Also called pike-perch, this species is generally re-stricted to main-stem Columbia River from the Canadian border to Portland and Colum-bia Basin lakes in Washington. Color is dark olive with mottled brassy specks. There are vermiculations on the side of the head. The lower jaw is flesh colored and there is a large black spot at base of last dorsal fin. The first dorsal fin has 12 to 15 spines, and the second dorsal has 19 to 23 soft rays. Scales along the lateral line, about 80 to 89. Walleye prefer cold lakes or rivers. They spawn in early spring in tributary streams or on gravel bars in lakes. Their primary food is small fish.

Sunfish

LARGEMOUTH BASS. (Micropterus salmoides). The largemouth is probably the most prized of the state's spiny rays. They are found in all sections of the state. Color is dark green over the back, with greenish-silver on sides. There is an indistinct dark band along the side. Belly is whitish. Mouth on the largemouth is big, extending beyond the hind margin of the eye in fish of 6 or more inches. The dorsal fins are sharply separated, and the largest has 9 or 10 spines, followed by 12 or 13 soft rays on the second dorsal. Anal fin usually has 3 short spines followed by 10 to 12 soft rays. Scale rows 58 to 69 along lateral line. Largemouth prefer weedy lakes or sloughs with weedy bottoms. Spawning takes place from early May through June when water temperatures are 60 to 68 de-grees. Males guard the eggs and young fish. Largemouth of 2 to 6 pounds are common in Washington. They eat fish, crayfish and frogs.

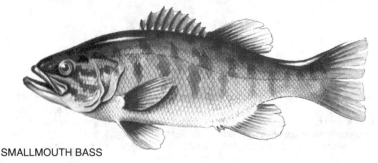

SMALLMOUTH BASS

SMALLMOUTH BASS. (Micropterus dolumiui). Most smallmouth are found E. of the Cascades, but there are a few lakes in W. Washington which carry the fish. It is dark green to pale olive-brown with some gold flecking. Sides are usually either lightly mottled or have vertical bars. They do not have a dark lateral band. The mouth is large but does not, when closed, reach the hind margin of the eye. Dorsal fins are separated by a shallow notch. The first dorsal has 9 to 10 spines and the second 13 to 15 soft rays. Scale rows along the lateral line, 67 to 81. Smallmouth like clear water with gravel bottoms, and sometimes are found in rivers. Spawning is during early summer in gravel nests. Most smallmouths in the state are under 3 pounds. Principal food is insect larvae, small fish and crayfish. Males tend the nest.

WHITE CRAPPIE. (Pomoxis annularis). There are white crappie on both sides of the Cascade Mountains. This species can take warmer, more turbid water than the Black Crappie. The white variety usually has 6 sharp spines on the dorsal fin, and is silvery in color. Several dark bands extend downward from the back. The fish may produce 2000 to 14,000 eggs, with spawning in summer. Most crappie are under 8 inches, but fish up to 16 inches have been taken in Washington. There are records of 5 pounders. Natural food of crappies include insects, worms, small minnows and crayfish.

BLACK CRAPPIE. (Pomoxis nigro maculatus). Black crappie prefer clear, weedy lakes and larger streams. They are not so plentiful in Washington as white crappie. The blacks are silvery olive with olive-green mottling, and have a dusky spot on the gill cover. The dorsal fin is continuous and has 7 or 8 spines along with 14 soft rays. There are 5 to 7 spines on the anal fin, followed by 18 or 19 soft rays. Black crappie seldom grow over 12 inches. Insects, crustaceans and small fish make up their diet. They spawn in early summer, with females producing 20,000 to 60,000 eggs. Colony nests are built in water of 3 to 8 foot depth.

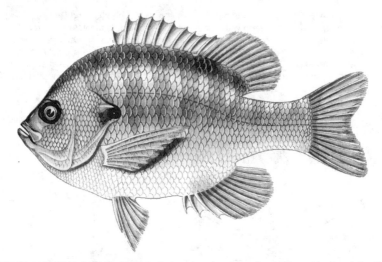

TRUE SUNFISH. Bluegill Sunfish (Lepomis macrochirus) and Pumpkin Seed Sunfish (Lepomis gibbosus) are the most important of the sunfish found in Washington. The bluegill may be easily identified by the blue-black color of the gill flap, plus the bluish tint of the gill cover. The last rays of the dorsal fin carry a dark spot. Pumpkin Seeds are bluish olive, with sides spotted with orange. Cheeks are orange with blue streaks. A bright red spot is located on the lower edge of the gill cover. Sunfish build nests in colonies and females deliver 12,000 to 27,000 eggs. Spawning is done in water of 12 to 40 inches in depth over gravel or sand bottoms. May through September, are spawning times. The males guard the nests. Sunfish are usually 7 to 8 inches or smaller, although some of 12 inches have been caught. Principal food of sun fish is insects, small crustaceans, water snails and fry of other fish.

Catfish

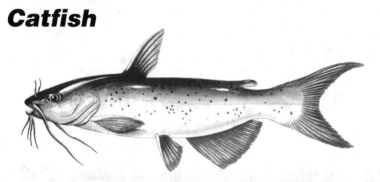

CHANNEL CATFISH. (Ictalurus puncta tus) and BLUE CATFISH (Ictalurus furca tus) are found in limited numbers in SE Washington in the Columbia and Snake rivers. Increasing numbers are being stocked in Western Washington waters. The blue catfish reach a weight of over 100 pounds, but nothing of this size has been reported from this state. The fish is slate-grey above and white below. The tail is deeply forked and the anal fin contains 30 to 36 rays. Channel catfish are smaller than blues. They are also slate-grey colored, but have many dark spots over their body, except sometimes in the case of large adults. Rays on the channel cat's anal fin number 24 to 30, and the fin is rounded along its free edge, whereas the blue's anal fin has a straight edge. Most channel cats are 12 to 16 inches although specimens of 12 to 15 pounds have been caught. The fish spawn in late spring or summer.

BULLHEAD CATFISH. Brown Bullhead Catfish (Ameiurus natalis) and Black Bullhead Catfish (Ameiurus melas), along with some Yellow Bullhead Catfish (Ameiurus natalis) are found throughout the state. They are easily recognized, having smooth, scaleless bodies and barbels or "whiskers" on chin and head. The dorsal has a sharp spine, as does each pectoral fin. Catfish to 4 pounds are taken, but the fish often are overcrowded and stunted. They spawn in early summer, with females depositing a gelatinous mass of eggs totaling from 2,000 to 10,000. Adult catfish herd their schools of young.

Location of Washington Counties

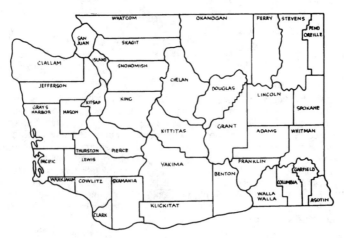

Washington Fish Species

Game Fish Species

LMB	Bass, Largemouth
RKB	Bass, Rock
SMB	Bass, Smallmouth
SB	Bass, Striped
BG	Bluegill
BH	Bullhead (General)
YBH	Bullhead, Yellow
BBH	Bullhead, Brown
BLB	Bullhead, Black
BUR	Burbot
CP	Carp
BCF	Catfish, Blue
CC	Catfish, Channel
FCF	Catfish, Flathead
AC	Char, Arctic
C	Crappie (General)
BC	Crappie, Black
WC	Crappie, White
EUL	Eulachon
SF	Flounder, Starry
AG	Grayling, Arctic
TMK	Musky, Tiger
SP	Perch, Shiner
YP	Perch, Yellow
NP	Pike, Northern
PS	Pumpkinseed
AT	Salmon, Atlantic
CK	Salmon, Chinook
CKS	Salmon, Summer Chinook
CH	Salmon, Chum
CO	Salmon, Coho
K	Salmon, Kokanee
SA	Salmon, Pacific Unknown
PK	Salmon, Pink
SO	Salmon, Sockeye
AMS	Shad, American
LFS	Smelt, Longfin
NSF	Squawfish, Northern
SS	Steelhead, Summer-Run
SW	Steelhead, Winter-Run
SH	Steelhead, Unknown race
GRS	Sturgeon, Green
WS	Sturgeon, White
SK	Sucker (General)
BRS	Sucker, Bridgelip
LRS	Sucker, Largescale
LNS	Sucker, Longnose
MNS	Sucker, Mountain
S	Sunfish (General)
GS	Sunfish, Green
BT	Trout, Brown
CT	Trout, Cutthroat General Unknown
CCT	Trout, Cutthroat Coastal Resident
SCT	Trout, Cutthroat Coastal Searun
LCT	Trout, Cutthroat Lahontan
WCT	Trout, Cutthroat West Slope
DB	Trout, Dolly Varden/Bull Unknown
BLC	Trout, Bull Trout (Char)
DVC	Trout, Dolly Varden (Char)
EB	Trout, Eastern Brook
GT	Trout, Golden
LT	Trout, Lake
RB	Trout, Rainbow Resident
RU	Trout, Rainbow Unknown race
TR	Trout, Unknown
WAL	Walleye
WM	Warmouth
WAG	White Amur-general
WAD	White Amur-diploid
WAT	White Amur-triploid
LW	Whitefish, Lake
WF	Whitefish, Mountain

Non-game Fish Species

CMO	Chiselmouth
LCH	Chub, Lake
TCH	Chub, Tui
DAC	Dace (General)
LED	Dace, Leopard
LND	Dace, Longnose
SD	Dace, Speckled
GF	Goldfish
LM	Lamprey (General)
PL	Lamprey, Pacific
RL	Lamprey, River
WL	Lamprey, Western Brook
MQF	Mosquitofish
OMM	Mudminnow, Olympic
PMO	Peamouth
P	Pickerel, Grass
SAN	Sandroller
COT	Sculpin (General)
CSS	Sculpin, Coastrange
MRS	Sculpin, Margined
MTS	Sculpin, Mottled
PSS	Sculpin, Pacific Staghorn
PTS	Sculpin, Piute
PRS	Sculpin, Prickly
RTS	Sculpin, Reticulate
RFS	Sculpin, Riffle
SHS	Sculpin, Shorthead
SLS	Sculpin, Slimy
TRS	Sculpin, Torrent
RS	Shiner, Redside
TSS	Stickleback, Three-Spine
TMT	Tadpole Madtom
TNC	Tench
PGW	Whitefish, Pygmy

Adams

COUNTY

Adams is not over-endowed with lakes, and fishing opportunities are limited, although the county ranks 16th in relative size among the state's 39 counties. The largest lake is Sprague with 1203 acres in Adams and 638 acres in Lincoln County. Cow and Rock Creeks drain the E. portion of Adams. Both the creeks are tributary to the Palouse River. Most of the W. half of the county is drained by Crab Creek. Adams is located in the SE portion of the state, and covers 1900 square miles. Highest point is situated NE of Ritzville at 2100 feet.

BLACK LAKES. Big Black covers 19 acres, while Little Black is 6 acres. Both lakes contain spiny rays, and are fed by an irrigation wasteway from Lower Goose Lake. They are located 8 miles NW of Othello. Gravel roads lead to Crab Creek, then it is a .05 mile hike to the lakes.

BUTTE LAKES. Three spiny ray lakes located 7.3 miles NW from Othello on S. side of Crab Creek on Columbia NWLR. Formed by seepage, they cover 30 acres.

CAMPBELL LAKE. Located 9 miles N. of Othello, a 115-acre private lake bounded on E. side by the E. Potholes Canal. It contains carp.

COW CREEK. Drains into Palouse River at Hooper Junction. Outlet of Middle, (Hallin) Cow and Finell Lakes. Few lateral roads. Contains eastern brook, German browns and rainbow. Spring months best time for the browns.

COW LAKE. Spiny rays and rainbow share this 226-acre enlargement of Cow Creek with numerous waterfowl. Contains perch, catfish, bluegills and largemouth bass. Dam at outlet. Has a public access site. Located 9.5 miles E. of Ritzville.

CRAB CREEK. (Lower). Meanders through portions of Columbia National Wildlife Refuge below Black Creek about 6 miles before entering Grant County and thence into Columbia River near Beverly. Few roads along this section. Best in May

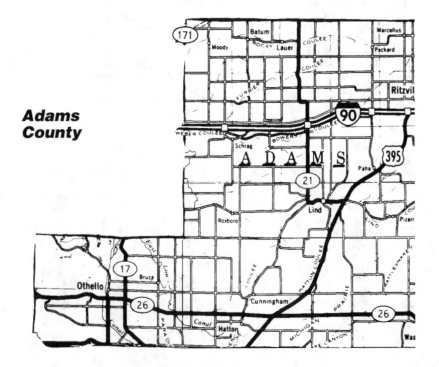

Adams
County

SMALLMOUTH BASS and channel catfish are primary fish in the Palouse River.

and June. Contains rainbow and German brown trout.

CRANE LAKE. Also known as Mallard or Long. About 15 miles E. of Ritzville with

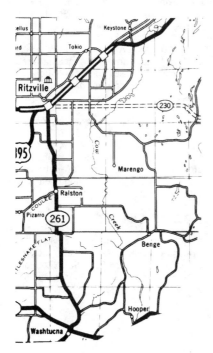

drainage into Palouse River. Contains spiny rays. Primarily a waterfowl lake.

DEADMAN LAKE. A spiny ray lake of 12.4 acres located about 5 miles NW from Othello and about 300 feet S. from Halfmoon Lake. Drainage to Crab Creek watershed.

FINNEL LAKE. Located 7 miles E. from Ritzville and 3 miles SW from Cow Lake. Contains largemouth bass, bluegill and brown bullhead.

FOURTH OF JULY LAKE. Ice fishing is popular in this 110 acre lake, which is usually managed as a winter lake. (74 acres in Adams County, 36 acres in Lincoln County). It holds rainbow. It drains to the Palouse River. Route is S. from Sprague on Hwy. 23 for 1 miles, turning W. on dirt road at Milepost I sign. Continue about 1 mile to cattle guard, turn right and take left fork of road 1 mile to lake.

HALFMOON, MORGAN, SHINER and **HUTCHINSON**. Chain of shallow lakes located adjacent to the McMannaman road about 6 miles NW of Othello on Columbia National Wildlife Refuge. Developed public fishing area on Morgan and on Halfmoon. Halfmoon and Morgan hold rainbow and Lahontan cutthroat. Shiner and Hutchinson are managed for bass. Outlet of lakes drain into Crab Creek. Easy access to all the lakes.

HALLIN LAKE. A 33.3 acre enlargement of Cow Creek located 11 miles E. from Ritzville. Contains a variety of spiny ray fish.

LINDA LAKE. Fed by irrigation water, Linda covers 99.2 acres and contains a variety of spiny rays. Location is 5.3 miles SW from Othello. Drainage to Scooteney Lake.

HAYS CREEK. Outlet of Halfmoon Lake which drains into Shiner Lake. It holds some rainbow and spiny rays.

HERMAN LAKE. This 33 acre lake is located 5 miles N. of Othello on private land. Lake contains rainbow. Route is via trail from Pit Lake parking area past Quail Lake to E. end of Herman. It is fed by Teal Creek.

LUGENBEAL SPRINGS CREEK. Rainbow planted stream which flows into N. end of Hallin Lake from the NE. It is about 4 miles long and heads in Lugenbeal Springs.

LYLE LAKE. Located 5 miles N. of Othello and 1200 feet SW of Herman Lake from which it is fed. Lyle is 22 acres and is planted with 'bows. Has public access area. Take McMannaman road from Othello for 4.5 miles, then drive NE on gravel road. Watch for signs.

McMANNAMAN LAKE. Lies 6 miles NW of Othello. Turn N. at E. end of Halfmoon Lake about 1.5 miles. Drive past sub-headquarters of Columbia N.W.R. McMannaman is 7 acres and is planted with rainbow. Noted as a spring and summer producer. Fed by Para Lake, (see Grant County) it drains into Morgan.

PALOUSE RIVER. April, May and June are best months for the Palouse where smallmouth bass are the favored fish. The river forms the south border of Adams County. It flows S. along the E. border of Franklin County and into the Snake. Channel cats also present.

PINES LAKE. Located 2000 feet S. of Fourth of July Lake and 3.5 miles S. of Sprague. Pines is a narrow, 120 acre lake planted occasionally with rainbow. Attracts waterfowl when water level is up. Drainage to Palouse River.

QUAIL LAKE. A 12 acre lake located just

E. of Herman Lake. A "catch and release" rainbow fishery. Approximately 1 mile walk to lake which is on the Columbia N.W.R., east of Herman Lake.

ROCK CREEK. Only 2.5 miles of Rock Creek are in Adams County, but this portion offers enjoyable stream fishing. A county road crosses the creek .05 miles from the Whitman County line near Paxton Station. Pleasant camping sites and drinking water at Weaver Springs. (Fine jump shooting for ducks along this stretch, too). Contains rainbow, German browns and smallmouth bass. July, August and September best fishing months.

ROYAL LAKE. Holds small spiny rays. Royal is a narrow, 101 acre lake and has perch, bass, sunfish, and catfish. Located 3 miles N. of state Highway 26 on Adams-Grant County line. County road adjacent to N. shore. Royal is used heavily by waterfowl.

SPRAGUE LAKE. Located 2 miles SW of town of Sprague. Highway 10 borders SE shore of this 1840 acre lake, (203 acres in Adams County with balance in Lincoln). Contains rainbow, cutthroat, brown trout, walleyes, largemouth bass, perch, crappie, catfish and smallmouth bass. May to September pegged best angling. Good winter fishing. Resorts on N. and S. ends of lake.

THREAD LAKE. A slim, 1.4 mile long lake of 29 acres adjacent to McMannaman road 3 miles N. of Othello. Fed by outlet of Lyle Lake. It holds rainbow and has a public access area.

WALL LAKE. This 15 acre lake is located 19 miles SE of Ritzville and 1 mile SE of Paxton Station. Wall is sometimes hit by both winter and summer kill of trout, but is planted with hardy Lahontan cutthroat. Route to Wall is to Paxton and taking private road S. from that point.

ADAMS COUNTY RESORTS

Sprague Lake: Sprague Lake Resort, Sprague, WA 99032. 509-257-2864; Four Seasons Campground, Sprague, WA 99032. 509-257-2332.

Asotin

COUNTY

The Snake River borders the NE and E. boundaries of Asotin, a mountainous county of 637 square miles. There are only 10 lakes covering 36 acres in Asotin. Best fishing is in the Blue Mountain's streams. Approximately two-thirds of the county drains E. via Alpowa and Asotin Creeks. The remainder drain into the Snake and Grand Ronde Rivers. Asotin is ranked 35th in size among Washington's counties. Highest point is Ray Ridge at 6191 feet.

ALPOWA CREEK. May to July is the best fishing period for this small Snake River tributary. Located in the Blue Mtns., Alpowa is easily accessible by roads. No public lands. It contains rainbow which are stocked regularly. (See Garfield County).

ASOTIN CREEK. Usually the only Asotin County stream receiving plants of legal rainbow, and these are placed into portions of the stream within Asotin W.R.A. Besides the 'bows, Asotin Creek carries whitefish. Top fishing comes from June on. The creek enters the Snake River at town of Asotin. Stream contains some summer steelhead, with best fishing for these fish in February and March in the stretch from mouth to deadline 400 feet below old Wash. Water Power Dam. Upper stretches of the Asotin above Lick Creek usually provide good fishing later in season. Branches of Asotin Creek include **GEORGE CREEK, SOUTH FORK, LICK FORK** and **CHARLIE FORK**. Route to upper portion of Asotin Creek is by good road through Asotin W.R.A which ends near the FS boundary.

CHARLIE CREEK. (Fork). Charlie Fork is rated "fair" for native rainbow early in the season. It is a tributary to Asotin Creek.

COTTONWOOD CREEK. May is best month for this small rainbow stream. The creek is a tributary of the Grand Ronde and is reached by driving up the Joseph Creek road from mouth of the Grand Ronde.

GRAND RONDE RIVER. An outstanding summer steelhead stream that also hosts

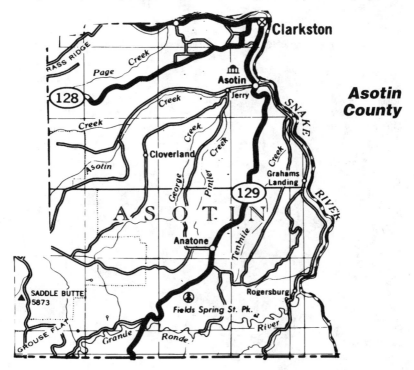

smallmouth bass and channel catfish plus some lunker native rainbow. This large stream heads in Oregon and flows E. across a corner of Asotin County before entering the Snake River. Most easily fished in Asotin County by driving S. from Asotin along the Snake River to mouth of Grand Ronde; down the Schumaker Grade from town of Anatone (inquire locally for directions); or upper reaches from Bogan's Oasis on the Asotin-Enterprise Highway, Hwy. 129. Peak fishing period for summer steelhead is in the fall from September into December.

JOSEPH CREEK. Only 4 miles of this small Grand Ronde tributary are in Washington. It holds rainbow and is usually best in September and October. It is best fished by driving upstream from mouth of the Grand Ronde about 5 miles.

RATTLESNAKE CREEK. Parallels Hwy. 129 before entering the Grand Ronde at the point the highway crosses the river. Contains rainbow and some summer steelhead. Best period is May and early June. The creek produces from its mouth to the headwaters.

SNAKE RIVER. Good roads follow this major tributary to the Columbia River in Asotin County. While best known for steelhead, the Snake also produces channel catfish, bass and sturgeon. Some of the best fishing stretches include around Silcott, just below mouth of Alpowa Creek; "Hog Pen" hole near U.S.G.S. gauging station; Dry Gulch, "High Land" hole in town of Clarkston; vicinity of Asotin, and numerous other good areas to mouth of Grand Ronde River.

TEN MILE CREEK. A small stream which empties into the Snake River about 7 miles S. of Asotin. It yields a few rainbow and steelhead. Best fishing early in May.

WENATCHEE CREEK. This small tributary of the Grand Ronde heads in the Blue Mtns. It joins the Grand Ronde about 1 mile before that river enters Oregon. Access is difficult, but fishermen may walk upstream from the road paralleling the N. side of the Grand Ronde about 1 mile before that river enters Oregon. Private property on lower 2 miles. It is rated as a fair rainbow prospect in May and June.

Rainbow have been stocked in several small county ponds including Evans, Golf Course, Headgate and Silcott.

ASOTIN COUNTY RESORTS

Snake River—Grand Ronde River: Beamers Hells Canyon Tours. Box 1243, Lewiston, ID 83501. 1-800-522-6966.

Grand Ronde River. (Lenny "G" Frasure Photo)

Benton

COUNTY

Dominating water from a fishing standpoint in the 1767 square mile Benton County is the lower Yakima River which flows through the central portion from W. to E., nearly dividing the county equally. The Columbia River, which forms

Benton's N., E. and S. boundaries, also provides fishing, but there are only 229 acres of lake water in the entire county outside the 33,756 acres of Wullula Lake on the Columbia River. The highest spot in the county is at 3629 feet in the Rattlesnake Hills.

COLUMBIA RIVER. Borders Benton County on the N., E. and S. Steelhead fishing from July through March, depending upon water conditions. Whitefish angling is best from September to December, with bass fishing tops from July to September. Most productive whitefish area is below Priest Rapids Dam. Bass fishing is best from A.E.C. reservation downstream. There is often good summer steelhead angling in the Richland-Ringold area, as well as in the Devil's Bend and Alder Creek drifts

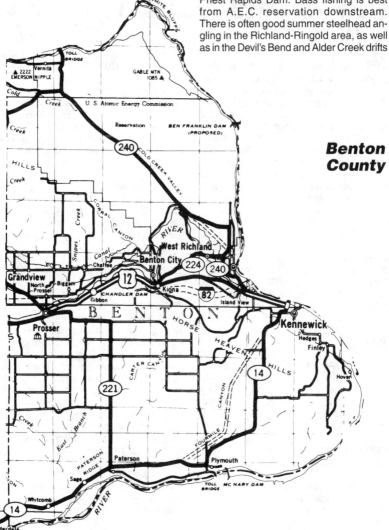

CLOVER ISLAND BOAT MARINA and recreational area on Lake Wallula. (Corps of Engineers Photo)

below McNary Dam. This same area is a popular sturgeon spot. In addition to these species, smallmouth bass, channel catfish, bluegill, pumpkinseed, crappie and brown bullhead provide fishing opportunities. Another fisheries is for walleye. Although walleyes can be caught throughout McNary and John Day Pools, popular areas are below McNary and John Day Dams. Boat launch facilities are at Crow Butte, Paterson, and Plymouth. Excellent smallmouth bass fishing can be found in the Columbia River and sloughs at Paterson, and largemouth and smallmouth fishing is good in the Hanford area and near the mouth of the Yakima River. Good largemouth bass fishing, as well as some fair crappie, perch, and brown bullhead action can be found in the Finley area. Channel catfish are caught throughout McNary Pool. Fish of 6 to 8 pounds are not uncommon. Columbia Park, which has 4.5 miles of river bank, is located at Kennewick. There are overnight camping facilities plus 4 boat ramps and boat docks at the park.

MITCHELL POND. A 3.7 acre pond located 13.5 miles SE of Kennewick and adjacent to the W. side of Lake Wallula. Formed by a railroad fill. Contains large and smallmouth bass, perch, crappie and catfish. Drains into Wallula.

MOUND POND. Formed by railroad fill adjacent to NW shore of Lake Wallula. Situated about 14.5 miles SE of Kennewick. Holds small and largemouth bass, perch, catfish and crappie. It is 34 acres. PIT PONDS. Ponds formed by a railroad fill. Both ponds hold small and largemouth bass,

perch, crappie and catfish, as do **PALMER** and **WALL PONDS** in the same vicinity.

SWITCH POND. Another "side lake" formed by a railroad fill along Lake Wallula. Located about 15.5 miles SE of Kennewick and 0.4 miles S. of **YELLEPIT POND**, which was also formed by a railroad fill. Both ponds hold small and largemouth bass, perch, crappie and catfish.

WALLULA LAKE. Reservoir backed up by McNary Dam on the Columbia River. About 40% of the reservoir's 38,800 acres are in Benton County. Best fishing is for spiny rays, plus blue and channel catfish during summer.

WELLSIAN POND. A pond of 2 acres located at W. city limits of Richland. Has been planted with rainbow.

YAKIMA RIVER. Benton County is divided about evenly by the Yakima River. Good roads run down both sides of the river offering access. Smallmouth bass fishing rated fair to good below Prosser in spring and summer. Whitefish angling is done during winter months. Best section of the Yakima in Benton County for whitefish is from Prosser to W. Richland and in vicinity of Horn Rapids dam, where there is a boat launch site. Whitefish angling is often good during October and November. Fishing for smallmouth bass and channel catfish is excellent in the lower Yakima River. The Richland area is a favorite area for these species. Channel catfish in the 8 pound class are not uncommon, but average size is 1 to 2 pounds. Smallmouth bass are generally under 1.5 pounds, but fish to 3 pounds and more are caught. Fair largemouth bass and crappie fishing can also be found on the lower Yakima near Richland.

YELLEPIT POND. A 36 acre pond formed by a railroad fill. Location is 15.4 miles SE from Kennewick. Connected by culvert to Lake Wallula. Holds many species of spiny rays.

Rainbow have been planted in several small county ponds and lakes including Caliche Lake, Columbia Pond, Columbia Park Lake, "H", Heart and Kiona.

PALMER POND is formed by railroad fills along Lake Wallula.

Chelan County

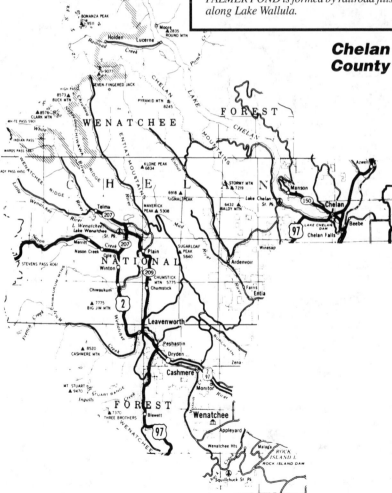

Chelan
COUNTY

Only 38 of Chelan's numerous lakes are located below 2500 feet elevation. The mountainous county is the 3rd largest in the state. Four major rivers—-the Stehekin, Chelan, Entiat and Wenatchee—drain Chelan County into the Columbia River. Bonanza Peak, at 9511 feet, is the most lofty point in Chelan, although there are many peaks over 8000 feet. Lake Chelan is the largest natural lake in the state.

AUGUSTA LAKE is located in a beautiful high meadow area at 6750 feet. It hosts cutthroat.

AIRPLANE LAKE. A 10 acre rainbow planted lake at 5350 feet 32 miles NW from Leavenworth on E. side of Mt. Saul. Drainage is to Indian Creek and White River.

AUGUSTA LAKE. Cutthroat inhabit this 25.7 acre lake on Icicle Ridge 8.8 miles NW from Leavenworth. Open shoreline. Elevation is 6750 feet. Augusta drains to Cabin Creek and Wenatchee River.

ANTILON LAKE. Originally a natural lake of about 20 acres, Antilon was dammed to create a 96 acre reservoir. (Including Long Jim Reservoir.) It is located about 5 miles N. of Manson on Grade Creek road past Roses and Wapato Lakes. Planted with brown trout.

BATTALION LAKE. This rainbow planted lake of 6.4 acres is situated at 5334 feet 3.4 miles SE from High Bridge Guard Station. It drains to Stehekin River.

BEEHIVE RESERVOIR. An 11.5 acre impoundment formed by a dam on upper Squilchuck Creek. Rainbow and eastern brook plants. Beehive is situated 8 miles SW of Wenatchee. Route is up Squilchuck Creek road from South Wenatchee about 10 miles to Squilchuck State Park, then NW 1.5 miles to the reservoir.

BIG JIM LAKES. Rainbow lakes of 4.3 and 4.5 acres at 6400 and 7000 feet on NE side of Big Jim Mountain, and 3300 feet NE from Augusta Lake. Drainage to Wenatchee River.

BLACK LAKE. (Wheeler Reservoir). Located 8.5 miles S. of Wenatchee on Wheeler Hill. Elevation is 3425 feet. The lake covers about 28 acres and holds rainbow and eastern brook. Summer is best fishing period. Private land and fishing is restricted.

BOULDER CREEK. An excellent fishing stream for rainbow of average size in July and August. The creek enters the Stehekin River about 1 mile above Lake Chelan. A trail leads up W. side of creek, touching the stream about 1 mile from mouth, then continuing to headwaters. Regular boat service from town of Chelan serves the community of Stehekin at end of Lake Chelan in N.C. Nat. Park.

BRIDGE CREEK. Enters Stehekin River at end of road leading from N. end of Lake Chelan. Rough road follows creek 4 miles to Bridge Creek Campground, then Cascade Crest Trail continues up creek to forks at Fireweed Campground. May also be reached by following Twisp River road from town of Twisp in Okanogan County to end of road where there is a campground, then climbing by trail about 5 miles over Twisp Pass and down E. fork of Bridge Creek. Top fishing for Bridge Creek rainbow and cutthroat comes in July and August. Trout are in the 8-10 inch range. Creek is in North Cascade National Park.

CANAAN LAKE. A 2.5 acre lake situated at 5500 feet at head of Royal Creek on SW side of Mt. Mastiff. It holds cutthroat. Drainage is to Nason Creek.

CAROLINE LAKES. Big Caroline Lake is at 5400 feet, 10.3 miles SW from Leavenworth in headwaters of Pioneer

Creek. Little Caroline Lake is 3.5 acres at 5900 feet and 2000 feet NW from Big Caroline. Both lakes have been cutthroat planted. Drainage to Wenatchee River.

CHELAN LAKE. Largest natural lake in Washington state, Chelan extends over 50 miles from town of Chelan to community of Stehekin at upper end. It averages about 1 mile in width, and maximum depth, off mouth of Big Goat Creek, is over 1500 feet. Regular boat service from Chelan calls at various points along the lake. Road up W. shoreline reaches as far as **TWENTY-FIVE MILE CREEK.** where there is a state park and resorts, before turning S. to wind through the mountains to Shady Pass and to drop down to the Entiat River road. Chelan has strikingly beautiful mountains rising steeply from the lake shore. It is not uncommon to spot mountain goats from boats. Most popular fish in Chelan are kokanee, although the huge lake also contains rainbow, cutthroat, Dolly Varden, lake trout, burbot, smallmouth bass and chinook salmon. Kokanee fishing sometimes starts as early as April, and these fish are caught all summer. Rainbow, cutthroat and Dolly Varden angling is best at mouths of the numerous creeks feeding Lake Chelan. Private boats may be launched at town of Chelan, Lake Chelan State Park, Manson, 25 Mile Creek Resort, Granite Falls Marina and the Cove Marina. There are re-

sort facilities at Stehekin, with saddle and pack horses, taxi and rental cars. Stehekin is reached only by boat, air or by hiking.

CHIWAUKUM CREEK. Drains into Wenatchee River above Tumwater Canyon 1 mile N. of Tumwater Campground on the Stevens Pass Hwy. Road follows creek about 2 miles upstream from mouth, then trail continues to Chiwaukum Lake. Series of beaver ponds in the creek below the lake cover about 10 acres and contain eastern brook, as does the creek itself. Rainbow also available.

CHIWAUKUM LAKE. Situated at 4950 feet, the 66 acre lake is fed by Larch and Cup Lakes. It holds a few cutthroat, but mostly eastern brook. Trail follows Chiwaukum Creek from campgrounds at end of road for about 8 miles to lake. **JASON LAKES** are located about 0.5 miles S. of Chiwaukum. They hold 7 to 9 inch cutthroat. No trail.

CHIWAWA RIVER. Empties into Wenatchee River 6 miles below Lake Wenatchee on Stevens Pass Hwy. about 15 miles W. of Leavenworth. Road parallels river approximately 25 miles upstream. Late June to mid-August is the best period for the stream's rainbow. Fall fishing can be very productive. There are summer steelhead and cutthroat in the river along

UPPER CHELAN LAKE is best reached by boat or float plane. The lake is over 50 miles long. (Joe Freet Photo)

COLECHUCK LAKE usually sheds ice by mid-June. Randy Carr is shown here making his way down to the rainbow and cutthroat lake. (Ben Crusan Photo)

with rainbow. Larger tributaries which offer fishing include Buck, Chickamin, Meadow, Marble, Phelps and Rock Creeks. Road ends at Trinity, and trail continues up to Buck Creek Pass. Excellent campgrounds along the road following the river.

CHORAL LAKE. Golden trout have been stocked in Choral, a 1.5 acre lake at 7200 feet. It lies about 35.5 miles NW from Entiat at head of Choral Creek. Drainage is to Entiat River.

CLEAR LAKE. Located about 9 miles S. of Wenatchee. The lake is at 3000 feet and covers 4.8 acres. It is stocked with eastern brook and rainbow and has a public fishing area. Drainage to Semilt Creek.

COLCHUCK LAKE. An 88 acre, deep lake at the head of Mountaineer Creek 10.5 miles SW of Leavenworth. It is cutthroat planted, and rainbow are self-sustaining. Route to the lake, which lies at 5570 feet elevation, is up Icicle Creek road W. from Leavenworth for 5 miles, then up Eight Mile Road for about 3 miles to Stuart Lake trailhead, then 2.5 miles to junction with Colchuck Trail, then 1.5 miles to lake. A trail follows Eight Mile Creek from about 4 miles to **EIGHT MILE LAKE** at 4450 feet, Rainbow, cutthroat and mackinaw in the 72 acre lake, which has a FS campground.

COMPANY CREEK. Joins the Stehekin River above Lake Chelan from the W. near an air strip. A good trail follows creek for about 6 miles before turning S. up Hilgard Creek. A brushy stream, Company Creek yields cutthroat, rainbow and eastern brook.

DOMKE LAKE. A 271 acre lake lying 21 miles by trail from Lucerne on W. shore of Lake Chelan. Rainbow are self-sustaining, cutthroat have been planted. Cabins, boats and camping sites. Reached by float plane or boat from Chelan to Lucerne. Best fishing usually comes from mid-June to mid-July, and again in fall months. The lake is fed by **EMERALD PARK CREEK** which provides fair fishing for cutthroat and rainbow.

DONALD LAKE. Rainbow stocked lake of 12.4 acres at 5800 feet. Location is 14.4 miles NW from Leavenworth. It drains to Wenatchee River.

DRY LAKE. (Grass). A 76.8 acre lake containing a wide variety of warm water fish including large bass, perch, sunfish, crappie and large brown bullheads. Location is 1.6 miles N. from Manson and about 1900 feet NW from Roses Lake from which it is fed. Drainage via Stink Creek to Lake Chelan.

EDNA LAKE. A 3.5 acre lake planted with golden trout. Location is 12.2 miles N. from Leavenworth at 6500 feet in headwaters of Index Creek. Drainage is to Wenatchee River.

EIGHT MILE LAKE. A 71.6 acre rainbow planted lake at 4450 feet, 10.5 miles SW from Leavenworth. It drains to Eight Mile Creek to Icicle Creek.

EILEEN LAKE. (Loch Eileen). Fall fishing is often most productive time in this 24 acre lake. Eileen is located about 9 miles E. of Stevens Pass at an elevation of 5200 feet. Stocked with rainbow and cutthroat which attain good size. Lake lies in semi-open meadow country. Reached by trail 1 mile above Julius Lake. (See Julius lake).

ELSEY LAKE. Golden trout have been planted in Elsey, a 16.4 acre lake at 6200 feet. Location is 18.7 miles NE from Stevens Pass and 11.5 miles NW from Lake Wenatchee. Drains to Napeequa River.

ENCHANTED LAKES. Group of golden trout stocked lakes of 4.6, 18.2, ll.8 and 23.3 acres at elevations of 6700 to 7060 feet. They are located about 10 miles SW from Leavenworth.   Drainage to Icicle Creek and Wenatchee River.

ENTIAT RIVER. A large stream which enters the Columbia River at town of Entiat. It is stocked regularly with rainbow and summer steelhead, with plants staggered through the season. Usually, trout fishing is best between the first of July and September. Fall months are best for the summer-run steelhead. Road parallels the Entiat about 40 miles to Cottonwood Campground past Myrtle Lake to headwaters. The Entiat is snow-fed, thus is colored during hot weather. Numerous tributaries offer fair to good fishing. They include Choral, Anthem, Snow Brushy, Cool and Ice Creeks.

ETHEL LAKE. Rainbow are present in Ethel's 15.6 acres at 5400 feet elevation. Location is 9.3 miles E. from Stevens Pass. Drainage to Nason Creek.

FISH CREEK. Enters Lake Chelan at Moore Point. Water taken during dry months from lower stretches for irrigation purposes. Upper reaches of the small creek, which is paralleled by trails up both N. and E. forks, yield cutthroat and rainbow of moderate size from June through August.

FISH LAKE. Situated 1 mile NE of Lake Wenatchee, Fish Lake fluctuates between 500 to about 600 acres. It has numerous small inlets and about 150 acres of marshy area at W. end. Has been planted with rainbow, brown trout and eastern brook. Also holds perch, small and largemouth bass. Resorts on lake. Road parallels entire N. shore.

FLORA LAKE. Cutthroat have been planted in Flora, a 10.7 acre lake. Elevation is 5900 feet. Location is 12.8 miles NW from Leavenworth in headwaters of S. Fork Chiwaukum Creek.

HEATHER LAKE. A lake of 89 acres situated at 3890 feet 8 miles N. of Stevens Pass. Reached by driving to end of road up Lake Creek on S. side of Little Wenatchee River and then heading up the Heather Lake road to Heather Lake trail head. Rough, steep trail for the last 1.5 miles. Total distance about 3 miles. Has been planted with both rainbow and cutthroat. Shoreline brushy, but good campsites along lake. **DONALD LAKE** lies 2500 feet W. of Julius at 5800 feet altitude and has been planted with cutthroat. No trail to lake. **GLASSES LAKE** lies 0.5 miles S. of Heather at 4750 feet elevation. The lake has been planted with cutthroat. It covers 24.5 acres. Fly fishermen do well at Glasses in August and September. Reached via Pacific Crest Trail by way of Smithbrook.

ICICLE CREEK. Tributary to Wenatchee River. Icicle road from Leavenworth heads S. and then W. and N. up creek. Campgrounds are spaced at intervals along the stream for about 20 miles. Icicle receives rainbow and summer steelhead plants.

KING LAKE. Situated at 6000 feet 36 miles N. from Leavenworth, the 12.2 acre lake has been planted with golden trout. It is fed by a glacier on NE side of Buck Mtn. Drainage is to Chiwawa River.

KLONAQUA LAKES. Lakes of 66 and 67 acres which lie at 5450 feet (Lower Klonaqua) and at 5500 feet (Upper Konaque) 19 miles W. of Leavenworth. Lakes drain into Icicle River, and both have been planted with cutthroat. Follow Icicle River road to end then strike trail up the Icicle about 2 miles to French Creek. Turn SW up French Creek trail about 6 miles, then W. 2 tough miles on Konaqua Lake trail to lakes. Dam at outlet of lower lake holds water back for irrigation use. August and September prime months for fishing. Rafts and campsites along the lakes.

LAKE CREEK. Drains Heather Lake and enters Little Wenatchee River at Lake Creek Campground. Road follows the creek for about 2 miles, and the trail parallels the stream to its headwaters at Heather Lake. August best for the small rainbow and cutthroat that Lake Creek holds.

LICHTENWASSER LAKE. Located at 4754 feet 3.3 miles north of Stevens Pass. Reached by 2.5 mile trail from E. end of old G.N.R.R. tunnel. Another route leads from end of Smithbrook road off Stevens Pass Hwy. 1 mile then a 1.5 mile scramble SW up the lake's outlet. Brushy along shoreline. The 22 acre lake produces cutthroat from mid-July on. **VALHALLA LAKE** lies at 5050 feet and covers 29 acres in a very scenic setting about 1 mile W. of Lichtenwasser. Trail access from Smithbrook. Valhalla holds cutthroat, some of large size. Good campsites at N. end of lake.

LILY LAKE. Located 9 miles S. of Wenatchee and 1 mile SE of Black Lake. The 15 acre lake was originally used for irrigation purposes. It gets regular plants of rainbow and eastern brook. Elevation is 3100 feet.

LITTLE WENATCHEE RIVER. Flows into SW end of Lake Wenatchee. FS road parallels river about 18 miles to end of road at Little Wenatchee Ford Campground. Several other fine campgrounds along the river. Trails lead up tributary stream and on from end of road to tie into Cascade Crest Trail. Water is slow along lower reaches with many beaver ponds which provide fishing for rainbow and cutthroat, as well as eastern brook. Fly fishermen love this one, particularly from August on. Regular plants of legal sized trout are made throughout the season. Some tributaries of the Little Wenatchee, including Rainy, Lake, Falls, Fish and Cady Creeks, offer fair to good fishing. Trails of varying condition follow these tributaries.

MAD RIVER. Enters Entiat River about 10 miles W. of town of Entiat. Road up Entiat River forks at Ardenvoir, then continues NW up the Mad River to Pine Flat campgrounds. Trail parallels river from this point to headwaters. The Mad receives plants of legal trout in lower stretches at intervals

through the year. Late spring is generally a good fishing period. Besides the 'bows, there are Dolly Varden and some cutthroat taken.

MEADOW CREEK. Rainbow are present in this stream which is a tributary to Jack Creek which joins Icicle Creek at Chatter Creek Campground. Route is S. and W. from Leavenworth on Icicle Creek road 15 miles, then S. by trail from camp ground for about 6 miles to junction of Jack and Meadow Creeks. Trails follow both streams.

MEADOW LAKE. (Galler Res.). Access is via a county right of way on this 36 acre spiny ray lake which holds brown bullhead and crappie. It is situated 1 mile SW from Malega which is 5 miles SE of Wenatchee on the Columbia.

MERRITT LAKE. A shallow lake of 7 acres situated on Nason Ridge at the head of Mahar Creek. Elevation is 5000 feet. Lake has been planted with eastern brook which are now self-sustaining. Reached by trail which leaves Stevens Pass Hwy. about 4 miles W. of Merritt. Approximately 3 miles by trail to lake. **LOST LAKE** is located 2900 feet N. of Merritt at 4900 feet. The 31 acre lake gets periodical cutthroat plants.

MIRROR LAKE. A 26 acre lake lying at 5490 feet about 4 miles SW of Lucerne on Lake Chelan. Route from Lucern is via Emerald Park and Mirror Lake trails, a total distance of 11 miles. (Lucern may be reached only by boat or float plane, or by trail over Cascade Crest from West. WA). The lake has had cutthroat plants and is said to hold some lunker rainbow.

MISSION CREEK. A small rainbow planted stream which is a Wenatchee River tributary which enters that river at Cashmere. Road from town parallels the popular creek for over 15 miles.

MYRTLE LAKE. About a 4 mile hike from end of Entiat River road is required to reach this 19 acre lake. Elevation is 3750 feet. Myrtle is host to eastern brook. Campsites and easy access to the lake.

NASON CREEK. The Stevens Pass Hwy. follows this creek from its headwaters near the summit to near the point it joins Lake Wenatchee's outlet just below the lake. Easily reached and fished, the lower Nason provides fair fishing for summer steelhead and planted rainbow which are planted at intervals during the season. Late summer is the best fishing period.

PESHASTIN CREEK. Blewett Pass Hwy. parallels the creek from the summit of the pass N. to its junction with the Wenatchee River just above Dryden. Lower stretches below Ingalls Creek provide best fishing for small rainbow and summer steelhead. Feeder streams, including the Scotty, Tronson, Negro, Shasher and Ingalls, yield small trout.

PRINCE CREEK. Enters Lake Chelan on N. side about two-thirds up the lake. Accessible by plane or boat only. Forest service campground at mouth. Trail follows creek upstream to headwaters. Small rainbow in lower section, with cutthroat in top stretches.

RAINBOW CREEK. Enters Stehekin River about 1 mile above head of Lake Chelan. Campground where Stehekin River road crosses Rainbow Creek near Rainbow Falls, a large creek which is often discolored by snow melt. Trail takes off road about 1 mile past Rainbow Falls, then swings back to parallel stream to head waters. Primarily a cutthroat show, but rainbow are taken also.

ROCK LAKE. Golden trout have been stocked in Rock which lies at 5600 feet. The lake covers 3.5 acres and drains to

EDNA LAKE, at a lofty 5000 feet elevation has been stocked with golden trout.

Nason Creek. Location is 7 miles NE from Stevens Pass on E. side of Rock Mountain.

ROSES LAKE. (Alkali). Located 1 mile N. of Manson above Lake Chelan and adjacent to Wapato Lake. A lake of 131 acres, Roses is noted for winter trout fishing through the ice. It is stocked with brown trout and rainbow and also holds warmwater fish. Resort and public access on lake.

SCHAEFER LAKE. An 83 acre lake which lies 8.5 miles N. from W. end of Lake Wenatchee at 5050 feet elevation. It has received cutthroat and offers small eastern brook. Chiwawa River road leads upstream 12 miles to Finner Creek Campground where a trail heads NW 6 miles to the lake.

SQUILCHUCK CREEK. A small rainbow stream which heads above Squilchuck State Park and flows NE approximately 12 miles to the Columbia River at South Wenatchee. A road from South Wenatchee follows the creek upstream to the park.

STEHEKIN RIVER. The principal tributary to Lake Chelan, the Stehekin drains a large area. A good road follows the river from the community of Stehekin to High Bridge, about 12 miles, and offers easy access. A rough road continues up stream another 10 miles or more. Boat and charter plane service, or trail, is the only means of reaching Stehekin. Taxi, resort and horse service is available at this point. The river often is colored, but holds Dolly Varden, rainbow and kokanee, as well as cutthroat. Late summer and fall is best fishing period. In North Cascade National Park.

SWIMMING DEER LAKE. A rainbow lake of 3 acres located on E. side of Cascade Crest at 2800 feet, S. from Josephine Lake. Drainage to Icicle Creek.

THREE LAKE. (Mud). A private reservoir of 33 acres located 5.5 miles SE of Wenatchee. It is fed by Stemilt Creek, plus drainage from Meadow Lake. There are some spiny rays including catfish in the lake.

TOP LAKE. (Summit). Lies 10 miles N. of Stevens Pass on the Cascade Crest. Top covers 7 acres, and is situated at an elevation of 4700 feet. It is planted with cutthroat and is reached via Top Lake trail over Shoofly Mtn. from Road No. 2713-A for 5 miles to lake.

TRAP LAKE. A lake of 11 acres situated at 5150 feet, Trap has been planted with cutthroat, and is also reported to contain a few lunker 'bows. About 12 miles via Cascade Crest trail from Stevens Pass, or 7 miles by way of Tunnel Creek from W. entrance of G.N. railroad tunnel in King County. This route passes **HOPE LAKE** which lies at 4400 feet at head of Basin Creek. Hope has been planted with cutthroat, but eastern brook reported.

TRAPPER LAKE. A beautiful mountain lake of 146 acres located 3 miles SE of Cascade Pass at 4165 feet. Inside North Cascade National Park, it drains via Cottonwood Creek into upper Stehekin River. Holds cutthroat of all sizes. Trapper is tough to reach. It is about 2 miles from end of rough road up Stehekin River via the lake's outlet.

TROUT LAKE. This 17 acre lake lies at 4850 elevation 5 miles by trail from Chatter Creek campground on Icicle River road. It holds rainbow and cutthroat and is located in a basin which offers good campsites. Drainage is to Icicle River.

TWENTY-FIVE MILE CREEK. Enters Lake Chelan at the end of the S. side road. A branch road S. leads about 5 miles along creek. Campground at point N. Fork joins Twenty-Five Mile Creek. Creek has kokanee, rainbow, cutts and eastern brook.

WAPATO LAKE. A 216 acre lake which lies just above the NE tip of Lake Chelan 2 miles N. of Manson, and adjacent to Roses Lake. Wapato is planted with eastern brook and rainbow and contains warmwater fish. Resorts and a public fishing area on E. end of lake. Road out of Manson parallels S. side of lake.

WENATCHEE LAKE. A natural, 5-mile long lake of 2445 acres situated at the head of the Wenatchee River 15 miles N. of Leavenworth. It holds rainbow, Dolly Varden and kokanee, and delivers best fishing in late spring and summer months. Reached by leaving Stevens Pass Hwy. at Cole's Corner on Hwy. 207 and driving S. about 3 miles to E. end of lake where Wenatchee State Park is located. Road up S. side of lake leads 3 miles to Glacier View

Campground. North shore road passes Lake Wenatchee ranger station, then forks at NW end of lake. Left hand fork follows Little Wenatchee River about 16 miles to road end at Little Wenatchee Ford Campgrounds. Right hand fork parallels White River 12 miles to end of road at White River Falls Campground. Resorts along Lake Wenatchee and FS improved campsites.

WENATCHEE RIVER. A large, beautiful stream heading in Lake Wenatchee and flowing 60 miles to join the Columbia River at Wenatchee. Highways parallel the river offering easy access for fishermen to work over rainbow, Dolly Varden, and whitefish, plus summer steelhead. Staggered plants of legal 'bows in Tumwater Canyon area. Several tributaries including Chiwaukum, Nason, Peshastin, Chumstick, Beaver and Mission Creeks plus the Chiwawa and Icicle Rivers provide fair to good fishing.

WHITE RIVER. Milky water hinders fishermen in this major tributary to Lake Wenatchee, but it is heavily fished above the N. Fork for rainbow and cutthroat. A road leaves the N. end of Lake Wenatchee and continues N. for 12 miles, paralleling the White. Three FS campgrounds are located on the road. Boulder, Panther, Indian and Napeequa Creeks, tributary to the White produce trout. The White is stocked with legal 'bows periodically.

CHELAN COUNTY RESORTS

Chelan Lake: 25-Mile Creek Resort, Chelan, WA 98816. 509-687-3610 Cannon's Resort, Chelan, WA 98816. 509-682 2932. The Cove Marina, Chelan, WA 98816. 509-687-3789. No. Cascades Lodge, Stehekin, WA 98852. 509-682-4711.

Fish Lake: The Cove Resort, Leavenworth, WA 98826. 509-763-3130.

Roses Lake: Paradise Lake Resort, Manson, WA 98831. 509-687-3444. Roses Lake Resort, Manson, WA 98831. 509-687-3179.

Wapato Lake: Kamei Resort, Manson, WA 98831. 509-687-3690. Paradise Resort, Manson, WA 98831. 509-687-3444.

Wenatchee Lake: Telma Resort, Star Rt., Wenatchee, WA 98801.

Clallam

COUNTY

Covering the N. tip of the Olympic Peninsula, Clallam County provides some of the state's best winter and summer steelhead and salmon fishing in a number of major rivers. It ranks 20th in size among the state's counties. Cape Alava is the most westerly point in the "lower 48" states. Nearly 500 of the county's 1787 square miles are inside Olympic National Park. Portions of the county receive over 200 inches of rain annually. Ozette Lake, 7787 acres, is the 3rd largest natural lake in the state.

AGENCY CREEK. Winter steelhead have been stocked in this Makah Indian Reservation short-run stream which enters the E. jaw of Neah Bay. Indian fishing license required for non-Indians.

ALDWELL LAKE. Formed by a NW Power & Light Co. dam on the lower Elwha River, Aldwell covers 320 acres. It is located 6 miles W. of Port Angeles on Hwy. 101. The lake contains rainbow, kokanee, eastern brook and some Dolly Varden around the inlet. Fall fishing is often excellent for rainbow and kokanee, while fly fishermen

score during summer months in the Elwha just above the lake.

BEAVER LAKE. Situated adjacent to the Sappho cutoff road 3 miles NE of Sappho. The 36 acre lake is brushy along shorelines. It delivers well for small cutthroat at season's opener, then slows. Some kokanee and yellow perch in the lake. Small car-top boats may be launched in lake from highway shoulder. Good fishing in outlet stream for 10 to 12 inch kokanee.

BIG RIVER. A small river that heads under Sekiu Mtn., Big River drains into Lake Ozette at Swan Bay. It comes on in fall months for sea-run cutthroat. Road to Lake Ozette parallels Big River for about 5 miles.

BLAKES PONDS. Three small ponds totaling about 1 acre which contain eastern brook. Location is 0.7 miles E. of Sequim on Bell Creek with drainage to Strait of Juan de Fuca.

BOGACHIEL RIVER. One of the Olympic Peninsula's major steelhead streams. It is joined by the Calawah River about 3 miles below Forks, then flows into the Sol Duc River to form the Quillayute River. Hwy. 101 parallels the Bogachiel for a number of miles, and roads extend up both sides for 6 or more miles above 101. The LaPush road comes within striking range of the river at a number of points, crossing the Bogachiel just above that river's junction with the Sol Duc. Heavily stocked with migrant-sized steelhead, the Bogy is known as an early producer for winter steelhead, then comes on late in year for larger

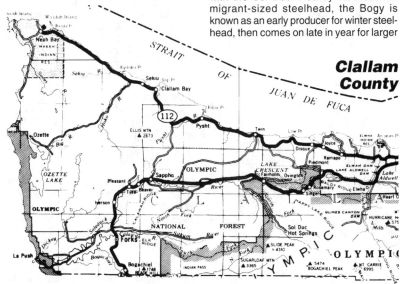

CALAWAH RIVER yielded this prime February steelhead for Toby Sprinkle.

native fish. It holds runs of chinook and silver salmon, summer steelhead and sea-run cutthroat. August, September and October are productive months for these fish. Public access and boat launch at confluence of Bogachiel and Sol Duc Rivers. State park with campsites where Hwy. 101 crosses Bogachiel.

CALAWAH RIVER. Major tributary to Bogachiel River, the Calawah contains winter and summer steelhead, chinook and silver salmon and sea-run cutthroat. The stretch below Hwy. 101 is difficult to fish

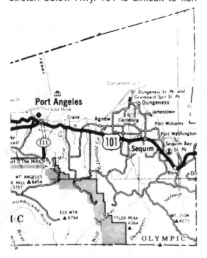

because of lack of roads, but a good road leaves 101 about 1.5 miles N. of Forks and parallels N. side of the Calawah 3.5 miles to where the N. and S. forks join. A rough road follows the Calawah's N. Fork about 12 miles over Schutz Pass and then drops down to pick up the Sol Duc River near Sappho.

CLALLAM RIVER. A small brushy stream which enters Strait of Juan de Fuca at town of Clallam Bay. Hwy. 112 roughly parallels the river for the lower 5 miles. Holds winter steelhead and salmon runs, but is best known for sea-run cutthroat in the fall.

DICKEY RIVER. Noted for fall sea-run cutthroat fishing, the Dickey is a short run river of approximately 20 miles that heads in Dickey Lake and flows into the Quillayute River about 1 mile from the ocean at Mora. The Dickey produces fair winter steelhead fishing. Road from Quillayute extends to the forks, and a trail from that point leads up the W. Fork to Lake Dickey.

DUNGENESS RIVER. Once one of the best streams for April and May late-run winter steelhead, but diversion of water for irrigation waters has diminished runs. It also has runs of chinook and pink salmon. The Dungeness crosses Hwy. 101 about 1.5 miles W. of Sequim. Road up W. side runs about 5 miles to state fisheries' hatchery. The Happy Valley road touches the E. side of the river 1 mile below the hatchery. Lower stretches of the Dungeness, below Hwy. 101 often produce late in the winter steelhead season. Road from Hwy. 101 about 3 miles E. of Sequim leads about 8 miles to Dungeness Forks FS Campground where Graywolf River joins the Dungeness. Forest service road continues up the Dungeness from the forks for about 10 miles.

EDUCKET CREEK. Small tributary to Waatch River on the Makah Indian Reservation, joining that river one mile S. of village of Neah Bay. Has had winter steelhead plants in recent years. Indian fishing license required.

ELWHA RIVER. The Elwha heads high in Olympic National Park on the slopes of Mt. Olympus, draining a tremendous territory before entering the Strait of Juan de Fuca at Angeles Point, a few miles W. of Port Angeles. Two dams gag what was probably once the greatest migratory fish river on the Olympic Peninsula, restricting steelhead and salmon runs to a mere 4 miles between the Strait and Lake Aldwell's Dam. Planted winter steelhead furnish good fishing in winter, with summer steelhead plants furnishing fish throughout the rest of the year when river is open. Sea-run cutthroat are also taken in the lower 4 miles of river. Upper stretches of the Elwha (See Olympic Nat. Park) offer some top fly fishing in the state. Resort at Hwy. 101 bridge.

GRAYWOLF RIVER. A brawling mountain stream that enters the Dungeness River at the Dungeness Forks FS Campground. A trail follows the river up into the park. The Graywolf holds steelhead, Dolly Varden, rainbow, salmon and eastern brook, with July, August and September best.

HOKO RIVER. A small, rain-fed stream which heads on the N. side of the Dickey-Hoko summit. A road near Sekiu on Clallam Bay leads upstream 2 miles past Hoko Falls, then a rough road turns SW for another 2 miles. Sometimes the Hoko provides good early winter steelheading in December. It holds sea-run cutthroat in fall months, but is plagued by low water periods during dry, summer months.

LIZARD LAKE. A cutthroat pond of 2 acres located 6 miles S. of Sekiu.

LYRE RIVER. The outlet to Lake Crescent, (see Olympic Nat. Park) the Lyre is crossed by Hwy. 112, 4 miles W. of Joyce. It offers fair to excellent steelhead fishing in December and January, and is usually fishable when other streams in the area are out of shape. Fishermen's trails follow the river upstream from Hwy. 112, and the river is also crossed near the lake by the Piedmont road.

DICKEY RIVER, an under-fished tributary to Quillayute River.

MILL CREEK. Tributary to Bogachiel River, this 5-mile-long stream contains sea-run cutthroat and has received steelhead and rainbow plants. It joins the Bogy about 1.5 miles above point where the Calawah enters that river.

MORSE CREEK. A small stream which has received winter steelhead plants. Location is 2 miles E. of Port Angeles where it is crossed by Hwy. 101. Deer Park road roughly parallels the stream on the E., S. of Hwy. 101.

OZETTE LAKE. The third largest natural lake in the state, Ozette is 8.5 miles long and averages 2 miles in width, covering 7,787 acres. It is located 15 miles by crow flight S. of Neah Bay, and 21 miles by good road from the Sekiu-Neah Bay road. Ozette holds cutthroat, with fall months best for this species, plus steelhead, sockeye salmon and perch. South end of the big lake produces most of the large fish. Trolling gang trolls with worms or eggs is effective technique. Primary tributaries are Big River and Umbrella Creek. The lake drains, via Ozette River, into the Pacific Ocean, a distance of about 4 miles. Road ends at a camping area and store. Trails start at this point into Olympic National Park to remote ocean beaches including the 3.5 mile hike to Cape Alava, the most westerly point in the contiguous United States.

PLEASANT LAKE. (Tyee). This 486 acre lake holds rainbow and cutthroat in addition to salmon and steelhead, and drains into the Sol Duc River. Turn off Hwy. 101 about 5 miles W. of Sappho on well-marked road. Rough boat launch area.

PYSHT MILL POND. An eastern brook pond of 1 acre which drains into Deep Creek. Location is 4.5 miles S. of Pysht. Road up Jim Creek from Hwy. 112 leads near the pond.

PYSHT RIVER. A small stream noted primarily for fall cutthroat fishing, although it has been planted with winter steelhead and produces these fish in December and early January. Hwy. 112 parallels the river for approximately 5 miles from Pillar Point state recreation area at mouth to 112's junction with the Sappho cutoff road. One mile S. on Sappho road a rough road heads SW following the Pysht for about 2 miles to headwaters.

SOL DUC RIVER combines beauty with productive fishing.

QUILLAYUTE RIVER. The largest river on the ocean side of the Olympic Peninsula, the Quillayute is formed by Bogachiel, Calawah, Sol Duc and Dickey Rivers. It is just 4 miles long and enters the ocean at LaPush. Roads to LaPush and to Mora follow both sides of the river, although bank access is difficult. Much of the river flows through Indian land, and is netted extensively. The Quillayute carries large numbers of steelhead and salmon as well as sea-run cutthroat. Fish tend to gang at point where Bogachiel and Sol Duc come together during low water periods. There is a public boat launch site and resort at this spot. Boating is the best method of fishing the river.

SAIL RIVER. Winter steelhead planted river of about 5 miles in length that joins Strait of Juan De Fuca E. of Kiachopis Point on Makah Indian Reservation. Indian fishing license required.

SEKIU RIVER. A small stream which enters the Strait of Juan de Fuca about 5 miles W. of town of Sekiu. The coast highway, 112, crosses the river at its mouth where a rough campsite is located. Contains a run of winter steelhead plus salmon and provides good fall cutthroat fishing.

SOL DUC. One of the best migratory fish rivers on the coast, the Sol Duc holds win-ter and summer steelhead, silver and chinook salmon, cutthroat and Dolly Varden in upper reaches. Hwy. 101 follows and frequently crosses the river from 4 miles W. of Lake Crescent for approximately 25 miles to 2 miles N. of Forks. The road to LaPush touches the river in several places, and the Mora road crosses the Sol Duc at its mouth. Sol Duc Hot Springs road at W. boundary of Olympic National Park off Hwy. 101 parallels the river into the park. A road bearing S. for 5 miles up the hot springs road follows the Sol Duc's S. Fork about 7 miles to headwaters under Pine Mtn. The Sol Duc yields winter steelhead from December through April, with late summer and fall months best for summer steelhead, cutthroat and salmon. Stocked with both summer and winter steelhead.

SOOES RIVER. Rises below Wahburn Hill 10 miles S. of Neah Bay. Receives winter steelhead and salmon plants. National fish hatchery with trap two miles upstream from mid-Makah Bay where the river empties. Indian fishing license required.

SUEZ CREEK. Heading in the hills N. of Lake Ozette, most of the Suez's productive water is within the Makah Indian Reservation. Reached by road from Neah Bay through the reservation or by boat where it enters the ocean at Makah Bay. Primarily a sea-run cutthroat stream, with a few steelhead and salmon.

SUTHERLAND LAKE. Producer of some large cutthroat trout. Sutherland also furnishes good fishing for kokanee. Small salmon plugs are effective for the big cutts. The lake is 360 acres and is located 12 miles W. of Port Angeles along Hwy. 101. Spring and fall months are most productive fishing periods. Sutherland is thought to have once been a part of Lake Crescent until a slide blocked it. Public access.

TWIN RIVERS. East and West Twin Rivers cross coast Hwy. 112 within a short distance of one another at the point they enter the Strait of Juan de Fuca 23 miles W. of Port Angeles. They provide limited winter steelhead fishing in winter months, and are fair for sea-run cutthroat in the fall. Smelt spawn on the fine gravel beach between the two streams. There are rough campsites here. A road follows East Twin about two miles, then swings W. to follow West Twin to its headwaters below Deep Creek fire station.

UNDI LAKE. A 15 acre lake located 5 miles SE of Forks. It is stocked with cutthroat. Drainage is to Bogachiel River. Turn right at N. end of Hwy. 101 bridge over Bogachiel and follow road short distance to lake.

VILLAGE CREEK. Short run creek on Makah Indian Reservation that flows into Strait of Juan De Fuca at village of Neah Bay. Planted with winter steelhead. Indian fishing license required.

WAATCH RIVER. Short-run winter steelhead planted stream on Makah Indian Reservation. Joins Makah Bay at Waatch Point. Indian fishing license required.

WENTWORTH LAKE. A 53 acre lake located 7.7 miles NW of Forks and reached via the Dickey River road. Drainage is into W. Fork of the Dickey. Wentworth contains planted rainbow. It receives light fishing pressure.

CLALLAM COUNTY RESORTS

Aldwell Lake: Elwha Fishing and Hunting Resort, Rt. 3, Box 464, Port Angeles, WA 98362. 457-7011.

Crescent Lake: See Olympic National Park.

Lyre River: Lyre River Park, Port Angeles, WA 98362. 928-3436.

Quillayute River: Three Rivers Resort, Forks, WA 98331. 374-5300.

WAATCH RIVER near ocean on Makah Indian Reservation.

Clark

COUNTY

Best fishing in Clark County is provided by migratory fish. The 65 square miles county is bordered by the Columbia River on the E. and W., and by the Lewis River on the N. It ranks 34th in the state in terms of size. All but a few lakes in Clark lie below 500 feet. Highest point in the county is the 4000 foot Silver Star Mtn. In addition to the Columbia and Lewis Rivers, the Washougal furnishes varied and excellent year around salmon and steelhead fishing.

BACHELOR'S SLOUGH. An arm of the Columbia River at Ridgefield which creates Bachelor's Island when joined by Lake River. Primarily a largemouth bass show from May to October, although sea-run cutthroat and some chinook and silver salmon are also taken in the late summer and fall months. Reached by boat from Ridgefield down Lake River about 1 mile, then turning upstream into the slough which is about 3 miles in length.

BATTLEGROUND LAKE. This 28-acre lake is situated in an old crater and its deep waters contribute to extended periods of good fishing. Battleground is planted with

rainbow and eastern brook, and produces from April into June. It is located 20 miles NE of Vancouver then 3 miles E. on Hwy. 503. State park offers campsites and boat launch.

BIG TREE CREEK. A small stream which flows into the E. Fork Lewis River at Moulton about 14 miles upstream from Battleground. Reported to hold large cutthroat early in the season. Tough access.

BURNT BRIDGE CREEK. Tributary to Vancouver Lake, this small creek flows through northern portion of City of Vancouver. Marginal fishing, except for sea-run cutthroat in lower reaches.

CAMPBELL LAKE. A 247 acre lake containing a variety of spiny ray fish including largemouth bass, perch, crappie and catfish. The lake is situated between Lake River and the Columbia River 2.5 miles S. of Ridgefield on Ridgefield National Wildlife Refuge. Hike of about 2 miles required to reach lake. For route check with Ridgefield NWR office in community of Ridgefield, phone 360-887-4106.

CANYON CREEK. Provides rainbow and cutthroat fishing in May and June. FS road N56 bears E. at Chelatchie Prairie off Hwy.

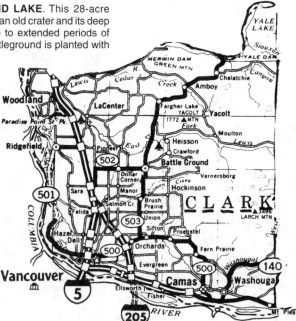

**Clark
County**

SALMON FISHING on the "Hog Line" below Bonneville Dam on Columbia River often is productive. (Clint Stockley Photo)

503 and follows the creek about 18 miles to point where Puny Creek joins Canyon Creek. There is an improved FS campsite approximately 10 miles from Chelatchie on Canyon Creek. During dry weather the upper reaches are sometimes closed to entry because of fire hazard. Canyon Creek enters the Lewis River N. Fork between Merwin and Yale Reservoirs. Rainbow have been planted.

CANVASBACK LAKE. Located on Batchelor Island 1 mile W. of Ridgefield, the 167 acre is host to yellow perch and brown bullhead. Drainage to Columbia River.

CARTY LAKE. A 42 acre lake adjacent to NW side of Ridgefield. It contains brown bullhead and yellow perch.

CEDAR CREEK. A small stream which joins the N. Fork Lewis River near Etna, 3 miles below lower end of Lake Merwin. Steelhead, jack salmon and cutthroat are taken at mouth of Cedar. Roads roughly parallel both sides of the creek which flows through community of Amboy. Sea-run cutthroat are also taken here. Cutts are best in fall months.

CHELATCHIE CREEK. A small, short-run creek fishable for approximately 4 miles from Chelatchie on Hwy. 503 to Amboy where it enters Cedar Creek. Rated fair in spring months for rainbow.

COPPER CREEK. Only 1 mile of Copper Creek is in Clark, with the rest in Skamania County. Reached by driving up the E. Fork Lewis River road to Sunset Falls on the county line. Bridge crosses the Lewis at this point, and FS road N412 swings S. upstream about 4 miles in Skamania County. May and June are best months for this stream's cutthroat. Fire closures sometimes restrict access. There is an improved FS campsite at Sunset Falls.

DEAD LAKE. Located 1 mile N. of Camas just W. of Hwy. 500, this 15 acre lake produces bass and other spiny rays. It lies 600 feet SW of Lacamas Lake. Drainage is into Washougal River via Lacamas Creek.

FARGHER POND A 3 acre lake containing planted brown trout. It is located 3.5 miles W. of Amboy, and adjacent to Fargher Lake, now dry. Drainage is into Rock Creek.

FIFTH PLAIN CREEK. Brown trout plants have made in this small stream which is reached by NE Ward Road out of Orchards. It drains to Lacamas Creek.

LACAMAS LAKE holds a variety of fish, has easy public access.

FLY CREEK. Drains into Canyon Creek above Chelatchie. Contains native cutthroat. Easily fished by following banks. Fly fishing is effective. Top fishing period is June, July and August.

GEE CREEK. Small stream heading E. of Ridgefield National Wildlife Refuge and entering refuge about 1 mile N. of refuge office in Ridgefield then flowing NW through a series of lakes to enter Columbia River. Fish species include largemouth bass, crappie, perch and catfish. Hiking is required to reach fishing water. Inquire at refuge headquarters in Ridgefield for map and refuge regulations.

GREEN LAKE. A 127 acre lake adjacent to E. side of Lake River at Knapp. Fish include perch and brown bullhead.

LACAMAS CREEK. The creek heads under Elkhorn Mtn., then meanders through farmland in lower reaches, flowing past community of Proebstel. May be reached by Orchards highway out of Vancouver or by Hwy. 500 out of Camas past Lacamas Lake which the stream feeds. Rated fair to good in May and June for planted brown trout, rainbow and some cutthroat. A sleeper portion of the creek is the short section that flows out of Lacamas lake (Round Lake) to drop down into the Washougal River.

LACAMAS LAKE. Formed by a dam on Lacamas Creek, this 315 acre lake produces good fishing for planted brown trout, and is productive in summer months for bass, perch, bluegills and planted channel catfish. There are also some cutthroat in the lake. The upper end of the lake is marshy and can provide top largemouth

bass fishing in September and October. Public boat launch site is located on the N. side on Leadbetter Road. Location is 1 mile N. of Camas adjacent to Hwy. 500. **ROUND LAKE** is connected to Lacamas by a narrow arm crossed by Hwy. 500 bridge. Round covers 32 acres and carries the same species of fish as does Lacamas. It is easily fished from shore in numerous spots.

LAKE RIVER. The outlet to Vancouver Lake, Lake River flows about 12 miles parallel to the Columbia River before joining that river at the lower end of Bachelor's Island. May be reached by highway out of Vancouver to Felida, about 8 miles, then W. 1 mile on Felida road to river, or from dock at town of Ridgefield at lower end of river. Lake River provides spiny ray fishing during much of the year, and also produces sea-run cutthroat and steelhead. **SALMON CREEK**, which is planted with winter steelhead, enters Lake River about 3 miles below Vancouver Lake. Boats are available at the Ridgefield town dock and at Felida Moorage. Private boats may be launched at Ridgefield, Felida or at Vancouver Lake.

LANCASTER LAKE. A 97 acre lake located on the NE border of Ridgefield NWR. Perch and brown bullhead present.

LEWIS RIVER. East Fork. One of the best migratory fish streams in SW Washington, the E. Fork holds substantial runs of both winter and summer steelhead (heavy plants of each) plus sea-run cutthroat and silver and chinook salmon. Winter steelheading is best from December through March at which time early summer or "springer" steelhead enter the river to provide sport into summer months. Late August into October is period for salmon and cutthroat fishing. The E. Fork is fairly accessible with a road roughly paralleling the river from the point Hwy. 5 crosses it near its mouth on through the town of LaCenter and upstream past Lucia, Horseshoe and Sunset Falls into the headwaters in Skamania County. (For N. Fork Lewis and Lakes Merwin and Yale see Cowlitz county).

LOST LAKE. Brown trout have been planted in Lost, a lake of 2 acres. Location is 7.5 miles NE from Yacolt and 2.5 miles E. from Tumtum Mountain. Drainage to Canyon Creek.

MUD LAKE. A spiny ray lake of 92 acres located on the Clark-Cowlitz County line 1 mile SW of Paradise Point state park. Fish species include largemouth bass and bluegills. Drainage to Lewis River.

POST OFFICE LAKE. A lake of 77 acres located on W. side of Lake River NW of Knapp. Fish include perch and brown bullhead. It drains to Columbia River.

ROCK CREEK. A small tributary to the Lewis River's E. Fork, joining that river about 1 mile upstream from Lewisville Park on the Lewis. Hwy. 503 NW of Heisson follows the creek for about 4 miles. Best fishing comes early in May and June for rainbow and some cutthroat.

ROUND LAKE. A variety of fish including black crappie, bluegill and channel catfish are found in this 16 acre lake. It is situated on W. side of Lake River SW of Knapp.

SALMON CREEK. A tributary to Lake River, Salmon Creek is crossed by Hwy. 5 about 4 miles N. of Vancouver. Lower reaches are slow, and produce a variety of spiny rays. The creek is planted with winter steelhead and provides steelheading in December and January, with cutthroat best in fall months.

SHANGHAI CREEK. Brown trout have been stocked in this stream. It is a tributary of Fifth Plain Creek. It is located N. of Robert L. Taylor Airport.

SIOUXON CREEK. Very tough access to this large creek which empties into the E.

WASHOUGAL RIVER provides migratory fish angling year-around.

side of Yale Lake at the head of a mile long inlet, 2 miles above Yale Dam. Road along E. shore of Yale crosses the inlet and rough fishermen's trails head up the creek. Private logging road to creek is often gated. Siouxon is not fished heavily and contains large rainbow and cutthroat.

VANCOUVER LAKE. A large lake 3 miles long and 2 miles wide covering 2858 acres, Vancouver is a top producer of a variety of spiny rays. It is easily accessible by highway, 3 miles NW of Vancouver and has a public fishing area. Paradise Point, 0.5 miles W. of Vancouver Junction, is a popular spot. Fish in the lake include largemouth bass, perch, crappie, and channel catfish. May, June and July are productive fishing periods, but anglers shouldn't neglect fall months. Drainage is into Columbia River via Lake River.

WASHOUGAL RIVER. One of the state's better migratory fish streams, the Washougal enters the Columbia River between Camas and Washougal. There is excellent shad fishing at the Washougal's mouth during all of June. The summer steelhead program is boosted by the hatchery on the Washougal's N. Fork, and plants of sunshine steelhead into the Washougal itself has developed this fishery. Winter steelhead are on tap from December through March, then the "springers" or early summer steelhead take over and are caught into fall months. Runs of silver salmon and some chinook salmon, along with jack salmon of both species, bolster fall fishing when permitted. There is a salmon hatchery on the upper river. An excellent road follows the Washougal for most of its length providing frequent and easy fishing access. **LITTLE WASHOUGAL** enters the main river from the W. about 4 miles from mouth. A road parallels the Little Washougal for much of its length. Some steelhead and trout fishing is available in the stream. **NORTH FORK OF WASHOUGAL** joins the Washougal river near the Clark-Skamania County line.

WIDGEON LAKE. Located on Batchelor Island 1 mile W. of Ridgefield, the 38 acre lake holds perch and brown bullhead. Drainage is to Columbia River.

WHIPPLE CREEK. Brown trout have been stocked in this Lake River tributary. The creek is crossed at Sara on NW 41st Ave., Vancouver.

Columbia
COUNTY

Fishing in Columbia County is primarily in small streams, with the exception of the Snake River, which forms its N. boundary. The county covers 862 square miles and rates 31st in size in the state. The 16 lakes listed for the county cover only 41 acres. Primary drainage for Columbia is into the Touchet River system and then into the Walla Walla River. The N. portion drains into the Snake via Tucannon River. Highest point in the county is 6401 feet at Oregon Butte SE of Dayton. The Blue Mountains occupy the S. part of Columbia.

BURNT FORK CREEK. The stream joins the S. Fork Touchet River at end of the S. Fork road. A trail takes off at this point and follows the stream to its headwaters under Griffin Mtn. S. Fork road is rough. The Touchet's S. Fork road is reached by driving E. on 4th street from Dayton, right across bridge at Signal Junction just E. of town.

BUTTE CREEK. Even though the creek is a tributary of Oregon's Wenaha River, all but 2 miles are in Washington. Upper reaches may be fished by taking trail from end of Godman Springs road at Teepee FS campground, and hiking about 4 miles down the E. Fork to junction with the main creek. Butte provides good rainbow fishing, but shouldn't be tried before July 4 because of snow. It is located in a highly scenic area.

CROOKED CREEK. Drainage is to Oregon's Wenaha River, but headwaters and most of the creek lie in Washington's Columbia and Garfield Counties. It is reached from Pomeroy via Pomeroy Grouse road (#40), or from Troy, Oregon, through Grouse Flat and past the abandoned Hunt school to end of road. Three Forks trail leads 3 miles to creek, where trails head both up and down stream. Trip best taken after July 4 because of snow conditions, with August, September and October best. Crooked Creek holds rainbow and eastern brook.

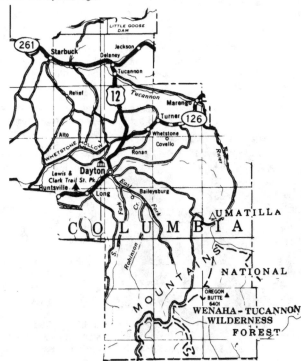

Columbia County

CUMMINGS CREEK. Enters Tucannon River from the E. about 10 miles up the Tucannon from Marengo where a side road (may be closed to vehicles) closely follows Cummings for 7 miles. The creek holds rainbow and some steelhead. It is rated best in May and June and gets 'bow plants. Best fishing is inside borders of the Wooten W.R.A.

DAM POND. Located just above Little Goose Dam off Snake River. Rainbow planted.

DAYTON JUVENILE POND. Small impoundment in town of Dayton. Receives annual rainbow plants.

GRIFFIN FORK. Tributary to Touchet river's S. Fork, reached by rough road up S. Fork of the Touchet which crosses the creek at its mouth. Trails lead upstream.

JIM CREEK. A small tributary of the E. Fork of the Touchet River, flowing into that river about 10 miles upstream from Dayton. A rough road leaves the E. Fork road at the Greiner Ranch and parallels the creek for approximately 4 miles. It is rated fair for rainbow during May and June.

LEWIS CREEK. Another E. Fork Touchet River tributary which enters the river 3 miles upstream from Jim Creek. The E. Fork road crosses the creek at its mouth and rough trails lead upstream. Lewis Creek may also be fished downstream by striking trail at Patrick Springs, 3 miles N. of Godman Springs FS campground. It is rated best in June, and carries rainbow and a few eastern brook.

ORCHARD POND. Small Snake River impoundment near Lyons Marina. Rainbow planted.

PATIT CREEK. The small creek flows into Touchet River at town of Dayton. A good road follows the creek for about 8 miles upstream, and another road continues up the N. Fork. Patit is so low during summer months that it offers marginal angling.

RAINBOW CREEK. A tributary of Butte Creek's W. Fork, Rainbow contains rainbow and delivers best fishing from June on. It is reached by a trail of 3 miles which leaves Godman guard station and heads down SW slope of Godman Peak. Low stream flows in late summer.

TYPICAL SNAKE River smallmouth bass displayed here by Dave Keech.

ROBINSON CREEK. This stream joins Wolf Creek near Mountain Home Camp, and then flows into the E. Fork of the Touchet River 5 miles SE of Dayton. A road from the mouth leads upstream 3 miles, then splits, with right fork continuing up Robinson Creek 2.5 miles. The other fork parallels **WOLF CREEK** for 6 miles to road end, and a trail continues up Wolf.

SNAKE RIVER. Good steelhead fishing is available in the Snake, a major year-around fish producer. Substantial plants of steelhead. Favored steelheading spots in Columbia County include the mouth of the Tucannon River. Choke Cherry Canyon (2 miles upstream on Little Goose Dam access road), and Lyons Ferry area. The Snake also offers smallmouth bass fishing during early spring and from July 1 to October 31. Some of the better Columbia County smallmouth areas include Lyons Ferry, mouth of Tucannon River, and sloughs and coves above Little Goose Dam. Riparia area just below Little Goose Dam is good also. Channel catfish are available in the Snake. They are most cooperative during early spring and again from July into October, and are found in the same areas as smallmouth bass and steelhead. Boat fishing is the best method of reaching the Snake's fish because of difficult access. The Snake forms the N.

county boundary between Columbia and Whitman Counties. Boat launching sites are located at Lyons Ferry and at mouth of Tucannon River. Sloughs and backwaters of the Snake provide excellent spiny ray fishing and are good for channel catfish in late summer. Sturgeon are taken throughout the year. Boat ramps, campsites and picnic areas are located near dams.

TOUCHET RIVER. The main river extends about 2 miles SE of Dayton in Columbia County where the S. and the N. Forks come together. The main stem continues into Walla Walla County where it joins the Walla Walla River near town of Touchet. Both forks are stocked with rainbow and Wolf Creek, a major tributary of the N. Fork, is also planted. The stream contains German browns, whitefish, summer steelhead and a few eastern brook in addition to the 'bows. Prime fishing time is from June on. There is beautiful, scenic territory along both forks with roads paralleling both streams to their upper reaches.

TUCANNON LAKES. Eight artificial lakes located on the Wooten W.R.A., 10 miles S. of Pomeroy along the Tucannon River, which are stocked with rainbow. The lakes include **SPRING, BLUE, RAINBOW, DEER, WATSON, BEAVER, BIG FOUR** and **CURL.** The lakes provide some of the best fishing in Columbia County during early season, but fishing pressure is heavy. They have public access areas. Spring Lake has been planted with eastern brook.

TUCANNON RIVER. A small river heading in the Blue Mtns. and flowing a total of 50 miles N. to town of Marengo then W. to enter the Snake River 5 miles below the town of Starbuck. Best fishing is in the section of river within the Wooten W.R.A. about 10 miles S. of Pomeroy, as heavy plants of rainbow are made here. Besides these trout, the Tucannon holds eastern brook, whitefish and planted summer steelhead, plus chinook salmon. A good road follows the Tucannon from the NW border of Columbia County for approximately 28 miles, with trail taking off from road end. Tucannon Campground is located at mouth of Hixon Canyon, about 17 miles S. of Marengo. The Tucannon is usually in fishable shape from June on. There is a little known fishery for rainbow to 5 pounds from Marengo downstream. The larger fish are very wary, but fly fishermen take them, particularly in fall months. Tucannon has received plants of steelhead in past few years.

WHITNEY CREEK. A tributary of Wolf Creek, Whitney enters that stream from the E. about 2 miles from the end of the Wolf Creek road. Planted rainbow are taken in lower stretches. There is a trail following the creek upstream for about 3 miles.

SPRING LAKE, one of eight lakes in the Tucannon Lakes chain on the Wooten WRA.

Cowlitz

COUNTY

Migratory fish are the mainstay of Cowlitz County's fishing. It is drained by the lower Cowlitz River plus the Toutle, Coweeman, Kalama and Lewis. All of these streams provide excellent steelhead fishing, with the exception of the Toutle which is recovering from the Mt. St. Helens' eruption, with salmon also available. Cowlitz County covers 1171 square miles. It ranks 28th in the state as to size, and the highest spot is Goat Mountain at 4965 feet.

ABERNATHY CREEK. Late summer and fall is best period for this small stream's planted sea-run cutthroat. Abernathy Creek enters the Columbia River 12 miles W. of Longview at Abernathy Point, with Hwy. 4 crossing the creek near its mouth. The Abernathy Creek road follows the stream for about 7 miles. Mouth of the creek as well as lower reaches are popular steelhead spots. Abernathy gets occasional winter steelhead plants. Boat launch ramp at mouth.

ALDER CREEK. Enters the N. Fork of the Toutle River approximately 22 miles E. of Castle Rock on Hwy. 504. Park at mouth of stream. A dirt road parallels the stream for about 3 miles, then trails continue upstream.

ARKANSAS CREEK. A meandering stream which joins the Cowlitz River from the W. opposite town of Castle Rock. Hwy. 411 crosses the creek 0.4 miles above its mouth, and county roads roughly follow Arkansas Creek and the N. Fork up Arkansas Valley. Early season fishing for rainbow is fair, with sea-run cutthroat fishing best from September on. Bass are available at mouth of the creek. Tributaries to Arkansas Creek include **DELA**, **METER** and **MONOHAN**. They offer fair early season rainbow fishing and some cutthroating later in year.

BLUE LAKE. An 8 acre cutthroat lake. FS Road 81 takes off near Cougar past Merrill Lake, then route is N. on FS Road 8123 approximately 2 miles to trailhead parking lot. Hike of .04 miles to lake.

CARLISLE LAKE. A rainbow planted lake of 20.3 acres located at Onalaska. Drainage is to S. Fork Newaukum River.

CASTLE CREEK. Heading in Skamania County, Castle Creek joins the Toutle's N. Fork about 7 miles below Spirit Lake. Weyerhaeuser logging road 3500 crosses the creek at its mouth, and a rough road follows Castle up W. side for 2 miles. A cut-

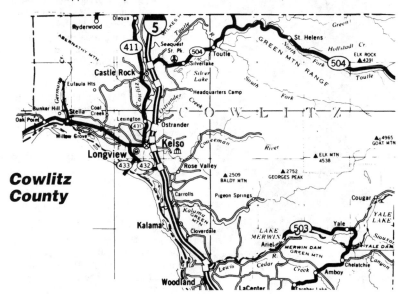

Cowlitz County

throat creek, Castle is brushy and snow-fed.

CASTLE LAKE. A 200 acre lake created by the 1980 Mt. St. Helens eruption and subsequent mudflow of debris down Toutle River Valley. Although the lake was not stocked it provides good fishing for rainbow. Access is via Weyerhaeuser Road 3000, then walking two miles down gated road. Area N. of lake closed to all entry.

COAL CREEK. A tributary to Coal Creek Slough which is crossed at its mouth by Hwy. 4 about 7 miles NW of Longview. Road parallels stream for about 4 miles. Coal Creek provides fair fly fishing for cutthroat early, and for sea-run cutthroat late in season. Receives winter steelhead plants. Boat launch at mouth at county dump.

COAL CREEK SLOUGHS. Hwy. 4 W. from Longview follows and crosses a network of Columbia River sloughs including Coal Creek Slough and others. There is a boat launch site at garbage dump where Coal Creek enters the slough. Early spring months as a rule are productive for crappie, perch and catfish. March and April are best for largemouth bass. In late May and early June spring freshets in the Columbia

RICH HORSFALL collected this steelhead from the Cowlitz River where it joins the Columbia River.

River back up water and flood these and other sloughs adjacent to the river.

COLDWATER CREEK. Drains into the N. Fork Toutle on Hwy. 504 about 42 miles E. of Castle Rock. Inlet and outlet of Coldwater Lake.

COLDWATER LAKE. Eruption of Mt. St. Helens May 18, 1980, blocked the S. Fork Coldwater Creek and created an 800 acre, clear water lake. Very limited bank access. New Hwy. 504 from Toutle leads to Coldwater Lake Visitor's Center near lake where information re: fishing and access is available. Parking area and boat launch (no gas motors) at lake which is planted with rainbow. Average length of fish in 1993 was 15.5 inches.

COLUMBIA RIVER BARS. Most popular fishing bars along the Columbia in Cowlitz County include Kalama, Woodland, Willow Grove, Johnson's Beach and the County Line Bar on the Cowlitz-Wahkiakum line. During summer months bar fishermen catch steelhead headed for upper Columbia tributaries, and also tap winter and spring steelhead, along with salmon. Cutthroat hit from August into October, while salmon fishing for chinook and silvers, plus jack salmon of both species, is productive from late summer through the fall. May is also a good jack month.

COUGAR CREEK. A short-run stream which empties into Yale Reservoir .04 miles E. of community of Cougar from the N. Rated just fair for small rainbow and cutthroat. Fished by trail along lower reaches from Yale Reservoir road. Cougar is a major spawning stream for Yale's kokanee. Campground near mouth.

COWEEMAN LAKE. A cutthroat lake situated at 2750 feet at head of Cowlitz River. It's 21.5 miles E. from Kelso and .05 miles N. from Elk Mtn. Lookout.

COWEEMAN RIVER. An excellent migratory fish river which joins the Cowlitz River just above that river's entry into the Columbia. Sustained plants of winter steelhead have built the Coweeman's winter steelhead production. Fine sea-run cutthroat fishing from August into late fall. Upper stretches of the river offer cutthroat fishing in May and June. Bottom portion of river above Hwy. 5 reached via road at end of Allen Street E. for about 4 miles on N.

SPRING CHINOOK from the Cowlitz River taken by Jerry P.L. Haupt.

side of river. The Rose Valley road which heads E. from Hwy. 5 about 4 miles S. of Kelso picks up Coweeman on the S. side and follows it for 13 miles. Major tributaries include Gobie, Mulholland, Baird and Skipper Creeks. A road follows the main Gobel Creek and the N. Fork for about 2.5 miles. This creek holds both rainbow and cutthroat, with the other Coweeman River tributaries primarily cutthroat streams.

COWLITZ RIVER. The largest tributary to the Lower Columbia River, the Cowlitz produces fish every month of the year. It is paralleled by Hwy. 5 on its E. bank and by Hwy. 411 along the W. side for most of its length in Cowlitz County. Bank fishing is done on both sides with the Olequa area on the W. side near the Cowlitz-Lewis County line 1 mile SE of Vader and the mouth of the river 3 miles S. of Longview favored spots, along with the mouth of the Toutle River. Much fishing is done from anchored boats in the big river, and trolling is popular. The river holds fine runs of winter steelhead which start in November and continue into April. There are spring chinook in the Cowlitz, along with fall chinook and silvers and jack salmon of both species. A highly popular sport is smelt dipping in spring months in the Kelso area when the temperamental fish decide to ascend the Cowlitz. Cutthroat fishing is good from July into November, about the same period for fall salmon. Tacoma dams at Mayfield and Mossyrock gag the middle portion of the Cowlitz. Boats may be launched at county park at Lexington 3 miles N. of Kelso on E. side highway and also at Castle Rock Fairgrounds. There are boat launch sites at the F&G Dept. fish hatchery and at the salmon hatchery. Hatcheries built below Mayfield help migratory fish runs. The river is planted with both winter and summer steelhead and cutthroat.

DEER CREEK. A small stream which joins the Toutle's N. Fork from the S. side about 27 miles E. of Castle Rock on Hwy. 504. Tough to reach, since highway runs along N. side of Toutle at this point, and only game trails along creek. Rated fair for cutthroat in fall months. Campsites downstream on S. side 3 to 4 miles at Hoffstadt Creek Park.

ELK CREEK. Enters Kalama River from the N. To reach the creek drive up Kalama River road to Pigeon Springs (about 16 miles) then continue on logging road 6000, when gates are open, about 8 miles where road crosses Elk Creek. Work upstream from here or drive another 1.5 miles to strike Elk Creek at higher point. Rated fair to good for rainbow and cutthroat.

FAWN LAKE. A 23 acre lake located at 3700 feet elevation at the headwaters of Shultz Creek, a tributary of Green River. Closest route is to turn N. up Coldwater Creek road off the Spirit Lake highway about 7 miles below Spirit Lake. The rough road bears N. crossing a branch of Maratta Creek, and continues approximately 3.5 miles to end. Fawn Lake lies 1 mile NE from this point. It contains both eastern brook and cutthroat. Campsites on Lake Hanaford and Elk Lakes in Skamania County are located 2 miles NE of Fawn.

GERMANY CREEK. Flows into the Columbia River at point Hwy. 4 crosses its mouth 11 miles W. of Longview. A road parallels the creek upstream N. for about 6 miles. Lower mile of Germany Creek produces some steelhead during winter season, and fall months are productive for sea-run cutthroat. The creek gets plants of winter steelhead and sea-run cutthroat.

GOBAR CREEK. Take Kalama River road on N. side 13 miles to Pigeon Springs. The creek enters Kalama River from the N. .05 miles above this point. A road follows Gobar Creek 4 to 5 miles upstream. Gobar has been termed a "picture stream" to fish, and produces rainbow and cutthroat along with summer steelhead, with May and June the best months. It comes on again in the fall.

GREEN RIVER. A large tributary of the Toutle's N. Fork which requires considerable work to fish, since few roads come close to it. It joins the N. fork on the N. side 20 miles from Castle Rock on Hwy. 504 at Maple Flat. Railroad bridge crosses the Toutle near mouth of the Green. Follow rough trail on S. side of Green River. Weyerhaeuser road 2500 extends to near junction on Miner's Creek with the Green.

HOFFSTADT CREEK. Enters N. Fork of Toutle River on N. side at community of St. Helens on Hwy. 504 about 24 miles from Castle Rock. **BEAR CREEK**, a tributary to Hoffstadt, is paralleled by a road.

HORSESHOE LAKE. This 79 acre lake lies in an old river channel of the N. Fork Lewis. It is planted with rainbow and brown trout and provides good fishing in April, May and early June. There are largemouth bass, yellow perch, brown bullhead and yellow bullhead present. It is adjacent to the S. city limits of Woodland. Boat launch site at park on lake.

HATCHERY CREEK. A Kalama River tributary joining that river at lower Kalama hatchery. Receives plants of winter steelhead.

KALAMA RIVER. A top producing migratory fish stream that delivers both winter and summer steelhead, which are planted, along with sea-run cutthroat. The Kalama enters the Columbia River a short distance N. of the town of Kalama. There is a public access and boat launch site at its mouth and at S. side of Modrow bridge. A good road parallels the river's N. side past Pigeon Springs. Summer steelies take a fly in this river, with July and August best. It may be fished from bank at numerous spots adjacent to road. Many fishermen boat the river. The river is spring fed. Trail No. 238 starts from trailhead at Kalama Horse Camp 8 miles N. of Cougar on FS Road 81. and follows the river upstream to the outlet of McBride Lake. Main tributaries include **LITTLE KALAMA, GOBAR** and **ELK CREEKS.** They furnish limited fishing during June and July.

KNOWLTON CREEK. A winter steelhead stream that joins Kalama River from the S. below Pigeon Springs.

KRESS LAKE. Brown trout, channel catfish, black crappie, bluegill warmouth, punkinseed, yellow perch and rainbow are present in Kress. Location is .04 miles N. of Kalama River road and .03 miles E. of Hwy 5.

LAKEVIEW PEAK LAKE. A 3 acre cutthroat planted lake 10.5 miles E. of Pigeon Springs on E. side of Lakeview Peak. Drainage to Kalama River.

LEWIS RIVER. (East Fork). See Clark County.

LEWIS RIVER. (North Fork). This river forms the boundary between Cowlitz and Clark Counties. It is followed by Hwy. 503 upstream 38 miles to the Cowlitz-Skamania County line at the E. end of Yale Reservoir. FS Road 90 continues along N. shore of Swift Reservoir and about 40 more miles up the N. Fork into Skamania County. There are three large reservoirs along the Lewis River's N. Fork—Merwin and Yale in Cowlitz County and Swift in Skamania County. Up to the base of Merwin Dam, which impounds Merwin, 10 miles upstream from Woodland, the N. Fork Lewis carries a variety of migratory fish. Winter steelhead enter the river from December into April when summer steelhead start to provide action. Large plants of both winter and summer steelhead are made. Spring chinook are taken from April into June, and sea-run cutthroat and fall chinook and silver salmon are caught from August into November. There is a boat launch site at end of Wyman road and at salmon hatchery on N. side of river.

McBRIDE'S LAKE. (Snowshoe Lake). Located 6 miles NE of Lake Merrill at 2700 feet adjacent to FS Road 81 which continues N. and E. past that lake. The 9 acre lake contains eastern brook and cutthroat.

MERRILL LAKE. (Trout). Lake is reached by leaving Hwy. 503 .07 miles W. of Cougar and driving up FS Road 81, 3 miles to the lake. The 344 acre lake lies at 1541 feet, and holds rainbow, browns, cutthroat and eastern brook. It drains N. into the Kalama River. D.N.R. boat launch and campsites.

MERWIN RESERVOIR. This 4089 acre Lewis River impoundment is located 10 miles E. of Woodland on Hwy. 503. Its depth, maximum 190 feet, aids in main-

LAKE MERWIN, an impoundment on Lewis River.

taining good to excellent fishing throughout the season. Merwin contains husky rainbow, yellow perch, juvenile coho salmon and tiger muskies. It also hosts cutthroat. The reservoir produces best in late summer and fall months. There is a boat launch site and boat dock at the park at Speelyai Bay near the E. end of the 12 mile long reservoir. County park boat launch. Resort facilities on N. shore about 5 miles above the dam.

MILL CREEK. Enters Columbia River 12 miles west of Longview near point where it is crossed by Hwy. 4. Holds both rainbow and cutthroat. In fall months Mill Creek delivers sea-run cutthroat. A road takes off upstream just W. of the creek's mouth and follows the stream for about 2 miles. Sea-run cutthroat are planted.

OSTRANDER CREEK. A small stream tributary to the Cowlitz River which crosses Hwy. 5 near community of Ostrander. Produces 'bows early in the year, and comes on for sea-run cutthroat in the fall. Paralleled for .05 miles by a road heading NE from top of hill in Ostrander.

SACAJAWEA LAKE. Situated in the City of Longview, this 48 acre lake receives plants of legal 'bows each year. It also contains brown trout, channel catfish and spiny rays. Drainage is to Columbia River.

SILVER LAKE. This large—2000 acre— shallow lake provides the best spiny ray fishing in Western Washington. Reached via Hwy. 504 about 6 miles E. of Castle Rock, Silver contains largemouth bass, crappie, perch, bluegills, catfish plus planted rainbow and cutthroat trout. During spring and early summer months bass are found close to the weedy shore lines, but they tend to move to deep water in the center of the lake later in the season. Perch are available most any time. May through July are prime crappie fishing periods, with June, July and August best for catfish. Trout are taken from Silver despite the spiny ray competition. There is a public boat launch site on the lake's N. shore, and rental boats, cabins and other facilities are available at resorts on the lake. Seaquest State Park is located near the NW end of Silver Lake.

SPIRIT LAKE. Post-Mt. St. Helens eruption

size of Spirit is 2500 acres, twice the original size. Thought to be barren after the blast, an 8 inch rainbow was netted in 1994. The lake is not presently being stocked, but is being studied to gauge its natural recovery.

TOUTLE RIVER. (Main). Formerly one of the state's best winter steelhead streams, the Toutle responded well to plants of summer steelhead. It was a top sea-run cutthroat and silver salmon stream and carried a big run of fall chinook prior to the eruption of Mt. St. Helens. The N. Fork Toutle's source is Spirit Lake. It is not known when the Toutle River will regain its former fish productivity, but it is showing encouraging signs of coming back. The Toutle crosses Hwy. 5 about 2 miles N. of Castle Rock and joins Cowlitz River within a short distance. There is good fishing at the mouth in the Cowlitz. Access is difficult along lower reaches, but a road branches N. from Hwy. 504 about 3 miles E. of Hwy. 5 to cross the Toutle on the Tower Bridge and continues upstream about 5 miles and dead-ends. The rough Burma Road leads upstream on N. side of river at Hwy. bridge. Hwy. 504 continues past Silver Lake to cross the Toutle at the Coalbank Bridge then continues up the N. Fork Toutle.

YALE RESERVOIR. Located 20 miles E. of Woodland on Hwy. 503, Yale is 8 miles long and covers 3801 acres, 2022 of which are in Clark County. The big reservoir was created by an earth dam on the Lewis River. Yale is cold and deep—up to 190 feet—and is a producer of large trout. Rainbow and kokanees are most plentiful, but there are also Dolly Varden and cutthroat present. Although a slow starter because of its cold water, Yale comes on strong in mid-summer and fall months. There are boat ramps at Saddle Dam, Yale and Beaver Bay. The Cougar Creek forest camp offers camping facilities.

COWLITZ COUNTY RESORTS

Cowlitz River: Barrier Dam Campground Salkum, WA 98582. 360-1985-2495.

Kalama River: Camp Kalama, Kalama WA 98625. 360-1673-2456.

Silver Lake: Anderson's Resort, 360-1274-6141. Streeter's Resort, 360-1274-6112. Silver lake Store and Resort, 360-1274-6201. All Silver Lake, WA 98645.

Check trail conditions

Because it is impossible to predict trail, snow and ice conditions, fishermen who plan high lake and stream trips should contact district offices of the US Forest and Park Service for information on waters located within forest and park boundaries. Also check for fire permit information and any special restrictions.

National Forests

MT BAKER—SNOQUALMIE. 21905-64th Ave. W., Mountlake Terrace, WA 98043. 206-775-9702.

GIFFORD PINCHOT. 6926 E. Fourth Plain Blvd., Vancouver, WA 98668. 360-750-5000.

OKANOGAN. 1240-2nd Ave. S., Okanogan, Wa. 98840. 509-826-3275.

OLYMPIC. 1835 Black Lake Blvd. SW, Olympia, WA 98502. 360-956-2400.

WENATCHEE. 301 Yakima St., Wenatchee, Wa. 98801. 509-662-4335.

COLVILLE. Federal Bldg., 765 S. Main St., Colville, Wa. 99114. 509-684-3711.

KANIKSU. Priest Lake Ranger Station, HCR 5, Box 207, Priest River, ID. 208-443-2512.

UMATILLA. 2517 SW Hailey Ave., Pendleton, Or. 97801. 503-276-3811.

National Parks

REGIONAL HEADQUARTERS. 909 First Ave., Seattle, WA 98104. 206-220-7450.

OLYMPIC. 600 E. Park Ave., Port Angeles, Wa. 98362. 360-452-9235.

MT. RAINIER. Tahoma Woods, Star Rt., Ashford, Wa. 98304. 360-569-2211.

NORTH CASCADES. North Cascades Complex, 2105 Hwy. 20, Sedro Woolley, Wa. 98284. 360-856-5700.

Phone 206/220-7450 for information on both National Forests and National Parks in Washington.

Douglas

COUNTY

Although 18th in size among the state's counties with 1862 square miles of area, Douglas County does not offer much fishing. Jameson Lake is an outstanding exception, however, furnishing excellent rainbow fishing in the spring and fall. The semi-arid county is bounded by the Columbia river on the W. Highest spot in the county, at 4244 feet, is located SW of Waterville. Douglas is drained by Foster Creek N. to the Columbia River, and Rock Island, McCartney and Douglas Creeks drain the S. portion, also to the Columbia.

DOUGLAS CREEK. A small stream which heads above the town of Douglas and meanders about 15 miles SE to Moses Coulee, then SW about 13 miles to join the Columbia River near the Chelan-Kittitas County line. The creek provides limited rainbow fishing, with best period from May to July. A road parallels Douglas down Moses Coulee. Another road follows the creek downstream from town of Douglas about 5 miles.

FOSTER CREEK. Located in N. Douglas County, Foster enters the Columbia River just below Chief Joseph Dam at Bridgeport. Hwy. 17 follows the creek 2 miles S. from Bridgeport, then swings E. to parallel Foster Creek's E. Fork to Leahy. A road heads S. up the W. Fork of Foster for about 10 miles to the headwaters. The stream holds eastern brook and brown trout and is rated best during June.

GRIMES LAKE. Located 8 miles SE of Mansfield, about 2 miles S. of Jameson Lake. The 150 acre lake is stocked with Lahontan cutthroat which adapt to alkaline

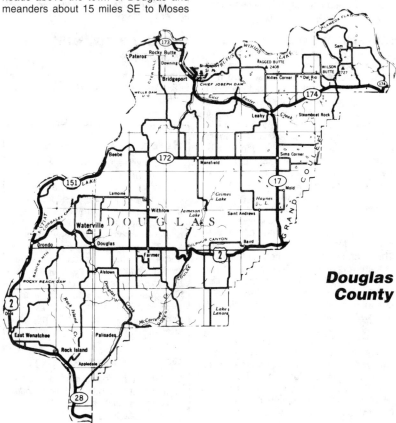

Douglas County

JAMESON LAKE public access on south end of lake.

waters. Light boats may be launched from shore.

JAMESON LAKE. One of the top rainbow lakes in the state, Jameson covers over 500 acres and is located near the head of Moses Coulee. It is heavily stocked with rainbow, and the lake's rich waters result in rapid growth. It is usually managed on a split season basis, opening in the spring and early summer, closed during the "bloom" of mid summer, and opened again early in the fall. Best fishing at Jameson is during April and May, and again in October. Foot-long trout are common, and 'bows of 3 to 5 pounds are not uncommon. There are resorts at both N. and S. end of the lake, and a public boat launch site at the S. end which is reached by leaving Hwy. 2 about 10 miles E. of Farmer and traveling N. up Moses Coulee 6 miles to lake. The N. end resort is reached via the town of Mansfield on Hwy. 172. Follow road out of Mansfield due S. 5.5 miles, then turn E. and S. about 4 miles to lake shore. Some Lahontan cutthroat present as a result of high water from Grimes Lake.

Several small Douglas County lakes and ponds adjacent to Rock Island Dam have been stocked with rainbow and largemouth bass. They include Pumphouse Pond and four Rock Island Ponds. Rufus Woods Lake, the 7800 acre impoundment behind Chief Joseph Dam which lies between Douglas and Okanogan Counties, had had eastern brook plants.

DOUGLAS COUNTY RESORTS

Jameson Lake: Jameson Lake Resort, 509-683-1141. Jack's Resort, 509-683-1095.

Before leaving home

Leave a schedule with a responsible person as to your exact fishing or hunting area; companions, along with color, model, license, and location of the car used; equipment carried, and return time (allowing extra time for possible problems you may encounter). The mentally prepared family at home will worry less about your being a little late if you carry and know how to use emergency overnight survival gear. You may be traveling alone, away from civilization, on foot. Be prepared for the worst the elements may offer.

Did you know?

Of all the trout species, the brown is the heartiest. It can withstand more pollution than any of its cousins.

FERRY

COUNTY

Lakes provide most of the fishing opportunities in Ferry County. The county covers 2259 square miles and is the 9th largest in the state. It is drained by the Kettle, San Poil and Columbia Rivers. Highest point in Ferry is at Cooper Butte, 7135 feet. The majority of lakes in the county are situated above 2500 feet elevation.

BARNABY CREEK. A producer of small eastern brook and rainbow, Barnaby is best in spring months. It heads under White Mtn. and flows into FDR lake across from Rice in Stevens County. Road N. from Inchelium up W. shore of Roosevelt Lake leads 10 miles to point the creek enters the lake. Lake Ellen road then heads E. and N. to follow creek 3 miles.

BOULDER CREEK. A tributary of the Kettle River, entering that stream approximately 10 miles upstream from its mouth. Boulder yields small eastern brook. A road leads W. from Hwy. 395 about 2 miles, then splits with roads paralleling both the N. and S. forks. There is an improved FS campground on the road near the headwaters of the N. Fork.

BOURGEA LAKE. Rainbow inhabit this 21.9 acre lake situated 4.6 miles S. from Inchelium. It drains to FDR Lake. It is reached by Twin Lakes Road, then Silver Creek and Covada Roads.

CADY LAKE. (Cody). Six acres in size, Cady is situated on the Colville Indian reservation 22 miles S. of Republic. It has been planted with eastern brook in past years.

CURLEW LAKE. This 869 acre lake receives plants of rainbow and eastern brook. It provides good fishing the entire season. Curlew is rich and trout gain weight rapidly. Largemouth bass are present. There are resort facilities and a public access on the lake. Hwy. 21 leads N. from Republic to and along the E. shore.

DAVIS LAKE. A cutthroat lake, Davis cov-

ers 17 acres and is located NW of Boyds on the E. flank of Thompson Ridge. Lake is accessible by a road which leaves Hwy. 395 at Boyds. The lake has a campground and is a fair producer all season.

DEADMAN CREEK. This Kettle River tributary carries small eastern brook and rainbow. It is easily fished as a road leaves Hwy. 395 just S. of Boyds and heads W. up the stream for over 15 miles.

ELBOW LAKE. A hook-shaped eastern brook lake of 51.2 acres located 13.5 miles N. from Inchelium on Elbow Lake road. Fed by Onion Creek, it drains to FDR Lake.

ELLEN LAKE. Ellen is planted with rainbow, and usually holds up throughout the

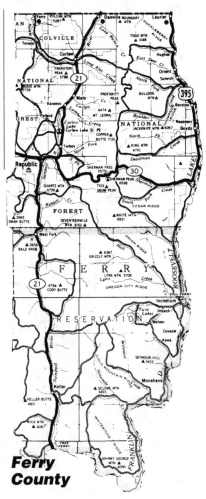

Ferry County

season. It covers 77 acres and is located 14 miles N. of Inchelium at an elevation of 2300 feet. There is an improved FS campground on E. end of lake. Ellen is reached by road up Barnaby Creek from Hwy. 395.

EMERALD LAKES. Pair of small lakes in Hoodoo Canyon about 22 miles E. from Republic and 4200 feet SE from Lily Lake. Planted with eastern brook.

EMPIRE LAKES. Three small lakes of 4, .06 and 1.5 acres at 3600 feet ll miles N. from Republic. They have been planted with eastern brook. Drainage is to Curlew Lake. North Empire Creek road from Hwy. 21 leads about 7 miles to lake.

FERRY LAKE. A rainbow producer which is planted regularly, Ferry offers good fishing through the season when it does not winterkill. It is located at 3329 feet elevation and covers 34 acres. Drainage is via Scatter Creek to the San Poil River. Ferry is reached by driving S. from Republic 9 miles on Hwy. 21, then W. up Scatter Creek about 7 miles to the lake.

FISH LAKE. A lake of 4 acres which lies at 3300 feet elevation 1 mile S. of Ferry Lake by road. Planted rainbow are available.

FROSTY MEADOW CREEK. Located on the Colville Indian reservation, the creek produces small eastern brook.

KETTLE RIVER. A large river which enters Ferry County from B.C. at town of Ferry, flows SE to Curlew, and then swings N. into B.C. again at Danville before re-entering the U.S. once more at Laurier. The river forms the E. boundary of Ferry County and is paralleled by Hwy. 395 to its mouth at FDR Lake near Kettle Falls. Fall is the best fishing time for the river's rainbow, while whitefish are taken in February. Some brown trout in lower river.

LA FLEUR LAKE. Located on the Colville Indian reservation 9 miles N. of Inchelium at 2250 elevation, La Fleur is 24 acres. It has been planted in past years with eastern brook and rainbow. **SIMPSON LAKES**, lakes of 21.9 and 9.6 acres at 2250 feet which lie just S. and E. of La Fleur, contain eastern brook.

LAMBERT CREEK. Entering Curlew Creek at Karamin a short distance above Curlew Lake, Lambert produces small eastern brook and rainbow throughout the season.

LONG LAKE. A 24 acre, narrow lake situated at 3250 feet elevation 11 miles S. of Republic. Route is S. from Republic 9 miles on Hwy. 21, then W. up Scatter Creek 7 miles to lake shore. Good late fall cutthroat fishing.

LONG ALEC CREEK. Joins the Kettle River at Curlew. A road follows the stream

SAN POIL RIVER holds both rainbow and eastern brook.

for several miles from the town. Contains small eastern brook and rainbow.

LYNX CREEK. The stream enters FDR Lake 1 mile N. of Inchelium. A road from that town follows the creek N. and W. about 5 miles to Seylor Valley where Hall and Spring Creeks join Lynx. The road continues 2 miles W. up Lynx. It is considered a fair bet for small eastern brook.

MUD LAKE. A shallow lake located about 1.5 miles NW of Republic. It varies in size and winter kills.

RENNER LAKE. A "deep" lake of 9.6 acres located I.8 miles W. from Barstow. Receives plants of brown trout and eastern brook. Drains to Kettle River. Reached via Hodson-Price and Lakin roads S. from Hwy. 395. Elevation is 2525 feet.

ROUND LAKE. An eastern brook lake of 52.1 acres which lies at 2275 feet on the N. side of Moon Mtn. about 5.5 miles W. of Inchelium. Round is on the Colville Indian reservation and is reached by taking the Cornstalk Creek road from Inchelium through Impach.

SAN POIL RIVER. Containing rainbow and eastern brook, the San Poil produces all season although spring and fall are best. The lower river is on Colville Indian land and is paralleled by Hwy. 21 most of its length from Republic about 58 miles to its junction with the Columbia. Wadeable during low water periods at riffles, the San Poil has numerous log jams which create deep pools and cover for trout of 3 pounds or more, although most are 6 to 10 inches. The W. Fork, which joins the main river from the W. about 16 miles S. of Republic, is a good producer during spring and summer.

SHERMAN CREEK. A rainbow stream and kokanee planted stream which produces small fish throughout much of the season. The creek enters FDR Lake on the Columbia River 9 miles S. of the Kettle Falls bridge. Hwy. 30 follows the main stem of Sherman Creek from its mouth to its headwaters under Sherman Creek Pass. S. Fork has eastern brook in its many beaver ponds.

SHERMAN LAKE. (Summit). A 3 acre lake situated at 5900 feet 1700 feet S. of Sherman Pass on the S. side. The lake winter kills.

SWAN LAKE. Located at 3641 feet elevation a few miles E. of the Okanogan County line, Swan covers 60 acres. There is an improved FS Campground on the E. shore. Eastern brook are planted annually. Swan is reached via Hwy. 21, 9 miles S. of Republic, then W. up Scatter Creek about 8 miles to the lake shore.

TONATA CREEK. A small Kettle River tributary, entering that stream 7 miles E. of Curlew on the Kettle River highway. A road leads upstream from a point 1 mile SE of the creek's mouth and continues upstream about 10 miles to headwaters near Kelly Mtn. Hosts rainbow and eastern brook.

TORODA CREEK. This stream offers good fishing for 'bows and eastern brook. It is paralleled by a road from its confluence with the Kettle River at community of Toroda to upper reaches in Okanogan County.

TROUT LAKE. A narrow, 8 acre lake 8.5 miles W. of Kettle Falls at SE end of Hoodoo Canyon. Elevation is 3000 feet.

TWIN LAKES. Two of Ferry County's best known trout lakes, offering rainbow. North Twin covers 744 acres, while South Twin is 97Z acres. A channel connects the lakes which lie at 2572 feet elevation. Twin Lakes are reached by road about 8 miles up Cornstalk Creek from Inchelium on FDR Lake. The lakes are on the Colville Indian reservation, with the Indians controlling fish management. There are resorts on both lakes.

WARD LAKES. Two lakes of 3 and 4 acres at 3625 feet 9.4 miles N. from Republic. They hold eastern brook. Drainage is via Bacon and Trout Creeks to Curlew Lake. They sometimes winter kill.

FERRY COUNTY RESORTS

Curlew Lake: Pine Point Resort, Republic WA 99166. 509-775-3643. Tiffany's Resort, Republic, WA 99166. 509-775-3152. Black's Beach, Republic, WA 99166. 509-775-3989. Fisherman's Cove, Republic, WA 99166. 509-775-3641.

North Twin Lake: Rainbow Beach Resort, Inchelium, WA 99138. 509-722-5901.

South Twin Lake: Log Cabin Resort, (Box 37) Inchelium, WA 99138. 509-1722 3543. South Twin Lake Resort, Box 146, Inchelium, WA 99138. 509-1722-3935.

FRANKLIN

COUNTY

Fishing is limited in Franklin County. The Palouse River forms the E. boundary, with the Snake River on the S. and the Columbia River on the W. Majority of Franklin County's lakes are man-made, created by seepage from drainage or by dams forming reservoirs. With 1276 square miles, Franklin is 27th in size among the state's counties.

CAMP LAKE. A 25 acre private lake formed by seepage, thus it varies in size. Camp is located 5.5 miles N. of Mesa. Route is S. on Canal Bank road at S. end of Scooteney Reservoir. Mixed species.

CHARLENE LAKE. Spiny rays are found in this 14 acre lake situated about 1 mile down the Snake River from Levey. It has public access.

CLARK POND The middle pond or lake in a string of 3 ponds located 5 miles SW of Mesa on the Ironwood road. It covers 49 acres, and hosts bass, perch, bluegill and carp. There is a public fishing area.

DALTON LAKE. This narrow, 30 acre lake is located 11 miles N. of Pasco on the Kahlotus road. Receives rainbow plants and also contains largemouth bass, small-mouth bass, yellow perch, black crappie and brown bullhead.

EMMA LAKE. A 20 acre lake formed by a railroad fill adjacent to backwaters of Ice Harbor Dam. Contains large and small-mouth bass, black crappie, yellow perch and brown bullhead. Location is about 7 miles NE from Ice Harbor Dam.

KAHLOTUS LAKE. (Washtucna). Originally a 321 acre lake, Kahlotus has shrunk in recent years. Fish species include largemouth bass, black crappie, bluegill, yellow perch and brown bullhead. It is located at the community of Kahlotus on State Hwy. 260, and has a public access area.

MESA LAKE. A 50 acre lake fed by irrigation water over-flow which lies 1 mile W. of Mesa. It has a public access on the W. shore, and carries largemouth bass, black crappie, yellow perch and brown bullhead.

SCOOTENEY RESERVOIR. (Eagle Lake). A 685 acre enlargement of Potholes Canal. There is a variety of spiny rayed fish including perch, bluegill, sunfish, crappie, small and largemouth bass along with Lahontan cutthroat. There are two sections in the reservoir of 425 and 260 acres connected by a canal. Overnight campground and concrete boat launch available. It lies

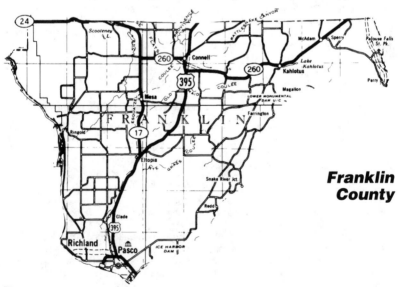

Franklin County

KAHLOTUS LAKE is located at community of Kahlotus.

13 miles SE of Othello on Hwy. 17 which passes close to NE tip. The siphon road leads to the lake.

SNAKE RIVER. Forms the boundary between Franklin and Walla Walla Counties. There is a 32-mile-pool, called Sacajawea Lake, which is formed by Ice Harbor Dam on the Snake about 10 miles E. of Pasco. Sacajawea backs up to the foot of Lower Monumental Dam. There is a great variety of fish in the Snake River including bass, crappie, channel and bullhead catfish, steelhead and salmon plus sturgeon. Boats may be launched at Sacajawea State Park at mouth of the Snake and at Levey Park approximately 10 miles from Pasco on the Kahlotus Road. Best fishing period is during summer months.

SULPHER LAKE. A 22 acre lake 7.5 miles west of Kahlotus in Washtucna Coulee. The lake is highly alkaline. This is a pretty fair waterfowl shooting spot. Route to the lake is approximately 7 miles E. of Connell on the Kahlotus Road.

WORTH LAKE. This 10 acre lake is located 7 miles W. of Mesa. Route to the lake is via Hwy. 170. Contains small spiny rays.

Several small lakes and ponds in Franklin County have been planted with rainbow. They include Flat Big Lakes, Marmes Ponds, Quarry Ponds, Railroad Ponds, and Riparia Lake.

Sharp, sharp, sharp!

Perhaps the most important thing that a fisherman can do to ensure more fish is to hone hook points. Hook manufacturers do a good job, but not all hooks come out of the box sharp enough to fish. In addition to touching up hooks on lures, new hooks should be sharpened if they won't stick in your fingernail.

Larger fish such as steelhead and salmon have extremely tough mouths. (Try jamming a hook past the barb into mouth of one of these fish lying on the bank.) Unless hook points are needle-sharp it is difficult to ram them past the barb. Hook hones work, but an ordinary automotive point file is handier.

What is a silver trout?

Land-locked sockeye salmon are the most plentiful "silver trout," although some Washington lakes have been stocked with silver salmon which are also referred to as "trout." Kokanee are another name for the fresh water sockeye.

Did you know?

The anablep, a fish that lives on the surface of the water, has eyes split in half. It sees other fish below and the birds above in one continuous picture.

GARFIELD

COUNTY

There are no natural lakes in Garfield, a county which ranks 33rd in size in the state with 717 square miles. Highest point in the county is Diamond Peak at 6379 feet. Best fishing is found in a few small creeks, but the county just doesn't offer much for anglers.

ALPOWA CREEK. Hwy. 12 picks up the creek's N. Fork about 18 miles E. of Pomeroy, and follows it 5 miles to the Asotin County line. Two miles W. of the county line a road heads SW up the Alpowa's S. Fork for about 5 miles. The small, clear stream contains native and planted 'bows, and receives plants on a regular basis. Best fishing comes during

early portion of the season before the stream gets too low.

BAKER POND. This 2 acre farm pond has public access through cooperation with the farmer, and is stocked with rainbow. It drains via Pataha Creek into the Tucannon River. Reached via Hwy. 128 and the Mountain Road.

BEAR CREEK. Located in Grouse Flat territory, Bear is reached via Troy, Oregon, or Mt. View road via Big Butte Clearwater Guard Station road. Contains rainbow. Limited water.

CROOKED CREEK. About 5 miles of this mountain stream is in Garfield County, with remainder in Columbia County. Lower few miles in Oregon. The area is within Wenaha-Tucannon Wilderness and no mechanized vehicles are permitted. The stretch in Garfield is reached by taking the road through Grouse Flat SW of Mt. View, W. past the abandoned Hunt school and the Evans and Neal ranches to road end. Three Forks trail from this point goes 3 miles and strikes Crooked Creek and the

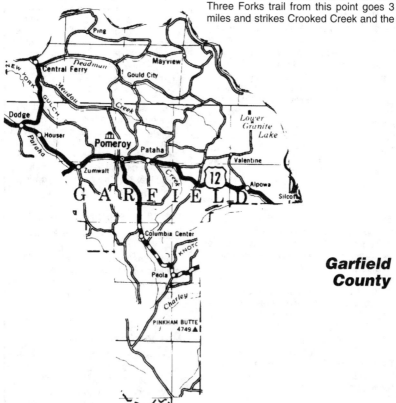

**Garfield
County**

CENTRAL FERRY state park on Snake River offers good boat docking/launching facilities.

trail which follows that stream both up and downstream. There is good rainbow fishing in the creek.

DEADMAN CREEK. Heads E. of Gould City 10 miles N. of Pomeroy, and flows W. to join the Snake River at Central Ferry. The creek is followed by good roads for over 15 miles, with another road paralleling N. Deadman Creek. It is a fair to good bet for spring rainbow fishing, with some large trout available.

PATAHA CREEK. Flows through town of Pomeroy, and closely follows Hwy. 12 W. and N. into Columbia County. Best fishing, however, is in upper reaches above Columbia Center reached by taking Hwy. 128 S. out of Pomeroy about 10 miles. Good for planted and native rainbow plus small eastern brook. Lower reaches infested with squawfish. Muddy roads during early part of the season often makes upper stretches of the Pataha tough to reach.

SNAKE RIVER. This large Columbia River tributary borders Asotin, Columbia and Walla Walla Counties at various points, as well as Garfield. From September through December the Snake is a summer run steelhead stream. It also offers good to excellent fishing for small-

mouth bass and channel catfish. The 'cats are on the increase. Early July into early November is the best time for these fish, although some are picked up from March on. Because the Snake covers such a big area with fish taken in many sections, anglers should check locally for hot spots. Some better areas include upper end in Garfield County via Silcott; lower end via Central Ferry; mid-reaches via Wawawai Grade road, Casey Creek road and Rice's Hill road.

TUCANNON RIVER. The top section of this river lies in Garfield County, and it offers some good fly water for rainbow. It also holds whitefish, but they don't come on until mid-season or later. Hwy. 128 heads S. from Pomeroy about 25 miles past Rose Springs to Teal Springs where a trail of about 2 miles continues S. to the Tucannon. There is a FS campground at Teal Springs, and the trail to the river takes off 1.5 miles E. of the campground.

Several small ponds in Garfield are planted with rainbow. They include Bakers, Casey, Cassey and Coles.

Grant

COUNTY

Grant is the 4th largest county in the state with 2807 square miles. It contains numerous seep lakes which provide top spring and winter rainbow angling. There are several outstanding spiny ray lakes in Grant, including Banks and Potholes. Highest elevation is 2800 feet. The 50 mile-long Grand Coulee is located in Grant County.

ALKALI LAKE. A 308 acre lake located between Blue and Lenore Lakes 9 miles N. of Soap Lake on Hwy. 17. It is located in lower Grand Coulee and was originally a part of Lenore. The highway and a dam now separate the lakes, which contain bass, perch, crappie, brown bullhead and rainbow. Public access.

ANCIENT LAKES. A group of 4 small lakes totaling about 15 acres that vary in size due to seepage. Drive W. of Quincy on Hwy. 28 for 4 miles, then S. on Road T.N.W. for

Grant County

1 mile, then right on road though breaks of Columbia. About 2 mile hike from gate. They hold rainbow, bass, crappie, walleye, bluegill, brown bullhead and perch.

BANKS LAKE. (Equalizing Reservoir). This 32-mile-long reservoir covers 27,000 surface acres and carries a wide variety of fish. It was formed by dams across Grand Coulee, with water being pumped from FDR Lake on the Columbia River. Fish species include stocked rainbow, kokanee, walleye, bass, perch, crappie, blue gill and scrap fish. Banks produces perch in the 1 pound class through the ice during winter, kokanee of 1 to 3 pounds, lunker bass and some rainbow. There are 5 public boat launch and fishing sites along the giant reservoir, along with several resorts. Coulee City is at the S. end of Banks and Grand Coulee at the N. end. State Hwy. 155 follows along the E. shore for the reservoir's full length. Banks is open year-around with spring and summer tops for the silvers (kokanee).

BEDA LAKE. This 45 acre lake contains rainbow and is located E. of Dodson road just S. of Winchester Wasteway. Difficult to fish from shore.

BLUE LAKE. Located 11 miles N. of Soap Lake on state Hwy. 17 which runs along the NW shore of the 536 acre lake. Blue is a natural lake and hosts rainbow, kokanee and browns. Easy access and a public boat launch area, plus resorts. **PARK LAKE** lies a few hundred yards NE of Blue and Hwy. 17 continues along its full length. It holds rainbow, and is 341 acres in size. Resort facilities.

BLYTHE, CORRAL and **CHUKAR LAKES.** Trio of lakes formed by seepage from Potholes Reservoir. Reached by road from W. end of O'Sullivan Dam. Boat launch site on Corral, an 80 acre lake, and on Blythe. Blythe covers 30 acres, as does Chukar. Blythe and Chukar are on Columbia National Wildlife Refuge. All contain rainbow, with spring fishing best, although Corral holds up into early summer.

BURKE LAKE. Located on Quincy W.R.A. 7.5 miles SW of Quincy. The 57 acre lake is planted annually with rainbow, and has 2 boat launch sites. Dusty, Quincy and Stan Coffin Lakes, plus Evergreen Reservoir, are grouped with Burke. To reach the recreation area drive S. from Quincy to county road 5NW, and then turn W. 2.5 miles. Stan Coffin Lakes plus Evergreen are managed as spiny ray waters.

CALICHE LAKES. A pair of lakes totaling 30 acres which lie adjacent to Hwy. 90 on E. side about 5.5 miles SW from George. Take Exit 143, then NE on Frontage road 1.4 miles. Upper Caliche is a good rainbow producer. They offer public access.

CANAL, HEART and **WINDMILL.** Three lakes that provide excellent spring and early summer rainbow fishing for trout to 16 inches. All 3 lakes have public boat launch sites. Size of Canal is 76 acres, while Heart is 20 acres, and Windmill, 33. Drive 3 miles E. from E. end of O'Sullivan Dam (road is along top of dam which forms Potholes Reservoir) and turn S. 4 miles to Heart Lake. Windmill and Canal Lakes are adjacent.

CASCADE, CLIFF, CUP, DOT, SPRING and **CRYSTAL LAKES.** A group of small lakes located on the Quincy W.R.A. W. of Burke Lake. They contain rainbow.

CASTLE LAKE. Castle lies 1 mile SW of Coulee City. It covers 12 acres and drains into Deep Lake which is 1.5 miles S. Hike of 0.5 miles, then down steel ladder over a cliff. Holds rainbow.

CHUKAR LAKE. (See Blythe lake).

CLEMENTINE LAKE. A 4 acre rainbow, bass and channel catfish lake located on Crab Creek W.R.A.

DENNIS CLAY tapped Rocky Ford Creek for this sizeable rainbow.

CORRAL LAKE. (See Blythe lake).

CRAB CREEK. Enters Grant County from Lincoln County at Marlin then meanders W. and S. to join Moses Lake at city of Moses Lake. It assumes identity again below Potholes Reservoir to flow through the seep lakes area and into Adams County and eventually empties into the Columbia River. Holds German brown, eastern brook and rainbow trout, but fishing is spotty. Roads cross and follow the creek at various points.

CRATER LAKE. A 25 acre lake situated 4 miles W. of Quincy. Spiny rays including black crappie, punkinseed, perch and yellow and brown bullhead are present.

CRATER SLOUGH. Located 3 miles W. of Quincy on Hwy. 28. The 15 acre slough offers perch, crappie and largemouth bass.

CRESCENT BAY LAKE. This artificial lake was formed by diking an arm of FDR Lake about 0.5 miles E. of city of Grand Coulee. It holds perch, crappie, walleye, large and smallmouth bass and whitefish. The lake covers 90 acres. It has a public access.

DEEP LAKE. Located in Sun Lakes state park, with a park road to W. end of lake. Deep is 1.5 miles long and covers 104 acres. It holds rainbow, mackinaw (lake trout) and kokanee. The park lies along state Hwy. 17 about 5 miles SW of Coulee City.

DRY FALLS LAKE. A beautiful lake lying at the base of vaulting cliffs in the N. part of Sun Lakes state park. A waterfall flowed over the cliffs in prehistoric times. The 99 acre lake is planted with rainbow and brown trout. Access area. Rental boats available at resort on Park Lake.

DUSTY LAKE. A "pocket" lake of 30 acres, surrounded on 3 sides by basalt cliffs, and located on the Quincy W.R.A. 7 miles SW of town of Quincy. Trail leads from Burke Lake about 0.5 miles to Dusty. It receives plants of 'bows and browns. Quincy recreation area may be reached by turning off Hwy. 28, 4 miles W. of town of Quincy and heading due S. 6 miles.

EPHRATA LAKE. A 25 acre lake formed by irrigation seepage located 4 miles NE from Ephrata. Rainbow planted. Drains to Rocky Ford Creek and Moses Lake.

EVERGREEN RESERVOIR. Located a few hundred yards S. of Burke Lake on the Quincy W.R.A. The 235 acre reservoir is 1.5 miles long. There are 3 boat launch sites on Evergreen, and fish species include walleye, largemouth bass, bluegill, perch, crappie and some rainbow.

FALCON LAKES. There are 5 small lakes in this group, covering about 15 acres. They are situated on the Columbia Wildlife Refuge near the W. end of O'Sullivan Dam. They contain rainbow.

FLAT LAKE. A 98.2 acre lake formed by irrigation water runoff about 6.5 miles S. from Quincy. It holds largemouth bass.

GOLDENEYE LAKE. Another Columbia Refuge rainbow lake. It lies 0.5 miles S. of O'Sullivan Dam and is fed by Falcon Creek. Reached by road turning S. from highway along top of dam.

GLOYD SEEPS CREEK. Plants of brown trout, eastern brook and rainbow have been made in this meandering stream.

GOOSE LAKES. Upper Goose is reached from the road leaving the highway at E. end of O'Sullivan Dam, about 3 miles from the highway. It has a public boat launch site and offers Lahontan cutthroat, walleye, perch, largemouth bass, brown bullhead and crappie plus occasional rainbow. LOWER GOOSE is separate but adjacent to Upper Goose. It also has a boat launch site and contains largemouth bass, black crappie, brown bullhead, perch and a few rainbow. Route to the lower lake is from the McMannaman road in Adams County. Upper Goose covers 112 acres, and Lower Goose, 50 acres.

"H" LAKE. A 7.2 acre lake situated 6.7 miles SW of Quincy on the Quincy W.H.A. about 1400 feet W. of outlet to Stan Coffin Lake. It holds bass and bluegill. See Burke Lake for route.

HAMPTON LAKES. Comprised of Upper Hampton lake (53 acres) and Lower Hampton (19 acres) plus a series of 6 smaller lakes referred to as Hampton Sloughs (12 acres). All are on the Columbia Refuge in the seep lake district below O'Sullivan Dam and contain rainbow. The road from the E. end of the dam leads to Upper Hampton.

HEART LAKE. (See Canal Lake).

DRY FALLS LAKE is located in Sun Lakes Park.

HERON LAKES. A pair of small lakes adjacent to S. side of O'Sullivan Dam, 2000 feet N. of Goldeneye Lake. Planted with eastern brook and rainbow.

HOURGLASS LAKE. A 2 acre rainbow planted seep lake between Cattail and Sago Lakes on the E. Canal road below O'Sullivan Dam. It is located on the Columbia Wildlife Refuge. Difficult access.

JUNE LAKE. A small, early season producer of rainbow. It lies just N. of the Windmill Lake group.

LEMNA LAKE. Lahontan cutthroat and rainbow have been stocked in this 3 acre lake. Location is 8.5 miles N. from Othella adjacent to W. shore of Shoveler Lake.

LENICE LAKE. A 100-acre rainbow and brown trout lake situated on Crab Creek W.R.A. **MERRY** and **NUNNALLY** lakes are located adjacent to Lenice. All are walk-in "quality" fishing waters.

LENORE LAKE. A 1400 acre lake located 4 miles N. of Soap Lake. Contains Lahonton cutthroat.

LIND COULEE WASTEWAY. A tributary drain that starts in the Warden area and leads to the Potholes Reservoir. Best fishing is during winter months for rainbow. It is open year around.

LONG LAKE RESERVOIR. (Billy Clapp Lake). Formed by a dam on the main Columbia Basin irrigation canal. Long Lake is 1010 acres and about 6 miles in length and lies in open sagebrush country 6 miles W. of town of Wilson Creek. The inlet plunges over a vertical 165 foot basalt cliff. The lake carries rainbow and kokanee plus many species of spiny rays including perch, crappie, bluegill and walleye. Good whitefish angling in the fall. It is on the Stratford W.R.A. and provides good goose shooting. There is a boat launch site.

MALLARD LAKE. An 8 acre lake located 10.1 miles N. from Othello. It contains large and smallmouth bass, black crappie, bluegill, pumpkinseed, yellow perch and brown bullhead. Drainage to Crab Creek.

MARCO POLO LAKE. A seep lake of 10 acres which lies about 0.5 miles N. of North Windmill Lake in a rock-walled coulee. Planted with rainbow.

MARTHA LAKE. A 20 acre lake formed in a gravel pit along S. side of Hwy. 90 1.3 miles NE of George on Frontage road. It gets 'bow plants **GEORGE LAKE** is on the N. side of the highway, and is planted with rainbow. George covers 8 acres. Rough boat launch site.

MEADOW and **SPRING CREEKS**. These small streams are in Sun Lakes park. They hold rainbow, brookies and brown trout.

MIRROR LAKE. Adjacent to the NE end of Park Lake in Sun Lakes state park. Mirror is a 4.5 acre lake which is planted with 'bows and eastern brook.

MOSES LAKE. This 6815 acre lake produces bluegill, largemouth bass, rainbow, large walleye, crappie, perch and smallmouth bass. The city of Moses Lake is adjacent to Lewis Horn and Parker Horn arms of the lake. Access is readily available at countless spots, and there is a public boat launch site, marina and resort.

NORTHRUP LAKE. A 3 acre rainbow lake located 2.9 miles S. from Electric City in a coulee. It drains S. to Northrup Creek and Banks Lake.

PARA-JUVENILE LAKE. Southern tip of Para lies in Adams County. The narrow, 12 acre lake is reached via the main Crab Creek road from O'Sullivan Dam through the seep lakes. It is fed by the Hampton Lakes and has been planted with rainbow and Lahontan cutthroat. The Grant County portions are in the Columbia Wildlife Refuge.

PARK LAKE. A natural lake of 341 acres located about 6 miles SW of Coulee City adjacent to state Hwy. 17. The NE third of Park is in Sun Lakes state park, and a road from the park follows the E. shoreline. Resort, public boat launching at park end of lake. Park lake carries rainbow and browns and produces well in spring and summer months.

PERCH LAKE. Located in NE end of Sun Lakes state park. The 15 acre lake is planted on regular basis with rainbow. Spring and summer are best fishing periods.

PILLAR LAKE. A 9 acre seep lake situated on the Columbia Wildlife Refuge. Contains rainbow and Lahonton cutthroat. It lies just below Soda Lake on the E. Canal road.

PIT LAKE. Rainbow are present in this 40 acre lake located 6 miles N. of Othello and adjacent to the S. side of Potholes Canal opposite Canal Lake.

POTHOLES RESERVOIR. One of the state's best spiny ray producers. The huge reservoir (28,200 acres at capacity) also holds large and smallmouth bass, perch, bluegill, black crappie, pumkinseed, large walleyes and is rainbow planted. Some of the 'bows caught here are giants. There is a resort at the W. end of O'Sullivan Dam, and 3 public boat launch sites at Lind Coulee (a long arm which reaches E. from the main Potholes), and at both ends of the dam. The reservoir holds thousands of ducks, particularly mallards. State park at S. end with campsites and boat launch.

LENICE LAKE came through for fly fisherman Kim Nakamura.

PRIEST RAPIDS RESERVOIR. Created by the Priest Rapids Dam across the Columbia River 29 miles E. of Yakima. About 59% of the 7700 acre pool is in Grant County, with 27% in Kittitas and 14% in Yakima County. It backs up to the foot of Wanapum Dam. There is a public boat launch site on the E. shore SW of Mattawa. The pool contains whitefish and steelhead plus salmon and spiny rays. **QUINCY LAKE.** A 62 acre lake on the Quincy W.R.A. area 7 miles S. of town of Quincy. It lies between Stan Coffin and Burke Lakes and has a public boat launch site. Rainbow are present.

RAINBOW LAKE. (Vic Myers). A man-made lake of 8 acres in Sun Lakes state park, and fed by seepage from Dry Falls Lake. Planted with rainbow. Best fishing in spring.

RED ROCK LAKE. A seepage lake of 180 acres. Holds bass, perch, pumpkinseeds, crappie and carp. Drive S. from Hwy. 26 at turn-off to Smyrna 1.3 miles, then E. on rough road. Primitive boat launch and camping area.

ROCKY FORD CREEK. A spring fed tributary to Moses Lake crossed by Ephrata—Moses Lake highway 4 miles from source. Total length of stream 6 miles. Fly fishing only. Premier stream for large rainbow.

ROUND LAKE. Privately owned lake of 110 acres situated 2 miles SW of community of Stratford. Contains bass and crappie.

SAGE LAKES. Two small lakes in the seep lake area below O'Sullivan Dam each about 5 acres and located 200 feet apart and 500 feet NE of Long Lake. They are on the Columbia Wildlife Refuge and are planted with 'bows and brown trout.

SAND LAKE. Largemouth bass and bluegill are present in this 28.4 acre lake. It lies adjacent to N. side of Frenchman Hills Wasteway in sand dunes area.

SHOVELER LAKE. A 6 acre rainbow and Lahontan cutthroat lake located 8.4 miles N. from Othello and 400 feet NW from Widgeon Lake.

SODA LAKE. Largest of the seep lakes below O'Sullivan Dam, Soda covers 155 acres. It hosts crappie, eastern brook, wall-

eye, whitefish, large and smallmouth bass, bluegill, perch and some large rainbow. It is reached by turning S. 1 mile from E. end of O'Sullivan Dam. A road parallels the open W. shoreline.

STAN COFFIN LAKE. This 41 acre lake is on the West Potholes W.R.A. It has a public boat launch site, and holds spiny rays including largemouth bass, black crappie, bluegill, perch, walleye, and brown bullhead.

SPRING LAKES. Two small rainbow lakes located about 500 feet W. from Crystal Lake on West Potholes Game Range. They lie 100 feet apart.

STRATFORD LAKE. (Brook Lake). A 427 acre enlargement of Crab Creek located 0.5 miles N. of state Hwy. 28 at community of Stratford. Road to W. tip of lake. Primarily a spiny ray and waterfowl lake.

SUSAN LAKE. A seep lake of 20 acres, Susan is planted with 'bows. Reached by turning S. from O'Sullivan Dam road 3 miles from E. end of dam, then traveling on dirt road about 2 miles.

TEAL LAKES. Both North and South Teal Lakes are on Columbia National Wildlife Refuge, and cover 22.5 and 28 acres respectively. They are planted with rainbow. The lower portion of South Teal is in Adams County.

THOMPSON LAKE. A lake of 13.6 acres located 7 miles SW from Electric City. Fish species include largemouth bass, black crappie and yellow perch.

TRAIL LAKE. This 6 acre lake holds black crappie, yellow perch and walleye. It is located about 3 miles S. from Coulee City.

VIRGIN LAKE. A 20 acre lake situated 0.5 miles E. of North Windmill Lake. It has been stocked with rainbow.

WANAPUM RESERVOIR. A 14680 acre pool formed by dam on Columbia 28 miles E. of Ellensburg. Some steelhead and salmon. Fair sturgeon fishing near Rock Island Dam. Boat launch sites at Hwy. 90 bridge and Crescent Bar.

WARDEN LAKE. Highway heading E. from O'Sullivan Dam passes close to N. end of lake 4.5 miles from E. end of dam. Short

YOUNG ANGLER scored with a husky rainbow from Vic Myers Lake. (Rainbow Lake).

road leads to public access area and boat launch at that point. Road to Susan Lake ties into S. end of lake. Warden covers 186 acres and contains rainbow, brown trout and perch.

WIDGEON LAKE. A 10 acre lake located between Sago and Upper Hampton Lakes below O'Sullivan dam. Receives rainbow plants.

WILLIAMS LAKE. Situated at head of Dry Coulee, the 11 acre lake is about 8 miles SW of Coulee City. No public access when water level is low. Holds largemouth bass, bluegill and cutthroat.

WILLOW LAKES. South Willow is 39.4 acres and contains black crappie, pumpkinseed, yellow perch and brown bullhead. It is located about 6.5 miles SE from city of Soap Lake and is an enlargement of Crab Creek. **NORTH WILLOW** is 6 miles SE from city of Soap Lake and holds the same species as Willow.

WINCHESTER WASTEWAY RESERVOIR. An enlargement of Winchester Wasteway. Fair largemouth bass, crappie, bluegill and perch angling. Two access areas on Winchester W.R.A. Head N. from George on Hwy. 283 to Road 5 NW, then

E. for 4 miles. Outlet flows SE to Desert W.R.A. and series of ponds which empty into SW side of Potholes Reservoir adjacent to state park.

WINDMILL LAKE. (See Canal Lake).

GRANT COUNTY RESORTS

Banks Lake: Coulee Playland, Electric City, WA 99123. 509-633-2671. Steamboat Rock State Park, Electric City, WA 99123. 509-633-2325. Big Wally's, Coulee City, WA 99115. 509-632-5504.

Blue Lake: Coulee Lodge, Coulee City, WA 99115. 509-632-5565. Blue Lake Resort, Coulee City, WA 99115. 509-632-5364. Sun Village Resort, Coulee City, WA 99115. 509-632-5664.

Moses Lake: Pier 4, Moses Lake, WA 98837. 509-765-0291. Big Sun, Moses Lake, WA 98837. 509-765-8294. Air Botel Resort, Moses Lake, WA 98837. 509-762-5485.

Park Lake: Sun Lakes Park Resort, Coulee City, WA 99115. 509-632-5291. Sun Village Resort, Coulee City, WA 99115. 509-632-5664.

Potholes Reservoir: Mar-Don Resort, Othello, WA 98843. 509-765-5061. O'Sullivan Sportsman Resort, Othello, WA 98843. 509-346-2447. Perch Point Resort & Store, Moses Lake, WA 98837. 509-766-9447.

The Caddis fly

Grains of sand, tiny stones, conifer tree needles or sticks forming a case make the home of caddisfly larvae easy to spot in freshwater lakes and streams. While the outside is thus protected, the interior is silk-lined. Females lay a gelantinous mass of eggs on plants or rocks under water. A sand or wood covering is built by the larva when it hatches, and this expands as the larvae grows. Food is furnished caddisfly larva by small acquatic animals, water plants and a variety of insects. Many flies have been tied by anglers to imitate this important fish food, and some fishermen collect them from rocks, pull them carefully from their cases and use them as live bait.

Grays Harbor
COUNTY

Fronted by the Pacific Ocean on the W., Grays Harbor's 1921 square miles include a portion of the S. Olympic Mountains and the N. slopes of the Willapa Hills. Highest elevation is 4965 feet near the headwaters of the Wynooche River. There are few lakes in Grays Harbor, but some excellent beaver pond fishing is available for sportsmen who explore small streams. The county offers some of the state's best steelhead fishing. The Chehalis, Satsop, Humptulips, Quinault and Wynooche rivers usually rate among the top 20 producers. Westport, an excellent sport salmon fishing spot, is situated at the W. jaw of Grays

Harbor itself. The county is 15th in relative size in the state.

ABERDEEN LAKE. A 64 acre lake formed by Van Winkle Creek and by water piped from the Wynooche River. Planted with rainbow, cutthroat, winter and summer steelhead, Aberdeen is best in April, May and October. City of Aberdeen operates a city park on the lake which is reached by heading N. 0.5 miles from Hwy. 12 about 2 miles E. of Aberdeen.

BEAVER CREEK. Cutthroat have been planted in beaver ponds along this small stream which joins Joe Creek 0.5 miles from Pacific Ocean at Pacific Beach State Park. Ocean Beach road follows lower stretches of stream.

BLACK CREEK. Enters Wynochee River 2.5 miles upstream from Hwy. 12 bridge on W. side. Turn NE from Wynochee Valley road to follow creek upstream. Black holds cutthroat.

BLACK RIVER. (See Thurston County).

CARLISLE LAKES. Group of 5 lakes in

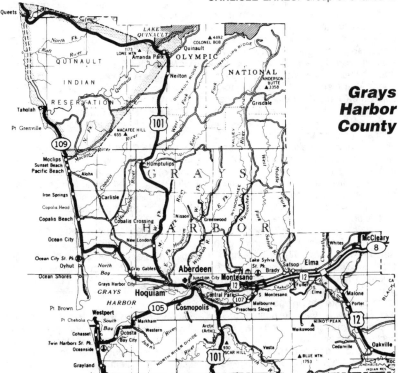

Grays Harbor County

LAKE ABERDEEN has a city park.

marshy area. They range in size from 0.7 to 4 acres. Location is 2.5 miles N. of Copallis Crossing. Cutthroat planted. Drainage is split between Damon and Cedar Creeks.

CEDAR CREEK. A Chehalis River tributary, joining that stream 3 miles NW of Oakville. The small creek produces cutthroat in May and June. A road leads E. from Hwy. 12 upstream for about 2 miles.

CHEHALIS RIVER. The county's major river, the Chehalis contains a wide variety of fish including chinook and silver salmon, steelhead, cutthroat, bass, sturgeon and shad. It heads in Lewis County and flows through the Chehalis Valley to Grays Harbor at Aberdeen. Good network of roads follow the Chehalis offering easy access in many spots and light boats may be launched at various points. Steelheading is best in December, January, February and March, with plunking popular from vicinity of Elma downstream. Sea-run cutthroat fishing starts around July 4 at mouth of Satsop River and downstream, and remains good into fall months. Trolling spinners and worms close to the Chehalis River's brushy banks is effective cutthroat technique. Silver and jack salmon come on in early September from mouth of the Satsop downstream, and chinook grab in October. The slough-like mouth of the Chehalis near Cosmopolis produces sturgeon, July being most productive. Summer months are best in upper stretches of the river above Oakville for shad. The Chehalis lends itself to drift hunting for ducks in the fall. The Chehalis provides the second largest fish spawning system in the state after the Columbia, with 1400

rivers and creeks in its drainage. Boat launch where the Montesano-Aberdeen Hwy. crosses the Chehalis.

CHENOIS CREEK. A cutthroat planted stream which enters North Bay at Chenois Creek settlement. It is crossed by Powell road close to its mouth. Beaver ponds along the creek have also been stocked with cutthroat.

CLOQUALLUM CREEK. A small stream that holds both steelhead and cutthroat. It joins the Chehalis River 1 mile upstream from South Elma. The Elma-Oakville road crosses Cloquallum at Elma's S. city limits, and a good road parallels the creek upstream. Fall is best for cutthroat, with December and January top steelheading period.

COPALIS RIVER. Enters Pacific Ocean at Copalis Beach. Access is tough, but the river may be fished upstream from the ocean. Rated just fair for cutthroat from July through October. It holds some steelhead.

COOK CREEK. Tributary to E. Fork Satsop. Receives winter steelhead plants. Beaver ponds along the creek have had rainbow plants. Road up Satsop's E. Fork crosses creek about 6 miles from Hwy. 8.

DAMON LAKE. A cutthroat planted lake of 15.7 acres located 2 miles E. of Copalis Crossing. Drainage is to Humptulips River.

DECKER CREEK. Enters the Satsop's E. Fork just below Schafer Park.

DELAZINE CREEK. A small, brushy tributary to the Chehalis River which provides good cutthroat fishing from July into October. Road to Weikswood leaves Chehalis River 2 miles E. of South Elma and follows creek about 8 miles. Difficult to fish.

DISCOVERY LAKES. (Klone Lakes). Series of 3 lakes of 2 to 5 acres on Discovery Creek planted with cutthroat. Situated 8.7 miles NE from Grisdale. Drainage to Wynoochee River. Elevation is 3200 feet.

DUCK LAKE. (Oyhut). This 3.5 mile long lake, located at Ocean Shores at N. side of entrance to Grays Harbor, has been planted with cutthroat, rainbow and salmon. Excellent largemouth bass fishing. Black crappie and bluegill present. Duck has two public access areas.

ELK RIVER. A cutthroat stream that comes on early in the summer and again in fall months. The stream is located about 1.5 miles W. of Ocosta. It produces fine fishing for sea-run cutthroat. It also has received winter steelhead plants. Turn S. from Hwy. 105 at Park's Store, drive about 0.5 miles to a point adjacent to the South Bay duck club.

FAILOR LAKE. An artificial lake of 60 acres formed by a dam on Deep Creek. Located 13 miles N. of Hoquiam on Hwy. 101 and then about 3 miles W. on a gravel road. Watch for sign on Hwy. 101. Stocked with rainbow and cutthroat, it produces primarily in April and May. Public boat launch site.

GRISDALE POND. A small cutthroat planted pond located 5.4 miles from former Camp Grisdale. Drainage to Wynooche River.

HOQUIAM RIVER. Flows into Grays Harbor at city of Hoquiam, with road following the river's E. bank for about 15 miles to headwaters. The Hoquiam produces steelhead in December and January, and

FALL CHINOOK taken from Chehalis River near Montesano on plugs.

sea-run cutthroat from July into fall months.

HUMPTULIPS RIVER. One of top steelhead streams in the state. Heavily stocked and heavily fished. The Humpy enters North Bay (Grays Harbor) NW of Hoquiam. It is crossed near mouth by Hwy. 109 and a road from the bridge heads upstream on E. bank of the river. Another road from Copalis Crossing follows the W. bank to the junction with Hwy. 101 at community of Humptulips. The Humpy produces steelhead from December into March. There are large numbers of silver and chinook salmon in the river from October into January. A salmon hatchery at mouth of Stevens Creek has boosted fishing. The stream provides excellent sea-run cutthroat angling from July into October. Both the E. and W. Forks of the Humptulips offer steelhead and cutthroat fishing. January is best steelhead month in the forks, with fall top cutthroating time. Access is difficult, but a road heading E. from Hwy. 101 about 1 mile S. of community of Humptulips roughly follows the E. Fork for 5 miles. Road up the W. Fork takes off E. from Hwy. 101 about 4 miles N. of Humptulips, first touching the stream near O'Brien Creek.

JOE CREEK. Flows into Pacific Ocean at Pacific Beach State Park on Hwy. 109. Has received both cutthroat and winter steelhead plants.

JOHNS RIVER. Primarily a sea-run cutthroat stream, Johns enters Grays Harbor about 2 miles NE of Ocosta. Hwy. 105 to Westport crosses the river at its mouth and a road parallels the W. bank for about 7 miles. A state F&W hunting area including a boat launch site is located 400 feet upstream from Hwy. 105. Summer and fall is best period for planted sea-run cutthroat. In recent years plants of winter steelhead has resulted in increasingly better steelheading.

MOCLIPS RIVER. A fall sea-run cutthroat and winter steelhead stream which flows into the Pacific Ocean at town of Moclips. Roads follow, at varying distances, both sides of the river, but access is not easy.

NORTH RIVER. The river heads and ends in Pacific County, but makes a big swing into Grays Harbor County. North is stocked with steelhead and delivers in December

SALMON ANGLERS line up on the Humptulips below salmon hatchery. (Harry F.H. Senn Photo)

and January, but is best known for excellent sea-run cutthroat and jack salmon fishing. Sea-run cutthroat have been planted. It is crossed by the Cosmopolis-Raymond Hwy. at Arctic about 15 crow-miles from its mouth. The Tokeland-Raymond road, which skirts the N. shore of Willapa Bay, crosses the mouth where there is a public boat launch site. North is best fished by boat upstream from mouth about 4 miles to falls for cutthroat and salmon in late July through October. A logging road extends downstream from Arctic to a point near the mouth.

POPE LAKES. Lakes of 3 and 7 acres that have been steelhead planted. Location is 4 miles SW of Hwy. 101 bridge across Quinault Lake's outlet. Drainage to Quinault River on Quinault Indian reservation.

PORTER CREEK. Sea-run cutthroat plants have been made in this Chehalis River tributary which enters that river at town of Porter on Hwy. 12.

PRAIRIE CREEK. Winter steelhead have been planted in this Quinault River tributary. The creek is crossed by Hwy. 10l about 1 miles W. of Lake Quinault. It

heads under Higley Peak on the Grays Harbor-Jefferson County line.

QUINAULT LAKE. A natural lake of 3729 acres on the Quinault Indian reservation situated 37 miles N. of Aberdeen and about 0.5 miles E. of Hwy. 101. It holds cutthroat, Dolly Varden and steelhead, as well as several species of salmon including the "Quinault" or sockeye. Fishing is regulated by the Indians, and fishing permits are required. (See resorts at Amanda Park and along S. shore of lake for permits). Two FS campgrounds on S. shore. Much of N. shore is in Olympic National Park, with campground at July Creek near E. end of lake. Full tourist facilities around the lake.

QUINAULT RIVER. The upper river flows into the E. end of Lake Quinault, with the lower river leaving the lake's W. end at Amanda Park under Hwy. 101 and flowing into Quinault Indian reservation and thence into Pacific Ocean. Upper reaches are open in season to fishing with roads up both sides of the river to the junction of N. and S. Forks. Winter and summer steelhead offer most of the action, with December, January and February the best winter steelheading period. July through September is top time for summer steelhead around and above Graves Creek inside the park. The upper river changes its course often. Boating is dangerous. Only way to fish the lower river is with Indian guides.

RAFT RIVER. Small size where Hwy. 10l crosses the upper river, but gains volume in lower reaches which are on Quinault Indian reservation. It hosts steelhead, cutthroat and several species of salmon. Rough road number 1700 heads W. 1.4 miles S. of Queets River on Hwy. 10l. It's 5.9 miles on Indian reservation to end of road which dead ends at old, derelict logging bridge which once spanned the river. The Raft enters Pacific Ocean at Tunnel Island. The road will be designated as State Hwy. 109 if built, leading to Tahola at mouth of Quinault River which is crossed by a state highway bridge. Indian fishing permit required on reservation.

SATSOP LAKES. A group of 5 lakes varying from 2 to 4 acres and located about 6 miles NE of Grisdale. There are numerous logging roads in this area, and project road 2222 runs within 0.4 miles of the lakes which have been stocked with rainbow and cutthroat.

SATSOP RIVER. A winter steelhead and cutthroat river which joins the Chehalis River about 3 miles S. of community of Satsop. The Satsop produces winter steelhead from December through March, and cutthroat from mid-July into October. It also holds good numbers of silver salmon which hit from November into February. Roads follow both sides of the river up stream from Hwy. 12 to junction of E. and W. Forks where there is a public boat launch site. The W. Fork is usually highly colored during winter steelhead season, and the E. Fork and its tributaries, along with the main river, provide most action. Road at E. end of Satsop River bridge leads upstream to Schafer State Park on the E. Fork, while road at Brady, 1 mile W. of bridge, leads upstream about 5 miles to junction of E. and W. Forks and follows W. Fork. Another branch of this road parallels the W. side of the E. Fork.

SHYE LAKE. A 9 acre lake located 12 miles NW from Hoquiam and a short distance S. from Copalis Crossing. The cutthroat lake drains to Humptulips River.

STUMP LAKE. A 23.2 acre lake situated 7.5 miles E. from Elma in old creek channel. The lake is filled with debris. It is stocked with both rainbow and cutthroat and drains into Cloquallum Creek. SYLVIA LAKE. A 31 acre lake situated 1 mile N. of Montesano, formed by a dam on Sylvia Creek. The lake is planted with rainbow

LOWER RAFT River close to Pacific Ocean.

WYNOOCHEE RIVER steelhead collected by Scott Steckler.

and cuthroat and produces best in April and May, and then again in September. There is a state park on the lake which provides campsites and a boat launch.

VANCE CREEK LAKE. A narrow, 3300 foot long lake of 9 acres located 1.5 miles SW from Elma in lower Vance Creek. Stocked with rainbow. Several beaver ponds along the stream have also been rainbow planted.

WILLABY CREEK. Has received winter steelhead plants. It flows into **LAKE QUINAULT** at Willaby campground on the Quinault Shore road.

WISHKAH RIVER. Joins the Chehalis River at its mouth at Aberdeen. Road from Aberdeen up both banks, but W. side road hugs the river and continues to headwaters. Best for sea-run cutthroat from July through the fall, but the Wishkah also contains winter steelhead and produces in December and January. Receives both cutthroat and winter steelhead plants.

WORKMAN CREEK. Primarily a cutthroat stream. Beaver ponds along upper reaches often provide excellent May fish-

ing, and then come on again in the fall. The small, brushy creek enters the Chehalis River 1.5 miles downstream from the South Elma bridge. Road from S. end of Chehalis River bridge leads about 5 miles S. up the creek.

WYNOOCHEE RIVER. Another large Chehalis River tributary which enters that river 1.5 miles S. of Montesano. Roads leave Hwy. 12 about 1 mile W. of Montesano to parallel both sides of the Wynoochee. The E. side road continues to the headwaters, although walking is required to reach the river in most stretches. The Wynooche produces steelhead during winter months, and also carries summer fish. It also provides good cutthroat angling in late summer and fall months. There is a public boat launch site on the E. side approximately 12 miles upstream from Hwy. 12, and another at Black Creek. The river gets both steelhead and cutthroat plants.

WYNOOCHEE LAKE. A dam on Wynoochee River 39 miles N. of Montesano has created this 1,120 acre, 4.4 mile long reservoir. Drive 1 mile W. of Montesano on Hwy. 101, then N. up Wynoochee River, following signs to dam. Several campgrounds are on the lake. Boat launch. Contains cutthroat, kokanee and rainbow.

ZIEGLER CREEK. Winter steelhead have been planted in this small stream which is crossed by the Shore road 0.5 miles S. of Lake Quinault into which it drains.

GRAYS HARBOR COUNTY RESORTS

Lake Quinault: Rain Forest Resort, Quinault, WA 98575. 1-800-562-0948. Lake Quinault Resort, Quinault, WA 98575. 360-1288-2362. Lake Quinault Lodge, Quinault, WA 98575. 360-1288-2571. Lake Motel, Amanda Park, WA 98526. 360-1288-2362.

Did you know?

The fisher cat, natural enemy of the porcupine, avoids the latter's quill-studded defense by burrowing up through the snow and attacking its victim from below, where there are no quills.

Island

COUNTY

Six islands in North Puget Sound comprise Island County. They cover 225 square miles, with Whidbey Island's 170 square miles accounting for most of the total. Camano Island is 40 square miles, with Smith, Strawberry, Ben Uhr and Hackney (Baby) Islands much smaller. The county doesn't have any major streams and relatively few lakes. Largest lake is Cranberry. Island is the smallest county in the state. Maximum elevation is found on Camano Island at 580 feet.

ADMIRALTY BAY POND. A rainbow planted pond located adjacent to Admiralty Bay on W. side of Whidbey Island.

CRANBERRY LAKE. Located at the N. end of Whidbey Island on Deception Pass state park, Cranberry is planted with rainbow and brown trout and also contains largemouth bass, yellow perch and brown bullhead. The lake covers 128 acres and drains into Rosario Strait. Usually offers some carry-over trout. April, May and June are best months. Full facilities including campsites, kitchens and boat ramps are available in the park.

DEER LAKE. A rainbow and cutthroat lake of 82 acres located 1 mile W. of Clinton on Whidbey Island. Deer gets regular plants and has a public boat launch site on E. shore. Resort facilities on the lake. Brown bullhead present.

DUGUALLA BAY LAKE. A 50 acre seep lake located adjacent to the Dugualla Dike road. The water receives rainbow plants. Fishing is best in the spring. The pond

Island County

GOSS LAKE receives plants of rainbow. (Lee Russell Photo)

hosts large numbers of shrimp which are feed for lunker 'bows up to 5 pounds. Drive N. from Oak Harbor on Hwy. 525, 3.7 miles to the Frostad road, then E. 2.6 miles to lake on Dugualla Dike road.

GOSS LAKE. (Camp). Situated 3 miles W. of Langley on Whidbey Island. The 55 acre lake contains rainbow and cutthroat and has a public boat launch area on NE end. It drains into Holmes Harbor. Goss is stocked annually and produces 'bows in the 8-11 inch range, with holdovers to 18 inches. Produces best in May, June and July.

GRAVEL PIT PONDS. Three small ponds stocked with cutthroat. One is located 0.5 miles N. of Hwy. 113 on the Keystone road, and the other two are located alongside Hwy. 113 just W. of intersection of the highway and the Keystone road.

HOLMES LAKE. A small rainbow planted pond near Freeland.

LONE LAKE. A 92 acre lake located 1 mile SE of Goss Lake and 2.5 miles SW of Langley on Whidbey Island. Lone is stocked regularly with rainbow and has a public fishing and boat launch site on E. shore. May to August is best fishing period. The rich lake's 'bows average 11-12 inches as yearlings and 14-18 inches as holdovers.

OLIVER LAKE. A 13 acre lake on SW side of Whidbey Island, located 1.5 miles NE of Double Bluff and about 900 feet from the beach. It is rated good for bass. Drainage is into Useless Bay.

ORR'S POND. (Martin Orr). This 1 acre pond lies 3300 feet SW of Whidbey Island's Columbia Beach. It has been planted with eastern brook trout. Considered only fair in April, May and June.

PONDILLA LAKE. A 3.7 acre lake containing catfish, yellow perch, largemouth bass and crappie and located 1200 feet N. of Partridge Point on the W. flank of Whidbey Island. Pondilla is 3.5 acres and produces spiny rays from May into August. Access is difficult. Best route is on Libby road to West Beach and then via a short trail which leads from parking lot on hill.

SILVER LAKE. A 15 acre lake which lies 5.4 miles E. of Oak Harbor on Whidbey Island. Silver holds bass and crappie, and has produced eastern brook in past years. It drains into Saratoga Passage. The lake is tough to reach. Easiest route is over private logging roads from Mariner's Cove. Public access is questionable.

ISLAND COUNTY RESORT

Lone Lake: Lone Lake Cottages, Langley, WA 98260. 360-321-5325

Jefferson

COUNTY

Almost 830 of Jefferson's 1879 square miles are inside Olympic National Park. The county ranks 17th in relative size in the state. It bridges the Olympic Peninsula from Hood Canal and Puget Sound on the E. to the Pacific Ocean on the W. There are relatively unknown lakes and small streams in some parts of this rugged county. Best fishing is for migratory fish in Jefferson's numerous fine steelhead, salmon and sea-run cutthroat streams. The Elwha and Dungeness Rivers drain a portion of the N. part through Clallam County into the Strait of Juan de Fuca, while the Hoh, Queets and Quinault drain the W. portion into the Pacific. The Duckabush, Dosewallips and Quilcene drain the majority of the E. part of Jefferson into Hood Canal.

ANDERSON LAKE. A 59-acre rainbow stocked lake located 8 miles S. of Port Town send on Anderson Lake road with state park boat launch. Beaver ponds situated downstream from lake on creek. They hold cutthroat and eastern brook. Drainage is to Chimacum Creek.

BROWN'S LAKE. Cutthroat have been stocked in this 3 acre lake which lies 7.5 miles W. of Port Ludlow and 1 mile NE from Tarboo Lake. (See Tarboo Lake for route). Drainage is to Tarboo Creek.

CHIMICUM CREEK. A small stream holding eastern brook and cutthroat. Turn N. from Hwy. 104 on the Center Valley road. The creek follows W. side of road closely for about 5 miles, then continues N. to drain into Port Townsend Bay just N. of Irondale.

CLEARWATER RIVER. A major tributary to the Queets which flows into that river approximately 6 miles from its mouth. The Clearwater provides winter steelhead fishing in December and January and sea-run cutthroat from July through September. It also hosts summer and fall chinook, fall coho and summer steelhead. Road to Clearwater heads N. from Hwy. 101 about 5 miles SE of the Queets River 101 bridge, crossing the Queets and following the Clearwater for 10 miles before dropping into the Hoh Valley.

CROCKER LAKE. Located 3.5 miles S. of Discovery Bay adjacent to Hwy. 101. The lake covers 65 acres and holds rainbow, perch, largemouth bass, and brown bullhead. Public boat launch site off highway shoulder. Crocker gets rainbow plants.

DEVIL'S LAKE. (Linger Longer). An 11 acre lake surrounded by timber and situated 2 miles S. of town of Quilcene at 844 feet elevation overlooking Quilcene Bay. Holds 'bows and cutts. Route is S. from Quilcene on Bonneville road, then short hike by trail to S. end of lake.

DOSEWALLIPS RIVER. Best known as a winter steelhead producer from December through March, but the Dose is also a sea-run cutthroat stream in late summer and fall months. In recent years steelhead

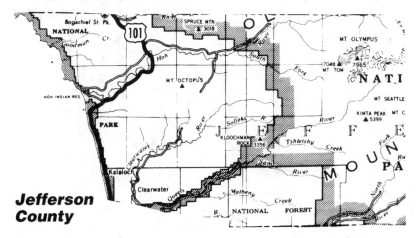

Jefferson County

have drastically declined for reasons unknown. There are limited numbers of summer steelhead available during summer and fall months. Plants of winter steelhead and cutthroat. State park at mouth where the Dosewallips enters Hood Canal. The river heads in Olympic National Park (see park section). A road follows the Dosewallips' N. bank approximately 13 miles to the park border and about 3 miles past that point. There is a FS campground along the river and another at end of road in park. During warm weather the Dosewallips is often milky from snow melt.

DUCKABUSH RIVER. Another Hood Canal winter steelhead and sea-run cutthroat stream which offers fair summer steelheading. It has suffered a decline in steelhead fishing similar to the Dosewallips. The Duckabush flows into Hood Canal about 3 miles S. of Brinnon. A road takes off from Hwy. 101 on N. side of the river, roughly paralleling the stream for about 7 miles. There is a FS campground at the 5 mile point. Access to the Duckabush is difficult and requires bucking brush in most spots. Plants of winter steelhead and cutthroat. The Duckabush heads high in Olympic National Park (see park section) and usually is fishable quicker after high water than other Hood Canal rivers.

FULTON CREEK BEAVER PONDS. Pioneer work is required to scout out the ponds. Turn NW from Hwy. 101 about 1 mile N. of Triton Cove on Hood Canal. Road crosses creek at approximately the 2 mile mark. Work upstream and down to locate ponds which hold cutthroat.

GIBBS LAKE. A 36.8 acre lake containing rainbow. Location is 7 miles NW from Port Ludlow and 3.5 miles SW from Chimacum. Drainage to Chimacum Creek.

GOODMAN CREEK. The creek enters the Pacific Ocean 6 miles N. of the Hoh River's mouth. It furnishes sea-run cutthroat angling from June through September. Goodman mainline road leaves Oil City road on N. side of Hoh River and heads N. to cross Goodman Creek. The stream receives winter steelhead plants.

GIBBS LAKE. A rainbow planted lake of 37 acres. Location is 7 miles NW from Port Ludlow and 3.5 miles SW from Chimacum. Also contains cutthroat, bass and coho. Drainage is to Chimacum Creek.

HOH RIVER. One of the state's top winter steelhead rivers and also one of the largest Olympic Peninsula streams. The Hoh heads high on the slopes of Mt. Olympus in Olympic National Park (see park section) and flows W. to join Pacific Ocean 15 air miles S. of Forks. It carries summer steelhead, cutthroat, Dolly Varden, spring

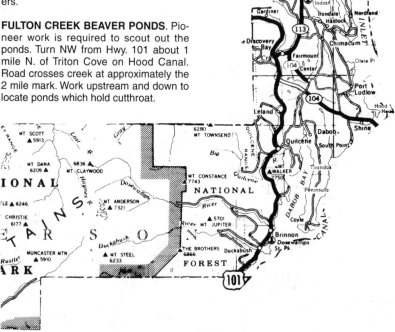

TROPHY STEELHEAD of 21.5 pounds was taken from Hoh River by John Truex.

and fall chinook, silver and jack salmon. Best fishing comes in December into April for winter steelhead, with late summer and fall months prime time for cutthroat, jack, silver and fall chinook, plus summer steelhead. Spring chinook are taken in May through August. Hwy. 101 follows the Hoh within striking distance for about 8 miles along the lower river's S. bank, then bridges the stream. One-half mile N. of the bridge the N. side road leads down river to Oil City on the Pacific Ocean. Two miles N. of Hwy. 101 bridge a hard-surfaced road heads upstream about 20 miles to end of road in Olympic National Park. Approximately 10 miles SW of Hwy. 101 bridge crossing the Hoh, a road leaves the highway to follow the S. side of the river to the Hoh Indian reservation at the river's mouth. The Hoh is planted with winter steelhead.

HORSESHOE LAKE. A 13 acre lake located 4 miles SW of Port Ludlow. Contains rainbow with a "fair" rating in spring and early summer. Hwy. 104 from NW end of Hood Canal bridge passes within 0.4 mile of Horseshoe's S. tip.

HOWE CREEK. Plants of cutthroat have been made in Howe, primarily in beaver ponds along its 5 mile length. The creek drains into Little Quilcene River. It is reached by driving N. from Quilcene on Hwy. 101 for 2 miles, then NW on FS road 2909 for approximately 3 miles, passing over Ripley Creek. Fish upstream from bridge, or drive 1 mile more to road junction, then turn N. on road which crosses upper portion of creek within 1.5 miles.

JUPITER LAKES. Four small lakes located on NE side of Mt. Jupiter 11 miles SW of Quilcene. Lake sizes are 0.5, 1.5, 3 and 6 acres. Cutthroat planted. Drainage is to Dosewallips River.

KALALOCH CREEK. A sea-run cutthroat stream, the Kalaloch crosses Hwy. 101 between the Queets and the Hoh Rivers and enters the Pacific Ocean at Kalaloch. July through September is best fishing period for the brushy creek. Access up and down stream from the highway is by rough trails.

LELAND CREEK. Outlet of Leland Lake, the 4-mile-long creek heads S. from the lake, paralleling the W. side of Hwy. 101 for about 3 miles before joining the Little Quilcene River 1 mile NW of town of Quilcene. Contains cutthroat.

LELAND LAKE (Hooker). Leland lies adjacent to Hwy. 101 about 4.5 miles N. of Quilcene. The 99 acre lake is planted with eastern brook and rainbow and also hosts spiny rays including some big largemouth bass and brown bullhead. Lunker'bows are taken here occasionally, as outlet is screened and carry-over trout are not uncommon. There is a public access site on the lake and a county park.

LENA LAKE. (Lower). A 55 acre lake in the headwaters of the Hamma Hamma River 15 miles N. of Hoodsport. Reached by taking road along Hamma Hamma River's N. side about 7 miles to Lena Creek campground, then 3.5 miles by trail to the lake. The lake contains rainbow and is reported to hold cutthroat and eastern brook. Campground on lake.

LOST LAKE. A rainbow planted lake of 7 acres situated 2.5 miles NW of South Point.

CLEARWATER RIVER gave up this bright steelhead for Wade Coaces.

Route is W. from W. end of Hood Canal bridge on Hwy. 104 for 4.5 miles, then S. about 4 miles, passing TWIN LAKES (Deep). PHEASANT LAKE, planted with eastern brook, is located 0.4 miles NE by trail. It hosts 'bows and covers 4.5 acres. MUD (2 acres), WAHL (22 marshy acres) and TULE (under 5 acres) LAKES are within 2 miles NW and NE of Lost.

LUDLOW CREEK. The creek drains E. from Ludlow Lake about 5 miles to enter Port Ludlow Harbor about 1 mile S. of town of Port Ludlow. Ponds along the creek have received both cutthroat and eastern brook plants. Largest pond lies 1 mile E. of Ludlow Lake. (See Ludlow lake for route).

LUDLOW LAKE. This eastern brook, rainbow and largemouth bass lake of 15 acres is situated 4.5 miles W. of Port Ludlow. Drive W. on Hwy. 104 from W. end of Hood Canal bridge for 8 miles, then turn N. about 0.4 miles where road passes within a few hundred yards of the lake's W. shore.

MOSQUITO CREEK. Steelhead and sea-run cutthroat are found in this small stream which enters the ocean N. of the Hoh River. Route is via the Oil City road along N. side of the Hoh to Goodman main line road which leads N. about five miles to cross the creek. The road continues to the Bogachiel River.

PENNY CREEK. Cutthroat have been stocked in ponds along this 4-mile-long creek which heads in a marshy area about 4 miles NW of Quilcene. The creek enters the Big Quilcene River at the U.S. Fish Hatchery about 2 miles SW of Quilcene. FS Road 2823 leads N. from hatchery 4 miles, closely following the stream.

QUEETS RIVER. (See Olympic National Park section).

QUILCENE RIVER. A fair to poor steelhead producer during December and January. Sea-run cutthroat grab from July to October. The Quilcene enters Hood Canal at the N. tip of Quilcene Bay. It is crossed by Hwy. 101 about 2.5 miles above its mouth, and is paralleled by the highway for 3 miles S. of the bridge. A road heads W. from town of Quilcene 1 mile, then S. to hit and follow the river about 2 miles. Receives steelhead and cutthroat plants with rainbow plants in upper stretches.

QUINAULT RIVER. (See Grays Harbor county).

RIPLEY CREEK. Cutthroat plants have been made in beaver ponds along this stream which is 2.5 miles long. It drains into the Little Quilcene River. Drive N. from Quilcene 2 miles on Hwy. 101, then NW on FS Road 2909 for 1.5 miles where road crosses creek. Work up stream to locate ponds, watching for beaver sign or patches of dead trees which indicate ponds.

SALMON RIVER. A major tributary of the Queets River heavily planted with steelhead by the Quinault Indians. Crossed by the upper Queets road near the Salmon River's mouth about 1.5 miles N. of Hwy. 101. The river heads on the Quinault Indian reservation and flows W. and then N. a short distance to enter Jefferson County, then joins the Queets River in Olympic National Park.

SANDY SHORE LAKE. This 36 acre private lake has been planted with rainbow and is reported to also host eastern brook and largemouth bass. Route is 8 miles W. of W. end of Hood Canal toll bridge, then S. for 1.5 miles on road which touches the lake's W. shore. No access.

SHINE CREEK. Cutthroat have been stocked in beaver ponds along the stream which is 3 miles long. It flows into Squamish Harbor 1 mile W. of Shine at W. end of Hood Canal bridge. Explorers may find trout by walking upstream and down from bridges crossing the creek twice on the South Point-Port Ludlow road which leaves Hwy. 104 and heads N. about 2 miles from Shine.

SILENT LAKE. Rainbow, cutthroat and eastern brook have been planted in this 11.9 acre lake in recent years. It is located 5.3 miles SE from Quilcene on E. side of Dabob Bay. Drainage to Hood Canal.

SILVER LAKES. Cutthroat lakes of 1 and 2 acres situated at head of Silver Creek 9 miles W. of Quilcene. They drain to Dungeness River.

SNOW CREEK. Winter steelhead plants have been made in this small stream wihich flows into S. tip of Discovery Bay. Cutthroat also available.

TARBOO CREEK. This cutthroat planted stream heads in Tarboo Lake and flows approximately 7 miles S. to enter Tarboo Bay 4 miles NE of Quilcene. Upper reaches may be fished from Tarboo Lake road. Lower stretch is easily reached by turning left from Chimacum-Quilcene road on a parallel road 0.5 miles S. of Hwy. 104. This road closely follows the last 3 miles of creek.

TARBOO LAKE (Cord). Rainbow, kokanee and cutthroat are taken from this 21 acre lake situated 1.5 miles SE of Crocker Lake. Tarboo is reached by taking the Chimacum-Quilcene road S. from Hwy. 104 leading from W. end of Hood Canal bridge 3 miles, then button hooking right and traveling 3 miles to lake. Public access. Tarboo is stocked regularly.

TEAL LAKE. Located 2 miles S. of Port Ludlow off Teal Lake road. It covers 15.3 acres and contains spiny rays. Rough boat launch. Drainage is to Port Ludlow Harbor.

THORNDYKE CREEK. Eastern brook are the attraction in this small stream. It heads in Sandy Shore Lake and flows 6 miles S. to enter Hood Canal at Thorndyke Bay 3 miles SW of South Point. Route is W. from Hood Canal bridge for 4 miles, then along South Point road for 1.5 miles, then along Thorndyke road for about 4 miles to crossing of Thorndyke Creek at large culvert. Brushy going down stream.

TOWNSEND CREEK. Lower 2 miles of this eastern brook planted stream has many falls and cascades, but upper reaches may be fished. It enters Big Quilcene River 5 miles W. of Quilcene and is approximately 7 miles long. It heads on the SE flank of Mt. Townsend. Drive W. from center of Quilcene to U.S. fish hatchery, then NW for 1 mile, then S. on FS Road 2812 which leads W. and then N. to follow E. side of the creek.

TWIN LAKE, UPPER. (Deep). A lake of 4.6 acres that contains largemouth bass. Location is 4.5 miles SW from Port Ludlow with drainage to Port Ludlow Harbor.

YOHO LAKE. Rainbow planted lake of 8.3 acres at 2350 feet elevation. It is located 3.5 miles N. of mouth of Sams River and drains to Clearwater River. DNR campground on lake. Easy access via 10.l mile well signed road leading E. from Clearwater road.

JEFFERSON COUNTY RESORTS

Hoh River: Hoh River Resort, Forks, WA 98331. 360-1374-5566. Westward Hoh Resort, Forks, WA 98331. 360-1374-6657. R&R Sport Center & RV Park, HC 80, Box 671, Forks, WA 98331. 360-1374-9288.

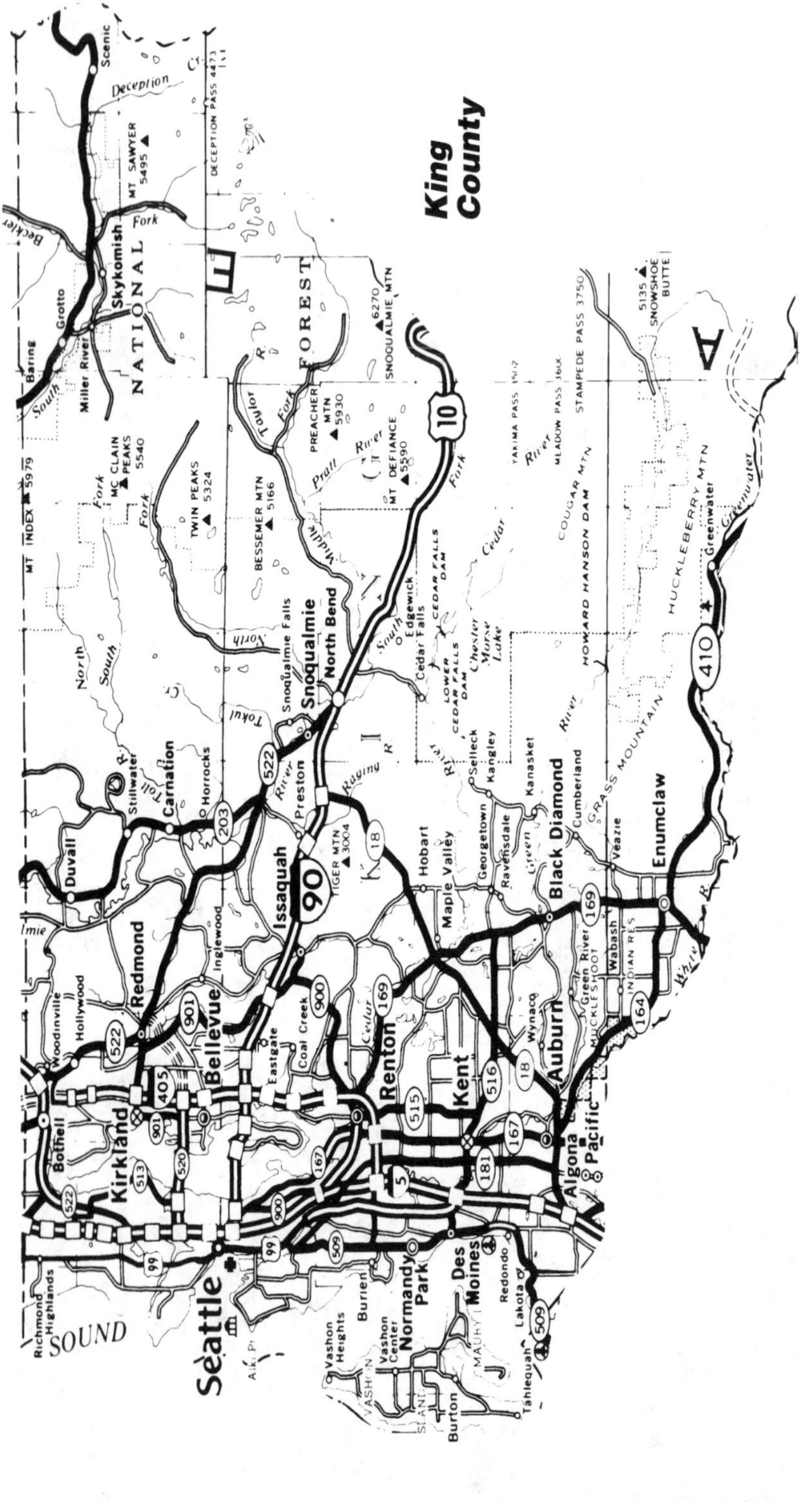
King County
Seattle
Kirkland
Bothell
Redmond
Bellevue
Issaquah
Renton
Kent
Auburn
Enumclaw
Black Diamond
Maple Valley
Snoqualmie
North Bend
Carnation
Duvall
Skykomish
Des Moines
Normandy Park
NATIONAL
FOREST
SOUND

King

COUNTY

There is the widest range of fishing opportunities in King, the 10th largest county in the state with a total area of 2206 square miles. Elevations vary from sea level on Puget Sound to Mt. Daniels at 7936 feet along the Cascade Mountain crest. There are over 750 lakes in the county, with 377 of these located over 2500 feet elevation. Primary drainage of King is via the Green, Cedar and Snoqualmie Rivers, with the Skykomish draining the NE portion and the White River draining the extreme S. Lake Washington at Seattle is the second largest natural lake in the state. Fishing is available for stocked rainbow in many of the county's lowland lakes from season opener into June. Numerous lakes hold kokanee, and this species provides action from May on. Spiny ray waters are plentiful, and bass, perch, crappie, catfish and other species offer summer fishing. The Green and Snoqualmie Rivers rank among the top winter steelhead producers in the state. Salmon fishing is available at Seattle's front door in Elliott and Ballard Bays on a year around basis.

ALICE LAKE. (Mud). Often hold-over rainbow are found in this 33 acre lake which lies at 875 feet elevation 2.5 miles S. of Fall City. Alice gets annual plants of 'bows and eastern brook and is heavily fished. There is a public access on the lake's E. tip. Route to Alice is due S. on Lake Alice road from Fall City for 1 mile. Difficult access.

AMES LAKE. An 80 acre lake situated 2 miles W. of Carnation. Ames is ringed with private homes. The lake has mixed species. Route is via Carnation Farm road N. from Carnation to Ames Lake road, then S. to lake. No public access.

ANGLE LAKE. Plants of legal rainbow help Angle early in the year, with kokanee, perch, largemouth bass and catfish picking up the slack in spring and summer months. Boat launching at county park. Angle is a lake of 102 acres and is located at Hwy. 99 S. at S. 194th about 12 miles from Seattle's city center.

ANGELINE LAKE. A beautiful mountain lake of 198 acres situated at 5100 feet 9.5 air miles S. of Skykomish in the Foss River group of lakes. It holds cutthroat. Route to the lake is E. on Hwy. 2 from Skykomish for 1.5 miles, then S. on the Foss River road for approximately 7 miles to road end. A trail starts here and passes **TROUT LAKE** (17 acres) rainbow, 2012 feet elevation at the 1.5 mile mark. **MALACHITE** (80 acres) rainbow, cutthroat, 4200 feet elevation, lies a short distance to the right 3.5 miles in from road end, while **COPPER** (148 acres) rainbow, cutthroat, eastern brook, 4000 feet elevation, is another 0.5 mile along the main trail. **LITTLE HEART** (29 acres) rainbow, cutthroat, 4250 feet elevation, and **BIG HEART** (191 acres) rainbow, cutthroat, 5100 feet elevation, are 6 and 8 miles in from road end. **CHETWOOT** (113 acres) rainbow, 5200 feet elevation, is located 1800 feet S. of Angeline. **AZURITE** (41 acres) cutthroat, is at 5100 feet elevation, **OTTER** (183 acres) cutthroat, 4400 feet elevation, and DELTA (47 acres) rainbow, cutthroat, 3500 feet elevation, are situated approximately 1 mile or less E. and N. of Angeline. Rough trails to these four lakes.

BASS LAKE. (Carlson). There are cutthroat, bass, crappie and perch in this 24 acre lake. It lies 3.5 miles N. of Enumclaw and 1700 feet SE of **BEAVER LAKE**, another spiny ray and rainbow pond of 13 acres. The lakes are reached by driving N. from Enumclaw on Hwy. 169 for 3.5 miles then W. about 0.4 miles to lakes. Bass Lake is first lake to left on SE 383rd St., and has a public access. No access to Beaver.

BEAVER LAKES. A series of three rainbow planted lakes totaling 82 acres. Largemouth bass, yellow perch and brown bullhead are present. Public fishing area on E. shore. Turn N. at light at Issaquah on Hwy. 90, then take first right road 1 mile, then left about 3 miles to SE 24th Street, then right for 1.5 miles to lake.

BEAR CREEK. (Big Bear). A small, Sammamish River tributary which heads near Ring Hill and flows SW about 6 miles. There is cutthroat fishing in lower reaches during the fall. Access is restricted in many areas. Popular area is around Redmond-Avondale road from Redmond N. to the Woodinville-Duvall highway which roughly parallels the stream. Receives cutthroat plants.

CHETWOOT LAKE is located at 5200 feet elevation.

BEAR LAKE. Situated at 3670 feet elevation, Bear is a 49 acre rainbow lake which lies in the headwaters of Taylor River. Route is NE from North Bend up the Middle Fork of the Snoqualmie River about 11 miles past Camp Brown guard station, then N. up Taylor River for 5 miles to road end. Trail continues 1.5 miles past Snoqualmie Lake to Bear.

BECKLER RIVER. Rainbow are stocked at intervals during the summer in the Beckler, with stocking dependent upon water conditions. The river enters King County from Snohomish County 5 miles N. of Skykomish and joins the Skykomish River at the town. A road leads upstream along the river into Snohomish County, offering easy access.

BIG CREEK. Limited numbers of rainbow are found in this small stream, tributary to the Snoqualmie River's N. Fork. The creek produces into fall months. It heads NW of Philippa Lake. Route is 12 miles N. of North Bend on the North Fork county road which crosses the mouth of the creek. Rough trails head upstream.

BITTER LAKE. A 19 acre lake inside Seattle's city limits at Greenwood Avenue and N. 133rd. Stocked with rainbow, cutthroat and eastern brook. It also holds largemouth bass, black crappie, yellow perch and brown bullhead. Access is limited.

BLACK LAKE. Rainbow plus a few cutthroat are available in Black, a 26 acre lake. Elevation is 1213 feet. Black usually starts slow, then picks up fishing momentum as waters warm. Drive N. from North Bend on the North Fork county road 6 miles to Spur 10 intersection, then left on main truck road (when gate is open) about 6 miles to lake's W. shore. MUD LAKE is located 1 mile N. along the main line. It covers 16 acres and holds rainbow.

BLACK DIAMOND LAKE. (Chub Lake). A 9 acre pond, planted with rainbow and also hosting numerous catfish. Situated 1 mile SW of Black Diamond at end of 248th Ave. SE. Access is difficult.

BOREN LAKE. A 15.3 acre lake located 4 miles N. of Renton. Rainbow planted with largemouth bass, yellow perch and brown bullhead also present. Drainage to May Creek.

BREWSTER LAKE. (Kerrs). A rainbow pond of 3 acres which lies 3.5 miles S. of North Bend. It is reached by turning S. from Hwy. 90 about 2 miles E. of North Bend and driving 2.5 miles on the Cedar Falls road, then W. about 1 mile on logging road. Private lake, poor fishing.

BRIDGES LAKE. The top lake in a series of three cutthroat and spiny ray lakes located about 6 miles NE of Snoqualmie. Bridges covers 34 acres; **KLAUS** is 62 acres. They drain via Ten and Tokul Creeks to the Snoqualmie River. To reach the lakes take the North Fork county road out of North Bend for 6 miles to Spur 10 intersection, then W. 1 mile (when Weyerhaeuser gate is open) to Road 3710, then N. for about 1 mile to NE tip of Klaus lake. Watch for trail sign. Trail continues from road end to **BOYLE** and Bridges Lakes, about 1.5 miles total.

BURIEN LAKE. Private property surrounds this 44 acre lake located on the SW outskirts of Burien. Reported to hold rainbow and spiny rays. SW 154th St. comes close to W. shore.

CALLIGAN LAKE. Both rainbow and cutthroat are found in this 361 acre lake which lies 9 miles NE of North Bend at 2222 feet elevation. It is reached by taking North Fork county road N. from North Bend 6 miles to Spur 10 intersection, then heading E. and N. on Spur 10 for 3 miles. Logging roads 14 and 14-D wind E. about 2 miles to NW tip of the lake. (Gates sometimes locked).

CALLIGAN CREEK. Drains Caligan Lake into the Snoqualmie's N. Fork, provides fair spring rainbow fishing.

CAROLINE LAKE. A 59.6 acre "deep" lake situated 6 miles from Snoqualmie Pass and 2000 feet W. from Upper Wildcat Lake. Rainbow planted. Drains to Derrick Lake and Middle Fork Snoqualmie River.

CEDAR RIVER. A large river which heads under Yakima Pass on the Cascade Crest and flows NW about 10 miles to enter the E. tip of **CEDAR LAKE**, (Chester Morse Lake) an artificial reservoir of 1682 acres formed by a dam on the river. The reservoir is used to store domestic water supplies for Seattle, and is closed to public entry. Downstream from Cedar Falls through Bagley Junction, Landsburg, Maple Valley and Renton where the Cedar enters the S. end of Lake Washington, fishing is permitted in season. There are sea-run cutthroat in the lower reaches during fall months and fair to good steelhead fishing from December through March. Receives winter steelhead plants. **ROCK CREEK**, a tributary of the Cedar, holds rainbow. It joins the river about 2.5 miles

E. of Maple Valley from the S. Roads follow along most of the lower Cedar River.

CHERRY CREEK. The creek heads in Cherry Lake near the King-Snohomish County line and flows W. to enter the Snoqualmie River 2 miles N. of Duvall. The brushy creek provides best fishing for eastern brook and cutthroat in beaver ponds along it's upper reaches. Road from Duvall heads E. up Cherry Creek for about 4 miles and rough trails continue.

CHERRY LAKE. Source of Cherry Creek, it is a 3 acre pond containing cutthroat and rainbow. Road from Stillwater on Hwy. 203 heads N. up Harris and Stossel Creeks for about 8 miles to cross upper Cherry Creek. A trail heads upstream about 1 mile to the lake.

CLEVELAND LAKE. A 2.5 acre rainbow lake at 4300 feet elevation located 3.4 miles SW from Skykomish on N. side of Cleveland Mtn. It drains to Miller River. **DRUNKEN CHARLIE LAKE** is 0.8 miles E. from Cherry Lake. It is 2.8 acres and contains rainbow and cutthroat. Difficult to reach.

CHARLIE LAKES. String of four lakes situated 8.5 miles S. from Skykomish on SW side of Camp Robber Valley at 3800 to 4200 foot elevations. Sizes are 2, 1.5, 3.5 and 4.5 acres. Rainbow planted.

CHETWOOD LAKE. A 113 acre lake at 5200 feet elevation located 10.8 miles S. from Skykomish and 1800 feet S. from **ANGELINE LAKE.** Holds rainbow. Drainage to W. Fork Foss River.

COAL CREEK. A tributary of the Snoqualmie River, entering that river at town of Snoqualmie. **KIMBALL CREEK** joins Coal 0.4 miles S. of Snoqualmie. Both streams get plants of rainbow and cutthroat.

COTTAGE LAKE. A 63 acre lake that receives rainbow plants. It also holds a variety of spiny ray species. Route is about 4 miles E. of Woodinville on the Woodinville-Duval Highway which skirts NE shore of lake. Public access.

COUGAR CREEK. Tributary to White River, Cougar holds rainbow and cutthroat and delivers fair fishing in summer and fall months. It is located 7 miles E. of

Enumclaw, and flows out of Cedar Lake. Beaver ponds in upper reaches offer cutthroat.

COUGAR LAKE. (Big). A 19.7 acre lake situated at 4123 feet 14 miles NE from North Bend. Planted with golden trout. **LITTLE COUGAR** lies 4900 NW from Big Cougar. Drainage to North Fork of Snoqualmie River.

CRATER LAKE. There are cutthroat and rainbow in this 17 acre lake which lies at 3500 feet in headwaters of Tolt River's S. Fork. Take Miller River road past Elizabeth Lake to road end. Trail continues 1 mile to lake's outlet stream. It's rough going .08 miles upstream to lake.

CRAWFORD LAKE. A 19.8 acre lake at 5350 elevation. It lies 1600 feet SE from **CHETWOOD LAKE.** It has received plants of golden trout.

DEEP CREEK. A small stream draining into the Snoqualmie River's N. Fork. It contains rainbow, eastern brook and cutthroat and provides fair to good fishing from May into October. It is reached by driving up N. Fork from North Bend to Lennox mine 5 miles from Spur 10 gate.

DEEP LAKE. Located 0.8 miles SW of Cumberland on the Kanaskat-Enumclaw road, Deep covers 39 acres and holds catfish, perch, crappie, cutthroat, rainbow and

HANCOCK LAKE produces best during fall months.

kokanee. The road touches the S. tip of lake. Boat launch, fishing docks.

DENNY CREEK. Tributary to the Snoqualmie River's S. Fork, the creek has a developed FS campground at its mouth about 18 miles E. of North Bend on Hwy. 90. The creek is rated fair for summer and fall cutthroat fishing. Trail No. 1014 from the campground leads upstream about 4 miles to **MELAWKWA LAKE** at the creek's headwaters.

DERRY LAKE. (Dairy). A 5 acre lake which holds eastern brook. Leave Hwy. 90 about 3 miles from North Bend's E. city limits and drive S. about 1.5 miles, crossing S. Fork of Snoqualmie enroute. The lake is located 0.5 miles E. of Edgewick.

DESIRE LAKE. (Echo). The 72 acre lake sometimes provides some hold-over trout at spring opening. It is planted with rainbow and cutthroat and also hosts largemouth bass, black crappie and yellow perch. There is a public access on the N. shore. To reach the lake drive 0.5 miles S. of Renton on 108th SE, then E. on 176th (Petrovitsky Road) to SE 184th St., then N. on 172nd SE, along W. shore.

DOLLOFF LAKE. Rainbow, largemouth bass, pumpkinseed, brown bullhead and perch are available in Dolloff, a 21 acre lake situated 1 mile E. of Federal Way. It has a public access on SE shore, and gets plants of legal rainbow. The Military Road parallels the W. shore.

DOROTHY LAKE. Rainbow planted lake of 290 acres at 3052 feet. Located 7.8 miles S. from Skykomish. Drains to E. Fork of Miller River.

DREAM LAKE. A rainbow lake of 35 acres located 17.5 miles NE from North Bend. Island of 0.5 acres in lake. Drains to Taylor River.

ECHO LAKE. An 11 acre lake which lies adjacent to Hwy. 99 just inside the King-Snohomish County line. It is stocked with rainbow and often carries a few hold-overs to 12 inches. Access is from power line road through county park.

ECHO LAKE. This 20 acre lake lies adjacent to Hwy. 90 about 2.5 miles SW of Snoqualmie. It contains rainbow plus cutthroat and largemouth bass. The lake may

DANDY CUTTHROAT spooned from Lake Sammamish by Ward Malernee.

be seen to the S. of the highway. There is no public access.

EDDS LAKE. Golden trout have been planted in this 10 acre lake at 4300 feet. It's located on N. side of Alaska Mtn. 4.5 miles NE from Snoqualmie Pass. Drains to N. Fork Snoqualmie River.

FENWICK LAKE. An 18 acre rainbow and spiny ray lake including largemouth bass, pumpkinseed, yellow perch and brown bullhead. Fenwick has a public access site on its W. shore. Route is via Hwy. 516 W. from Kent across Green River, then S. on Lake Fenwick road 0.5 miles to lake. **FISH LAKE.** Both rainbow and cutthroat are present in this 17 acre lake. It has a public access, and lies 1.5 miles SW of Cumberland about 0.5 miles W. of the Kanaskat-Enumclaw road. **DEEP LAKE** is situated 1 mile E.

FIVE MILE LAKE. Public access is through park on this 38 acre lake. Five Mile is stocked with rainbow, and has largemouth bass. It is located about 1.5 miles NE of Milton. The Military Road skirts E. side of lake where the park is located.

FOSS RIVER. A mountain stream heading in NE King county under the Cascade Crest, the Foss flows N. to junction with the Tye River 2 miles E. of town of Skykomish. (The Beckler River joins these streams 1.5 miles W. of their junction and the three rivers then form the S. Fork of the Skykomish River). A road leads E. from Skykomish 2 miles and swings S. to follow the Foss 4 miles to junction of W. and E. Forks, then continues about 2 miles up the W. Fork. The Foss is a rainbow stream and provides fair fishing from May into October. It receives staggered plants of legal rainbow.

GENEVA LAKE. Anglers working this 29 acre lake are surprised occasionally by husky hold-over rainbow. Geneva is planted with 'bows, and has a public access on the SW shore. The lake is reached by taking Military Road 3 miles SW from Auburn to junction with 342nd, then W. for 0.5 miles to corner of S. 38th and S. 344th. **LAKE KILLARNEY** is located across the street.

GRANITE CREEK. A tributary of the Snoqualmie River's Middle Fork, Granite provides fair to good cutthroat fishing in late summer and fall months. It enters the stream approximately 5 miles NW of North Bend's airstrip with a road up the river's S. bank crossing the mouth. The creek drains **GRANITE LAKES** of 9 and 14 acres situated 8.8 miles SE of North Bend at 3660 and 2950 feet. Rainbow planted.

GREEN LAKE. Located in the center of Seattle. Green is 255 acres and is planted with rainbow and brown trout. Largemouth bass, yellow perch and brown bullhead are also present. It provides good to fair angling through much of the year, with late summer and fall particularly productive. Rental boats are available on Green and small boats may be launched from various points during spring and early summer months. The lake lends itself to bank fishing with public access surrounding entire lake.

GREEN RIVER. One of the state's top winter steelhead streams, but is heavily netted by Indians. There is good summer steelheading, also. It furnishes trout fishing in its upper reaches near Lester after spring snow run-off. The big river heads under Blowout Mtn. on the Cascade Crest and flows N. and W. through the rugged Green River Gorge between Kanaskat and Kummer, then through Auburn and Kent in the flat, lower valley. From the Renton Junction downstream to Elliott Bay the river is known as the Duwamish. Lower reaches of the river up to Flaming Geyser Park, about 3 miles S. of Black Diamond, are easily fished in many places with roads paralleling both banks for much of its length. The upper valley includes approximately 50,000 acres of public U.S. FS service land. Access is blocked from the W. by City of Tacoma gates which uses water behind the federally-built Howard Hanson Dam on the upper Green for commercial and domestic use. Route to the upper valley from Puget Sound region is over Snoqualmie Pass and past **KEECHELUS LAKE** on Hwy. 90, then W. over Stampede Pass and down into the head of Green River valley. Get a FS map of the North Bend district to determine what portions of river touch public land. The upper river is open to fishing in season on public land.

GREENWATER RIVER. A medium sized stream which joins the White River at the community of Greenwater where the mouth is bridged by Hwy. 410 about 17 miles E. of Enumclaw. An excellent road leads upstream, taking off from Hwy. 410 at a truck overpass 2 miles SE of Greenwater. This road continues upstream approximately 10 miles offering easy access to the river's rainbow, cutthroat and occasional eastern brook which bite best from mid-summer

into late fall. There is a campsite at Himes Camp, about 7 miles in. This area is popular with mushroom pickers. Trail No. 1176 from Himes Camp leads SE 2 miles to **MEEKER LAKES** which lie on the King-Pierce County line at 2780 feet elevation. They are 4 and 6 acres and contain cutthroat, rainbow and eastern brook.

GROTTO LAKE. A deep, 4 acre rainbow lake which lies at 3900 feet on NE side of Grotto Mtn. Drains to S. Fork Skykomish.

HALLER LAKE. A 15 acre resident-surrounded lake located at Meridian and N. 125th in Seattle. It holds rainbow, largemouth bass and brown bullhead. Public access is via street ends at W. and N. ends of the lake.

HANCOCK LAKE. A 236 acre lake which lies at 2172 feet elevation. Hancock carries rainbow, eastern brook and cutthroat. It is reached by driving N. of North Bend on the North Fork county road for 6 miles to the Spur 10 intersection, then E. on Spur 10 for 0.5 miles to Spur 13 which leads approximately 2 miles to the lake's W. tip. Locked gates sometimes bar access. Best fishing is in fall.

HANSEN CREEK. A cutthroat stream, Hansen does best in summer and fall. It drains Scout Lake and flows N. to join the

LAKE MORTON gets a look-over by Mark Lewis.

Snoqualmie River's S. Fork at the Bandera emergency airstrip on Hwy. 90 about 7 miles W. of Snoqualmie Pass. Bandera Road No. 222 leaves Hwy. 90 at Camp Mason, 11 miles E. of North Bend, and continues 5 miles to junction of Hansen Creek road. Drive up Hansen Creek, park and hike 1.5 miles on rough trail to **SCOUT LAKE** at 3850 feet. It holds cutthroat and 'bows.

HEART LAKES. Big Heart at 5100 feet elevation and 190.7 acres lies 9 miles S. of Skykomish. **LITTLE HEART** is at 4250 feet and covers 28.6 acres. Both rainbow planted. They drain to W. Fork Foss River.

HESTER LAKES. Big Hester, 66.6 acres, carries rainbow. It is located at 4050 feet 5.8 miles N. of Snoqualmie Pass in headwaters of S. Fork Dingford Creek. **LITTLE HESTER** has been planted with golden trout. It is a 9.5 acre lake at 4200 feet and lies 700 feet W. from Big Hester. Both drain to Middle Fork Snoqualmie River.

HOLM LAKE. (Nielson). Rainbow and largemouth bass present in this marshy, 19 acre lake which lies 4 miles E. of Auburn. Auburn-Black Diamond road from that city leads due E. across the Green River then right at end of bridge on Lake Holm road for about 2 miles. Public access.

HOLOMAN LAKE. Rainbow planted lake located 4.8 miles SW from Index at 3650 feet. Drains to N. Fork Taylor River.

HORSESHOE SLOUGH. A 7.1 acre lake containing largemouth bass and yellow perch. Location is 4.5 miles N. from Fall City adjacent to Snoqualmie River.

HULL LAKE. A 5.7 rainbow and cutthroat lake at 822 feet located 9.5 miles N. from Snoqualmie. Drains to Snoqualmie River.

ISLAND LAKE. Covers 17.4 acres and holds 'bows. It is situated at 4200 feet 13 miles SE from North Bend. Drainage is to Talapus Lake.

ISSAQUAH CREEK. Entering the S. end of Sammamish Lake, Issaquah provides fair to good spring angling for cutthroat and rainbow, and fair winter steelheading. There are a few sea-run cutthroat taken in fall months. Roads along the stream provide easy access, although much of the land is privately owned and permission is needed. The creek heads NE of Hobart and flows N. about 10 miles to join the lake.

JANICKE SLOUGH. An "U" shaped lake of 10.2 acres located 2 miles N. from Fall City. It contains largemouth bass and yellow perch. Drainage to Snoqualmie River.

JONES LAKE. (Fourteen). A brushy-shored lake of 23 acres which contains rainbow bass, crappie, catfish and perch, Jones is situated 0.5 miles S. of Black Diamond and drains into Rock Creek. It lies close to the W. side of Hwy. 169. Tough access.

JOY LAKE. Covering 105 acres, Joy is planted with rainbow and produces well in April and May. It is reached by driving 2 miles N. of Carnation on Hwy. 203 to Stillwater turning NE up Harris Creek for 1 mile, then E. 1 mile to Joy where Lake Joy road encircles the lake. Small boats may be launched at NW shore.

JUANITA LAKE. (Wittenmeyer, Mud). A 3 acre pond which offers bass and crappie, Juanita is located at Firloch about 1.5 miles NE of town of Juanita. A good fishing lake for kids.

KATHLEEN LAKE. (Meadow). A 39 acre lake which lies 4 miles E. of Renton, Kathleen holds rainbow, plus perch and bass. It drains into May Creek. Take SE 128th street E. from Renton about 3 miles to Lake Kathleen road, then S. for 0.5 miles to lake. Access is restricted.

KERRS LAKE. (Brewster). Cutthroat are found in this 3 acre lake with is located 3.4 miles S. from North Bend. Drainage is to S. Fork Snoqualmie River.

KILLARNEY LAKE. The lake is 31 acres and has a public access on the NE shore. It is located 3 miles W. of Auburn on Military Road to 342nd street, then W. 0.5 miles to corner of S. 38th and S. 344th. It is planted with rainbow and cutthroat and also contains largemouth bass, bluegill, yellow perch and brown bullhead. **LAKE GENEVA** is across the street.

KINGS LAKE. Kings is a 3 acre eastern brook lake which is surrounded by over 50 acres of peat bog swamp. It lies 1 mile W. of **BOLYE LAKE.** Fishing is best in spring and fall. (See Bridges Lake for route). Ten Creek fire road passes within 100 yards of lake.

KULLA KULLA LAKE. A mountain lake of 60 acres which lies at 3765 feet elevation on E. slope of Mt. Defiance. The lake holds cutthroat and rainbow and is reached by the Pratt Lake trail system which leaves Hwy. I-90 approximately 0.8 miles W. of the Asahel Curtis FS picnic area. The trail forks just above the highway with the Pratt Lake trail leading W. about 2.5 miles to **TALAPUS LAKE** at 3780 feet. Lake may also be reached from Mason Lake and by a trail which leaves I-90 about 15 miles E. of North Bend. Watch for sign. This lake holds small eastern brook.

OLALLIE LAKE, which is 17 acres, lies 2400 feet NE of Talapus. It holds rainbow and cutthroat also. It is best reached from Talapus. The trail leads N. about 2 miles to **PRATT LAKE** at 3385 feet. Pratt contains eastern brook. The main trail continues W. for 1.5 miles to pass between **RAINBOW LAKE**, a rainbow lake of 6 acres at 4270 feet, and **BLAZER LAKE** which holds rainbow and is of similar size. Blazer's elevation is 4060 feet. Approximately 0.8 miles farther W. a side trail leads 0.4 miles S. to **MASON LAKE**. This lake covers 33 acres and lies at 4180 feet elevation. It holds rainbow. Another rainbow lake, **LITTLE MASON**, is located 1200 feet SW of Kulla Kulla Lake at 4260 feet. Because of the elevation, these lakes do not provide good fishing until mid-June or later. Fall months are often excellent, snow conditions permitting. The lake system is also reached via Mason Lake. FS road 9030 leads W. and N. from I-90 across from air strip for about 5 miles, doubling back E. on FS 9031 for 0.5 miles where a trail leads 1 mile to Mason.

LANGLOIS LAKE. Anglers are sometimes surprised in Langlois with hold-over rainbow. The lake is deep, 98 feet maximum, and covers 40 acres. It has a public access on the SE shore, and receives annual plants of 'bows. Route to lake is S. from Carnation 0.5 miles on Hwy. 203 then E. for 1 mile on the Langlois Lake road, (NE 32nd).

LARSEN LAKE. A 7.3 acre lake holding largemouth bass and yellow perch. It is located 3 miles E. from Bellevue and drains to Lake Washington.

LENNOX CREEK. Tributary to the Snoqualmie River's N. Fork, Lennox is a rainbow and cutthroat stream which yields best in fall months. It joins the Snoqualmie

about 18 miles NE of North Bend where the North Fork county road swings SE to follow Lennox upstream for 7 miles.

LEOTA LAKE. (Summit). A 10.1 acre lake situated 2 miles E. of Woodinville adjacent to the S. side of the Woodinville-Duval Hwy. It contains rainbow, largemouth bass, bluegill, black crappie, yellow perch and brown bullhead. Access is difficult.

LODGE LAKE. Rainbow lake of 9.3 acres located 1.5 miles SW from Snoqualmie Pass. Empties into Lodge Creek to S. Fork Snoqualmie River.

LOOP LAKE. Planted with eastern brook, Loop is a 35.7 acre lake situated 2.8 miles E. from Carnation. Drains to Tolt River.

LUCERNE-PIPE LAKES. The pair of lakes are connected by a narrow neck. Lucerne is 16 acres and Pipe covers 52 acres. The lakes rainbow come on in spring, but best fishing is for the lakes perch and bass. Cutthroat and catfish are also present. Location is approximately 7 miles E. of Kent on Hwy. 516, then N. 0.4 miles on 213th Place SE to lakes. Access is from street end located between the lakes.

MALACHITE LAKE. A cutthroat planted lake of 79.7 acres at 4200 feet. Location is 7.4 miles S. from Skykomish. Drains to W. Fork Foss River.

MALONEY LAKES. Group of three small lakes at 4000 feet located 2.8 miles S. from Skykomish. They outlet to S. Fork Skykomish. Planted with rainbow and cutthroat.

MARGARET LAKE. (Marion). Planted with cutthroat, Margaret sometimes starts slow, but picks up fishing tempo in summer and fall months. Cutts of 9-12 inches are common in this 44 acre lake. Drainage is via Margaret Creek to Snoqualmie River. The lake is reached by driving 3.5 miles E. from the N. city limits of Duvall, then N. 2 miles to the lake's W. shore where there is a public access.

MARIE LAKE. A cutthroat lake, Marie is 10 acres and produces in the spring, but is best in late summer and fall. It is located 2 miles E. of Fall City. Drive E. from the town on the Fall City Snoqualmie Hwy., then turn N. for 1 mile to W. end of the lake. Marie has a boggy shoreline.

MOOLOCH, NADEAU and SMC lakes.

MARMOT LAKE. Although this 135 acre lake lies in King County, best route is to drive to end of the Cle Elum River road approximately 33 miles N. of town of Cle Elum. Follow the Cascade Crest trail past Hyas Lake to Deception Pass, 5 miles from road end. Trail to Marmot leads NW from the pass for 3 miles, then another steep 0.5 miles on a fishermen's trail to the lake at 4900 feet elevation. There are cutthroat in Marmot. **CLARICE LAKE** lies at 4500 feet about 1 mile of tough going N. of Marmot. It is a 41 acre eastern brook lake.

MARTEN LAKE. There are rainbow in this 40 acre lake which drains into the Taylor River. Elevation of the lake is 2959 feet. Marten is reached by leaving Hwy. 90, 3.2 miles E. of North Bend and driving up the Snoqualmie River's Middle Branch for 15 miles to Camp Brown. A road branches N. and crosses Marten Lake's outlet at the 3.5 mile mark. From here it is a scramble of 1 mile NW up the stream to the lake. DREAM LAKE is reached by continuing on the road 2 miles past Marten's outlet to Big Creek, then toughing it up the creek 1.5 miles to Dream which lies at 3800 feet and offers rainbow. The lake covers 35 acres.

MARTIN CREEK. Rainbow and cutthroat are taken from Martin, a Tye River tribu-

tary. Access is difficult via an abandoned trail up the stream from its mouth at Tye Canyon FS campground located 7 miles E. of Skykomish on the N. side of the Tye.

MASON LAKE. Big Mason covers 32.6 acres and lies at 4180 feet l2 miles SE from North Bend. **LITTLE MASON**, 4.3 acres, is located 1250 feet NW. Both get rainbow plants and drain to S. Fork Snoqualmie.

MAUD LAKE. A cutthroat planted lake of 2.1 acres located 8 miles N. from North Bend at 1140 feet. It drains to North Fork Snoqualmie.

McDONALD LAKE. A bass lake of 18 acres located 6 miles E. of Renton and 0.5 miles SE of Kathleen Lake. Drainage is into Issaquah Creek. Route is E. from Renton 4 miles on SE 128th street, then S. for 1 mile on 196th Ave. SE which runs close to W. side of lake.

McLEOD LAKE. Rainbow, eastern brook and cutthroat inhabit McLeod, a 13 acre lake which lies at 1006 feet elevation 5 miles N. of North Bend. It drains into Tate Creek and the N. Fork Snoqualmie River. Take county road N. for about 4.5 miles from North Bend, and take spur road H-10 for 0.4 miles E. to lake shore.

MEADOWBROOK SLOUGH. Three segments make up this 13.9 acre slough. It holds largemouth bass and yellow perch. Location is 1 mile E. fom Snoqualmie with drainage to Snoqualmie River.

MELAKWA LAKES. Lower Melakwa is at 4490 feet 3 miles NW from Snoqualmie Pass. It covers 7.9 acres and is fed by **UPPER MELAKWA**, a lake of 1.8 acres situated 300 feet N. Both hold rainbow and drain to Pratt River.

MERIDIAN LAKE. Rainbow furnish early season action in Meridian, while kokanee pick up fishing slack in mid-summer months, along with large and smallmouth bass, pumpkinseed, yellow perch and brown bullhead. The lake is 150 acres and has a small public access on its E. shore. A county park also offers boat launching facilities at 27103-148th SE. Meridian is located 4 miles E. of Kent on Hwy. 516. It drains to Soos Creek.

METCALF SLOUGH. Actually a series of marshy ponds covering about 5 acres and holding eastern brook and cutthroat. Metcalf is situated at the head of Ten Creek, 6.7 miles N. of North Bend. Drainage is to **METCALF LAKE**, a 6 acre pond which carries the same species of fish and is located at the slough's S. end. It drains to Snoqualmie River.

MILLER RIVER. A tributary of the Skykomish River's S. Fork, entering that stream 2 miles W. of town of Skykomish, the Miller provides fair rainbow fishing in October. Money Creek FS campground is situated near the Miller's mouth. FS road 6412 leads up the Miller 9 miles where trail 1072 extends 1.5 miles to **DOROTHY LAKE**. There are two FS campgrounds on this stretch adjacent to the river and road.

MONEYSMITH LAKE. Bass, perch, crappie and catfish are found in this 22 acre lake which lies 4 miles E. of Auburn and 0.5 miles S. of Holm Lake. Exceptionally large perch have been taken from this shallow lake in past years. Route is E. of Auburn on Auburn-Black Diamond road, crossing Green River and turning E. on Lake Holm road (336th) about 2 miles to Moneysmith road, then S. to lake.

MOOLOCK LAKE. 45 acre rainbow and cutthroat lake situated at 3903 feet about 1.5 miles SE of **HANCOCK LAKE'S** E. tip.

SNOW LAKE—A rainbow and cutthroat producer.

NADEAU LAKE lies adjacent to Moolock's S. shore. It is 19 acres and contains rainbow. S.M.C. LAKE is 41 acres and is located at 3702 feet elevation immediately to the S. of Nadeau. It holds rainbow. Spur 12 from the Spur 10 intersection about 6 miles N. on the county road from North Bend leads to within about 1 mile of the W. shore of S.M.C. Lake. Gate leading to this spur is sometimes locked.

MORTON LAKE. A rainbow and kokanee planted lake of 66 acres, Morton has a public access on its NW shore and is rated good in April. Route is E. from Auburn on Hwy. 516 for about 3.5 miles, then S. on Covington Way SE to SE 284th to 290th for 2.5 miles, then right on 188th Ave. SE for 1 mile to NW end of lake.

MURPHY LAKES. A pair of mountain lakes. Lower Murphy, 4300 feet elevation and 3.5 acres; Upper Murphy, 4500 feet, 7 acres, which lie at head of Murphy Creek 1.5 miles S. of Scenic on the Stevens Pass Hwy. The lakes hold rainbow and cutthroat. Best route is to follow the ridge on W. side of Murphy Creek S. to the lakes. No formal trail. **MYRTLE LAKE**. Rainbow planted lake of 18 acres which lies at 3950 feet 8.5 miles N. from Snoqualmie Pass. Fed by **LITTLE MYRTLE** LAKE 2800 feet S. of Big Myrtle. Lakes drain to North Fork Snoqualmie River.

NEWAUKUM CREEK. This Green River tributary heads under Enumclaw Mtn. and flows W. of the N. side of town of

Enumclaw, then N. a total of approximately 15 miles. It contains rainbow, cutthroat and a few steelhead. County roads cross and follow the stream at various points, providing relatively easy access.

NORDRUM LAKE. Cutthroat are present in Nordrum, a 60 acre lake situated at 3800 feet elevation 17 miles NE of North Bend in the headwaters of the Taylor River's S. Fork. **JUDY LAKE** is located 1500 feet W. of Nordrum. It covers 10 acres and is fed by underground outlet from Nordrum. **CAROLE LAKE**, 11 acres lies 3000 feet W. of Nordrum. ROCK and **LUNKER LAKES,** 9 and 3 acres, are in the same group. These lakes contain brown trout, cutts and rainbow. Route to the lakes is NE up the Snoqualmie River's Middle Fork from Hwy. 90 just 3.2 miles SE of North Bend, to mouth of the Taylor River, about 15 miles where there is a FS camp. The road NE up the Taylor River for 10 miles has been closed by a bridge washout. Nordrum Lake trail 1004, takes off from this point and continues 4 tough miles to Nordrum where there are campsites. Fishermen's trails lead to other lakes in the basin.

NORTH LAKE. A 55 acre rainbow lake which has a public access on its W. shore. North is located 3 miles W. of Auburn. It drains into Commencement Bay via Hylebos Creek. The lake is reached by driving past Federal Way on Hwy. 99 N. for 2 miles to Kitts Corner, then E. on S. 336th St. for 0.7 miles, then N. on 30th Ave. S. to W. shore of lake.

PANTHER LAKE. A 33 acre lake which hosts perch, bass and other spiny rays. It is located 2 miles N. of Kent on Hwy. 515 then E. for 0.5 miles on 204th St. to S. end of the lake.

PARADISE LAKE. There are cutthroat and rainbow in Paradise, an 18 acre private lake located 5 miles NE of Woodinville. The lake drains into Bear Creek and then into the Sammamish River. Route is E. from Woodinville 4.5 miles, passing Cottage Lake, then N. on Paradise Lake road 1.5 miles to S. side of lake.

PETERSON LAKE. A 10 acre lake located 1 mile SE of Spring Lake. Holds rainbow, perch, catfish and cutthroat. Drains to Cedar River.

PHANTOM LAKE. Located 3.5 miles SE of Bellevue. It covers 63.2 acres and drains to Lake Sammamish. Phantom has a road, SE Phantom Way, along its N. shore. Contains largemouth bass, black crappie, pumpkinseed, yellow perch and brown bullhead. Difficult access.

PHILLIPA LAKE. Phillipa is a mountain lake of 121 acres which holds rainbow. It lies at 3346 feet elevation at the headwaters of Phillipa Creek, a tributary of the Snoqualmie River's N. Fork, 11 miles NE from North Bend. Drains to North Fork Snoqualmie River. **ISABELLA LAKE** covers 12 acres and is located 700 feet E. of Phillipa. It has cutthroat. The lake is reached by driving N. from North Bend on the North Fork county road to Spur 10 Junction, about 6 miles continuing N. on the county road for another 8 miles where Spur 16 leads E. and S. up Brannon Creek for about 1.5 miles. Phillipa is located a rough 2 miles up the creek. There is no regular trail.

PINE LAKE. Rainbow, German brown, cutthroat and eastern brook are planted in Pine, an 88 acre lake situated 4 miles N. of Issaquah. It also has largemouth bass. Pine starts slow, but usually holds up for fishing during the season. To reach Pine turn N. at Issaquah from Hwy. 10 for 0.4 miles, then right or NE for 1 mile, taking left fork N. for 2.5 miles to the shore on 226th Ave. SE. County park on E. shore with boat launch and picnic area. Drains to Lake Sammamish.

PRATT RIVER. A tributary of the Middle Fork of Snoqualmie River, Pratt holds small rainbow, cutthroat and a few eastern brook. It is a turbulent mountain stream and offers best angling from mid- summer into fall. Follow Middle Fork Snoqualmie road (see Snoqualmie River for route) for about 9.5 miles where road touches W. side of Middle Fork. Cross Snoqualmie and strike trail 1007 up Pratt for about 4 miles. Rough campsites along stream.

PRESTON MILL PONDS. A pair of 2 acre rainbow ponds which drain into Raging River. The ponds are located at the community of Preston.

PTARMIGAN LAKE (Upper). Golden trout have been planted in this deep lake of 12.8 acres situated at 5000 feet. Drains to **LOWER PTARMIGAN**, 28 acres, located 800 feet SW of Lower Ptarmigan 7.8 miles

SE from Skykomish. Lakes drain to Deception Creek and Tye River.

RAGING RIVER. Primarily a winter steelhead stream, Raging River receives steelhead plants in its lower reaches. The river clears quickly and is often fishable when larger rivers are dirty. It joins the Snoqualmie River at Fall City, and a road from that town leads SW up Raging for 4 miles to Hwy. 90, continuing another 2 miles upstream.

RATTLESNAKE LAKE. Stocked with rainbow, this lake is around 100 acres when full, but fluctuates in size. It lies at 911 feet elevation. Take Cedar Falls road from Hwy. 90 at North Bend's E. city limits and drive S. 4 miles to E. shore of lake.

RAVENSDALE CREEK. Spring and summer months are best for Ravensdale Creek's cutthroat and rainbow. The brushy creek meanders about 3 miles SW from Ravensdale (Beaver) Lake, crossing under Hwy. 169 to enter the S. end of Sawyer Lake.

RAVENSDALE LAKE. (Beaver). Ravensdale is a brush-lined lake of 18 acres which offers fair to good rainbow and cutthroat angling in spring and fall. A road from Black Diamond leads N. for about 2 miles to E. side of the lake. The N.P. railroad skirts the SE shore.

RED CREEK. A late summer producer of small eastern brook. Red Creek is a tributary of the White River. It is reached by driving 6 miles E. of Enumclaw on Hwy. 410 which crosses the stream.

REID SLOUGH. Covering 3.4 acres, Reid is located 1.4 miles N. from North Bend. It contains largemouth bass and yellow perch. Drainage to Snoqualmie River.

RETREAT LAKE. (Thirty Two, Fish). Rainbow, cutthroat and kokanee are available from Retreat. The 53 acre lake also holds perch and crappie. It is located about 2 miles E. of Ravensdale. Road from Summit on Hwy. 169 approximately 4 miles S. of Maple Valley, heads E. 3.5 miles to W. end of lake which is nearly encircled by SE 276th and SE 280th. No public access.

ROCK CREEK. Rainbow are present in Rock Creek, a tributary of Cedar River which joins the stream 3 miles upstream from Maple Valley. The stream offers limited cutthroat fishing in the fall.

ROCK LAKE. A 23 acre lake stocked with brown and rainbow trout. Elevation is 4400 feet. Location is 5 miles S. from Skykomish with drainage to W. Fork Foss River.

ROUND LAKE. A pond of 2.6 acres holding largemouth bass. It is located about 2 miles E. from Issaquah, draining to Issaquah Creek.

RUTHERFORD SLOUGH. Also known as Fall City Slough, Rutherford covers 18 acres and lies 0.5 miles N. of Fall City adjacent to Hwy. 203. It contains rainbow and largemouth bass, with April, July and August best fishing months. An unusual feature of the slough is that a small lake is located on an island.

SAMMAMISH LAKE. The widest variety of fish are available in Sammamish, including large and smallmouth bass, perch, catfish, cutthroat, kokanee, rainbow, salmon and steelhead. The lake is 8 miles long and covers 4897 acres. Cutthroat hit in the spring and fall, with kokanee coming on in May. Sammamish is deep, 100 feet maximum. The N. end is marshy and offers good early morning and evening bass fishing when water level drops in mid-summer. Boats may be launched at the lake's S. end at state park. Roads parallel both shores, leading from Hwy. 90 a few miles E. of Bellevue. Sammamish is open to fishing year around.

SAMMAMISH RIVER. The Sammamish flows NW from N. end of Sammamish Lake to enter Lake Washington at Kenmore where a public boat launch site is located at the Kenmore bridge. The sluggish, ditch-like stream carries a fair run of winter steelhead, and offers sea-run cutthroat in spring and fall. Road from Bothell to Redmond affords easy access at many points.

SAWYER LAKE. There are kokanee, rainbow, small and largemouth bass, crappie, perch and catfish in Sawyer, a year around lake of 279 acres. Spring and fall are best for spiny rays and cutthroat, while kokanee hit from May into mid-summer. Occasionally the kokanee hit in early spring. There is a resort on the lake and public access at the county park on the W. shore which is reached by driving 7 miles E. from Kent on Hwy. 516 to 216th Ave. SE, then S. for 1.5 miles to SE 296th, then keeping right to launch area which is second road past fish screen on outlet stream.

SECOND LAKE. A rainbow and cutthroat planted lake of 2.5 acres located 3 miles E. from Enumclaw. Drainage to White River.

SHADOW LAKE. The lake covers 50 acres and has a public access on its N. shore, plus a resort. Route to Shadow is E. about 5 miles from Renton on Hwy. 169 to 196th Ave. SE then S. for 4 miles to NE side of the lake. Shadow gets rainbow plants and also contains largemouth bass, black crappie, pumpkinseed and yellow perch.

SHADY LAKE. (Hostak, Mud). Shady is a 21 acre lake which lies 5 miles SE of Renton. It gets rainbow and cutthroat plants and has a public access on its S. shore. Route is S. from Renton on 108th Ave. SE to 176th (Petrovitsky Road) then E. for about 5 miles to SE 192nd which circles lake.

SIKES LAKE. Eastern brook have been planted in Sikes, a 14 acre lake located on Carnation Farm, N. of town of Carnation. The lake also contains brown bullhead. Drainage is into Snoqualmie River.

SKYLINE LAKE. A 2 acre rainbow lake at 4950 feet elevation. Location is 1 mile N. from Stevens Pass. Drainage to Tye River.

SKYKOMISH RIVER. (South Fork). The S. Fork is formed by the Foss, Tye and Beckler Rivers which join 1 to 2 miles E. of town of Skykomish. The Miller River and Money Creek, other major tributaries, enter the Sky about 2 miles W. of Skykomish. Plants of legal rainbow are made at intervals from June into August depending upon water flows. Sunset Falls, located 2 miles upstream from the S. Fork's confluence with the N. Fork near Index junction in Snohomish County, blocks migratory fish. During fall and early winter months salmon, steelhead and cutthroat which collect under the falls are trapped and trucked around the barrier. The river above the falls provides good to excellent rainbow fishing in mid-summer. The Stevens Pass Hwy. closely follows the S. Fork from Index SE to Skykomish, then continues to the pass along the Tye River. (The N. Fork and main Skykomish are in Snohomish County). The river also produces summer steelhead.

SNOQUALMIE LAKE. There are rainbow, cutthroat and eastern brook in Snoqualmie Lake which lies at 3225 feet elevation in the headwaters of Taylor River. The 126 acre lake is reached by driving E. from North Bend on Hwy. 90 for 3.2 miles then turning N. off the highway to FS road 56, continuing for 12.7 miles to major road fork. Hike N. up Taylor River 7 miles to road end. Trail 1002 takes off from here 2.5 miles to

SAMMAMISH RIVER easily accessible and fished.

the lake. The trail continues 1 mile to **DEER LAKE**, a 46 acre rainbow and cutthroat lake at 3630 feet where there are campsites, and BEAR, 49 acres at 3670 feet elevation which is adjacent to E. side of Deer. Bear holds rainbow and cutthroat. One mile E. by trail lies **DOROTHY LAKE** at 3052 feet. It covers 290 acres and contains cutthroat and eastern brook. There are several campsites on this lake which drains into the Miller River's E. Fork. The other lakes empty into the Taylor River drainage.

SNOQUALMIE RIVER. (Main River). The main river is formed by the N., Middle and S. Forks which join about 1 mile E. of the town of Snoqualmie, then plunges over Snoqualmie Falls below the town. Winter steelhead are the big attraction from the falls downstream to the river's junction with the Skykomish River in Snohomish county. Liberal plants of migrant steelhead in Tokul Creek, Raging and Tolt Rivers, boost the river. Summer steelhead are planted in the Snoqualmie and Tolt, which joins the Snoqualmie near Carnation, and action starts about July 4 at the mouth and below for the sunshine steelhead. Winter steelheading kicks off in December and continues into March. Sea-run cutthroat are available from mid-July into fall. The river may be fished from the beach since roads follow its E. side for most of its length. There are boat launch sites just below Tokul Creek on the E. side and at mouth of Raging River at Fall City, plus an area at mouth of the Tolt.

SNOQUALMIE RIVER. (North Fork). Rainbow, cutthroat, whitefish and a few Dolly Varden are found in the N. Fork. The county road N. from North Bend follows the stream for 15 or more miles, then swings SE for 4 miles up Lennox Creek.

SNOQUALMIE RIVER. (Middle Fork). Good populations of cutthroat plus a few rainbow available for anglers who work for their fish. Good from mouth to source. The river is paralleled by a road which leave Hwy. 90 just 3.2 miles E. of North Bend, continuing NE on FS road 56 for 15 miles to Taylor River FS campground, then E. and S. for 11 miles to road end on the Cascade Crest. Dingford Creek campground is located 5 miles upstream from Taylor River campground.

SNOQUALMIE RIVER. (South Fork). This fork of the Snoqualmie River has good

numbers of cutthroat plus a few 'bows. Trout to 14 inches are available. There is easy access along the stream since Hwy. 90 follows it closely from North Bend upstream for 20 miles to Snoqualmie Pass. There are campsites at Asahel Curtis, Denny Creek and Commonwealth FS campgrounds along the upper stretch of river.

SNOW CREEK. A tributary of the upper Green River, Snow flows into the river 5 miles NE of Lester. It produces a few small cutthroat during summer months. Route is over Stampede Pass from Hwy. 90.

SNOW LAKE. Located at 4016 feet elevation, Snow is a 160 acre rainbow and cutthroat lake, which lies 3 miles NW of Snoqualmie Pass in the headwaters of the Snoqualmie River's Middle Fork. Trail 1013 starts at Alpental ski area and continues 4 miles to lake. Trail forks at Snow Lake with one fork dropping into the Middle Fork of Snoqualmie River for 7 miles to Goldmeyer Hot Springs. The other fork continues 0.5 miles to **GEM LAKE** at 4857 feet. It contains rainbow.

SOUPHOLE LAKE. A cutthroat planted lake of 3.4 acres at 820 feet on the King-Snohomish County line 4.5 miles NE from Duvall. Drainage to Lake Margaret.

SOURCE LAKE. Planted with cutthroat, the lake lies at 3750 feet 2.7 miles NW from Snoqualmie Pass on NE side of Bryant Peak. Drains to S. Fork Snoqualmie River.

SPOOK LAKE. An eastern brook planted, marshy lake of 19.5 acres 2.5 miles SE from Tolt. Drains to Tolt River.

SPRING LAKE. (Otter). Planted with rainbow and cutthroat and also holds largemouth bass, yellow perch and brown bullhead. The 68 acre lake drains via Peterson Creek into Cedar River. It has a public access on its W. shore. Location is 5 miles SE of Renton on Hwy. 169, then S. for 1.5 miles to NE tip of the lake on 196th SE.

STAR LAKE. April and May are productive months for Star Lake's planted rainbow. It also has largemouth bass, yellow perch and brown bullhead. The lake covers 34 acres. Public access is gained via S. 277th on the S. shore. Star is reached by driving S. from Kent's S. city limits on Military Road to S. 277th, then E. I.5 miles

to lake. Catfish, largemouth bass and kokanee are also present.

STEEL LAKE. Steel is 46 acres and is located 4 miles NW of Auburn. Public access
is through county park at S. 312th at 24th
S. Federal Way. The lake hosts planted
rainbow, largemouth bass, pumpkinseed,
yellow perch, black crappie and brown
bullhead. It drains to Hylebos Creek.

STICKNEY SLOUGH. Located in an old
river channel, Stickney covers 5.6 acres
and contains largemouth bass and yellow
perch. Location is 3 miles NW from Fall
City. Drainage to Snoqualmie River.

STOSSEL CREEK. Cutthroat and rainbow
are found in Stossel, a brushy stream which
heads under Platts Lookout on the
King-Snohomish County line and flows 6
miles S. to join the Tolt River 5 miles NE of
Carnation. Upper reaches of the creek are
reached by heading N. and E. from
Stillwater, on the Duvall-Carnation road, for
5 miles. **STOSSEL LAKE,** (Langendorfer)
lies at the head of the creek. It is 5 acres
and is said to hold cutthroat.

SUNDAY CREEK. Tributary to the upper
Green River, Sunday Creek provides rainbow action in early summer and again in
the fall. It enters the Green 2 miles E. of
Lester. and is paralleled by FS road 54 from
near the summit of Stampede Pass for
about 5 miles.

SUNDAY CREEK. A spring and fall rainbow producer, this Sunday Creek drains
Sunday and the Loch Katrine Lakes and
flows into the Snoqualmie River's N. Fork.
Has received winter steelhead plants.

SUNDAY LAKE. Located 13 miles NE from
North Bend at 1865 feet elevation at head
of Sunday Creek. The lake covers 21 acres
and contains cutthroat, eastern brook and
rainbow. Lower or **LITTLE SUNDAY** Lake
holds the same species of fish. It is a 2
acre pond. There are campsites on the
lakes. **LOCH KATRINE** is a 51 acre rainbow lake located 1 mile NW of Little Sunday Lake. The brushy-shored lake has a
campsite at its outlet, and is best from July
on. The lake may be reached by a logging
road which runs close to the lake's outlet.
UPPER LOCH KATRINE LAKE is located
at 4250 feet and 4500 feet S. of Loch
Katrine. It is 24 acres and holds cutthroat
and rainbow. Best route is to head cross
country SW from S. end of Sunday Lake
about 1.5 miles. It's a rough trip.

SURPRISE LAKE. Eastern brook are
found in Surprise. The 28 acre lake lies at
4600 feet. **GLACIER LAKE,** another
brookie lake, is located 1 mile S. Glacier's
elevation is 4900 feet and it covers 60
acres. The lakes are reached by trail heading S. from Scenic, on the Stevens Pass
Hwy. for 4.5 miles. There are campsites
on both lakes.

STEELHEAD PLUNKING popular on Snoqualmie River.

SURVEYORS LAKE. A rainbow stocked lake of 5.1 acres at 3980 feet elevation 2 miles S. from Snoqualmie Pass. Drainage to Rockdale Creek.

SWANS MILL POND. Swans is a 5 acre pond located 1.5 miles NE of Joy Lake. It contains eastern brook and cutthroat and drains into Stossel Creek.

T'AHL LAKE. Golden trout have been stocked in this high mountain lake of 6.5 acres. It lies at 5200 feet about 10 miles SE from Skykomish. Drainage is to Necklace Valley and E. Fork Foss River.

TALAPUS LAKE. Situated at 3270 feet the lake covers 17.8 acres and has been planted with brown trout. It lies 4.7 miles W. from Snoqualmie Pass. Drainage is to S. Fork Snoqualmie River.

TATE CREEK. A tributary of Snoqualmie River's N. Fork, Tate holds rainbow and eastern brook. It produces small trout from spring into fall. Route to Tate is up the North Fork road 1 mile from the mouth of the Snoqualmie's N. Fork.

TAYLOR RIVER. A major tributary of the Snoqualmie River's Middle Fork, the Taylor provides fair to good rainbow and cutthroat angling from July into fall months. Route is E. from North Bend on Hwy. 90 for 3.2 miles, then N. to and up FS road 56 for 12.7 miles on a rough road. Road blocked at Taylor River near mouth. Walk or trail bike. Trail at road end leads 2 miles to Snoqualmie Lake, the river's source.

TERRACE LAKES. Lakes of 2 and 1.8 acres which contain rainbow. They lie at 5200 and 5300 feet 7 miles S. from Scenic on SW side of Terrace Mtn. Drainage is to Tye River.

THOMPSON LAKE. (Horseshoe). Thompson is a rainbow lake of 47 acres situated at 3650 feet elevation. Drainage is to the Pratt River. Shortest route is N. from Hwy. 90 along Middle Fork of the Snoqualmie River for 3.5 miles where a rough road leads E. along Granite Creek to and past Granite Lakes. A trail takes off from a logging road above Granite for 1.5 miles E. to Thompson Lake. At the head of Granite Creek are **LOWER GRANITE LAKE**, a 9 acre lake at 2950 feet elevation, and **UPPER GRANITE**, 15 acres at 3060 feet. The lakes are close together and have been

TOLT RIVER steelhead beached by Milt Keizer.

planted with rainbow. Logging road up Granite Creek at the 2.5 mile mark passes within 0.4 miles of E. side of the lakes. Maze of roads in this area complicate the route. It's a 4x4 rig show.

TOKUL CREEK. Beaver pond fishing in upper reaches of Tukul Creek for cutthroat, eastern brook and rainbow is fair to good during early summer and again in the fall. There is winter steelheading in lower stretch. The creek heads 8 miles N. of Snoqualmie. A road heads N. up the creek, leaving the highway 1 mile NW of town of Snoqualmie at the power house. Gates block road much ot the time. It leads upstream about 7 miles. Upper stretches may be reached by driving N. from North Bend on the North Fork county road 6 miles to Spur 10 intersection. A logging road leads W. for 2.5 miles to the stream. Locked gates often block this road. **BEAVER** and **TEN CREEKS** are small, brushy tributaries of Tokul, entering high. They offer best fishing in small beaver ponds and contain cutthroat with some eastern brook. Tokul enters the Snoqualmie River about 1 mile below Snoqualmie Falls.

TOLT RIVER. Both summer and winter

steelhead stack in the Tolt which joins Snoqualmie River 0.5 miles SW of Carnation. Winter steelheading is primarily in lower 6 miles. A road from center of Carnation leads upstream 4 miles NE on the river's W. side to a public access area at road end. The river may be fished up and downstream from this point. December, January and February are best for the Tolt's planted winter fish, while July into October are summer steelheading months. There is a popular public fishing area at mouth of the Tolt reached by turning W. for 0.4 miles off Hwy. 203 at the Tolt River bridge at S. outskirts of Carnation. Access to N. and S. Forks of the Tolt is complicated by restrictions by City of Seattle and by Weyerhaeuser Co. which sometimes locks gates leading to the river. The forks may be reached by leaving Hwy. 203 at Stillwater, 2 miles N. of Carnation and driving about 5 miles N. and W. past Joy and Moss Lakes, then walking E. about 1 mile.

TOP LAKE. A 5 acre lake at 4500 feet 3.8 miles S. from Skykomish. Planted with rainbow and cutthroat. Drainage to Evans Lake and Foss River.

TRADITION LAKE. Tradition is a spiny ray lake—yellow perch—of 19 acres which lies 1.4 miles E. of Issaquah. Drainage is into Issaquah Creek. Elevation of the lake is 490 feet, and it is reached by driving E. from Issaquah 2 miles, then turning SW on a rough road 0.4 miles to the lake which is located under the power line. Difficult access.

TROUT LAKE. (Jovita). An 18 acre rainbow lake, Trout is located 2 miles NE of Milton. It also holds spiny rays. Public access is gained from a county road and on the lake's S. shore. Route is E. from Milton on S. 348th street 0.5 miles, then NE on a county road to the W. side of the lake at 43rd S. and 376th. Trout is situated 0.4 miles S. of **FIVE MILE LAKE.**

TWELVE LAKE. (Cow). Rainbow are stocked in Twelve which also holds largemouth bass, pumpkinseed, yellow perch and brown bullhead. It is a 43 acre lake which lies 1.5 miles NE of Black Diamond and has a public access on its S. shore. Take Green River Gorge road E. from town to 270th Place SE and turn left to W. tip of lake.

TYE RIVER. The Tye is a major tributary of the Skykomish River's S. Fork joining the river at outskirts of town of Skykomish.

The Stevens Pass Hwy. follows the Tye for its entire length to headwaters at summit of Stevens Pass. Plants of legal rainbow are made at intervals in the Tye from June to August, depending upon water levels.

UNION LAKE. A 598 acre lake situated in the heart of Seattle. The lake holds rainbow, migrating steelhead and salmon, cutthroat, bass, crappie and perch. It is fed by a canal from Lake Washington and drains into Puget Sound through the Ballard Locks.

WALKER LAKE. (Crow). Walker is a 12 acre lake which hosts rainbow, cutthroat, and pumpkinseed. Route to the lake is 0.5 miles SW of Cumberland then E. 1 mile to the lake which is circled by a road. There is a public access area on the lake's SW shore.

WASHINGTON LAKE. A natural lake of 22,138 acres, Washington is 20 miles long and is located on the E. side of Seattle. It is fed by the Cedar and Sammamish Rivers, plus smaller streams, and drains into Union Lake. The lake contains rainbow, cutthroat, kokanee, large and smallmouth bass, catfish, crappie, perch, along with migrating steelhead and salmon. It is 209 feet deep at deepest point, and is reported to hold a few mackinaw. The lake is open year around and is under-fished. Those who have studied the huge lake make consistently good catches. Trout fishing is best October through April, with kokanee starting in May. Bass cooperate from May through August and again in late fall. Silver and chinook salmon concentrate at the mouths of Sammamish and Cedar Rivers from September into November. Sea-run cutthroat are in these areas during same period. Top bass area for both large and smallmouths, along with crappie, is in Union Bay near the U. of W. Stadium and in inlets of the arboretum. Waters around Juanita are good for largemouth. There are several public access areas around the lake including sites at mouths of Cedar at the S. end and Sammamish at the N. end, under the W. end of the old floating bridge, at town of Kirkland, plus several other areas in city parks. There are public fishing docks at various points around the lake.

WILDCAT LAKES. Upper Wildcat Lake covers 54 acres and carries rainbow and cutthroat. It is located at 4218 feet elevation 5.4 miles NW of Snoqualmie Pass. **LOWER WILDCAT** is 19 acres and lies at

OPENING DAY on Lake Wilderness draws crowds.

3880 feet about 1500 feet E. of the upper lake. It has rainbow and cutthroat. Shortest route is NE up the Snoqualmie River's Middle Fork from Tanner on Hwy. 90 for 16 miles to Wildcat Creek, then SW up the creek 2 miles to the lower lake. Upper Wildcat is 0.4 miles W. up the inlet stream.

WILDERNESS LAKE. There are planted rainbow and kokanee in Wilderness. The lake is best in April and May. It is 66 acres and lies 2.5 miles S. of Maple Valley at 470 feet elevation. Public access is through county park at 22601 SE 248th St. Route is S. from Maple Valley 1.5 miles on Hwy. 169 continuing S. on 228th Ave. SE to N. tip of lake.

WISE CREEK. A tributary of the Middle Fork of the Snoqualmie River, Wise produces rainbow and cutthroat from mid-summer into fall. It has been fry planted in past years. It enters the river 1.5 miles downstream from the mouth of Taylor River.

WITTENMEYER LAKE. A 3 acre lake containing largemouth bass and yellow perch. Location is 1.5 miles NE from Juanita. Drainage to Lake Washington.

WINDY LAKE. A 5.7 acre lake that holds planted rainbow. It is located at 4186 feet elevation about 5 miles NW from Snoqualmie Pass. Drainage is to Kaleetan Lake and Pratt River.

KING COUNTY RESORTS

Green Lake: Green Lake Boathouse, 206-527-0171.

Green River: Green River Gorge Resort, Enumclaw, WA. 866-2302.

Sammamish Lake: Vasa Park, Bellevue, WA 98009. 206-746-3260.

Alexander's Beach Resort, Issaquah, WA 98027. 641 -5803.

Sawyer Lake: Lake Sawyer Resort. 30250-224th Ave. SE, Kent, WA 98131. 206-886-2244.

Shadow Lake: Foss' Shadow Lake Park, Renton, WA.206- 631-2440.

Snoqualmie River: Snoqualmie River Campground. 206-652-7083.

Washington Lake: Rainier Beach Moorage, Seattle, WA 98101. 206-725-9271.

Remove line twists like this

If a fishing line is twisted, this can be remedied by simply dragging the line in the water behind a boat. The water flowing over the line will take the twist out of it.

KITSAP

COUNTY

Most of Kitsap's 469 square miles are bordered by Puget Sound or Hood Canal waters. The county is relatively flat, with highest elevation being Gold Mountain at 1761 feet. It has countless beaver ponds which have been planted regularly over the years with cutthroat and eastern brook, plus some rainbow. Largest lake is Long which covers 314 acres. Bainbridge and Blake Islands are both in Kitsap. The county ranks 36th in relative size in the state.

BEAR LAKE. Marshy shore lines surround this private 12 acre bass lake which lies 3.8 miles E. of Belfair. Drainage is to Case Inlet. Road from S. border of Bremerton Airport leads 1 mile to lake's W. shore. No public access.

BIG BEEF CREEK. Rated "good" for sea-run cutthroat from July to October, the creek also holds limited numbers of winter steelhead in December, January and February. It heads near Tahuya Lake and flows N. to enter Hood Canal at Big Beef Harbor, 2 miles NE of Seabeck. A road from the mouth heads upstream for about 0.5 mile.

BAINBRIDGE ISLAND LAKE. (Grazzam). Located on W. side of Bainbridge Island,

Kitsap
County

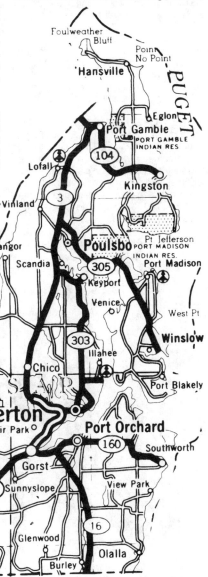

the 12.7 acre lake is planted with rainbow. Drainage is to Port Orchard.

BUCK LAKE. Located near tip of Kitsap Peninsula approximately 1.5 miles SW of Hansville, Buck is stocked with rainbow. It has a public access on its E. shore. County road from Hansville leads to the lake.

BURLEY CREEK. Flows into Burley Lagoon at head of Henderson Bay. It's a short run stream of about 5 miles. Hwy. 16, flanks the E. side for most of its length. Steelhead and cutthroat are available.

COULTER CREEK. This creek heads E. of the Bremerton Airport and is fed in part by Kriegler Lake. It flows SW into Mason County, and yields fair cutthroat angling from July into October. Road from mouth follows creek for about 2.5 miles.

CURLEY CREEK. Outlet of Long Lake, Curley flows NE for 2.5 miles to join Puget Sound at South Colby. The small stream produces sea-run cutthroat in spring and fall months, and has been planted with winter steelhead. Road from South Colby, located between Port Orchard and Harper on Hwy. 160 follows Curley Creek upstream to Long Lake.

FAIRVIEW LAKE. (Therese). A private

lake of 7.5 acres which contains largemouth bass and brown bullhead plus some rainbow. It is located 6.7 miles SW of Port Orchard. Drainage to Case Inlet.

FLORA LAKE. Privately owned, Flora covers 6.5 acres and holds rainbow, largemouth bass and brown bullhead. It is situated 5 miles SW of Port Orchard with drainage to Sinclair Inlet.

GLUD PONDS. Three small ponds located 3.8 miles S. of Keyport on Steel Creek. Ponds have been stocked with rainbow and cutthroat. Drainage is to Burke Bay.

HORSESHOE LAKE. Planted rainbow boost this 40 acre lake. It also holds brown bullhead. Horseshoe is best in April and May. Route to lake is S. on Hwy. 16 from Port Orchard for 7 miles, then W. 2 miles through Burley, and S. again 1 mile to the W. shore of Horseshoe where there is a public access site. Drainage via Bear Creek.

ISLAND LAKE. Located 2 miles SW of Keyport on Hwy. 303, Island is nearly encircled by county roads. The lake covers 43 acres and receives plants of rainbow. It contains brown bullhead. Private boats may be launched from a county road access on E.side. Drainage to Barker Creek.

TAHUYA RIVER's mouth draws steelhead anglers.

KITSAP LAKE. A rainbow lake of 238.4 acres, Kitsap produces throughout the season, and sometimes produces large trout in early spring. It has a public access on the W. shore. Kitsap is located 1 mile W. of Bremerton with Hwy. 3 running close to the lake's N. tip. County roads circle the lake. Kitsap produces cutthroat through much of the year, and also holds largemouth bass, bluegill and brown bullhead. It drains to Kitsap Creek.

LONG LAKE. A 314 acre, narrow lake that stretches 2 miles in length. Long contains cutthroat, largemouth bass, catfish, crappie, bluegill steelhead and salmon. Inlet is Salmonberry Creek, and outlet is Curley Creek. There is a public access on lake's W. shore. Fishing is best from May through September. The lake is located 3.5 miles SE of Port Orchard, with county roads from East Port Orchard leading to and around lake.

LUDVICK LAKE. A 2 acre lake located in headwaters of Dewatto River 2 miles S. from Holly. It contains largemouth bass and native cutthroat. **MISSION LAKE.** The lake is planted with rainbow and is noted as a lake which offers hold-over trout each spring. Brown bullhead are also present. It is 88 acres and has a public access on its N. shore. Route to Mission is S. from Gorst on old Belfair highway to Bear Creek store, then right on Bear Creek road for 3 miles to Mission Lake road. **MISSION POND**, which covers 4 acres, lies 2000 feet SE of Mission Lake. It contains cutthroat and catfish and drains into Union River via Bear Creek.

PANTHER LAKE. (No Fish). It really does have fish-rainbow-which are planted, and brown bullhead. The lake covers 104 acres and is situated 10 miles W. of Bremerton. Panther produces in the spring and again in the fall, and drains into Panther Creek and then into the Tahuya River. Approximateiy 30 acres of this lake is in Mason County. Panther is reached by driving S. on the old Belfair highway from Gorst to Bear Creek Corner, then right on Bear Creek road to lake. Public access located on S. shore.

SCOUT LAKE. (Tin Mine). Rainbow, cutthroat and eastern brook are found in Scout, a private 3 acre pond. It is located 2 miles SW of Wildcat Lake, with drainage into Tin Mine Creek to Tahuya River.

SQUARE LAKE. A rainbow lake of 8 acres located 4.5 miles SW of Port Orchard. It provides fair spring largemouth bass fishing. Situated in state park of 237 acres. Gravel boat launch. Drainage is via a swampy area to Square Creek and Sinclar Inlet. at SE end of lake.

TAHUYA LAKE. A peat bog lake of 17.9 acres which contains largemouth bass. Location is 5 miles S. from Seabeck. It drains to Tahuya River.

THREE FINGER CHAIN BEAVER PONDS. Cutthroat planted ponds located W. of Hintzville cut-off. Drive W. on Bear Creek road across Tahuya River about 0.8 miles, then right on Hintzville road. Many roads and trails leading from this road touch the ponds along their several miles of length. Roads may not be open to vehicles. Large cutthroat have been taken from these ponds.

TIGER LAKE. Only 6 of Tiger's 109 acres are in Kitsap County, with the rest in Mason County. It is a planted rainbow and cutthroat lake that does very well for anglers from spring opener into summer. Road from S. end of Mission Lake leads 0.5 miles to N. tip of Tiger. The lake has a public access on N. side.

WILDCAT LAKE. Public access on Wildcat's N. shore and a county campground on E. shore. The lake is 117 acres and gets plants of rainbow. Largemouth bass and brown bullhead are also present. It usually does well in the spring, and then comes on strong during the fall. Outlet is Wildcat Creek which drains into Dyes Inlet. The lake is located 6 miles NW of Bremerton. Best route is 3 miles NW of Bremerton on Hwy. 3, then W. and N. on Seabeck highway up Wildcat Creek for 2.5 miles, then S. for 1.5 miles to the lake which is ringed by a road.

WYE LAKE. (Y). A rainbow planted lake of 38 acres, situated 3.5 miles SE of Belfair. It also holds brown bullhead. There is a public access on S. shore of Wye. The lake is reached by turning S. from Hwy. 3 about 2 miles W. of Gorst at head of Sinclair Inlet, driving 3 miles S. passing through Sunnyslope, then W. 0.5 miles, and S. again 2.5 miles to Wye, passing Bear Lake enroute. A road circles Wye. Drainage is to Case Inlet.

Kittitas

COUNTY

Centered in the state, Kittitas is mountainous over much of its 2341 square miles. Mt. Daniel on the Cascade Crest is highest point at 7986 feet. The Yakima River and its tributaries drain most of Kittitas. Of the 200-plus lakes in the county, over 150 are situated over 2500 feet elevation. Largest natural lake is Waptus with 246 acres. Best trout fishing is after July 1 in the alpine lakes, with fall months best. The portion of Yakima River in Kittitas provides excellent fishing for

large trout. Some of the most productive water lies in steep canyons between Cle Elum and Ellensburg. Kittitas is the 7th largest county in the state.

ALASKA LAKE. A 35 acre lake located 3.8 miles NE of Snoqualmie Pass at an elevation of 4230 feet. It is fed by Ridge Lake with drainage to upper Gold Creek and Keechelus Lake. The lake holds cutthroat and is reached by the Gold Creek trail which is accessed via the Hyak exit from Hwy. 90 to FS road 2202. Turn left after crossing Gold Creek and proceed up Gold Creek Valley and follow road to trail.

BAKER LAKE. (Thetis). There are planted rainbow and small eastern brook in this 5 acre lake which lies at 4220 feet in headwaters of Thetis Creek. Drainage is to Kachess. Route is 3 miles N. from Hwy. 90 on Lake Kachess road to microwave sign, then left to tower on road, then buck brush 0.5 miles down hill to lake. Campsites and rafts on lake.

BOX CANYON LAKE. Lake of 1.6 acres planted with cutthroat. Elevation is 4500 feet

Kittitas County

and location is 6.5 miles E. from Snoqualmie Pass. Drainage to Kachess River.

BULLFROG POND. A rainbow planted 2.9 acre pond adjacent to W. side of Bullfrog cutoff road on E. side of Cle Elum River.

CABIN CREEK. Contains both eastern brook and rainbow. June and July are best fishing months for the small creek which is a tributary to the upper Yakima River. Take Cabin Creek road E. out of Easton for about 3 miles. The road crosses the creek near the old logging camp of Upham. The road continues upstream for several miles.

CARIBOU CREEK. May and June are top fishing months for this rainbow stream. It is located E. of Ellensburg where it bisects the irrigated valley before emptying into the Yakima River. Drive E. on Hwy. 90 about 6 miles from Ellensburg to Caribou road which follows the creek for a few miles.

CHIKAMIN LAKE. A rainbow lake of 18.3 acres located 6.5 miles NE of Snoqualmie Pass on Cascade Crest. Elevation is 5785 feet. Drainage to Cooper River.

CLE ELUM LAKE. Enlarged by dam on natural lake on Cle Elum River, the lake covers 4810 acres and hosts rainbow, cutthroat, kokanee, Dolly Varden, eastern brook, whitefish and burbot. It comes on

for 8-10 inch kokanee after June 1. An occasional mackinaw to 20 pounds is caught by trollers. Trolling is most effective fishing method for most species in the lake. The big reservoir stretches for nearly 8 miles, and the road to Salmon La Sac touches it at a number of spots. Boats may be launched at Wishpoosh and at Bell, Morgan and Dry Creeks. Elevation of the lake is 2223 feet, and it is situated 7.3 miles NE of Cle Elum on the Salmon La Sac road.

CLE ELUM RIVER. Easy access is available on the upper section from Cle Elum Lake upstream to within about 2 miles of the river's source at Hyas Lake. The top section is not stocked with rainbow until July when snow run-offs are completed. Large tributaries, including Cooper and Waptus Rivers and Fortune Creek, offer additional fishing. Best fishing comes early in May, and then again in July, August and part of September. Excellent campsites at Salmon La Sac FS campground. Lower sections of the Cle Elum River are rated "fair" for rainbow in May and June.

COLE CREEK. Contains eastern brook, and is most productive in May and June. The creek is located about 5 miles SW of Easton and is a tributary of Cabin Creek. It is reached by driving S. up the Cabin Creek road.

COLEMAN CREEK. Most productive period for this small stream, a tributary to Naneum, is May and June. Route to the creek is via the Fairview road which leaves Hwy. 90 about 4 miles E. of Ellensburg.

COOKE CREEK. A small stream ranked "good" for rainbow. It gets the nod in May and June. Best stretch is on N. edge of valley adjacent to irrigated area. Cooke drains into Wipple Wasteway near S. end of Kittitas valley and may be reached by driving up the Cooke canyon road 8 miles E. and 7 miles N. of Ellensburg.

COOPER LAKE. The 120 acre lake contains rainbow, cutthroat and kokanee. It lies at 2788 feet elevation 3.5 miles NW of Salmon La Sac. There are several campsites on the shores. To reach Cooper, turn left on Cle Elum River road 1 mile S. of Salmon La Sac on road 229. Boat launch. Prime fishing time is June, July and October.

COTTONWOOD LAKES. Upper lake is 1.5 acres. and the lower lake covers 8.3 acres.

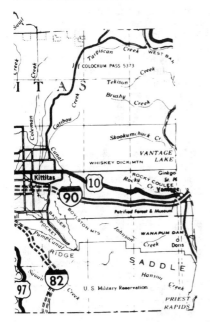

CLE ELUM LAKE covers 4810 acres.

Elevation of the lakes is 3900 feet They drain into Lost Lake and thence into Keechelus Lake. The Cottonwoods have been planted with cutthroat, brookies and rainbow. Drive up the Lost Lake road from Stampede Pass road and continue about 1 mile past Lost to Mirror Lake trail. Walk about 0.5 miles. The lakes are brushy and difficult to fish from shore. **MIRROR LAKE** lies 0.5 miles W. of Cottonwood at 4195 feet. It holds chunky rainbow and cutthroat. From Mirror Lake the Cascade Crest trail leads another 0.5 miles to **TWILIGHT LAKE** which holds cutthroat.

DEEP LAKE. A 52 acre lake located 9.5 miles N. of Salmon La Sac at 4450 feet. Reached by driving up Cle Elum River past Fish Lake guard station 2 miles. Trail crosses river and continues 2.5 miles S. past Squitch Lake to Pacific Crest trail, then down to the lake. Total distance 7.5 miles. Lake has open shores and fine campsites. It is planted with rainbow. Best fishing is from mid-August through fall. Another 6 lakes may be reached with short hikes from Deep. **PEGGY'S POND** lies 2700 feet N. of Deep at base of Cathedral Rock at 5600 feet. The 5 acre pond has been planted with cutthroat. **DEER LAKES**, 1 and 4 acres, are situated 2400 feet S. of Deep at 4600 feet. They hold rainbow. **CIRCLE LAKE** is at 6100 feet and lies 0.8 miles W. of Deep. It is cradled in a deep bowl, covers 48 acres, and contains 'bows. It usually is frozen until late August. **VINCENTE LAKE** is at 5700 feet and is situated 1.4 miles SW of Deep. It is 11 acres and contains cutthroat.

DIAMOND LAKE. Cutthroat are present in this 5.1 acre lake which lies at 4950 feet 4 miles NW from Salmon La Sac on Polallie Ridge. Drainage is to Hour Creek.

EASTON LAKE. May and June are top fishing months at Easton, a 237 acre reservoir located 0.5 miles NW of Easton. It is formed by a dam on the Yakima River, and is also fed by Kachess River. Rainbow and brown trout are planted. Other species of fish in Easton include cutthroat and eastern brook. Lake Easton state park is situated on the N. shore of the lake, offering boat launch facilities plus cabins and overnight camping.

EASTON PONDS. Both brown and rainbow trout have been stocked in these ponds, the largest of which is 12.7 acres. They are located adjacent to E. side of Easton on S. side of Yakima River. The ponds are former gravel pits. Drainage to Yakima River.

FIO RITO LAKE. A 54 acre lake located 5 miles S. of Ellensburg just E. of Hwy.I-82. Rainbow and brown trout planted with brown bullhead and pumpkinseed also present. Public access.

FISH LAKE (Tucquala). Popular lake of 63 acres located 7.5 miles N. of Salmon La Sac. It is a narrow, shallow and weedy lake, and most fishing is done in channels. Fish lake holds rainbow and eastern brook. Small boats may be launched adjacent to the road, where there are good camping spots. Meadows around the lake some years furnish good huckleberry picking in August and September.

FRENCH CABIN CREEK. Yields rainbow in July and August. It drains into upper Cle Elum River 0.4 miles N. of Cle Elum Lake. To reach the creek drive N. on Salmon La Sac road crossing Cle Elum River on French Cabin Creek road #2211.

GLACIER LAKE. Golden trout have been stocked in this 2.8 acre lake at 4780 feet. It lies 2800 feet NW from **LILLIAN LAKE** on Rampart Ridge. It outlets to Gold Creek.

GOLD CREEK. Leave Hwy. 90 at Hyak exit to FS road 2202 and follow road up creek about 2 miles upstream. A trail continues up the creek for another 5 miles to JOE LAKE, the source of Gold Creek. Summer and fall are top fishing periods for the creek's cutthroat. Joe Lake is at 4624 feet and covers 30 acres. It has been planted with cutthroat and rainbow. Last 1.5 miles to lake are tough.

GOLD LAKE. A rainbow planted lake of 2.8 acres at 4780 feet. It lies 2800 feet NW from **LILLIAN LAKE** on Rampart Ridge. It outlets to Gold Creek.

HANSEN'S PONDS. A pair of rainbow and brown trout planted ponds situated at Cle Elum just S. of Hwy. 90. Public access.

HUDSON CREEK. Eastern brook are present in this Yakima River tributary. Summer is best fishing time. Route to the creek is via Cabin Creek road about 5 miles W. of Easton off Hwy. 90 on exit 63.

HYAS LAKE. A short hike of about 1.5 miles from end of Fish Lake road along upper Cle Elum River 11 miles N. of Salmon La Sac leads to the lake. It holds eastern brook and is rated fair from late July through September. Lake is at 3550 feet elevation and covers 124 acres.

KACHESS LAKE. Contains kokanee, rainbow, cutthroat, Dolly Varden, mackinaw and a few fresh water lingcod, (burbot). The lake extends over 10 miles and covers 4540 acres when full. It was created by a dam on Kachess River. By early June Kachess starts to deliver kokanee of 8-9 inches. Exit ramp from Hwy. 90 about 2 miles E. of lower end of Keechelus Lake leads to W. shore of Kachess where a re-

sort and several FS campgrounds are located. Road reaching half-way up E. shore of lake takes off from Hwy. 90 just W. of Easton. FS trail on W. side of lake parallels **LITTLE KACHESS**, connected with the big lake by a narrow neck. Tough, brushy route NW up **MINERAL CREEK** to **PARK LAKES**, about 5 miles from N. end of Kachess. Logging road and trail heads W. from Lake Kachess forest camp 4 miles to **SWAN LAKE** at 4040 feet. The 7 acre lake has been planted with cutthroat and rainbow. Several good camp areas. **ROCK RABBIT LAKES** are 2 small ponds located 1300 and 1800 feet S. and SW of Swan. **STONES THROW LAKE** is another pond just 1800 feet NW of Swan. Fishing in these tiny lakes is for small cutthroat. Best fishing comes after first of July.

KACHESS RIVER. Connects Kachess Lake with Lake Easton. Produces a few rainbow early in the season. Occasional kokanee taken.

KEECHELUS LAKE. Located 3 miles SE of Snoqualmie Pass. Hwy. 90 parallels E. shore of the 2560 acre reservoir which was created by a dam on the Yakima River. After June 1 kokanee in the 10-12 inch range start hitting. Other fish species include rainbow, cutthroat, Dolly Varden, and limited numbers of burbot. FS campground is located on Yakima River. Use Hwy. 90 exit 62. Boats may be launched at site on Hyak side of lake.

KENDALL PEAK LAKES. Series of 3 lakes of 2.1, 3.8 and 6.6 acres at head of Coal Creek about 1.8 miles E. from Snoqualmie Pass. Elevations range from 4380 to 4780 feet. Rainbow present.

LAURA and **LILLIAN LAKES.** It requires a tough scramble of 2.5 miles up Rocky Run Creek from Rocky Run guard station on Keehelus Lake to reach these lakes. Lillian can be reached by hiking 6.5 miles from FS road 2112 on trail number 1332. A poor trail climbs from 2517 feet to 4410 feet at Laura and to 4800 feet at Lillian, which is a 17 acre lake containing rainbow. Laura covers 3 acres and lies 700 feet SW of Lillian. It is stocked with rainbow.

LAVENDER LAKE. A 26 acre rainbow and brown trout lake located 2 miles E. of Easton at East Nelson interchange.

LEMAH LAKE. Golden trout are present in this small (0.5 acre) lake 8 miles NE from

Snoqualmie Pass. Elevation is 3900 feet. Drainage is to Pete Lake and Cooper River.

LOST LAKE. Overlooks Keechelus Lake from W. side. Reached by leaving Hwy. 90 at the Stampede Pass exit at lower end of Keechelus, and driving 1 mile to Lost Lake road fork. Turn W. for 4 miles to lake shore. Unimproved but pleasant campsites at E. end of 144 acre lake. Rough boat launch site. Lost contains cutthroat, eastern brook, plus kokanee. Elevation is 3089 feet. Road continues about 1.5 miles where trail to **MIRROR** and **COTTONWOOD LAKES** starts.

LOST LAKE. Take road W. up Taneum Creek from Hwy. 90 about 4 miles NW of Thorp for 11 miles to FS road 1905, then 8 miles to FS road 1807 for 4 miles to Buck Meadows. Lake is located 1.5 miles by trail SW of this point. Elevation is 4820 feet, and the lake is 9 acres. Eastern brook and cutthroat are caught with July and early August the best. Trail continues SE 1.4 miles to **MANATASH LAKE** at 5000 feet. This lake covers 23 acres and lies in a timbered bowl. A trail leaves Buck Meadows and leads another 1.5 miles past Lost Lake. Total hiking distance is 4.1 miles. Manastash holds eastern brook, some of good size, although average size is 8-10 inches. The lake is slowed by heavy algae growth in late summer. Good camping spots along the open shore.

MICHAEL LAKE. (Round). Drive past Salmon La Sac and Fish Lake to Cathedral Rock trail which bridges Cle Elum River. Hold to left up Trail Creek about 3.5 miles where trail forks E. 3.5 miles to Michael. Elevation is 5100 feet. The 17 acre lake has been planted with rainbow and fishing is easy from open shore line. **LAKE TERENCE** lies about 0.8 miles SW of Michael at 5550 feet. Trail crosses outlet of Michael Lake and continues SW. Terence contains rainbow and covers 14 acres.

MILK LAKE. Road leads to lake from Hwy. 410 from take-off point 0.5 miles S. of Little Naches campground. The lake is 3 acres, lies at 4700 feet, and contains rainbow and eastern brook. Camping on lake.

MIRROW LAKE. A deep, rainbow lake of 29 acres at 4195 feet 5.8 miles S. from Snoqualmie Pass and 1400 feet SW from **COTTONWOOD LAKE**. It drains to Lost Lake and Roaring Creek.

NANEUM CREEK. Upper stretches produce native cutthroat of 7-10 inches, while rainbow furnish action in lower reaches. Most productive time is late May and June, with best rainbow fishing in the portion of creek from city of Ellensburg intake downstream. Small cutthroat and rainbow are available above intake. Naneum is a tributary of Yakima River and is reached via the Naneum road. Gate on private land near power lines. Other routes are Jeep

JACK HOYT presents a fly to Hansen Pond trout.

roads from Clockum road and trails from Table Mtn.

NANEUM POND. A rainbow planted 1.5 acre pond 0.2 miles N. from Hwy. 10 and adjacent to E. side of Naneum road about 4 miles E. of Ellensburg. Drainage to Yakima River.

PETE LAKE. Cooper Lake road from Salmon La Sac comes within 3 miles of the lake which is situated at 2980 feet and covers 37 acres. It is a beautiful mountain lake that yields rainbow and an occasional eastern brook. Good undeveloped camping areas along the lake.

PARK LAKES. Rainbow lakes of 9.8 and 10.8 acres situated 6 miles E. from Snoqualmie Pass on SW side of Chikamin Ridge. Elevations are 4510 and 4700 feet. Outlet to upper Mineral Creek.

RACHEL LAKE. This 27.3 acre lake contains cutthroat. It is located 4 miles NE from Snoqualmie Pass on Ramport Ridge. Drainage to Box Canyon Creek.

RIDGE LAKE. Elevation of this 2.3 acre, golden trout stocked lake is 5220 feet. Location is 3.5 miles NE from Snoqualmie Pass and 1700 feet W. from **ALASKA LAKE** to which it drains.

SPADE LAKE. Strike trail at Salmon La Sac to **WAPTUS LAKE** 8.5 miles, turn left and follow Spinole Creek trail 1 mile to P.C. trail. Turn left on P.C. trail 1.5 miles to Spade Lake trail which leads a steep 3 miles to lake at 5050 feet. Spade covers 122 acres and holds cutthroat.

SQUAW LAKE. A 12.4 acre lake which hosts rainbow. Elevation is 4850 feet and location is 9 miles N. from Salmon La Sac. Outlet is to Cle Elum River.

STIRRUP LAKE. Rainbow inhabit this 9.1 acre lake at 3550 feet. Location is 3.5 miles W. from Stampede Pass on E. side of Cascade Crest at Meadow Pass. Drainage is to Meadow Creek.

SUMMIT CHIEF LAKE. Golden trout have been stocked in this 6.5 acre lake at 6500 feet. It lies 10.5 miles NW from Salmon La Sac and about 0.8 miles S. from Summit Chief Mtn. Drainage is to Waptus River.

SWAN LAKE. Cutthroat are present in

Swan, a 7.4 acre lake at 4640 feet. It lies 5.8 miles SE from Snoqualmie Pass in headwaters of Gate Creek.

SWAUK CREEK. Follows Blewett Pass for about 15 miles and drains into Yakima River. It is easily accessible and hosts rainbow, cutthroat and a few eastern brook. Best fishing is early in the season. There are campsites and motels available.

TANEUM CREEK. Joins Yakima River 2 miles N. of Thorp, with a road paralleling the creek about 12 miles to its headwaters. Taneum produces rainbow in May, June and July.

TANEUM LAKE. Rough road leads from Gnat Flat to Quartz Mtn. lookout where a trail leads one mile to S. shore of the 3.1 acre lake. Contains rainbow. Elevation is 5266 feet. Drainage to headwaters of Taneum Creek.

TEANAWAY RIVER. Enters Yakima River 1 mile E. of junction of Blewett Pass cut-off with Hwy. 90. A secondary road leaves the pass highway 3 miles from junction and follows river NW to Casland. The Teanaway splits into 3 forks here. Road up Middle Fork continues for 3 miles then trail takes off to headwaters near Jolly Mtn. Road up W. Fork climbs over the ridge and drops to Lake Cle Elum. Road follows N. Fork for 16 miles with branch roads offering access to tributaries including **INDIAN, JACK** and **STAFFORD CREEKS.** Other N. Fork tributaries are **JUNGLE, BEVERLY** and **DE ROUX CREEKS.** The Teanaway contains rainbow and cutthroat. It delivers best from June through August. By mid-August water levels are usually too low for good fishing. The stream is wadeable.

THREE QUEENS LAKE. A golden trout planted lake of 1.5 acres at 5390 feet near SE end of Chikamin Ridge about 7 miles W. from Salmon La Sac. It outlets to Kachess River.

TERRACE LAKE. Terrace receives rainbow plants and is located 4 miles N. from Salmon La Sac at 5550 feet. It is on W. side of Davis Mtn. with drainage to Waptus River.

THORPE LAKE. Both rainbow and cutthroat occupy this 4.4 acre lake. It is located 1.1 miles N. from Thorpe. Outlet to Yakima River.

SPADE LAKE contains cutthroat.

TUCQUALA LAKE. Eastern brook and cutthroat are found in this 63 acre lake at 3225 feet. It lies in a narrow valley 7.5 miles N. from Salmon La Sac with drainage into Cle Elum River.

TWIN LAKES. A pair of small lakes, 4.2 and 1.6 acres situated 4.8 miles S. from Snoqualmie Pass in headwaters of Cold Creek. They contain rainbow and outlet via Cold Creek to Lake Keechelus. **VENUS LAKE.** Situated 1900 feet N. of **SPADE** at 5600 feet. It covers 56 acres and holds cutthroat in the 8-12 inch range. No trail.

WAPTUS LAKE. A well-defined trail heads N. from Salmon La Sac 9.5 miles to the lake at 2980 feet. Waptus is a deep lake of 246 acres containing rainbow and eastern brook. Trail follows N. shore. There are a number of undeveloped camping sites along both sides of the lake. Waptus is often used as a base camp since numerous other lakes are within a short walk.

WAPTUS RIVER. The outlet of Waptus Lake which empties into Cle Elum River 1.5 miles above Salmon La Sac. A beautiful mountain stream which holds rainbow and eastern brook. Trail to **WAPTUS LAKE** runs close to the river for the last 5 miles where the best fishing is found. August is top angling month.

WILSON CREEK. Flows through Ellensburg and has been used by that city for domestic water. For about 1.5 miles it joins Naneum Creek and assumes identity of that creek until it forks again in lower reaches. Accessible by road along much of its length. Wilson produces rainbow in May and June.

YAKIMA RIVER. One of the best streams in the state for large trout, other than steelhead. Easily reached at countless points along the 90 miles from the lower end of Keechelus Lake to city of Yakima. The upper river above Ellensburg produces rainbow, cutthroat and eastern brook from May to October, depending upon water flow. Fall is prime fishing time. Below Ellensburg there are a few German browns in addition to the other species. The Yakima offers excellent whitefish angling in winter months. Top whitefish areas include the entire stretch from Cle Elum to Yakima County line. Boat float trips through canyon stretches particularly in the fall are the most effective method of locating trout. Access and boat launch areas are located at the Roza Pool, mouth of Squaw Creek and at mouth of Umtanum Creek.

KITTITAS COUNTY RESORTS

Lake Easton: Lake Easton Resort, Easton WA 98295. 509-656-2255. Lake Easton State Park, Easton, WA 98295. 509-656-2230.

Lake Kachess: Kachess Resort, Easton WA 98925. 509-656-2209.

KLICKITAT

COUNTY

The Klickitat River is the top fishing water in Klickitat County, with the stream ranking high as a summer steelhead producer. White Salmon River treats trout fishermen well. The county, with 1932 square miles, is mountainous and rates 14th in size in the state. Most of the W. portion of Klickitat drains to the White Salmon River, while the Klickitat River drains the S. part. Highest point in the county is 5823 feet near Indian Rock.

BLOCKHOUSE CREEK. Legal plants of 'bows are made in this spring-fed creek which crosses Hwy. 141 at Blockhouse. It flows through farm lands 8 miles W. of Goldendale before entering the Little Klickitat River.

BLOODGOOD CREEK A short-run creek which flows S. through Goldendale golf course and enters Little Klickitat River at W. city limits of Goldendale. It receives legal-sized rainbow plants.

BOWMAN CREEK. Headwaters of Bowman are in the Simcoe Mtns. N. of Goldendale. The rainbow planted stream flows SW to meet the Little Klickitat River.

It may be reached by driving W. from Goldendale on Hwy. 142 for 16 miles. It also crosses the Goldendale—Glenwood road. There are two campgrounds on the creek in the mountains N. of Goldendale.

CHAMBERLAIN LAKE. An 80 acre lake located 0.5 miles W. of Lyle adjacent to the Columbia River. It is formed by a railroad fill. Contains small and largemouth bass, black crappie and brown bullhead.

HORSE THIEF LAKE. Formed by backwaters of The Dalles' Columbia River dam, Horsethief is situated 2.5 miles NE from The Dalles dam. The lake gets substantial rainbow plants and is connectecd to the Columbia by a culvert. Boat launch and picnic, camping areas at state park, 6 miles E. Lyle on Hwy. 14.

JEWITT CREEK. A small stream which flows through the community of White Salmon to enter the Columbia. It is planted with legal 'bows just prior to season opening.

KLICKITAT RIVER. One of the state's major summer steelhead streams, and also a salmon producer near mouth at Lyle where the Klickitat enters the Columbia. From July to October is best steelhead period, depending upon color of water which is often out of shape from snow melt from Mt. Adams during hot weather. Cutthroat and rainbow are also taken in the river, along with whitefish. An excellent road

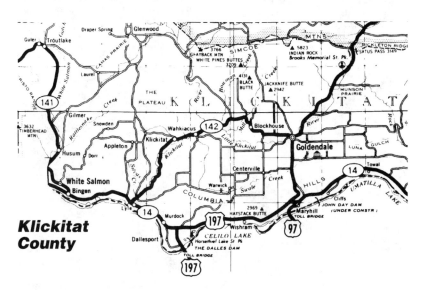

Klickitat County

follows the E. bank upstream from Lyle through the town of Klickitat and on past Wahkiacus, offering easy access. The Klickitat is planted with summer steelhead. The **LITTLE KLICKITAT**, which gets rainbow plants, joins the main river from the E. about 2.5 miles NE of Wahkiacus.

LOCKE LAKE. A fluctuating lake in size of around 20 acres which lies 3 miles E. of Bingen. Locke is bisected by Hwy. 14. It contains rainbow, large and smallmouth bass, black crappie and brown bullhead.

MAJOR CREEK. Hosts native populations of eastern brook and rainbow. Major enters Columbia River 5 miles upstream from Bingen. Best fishing is early in the season.

MILL CREEK. A brushy stream tributary to the Little Klickitat River. It flows parallel to and between Blockhouse and Bowman creeks. It is reached via Hwy. 142 about 11 miles W. of Goldendale, or 12 miles N. of Goldendale on the Cedar Valley road. Mill gets plants of legal 'bows.

NORTHWESTERN LAKE. A 97 acre lake (50% of the lake is in Skamania County) formed by a dam on the White Salmon River 3 miles N. of town of White Salmon. Northwestern yields rainbow in April, May and June, as well as cutthroat. Resort facilities.

POTHOLE LAKE. Cradled in an extinct crater, Pothole covers 8 acres and lies at 2300 feet elevation 6 miles N. of Goldendale. There is no apparent inlet or outlet. Pothole contains rainbow, brown trout and eastern brook. It is rated good for

KLICKITAT RIVER is a top summer steelhead stream.

these trout in April and May. **CARP LAKE**, a 21 acre lake, is located 1 mile NW of Pothole Lake and 7 miles N. of Goldendale adjacent to a county road from that town. The lake holds spiny ray species.

RATTLESNAKE CREEK. A tributary to the White Salmon River, joining that stream at the community of Husum on Hwy. 141 from the NE Easy access is afforded along the W. side of the Rattlesnake for about 5 miles upstream. Primarily an early season show for small rainbow and eastern brook.

ROCK CREEK. This small, rainbow stream is located 20 miles E. of Goldendale on the Bickleton road. Some sections of the stream dry up in summer months, but it affords good fishing from opening day into June. A county road parallels the creek for 12 miles, and two camping areas are situated along the stream. Good smallmouth bass fishing, with some crappie, bluegill, salmon and steelhead taken in the 5 acre enlargement at point the stream enters the Columbia River about 10 miles upstream from John Day Dam and adjacent to Hwy. 14. There is a Corps of Engineers boat launch and park at mouth of Rock Creek.

ROWLAND LAKE. (DuBois). Located adjacent to the N. shore of Bonneville Pool 4 miles E. of Bingen and bisected by Hwy.

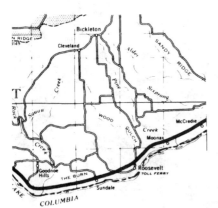

14, Rowland covers 84 acres. It holds eastern brook and rainbow, plus large and smallmouth bass, black crappie, bluegill, yellow perch and brown bullhead. It has a public access on N. shore.

SPEARFISH LAKE. Size of this Columbia River seepage lake ranges from about 10 to 20 acres. It is located 1 mile N. from The Dalles Dam and is also fed by Five Mile Creek. It gets rainbow and brown trout plants. Light boats may be launched along the shore. **LITTLE SPEARFISH LAKE**, about 6 acres, is situated 300 feet SE of Big Spearfish. It contains bass and crappie.

SPRING CREEK. A spring-fed creek which starts at Goldendale fish hatchery 4 miles W. of Goldendale and flows 8 miles SW to join the Little Klickitat River. Good plants of rainbow, but heavy fishing pressure. Some stream bank access.

TROUT LAKE. Once a large lake, but silting has reduced Trout Lake to about 10 acres. It lies 0.5 miles NW of town of Trout Lake and holds rainbow.

TROUT LAKE CREEK. Heading in Skamania County, Trout Lake Creek flows SE to empty into Trout Lake 0.5 miles NW of town of Trout Lake. A good road from the town follows the creek NW to the county line where a FS campground is located. It is brushy fishing. The creek is slow below the campground but offers eastern brook,

some of good size. Faster water upstream provides rainbow.

WHITE SALMON RIVER. A large stream joining the Columbia 1.5 miles W. of town of White Salmon. An excellent road follows the river about 35 miles upstream to the headwaters near Swampy Meadows. A fair rainbow river in upper reaches, with salmon and steelhead fishing opportunities in lower 3 miles of river below Northwestern Dam. Receives winter and summer steelhead plants. Boat launch at mouth controlled by Indians.

KLICKITAT COUNTY RESORTS

Northwestern Lake: Northwestern Lake Resort, White Salmon, WA 98672. 509-493-2802.

Horse Thief Lake State Park. 509-767-1159.

Study, then fish

Careful! Read the official fish and game regulations BEFORE heading afield, or you may be telling it to the judge. The regulations are free at sport shops and marinas.

Did you know?

The California condor is America's largest soaring bird.

WHITE SALMON RIVER boat launch at mouth.

Lewis

COUNTY

The largest county in W. Washington and the 6th largest in the state, Lewis covers 2447 square miles. Most of the E. part of Lewis is mountainous, with Old Snowy Mountain on the Cascade Crest at 7950 feet the highest point. Over 50 square miles of Lewis lies within Mt. Rainier National Park. Most of the county's drainage is via the Cowlitz and Chehalis River systems. Of the over 200 lakes in Lewis, 142 are situated at elevations at or over 2500 feet. There are many streams of varying sizes in the county in addition to the lakes.

AIRPORT LAKE. A 4 acre lake situated 2.5 miles S. from Centralia and on NE side of airport. It holds largemouth bass.

ALDER LAKE. (See Pierce county).

ART LAKE. A 1.5 acre lake at 4000 feet located 3 miles E. from Packwood. The cutthroat planted lake drains to Lake Creek and Cowlitz River.

BEE TREE LAKE. Formerly a 10 acre lake, but requires replacement of a dam to become a good fish producer. Route is FS road 123 S. from Randle crossing Cowlitz River to FS road 112 then to FS road 111.

Lake may be seen from high point on road 111 S. of lake.

BIG CREEK. A large stream which enters the Nisqually River about 1.5 miles SE of National. An all-weather road leaves Hwy. 706 0.5 miles E. of National and follows creek 9.4 miles to a point just short of Cora Lake, the source of Big Creek. Big Creek has rainbow, cutthroat and some eastern brook. It produces best in June and July. Several camping spots.

BERTHA MAY LAKES. Upper lake covers 30 acres and lies at 4000 feet. Lower lake is 6 acres at 3700 feet 7 miles SE from National on NE side of Sawtooth Ridge and 1000 feet NE from Big Bertha May. Both lakes contain rainbow. Drainage is to Pothole Lake and Teeley Creek.

BLUE LAKE. A clear, eastern brook and 'bow lake of 127.9 acres, situated at 4050 feet. Reached by FS road 123 from Randle SE for 15.5 miles to trail marker, then 3 mile hike to lake.

BLUFF LAKE. Cutthroat have been stocked in Bluff at 3900 feet. Location is 7 miles NE of Packwood near N. end of Coal Creek Mtn. Drains via Purcell Creek to Cowlitz River.

BORST LAKE. An artificial lake of 5 acres located at Fort Borst park in Centralia. Stocked with rainbow.

BUCK CREEK BEAVER PONDS. Rated

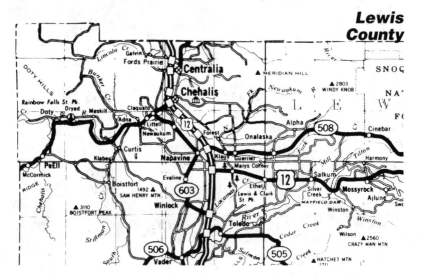

Lewis County

COWLITZ RIVER spring chinook boated by John Waters.

CARLISLE LAKE. A spring producer of 20.3 acres for rainbow with public access area. Located 0.4 miles west of Onalaska off Hwy. 508. Planted with rainbow and brown trout. It also holds largemouth bass and bluegill.

CARLTON CREEK. Take Hwy. 12 NE of Packwood 9 miles. Turn E. on FS road 4400 0.5 miles before entering Mt. Rainier National Park. Drive 8 miles to end of road. Follow trail up creek. Rainbow and cutthroat trout.

CHAMBERS LAKE. Located 11.5 miles SE of Packwood, the lake holds 'bows, brown trout and eastern brook and has many beaver ponds around inlet. Feeds Chambers Creek, a tributary to the upper Cispus. Lake is 14.4 acres. Elevation is 4525 feet, thus Chambers is late starter, and is best after July 1. FS road 2100 about 2.5 miles SE of Packwood heads S. up Johnson Creek 10 miles past Hugo Lake.

CHEHALIS RIVER. (Upper). Rated fair for rainbow and cutthroat in May and June with Pe Ell area good for March steelheading. Hwy. 6 follows the river E. from Dryad Junction past Rainbow Falls state park (1 mile) to join Hwy. 5 at town of Chehalis. The river then swings N. past Centralia and Fords Prairie.

CISPUS RIVER. Produces rainbow and cutthroat from May to August. Cross Cowlitz River at Randle and take FS road 2500 to lower Cispus. FS road 2300 leads

as "fair" for cutthroat with top period in May and June. Situated 2 miles above East Canyon along the Cispus road. They drain into the Cispus River.

BUTTER CREEK. Reached by crossing Cowlitz River at Packwood N. on FS road 5200 and continuing about 2.5 miles to FS road 5270 which leads E. and N. upstream for over 7 miles. Contains rainbow, eastern brook and cutthroat.

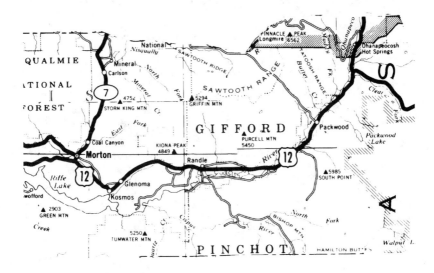

to upper Cispus via roads 2100 and 2160 to Walupt Lake, a total distance of about 40 miles. FS campgrounds located at Tower Rock, North Fork, Cat Creek and Walupt Lake. Road leads up N. fork of the Cispus about 10 miles, with roads also up such major tributaries as Quartz Creek, Iron Creek and Yellow Jacket Creek. N. Fork Cispus is planted with rainbow.

CLEAR FORK. (Cowlitz River tributary). Contains rainbow, cutthroat and eastern brook and is best from mid-summer on because of elevation. Reached via Hwy. 12 through and past Packwood 4.5 miles to FS road 4600. Travel road 4600 for 8 miles to the Clear Fork trailhead. Trail to **LILY LAKE** up Little Lava Creek leads 2 miles from road end. Substantial plants of rainbow usually made after snow run-off each year.

COAL CREEK. A small mountain stream which enters the Cowlitz 4 miles NE of Packwood. Cutthroat and rainbow are taken in spring and early summer months. Rough fishermen's trails follow up the creek which heads in **BEAVER** and **LOST LAKES.** FS road 4610 follows middle stretch.

CORA LAKE. Rainbow inhabit this deep, 28 acre lake at 3900 feet. It is located 9.4 miles SE from National and 0.5 miles NW from High Rock on end of Sawtooth Ridge. Drains via Big Creek to Nisqually River.

COWLITZ RIVER spring chinook.

COWLITZ RIVER. One of the state's major streams is blocked by Mayfield and Mossyrock dams. The big river yields rainbow and cutthroat, along with salmon and steelhead. Excellent salmon and steelhead fishing below salmon hatchery where there is a public access and boat launch site. Another public access and boat launch site at F&W department hatchery downstream from salmon hatchery. Turn S. off Hwy. 12 near Salkum to reach these areas. Heavy plants of steelhead and salmon below Mayfield are returning runs to the lower river. The river below Toledo offers excellent sea-run cutthroat fishing during August and September. The upper river gets plants of legal rainbow. The Cowlitz joins the Columbia at Longview. Boat launch at Toledo and at I-5.

CORTRIGHT CREEK. Joins Clear Fork of the Cowlitz 1 mile NE of La Wis Wis campground on Hwy. 12 just N. of Packwood. FS road 4500 up Cortright leaves Hwy. 12 about 1 mile E. of Ohanapecosh Junction, paralleling the creek for 3.5 miles. Contains cutthroat, eastern brook and rainbow.

DAVIS LAKE. An 18 acre lake holding rainbow, cutthroat, largemouth bass and bluegill. It is situated 1.5 miles SE of Morton at 940 feet elevation. Roads from center of Morton run along both N. and S. sides of the lake. Drainage is to Tilton River. April, May and June are considered best fishing months. Drainage is to Simmons Creek and Cowlitz River.

DECEPTION CREEK. Reached via Johnson Creek road off Hwy. 12 about 2.5 miles S. of Packwood and then 6 miles SE up Johnson Creek on FS road 2100 to FS road 2130 turning sharply NW up Deception Creek 2.5 miles. A small rainbow and cutthroat stream that has been stocked with rainbow.

DUMBELL LAKE. A cutthroat planted lake of 41.6 acres at 5200 feet 3.8 miles N. from White Pass on Cascade Crest. Drainage to **BUESCH LAKE**.

ELK CREEK. A producer of cutthroat in May and June. The creek enters the Chehalis River at Doty.

EMERICK LAKE. (Airport). Varying in size from 4 to 7 acres, this narrow bass and catfish lake lies adjacent to the SW side of the Chehalis airport.

UPPER AND LOWER Bertha May Lakes and Granite Lake.

FRYING PAN LAKE. A mountain lake on the Cascade Crest at 4850 feet altitude and 6.5 miles N. of White Pass. The 23 acre lake holds rainbow, cutthroat and eastern brook and is reached via the Cascade Crest trail. Adjacent **LITTLE SNOW LAKE** has brookies.

GLACIER CREEK. Outlet of **GLACIER LAKE** The small stream enters Johnson Creek 4.5 miles upstream from confluence of Johnson Creek road which leaves Hwy. 12 about 3 miles SW of Packwood crosses Glacier Creek at its mouth. Trail up N. bank extends 2 miles to Glacier Lake. The creek has been planted with cutthroat and also contains some rainbow and eastern brook.

GLACIER LAKE. Located in headwaters of Glacier Creek and reached via a 2 mile hike E. to the 19 acre lake which lies at 3000 feet. Glacier Lake has cutthroat and eastern brook.

GOAT CREEK. Heading high in the Goat Rocks Wilderness Area on the Cascade Crest at Goat Lake, much of this beautiful creek flows through meadows. Cutthroat are colorful 10-12 inches. Best fishing for cutthroat and some fine rainbow from mid-July through September. Route is up Johnson Creek on FS road 2100 leaving Hwy. 12 about 3 miles W. of Packwood, approximately 11 miles NE to Chambers Lake road.

GOAT LAKE. A 10 acre lake at 6900 feet elevation at head of Goat Creek. No report of fish.

GRIMM CREEK. Located S. of Mary's Corner and crossed by Hwy. 12. The creek produces a few cutthroat with best months May and June.

HANNAFORD CREEK. Enters Skookumchuck River 1.5 miles N. of Centralia. It contains cutthroat and delivers during May and June. Road turning E. from Hwy. 507 at creek's mouth follows up the stream for about 10 miles.

HORSESHOE LAKE. Located 1.5 miles SW of Centralia, the 4 acre lake holds spiny rays. It lies close to W. side of Chehalis River.

HUGO LAKE. The 1.5 acre lake lies adjacent to E. side of Johnson Creek on FS road 2100 about 11 miles from Hwy. 12 approximately 1 mile S. of Packwood. It has been planted with both rainbow and cutthroat.

IRON CREEK. Rainbow are available in this Cispus River tributary. FS road 2510 from the road up S. side of Cispus River leads up the creek for over 5 miles. FS campground at creek's mouth.

JACKPOT LAKE. Cutthroat planted 5.5 acre lake at 4450 feet 9.8 miles S. from Packwood. Drainage is to Jackpot Creek and N. Fork Cispus River.

JESS LAKE. (Pipe). An 8.5 acre cutthroat lake situated 4.4 miles N. from White Pass and 2000 feet NW from **DUMBELL LAKE.** Elevation is 5175 feet. Drainage is to Summit Creek and Ohanapecosh River.

JOHNSON CREEK. A major tributary of the upper Cowlitz, entering that river 3 miles SW of Packwood. FS road 2100 leads from near mouth upstream 12 miles to headwaters of Johnson Creek, then drops down into Cispus River drainage. Top fishing for rainbow, eastern brook and cutthroat is from mid-summer into fall. Tributaries include Glacier, Deception, Middle Fork, Jordan and Mission Creeks. All may be fished upstream from Johnson Creek road.

JUG LAKE. An excellent eastern brook lake of 28 acres located 2.5 miles NE of Soda Springs forest camp. Best in July and August. Elevation is 4550 feet.

KNUPPENBURG LAKE. (Kuppenheimer). Brown trout are the attraction in this 4 acre lake. It lies at 4200 feet 1.5 miles S. of White Pass and adjacent to S. side of Hwy.

12. Drainage is into Cowlitz River. FS picnic site adjacent to lake.

LA CAMAS CREEK. Enters the Cowlitz River 1 mile S. of Vader with Hwy. 506 crossing the creek's mouth. A county road follows the N. side 3 miles upstream where Hwy. 5 crosses the creek. Contains rainbow and cutthroat, with early season fishing best, although some cutthroat are found in fall months.

LAKE CREEK. Outlet of Packwood Lake, flowing NW about 5 miles to join Cowlitz River 2 miles NE of Packwood at which point Hwy. 12 crosses Lake Creek. Rough fishermen's trails lead upstream to good rainbow fly water. The creek may be fished downstream from Packwood Lake. Mid-stretch is rough going.

LILY LAKE. Large brookies and rainbow in this 25 acre lake which lies at 3750 feet 3.8 miles W. of White Pass in Goat Rocks Wilderness Area. Take FS road 46 N. of Packwood to road end. Hike of 2 miles to lake. Drainage is to Clear Fork, Cowlitz River.

LINCOLN CREEK. Tributary to Chehalis River, joining the Chehalis near Galvin. A deep, brushy creek which produces cutthroat, rainbow and a few steelhead.

RIFFE LAKE, a 23-mile-long reservoir on Cowlitz River.

Reached by turning W. from Harrison Ave. at Fords Prairie through Galvin and continuing upstream to road paralleling Lincoln Creek about 15 miles. Good jump shooting for ducks along the creek. October sometimes productive for sea-run cutts.

LITTLE NISQUALLY RIVER. Flows into the S. arm of **ALDER LAKE** close to the S. Lewis-Thurston County border. FS road 147 heading NW from Hwy. 7 about 2 miles N. of Mineral through Pleasant Valley skirts S. shore of Alder Lake to mouth of the Little Nisqually. The road continues up Little Nisqually past **DUCK** and **GOOSE LAKES** to complete a loop back to Hwy. 7 near Mineral. Mid-June through September are best months for the Little Nisqually's rainbow and cutthroat. West Fork of Little Nisqually offers good to excellent cutthroat angling in top reaches.

LONE TREE LAKE. A 2.5 acre cutthroat lake at 3500 feet. Location is 6.8 miles SE from Randle on N. side of Lone Tree Mtn. It drains to Camp Creek and Cispus River.

LONG LAKE. Brown trout are the attraction in this 6 acre lake at 4000 feet. It lies 6.5 miles W. from Packwood. Drainage to N. Fork Willame Creek and Cowlitz River.

LOST HAT LAKE. Cutthroat planted lake of 3 acres at 4500 feet. Location is 3.4 miles NE from Packwood Lake's outlet. It drains to Lava Creek to Clear Fork of Cowlitz River.

MAYFIELD LAKE. A 13 mile-long reservoir of 2200 acres formed by a Tacoma dam on the Cowlitz River 13 miles NE of Toledo on Hwy. 12. Road along N. shore of lake leads to Mayfield state park. Species of fish include rainbow, cutthroat, coho salmon juveniles, tiger muskies, yellow perch and a few crappie, bass and brown bullhead. There are boat launch facilities located at both state and county parks and at resort.

MINERAL CREEK. Enters Nisqually River 2 miles E. of top end of **ALDER LAKE**. Road from Elbe on Hwy. 706 leads S. past Mineral Lake then SE about 12 miles to creek's headwaters. Railroad track follows Mineral Creek from its mouth upstream 3 miles to town of Mineral. Good in lower reaches for rainbow and cutthroat early in year, with top stretches better later in season.

MINERAL LAKE. Located 3 miles S. of Elbe at town of Mineral. The lake covers 277 acres and is planted with rainbow, cutthroat and brown trout. Good early in season. Public access and resort facilities on the lake.

MOSS LAKE. A cutthroat stocked lake of 3.5 acres located 1000 feet SW from **NEWAUKUM LAKES** Lakes at 3024 feet elevation. Drainage to S. Fork Newaukum River.

MUD LAKE. A 7.5 acre lake at 4850 feet situated on NW side of Hamilton Buttes and 3.8 miles E. from Blue Lake. It carries cutthroat.

NEWAUKUM LAKE. Brown trout have been planted in this 17 acre lake at 3000 feet 13 miles NE from Onalaska at head of S. Fork Newaukum River.

NEWAUKUM RIVER. A small river that furnishes rainbow, steelhead, cutthroat and salmon fishing. The Newaukum enters Chehalis River at town of Chehalis, and county roads follow the river S. for 5 miles where Hwy. 5 crosses. Hwy. 508 parallels the Newaukum E. to vicinity of Onalaska. It receives plants of sea-run cutthroat, and the S. Fork is good for fly fishing from mid-June to mid-July.

NISQUALLY RIVER. (See Pierce county).

PACKWOOD LAKE. A large mountain lake of 452 acres which lies at 2858 feet elevation 8.5 miles E. of town of Packwood. Some large 'bows taken here. Mid-June through September is best fishing period. Road from Packwood ranger station heads E. for about 4.5 miles and an easy trail continues 3.5 scenic miles to the lake. There are FS campgrounds at N. end of the lake, and there is a resort. Trail from N.end of Packwood Lake leads 4 miles E. to **LOST LAKE** at 5100 feet elevation. The 21 acre lake holds 'bows.

PLUMMER LAKE. An old gravel pit site now a lake of 12 acres located on W. side of city of Centralia. Stocked with rainbow and brown trout and rated fair in the spring.

QUARTZ CREEK. Drive S. from Randle on road 2500 across Cowlitz and Cispus Rivers to Road 2600 which follows up Quartz Creek for about 8 miles to its source in Skamania County. Quartz holds cutthroat and rainbow with June into September usually the best fishing months.

RIFFE LAKE. A 23-mile-long reservoir formed by a Tacoma dam on the Cowlitz River. It has 52 miles of shoreline and contains landlocked coho salmon, rainbow, brown trout, small and largemouth bass, black crappie, brown bullhead and bluegill. Hwy. 12 crosses the Cowlitz River 2 miles from W. tip of Riffe, then follows NW shore of lake for 3 miles. FS road 1203 takes off from Hwy. 12 at E. end and parallels E. shore of reservoir. County road from community of Mossyrock leads E. and S. to touch Riffe in two places on SW shore. Boat launches are at parks on both ends of lake.

SALMON CREEK. Joins Cowlitz River 1 mile SW of Toledo and crossed by the old highway bridge 1 mile E. of the mouth. Produces rainbow early in the season, with sea-run cutts in late summer and fall. Access is limited in bottom stretches. Hwy. 505 E. from Toledo crosses middle portions of the Salmon, and a road from SE end of Mayfield Lake turns S. at Winston to headwaters.

SILVER CREEK. A Cowlitz River tributary which offers good to excellent rainbow fishing for anglers willing to walk. FS road 75 leading from Randle ranger station head N. about 4 miles on the creek's W. side before dropping within 0.4 miles of Silver. One mile E. of the ranger station FS road 47 leaves the highway to head N. along E. bank of the creek by-passing a tough canyon. July and August are the most productive months.

SKATE CREEK. Heads in N. Lewis County at Bear Prairie and flows S. to join the Cowlitz River at Packwood. A large creek with numerous tributaries, Skate gets rainbow plants, and also hosts cutthroat. FS road 5200 from Packwood crosses the Cowlitz and heads N. about 10 miles to headwaters of Skate, closely following the stream. Series of beaver ponds containing cutthroat are located along the creek on Bear Prairie.

SKOOKUMCHUCK RIVER. Primarily a winter steelhead stream with excellent fishing toward end of season. It has been planted. The river joins the Chehalis at W. city limits of Centralia. Hwy. 507 N. from Centralia follows the river to Bucoda, then

a county road leads E. upstream for several miles. Dam on upper river.

SMITH CREEK. FS road 2100 leaves Hwy. 12 about 3 miles SW of Packwood to follow Smith Creek for 9 miles. The Cowlitz River tributary gets a "fair" rating for rainbow and cutthroat during summer months.

SNOW LAKE. Cutthroat have been stocked in Snow, an 8 acre lake at 4975 feet 6 miles N. from White Pass. Drainage to Summit Creek and Ohanapecosh River.

ST. JOHN LAKE. Golden trout have been stocked in St. John which is located 9.5 miles S. from Packwood. It is a "deep" 3 acres. It drains to St. John Creek to N. Fork Cispus River.

SUMMIT CREEK. The creek heads just under the W. summit of the Cascade Crest and flows W. to enter the Ohanapecosh River 2 miles S. of Mt. Rainier National Park border. Stocked with rainbow, Summit yields trout from July into October. One mile E. of the junction of the Cayuse-White Pass highways FS road 4510 heads N. and E. about 2 miles to Summit Creek campground and another 3 miles to Soda Springs campground at road end. Trail from here leads E. up the creek to Jug and Frying Pan Lakes.

SWAFFORD POND. A 240 acre pond formerly used for rearing steelhead. It now contains bass, bluegill, rainbow, brown trout, crappie, brown bullheads and channel catfish. Location is adjacent to Riffe Lake at Mossyrock.

TATOOSH LAKES. Lakes of 2.5 and 10 acres 7.5 miles N. from Packwood at 5000 feet on NE side of Tatoosh Ridge. They are stocked with rainbow.

TILTON RIVER. Upper Tilton is planted with rainbow and is a good trout producer in June, July and August. Hwy. 508 leads along the upper river through Morton.

WALUPT LAKE. Both rainbow and cutthroat are available in this 384 acre lake. Walupt is situated at 3927 feet elevation 3 miles W. of the Cascade Crest. It produces rainbow as soon as ice goes off in early summer and continues to offer action into fall months. There are 4 FS campground sites at the NW end of Walupt and a boat ramp. Route is via FS road 2100 which leaves Hwy. 12 about 3 miles SW of Packwood, driving 13 miles S. to FS road 1114, then 4.5 miles E. to lake shore.

WILLAME CREEK. Enters Cowlitz River 4 miles SW of Packwood. The rainbow stream is reached by crossing the Cowlitz at Packwood and driving N. for 4 miles on FS road 5200 to FS road 4200 which follows the stream about 1 mile. FS road 4730 then leads SW for about 2.5 miles along Willame Creek to within a short distance from the N. side of **WILLAME LAKE** at 3650 feet. FS road 4740 from FS road 4700 extends to **LONG LAKE** which lies at 4000 feet. Long, a rainbow lake, covers 6 acres.

WINSTON CREEK. Planted with rainbow in April and May, Winston delivers good fishing. It flows into the S. tip of Mayfield Lake and is easily reached by a road which heads S. from Hwy. 12 where that highway crosses to E. side of the lake. Winston Creek road follows the stream for about 5 miles SE. Good cutthroat to 16 inches in brushy sections. Ponds along the creek also get rainbow plants.

WOBBLY LAKE. A cutthroat and eastern brook lake of 8 acres situated 13 miles S. of Randle. Reached by FS road 22 then road 2208 up North Fork Cispus River 10 miles E. of North Fork guard station near Cispus Forks, then by 2 mile trail up Wobbly Creek to lake. Wobbly produced a state record 9 pound eastern brook in 1988.

WRIGHT LAKE. (Little Fritzie). A 3 acre lake holding cutthroat and rainbow. Wright is located 9 miles SE of Packwood at 3100 feet. It drains into Johnson Creek.

YELLOW JACKET PONDS. Rainbow are stocked in these 2 ponds located 10.1 miles from Randle via FS road 23 and 28 near the junction of the Cispus and Yellow Jacket Rivers.

LEWIS COUNTY RESORTS

Mayfield Lake: Mayfield Lake Resort, Mossyrock, WA. 360-985-2357.

Mineral Lake: Mineral Lake Resort, Mineral, WA. 360-492-5367.

Packwood Lake: Packwood Lake Resort, Packwood, WA. 360-494-9220.

Riffe Lake: Riffe Lake Campground, Mossyrock, WA. 983-8122.

Fish dislike human smell

Do fishermen really stink? There is evidence that migratory steelhead and salmon not only don't appreciate the smell of humans, but will leave the scene if possible when subjected to that smell.

Fish biologists at Bonneville Dam on the Columbia River noted this aversion of fish to man smell while working around the fishways. While both salmon and steelhead would swim and jump around men, when someone would put a bare hand in the water, all fish movement would stop for at least 30 minutes. Fish workers put this B.O. factor to work on several occasions when zestful spring Chinook salmon were ascending the fish ladders. The energy-packed springs were jumping so high in the low-ceilinged ladders that they were breaking the expensive overhead lights. A hand in the water at top of the ladder put the salmon down .

British Columbia fish biologists, working on silver salmon counts on the Stamp River, had a similar experience. The silvers were going over a counting ladder at a steady clip until one of the biologists waded bare footed into the river above the ladder. All fish movement immediately stopped. Intrigued, the men made some tests. A ten minute check of salmon over the ladder came up with 34 fish. They then immersed bare hands in the water for one minute, following this with another ten minute check. Only four fish passed them during this period.

The biologists tested a number of solutions to determine whether foreign organic substances spooked the fish. After several months of such tests they concluded that with the exception of hand rinses, no solution showed sufficient effect on the migratory rate.

Biologists have figured for years that it is the olfactory organs of salmon and steelhead which enable them to "home" to the stream where they spent their pre-ocean years. Evidently this same highly developed sense of smell comes into play with fish's aversion to human smell.

In view of these findings, fishermen might consider pulling on gloves before baiting. It could be the considerate thing to do.

Lincoln
COUNTY

Although there are 2335 square miles in Lincoln, making it the 8th largest county in the state, fishing is limited. Many small lakes and ponds in the county contain water in the spring and early summer only. Drainage is via Crab Creek watershed into the Columbia River. Coffee Pot Lake is an excellent spiny ray producer.

BASS LAKES. Two small lakes of 2 and 3 acres located within 800 feet of one another, and 1.5 miles S. of Sprague with drainage to the Palouse River. They hold spiny rays.

COFFEE POT LAKE. One of the district's top spiny ray lakes offering largemouth bass, crappie, yellow perch, catfish, bluegills and sunfish. Coffee Pot covers 316.9 acres, and is formed by an enlargement of Lake Creek. It's about 3 miles long. It is located 12 miles NE of Odessa and is reached by taking Hwy. 21 from Odessa N. for 5.5 miles then continuing straight ahead on county road 6.5 miles, then E. about 5 miles to lake. Crab Creek drainage.

CRAB CREEK. Forms the principal drainage for Lincoln County. Crab Creek heads in NE Lincoln, receiving water from seepage and numerous small creeks. It flows SW to within 2 miles of the Adams County line, then swings W. to enter Grant County, picking up volume as it goes. The creek contains rainbow and some German brown trout and produces best during the spring and summer.

COTTONWOOD CREEK. A small stream which flows E. from Davenport for about 5 miles to join Hawk Creek. Planted with rainbow.

DEER LAKE. (Deer Springs). An enlargement in Lake Creek located ll miles NE from Odessa and 1 mile below **COFFE POT LAKE** along Lake Creek. The lake covers 60 acres and is planted with rainbow. It also holds largemouth bass and other spiny rays. Rough campsites along N. end. Deer produces best during the early part of the season.

Lincoln County

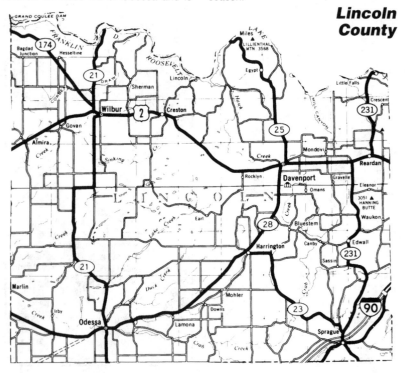

PACIFIC LAKE is enlargement of Lake Creek.

DOWNS LAKE. (See Spokane county).

FISHTRAP LAKE. A narrow, 3-mile-long lake of 195 acres (22 acres in Spokane County) situated 6.5 miles E. of Sprague. Fishtrap is rainbow planted. It has a public boat launch area. Drive NE from Sprague on Hwy. 90 for 3 miles, then turn E. 6 miles to lake. An outstanding trout lake in the county. Drainage to Negro Creek and Palouse River.

"H" LAKE. A 26 acre lake located 5.8 miles S. from Wilbur.It contains largemouth bass, black crappie and bluegill.

HAWK CREEK. Rises near Davenport and flows W. and N. about 20 miles to empty into FDR Lake below Hawk Creek Falls. Roads NW from Davenport follow most of the creek's course. Hawk is figured a good May and June bet for planted rainbow and a few eastern brook.

ICE HOUSE LAKE. Largemouth bass are present in this 5.3 acre lake which is located 1.5 miles E. from Almira on E. side of Hwy. 2.

INDIAN CREEK. Joins Hawk Creek 1.5 miles S. of Hawk Creek Falls. The Indian Creek road follows the rainbow planted stream E. and S. upstream for about 10 miles.

PACIFIC LAKE. Another enlargement in

Lake Creek's channel, Pacific is 1.8 miles long and is 129 acres. It is reached via Hwy. 2 N. from Odessa 2.5 miles, then W. and N. 5 miles on county road which crosses W. end of lake. Public boat launch site near W. end. Spiny rays are the attraction. **TULE LAKE,** 126 acres, lies 0.4 of a mile S. of Pacific. The two mile-long lake has spiny rays.

SHERMAN CREEK. Road from Hwy. 2, 4 miles E. of Wilbur heads N. up Sherman Creek for about 6 miles to settlement of Sherman. The stream gets rainbow plants.

ROOSEVELT LAKE. (See Stevens county).

SPRAGUE LAKE. Much of this lake is in Adams County, but 637 acres are within Lincoln County. The N. end of the lake is only 1.5 miles SW of town of Sprague, and Hwy. 90 follows the E. shore. There is a resort at N. end. Sprague contains largemouth bass, smallmouth bass, walleye, bluegill, perch, rainbow, crappie and catfish and is best from May to September. It is also good for perch and bluegill during the winter through the ice.

TWIN LAKES. Lower Twin with 45 surface acres is the larger of this pair of lakes which are enlargements of Lake Creek in SW Lincoln County. Upper Twin covers 39 acres. They are situated 15 miles NE of Odessa and about 2 miles up Lake Creek from **COFFE POT LAKE**. County road passes 0.5 miles W. of Lower Twin. Both lakes hold largemouth bass, crappie and perch, with rainbow present in Upper Twin. The lakes are 500 feet apart.

WALL LAKE. (Big). A 32.2 acre lake located 10.5 miles NW from Harrington. It contains large and smallmouth bass, black crappie, pumpkinseed and yellow perch.

WEDERSPAHN LAKE. A 13.8 acre lake about 5.4 miles N. from Odessa in Lake Creek channel. Fish species include large and smallmouth bass, black crappie, yellow perch and pumpkinseed.

WILSON CREEK. Receives occasional plants of rainbow and delivers fair fishing in the spring. Wilson drains into Crab Creek.

LINCOLN COUNTY RESORTS

Roosevelt Lake: Ft. Spokane Store, 509-725-5783. Lakeview Marina, Wilbur, WA 99185. 509-647-5755. Seven Bays Resort, Davenport, WA. 509-725-1676.

Sprague Lake: Sprague Lake Campground, Sprague, WA 99032. 257-2864. Bob Lee Campground, Sprague, WA 99032. 509-257-2362.

Fish Trap Lake: Fish Trap Lake Resort, Sprague, WA 99032. 509-235-2284.

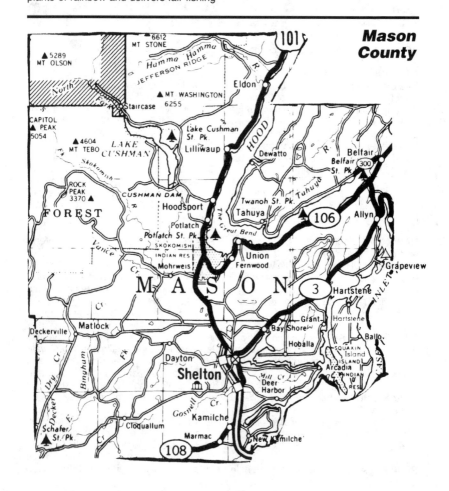

MASON
COUNTY

Mason county contains fishing to suit all tastes. A section of the 1052 square mile county fronts on Puget Sound, and another portion touches Hood Canal. There is salmon fishing on a year-around basis in these sheltered waters. The Skokomish, Hamma Hamma and Tahuya Rivers, which hold winter steelhead, sea-run cutthroat and salmon in season drain the N. and E. parts of Mason to Hood Canal. The Satsop River system drains the S. and W. portions to the Chehalis River. There are plenty of lakes in Mason, over 200, but some of the county's best fishing is in countless beaver ponds which require exploration up small creeks to locate. Mason County rates 29th in size in the state. Highest point is 6612 feet on Mt. Stone.

ALDRIDGE LAKE. Located 1.5 miles S. of Dewatto overlooking Hood Canal. Road W. at top of hill above Dewatto leads 1 mile to lake. Aldridge is 9 acres and is planted with rainbow. It is best in spring and early summer and has a public access and DNR campground. Drains to Hood Canal.

ARMSTRONG LAKE. An eastern brook and rainbow lake of about 4 acres or larger which lies 2.8 miles NE of Eldon. Logging road 1 mile N. of Eldon heads W. up hill 1.5 miles, then rough track leads N. 1.5 miles to lake. Occasional large trout taken here.

BATHTUB LAKE. A 2 acre eastern brook pond which lies 4 miles S. of Union. Drive S. from Union up hill for 4 miles, then turn E. and N. for 0.5 miles to lake.

BENSON LAKE. Rated fair to good for cutthroat, kokanee and rainbow in the spring and fall months. Benson covers 81 acres. Public access on lake which is reached via Hwy. 3 heading NE from Shelton 11.5 miles, then N. on county road 2.2 miles. Benson is 1.3 miles from E. side of **MASON LAKE**. Drainage is to Oakland Bay.

BINGHAM CREEK. Tributary to Satsop River's E. Fork. Crossed by

SKOKOMISH RIVER delivers fine March steelhead.

Matlock-Shelton road 1.5 miles E. of Matlock, with road turning S. 0.5 miles to parallel both Bingham and Outlet Creeks for about 5 miles. Bingham is tough to reach but provides good cutthroat fishing in mid-summer and fall.

BLACKSMITH LAKE. Largemouth bass are the attraction in this 18.3 acre lake. It is located 5.5 miles NW from Belfair. Drainage is to Tahuya River.

BUCK LAKE. (Wildberry). Located near hook of Hood Canal 1.5 miles NW of Tahuya. The 8.1 acre lake receives rainbow plants. Maze of roads in this area termed the "Oak Patch." Watch for signs. Drainage is to Hood Canal.

CADY LAKE. A 15 acre lake situated 2 miles SE of Dewatto adjacent to S. side of road up the hill. Cady is planted with rainbow and cutthroat and has a public access area. It drains to Dewatto River.

CAMP POND. A 6 acre rainbow lake located 4 miles NW of Belfair. Largemouth bass are present. Has DNR campground. Route is N. from Hood Canal on El Fendahl road past Oak Patch Lake.

CARSON LAKE. An 8 acre lake holding eastern brook. Located 3 miles SE of Union with drainage to Mason Lake via Shumocher Creek. Drive S. from Union up the hill for 2 miles, then turn E. for 2 miles, then S. where rough road leads close to lake's W. shore.

CLARA LAKE. (Don). Rainbow and cutthroat are found in this 17 acre lake situated 1.5 miles S. of Dewatto and 0.5 miles W. of road up the hill out of Dewatto. Clara has a good public access. Drainage to Hood Canal.

COLLINS LAKE. A 4 acre private lake that yields eastern brook and rainbow, along with largemouth bass and brown bullhead. Collins is located 0.5 miles S. of Erdman Lake 5 miles NE of Tahuya. Loop road from Tahuya N. and E. down Stimson Creek passes between Erdman and Collins. **HOWELL LAKE**, 10 acres, is located 0.5 miles S. of Collins and is rainbow planted. It has a DNR campground. Both lakes drain into Tahuya River.

COULTER CREEK. Flows into North Bay at head of Case Inlet 3 miles S. of Belfair. Good cutthroat fishing. A road extends N. from Hwy. 3 up the creek.

CRATER LAKE. (Haven). Located 2 miles W. of former Camp Govey above the S. Fork of the Skokomish River. Network of logging roads lace this area, and roads pass along both N. and S. shores of Crater Lake. Kokanee and eastern brook are present.

CUSHMAN LAKE. Formed by a Tacoma dam on the Skokomish River's N. Fork, Cushman is 8.5 miles long and covers 4003 acres. It holds a variety of fish including rainbow, cutthroat, eastern brook, largemouth bass, kokanee and land-locked chinook salmon. Best known for kokanee fishing with trolls and worms from mid-June into September. There is a resort at the S. end of the lake with full facilities, a state park with camping and boat launch facilities 2.5 miles N. on Cushman's E. shore. **STANDBY LAKE** lies adjacent to the SE end of Cushman. The 15 acre man-made lake contains cutthroat. Another reservoir, **KOKANEE LAKE** of 70 acres formed by the lower Tacoma dam, is located 1 mile S. It had been planted with rainbow, cutthroat and kokanee, and drains to N. Fork Skokomish River. No fish passage facilities on either dam. Access is difficult. Road to Cushman leaves Hwy. 101 at Hoodsport heading W. and N. to follow the lake. Cushman Lake is unique in that chinook salmon, which were trapped when the Tacoma dams were built in the 1920's, have survived and spawned in the Skokomish River feeding the lake. Adult, 5-year fish estimated at 20 pounds, have been observed while spawning and scale-checked for age.

DECKER CREEK. Tributary to the Satsop River's E. Fork, joining that river in Grays Harbor County just below Schafer State Park. Upper reaches of Decker are crossed by a road leading NW from Matlock about 2 miles. Some cutthroat available.

LAKE CUSHMAN formed by Tacoma dam on Skokomish River.

DEER LAKE. (Seymour). Contains rainbow. Deer is 12 acres and lies 10.8 miles NE of Shelton and 2 miles S. of Benson Lake, about 0.4 miles E. of Hwy. 3. Drainage is into Pickering Passage.

DEVEREAUX LAKE. (Trout, Deborah, Lakewood). A lake of 100 acres, Devereaux has a public access and gets rainbow, kokanee and cutthroat plants. Location is 1.5 miles NW of Allyn and 3 miles S. of Belfair. Hwy. 3 runs S. from Belfair and adjacent to NE shore of the lake.

DEWATTO RIVER. Sometimes this small stream offers fine winter steelhead fishing in December and January. It is planted occasionally with winter steelhead and cutthroat. The Dewatto gives sea-run cutthroat in lower reaches from summer through fall months, and some years hosts lunker silver salmon at its mouth in Dewatto Bay from October into December. It heads in Kitsap County and flows SW about 8 miles in Mason County to enter Hood Canal at community of Dewatto. A road follows the river upstream from its mouth.

DRYBED LAKES. Upper lake covers 4.5 acres; lower lake 7 acres. They carry planted rainbow and eastern brook. Head N. from Matlock, keeping right at first forks, and drive about 4 miles. Turn left (W.) for 1 mile, then right for 2.5 miles on Road 2255 to S. end of lower lake.

ELK LAKES. Formed by a natural obstruction in Jefferson Creek, Upper Elk is 3 acres, while Lower Elk covers 6 acres. Primarily eastern brook with a few 'bow and planted cutthroat. Road up Jorsted Creek, which leaves Hwy. 101 approximately 4 miles N. of Lilliwaup, swings N. to follow Hamma Hamma River, then a branch turns W. 2.5 miles up Jefferson Creek to **JEFFERSON LAKES.** Lower Jefferson covers 10 acres. Upper Jefferson is 3 acres and is situated 800 feet SW from the larger lake. Rainbow, eastern brook and cutthroat have been planted here.

ERICKSON LAKE. A narrow lake of 15 acres which holds cutthroat. Route to lake is N. from Belfair 4 miles up Union River, then W. and N. for 8 miles, then S. for 0.4 miles on road along Erickson's E. shore.

FORBES LAKE. Largemouth bass are present in Forbes, a 38.4 acre lake located

6 miles E. from Shelton. It drains to Mill Creek.

GOAT RANCH LAKE. A marshy lake of 20 acres located 3.5 miles NW from Belfair. Has received rainbow and cutthroat plants.

GOLDSBOROUGH CREEK. Small stream flowing through town of Shelton. Stocked with winter steelhead and cutthroat. Can be productive for steelhead in early December.

GOOSE LAKE. Rainbow planted lake of 9 acres located 2 miles NW from Shelton and 1500 feet W. from Hwy. 101. Drains to Swamp Creek to Goldsborough Creek.

GRASS LAKE. A 2.5 acre lake holding stocked rainbow, cutthroat and eastern brook. Located about 3 miles NE from Tahuya.

HAMMA HAMMA RIVER. Produces winter steelhead and sea-run cutthroat in the lower 3 miles above Hood Canal where a falls blocks migratory fish just above the noted "Blue Hole". Access is limited in lower reaches. Top stretches have been planted with rainbow and provide fair fishing in May and June. A road 1.5 miles N. of Eldon leaves Hwy. 101 to meet the Hamma Hamma 3.5 miles upstream from its mouth, and then parallels the river for about 8 miles. FS campgrounds are located at mouths of Cabin and Lena Creeks. Poor steelhead production in past few years.

HANKS LAKE. A 27 acre lake, largest in a series of small lakes, holding rainbow and largemouth bass. Route is N. from Shelton 3 miles on Hwy. 101, then W. on Matlock road 6 miles, then N. 1 mile to W. side of lake. **LITTLE HANK** Lake lies 500 feet S. Bass and catfish in little Hanks.

HATCHERY LAKE. Both rainbow and cutthroat have been planted in this peat bog lake of 10.7 acres. Location is 6.5 miles N. from Shelton. Drainage to Skokomish River.

HAVEN LAKE. (Carstairs, Call). A lake of 70 acres that contains rainbow, cutthroat and kokanee. Haven has a public access area. It produces well both in the spring and again in the fall. It is located 7.5 miles W. of Belfair between Wooten and Erdman Lakes. Hwy. 300 leads SW from Belfair 4 miles then heads N. and W. up Stimson creek about 6 miles to the lake.

ISABELLA LAKE. A 208 acre lake located 2.5 miles S. of Shelton and 1 mile W. of Hwy. 101. Isabella has a public access, and is planted with rainbow, which offer spring action, and also with sea-run cutthroat. Outlet is via Mill Creek to Hammersley Inlet. Sea-run cutthroat ascend the creek in fall months. Other species include kokanee, largemouth bass and brown bullhead.

ISLAND LAKE. One of the few Western Washington lakes offering smallmouth bass, Island is a clear, 109 acre lake located 2.5 miles N. of Shelton. It also hosts rainbow, largemouth bass, catfish and some large perch. A road turns E. at the airport adjacent to Hwy. 101 about 1.5 miles N. of Shelton 1 mile to Island Lake. Public access on E. shore.

JIGGS LAKE. A 8.8 acre lake situated 1.5 miles NE from Tahuya. It contains largemouth bass and yellow perch. Drainage is to Tahuya River.

LENA CREEK. Produces rainbow in midsummer months. The outlet of Lena Lakes entering the Hamma Hamma River 8 miles W. of Hwy. 101 on the N. bank Hamma Hamma road. Trail upstream from mouth 4 miles to Lower Lena Lake in Jefferson county. FS campground at mouth.

LILLIWAUP CREEK. High falls block the stream 1 mile from mouth, but fair sea-run cutthroat fishing in this stretch. Upper reaches are primarily a series of beaver ponds. (See Lilliwaup Swamp).

LILLIWAUP SWAMP. A series of beaver ponds sprawled over a large area in the headwaters of Lilliwaup Creek 6 miles N. of Hoodsport. Estimated at 25 acres total. Fishing these ponds requires pioneer work. Easiest route is W. and N. up Lake Cushman road from Hoodsport past Price Lake turnoff (about 7 miles) another 1.4 miles and head NE on good gravel road 2 miles. Then work out rough roads S. Fair fishing in spring and fall months in these ponds for eastern brook and cutthroat.

LIMERICK LAKE. An 80 acre lake created by a dam on Cranberry Creek. Planted occasionally with rainbow and hosting largemouth bass, yellow perch and brown bullhead. Public access. Located about 4 miles N. of Shelton and 3.5 miles SE of Cranberry Lake. Drive NE of Shelton on Hwy. 3, then turn W. from highway at Bayshore and follow signs to lake. Bass also present, along with perch.

LOST LAKE. This 121 acre lake gets rainbow and kokanee plants and offers a public access. Brown bullhead present. It is located 8 miles SW of Shelton on a county road between Shelton and Elma, then N. for 0.5 miles to E. shore.

MAGGIE LAKE. The lake covers 22 acres and carries rainbow. It has a public access area and is situated 2.4 miles NE of Tahuya. A road from that community heads N. for 2 miles to W. shore of Maggie.

MASON LAKE. One of the county's larger lakes, Mason covers 996 acres. It carries rainbow, kokanee, cutthroat, largemouth bass, yellow perch and brown catfish, and has a public access. Mason comes on in the spring and again in fall months. Route is 11.5 miles NE of Shelton on Hwy. 3, then W. for 3.5 miles on a country road. County park on lake.

MILLER MARSH. A beaver pond type lake of 15 acres carrying cutthroat. It is located at head of Eagle Creek with drainage into Hood Canal. It lies .08 miles E. of **OSBORN LAKE** and is reached by road up Jorsted Creek from Hwy. 101 about 4.5 miles N. of Lilliwaup.

NAHWATZEL LAKE. Holds some large cutthroat in addition to smaller rainbow, cutthroat and largemouth bass. A 268 acre lake located 11 miles W. of Shelton alongside Shelton-Matlock road. Produces both early and late in the season. Nahwatzel has a public access plus resort facilities.

PANHANDLE LAKE. Rainbow have been stocked in Panhandle's 14.4 acres. It is situated 8 miles SW from Shelton with drainage to Goldsborough Creek and Oakland Bay.

PANTHER LAKE. The lake covers 103 acres with 30 acres in Mason County and the remainder in Kitsap. Panther contains rainbow and has a public access. Panther is situated 10 miles W. of Bremerton.

PHILLIPS LAKE. This 112 acre lake usually starts fast, delivering planted 'bows. It has a public access site and is reached via Hwy. 3, 7.7 miles NE of Shelton, then E. 1.5 miles past **SPENCER LAKE** to Phillips Lake road which leads 1.5 miles to the lake.

MASON LAKE has county park.

PINE LAKE. Situated in headwaters of Pine Creek at 2250 feet elevation. Pine covers 7 acres and hosts rainbow. It is rated fair to good during summer. Route is up S. Fork of Skokomish River past the former Camp Govey and Brown Creek campground, driving 5 more miles NW, then 3.5 miles W. up Pine Creek to lake.

PRICE LAKE. Has produced some large eastern brook along with rainbow. Price is a shallow, weedy lake of 61 acres reached by the Lake Cushman road 7 miles N. of Hoodsport, then E. 1.5 miles to the lake. Outlet drains into Lilliwaup Creek, and beaver ponds along its 1 mile length furnish good spring and fall fishing for eastern brook and some cutthroat.

ROBBINS LAKE. (Robinson). A 16 acre lake 1.5 miles S. of Dewatto in the "Oak Patch". Robbins is a spring producer for planted rainbow. DNR picnic and boat launch sites on E. shore.

ROSE LAKE. Rainbow and cutthroat plants made in this 8.5 acre lake located 4 miles SW of Potlatch. Leave Hwy. 101 1.4 miles S. of Potlatch and turn W. for 1.5 miles, then S. for about 4 miles passing **STEVENS LAKE** (Steve's), an 8.5 acre rainbow lake, enroute.

SHOE LAKE. Just 6 acres in size, but a fair spring lake for eastern brook and rainbow. The lake lies 8.5 miles W. of Belfair between **TEE** and **HAVEN LAKES**.

SIMPSON LAKE. Largemouth bass and brown bullhead are present in this 29.4 acre lake located 9.5 miles N. from Elma. It drains to E. Fork Satsop River.

SKOKOMISH RIVER. Largest of Hood Canal rivers. It produces migratory fish including winter and summer steelhead, sea-run cutthroat, silver, chinook and chum salmon. The Skokomish enters Hood Canal at its "hook" in Annas Bay about 10 miles N. of Shelton. It provides cutthroat action for fly fishermen in tidal reaches in spring and fall months. December into April is winter steelhead period, with limited summer steelhead fishing from July into October. Jack and adult salmon are available from late August through October. North Fork of the Skokomish is blocked by a Tacoma dam and forms Lake Cushman. It contributes little water to the main river. The South Fork is readily fished from the S. side. The Skokomish Indian reservation reaches from the mouth to 0.4 miles above Hwy. 101. The Skokomish gets periodic plants of winter steelhead. Upper stretches of the S. Fork may be fished by turning W. before crossing the river on Hwy. 101 and continuing up stream past the former Camp Govey on logging roads. There is a FS campground at mouth of Brown Creek above Camp Govey.

SPENCER LAKE. A fine rainbow lake of 220 acres that often holds carry-over trout. It also has largemouth bass. The lake is located 7.7 miles NE of Shelton on Hwy. 3, then .03 mile to right on county road, then right 1.2 miles to public access. Spencer has held up well into the season in past years.

SPIDER LAKE. A narrow, 23 acre cutthroat and eastern brook lake in the Skokomish River's headwaters. Reached by logging road which heads N. from former Camp Govey on Skokomish River's S. Fork, past FS campground at Brown's Creek, then due W. about 6 miles to lake at an elevation of 1290 feet.

STUMP LAKE. Situated approximately 13 miles SW of Shelton and 3 miles S. of the Shelton-Elma road along Cloquallam Creek. The snag-filled lake has cutthroat and eastern brook and offers bass fishing. Light boats may be launched along the shore.

TAHUYA RIVER. A short-run, brushy stream that rises in the "Oak Patch" maze of lakes 10 miles NW of Belfair. Best known as a sea-run cutthroat river in the fall, the Tahuya also yields some winter steelhead in December and January. It drops into fishable shape quickly after heavy rains, and drains into Hood Canal.

TEE LAKE. Covering 38 acres, Tee has a public access and is located 2.5 miles SE of Dewatto between **SHOE** and **CADY LAKES**. It holds rainbow, bass and perch.

TIGER LAKE. Most of this lake's 109 acres are in Mason County, with remainder in Kitsap. Tiger is planted with rainbow and has access on N. shore. Drive up Union River road from Belfair for 4 miles, then turn left 2 miles to S. end of lake.

TRAILS END LAKE. (Prickett). A rainbow lake of 68 acres, it is situated 6 miles SW of Belfair. Brown bullhead present. It has a public access. Route is SW for 5 miles from Belfair on Hwy. 106, then S. 1.5 miles to lake.

TRASK LAKE. Produces rainbow at start of season. Trask is 13 acres, and is located 10 miles NE of Shelton and 1 mile N. of **MASON LAKE.** Private lake.

TWIN LAKES. (Spider). Big Twin is 15 acres and adjoining Little Twin is 5 acres. The lakes hold 'bows and brookies and are in the "Oak Patch" cluster of lakes 7 miles NW of Belfair and 1.5 miles NE of Wooten

Lake. Big Twin has a boat launch site, and a DNR campground.

UNION RIVER. Principally a sea-run cutthroat stream in the spring and early fall, with some winter steelhead action in December and January. The Union flows into the end of Hood Canal close to Belfair. It is paralleled by a road upstream from its mouth for several miles.

WEST LAKE. A marshy lake of 16.5 acres that contains brown bullhead. It lies 13 miles NW from Shelton.

WOOD LAKE. A rainbow planted lake of 10 acres situated 2 miles N. of Tahuya and 0.5 miles NE of **BUCK LAKE.** Watch for signs in maze of roads.

WOOTEN LAKE. This 69 acre lake has a reputation for producing large, hold-over rainbow and often comes on strong in the fall. It gets plants of 'bows and cutthroat and has a public fishing area. Wooten is reached by driving SW from Belfair on Hwy. 300 about 5 miles, then turning N. 2 miles up Stinson Creek, and W. about 5 miles to lake. It sits between **HAVEN** and **BENNETTSEN LAKES** in the "Oak Patch".

MASON COUNTY RESORTS

Cushman Lake: Lake Cushman Resort, Hoodsport, WA 98548. 1-800-588-9630.

Nahwatzel Lake: Lake Nahwatzel Resort, Shelton, WA 98584. 360-426-8323.

Spencer Lake: Spencer Lake Tavern, Shelton, WA 98584. 360-426-2505.

Tahuya River: Summertide Resort & Marina, Belfair, WA 360-275-2268.

Gang trolls are effective

Bait fishermen may want to use a small, light-weigh gang troll. A leader of 12 to 18 inches is tied behind the spoons. Three to six pound test leader is sufficient for most trout angling. Worm hooks in sizes four to eight are common. They are either tied in tandem or singly. Some fishermen bait the top hook with worms, permitting the worm to trail over the bottom, egg-baited hook.

OKANOGAN

COUNTY

Bordered on the N. by British Columbia, Okanogan is the largest county in the state with 5332 square miles. There are over 930 lakes in the county, and 534 of these are located over 2,500 feet elevation, with 215 of this group situated at or over 4000 feet. Highest point in Okanogan is North Gardner Mtn. at 8956 feet. This E. Central County provides some of the best lowland lake fishing in the state, in addition to good fishing in countless mountain lakes. There is good stream fishing, also, with substantial plants made in creeks and rivers after the spring snow run-off and then at intervals through the summer. Most of W. Okanogan is drained by the Methow River system, while the Okanogan River drains the central and N. portion.

AENEAS LAKE. An excellent spring and fall rainbow planted lake. Carry-over trout in the 15 inch class are available in the 60 acre lake. Aeneas has a public access and is located 3.5 miles SW of Tonasket with a road from town crossing the Okanogan River leading to the lake, then S. 0.5 miles to FS road 9410.

ALTA LAKE. Heavy plants of rainbow are

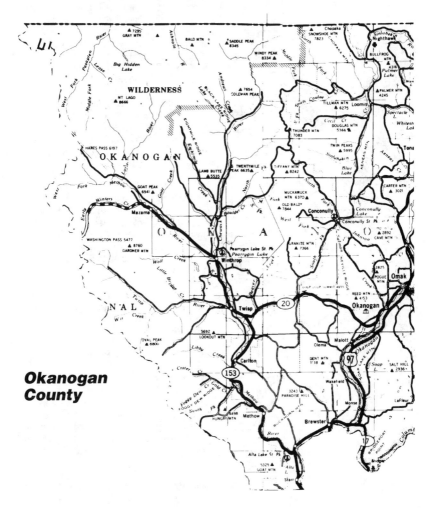

Okanogan
County

made each year in Alta, and the lake comes through despite heavy early pressure. It covers 187 acres and lies 1.5 miles W. of Pateros on Hwy. 153, then S. for 2 miles to lake. There is a state park at Alta with boat launching and camping, plus several resorts.

ANDREWS CREEK. A 'bow and cutthroat stream which enters Chewack River at Andrews Creek campground 19 miles N. of Winthrop on Chewack River road. A trail follows the stream upstream 13 miles to headwaters under Remmel Mtn. in Pasayten Wilderness.

BARNSLEY LAKE. This private 9 acre lake suffers from winter kill. It is located 1.5 miles SW of Winthrop.

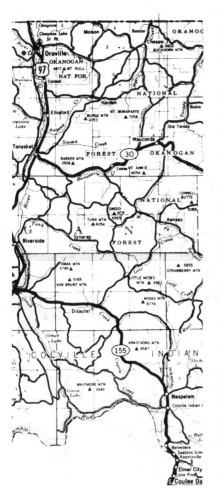

BEAVER LAKES. A pair of lakes holding rainbow and brookies. "Big" Beaver is 30 acres with the 5 acre "Little" Beaver situated 100 ft. E. The lakes are at 2700 and 2675 elevation, and offer best fishing in late spring. They are reached via Hwy. 20 about 18 miles E. of Tonasket, then N. 12 miles past **BONAPARTE LAKE** to Big Beaver where there are two FS campgrounds. County road 9480 from Little Beaver leads 0.5 miles to **BETH LAKE**, 13 acres, which has rainbow and cutthroat. Boat ramp on Big Beaver Lake. FS campground and boat launch on Beth, also.

BLACK LAKE. A 66 acre lake at 4000 feet which contains rainbow. Drive N. from Winthrop about 20 miles up Chewack River to FS road 51, then NW for 2.5 rough miles to road end. Lake Creek trail continues 4 miles to lake. **HALFMOON LAKE**, 15.5 acres, lies 2700 feet above Black Lake 1.4 miles cross country W. of Black Lake in Pasayten Wilderness. It has cutthroat. **KIDNEY LAKE**, a 12.5 acre cutthroat lake is 1 mile S. from Halfmoon.

BLACK PINE LAKE. An 18 acre lake which lies at 3900 feet. It is planted with eastern brook. Drive 4 miles W. from Twisp on S. side of the Twisp River, then about 6 miles S. up Poorman Creek road to lake. Campground.

BLUE LAKE. Located at the head of Sinlahekin Valley on the Sinlahekin W.R.A. at 1686 feet elevation. A lake of 186 acres which holds 'bows. Reached by leaving Hwy. 97 about 5.5 miles N. of Riverside and driving W. 8.5 miles past **FISH LAKE** and another 4 miles N. to Blue Lake. Boat launch area.

BLUE LAKE. Lake of 110.6 acres located 5 miles SW of Oroville. Blue has been stocked with eastern brook, rainbow and Lahontan cutthroat.

BONAPARTE LAKE. Produces kokanee, eastern brook, 'bows and mackinaw. Late spring through summer months offer good fishing in this 158 acre lake which lies at 3554 feet elevation. FS campground at lake's S. end, plus resort facilities. Route to Bonaparte is E. from Tonasket on Hwy. 30 for 20 miles, then due N. for 6 miles up Bonaparte Creek on FS road 32. Boat ramp on lake.

BONNER LAKE. (Ward). Largemouth bass

and black crappie are found in this 15.7 acre lake which is located about 2.4 miles N. from Twisp. It drains to Methow River.

BOULDER CREEK. A tributary to the Chewack River which joins that stream 7 miles N. of Winthrop. Boulder is paralleled by road from its mouth. Road from Winthrop heads N. for 7 miles on E. side of the Chewack River to cross Boulder at its mouth. Brookies present.

BUCK LAKE. There is a FS campground on this 15 acre lake situated at 3247 feet elevation 9 miles N. of Winthrop. It has been rainbow planted. Some largemouth bass and brown bullhead present. A small pond lies 800 feet S. of Buck. Route is N. from Winthrop up W. side of Chewack River 9 miles to Eight Mile road junction on left, then 0.4 miles W. to Buck Lake road for 2 miles to lake. Frequent winter kills.

BUCKSKIN LAKE. A cutthroat planted lake of 11.6 acres at 6000 feet elevation located about 33 miles NW from Winthrop on SE side of Buckskin Point. Drainage to Pasayten River.

BUFFALO LAKE. (Annum). This 542 acre lake is situated on the Colville Indian reservation. It contains rainbow, silver salmon and spiny rays. Good fishing through summer months as the lake is 121 feet deep at one point. Some large rainbow are taken in Buffalo. The lake has resort facilities and a public access on the W. shore. It is reached via Hwy. 155 about 12 miles SE of Nespelem, then E. 5 miles to lake on Buffalo Lake road.

BUZZARD LAKE. A private 15 acre lake which lies at head of Little Loup Loup Creek at 3380 feet elevation. Buzzard holds rainbow.

CAMPBELL LAKE. Located on Methow W.R.A., it holds 'bows, covers   11 acres and has a public access site. Route is SE from Winthrop 1.5 miles on road following E. side of Methow River, then E. about 4 miles to N. tip of lake.

CASTOR LAKE. Rainbow inhabit Castor, a 17.9 acre lake located 3.7 miles NW from Riverside.

CHEWACK RIVER. Considered a fair bet for rainbow in summer and fall months. Also contains whitefish, steelhead and cutthroat. Chewack joins the Methow River at town of Winthrop. Roads follow both sides of the stream, with the W. side road leading over 20 miles upstream. There are 7 FS campgrounds along this stretch. The Chewack gets plants of 'bows at intervals during

LAKE CHOPAKA yields chunky rainbow for Trish Bottcher. (Blair Alexander Photo)

summer. A trail follows river N. from 30 Mile campground into Pasayten Wilderness.

CHILIWIST CREEK. This stream has been planted with eastern brook. Route is 2 miles SW of Molott on W. side of Okanogan River then W. on road which follows the creek about 5 miles.

CHOPAKA LAKE. Road from Loomis heads N. up Chopaka Creek about 7 miles to lake, which has a public access and a DNR campground. Chopaka is a rainbow planted lake. It is 1.5 miles long and covers 148 acres.

CONCONULLY LAKE. An irrigation reservoir of 450 acres created by a dam in Salmon Creek. It gets plants of rainbow. Fluctuations in water levels are common. There are resort facilities plus a state park with a boat launch and camping located at N. end of the reservoir. Route to Conconully is 15 miles NW from town of Okanogan up Salmon Creek.

CONNERS LAKE. A small eastern brook planted lake located on Sinlahekin W.R.A. Gravel boat ramp.

COPPER LAKE (Silver Nail). A 5.4 acre rainbow pond which lies 4 miles N. of Oroville adjacent to W. side of Hwy. 97.

COUGAR LAKE. Planted with rainbow, Cougar is 3 acres and is located on Methow W.R.A., 1.5 miles N. of **CAMPBELL LAKE** road. Turn left 1 mile after crossing Bear Creek enroute to Campbell Lake. Public access.

CRATER LAKE. Located at 6900 feet elevation 14 miles SW of Twisp. The 13 acre lake holds 'bows and cutts. Drainage is to Methow River via Gold Creek. Route to this walk-in lake is 6 miles NW of town of Methow, then 10 miles W. up Gold Creek road and up Crater Creek where a trail takes off up Crater Creek 3.5 miles to the lake. Because of its elevation, Crater is a late summer and fall show.

CRAWFISH LAKE. Located partly on the Colville Indian reservation, Crawfish covers 80 acres, has brook trout and some rainbow. It lies at 4475 feet. Route is via road up E. side of Okanogan River 12 miles, then E. about 14 miles up Tunk Valley to the lake. There is a FS campground on the lake's NE shore plus a boat ramp.

CRUMBACHER LAKE. Eastern brook are planted in this 4.6 acre pond. It is located adjacent to W. side of Hwy. 97 approximately 7 miles N. of Riverside.

CUB CREEK. Brookies have been stocked in beaver ponds along this Chewack River tributary. Follow W. side of Chewack River 5 miles N. from Winthrop, then take FS road 375 NW along the creek for 10 or more miles. Watch for marshy areas.

DAVIS LAKE. This 39.3 acre lake is planted with rainbow. There is a public access in addition to a resort. Davis is located 4 miles SE of Winthrop. Take road on E. side of Methow River about 1 mile S. from town then E. and S. about 2 miles to N. end of lake.

DIBBLE LAKE. (Garrett). Rainbow planted lake covering 5.3 acres. Location is 3.4 miles S. from Winthrop.

DUCK LAKE. (Bide-a-Wee). A mixed species lake which has received rainbow and bluegill plants. It also has largemouth bass, black crappie and pumpkinseed. The 29 acre lake is located 3 miles N. of Omak and 1 mile W. of Omak airport. Road from Omak leads N. to lake. Inlet is a canal from Salmon Creek.

DUFFY LAKE. A 9 acre lake situated at 6500 feet. Some large cutthroat plus eastern brook reported. Take FS road 4420 about 10 miles W. of town of Twisp up Oval Creek to Oval Creek trail. Hike 4.5 miles S., then cross country E. for 1 mile. **OVAL LAKES** lie at head of Oval Creek, 7 to 9 miles by trail. The lakes are 18, 8 and 21 acres and contain cutthroat and rainbow. Elevation of lakes 6200 to 6600 feet.

EARLY WINTERS CREEK. Tributary to Methow River which joins that stream 1.5 miles NW of Mazama. There is a FS campground at this point. North Cascades Hwy. follows creek upstream for 13 miles. The stream carries rainbow and cutthroat. A trail heads SW 2.5 miles up Cutthroat Creek to **CUTTHROAT LAKE,** a 9 acre lake at 4935 feet which holds small cutthroat.

EIGHT MILE CREEK. Carries both rainbow and eastern brook plus summer steelhead with a "fair" rating during late spring and summer months when it gets plants. The creek joins Chewack River 8 miles N. of Winthrop, and a road follows along its

CONCONNULLY LAKE, a 450 acre reservoir.

banks for over 15 miles upstream. There are 4 FS campgrounds along Eight Mile.

ELL LAKE. Rainbow are present in this 21 acre lake. It is situated in the Aeneas Valley, 17 miles SE of Tonasket adjacent to Hwy. 20. Ell is managed as a "quality" lake. **LONG** and **ROUND LAKES** are close to Ell along the highway. All 3 lakes have public access areas and hold rainbow which provide fly fishing. Long is 16 acres and Round covers 20 acres.

FAWN LAKE. Cutthroat have been stocked in Fawn, a 5.8 acre lake at 5500 feet. It is located 29.5 miles N. from Winthrop near Ashnola Pass. Drainage is to Lake Creek.

FISH LAKE. Most of this 102 acre lake is located on the Sinlahekin W.R.A. about 4.5 miles NE of Conconully on county road 219. Fish has a public access area at E. end and is stocked with rainbow. Route is on county road 4015 E. of Conconully along N. shore of **CONCONULLY LAKE** past Sugar Loaf campground to lake shore.

FORDE LAKE. A 24 acre reservoir on Sinlahekin W.R.A. located 6 miles S. of Loomis. Eastern brook. Public boat launch site.

FRENCH CREEK. Enters Methow River at N. town limit of Methow. Beaver ponds along stream offer marginal fishing for brookies. Road from Methow follows creek NE about 5 miles from town.

FRY LAKE. (Loon). Located 200 feet W. of **DUCK LAKE** about 3 miles N. of Omak. It is 10 acres in size and holds mixed species.

GOLD CREEK. A tributary of the Methow River which enters that river 6 miles NW of town of Methow. Small rainbow are taken from this beautiful creek from mid-June on. Access is easy as a road parallels the N. bank about 10 miles to the headwaters. There is a FS campground at point Foggy Dew Creek joins Gold Creek 5 miles from the Methow Hwy. Gold gets plants of rainbow throughout the summer.

GOLD LAKES. A pair of eastern brook lakes on the Colville Indian reservation 14 miles N. of Nespelem up the Nespelem River. The upper lake is 19 acres, with Lower Gold covering 11 acres. May is best angling month.

GOOSE LAKE. (Big). Located on Colville Indian reservation 17 miles W. of Nespelem. The 181 acre lake has bass and crappie, and usually is best in summer months. Road from SW end of **OMAK LAKE** leads 5 miles to Goose. Low water level has hurt fish population.

GOOSE LAKE. (Little). An 8 acre lake which lies 6.5 miles SE from town of Okanogan adjacent to the road past the Okanogan airport. Little Goose has received plants of eastern brook and rainbow in the past. It is on the Colville Indian reservation. Public access.

GREEN LAKE. (Upper). Located 5 miles N. of town of Okanogan. Green covers 44 acres and boasts a public access. Route is up Salmon Creek NW of Okanogan 4.5 miles then N. about 2 miles to lake. Holds rainbow and eastern brook. **LOWER GREEN** is located 1500 feet S. of Upper Green. It is 9 acres.

HESS LAKE. A narrow, 6 acre lake in Scotch Creek planted with rainbow. Location is 6.2 miles W. from Riverside. Drainage to Johnson Creek.

HORSESHOE LAKE. Lahontan cutthroat have been planted in this 28.7 acre lake in recent years. Location is 5.2 miles NW from Riverside. Accessed off the Coulee Creek road. Drainage to Okanogan River.

INDIAN DAN LAKE. A 13.8 acre lake located in Indian Dan Canyon 3.9 miles W. from Brewster. It contains largemouth bass and bluegill.

LEADER LAKE. 159 acre reservoir located 9 miles W. of Okanogan off Hwy. 20. Planted rainbow. DNR campground and boat launch on SW shore.

LOST CREEK. The creek produces small rainbow and eastern brook from early summer into fall. It is located about 24 miles SE of Tonasket on the Aeneas Valley road, and is a tributary to the San Poil River's W. Fork. A road 1 mile W. of Aeneas leads S. up the creek over 10 miles with a FS campground 2 miles up the creek.

LOST LAKE. A 46 acre lake located 6 miles N. of **BONAPARTE LAKE**, about 30 miles NE of Tonasket. Route is via Hwy. 20 for 17 miles E. from Tonasket and then N. about 13 miles to the lake. There is a FS campground at the lake's N. end. Lost holds rainbow and eastern brook. Boat launch sites.

LOUIS LAKE. Cutthroat and rainbow, some large, may be found in this 27 acre lake. Elevation is 5300 feet. Route is 22 miles W. of town of Twisp along Twisp River

to South Creek campground, then hike 2 miles along South Creek to Louis Creek trail and another 3 miles to lake.

LYMAN LAKE. Eastern brook are present in this 3.5 acre lake situated 2.5 miles SW from Aeneas. It drains to Lyman Creek. It has a FS campground and boat ramp.

MARPLE LAKE. (Bench, Rainbow). Winter kill hinders this 3 acre private pond which contains rainbow. It lies 15 miles SE of Tonasket up the Aeneas Valley.

McGINNIS LAKE. A 115 acre lake on the Colville Indian reservation. Drive 7 miles S. of Nespelem on Hwy. 155, then E. and S. past **REBECCA LAKE** 5 miles to W. tip of McGinnis. The lake carries eastern brook and has a public access area.

METHOW RIVER. Starts high on E. side of the Cascade Crest at the head of Methow Valley. A good road parallels the river from Pateros on the Columbia River upstream approximately 50 miles. There are 5 FS campgrounds along upper stretches of the Methow above Mazama. The river gets plants of legal 'bows upstream from mouth of Lost River at intervals during the season as well as steelhead plants. It produces whitefish during winter months in addition to steelhead.

MOCCASIN LAKE. A lake of 33 acres lo-

PEARYGIN LAKE often has carry-over rainbow.

SIMILKAMEEN RIVER is best in spring and fall.

cated 4 miles S. of Winthrop. Road from town leads past Twin Lakes, swinging W. 1 mile to a parking area on **PATTERSON LAKE** road. It is a 1 mile walk from this point. There are husky rainbow in the lake.

MOLSON LAKE. A 20 acre lake that provides fair fishing for rainbow, but is prone to winter kills. Molson lies adjacent to E. side of **SIDLEY LAKE** about 11 miles E. of Oroville. Take Tonasket creek road 8 miles E. from Oroville, then N. 5 miles through community of Molson to Molson Lake.

OKANOGAN RIVER. A large Columbia River tributary that flows S. from Osoyoos Lake on the U.S.-Canada border. It yields smallmouth bass in the Oroville area and also between Riverside and Tonasket. The river also holds whitefish and steelhead which are planted as smolts. Night fishing is effective for the bass and trout. Hwy. 97 leads N. from mouth of Okanogan River at Brewster along the river to the Canadian border offering easy access.

OMAK CREEK. Flows into Okanogan River at town of Omak from the E. Hwy. 155 roughly follows the creek's N. side about 20 miles through Disautel. June through August is best period for the creek's small rainbow and eastern brook. It is on the Colville Indian reservation. It has received steelhead plants.

OMAK LAKE. A 3242 acre body of water situated 7 miles SE of Omak at 950 feet elevation on Colville Indian reservation. A mixed species lake that has been stocked with cutthroat and rainbow. Resort facilities.

OSOYOOS LAKE. A lake of 2036 acres situated 1 mile N. of Oroville adjacent to Hwy.97 on the U.S.-Canada border. The lake contains a wide variety of fish including small and largemouth bass, kokanee, rainbow, and various panfish. There is a state park with boat launch and camping area on lake.

OPAL LAKES. String of 3 cutthroat planted lakes at head of Opal Creek 16.5 miles SW from Twisp. Sizes are 8, 21.3 and 21 acres. Elevations are 6200 to 6500 feet. Drainage to Opal and Eagle Creeks to Twisp River.

PALMER LAKE. A large, natural lake of 2063 acres which carries a variety of fish including large and smallmouth bass, kokanee, rainbow, catfish, crappie and fresh water ling. Lings (burbot) are caught through the ice in winter. Public access at S. end of lake plus a resort, with a picnic site at NE end. Road heads N. from Loomis 4 miles to Palmer's S. end, then closely follows E. shore.

PATTERSON LAKE. A rainbow and eastern brook producer of 143 acres located 7 miles SW of Winthrop. Patterson has a resort and public access and is stocked with rainbow. Road at Winthrop's S. town limit leads past **TWIN LAKES** then button-hooks N. to Patterson.

PEARRYGIN LAKE. Generally holds husky carry-over rainbow in addition to current plants. The lake has resorts, a state park with boat launch and camping, and a F&W department boat launch site. It is located 1.5 miles NE of Winthrop. A road from center of town leads to turn-off to the lake.

PROCTOR LAKE. This 7 acre lake has received both rainbow and eastern brook plants. It is located 3.5 miles N. from Omak and about 300 feet N. of Duck Lake. Drainage is to Okanogan River watershed.

RAMON LAKES. Three small cutthroat planted lakes of 2 to 3 acres at elevations of about 7000 feet in headwaters of Ramon Creek on N. side of Sheep Mountain. They lie about 700 feet S. of U.S.- Canada border. Drainage is to Ashnola River.

RAT LAKE. An irrigation reservoir of 62.5 acres formed by a dam in Whitestone Creek. It carries rainbow and brown trout. Rat is reached by driving 3.5 miles N. from Brewster up Swamp Creek, then taking road N. up Whitestone Creek 2 miles to the lake which has public access.

REMMEL LAKE. Cutthroat have been stocked in this 13.2 acre lake. It is located about 33.5 miles N. from Winthrop at 6500 feet. It lies 2.2 miles N. from Remmel Mtn. Drainage is to Chewack River.

ROCK LAKES. Two lakes of 3.5 and 4.5 acres located 11 miles NW of Okanogan. Route is via Loup Loup road, then on Rock Lakes road. DNR campground. Eastern brook planted.

ROUND LAKE. A lake of 20.3 acres in Aeneas Valley 16 miles E. from Tonasket. It receives rainbow plants. Drainage is to W. Fork San Poil River. Public access.

ROWEL LAKE. Both eastern brook and rainbow are available in 4 acre Rowel. Location is 10.5 miles N. from Brewster in Rowel Canyon. It drains to Whitestone Creek.

SALMON CREEK. Flows into the N. end of Conconully Reservoir at town of Conconully. A good road follows the creek upstream about 8 miles to Salmon Meadows FS campground with 4 other campgrounds along this stretch. Salmon Creek holds rainbow and eastern brook. Lower portion of the creek flows from S. end of **CONCONULLY RESERVOIR** SE about 15 miles to join the Okanogan River at Okanogan. The Okanogan-Conconully road parallels the creek most of its length.

SALMON LAKE. (Upper Conconully Reservoir). Rainbow are planted in this 272 acre lake which lies 1500 feet SW of Conconully Reservoir in town of Conconully. A road leads from town about 4 miles up N. shore of the narrow lake to Sugar Loaf FS campground at tip of lake. There is a public access site on Salmon, plus a resort.

SAN POIL RIVER. West Fork. Heads in the hills N. and S. of Long, Round and Ell Lakes about 17 miles SE of Tonasket. Road up Aeneas Valley follows the San Poil about 10 miles from the river's junction with Aeneas Creek E. and S. through Aeneas and into Ferry County. There is a FS campground 2 miles inside the Okanogan County line. The river contains eastern brook and rainbow and is best in late spring months.

SASSE LAKE. A 6 acre reservoir on the Sinlahekin WRA, about 1 mile NE of the

outlet of **FISH LAKE.** Sasse is subject to summer kill and is not planted.

SCHALLOW POND. Formed by a dam across Fish Lake's outlet. The 10 acre pond lies 4.5 miles NE of Conconully on the Sinlahekim WRA. It holds rainbow and eastern brook.

SCHEELITE LAKE. A small high mountain lake planted with golden trout. Location is about 2 miles S. of U.S.-Canada border between Scheelite Pass and Bauerman Ridge.

SIDLEY LAKE. Located 1 mile S. of the U.S.-Canada border 1 mile NW of community of Molson. The lake covers 108 acres and lies at 3675 feet elevation. Sidley gets Lahontan cutthroat and rainbow. There is a public access plus a resort on the lake, and it may be fished from the open shores.

SILVER LAKE. This 3 acre lake had been stocked with cutthroat. It lies 16 miles SW from Twisp and 1.9 miles NE from Eagle Pass at 5550 feet. It drains to Eagle Creek.

SIMILKAMEEN RIVER. Enters the U.S. from British Columbia 6 miles N. of Palmer lake, and flows about 25 miles S. and E. to enter the Okanogan River at Oroville. A road NW from Oroville closely follows the river. The Similkameen carries rainbow, steelhead and whitefish, and delivers best fishing in spring and fall. Prime fishing water between Nighthawk and Oroville. An old hydroelectric dam near Oroville blocks steelhead and salmon from potential spawning areas upstream.

SOUTH CREEK. A Twisp River tributary which holds cutthroat. It enters the Twisp at South Creek FS campground approximately 22 miles W. and N. of town of Twisp. A trail follows the stream for about 5 miles.

SPECTACLE LAKE. An excellent fishing lake for rainbow, Spectacle is 314 acres. It has several resorts and a public access area. Location is 2.5 miles E. of Loomis. Produces throughout season.

STARZMAN LAKES. Lakes of 8 and 5.5 acres which hold eastern brook and rainbow. Head N. from Brewster on road to Wakefield 1.5 miles, then turn left to follow Starzman Creek 8 miles to S. end of Lower Starzman.

STEVENS LAKE. An 11 acre lake located

in Horse Springs Coulee. It contains eastern brook. Stevens is reached by road on W. side of Okanogan River in town of Tonasket which leads 8 miles SW and then N. to mouth of Horse Springs Coulee where a rough road continues N. 3 miles to lake. Sometimes winter kills.

SUGARLOAF LAKE. (Pine Tree). Eastern brook have been planted in this 6 acre lake. Location is 750 feet N. from Salmon Lake in town of Conconully.

SUMMIT LAKE. Rainbow are the attraction in this 9.9 acre lake located about 11.5 miles NE of Nespelem near head of Coyote Canyon. Drainage to Omak Creek.

TORODA CREEK. The stream heads N. of Wauconda 20 miles E. of Tonasket on Hwy. 20, and flows NE about 20 miles to join the Kettle River at Toroda in Ferry County. A road follows Torada Creek for its full length from Wauconda to Toroda, but private property hampers access. Best for planted eastern brook in the spring. The creek has a few rainbow.

TURNER LAKE. A narrow, 2300 foot lake of 16.5 acres which lies at 4164 feet. Turner winter-kills and is not planted. It is located S. of Wauconda.

TWIN LAKES. Adjoining rainbow-planted lakes of 77 and 24 acres located 4 miles SW of Winthrop. Before entering town turn W. from Hwy. 20 for 1 mile, then S. for 2 miles to Big Twin which has been planted with Lahontan cutthroat. Public access on both lakes with resort facilities on the larger lake. Best fishing is usually during spring.

TWISP RIVER. A major tributary of the Methow River which enters that stream at town of Twisp. A good road parallels the Twisp for over 25 miles W. and N. of the mouth, and 5 FS campgrounds are located at intervals along the river's banks. Many tributaries, including Poorman, Newby, Coal, Little Bridge, Buttermilk, Lime, Eagle, War, Williams, Reynolds, South and North Creeks offer additional fishing opportunities for rainbow, steelhead and cutthroat. Fishing is best from the end of June through fall months. Plants of rainbow and during the year in the Twisp above War Creek. The river also receives steelhead plants.

VARDEN LAKE. A cutthroat planted lake covering 4.5 acres. Location is 17.5 miles NW from Silver Star Mtn. Drainage to Varden Creek, Early Winters Creek and Methow River.

SIDLEY LAKE holds Lahontan cutthroat.

WANNACUT LAKE. A slightly saline lake of 411 acres that holds up for fishing into summer because of its depth, 158 feet at deepest point. Wannacut produces chunky rainbow and is planted regularly, and usually has carry-over trout. There are resort facilities on the lake plus a public access. Route to Wannacut is S. from Oroville 2.5 miles on W. side of Okanogan River, then W. 3 miles past Blue Lake to north tip of Wannacut.

WAR CREEK. A cutthroat and 'bow stream which joins the Twisp River at War Creek FS campground about 15 miles W. of Twisp. A road extends 2 miles up War Creek with a trail then following the creek about 10 miles to headwaters at War Creek Pass.

WASHBURN LAKE. Located 2.1 miles NE from Loomis, Washburn covers 12.8 acres and hosts planted eastern brook along with bluegill. It drains to Spectacle Lake.

WHITESTONE LAKE. This 169 acre lake contains crappie, perch, pumpkinseed, catfish and bass and is reached by driving N. from Tonasket on W. side of the Okanogan River 4.5 miles, then W. for 3 miles to Whitestone. Public access.

WOLF CREEK. (Little). Brookies have been stocked in this small stream's beaver ponds. It is reached by driving W. from bridge S. of Winthrop, bearing right at Twin Lakes turn-off. It also holds rainbow and cutthroat.

OKANOGAN COUNTY RESORTS

Alta Lake: Alta Lake State Park, Pateros, WA 98846. 509-23-2473. Otto's Resort, Pateros, WA 98846. Whistling Pines, Pateros, WA 98846. 509-923-2548.

Big Twin Lake: Big Twin Lake Resort, Winthrop, WA 98862. 509-996-2650.

Bonaparte Lake: Bonaparte Lake Resort, Tonasket, WA 98855. 509-486-2828.

Buffalo Lake: Reynold's Resort, Nespelem, WA 99155. 509-633-1092.

Conconully Reservoir: Shady Pines Resort, Conconully, WA 98819. 509-826-2287. Liar's Cove, Conconully, WA 98819. 509-826-1288.

Conconully Lake: Conconully Lake Resort, Conconully, WA 98819. 509-826-0813.

Davis Lake: Davis Lake Campground. 509-996-2169.

Palmer Lake: Chopaka Resort, Loomis WA 98827. 509-223-3131.

Patterson Lake: Sun Mtn. Resort Winthrop, WA 98826. 509-996-3169.

Pearrygin Lake: Derry's Resort, Winthrop, WA 98826. 509-996-2322.   Pearrygin Lake State Park, Winthrop, WA. 996-2370. 5-Y Resort, Winthrop, WA 98862. 509-996-2448.

Spectacle Lake: Spectacle Lake Resort, Loomis Rt., Tonasket, WA 98855. 509-223-3433. Spectacle Falls Resort, Tonasket, WA 98855. 509-223-4141. Rainbow Resort, Tonasket, WA 98855. 509-223-3700.

Twin Lakes: Big Twin Campground, Winthrop, WA. 98826. 509-996-2650. Wannacut Lake: Sun Cove Resort, Oroville, WA 98844. 509-476-2223.

Trolling techniques

Light leaders of three to six pound test in lengths of three feet or more are commonly used. If fly lines are employed, longer leaders are in order. Small spoons are ideal for trolling and are proven fish catchers. Heavy leaders may kill action of light spoons, however. Check action of the spoon along side the boat at varying speeds to determine how it should be fished. When spoon is regulated, play out about 40 to 60 feet of line, starting shallow and close to shore, and lengthening line to send lure deeper. Trolling is effective on the surface during morning and evening hours, but usually it is necessary to fish deeper during middle of day. Keel type sinkers for 1.8 to 1/4 ounce should be enough.

Did you know?

The Golden Dorado of Paraguay, Brazil and Argentina, a highly prized game fish among fishermen, reaches weights in excess of 70 pounds.

PACIFIC

COUNTY

There are several small but excellent winter steelhead, salmon and sea-run cutthroat streams in Pacific, a 970 square mile county which ranks 30th in size in the state. The Willapa, Naselle, North and Nemah Rivers all produce in season. Productive lakes are not overly plentiful, and most are located on Long Beach Peninsula which fronts on the Pacific Ocean. Pacific County's highest point is about 3,000 feet near the Grays River's headwaters. The Willapa River drains the central portion of the county into Willapa Bay, and the Naselle River drains the S. part to Willapa Bay.

ALDER CREEK. A small cutthroat stream which enters the Naselle River's E. Fork just above the point where it joins the N. Fork of the Naselle. Road from town of Naselle leads E. and N. up the N. Fork with logging roads providing access to about 5

miles of the creek. Best fishing in this small, brushy stream is during late summer and fall.

BEAR RIVER. Fair fishing for cutthroat in the fall, with limited steelhead action in lower reaches of the river during December and January. Hwy. 101 crosses Bear River at its mouth at Willapa Bay. The river may be fished upstream for a short distance from Hwy. 101. Access to the upper river is limited, but a road 1 mile E. of Illwaco leads E. 2 miles, then NE 2.5 miles to touch the stream.

BLACK LAKE. A 30 acre lake located 0.5 miles N. of Ilwaco. Stocked with rainbow and also hosting largemouth bass, yellow perch and brown bullhead. Drainage is to Cranberry Marsh and Willapa Bay.

BREAKER LAKE. Lagemouth bass and yellow perch are available in this 20.3 acre lake. It is located 1.5 miles N. from Long Beach and drains into Pacific Ocean.

CANYON CREEK. Tributary to the S. Fork of Palix River which furnishes fair cutthroat fishing. The brushy creek may be reached by taking a road at South Bend's W. city

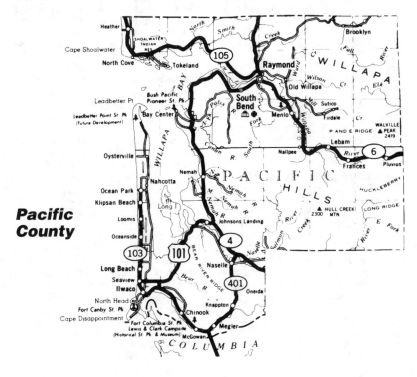

Pacific County

PALIX RIVER flows under Highway 101 bridge near Willapa Bay.

limits and heading N. for about 5 miles where the road meets and follows the creek for about 2 miles.

CASE POND. A 2 acre pond located 1 mile E. of Raymond. Planted with legal rainbow for juvenile fishing.

CEDAR RIVER. Empties into Willapa Bay 4 miles E. of North Cove on Hwy. 105. Logging roads follow the river upstream. Sea-run cutthroat are taken in fall months.

CLAM LAKE. A 10 acre lake that holds bass, crappie and perch. It is located 2.4 miles N. of the community of Long Beach on the North Beach Peninsula. A road runs close to the N. tip of the lake.

CRANBERRY LAKE. A spiny ray lake of 18 acres, containing largemouth bass and yellow perch, which lies 3.5 miles N. of Long Beach. Outlet drains into Willapa Bay. A county road parallels the W. shore of the lake.

DEER LAKE. Largemouth bass and yellow perch are found in Deer, a 7.6 acre lake located 2 miles N. from Long Beach. It drains to Pacific Ocean.

FALL CREEK. Joins upper North River at Brooklyn in NE Pacific County. A cutthroat stream that does best in fall. The road to Pack Sack Lookout follows the creek S.

from Brooklyn for about 2 miles. A maze of logging roads head SE from the lookout to lead to upper reaches of Fall Creek.

FORT CANBY LAKE. (O'Neil). A shallow, stumpy lake of 10 acres which lies about 2 miles SW of Ilwaco at Fort Canby. Contains bass and a few rainbow. The road to the jetty at the N. jaw of the Columbia River passes S. of the lake.

FRESHWATER LAKE. A 5.1 acre lake containing yellow perch and largemouth bass. It is located 5 miles N. from Long Beach. Drainage is to Willapa Bay.

GILES LAKE. This 18 acre lake on the North Beach Peninsula holds bass, perch and crappie. It is located 2.5 miles N. of Long Beach. County roads run close to N. and E. shores of the lake.

GOOSE LAKE. (Mallard). The northern lake in the string of lakes located N. of the town of Long Beach on the North Beach Peninsula. Goose covers 5 acres and hosts spiny rays. Other lakes in the chain include Lost, Island, Tape, Cranberry, Clam, Briscoe, Deer, Breaker, Clear and Tinker. County roads from Hwy. 103 lead to the lakes.

ISLAND LAKE. This 55 acre lake has a public access and produces through the summer for largemouth bass and yellow perch. It is located 4 miles S. of Ocean Park on the North Beach Peninsula with a road leading E. from Hwy. 103 to the lake.

LITSCHKE LAKE. Largemouth bass and yellow perch are present in this 5.2 acre lake situated 4 miles N. from Long Beach. It drains to Willapa Bay.

LOOMIS LAKE. A narrow, 2.5 mile long lake of 150 acres situated 2.5 miles S. of Ocean Park. One of the better rainbow lakes in the county with fishing fair to good from April into August. Best month is May. Yellow perch present. Loomis has a public access and it gets regular 'bow plants.

LOST LAKE. A small lake which holds yellow perch. It is located 1.7 miles SE from Klipsan Beach. Drainage is to Pacific Ocean.

MILL CREEK. Tributary of the Willapa River which joins that river 3 miles SE of Raymond. Mill Creek furnishes some cutthroat activity in the fall. Road from Raymond heads SE up the creek for over 5 miles.

NASELLE RIVER. Produces winter steelhead in December, January and February, responding well to plants. The Naselle enters Pacific County from Wahkiakum County 3.5 miles E. of the town of Naselle and flows NW about 10 miles to Chetio Harbor in Willapa Bay. Hwy. 101 crosses the river at its mouth and Hwy. 4 follows the N. bank for about 7 miles, with a secondary road continuing along the river to its headwaters. The Naselle also yields sea-run cutthroat from July through the fall. Public boat launch site in town of Naselle. The Naselle offers jack and adult chinook and silver salmon from August through December. Silvers the late fish. A few white sturgeon are taken in lower reaches from late fall into spring.

NEMAH RIVER. There are 3 forks of the Nemah, all emptying into Willapa Bay between Bay Center and Johnson's Landing on Hwy. 101. The N. Fork of the Nemah gets most fishing attention and is paralleled by a road upstream for over 5 miles. Logging roads follow the middle Nemah for approximately 5 miles, while Hwy. 101 runs along the S. Fork. Plants of steelhead in the Nemah's N. Fork have produced good steelhead fishing in December, January and February. Sea-run cutthroat are found

in tidal reaches of all three forks with best fishing in the fall.

NORTH RIVER. An excellent sea-run cutthroat stream from late July into September, with early winter months fair for planted steelhead. The slow-moving river heads in Pacific County, then runs into Grays Harbor County and back to Pacific to flow SW to Willapa Bay 8 miles E. of North Cove on Hwy. 105. There is a public boat launch site at mouth of Smith Creek which joins North River in its tidewater area. Hwy. 101 crosses the stream in Grays Harbor County with a logging road following the stream downstream to near its mouth. Easy method of fishing the river is to launch a boat at mouth of Smith Creek and to follow an in-tide upstream about 4 miles to the falls. August and September are good periods for sea-run cutthroat and jack salmon in the lower river. Watch the channel buoys.

PALIX RIVER. The river heads in the hills S. of South Bend and meanders about 7 miles SW to empty into an arm of Willapa Bay 2 miles SE of Bay Center. Hwy. 101

WILLAPA RIVER yields a nice sturgeon near Raymond.

crosses the Palix at its mouth. A boat launch site is located here. A network of logging roads runs between the Palix River's Middle and S. Forks. A few winter steelhead are caught in lower reaches during December and January, and sea-run cutthroat grab in fall months. Public boat launch on the lower river adjacent to Hwy. 101.

RADAR PONDS. A pair of small, 3.2 and 4.6 acres, eastern brook and cutthroat ponds located N. of Naselle near the radar station. Head NW of Naselle 1.5 miles on Hwy. 4, then turn N. up Holm Creek for about 3 miles.

RUE CREEK. Enters Willapa River's S. Fork about 1 mile W. of Menlo. Road from Menlo leads S. up the creek for about 4 miles. Rue holds cutthroat with best fishing for cutts in late summer and fall.

SALMON CREEK. This cutthroat stream joins the Naselle River 1 mile E. of town of Naselle. Salmon Creek is followed by Hwy. 4 about 3 miles E. from its mouth, then NE in and out of Wahkiakum County and on up to Salmon Creek's headwaters.

SKATING LAKE. A long (2.5 miles) lake covering 66 acres. It holds yellow perch. Location is 1 mile S. of Oysterville.

SOUTH BEND POND. Rainbow are stocked in this 1.8 acre pond situated 1.4 miles W. from South Bend. It drains to Willapa River.

SMITH CREEK. Holds planted winter steelhead early in the season in its lower stretches, but is best known as a sea-run cutthroat and jack salmon producer. Smith Creek flows into Willapa Bay at mouth of North River, and is crossed at its mouth by Hwy. 105. There is a boat launch site at this point. August and September are cutthroat and jack salmon months. Upper stretch of the creek is crossed by Hwy. 101 between Raymond and Aberdeen and a road 1 mile S. of this point continues E. to the creek's headwaters.

TAPE LAKE. Yellow perch are found in Tape which covers 9.9 acres. Location is 4 miles N. from Long Beach with drainage to Willapa Bay.

TINKER LAKE. An 11 acre lake situated adjacent to NE side of Long Beach. It holds

largemouth bass and yellow perch. Drainage is to Willapa Bay.

TRAP CREEK. A tributary to Willapa River, joining this stream 10 miles SE of Raymond. Hwy. 6 crosses Trap Creek's mouth, and logging roads follow up stream about 5 miles to headwaters near Trap Creek Lookout. The creek is considered a fair bet for cutthroat in the fall.

WILLAPA RIVER. Plants of winter steelhead help this stream produce in December and January. The Willapa heads in SE Pacific County and flows NW about 30 miles before entering the N. tip of Willapa Bay below South Bend. Hwy. 6 heading SE from Raymond to Chehalis parallels the Willapa for many miles. Besides steelhead the river contains sea-run cutthroat from July into October, and also hosts jack salmon during the same period. The Willapa's S. Fork enters the main river at Raymond where a road follows the stream S. about 5 miles. The S. Fork holds planted winter steelhead and cutthroat. There is a public boat launch site at town of Willapa.

WILSON CREEK. A tributary to Willapa River which joins that stream at town of Willapa. There is a public boat launch site at mouth of creek. Wilson Creek is primarily sea-run cutthroat water. Roads follow the creek E. upstream to its headwaters.

Dobson Fly

Larvae of dobson flies are called hellgrammites by fisherman, and are a popular live bait for a variety of fish. Most dobson fly activity takes place at night. Eggs are laid on rocks close to the edge of fresh water or on leaves of plants overhanging the water. Larvae crawls or drops into the water where they live for three years, preying on other aquatic insects before crawling out of the water to lay eggs.

Did you know?

The zebra fish, sometimes called the turkeyfish, spreads its long fins like feathers of a strutting gobbler, while swimming through warm waters of the Indian and Pacific Oceans. Hidden among the lacy frills, the zebra fish has 18 needle-like poison spines and many skin divers are stung when they reach out to touch it.

PEND OREILLE COUNTY

Pend Oreille county occupies the extreme NE corner of the state. It covers 1428 square miles and ranks 25th in relative size. The county is drained by the Pend Oreille River which enters Washington from Idaho and flows into the Columbia River in Canada near the U.S.—Canada border. There are over 170 lakes listed for Pend Oreille County, and 106 of them lie at or above 2500 feet. Highest point is Gypsy Peak at 7318 feet.

BEAD LAKE. A 720 acre lake which lies in a beautiful mountain setting at 2850 feet elevation NW of Newport. There are mackinaw, kokanee and burbot in the lake which is reached by crossing the Pend Oreille River to the E. bank from Newport, then driving 8 miles NW to the S. shore of the lake. To gain access walk from FS boundary on S. side of lake on Bead Lake trail. No boat access.

BOUNDARY LAKE. Rainbow are present in this 9 acre lake which lies adjacent to Hwy. 31 about 10 miles N. of Metaline Falls. It is located just inside the U.S.-Canada line.

BOUNDARY RESERVOIR. A 1600 acre reservoir formed by a dam on the Pend Oreille River about 8.8 miles N. from town of Metaline Falls. City of Seattle was the dam builder. Largemouth bass and yellow perch present. Picnic and boat launch areas.

BOX CANYON RESERVOIR. Pend Oreille PUD built the dam on Pend Oreille River to create the 6000 acre reservoir. Location is 2.8 miles N. from Ione. Fish species include largemouth bass, black crappie, yellow perch and brown bullhead.

BROWN'S LAKE. One of the state's better "fly fishing only" lakes, Brown's holds cutthroat and occupies 88 acres. The lake is reached by crossing the Pend Oreille River at Usk on Hwy. 31, driving N. 5 miles, and then NE about 6 miles to S. shore of

the lake where a FS campground and boat launch ramp are located. A fish viewing platform that is handicapped accessible is located 0.5 miles E. on inlet stream. It can be reached by road. Best to view cutthroat spawning in April. Elevation is 3450 feet, and best fishing periods are spring and fall.

CALDWELL LAKE. An eastern brook

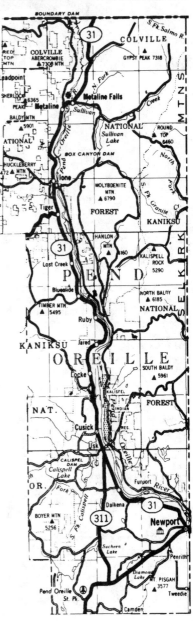

BOUNDARY RESERVOIR extends 17 miles behind Seattle City Light dam on Pend Orielle River. (Seattle City Light Photo)

planted lake of 14.8 acres located 7.4 miles SE from Ione. Drainage to Scotchman Lake to Pend Orielle River.

CARL LAKE. A 7 acre lake stocked with eastern brook. Route is Tiger-Colville road from town of Tiger for 4 miles, then S. on rough road 1.5 miles to lake.

CHAIN LAKE. An enlargement of Little Spokane River covering 77.6 acres in a 1.2 mile stretch of two connected segments. It has yellow perch and largemouth bass. Location is 3.6 miles NE from Elk.

CONGER PONDS. Pair of small ponds of 3.2 and 5.3 acres in headwaters of Trimble Creek 5 miles NW from Cusick. Planted with rainbow and eastern brook.

COOKS LAKE. Rainbow stocked lake which lies at 3075 feet. It covers 20 acres. Road past **BEAD LAKE** leads 5 miles to Cooks. Location is 5.2 miles NE from Usk.

CRESCENT LAKE. A 21.6 acre lake located 9 miles N. of Metaline Falls adjacent to W. side of Hwy. 31. Crescent is stocked with rainbow and offers fair angling from July to October. Pumpkinseed also present. Campground, picnic area and small boat launch on S. shore.

DAVIS LAKE. This 145.9 acre lake at 2150 feet offers eastern brook, rainbow and kokanee, plus largemouth bass. It has a public access area and is reached by driving 5.7 miles S. of Usk on Hwy. 311. Davis comes on early and then again in fall months.

DIAMOND LAKE. There is a public access plus resorts on Diamond. Route is 7 miles SW of Newport on Hwy. 2 which parallels the SE shore of the lake. The 754 acre lake at 2360 feet has rainbow and cutthroat plus largemouth bass. It drains to Sacheen Lake.

FAN LAKE This 72.9 acre lake has a public access and lends itself to fly fishing for cutthroat and rainbow. It is located 8 miles NE of Deer Park, 2.5 miles W. of Hwy. 195 at 1930 feet. Best fishing is in spring and fall.

FRATER LAKE. An 11 acre cutthroat planted lake located 6.5 miles S. of Ione on Hwy. 311, then 6 miles SW on Hwy. 294. Drainage is into **LEO LAKE**, and most productive fishing comes during spring and September and October. Small boats may be launched from lake's shore.

GOOSE CREEK. A remote creek which

flows into the upper West Branch inside the Idaho line. Top stretch of the creek carries small cutthroat and eastern brook and is crossed by the road running NE from Usk 16 miles between North and South Skookum Lakes. A rough fishermen's trail heads upstream.

GRANITE CREEK. Only the upper reaches of this Priest Lake tributary are in Washington. Check for restrictions.

HALFMOON LAKE. (Moon). A 14 acre lake which contains small eastern brook. It is located 7.5 miles NE of Usk at head of Halfmoon Creek. A road parallels E. shore of the lake. Cutthroat plants have been made in Halfmoon. Spring and fall offer best fishing.

HARVEY CREEK. The creek heads in Bunchgrass Lake on the E. slope of Molybdenite Mtn. and flows NW into Sullivan Lake. Best fishing for the creek's rainbow and cutthroat comes after July 1. Route is road from Ione about 7 miles NE toward **SULLIVAN LAKE**, then E. and S. up Harvey Creek 8 miles to Bunchgrass Lake at 4950 feet.

HORSESHOE LAKE. Kokanee and rainbow along with largemouth bass, crappie, perch, sunfish and catfish inhabit this 128 acre lake. It is a steady producer of medium sized kokanee. The lake lies in a deep bowl, and is reached via road from S. end of **ELOIKA LAKE** in Spokane County 8 miles to lake shore. There is a public access on Horseshoe. Elevation is 1975 feet.

IONE MILL POND. This 37 acre lake lies adjacent to W. side of Hwy. 31 at Ione. Marginal fishing.

KINGS LAKE. Arctic grayling have been stocked in this 53.2 acre lake which lies at 3250 feet 6.5 miles NE from Usk. Major species in lake are planted cutthroat. Drainage is to Skookum Creek.

LAKE OF THE WOODS. An 8 acre lake stocked with rainbow. It lies at 2400 feet about 6 miles E. of Camden on Spring Valley road. Access problems.

LEADBETTER LAKE. (Loon). A producer of eastern brook covering 22 acres. Leadbetter is situated 5 miles N. of Metaline Falls on the road running along the W. side of Pend Oreille River. Private.

LEAD KING LAKES. Rainbow and eastern brook planted lakes of 4.2 and 2.4 acres at 2550 feet. Location is 5.5 miles N. from Metaline Falls and about 1.9 miles N. from **LEADBETTER LAKE.**

LEO LAKE. A cutthroat lake of 39 acres which lies adjacent to the S. side of Hwy. 294 at the Pend Oreille-Stevens County line. Leo offers action during spring and fall. FS campground and boat launch at N. end of lake.

LITTLE SPOKANE RIVER. (East Fork). Crossed by Hwy. 195 about 4 miles SW of Newport, the river flows SW to feed Chain Lake, and continues out of the lake into Spokane County. A road and a R.R. parallel the Little Spokane for 6 miles or more. The river holds small eastern brook. **WEST FORK LITTLE SPOKANE RIVER** flows SE from Sacheen Lake into Trout Lake, then into Horseshoe and upper Fan Lake before crossing the line into Spokane County and into **ELOIKA LAKE.** The river contains eastern brook, rainbow, plus spiny rays in the stretch between Horseshoe and Eloika Lakes.

LITTLE LOST LAKE. Eastern brook and

LINDA AKERLUND displays largemouth bass taken from Campbell Slough along Pend Orielle River. (Bill Akerlund Photo)

rainbow have been stocked in the 5.7 acre lake at 3150 feet. Location is 5.5 miles N. from lone at head of Lost Lake Creek. It drains to Pend Orielle River.

LOST CREEK. Rainbow and brook trout are available in this small stream, a tributary of Pend Oreille River S. of Tiger. Series of beaver ponds along the creek.

LOST LAKE. An eastern brook lake of 22.1 acres situated 9 miles NW from Elk and 1.1 miles W. from **TROUT LAKE.** Drainage is to W. Branch Little Spokane River.

LUCERNE LAKE. (Yorke). Eastern brook are present in this 17 acre lake. Location 8 miles N. of Metaline Falls on the W. side of Hwy. 31 about 0.4 mile S. of **CRESENT LAKE.** Private lake.

MARSHALL LAKE. Plants of cutthroat maintain this 188 acre lake which is fed by Marshall and Burnt Creeks. It also has had arctic grayling plants. Route is across the Pend Oreille River at Newport, then 6.5 miles NW to S. end of lake. Marshall holds up well throughout the season and has a public access site and resorts.

MEADOW LAKE. A 4.1 acre lake in a peat bog area about 20 miles NE from Colville

at elevation of 3450 feet. Planted with eastern brook. It drains to Columbia River.

MILL CREEK. A tributary of the Pend Oreille River, joining the stream at Babbitz Landing on County East Side highway, 14 miles N. of Usk. Mill Creek is followed upstream 6 miles by a road on the N. bank. It hosts small eastern brook and cutthroat, and produces best angling during late summer.

MUSKEGON LAKE. Cutthroat are the attraction in this 7.5 acre lake. Elevation is 3450 feet. It lies 16 miles SE from Metaline Falls and about 1300 feet W. from Washington-Idaho border. Drainage is to Priest River.

MYSTIC LAKE. A 17 acre lake stocked with cutthroat. Elevation is 2975 feet, and route is 4 miles beyond **BEAD LAKE** on the Bear Paw road. Good camp site, heavily used.

NILE LAKE. Both rainbow and eastern brook plus cutthroat are found in Nile, which lies at 3190 feet elevation and covers 23 acres. Route is 5 miles SW of Tiger where the lake is situated adjacent to E. side of Hwy. 294. Nile is considered a good fly fishing prospect in June and September. Small boats may be launched along shore.

DAVIS LAKE along Hwy. 311 contains rainbow, eastern brook and kokanee.

NO NAME LAKE. Planted with cutthroat, this 15 acre lake is located 1 mile past **BEAD LAKE** off Bear Paw road. FS campsites.

PARKER LAKE. A 22.1 acre lake adjacent to 27 acre marsh. Parker has been planted with rainbow and eastern brook. Dispersed campsites on FS land. It is reached by traveling 3.5 miles up Cusick Creek Road (County Road 2441) from intersection with Hwy. 20 approximately 6 miles N. of town of Cusick.

PETIT LAKE. A cutthroat lake of 10 acres located at 3975 feet on the N. flank of Diamond Peak. It is reached by a road up LeClerc Creek's E. Branch from town of Ruby on Hwy. 31.

PEND OREILLE RIVER. A major river which heads in Idaho's Pend Oreille Lake. It flows W. to enter Washington at Newport, continuing N. the length of Pend Oreille County. It enters B.C. 10 miles N. of Metaline Falls and then joins the Columbia River. Hwy. 31 follows the river for its entire run in Washington, offering easy access at frequent points. The river contains many species of fish including spiny rays, rainbow, whitefish, cutthroat, German browns and bass. Fishing holds up throughout the year.

POWER LAKE. (Power Dam). A 55 acre reservoir created by a dam on Kalispell Creek's N. Fork. Both rainbow and eastern brook are taken here from May on. Elevation of the lake is 2421 feet. Route is SW from Usk about 7 miles past Calispell Lake. Water levels fluctuate.

PRIEST RIVER. (Lower West Branch). A pretty stream which delivers small cutthroat and eastern brook throughout the season. Best route is to follow Hwy. 57 N. from town of Priest River in Idaho, turning NW up the river at Falls RS. This road continues upstream to the river's headwaters before swinging W. and S. to Usk on Washington's Hwy. 31.

RUBY CREEK. Both eastern brook and rainbow have been planted in this stream's beaver ponds. The creek enters Pend Orielle River at Blueside. Ruby Creek road leads from Hwy 20 S. and W. to follow creek.

SACHEEN LAKE. Eastern brook, brown trout and rainbow are found in this 319 acre lake. It is reached by driving 11 miles SW from Newport on Hwy. 195 then N. for 4 miles to the lake on Hwy. 311. There are resorts on Sacheen plus a public access area on the NE shore. Elevation is 2250 feet.

SALMO RIVER. (Upper). Located in NE corner of the county, heading under Little Snow Top Mountain on the Idaho line, and flowing NW about 6 miles to enter B.C. From Metaline Falls take FS road 302 E. up Sullivan Creek for about 11 miles to FS Road 654. Follow this road about 12 miles to trail 506 which leads 3 miles to river.

SKOOKUM LAKES. Plants of eastern brook boost South Skookum (32 acres) and North Skookum (38 acres). South Skookum has also received rainbow plants. Both lakes lie at slightly over 3500 feet elevation, 6 and 7 miles N. of Usk on Hwy. 31. Road follows Skookum Creek upstream. Mid-May is best fishing period. There is a FS campground and boat ramp on South Skookum, and a state campground on **NORTH SKOOKUM**, as well as a resort.

SLATE CREEK. A producer of small cutthroat, brook trout and rainbow through much of the season, Slate is a tributary of Pend Oreille River, joining that stream 6 miles N. of Metaline Falls. Hwy. 31 crosses the creek near its mouth, and a road leads up the N. bank for about 6 miles.

SULLIVAN LAKE. Route is up Sullivan Creek from Metaline Falls about 4 miles past **SULLIVAN MILL POND**, then 2 miles S. where FS road 303 parallels the W. shore for 3.5 miles. The lake has kokanee. Some large browns, brookies and rainbow available. There are FS boat launches and campgrounds at both ends of the 1290 acre lake. Road continues SW back to Hwy. 31 at Ione.

TACOMA CREEK. Crossed by Hwy. 31 about 3.5 miles N. of Cusick, the small stream yields eastern brook, rainbow, brown trout and cutthroat. Roads follow the creek upstream for several miles.

TROUT LAKE. A private 95 acre lake that holds rainbow, eastern brook, perch, bass and sunfish. Trout turns out a few large 'bows early each year. Road heads NW for 4 miles to lake from Hwy. 195 at Pend Oreille State Park.

VANES LAKE. Eastern brook have been stocked in Vanes, a 4 acre lake at 3000 feet. Location is 1 mile N. from **NO NAME LAKE** in marshy area.

WEST BRANCH PRIEST RIVER. (Lower). Rated fair for eastern brook and cutthroat, the stream is reached by driving N. from town of Priest River in Idaho 12 miles on Hwy. 57 to Falls ranger station, then NW up the stream into Washington, where the road runs along the river for approximately 10 miles. **UPPER WEST BRANCH** is reached via a road NW from Idaho's Hwy. 57 N. of Priest River. A road follows river for about 7 miles in Washington through Squaw Valley. Eastern brook and cutthroat are present. Rough campsites along stream.

YOCUM LAKE. Plants of cutthroat are made in this 41 acre lake which lies at 2875 feet elevation. It is reached by following Le Clerc Creek's W. Branch road 6 miles then W. for about 3 miles to lake shore. Unimproved campsite at lake.

PEND OREILLE COUNTY RESORTS

Diamond Lake: Diamond Lake Resort, Newport, WA 99156. 509-447-4474. Shadow Bay Resort, Newport, WA. 509-447-3332.

Marshall Lake: Marshall Lake Resort, Newport, WA 99156. 509-447-4158.

North Skookum Lake: Skookum Chinook, Newport, WA 99156. 509-447-4158.

Pend Oreille River: Blueside Resort, Usk, WA. 4509-45-1327.

Sacheen Lake: Cedar Creek Lodge, Newport, WA 99156. 509-447-3212. Sacheen Lake Resort, Newport, WA 99156. 509-447-3485. Circle Moon, Newport, WA 99156. 509-447-3735.

Sullivan Lake: Sullivan Ranger District. 509-446-2681.

> ### Did you know?
>
> Heaviest flying bird of North America is the trumpeter swan, with maximum weights of 40 pounds

---

Slick up spoons

All it requires is elbow grease to shine the spinners, gang trolls and spoons that have been rusting and tarnishing in your tackle box. They are supposed to attract fish, remember? Some smart operators run the lures in with a silver polishing session at home. Spouses who go along with this are truly lovable creatures.

Watch slippery logs

When you fall it (and who doesn't?), take off your wet clothes, wring them as dry as possible and put them on again. Sure, it's a bit chilly, but why did you walk out on that slippery log?

Pierce County

PIERCE

COUNTY

The topography of Pierce County ranges from sea level to Mt. Rainier, 14,410 feet, the highest point in the state. Pierce covers 1789 square miles and ranks 19th in size among the 39 counties. About 323 square miles lie within the boundaries of Mt. Rainier National Park. Approximately one-half of the lakes are located above 2500 foot elevation. The Puyallup and Nisqually River systems drain all but the NE portion which is drained by White River.

ALDER LAKE. Reservoir formed by a Tacoma power dam on the Nisqually River totaling 2931 acres, with about 1700 acres in Pierce, 1117 acres in Thurston and 124 acres in Lewis County. Best fishing for rainbow and kokanee at upper end of lake. It also holds black crappie, largemouth bass, yellow perch and catfish. Tacoma City Light has public access and boat launch sites on the lake. DNR has campsites and launch ramp. There is also a resort. Hwy.

7 about 5 miles S. of Eatonville follows along Alder's N. shore.

AMERICAN LAKE. A 1125 acre lake situated 8 miles SW of Tacoma which produces rainbow, cutthroat, kokanee, perch, crappie, brown bullhead, rock bass and largemouth bass, holding up well into the season. Usually rainbow in the 7-9 inch class offer action in April, with kokanee coming on in mid-May. There is good fall kokanee fishing in American, and the lake holds some large rainbow. Resort on the lake's E. shore and a large public access area near Camp Murray, plus another public access located on N. end. Take Camp Murray-Madigan exit W. from Hwy. 5 for 1 mile to lake.

BAY LAKE. An excellent rainbow producer covering 119 acres. The lake is shallow and rich and yields 'bows to 16 inches. It has a public access. Route is over the Narrows Bridge from Tacoma to Purdy, then W. and S. on Hwy. 302 about 7 miles to Key Center where a road heads due S. for 7 miles past Home to the lake.

BEAVER CREEK A tributary of the Big Mashell River, entering that stream 4 miles E. of Eatonville. Beaver holds cutthroat and rainbow. Road from Eatonville leads up the Mashell about 3 miles, then swings SE to parallel Beaver Creek for 2.5 miles.

BENBOW LAKES. Chain of 5 lakes including Whitman, Byron, Upper and Lower Twin plus an unnamed lake. All are private except Whitman, a 29 acre lake which has a

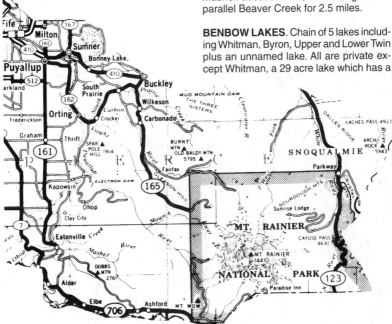

public access and contains rainbow, cut-throat and spiny rays. Lakes are located 2.5 miles W. and S. of Kapowsin.

BONNEY LAKE. Some hefty rainbow trout are sometimes taken in this 17 acre lake, along with largemouth bass and pumpkin-seed. It has a public access site and is lo-cated 2.5 miles SE of Sumner on Hwy. 410, then N. for 1 mile on Myers road to 77th SE, then E. to circle lake.

BOWMAN LAKE. Contains rainbow and spiny rays. It covers 11 acres and lies 4.5 miles SE of Auburn. Drainage is to the Stuck River.

CARBON RIVER. A heavily silted stream that rises from a glacier in Mt. Rainier Na-tional Park and flows NW to join Puyallup River about 3 miles N. of Orting. Receives winter steelhead plants.

CARNEY LAKE. A rainbow lake of 39 acres with about 18 acres in Kitsap County. April, May and June are top months. Carney is located 4 miles N. of Vaughn on the Pierce-Kitsap County line. It has a pub-lic access.

CARTER LAKE. A 6.3 acre marshy lake located 0.5 miles SW from Ponders on McChord AFB. Planted with rainbow.

CHAMBERS CREEK The creek produces eggs for the state's winter steelhead pro-gram. Poor fishing. It heads in Steilacoom Lake and flows W. to enter Puget Sound near town of Steilacoom. Good sea-run cutthroat fishing at mouth in fall.

CHAMBERS LAKE. An 80 acre marshy lake formed by a dam on Muck Creek. Lo-cated 1 mile NE of Roy on Ft. Lewis mili-tary reservation. Chambers holds rainbow, cutthroat and largemouth bass.

CLARKS CREEK. A tributary of Puyallup River which rises from Maplewood Spring SW of Puyallup and joins the Puyallup River from E. side a few miles W. of town. Favored steelhead hole at mouth of Clark, with some sea-run cutthroat. A road follows the W. bank upstream. Receives winter steelhead plants.

CLEAR LAKE Stocked with rainbow and kokanee, Clear is a 155 acre lake with a public access and resort facilities. It is situ-ated 5.5 miles N. of Eatonville on W. side of Hwy. 7. A road borders much of the lake.

CLEARWATER CREEK. Reached via Hwy. 410 about 10 miles E. of Enumclaw, then S. on logging roads which follow creek upstream. The Clearwater joins White River on the Pierce-King County line. It

LAKE JOSEPHINE is located on Anderson Island. (Carol Crusan Photo)

produces rainbow and cutthroat in spring and summer months.

CRESCENT LAKE. A rainbow and cutthroat planted lake of 47 acres located 4 miles N. of Gig Harbor. It has a public access area.

ECHO LAKE. A 61.4 acre lake reached via a 5 mile trail from summit of Corral Pass. Drained by upper Greenwater River. Has cutthroat in 7-8 inch range. Road to Corral Pass heads E. from Hwy. 410 at Silver Springs. Elevation is 3819 feet.

DALLES LAKES. Pair of small lakes, 2.5 and 0.8 acres, 7 miles SE from Greenwater at N. end of Dalles Ridge. Elevation is 4550 feet. Drainage to White River.

DECOURSEY POND. A small rainbow planted pond located 4 miles SE of Tacoma on Pioneer Road. It drains to Clark Creek and Puyallup River.

EAST LAKE. A cutthroat planted lake of 4 acres located about 15 miles SE from Enumclaw on N. side of Cayada Mountain. It drains to Carbon River. Elevation is 4000 feet.

EATONVILLE POND. Rainbow are stocked in this 4 acre pond located 0.5 miles S. from Eatonville. Drainage is to Mashel River.

FLORENCE LAKE. Located on Anderson Island in lower Puget Sound, this 66.5 acre lake has received brown trout and rainbow plants. It also holds largemouth bass and bluegill.

FOREST LAKE. A 6.3 acre lake containing brown trout and rainbow, along with rock bass and pumkinseed. It lies 3.4 miles S. from Orting and drains to Puyallup River.

GEORGE POND. A 1.6 acre pond containing cutthroat. Location is 26 miles SE from Enumclaw on N. side of Noble Mtn. at 5470 feet. Drainage is to Greenwater River.

GRAVELLY LAKE. Access to this 148 acre lake is difficult since private homes ring entire lake. Gravelly contains spiny rays and is situated 0.5 miles NW of Ponders.

GREENWATER LAKES. (Meeker). Located on Pierce-King County line. Upper lake covers 6 acres, with the lower lake 4 acres. They drain into Greenwater River and hold eastern brook, cutthroat and rainbow. A trail leads SE from Himes Camp approximately 8 miles up Greenwater River road from Hwy. 410 about 2 miles to the lakes. Elevations are 2780 and 2846 feet.

HARTS LAKE. Fair spiny ray fishing for bass, crappie, pumpkinseed, perch and yellow and brown bullhead with plants of rainbow aiding spring angling. Hart is a 109 acre lake and has resort facilities and a public boat launch area. Road leads SE from McKenna about 5 miles to the lake.

LITTLE HART LAKE, 10.6 acres, lies 600 feet S. from Harts. It contains brown bullhead.

HELEN'S LAKE. Rainbow are present in Helen's which covers 5 acres. It lies ate 4000 feet 7.5 miles NE from National. Drainage is to Puyallup River.

HERRON LAKE. A private 10 acre rainbow lake adjacent to Case Inlet 1 mile S. of the community of Herron.

HILLE LAKE. Rated just fair fishing. The 3 acre pond has rainbow and spiny rays. It lies adjacent to the E. side of Lake Tapps' N. end.

HORSESHOE LAKE. Located 3 miles N. of Eatonville at SW end of **OHOP LAKE** on Northwest Trek. No fishing access. The lake is 12 acres in size and carries spiny rays.

JOSEPHINE LAKE. Situated on the E. shore of Anderson Island, Josephine covers 72 acres and hosts bass and other spiny rays.

KAPOWSIN LAKE. Primarily a spiny ray lake which is bolstered with spring plants of legal-sized rainbow. Fish species include largemouth bass, rock bass, black crappie, bluegill, pumpkinseed, yellow perch and brown bullhead. The lake is located at community of Kapowsin with resorts on the SW and N. shores. Kapowsin often comes on in early fall months for fly fishermen for large rainbow. St. Regis Co. maintains a boat launch site and campground on N. end of lake.

KREGER'S LAKE. (Alder). Located 1 mile SW of **SILVER LAKE** and 5.5 miles W. of Eatonville. The lake contains bass and is 42 acres in size. It drains into Nisqually River. Private lake.

LILLY LAKE. A 10 acre lake which lies at 4080 feet elevation. Holds cutthroat and rainbow. Drainage is into Clearwater River. Easiest route is up W. Fork White River road to road end at Martin Gap, then 6 or 7 miles W. cross country.

LOUISE LAKE. (Balch). Planted rainbow keep this 39 acre lake going into June. It also holds largemouth bass and brown bullhead. Louise lies in a bowl 1.5 miles SE of Steilacoom with access via Old Military Road to 99th Ave. SW to Lake Louise Drive which circles lake.

MASHELL RIVER. Cutthroat and rainbow, plus steelhead are available in this Nisqually River tributary. Road from Eatonville leads upstream for about 7 miles. The **LITTLE MASHELL** joins the Big Mashell 1 mile S. of Eatonville with a road following the stream to its headwaters, about 8 miles. There is a waterfall 1 mile above its mouth. The stream contains rainbow and cutthroat.

MORGE LAKES. Trio of lakes at 4400 feet covering 1.5, 3.0 and 2 acres. They are located 4.4 miles NE from National at head of Busywild Creek. They contain cutthroat. Drainage is to Nisqually River.

MUCK CREEK. The creek flows through town of Roy and then W. for 4 miles inside Fort Lewis military reservation to enter Nisqually River. Fishing is marginal, although there is a good winter steelhead hole at its mouth. There are some sea-run cutthroat available in fall months.

MUD LAKE. A private spiny ray lake of 20 acres located 4 miles NW of Eatonville and 1 mile W. of Clear Lake. A road leads from Hwy. 7 about 1 mile W. to the lake.

NATIONAL MILL POND. Cutthroat are present in this 9 acre pond which lies adjacent to N. side of Nisqually River at National.

NISQUALLY LAKE. Located on the Fort Lewis military reservation 4 miles NW of Roy. It holds rainbow and varies from 40 to 100 acres.

NISQUALLY RIVER. The Nisqually River forms the boundary between Pierce and Thurston Counties. The large, glacial stream heads in Mt. Rainier National Park and flows W. to empty into Puget Sound between Tacoma and Olympia. The

STEELHEAD PLUNKING at mouth of Clark's Creek on Puyallup River.

Nisqually's lower reaches below Tacoma's Alder dam are fished most often, as glacial bleed colors the upper portions. Best known for winter steelhead, with top periods in December, January and late March and April, seasons permitting. The Nisqually also offers excellent sea-run cutthroat fishing from mid-summer into fall for the lower few miles. Indians net the lower river for salmon and steelhead on their reservation.

OHOP LAKE. A narrow, 2.4 mile-long lake of 235 acres which offers early rainbow fishing due to spring plants of legal 'bows. When the water warms, Ohop provides good to excellent angling for bass, crappie, perch and brown bullhead, and then comes on for larger 'bows in fall months. The lake has a public access and is located 1.5 miles N. of Eatonville, with a road hugging the entire W. shoreline.

ORTING LAKE. (Forest). A 4 acre pond containing rock bass. It is situated about 2 miles NE of Orting. Drainage of the marshy lake is to the Puyallup River. Foot access only.

PUYALLUP RIVER. One of the state's best winter steelhead streams which yields the big sea-run rainbow from December into March in lower stretches. Roads parallel both banks of lower river from Sumner to Tacoma offering easy access. Sea-run cutthroat are available in late summer and fall months low in the river, and there is limited rainbow fishing in upper Puyallup. The river heads high on Mt. Rainier from a glacier which contributes to the river's milky appearance. Major tributaries include the White and Carbon Rivers and South Prairie Creek. Road from Orting to Electron parallels the Puyallup and a rough road continues SE upstream for a few miles.

PITCHER MT. LAKE. A rainbow lake of 7 acres located 1.8 miles W. from **SUMMIT LAKE** on NW side of Pitcher Mtn. Elevation is 4650 feet. It drains to Carbon River.

RAPJOHN LAKE. There are brown trout and rainbow in this 56 acre lake, plus largemouth bass, black crappie, pumpkinseed, yellow perch and brown bullhead. It is spring planted with legal 'bows. Rapjohn has a public access and resort facilities. It is located about 5 miles NW of Eatonville between Hwy. 7 and 161.

ROY LAKE. (Muck). A private lake of 26 acres which lies 0.5 miles NE of Roy. It holds spiny rays.

SECUALLITCHEW LAKE. Located on Fort Lewis military reservation 1.5 miles NE of Dupont. The lake covers 81 acres and has been planted with silver salmon. Drainage is through Edmond Marsh to Puget Sound. It also holds rainbow.

SILVER LAKE. Anglers are offered a variety of fish in this 138 acre lake. It contains rainbow, perch, bass, brown bullhead, pumpkinseed and black crappie. Silver furnishes fair to good fishing, from May into September. There is a resort on the lake which lies adjacent to Hwy. 7 about 5 miles W. of Eatonville.

SNELL LAKE. A 2 acre rainbow lake 1.4 miles SE from Wilkeson. It drains to Wilkerson Creek.

SOUTH PRAIRIE CREEK. Rainbow and a few winter steelhead are available in South Prairie, along with some cutthroat. The creek heads in the Three Sisters area SE of Mud Mtn. Dam and flows W. to join the Carbon River 2 miles N. of Orting. It is crossed by the Buckley-Wilkeson highway and road from Buckley heads S. 2 miles, then E. about 10 miles to headwaters.

SPANAWAY LAKE A popular resort lake located 0.5 miles W. of community of Spanaway on Hwy. 7 S. from Tacoma. It contains perch, small and largemouth bass, brown bullhead, pumpkinseed, and crappie, and is boosted with spring plants of legal 'bows and cutthroat. Spanaway covers 262 acres. A county park at the lake's NE end offers public access and a boathouse. Drainage is to Spanaway Creek to Clover Creek into Steilacoom Lake.

STEILACOOM LAKE. A year-around lake which offers a few large rainbow plus largemouth bass, rock bass, cutthroat and brown bullhead. Poor fishing. Steilacoom is 313 acres and is located 3 miles E. of town of Steilacoom. Interlaken Drive SW bridges the lake in the middle.

SUNSET LAKE. An artificial lake of 7.7 acres situated 1.5 miles E. of Wilkeson. It has received rainbow plants. Drainage is to Sunset Creek and South Prairie Creek.

SPANAWAY LAKE dawn on opening day. (Ernie Wolcott Photo)

SURPRISE LAKE. Located about 1.5 miles E. of Milton adjacent to the S. side of Hwy. 514. A county road, 9th St. NW, parallels the W. shore. Surprise is a lake of 30 acres. It is planted regularly with rainbow and also offers spiny rays including bass. Best fishing comes in April, May and June.

TANWAX LAKE. There are resorts and a public access site on this 173 acre lake which holds bass, perch, pumpkinseed, crappie, brown bullhead, eastern brook and rainbow. The lake comes on early for planted rainbow, produces spiny rays during summer, and gives with larger rainbow in fall. It is located close to E. side of Hwy. 161 SW of Kapowsin.

TAPPS LAKE. Formed by flooding a group of 7 small lakes with a diversion from the White River, thus making a power reservoir of 2296 surface acres with numerous inlets. The lake is situated 3 miles NE of Sumner and a maze of roads follow and meet the shore line at many places. It holds spiny rays, kokanee and rainbow and offers fair fishing from May into August.

TULE LAKE. A 31 acre rainbow lake which lies 1.5 miles SE of **HARTS LAKE**. It also carries largemouth bass, black crappie, yellow perch and brown bullhead. Road from McKenna leads SE about 7 miles to lake's E. shore, passing Harts Lake. Tule also contains spiny rays and cutthroat.

VOIGHT CREEK. A small tributary of the Carbon River, joining that stream at Orting. Rated fair for rainbow and cutthroat. A road leaves Hwy. 162 at Crocker 2 miles E. of Orting and follows the creek upstream for about 11 miles to junction with McGuire Creek.

WAPATO LAKE. This 28 acre lake is located in Tacoma and is stocked with rainbow, and also holds pumpkinseed and brown bullhead. City park is situated on lake. Alaska Street runs along W. shore.

WAUGHOP LAKE. (Mud). A marshy lake of 21.7 acres that contains rainbow. It is situated 1.5 miles E. from Steilacoom and drains into Puget Sound.

WEST LAKE. (Hidden Lake). Rainbow have been stocked in West, a 6 acre lake 7 miles NE from National. It lies at 4600 feet and drains to South Puyallup River.

WHITE RIVER. (Stuck). The milky glacial color for which the river is named restricts fishing in the White. The river serves as the boundary between Pierce and King Counties for much of its length. It enters Puyallup River at Sumner, and is best known as a winter steelhead stream in its lower reaches. There are some whitefish, cutthroat, Dolly Varden and rainbow in upper portion of the White which is paralleled for many miles by Hwy. 410. A road leaves the highway about 3 miles SE of Greenwater to cross the White and to follow river's W. Fork for 11 miles to within 1 mile of Mt. Rainier National Park's N. boundary.

WHITMAN LAKE. A 29.6 acre rainbow planted lake 6.5 miles N. from Eatonville. Largemouth bass, pumpkinseed, yellow perch and brown bullhead are also present. It the largest of the Benbow group of lakes. It has a public access and drains to Tanwax Creek.

PIERCE COUNTY RESORTS

Alder Lake: Eagle's Nest Motel, La Grande, WA 98348. 360-569-2533.

American Lake: Bill's Boathouse, Tillicum, WA 98492. 360-588-2594.

Clear Lake: Big Foot Tavern, Eatonville, WA 98328. 360-832-6900.

Deep Lake: Deep Lake Resort, Olympia, WA. 98512. 360-352-7388.

Kapowsin Lake: Whitehawk, WA 98360. 360-893-2748.

Spanaway Lake: Spanaway Lake Park Boathouse, Spanaway, WA. 360-531-0555.

Silver Lake: Henley's Silver Lake Resort, Eatonville, WA 98328. 360-832-3580.

Tanwax Lake: Tanwax Lake Resort, Eatonville WA 98328. 360-879-5533. Rainbow Resort, Eatonville, WA. 360-879-5115.

San Juan

COUNTY

All of San Juan County is made up of islands. It is figured at 265 square miles, ranking 38th among Washington's 39 counties, but actual land area is only 172 miles, the smallest of any county in the state. The three largest islands are Orcas, San Juan and Lopez. There are over 400 islands within the county. Largest lake is Mountain on Orcas Island. There are no important streams. Salmon fishing is good, and some of the state's largest feeder chinook (blackmouth) are caught at N. end of San Juan and off Orcas Island during winter months. Highest point in the county is 2409 feet at Mt. Constitution on Orcas.

CASCADE LAKE. Located 3.5 miles SE of East Sound in Moran State Park on Orcas Island. This 171 acre lake holds cutthroat, rainbow and kokanee. Usually a fast rainbow and cutthroat starter at season's opener, with kokanee coming on later. Some lunker cutthroat caught here each year. April through July pegged as best fishing. Rental boats available at park on N. shore. Public boat launch site.

EGG LAKE. A tiny lake of 7 acres on San Juan Island. It delivers rainbow in fair fashion in April and May. Largemouth bass are present. It has public access area adjacent to road on W. shore. Located 900 feet W. of Sportsman's Lake on Egg road.

HUMMEL LAKE. A 36 acre, very rich lake in the N. portion of Lopez Island. Although it drops to a 5 or 6 foot depth in dry years, Hummel produces some extra nice rainbow. Stocked regularly. It also contains largemouth bass and bluegill. Take main road from ferry landing about 3 miles to lake shore. Public access on N. shore.

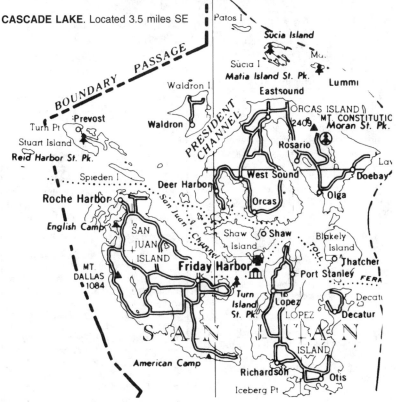

MOUNTAIN LAKE on Orcas Island is in Moran State Park.

KILLEBREW LAKE. Planted with cutthroat, Killebrew is 13 acres and has a public access. It also holds largemouth bass and bluegill. Route is N. from town of Orcas on Orcas Island on Dolphin Bay road for about 4 miles. Drainage is to Grindstone Harbor.

MOUNTAIN LAKE. This 198 acre lake comes on strong in June, July and September. It holds rainbow and kokanee. Located 4.4 miles SE of East Sound on Orcas Island in Moran State Park. Good campgrounds and rental boats on lake. Small boats may be launched from SW shore. Mountain Lake serves as water supply for communities of Doe Bay and Olga.

SPORTSMAN'S LAKE. A 66 acre lake situated 3.5 miles NW of Friday Harbor on San Juan Island. This spring-fed lake is a top largemouth bass lake. Best fishing usually comes in fall when water level retreats from brushy shoreline. Public access area on N. side.

TWIN LAKES. A pair of small lakes of 8 and 3 acres situated 3500 feet by trail N. of Mountain Lake on Orcas Island. Holds both rainbow and cutthroat. May be fished from shore.

SAN JUAN COUNTY RESORT

Cascade Lake: Moran State Park, Eastsound, WA. 360-376-2326.

Freeze Fish In Water For Best Results

For better tasting frozen fish, freeze them in water so as to retain moisture. Fish may be placed in a cake pan, covered with water and frozen. When ice is solid a sharp rap will release the pan for cake baking and the fish, or fillets of fish, are encased in an easy-to-stack block of ice.

Stonefly

Stoneflies vary in color, depending upon the species, but most often are green, yellow or brown. Fly fishermen seem to favor the "browns", and pattern both wet and dry flies after this color. Stoneflies are not great flyers, but are sometimes noted in awkward flight over fresh water. Stonefly nymphs grow to three inches in length or more, and feed on other aquatic insect nymphs and larvae. They are an important food source for fresh water fish.

Skagit

COUNTY

The Skagit River, one of the state's top producers of winter steelhead, dominates fishing in Skagit County, although over 280 lakes offer trout and spiny ray fishing. The county covers 1775 square miles and ranks 22nd in size in the state. Nearly three-fourths of Skagit County is mountainous with highest point the 9200 foot Mount Buckner on the Cascade Crest. The Skagit River drains most of the county, with Samish River draining the W. part.

ALDER CREEK. Tributary to the Skagit River crossed by Hwy. 20 about 1.5 miles E. of Hamilton. Limited cutthroat fishing.

ARROWHEAD LAKE. A 14.9 acre rainbow lake at 4500 feet located 9.5 miles SE from Marblemount. Drainage to Cascade River.

BACON CREEK. Enters the Skagit 5 miles NE of Marblemount. Bacon is a favored fly fishing stream for rainbow and some eastern brook in top stretches. A road leaves Hwy. 20 at Bacon Creek Siding to head N. upstream for 5 miles and into Whatcom County. Picnic area at creek's mouth.

BASIN LAKE. Rainbow lake of 2.5 acres located 8 miles SE from Marblemount at 4200 feet. It drains to Cascade River.

BEAR CREEK. A small creek that flows into **SHANNON LAKE** from the W. at the Bear Creek power house, about 6 miles N. of Concrete on the Baker Lake road. It produces small cutthroat and rainbow early in the season.

BEAR LAKE. A 2 acre lake which lies at 3900 feet at headwaters of Irene Creek. It has had plants of cutthroat. Route is E. from Marblemount across the Skagit and up the Cascade River road about 8 miles to Marble Creek campground, crossing the Cascade and taking an old trail to lake.

BEAVER LAKE. Rainbow plants aid this 73 acre lake which is fed by **CLEAR LAKE** It also hosts largemouth bass and brown bullhead. Beaver has a public access on its W. shore and is situated 1 mile SE of village of Clear Lake.

BIG LAKE. Plenty of variety is offered anglers in Big, a 545 acre lake located 5 miles SE of Mt. Vernon. Hwy. 9 skirts the lake's E. shore. A public access is located on W. side, and resort facilities are available. Fish species include rainbow, cutthroat, bass, perch, brown bullhead and crappie. Big lake produces some large bass and holds up well through the season.

BOULDER LAKE. Rainbow are present in Boulder's 55 acres. It lies 13.5 miles NE from Darrington on SW flank of Hurricane Peak at 5000 feet. Drainage to Suiattle River.

BULLAR LAKE. A 2 acre pond planted with rainbow. It lies at 3500 feet 4.5 miles

Skagit County

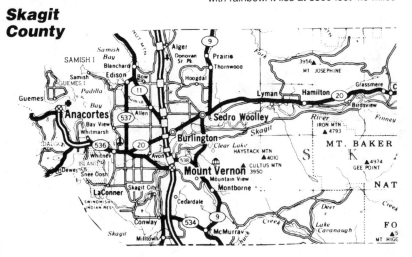

SE from Marblemount. Drainage to Cascade River.

CAMPBELL LAKE. Located on Fidalgo Island, 5 miles S. of Anacortes, with the Deception Pass Hwy. touching the lake's E. tip. Campbell holds bass, perch, brown bullhead, rainbow, and has a resort and a public access on N. side. It is fed by **ERIE LAKE**.

CANNERY LAKE. Yellow perch and brown bullhead are present in this 18 acre lake which is located 3 miles W. from Anacortes and adjacent to beach at Shannon Point. It drains to Guemes Channel.

CAREYS LAKE. Cutthroat and some rainbow are found in this 4 acre lake which lies 1 mile NE of Hamilton. It drains into Hamilton Slough.

CASCADE RIVER. Produces steelhead, rainbow, cutthroat and Dolly Varden. It also carries salmon. The Cascade joins Skagit at Marblemount, where a road heads E. and S. for about 20 miles to within 2 miles of Cascade Pass on Cascade Crest which is reached by trail. The trail drops into upper Stehekin River in Chelan County. There are FS campgrounds at Marble Creek and Mineral Park along this stretch. Summer steelhead have been planted in Cascade.

CASKEY LAKE. A private 5 acre eastern brook and rainbow lake which has brown bullhead. It is located 6 miles S. of Rockport on W. side of Sauk River into which it drains.

CAVANAUGH LAKE. This 844 acre lake is a slow starter, but delivers for fall fishing. It carries rainbow, cutthroat, kokanee and a few eastern brook. The lake has a public access on the SE shore, plus a resort. Route to the lake is E. from Arlington on Hwy. 9 for 0.4 miles past Pilchuck Creek, then right on creek for about 14 miles to lake. Road continues SE from E. end of lake 5 miles to Oso on Darrington Hwy.

CLEAR LAKE. A 223 acre lake which lies 3 miles S. of Sedro Woolley at community of Clear Lake. It holds rainbow, perch, yellow perch and brown bullhead, and has a resort. A public access is on the N. shore. Drainage is into **BEAVER LAKE**.

CLIFF LAKE. Rainbow are present in Cliff, a 5 acre lake at 4800 feet located about 12 miles from Marblemount. It drains to Suiattle River.

CRANBERRY LAKE. (Little). Largemouth bass are found in Cranberry's 26.8 acres. Location is in Anacortes city limits.

CUB LAKE. A rainbow planted lake of 11 acres situated about 25 miles E. from Darrington. Drains to **ITSWOOT LAKE**. Elevation is 5400 feet.

CYCLONE LAKE. Golden trout plus rainbow have been stocked in Cyclone's 55.5 acres. Elevation is 5300 feet and location is ll.5 miles SE from Marblemount at head of Found Creek. Drainage to Cascade River.

DAVIS SLOUGH. Both cutthroat and rain-

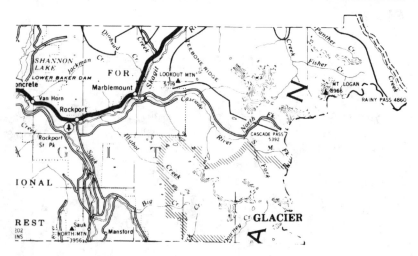

BEN CRUSAN with cutthroat from Anjar Lake.(Matt Aldred Photo)

bow are taken from this 7 acre slough. It lies adjacent to the S. side of Hwy. 20 about 1.8 miles E. of Hamilton. Closed much of the time because it is used for rearing steelhead smolts.

DAY CREEK. Feeds into the Skagit River across from Lyman. Summer steelhead are caught in late summer and fall months. Some sea-run cutthroat are taken. Road from S. side of the Skagit parallels Day Creek high on the ridge on W. side upstream to **DAY LAKE**, about 7 miles, with a rough section about halfway at Rocky Canyon.

DAY LAKE. Best route to this 136 acre lake is from Oso on Hwy. 530 along the Stillaguamish River 4 miles NW to Cavanaugh, then about 8 miles N. to Day. The lake carries rainbow and eastern brook, with beaver ponds at the head of the lake best for brookies.

DEVILS LAKE. An eastern brook lake of 31 acres which lies at 826 feet elevation about 6 miles SE from Mt. Vernon. The outlet, Devils Creek, contains eastern brook and a few cutthroat, but it is tough going along brushy creek. Land around the lake is privately owned. No access.

ENJAR LAKE. Cutthroat share this 12 acre lake with golden trout. Enjar is located 1.5 miles N. of Snowking Mtn. at 4300 feet and 3 miles E. of **SLIDE LAKE** which is 8 miles SE from Marblemount. A faint trail leads about 2 miles up Slide Creek to Enjar.

ERIE LAKE. Located on Fidalgo Island 2 miles S. of Anacortes. A good rainbow producer of 111 acres which offers both a resort and a public access which is on the SE end. Route to lake is 9 miles W. of Mt. Vernon on Hwy. 536, then S. on Hwy. 525, then W. past **CAMPBELL LAKE** about 1.5 miles, to lake shore.

EVERETT LAKE. An 8 acre lake which lies 1 mile E. of Concrete with drainage into **SHANNON LAKE** via Everett Creek. The lake holds rainbow, eastern brook and cutthroat. Cross Baker River, then turn N. about 1 mile to lake.

FALLS LAKE. The lower lake covers 60.4 acres at 4200 feet elevation and Upper Falls, at 4500 feet, is 22.4 acres. They both have been stocked with rainbow. Location is 4.7 miles SE and 5.4 miles S. of Marblemount. Drainage is to Cascade River.

FINNEY CREEK. A Skagit River tributary, Finney enters that river on S. side about 1 mile upstream from Birdsview. Rated fair for rainbow in July and August. It carries a few summer steelhead. Cross Skagit on Dalles Bridge at Concrete then drive upstream 8.5 miles, then SW up Finney Creek. Road continues upstream 7 miles.

FLY LAKE. A 2 acre rainbow planted lake which lies at 4000 feet 7.4 miles SE from Marblemount. It drains to Cascade River.

FLUME CREEK PONDS. Series of beaver ponds located 5 miles S. of Rockport on W. side of the Sauk River. The ponds, totaling 4 acres, produce eastern brook in April and May. Route is up Flume Creek 1.5 miles from road on W. side of the Sauk.

FRIDAY CREEK. Tributary of Samish River, joining that river just above old Hwy. 99 bridge. The creek contains sea-run cutthroat, rainbow and steelhead. Friday Creek drains **SAMISH LAKE**.

GEE POINT LAKE. A 4 acre lake planted with rainbow. It lies at 4100 feet 8.5 miles SE from Concrete. **LITTLE GEE**, 1.5 acres, lies 4750 feet SE. Lakes drain to Skagit River.

GRANDY LAKE. A cutthroat lake that does well for fly fishermen in spring and again in fall. The cutts are in the 9-10 inch range. The lake is 56 acres and is reached by traveling up Baker Lake Hwy. 4 miles from Hwy. 20. Small boats may be launched from N. shore.

GRANITE LAKES. Big Granite is one of the few grayling lakes in Washington state. (Catch and release). It is a deep, 144 acre lake which lies at 5000 feet at head of Boulder Creek, 7 miles SE of Marblemount. Granite Lakes No. 1, 2 and 3 are 4, 7 and 38 acres. They hold cutthroat and rainbow. Route is up Boulder Creek logging road to last crossing. Hike up E. side of main creek to Big Granite off upper road. It's a STEEP 0.5 mile scramble.

HAWKINS LAKE. Rainbow have been stocked in Hawkins, a lake of 7 acres at 3500 feet. It is situated 9.4 miles NE from Oso with drainage to Deer Creek.

HEART LAKE. (Hart). A rainbow lake of 61 acres located about 1 mile S. of Anacortes. A road from town runs along the lake's E. shore where there is a public access.

HILT LAKE. A marshy lake of 3 acres which holds eastern brook. Cross Skagit River at Rockport, drive S. for 1.5 miles then turn E. and S. for about 5 miles to power line road which is close to N. end of lake.

JACKMAN CREEK. Best fishing in this Skagit River tributary is in July and August for cutthroat. There is an excellent winter steelhead drift at creek's mouth. Upper stretch is reached by taking a road 2 miles E. of Concrete, past Everett Lake, and then NE up creek for about 4 miles. A few cutthroat are reported in upper river.

JORDAN CREEK. Enters Cascade River about 0.5 miles above that river's junction with Skagit at Marblemount. Jordan is best in mid-summer and fall months for cutthroat and rainbow. A logging road on the creek's E. bank leads upstream for 4 miles to within 0.5 miles of **FALLS LAKE.** The 60 acre lake lies at 4200 feet elevation and drains into Jordan Creek via a cascading outlet. Both the lower lake and the upper (22 acre) lake offer cutthroat.

JORDAN LAKES. The lower lake is 59 acres and lies at 4150 feet. Upper Jordan covers 65 acres and elevation is 4550 feet. It is 2300 feet E. of the lower lake. Both have been planted with cutthroat. Route is up trail from end of logging road up Jordan Creek. Hike is about 4 miles.

CLEAR LAKE holds rainbow as well as a variety of spiny ray species.

GRANITE LAKE grayling caught and released by Richard Cole. (Ben Crusan Photo)

JOSEPHINE LAKES. The upper lake covers 3 acres, and lower Josephine is a 2 acre pond. Upper lake contains eastern brook and lower lake has cutthroat. They are located 5 miles NE of Hamilton at an elevation of about 3000 feet a short distance E. of Mt. Josephine. Road from Hamilton leads NW to Jones Creek and then corkscrews NE about 6 miles to Mt. Josephine. Tough 0.4 mile hike E. from there.

LA RUSH LAKE. Boggy lake of 3 acres which has been rainbow planted. The lake lies 7.4 miles SE from Marblemount at 3200 feet. It drains into the Cascade River.

LIZARD LAKE. Eastern brook are found in this 2 acre lake which is located 2.8 miles N. from Blanchard. **LILY LAKE**, also 2 acres, lies 2200 feet S. from Lizard. The lakes drain via Oyster Creek to Samish Bay.

LOUISE LAKE. (White Lake). A rainbow lake of 6 acres at 5000 feet located 8.7 miles S. from Marblemount. It drains to Sauk River.

MARTIN LAKE. Rainbow inhabit this 10 acre lake located 5 miles S. from Marblemount at 4650 feet. Drainage is to Skagit River.

McMURRAY LAKE. This 160 acre lake has a public access area on its SE shore

and a resort. It is located adjacent to the E. side of Hwy. 9 about 9 miles NW of Arlington. It contains planted rainbow, yellow perch and black crappie.

MINKLER LAKE. A narrow, slough-like 37 acre lake which holds cutthroat and bass. The lake lies along Hwy. 20's S. side 3.5 miles E. of Sedro Woolley.

MUD LAKE. An 8 acre bass, crappie, yellow perch and brown bullhead lake situated in the community of Clear Lake.

NOOKACHAMPS CREEK. Flows N. from Big Lake about 6 miles to enter Skagit River near Burlington. The E. Fork of creek enters main creek from the E. near community of Clear Lake. Nookachamps provides early fishing for rainbow and cutthroat, with cutthroat action again in fall months. Roads follow creek most of its length. Road from Clear Lake leads past Beaver S. to cross the E. Fork.

NOOKSACK RIVER. (South Fork). July and August are best months for this stream's rainbow. Route is NW from Hwy. 20 at Hamilton about 6 miles up Jones Creek through Scott logging works, then E. to follow Nooksack 12 miles upstream nearly to Whatcom County line. Trails from this point head E. up Wanlick Creek 3 miles, and N. along S. Fork to its headwaters at **ELBOW LAKE**. Access sometimes restricted on the logging road. Another route to upper South Fork is via Rocky Creek road which leaves Baker River road just below Baker Dam in Whatcom County.

NEORI LAKE. Rainbow plants boost Neori, a lake of 13 acres which lies about 12 miles SE from Marblemount. It drains to Cascade River. Elevation is 4400 feet.

PASS LAKE. A fly fishing only lake of 99 acres which lies adjacent to Hwy. 525 at N. end of Deception Pass bridge to Whidbey Island. There are large rainbow and cutthroat in lake, with most in the 10-12 inch range. Other species include Atlantic salmon and brown trout. Boat launch facilities and campsites are located in Deception State Park at the lake's W. end.

PHEBE LAKE. Located near center of Cypress Island. Phebe is the largest, at 15 acres, of 3 adjoining lakes. It holds cutthroat, rainbow and kokanee. It is reached by trail 1 mile from Strawberry Bay on the island's W. flank, or by private logging road from E. shore.

PILCHUCK CREEK. The stream has been planted with winter steelhead. It heads N. of **CAVANAUGH LAKE** and is readily fished from a N. bank road which closely follows creek in Skagit County. Road leads NE up Pilchuck from Hwy. 9 N. of Arlington.

PRAIRIE LAKES. The lower lake covers 5 acres and upper Prairie is 3 acres. The lakes lie at 1500 and 1600 feet elevation 8.5 miles NE of Darrington on slopes of Prairie Mtn. They have been stocked with rainbow and also carry eastern brook. Logging road leads from Sauk Prairie road via Darrington to lakes. Drainage is to Suiattle River.

SAMISH RIVER. This small stream produces well for both winter steelhead and sea-run cutthroat. It is easily waded except in lower reaches where it enters Samish Bay at Edison. This lower portion is excellent for cutts in late summer and fall. Steelheading is best in December, January and February. Most popular steelheading area is from old Hwy. 99 downstream for about 3 miles. Plants of steelhead boost the Samish. Sea-run cutthroat are also found in upper reaches. There is a state fisheries' installation on Friday Creek just above that creek's junction with the Samish, with some closed waters at this point. The Samish is bridged below Hwy. 99 at Allen, at Thomas road,

at Farm to Market road and at its mouth at Edison. One mile N. of Hwy. 99 bridge a road turns E. and N. to follow river to its headwaters in Whatcom County.

SAUK RIVER. (Lower River). A large glacial tributary of Skagit River which joins that stream just below town of Rockport. The Sauk carries both winter and summer steelhead, plus Dolly Varden, sea-run cutthroat, spring and fall chinook and silver salmon. Winter steelheading is good from mid-December into March, with trophy steelhead taken each season. Limited summer steelhead action comes in late summer and fall months. Road up Sauk's E. side crosses Skagit at Rockport and follows upstream past Darrington and into Snohomish County. A road leads downstream from the old government bridge 5 miles from the mouth along W. side. The river is swift and dangerous to boat. The Suiattle River enters Sauk 11 miles upstream from Rockport.

SHANNON LAKE. Formed by a Puget Sound P&L Co. dam on the Baker River just N. of Concrete. The reservoir covers 2148 acres and is fed by Rocky, Sulpher, Bear, Thunder, Everett and Three Mile Creeks, plus the Baker. Shannon holds rainbow, Dolly Varden, cutthroat, silver and sockeye salmon. Reached by turning N. from Hwy. 20 about 0.4 miles after crossing Baker River at Concrete. The road follows E. shore for approximately 8 miles, then crosses the narrow neck between Shannon and Baker Lake in Whatcom County. A boat launch area is situated near mouth of Everett Creek on E. side of lake. Best fishing period in Shannon is May, June, September and October.

SAUK LAKE. Rainbow have been stocked in Sauk Lake's 10 acres. The lake is at 4025 feet 7 miles E. from Concrete. It drains to Skagit River.

SHELF LAKE. A 3.5 acre lake holding rainbow. Elevation is 4050 and location is 9 miles NE from Oso and 1100 feet SW from **HAWKINS LAKE**. Drainage to Deer Creek.

SIXTEEN LAKE. Planted cutthroat and rainbow are available in this 42 acre lake. The lake has a public access on the W. end. Drive 2 miles E. of Conway on Hwy. 534 where a F&W department sign marks the turnoff from Hwy. 534. The lake is situated about 0.4 miles N.

SKAGIT RIVER. One of the state's best producers of winter steelhead, the Skagit heads in Canada, is blocked by 3 Seattle power dams in Whatcom County, and enters Skagit County 2 miles downstream from Newhalem. The N. Fork flows into Skagit County 2 miles downstream from Newhalem. The N. Fork flows into Skagit Bay 2 miles S. of La Conner, and S. Fork empties into same bay at Milltown on Skagit-Snohomish County line. The Skagit receives planting help by way of both winter and summer steelhead plants. The river also holds large runs of fall salmon, including chinook and silvers, along with spring or summer chinook. In odd-numbered years the Skagit hosts big numbers of humpy salmon. Sea-run cutthroat and Dolly Varden are common throughout river and at its mouth. The N. Fork's mouth is favored spot for large chinook, silvers and humpies in summer months, and also provides good winter steelhead, Dolly Varden and cutthroat fishing for trollers. A resort near mouth offers rental boats and a boat launch ramp. Access is no problem along the Skagit, with roads roughly paralleling both sides. Easiest way to fish Skagit is by boat but care should be taken as the river is deep, swift and cold. Professional guides are based around Sedro Woolley.

SKARO LAKE. The 12 acre lake, which is surrounded by cliffs, receives rainbow plants. Elevation is 4450 feet and location is about 12 miles SE from Marblemount and 2500 feet SW from Found Lake. It drains to Cascade River.

SLIDE LAKE. A 37 acre lake at 3300 feet which hosts rainbow. Location is 8 miles SE from Marblemount with drainage to Skagit River.

SNOW KING LAKE. A rainbow lake of 26.3 acres at 4600 feet about 13 miles SE from Marblemount. It is fed by **CYCLONE LAKE** and drains to Cascade River.

SPRINGSTEEN LAKE. Cutthroat are the attraction in this 19.2 acre lake at 3550 feet. It lies 7.5 miles NW from Concrete and 0.8 miles SW from Washington Monument (Mtn.) Drains to S. Fork Nooksack River.

SUIATTLE RIVER. Bad silting conditions make this Sauk river tributary tough to fish. Much of the upper Suiattle is in Snohomish County. There are rainbow, Dolly Varden and cutthroat in river, and it is likely that the river carries at least a few steelhead and summer chinook salmon. Road down the Sauk's E. bank hits Suiattle about 6 miles N. of Darrington, and then swings E. and S. to follow stream about 20 miles and into Snohomish County. There are FS

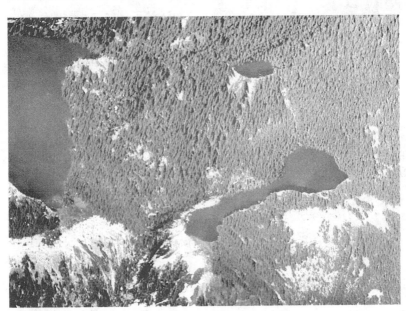

LOWER GRANITE Lake, center, with Upper Granite at right.

campgrounds at Buck, Downey and Sulfur Creeks, all in Snohomish County.

SUMNER LAKE. An 8 acre, marshy lake that contains rainbow and spiny rays. It is located 2.8 miles NE of **MCMURRAY LAKE** and drains into Big Lake.

TEN LAKE. Eastern brook, cutthroat, kokanee and rainbow are present in Ten. It covers 16 acres, with drainage via Carpenter Creek. Take Devil Mtn. Lookout road from Big Lake 3 miles SE of Mt. Vernon. The road passes close to the lake. A trail starts at gate and heads down hill 0.4 miles to the lake.

TEXAS PONDS. Take road N. from Darrington 6 miles on Sauk's W. bank, then NW 2 miles to the 6 acre ponds which lie

CHARLOTTE FRENCH caught this late season Skagit River steelhead.

at 1500 feet. They hold eastern brook, some of excellent size.

THUNDER CREEK. A tributary of **SHANNON LAKE**, flowing into lake from E. The creek furnishes fair rainbow and cutthroat angling in May and June. Route is up E. shore of Shannon Lake 4 miles N. from Concrete, then E. on rough road about 5 miles to mouth of Survey Creek.

TUPSO LAKE. Located at head of Grade Creek at 4500 feet, this 4 acre lake holds planted rainbow. It lies 9.5 miles N. of Marblemount with drainage to Suiattle River.

VOGLER LAKE. There is a public access area on this 3 acre eastern brook and rainbow pond. It is situated 3 miles N. of Concrete adjacent to W. side of Baker Lake road.

WHALE LAKE. A 50.1 acre lake which has received rainbow plants. Location is 9 miles SE from Marblemount at 4600 feet. Drainage is to Cascade River.

WHISTLE LAKE. a 29.7 acre lake 3.5 miles S. from Anacortes on Fidalgo Island. It gets cutthroat plants and contains largemouth bass and yellow perch. Drainage to Skagit Bay.

WING LAKE. A remote lake of 15 acres which lies near Cascade Crest 2.8 miles S. from Mt. Arriva at 6400 feet. It has been stocked with rainbow. Drainage is to headwaters of Granite Creek and Ross Lake.

SKAGIT COUNTY RESORTS

Big Lake: Big Lake Resort, Rt. 5, Mt. Vernon, WA 98273. 360-422-5755.

Campbell Lake: Lunz's Resort, Anacortes, WA 98221. 360-293-6316.

Erie Lake: Lake Erie Grocery & Trailer Park, Anacortes, WA 98221. 360-293 2772.

McMurray Lake: Lake McMurray Resort, Mt. Vernon, WA 98273. 360-445-4555.

Skagit River: Blake's Skagit Resort, 1171-A Rawlins Rd., Mt. Vernon, WA 98273. 360-445-6533.

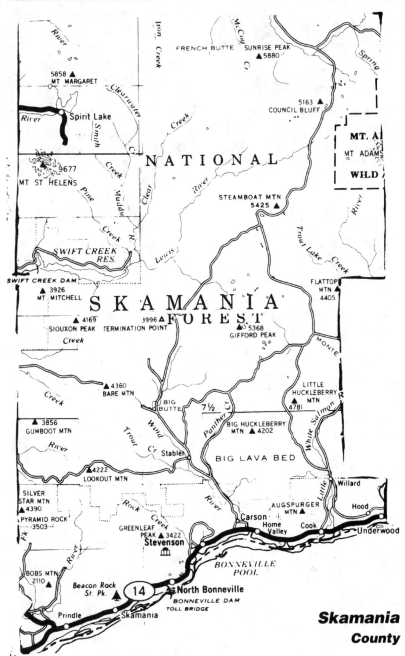

5858 ▲
MT MARGARET

Spirit Lake

▲ 9677
MT ST HELENS

FRENCH BUTTE   SUNRISE PEAK
▲ 5880

5163 ▲
COUNCIL BLUFF

MT. A
MT ADAMS
WHLD

N A T I O N A L

STEAMBOAT MTN
5425 ▲

SWIFT CREEK
RES.

SWIFT CREEK DAM
▲ 3926
MT MITCHELL

FLATTOP
MTN
4405

S K A M A N I A

▲ 4169   3996 ▲ F O R E S T
SIOUXON PEAK TERMINATION POINT   ▲ 5368
                                      GIFFORD PEAK

Creek

MONTE

▲ 4360
BARE MTN

▲ 3856
GUMBOOT MTN

BIG
BUTTE   7½

LITTLE
HUCKLEBERRY
MTN
4781 ▲

BIG HUCKLEBERRY
MTN ▲ 4202

▲4222
LOOKOUT MTN

Stabler

BIG LAVA BED

SILVER
STAR MTN
▲ 4390

PYRAMID ROCK
3503

GREENLEAF
PEAK ▲ 3422
Stevenson

AUGSPURGER
MTN ▲

Willard

Hood

Carson
Home
Valley   Cook

Underwood

BOBS MTN
2110 ▲

Beacon Rock
St. Pk. ▲

14   North Bonneville

BONNEVILLE
POOL

Prindle   Skamania

BONNEVILLE DAM
TOLL BRIDGE

Skamania
County

SKAMANIA

COUNTY

Majority of Skamania County's 1691 square miles are in the Cascade mountain range. Mt. St. Helen's summit, 8363 feet, is the highest point in the county. Three areas hold most of Skamania's lakes. One area between North Bonneville and Stevenson contains over 60 natural, rock-bound (for the most part) lakes. The Indian Heaven region, about 25 miles N. of the Columbia River, has over 175 lakes of varying sizes. The third area has over 40 lakes, most at elevations of 4000 to 5000 feet. This region is between the headwaters of Green River and Toutle River's N. Fork. In addition to over 300 lakes, Skamania county has such fine migratory fish streams as the Wind, Big and Little White Salmon and the upper reaches of Washougal River. The county is 24th in size in the state.

ASHES LAKE. This 51 acre lake offers large and smallmouth bass. It lies 1.8 miles SW of Stevenson. **LITTLE ASHES LAKE** is a rainbow planted pond covering 2 acres. It is located 2 miles SW of Stevenson adjacent to the N. side of Hwy. 14 and can be fished from the shore. It produces best in April and May.

BASS LAKE. Rainbow planted, but high water from the Columbia River has added spiny rays, including largemouth bass, to the lake's 10 acres. It is located NW from North Bonneville. Drains to Greenleaf Slough.

BEACON ROCK LAKE. (Riddell). A 1.5 acre lake that has been planted with eastern brook. Location is 4.5 miles SW from North Bonneville and 1500 feet S. from Beacon Rock. Drains to Columbia River.

BEAR CREEK. Flows from St. Helens Lake 1.5 miles S. into Spirit Lake.

BEAR LAKE. A rainbow lake of 8 acres situated 2.5 miles SW of Cultus campground at 4750 feet elevation. Route is W. from community of Trout Lake in Klickitat County on FS road 24 for 16 miles to Cultus Creek campground. It is a 3 mile hike to

the lake. **ELK**, **CLEAR**, **LEMEI** and **DEER** Lakes are within a 0.5 mile radius from Bear.

BIG CREEK. Reached by FS road 90 at E. end of Swift Reservoir about 7 miles where road crosses stream. FS road 72 encounters the creek upstream. Big Creek, which drains into Lewis River, holds 'bows.

BLACK CREEK. An eastern brook stream that produces best from July on in beaver ponds along upper creek. It is an upper Wind River tributary and is reached by driving up Wind River NW from Carson for 9 miles, then NE up FS road 60, 7 miles to Black Creek.

BLUE LAKES. Series of three small eastern brook and cutthroat lakes. Take Ash Lake road from Hwy. 14 about 1.5 miles W. of Stevenson to Blue Lakes road, then to gravel pit parking area where trail begins.

BLUE LAKE. Located in Indian Heaven area, the 12 acre lake contains eastern brook. Route is 4 miles up Wind River from Carson, then N. and E. on FS road 60 for about 10 miles to FS road 6048, then 3 miles to Red Mt., elevation 4968 feet. Trail leads approximately 5 miles along Cascade Crest trail to W. side of lake at 4640 feet.

BLUFF LAKE. A 5 acre lake located 3.5 miles N. of Beacon Rock and 5.7 miles W. of North Bonneville. Holds a few rainbow, cutthroat and bass and drains into Woodward Creek.

BRADER LAKE. Three acre lake which has been planted to eastern brook. Location is about 19 miles N. from Carson and 1200 feet SE from **EUNICE LAKE**. Wind River drainage.

CHAIN OF LAKES. A string of approximately 10 small lakes that hold eastern brook and brown trout. Largest lakes in the chain are 6 and 9 acres, and elevation is 4300 feet. Route is up FS road 123 from Randle to **TAKHLAKH LAKE** campground. A road leads 1 mile N. from this point to lakes and campground. Drainage is to Cispus River.

CLEAR LAKE. A 13 acre lake located at 4800 feet elevation 2 miles SW of Cultus Creek campground. (See Bear Lake). A 2.5

mile hike is required to reach the eastern brook, rainbow and cutthroat lake.

COMCOMLY LAKE. A 5 acre lake at 4500 feet 1.4 miles E. from Wapiki. It holds eastern brook and drains to White Salmon River.

COUNCIL LAKE. This lake is 48 acres and offers eastern brook, rainbow and cutthroat. It lies at 4200 feet. There is a campground at the lake's S. tip. Location is 24.5 miles SE from Randle. Council is reached by driving SE from Randle at the N. Fork campground at forks of the Cispus River on FS road 123, then S. up main Cispus 20 miles, still on FS road 123, to lake. Elevation is 4200 feet. Lake drains to Cispus River.

CULTUS CREEK. A small, brushy stream that heads under Bird Mt. and flows NE to join Trout Lake Creek. Drive SW from Trout Lake on Hwy. 141 for 7 miles to Peterson guard station, then N. on FS road 24 for 9 miles to Cultus Creek campground. The creek contains eastern brook.

CULTUS LAKE. Situated 500 feet SW from Deep Lake at 5000 feet. Cutthroat planted. Drainage to White Salmon River.

BEACON ROCK moorage on Columbia River at base of Beacon Rock. (Dept. C.& E. Dev. Photo)

DEADMAN'S LAKE. This 34 acre lake puts out eastern brook. It lies at 4330 feet elevation and has a maximum depth of 60 feet. Leave Hwy. 12 at Randle and drive S. on FS road 25 to FS road 26, then S. approximately 10 miles to Goat Mt. trail head. Hike in via Goat Mt. trail 213. **DEEP LAKE** lies 1 mile E. of Deadman's at 3963 feet. It holds eastern brook.

DEE LAKE. Eastern brook and cutthroat are present in Dee, a 2.5 acre lake at 4500 feet located about 20 miles N. from Carson. It drains to Wind River.

DEEP LAKE. A 6 acre rainbow and cutthroat lake located at 4950 feet elevation 1.7 miles SW of Cultus Creek campground. (See Bear Lake). Drainage to White Salmon River.

DEER LAKE. Eastern brook and cutthroat are present in this 5 acre lake. It lies at 4800 feet 2.5 miles SW from Cultus Creek campground. (See Bear lake). Drainage to N. Fork Lewis River.

DRANO LAKE. Bonneville Dam backwater created this 220 acre enlargement of the mouth of the Little White Salmon River. Location is 7 miles W. of town of White Salmon adjacent to N. side of Hwy. 14. Steelhead and salmon are taken at mouth in season.

ELK LAKE. Both rainbow and cutthroat have been planted in Elk's 13 acres. The lake lies at 4700 feet 2.5 miles SW from Cultus Creek guard station. It drains to N. Fork Lewis.

EUNICE LAKE. A 6.5 acre lake planted with eastern brook and cutthroat. Elevation is 4500 feet and location is 19.5 miles N. from Carson. It outlets to Wind River.

FOREST LAKE. (Doris). Located on Skamania-Cowlitz County line at 3900 feet. It contains brown trout and cutthroat. Location is 6.5 miles NW from **SPIRIT LAKE** outlet N. of Coldwater Ridge visitor's center. Access is off Weyerhaeuser road 3500.

FRANZ LAKE. Covering 99 acres, Franz lies 7 miles SW from North Bonneville along N. side of Columbia River. It contains largemouth bass and brown bullhead.

EAST CANYON CREEK. Both cutthroat and rainbow are taken from this creek which is paralleled by road for all of its 10 mile length. Reached by driving SE from Randle on FS road 123 to North Fork campground at forks of Cispus River, then up main Cispus for about 7 miles where FS road 123 continues to creek. Unimproved camp sites along creek.

FALLS CREEK. Take Wind River road NW from Carson. 4 miles to FS road 65, then N. on road 65 for 14 miles to where road crosses stream's upper reaches. Falls Creek contains eastern brook and rainbow.

FISH LAKE. (Little Fish). Elevation of this 4 acre eastern brook and cutthroat lake is 3800 feet. It lies 1.5 miles NE of Steamboat Mt. and about 18 miles NW by FS road 88 from **TROUT LAKE.** FS road 8845 leads W. 1 mile from 88 to lake.

FORLORN LAKES. Situated 1 mile N. of Goose Lake's E. end 19 miles N. from Stevenson, with a good road threading among lakes. Largest of lakes covers 14 acres. Elevation of group ranges from 3500 to 3700 feet. They have been planted with brown trout, rainbow and eastern brook and furnish best action in August and September.

FROG LAKE. (School House). Located 4 miles E. from Carson adjacent to road. The 4 acre lake has had eastern brook stocked, but contains a variety of spiny ray fish. It drains to Columbia River.

GHOST LAKE. A cutthroat and eastern brook lake of 5 acres located at 3767 feet elevation. Route is FS road 99 to Bear Mt. viewpoint. Take Boundary trail 1 on N. side of road for 0.5 miles to Ghost Lake spur 1-H. on trail #1 to trail #181, and then 1 more mile to lake. **STRAWBERRY LAKE**, which covers 10 acres and lies at 5374 feet, is 0.5 miles NE of Ghost. It contains eastern brook.

GILLETTE LAKE. Eastern brook have been stocked in this 3.5 acre pond which is located about 1.5 miles N. of North Bonneville adjacent to a power line road.

GOOSE LAKE. A brown trout producer covering 58 acres and lying at 3050 feet 13 miles N. from Carson. Small boats may be launched from FS campground on lake. Lava beds are adjacent to Goose. Route is N. on FS road 60 about 20 miles from Wind River road to lake shore. It drains to White Salmon River.

GRANT LAKE. An 11 acre lake located 5 miles E. from Carson and adjacent to N. side of Hwy. 830. It holds largemouth bass and brown bullhead.

GREENLEAF LAKE. (Slough). Located 1

MEDICARE BAR on Drano Lake at mouth of Little White Salmon River is easy time fishing for steelhead and salmon.

mile W. from North Bonneville along Hwy. 14. Greenleaf is 48 acres. It holds spiny rays. A road from NE end of lake follows N. shore.

HAMILTON CREEK. Tributary to Columbia, entering river 2 miles W. of North Bonneville at W. end of Greenleaf Slough. Hamilton receives winter steelhead and cutthroat plants. Best steelheading period is during December and January. A rough road follows the stream from mouth upstream about 5 miles.

HANAFORD LAKE. (Frances). One of the group called **FAWN LAKES** situated at 3900 to 4000 feet N. and W. of Elk Prairie at headwaters of Coldwater Creek. (Fawn Lake itself is located 1 mile W. of the Skamania-Cowlitz line). Other lakes are **FOREST** and **ELK**. Hanaford is 23 acres and has cutthroat, eastern brook and rainbow. Elk covers 30 acres, and Forest, 8. They also hold brookies and 'bows. They are located on Weyerhaeuser land N. of Coldwater Ridge visitor's center. Access is off the company's 3500 road. Check with company for information on access routes.

HEMLOCK LAKE. (Trout Creek Reservoir). An artificial lake of 14 acres in Trout Creek located 7.5 miles N. from Stevenson. Has had eastern brook plants.

HIDDEN LAKES. Two adjacent lakes at 4050 and 4100 feet 1 mile E. from Cultus Creek guard station. They are 5 and 10 acres and contain eastern brook. Drainage to White Salmon River.

HORSESHOE LAKE. A brookie lake of 24 acres at 4150 feet elevation. FS campground is situated on lake's E. shore. Route is up Cipus River out of Randle on FS road 123 past **TAKHLAKH LAKE**, then 7 miles NE on FS road 101. **GREEN MOUNTAIN LAKE** is located 2000 feet NW of Horseshoe. It is 4 acres and has been planted with eastern brook.

ICE HOUSE LAKE. (Bridge). A 3 acre brown trout and rainbow pond. It is located 2.5 miles SW of Stevenson and across highway from Bridge of Gods on Columbia River.

INDIAN HEAVEN LAKES. Perhaps 50 lakes and ponds along the Cascade Crest trail are included in this group which offer a beautiful region for a combination

hiking-fishing trip. Best route to the lake dotted plateau is to take FS road 24 from Mt. Adams RS at Trout Lake to Cultus Creek campground, then strike trail 33, Indian Heaven trail, and hike SW. Major lakes in the group include Blue, Bear, Elk, Clear, Deer, Cultus and Deep. (See individual listings).

KIDNEY LAKE. This 12 acre cutthroat and rainbow planted lake is situated 1 mile N. of North Bonneville on power line. Because of its depth, 59 feet at deepest point, the lake holds up well into summer. It seeps to Columbia River.

KWADDIS LAKE. Eastern brook and cutthroat have been stocked in this 3.5 acre lake. It is located at 4300 feet, 19 miles N. from Carson. Drainage to McClellan Meadows.

LARSON LAKES. (Nelson). A string of 3 lakes of 1 to 3 acres located 4 miles N. of Home Valley. They hold eastern brook and rainbow. Road from Home Valley leads NE about 6 miles to lakes.

LAVA LAKES. There are 7 small lakes in this group, with surface acres estimated at 4 acres. They are situated on the power line 1.7 miles NW of Stevenson and host eastern brook, rainbow and cutthroat. **FRENCH LAKE**, 2 acres, **BIG** and **LITTLE MAIN LAKES**, 3 and 2 acres, and **SARDINE LAKE**, 2 acres, are within a short distance of Lava Lakes. These small ponds carry rainbow. Sardine has cutthroat in addition to rainbow.

LEMEI LAKE. Small lake located on W. side of Lemei Rock at 5000 feet. Stocked with eastern brook, it drains to N. Fork Lewis River.

LEWIS RIVER. (North Fork). Upper stretches of the river provide fair to good rainbow and cutthroat fishing in late summer months. Some large trout are caught near mouth of river where it enters E. end of **SWIFT RESERVOIR**. FS road 90 leads from this point about 18 miles up the river's S. side past upper Lewis River falls. Lower Falls campground is at mile 14. Trailhead here for Lewis River trail 31 which follows length of river from Curly Creek to upper falls.

LILY LAKE. (Hamilton Creek Pond). Eastern brook have been planted in Lily which covers 8 acres. The lake lies 7 miles W. of

FORLORN LAKES deliver best in late summer and early fall.

Stevenson and drains into Hamilton Creek. Best route to lake is via Beacon Rock Hill road to Three Corner Rock road and then 3 miles N.

LITTLE WIND RIVER. Flows into Wind River from the E. just above mouth at Carson. The stream is wadeable and carries a few steelhead in lower reaches. Home Valley road leads to power line road which extends to mouth of Little Wind River.

LOST LAKE. An 8 acre lake which holds eastern brook. It is located 3 miles by trail W. of road end at Government Mineral Springs where Trapper Creek enters the Wind River. Elevation of the lake is 3760 feet. It is a tough hike.

MEADOW CREEK. Reached by road 25 miles up Wind River from Carson, passing Paradise Creek campground enroute. Meadow Creek meanders through Lone Butte Meadows for about 4 miles before emptying into Rush Creek near the road crossing. The creek provides rainbow and eastern brook fishing and access is relatively easy in meadow area. Road through Lone Butte Meadows button-hooks E. and S. again to pass **SURPRISE LAKES** and Cold Spring campground and crosses upper portion of creek. Meadow Creek campground is located at this point. Top fishing period is during July.

META LAKE. The 9 acre lake supports eastern brook and is located at 3580 feet elevation E. of Spirit Lake's inlet. An interpretive trail provides information about the eruption and how aquatic life survived. Access is 0.5 miles S. on road 99 from intersection of FS roads 26 and 99.

MOSELY LAKES. There are 5 small lakes in this group. Location is 2 miles W. of Stevenson, and drainage is into Rock Creek. The lakes cover about 3 acres and had plants of eastern brook and rainbow in past years. Early season fishing is best. Route to lakes is on Ash Lake road from Hwy. 14 to the Blue Lake road.

MOSQUITO LAKES. Fall fishing is productive period for eastern brook in both big and little Mosquito. The larger lake covers 24 acres; the smaller, 5 acres. From Peterson guard station W. of Trout Lake, drive 15 miles N. on FS road 24 where road touches E. tip of Big Mosquito. Elevation is 3900 feet and drainage is to Trout Lake.

MOUSE LAKE. A mostly shallow lake of 9 acres at 4500 feet 18.5 miles SE from Randle. It has received cutthroat plants. Drainage is to Cispus River.

MUDDY RIVER. Considered a good bet for fall rainbow and cutthroat fly fishing. The Muddy, which is glacial-fed and cloudy much of the year, enters upper end of **SWIFT RESERVOIR**, at which point FS road 25 follow river N. for about 4 miles, offering access after a hike of about 1 mile except at bridge. Clearwater FS campground is located along this stretch of river. Major tributaries of the Muddy offering good angling for cutts and rainbow from mid-summer on are **CLEAR CREEK, CLEARWATER CREEK**, and **SMITH CREEK**. FS road 93 crosses Clear Creek, the best fishing stream, about 1 mile from mouth and a rough road, 9303, parallels the creek for about 4 miles. Some whitefish are present in these streams. **PINE CREEK** joins the upper end of Swift about 0.5 miles below mouth of Muddy River, roughly paralleled by a road NW for 8 miles. It contains rainbow and cutthroat, but fishing is poor.

NORTHWESTERN LAKE. A 97 acre reservoir in White Salmon River located 2.7 miles N. of town of White Salmon. Lake is 2 miles long and contains eastern brook, rainbow and cutthroat. Half the lake lies in Klickitat County. Turn N. at Underwood from Hwy. 14 to follow White Salmon River to lake which has resort facilities.

OBSCURITY LAKE. A 10 acre eastern brook lake at 4337 feet in the Mt. Margaret back country area. Access from Norway Pass trailhead on Lakes Trail 211, a hike of about 6 miles. Permit camping only. Information from National Volcanic Monument headquarters.

OLALLIE LAKE. (Sheep). Drainage of this 15 acre lake is via Sheep Creek to the Cispus River. The lake contains eastern brook, brown trout and cutthroat and lies at 4250 feet elevation 27 miles SE of Randle on FS road 123. Campground on lake. Late season fishing is best.

PANHANDLE LAKE. A 15 acre lake which lies at 4520 feet 10 miles by trail over Norway Pass on Lakes trail 211, approximately 7 miles. Permit camping only. Eastern brook and rainbow in lake.

PANTHER CREEK. May is prime fishing time for this creek's rainbow. The stream also holds cutthroat and steelhead. It is a major tributary of Wind River, entering that stream 4 miles from Columbia River. FS road 65 heads N. and E. from Wind River road 4 miles upstream from Carson and follows Panther for approximately miles.

Mouth of Panther where it enters Wind is a favored steelheading spot.

PLACID LAKE. Cutthroat inhabit this 19 acre lake which lies at 4000 feet elevation 1 mile SE from Lone Butte which is 4791 feet in elevation. Route is N. from Carson up Panther Creek on FS road 65, then 1 mile E. on FS road 420 where the trail begins.

ROCK LAKE. A 2 acre eastern brook pond in Indian Heaven region about 23 miles N. of Stevenson. Drainage to Wind River.

RYAN LAKE. No fish survived Mt. St. Helen's eruption.

SOUTH PRAIRIE LAKE. A marshy 14 acre lake located 9.5 miles N. of Willard on NE side of Big Lava Bed. Stocked with eastern brook. Drainage to White Salmon River.

ST. HELEN'S LAKE. A casualty of the Mt. St. Helen's eruption, the lake basin is closed to all public access and is reserved for research purposes.

SHOVEL LAKE (African). A 21 acre lake at 4653 feet elevation which hosts eastern brook. It is reached from Norway Pass trailhead on Lakes Trail 211, approximately 8 miles. Permit camping only.

SNOW LAKE. (Burgoyne). Located 1 mile W. of Shovel Lake at 4700 feet. No fish.

SPIRIT LAKE. Once one of the state's most beautiful lakes, Spirit was devastated by the eruption of Mt. St. Helens on May 18, 1981. Information on the Mt. St. Helens National Volcanic Monument, of which Spirit Lake is a part, is available at a visitor's center which may be reached via exit 68 off 1-510 miles S. of Chehalis, then E. on Hwy. 12 to old 99 Hwy. Turn S. at this point for 1.5 miles to Lewis and Clark State Park. At S. boundary of park a forest service sign indicates entrance to the visitor's center. Display in the center interpret events related to the eruption. A documentary film, "The Eruption of Mt. St. Helens" is shown at regular intervals. The center is open 7 days a week except for holidays. Information is also available at Coldwater Ridge Visitor's Center located just 7 miles from Mt. St. Helen's crater.

STEAMBOAT LAKE. Brown trout and eastern brook are the attraction in this 9 acre lake located 13 miles NW from Trout Lake. Elevation of Steamboat is 4050 feet. A rough road leads 2.5 miles E. from Mosquito Lake guard station to N. end of lake. Mosquito is 17 miles NW of Peterson guard station on FS road 24.

STRAWBERRY LAKE. An eastern brook lake of 10 acres at 5374 feet. See **GHOST LAKE** for access.

SURPRISE LAKES. There are about 15 small lakes and ponds in the Surprise group of lakes located 2.5 miles S. of Mosquito Lake guard station. Some of the shallow lakes contain eastern brook. There is a campground adjacent to lakes.

SWIFT RESERVOIR. An excellent producer of rainbow. particularly in late summer and fall months, Swift is a deep, 4589 acre reservoir formed by a dam on the Lewis River's N. Fork. It is 10 miles long with boat launches at each end accessed by FS road 90. Besides 'bows Swift contains brown trout, cutthroat, kokanee and Dolly Varden. Hwy. 503 leads about 25 miles NE from Woodland past **MERWIN** and **YALE RESERVOIRS** on the N. Fork, then county road 16 through Cougar, and then FS road 90 for 18 miles to end of reservoir.

TAKHLAKH LAKE. Cutts and eastern brook are present in Takhlakh. It covers 35 acres and lies at 4350 feet elevation in scenic territory 24.5 miles SE from Randle. Route is up Cispus River SE of Randle on FS road 123, then N. for 1.5 miles on FS road 101 to lake which has a campground.

THOMAS LAKE. Thomas is a shallow, 10.5 acre lake situated at the head of Outlaw Creek 19 miles N. of Carson. It has been planted with eastern brook and rainbow. FS road 65 up Panther Creek, which heads N. from Wind River road 4 miles N. of Carson, extends to within 0.5 miles of the lake's W. shore. Thomas Lake trail 111 continues from there. Drainage to Wind River.

TRADEDOLLAR LAKE. Twelve acres in size, Tradedollar is a cutthroat lake which lies at 3552 elevation. Access by Weyerhaeuser road 3500 to Elk Prairie past **FAWN, HANFORD**, and **ELK LAKES** to within a short distance from Tradedollar.

TROUT CREEK. An easy to-reach tributary of Wind River, Trout Creek can be accessed from Carson about 7 miles NW on Wind River road, then 1 mile W. on Hemlock road to FS road 43 which parallels Trout Creek about 5 miles. **HEMLOCK LAKE**, a shallow 16 acre lake at junction of Hemlock road and FS road 43 is stocked

SWIFT RESERVOIR extends ten miles behind a dam on Lewis River. (Western Ways, Inc. Photo)

with rainbow and eastern brook. Main-stem Trout Creek produces steelhead, and beaver ponds on upper creek hold eastern brook. Wild steelhead release only above Hemlock Reservoir.

TROUT LAKE CREEK. Heading under Steamboat Mt., Trout Lake Creek flows SE about 18 miles through community of Trout Lake in Klickitat County to join the White Salmon River near that town. FS roads 88 and 8810 NW of Trout Lake follow creek for much of its length. It holds 'bows, brookies and cutthroat, with best fishing period in July and August. Trout Lake Creek campground is located on Skamania-Klickitat County line on FS road 88.

TUNNEL LAKE. (Stump, Mud). A rainbow stocked lake of 13 acres which lies adjacent to Hwy. 14 on the Columbia River about 2 miles E. of Cook. Tunnel may be fished from shore. It produces best in spring months.

VENUS LAKES. Rainbow and cutthroat lakes of 8 and 12 acres on E. side of Mt. Venus in Mt. Margaret area at 4600 and 4920 feet. Drainage to Green River. No trail, no camping allowed.

WAPIKI LAKE. Rainbow and cutthroat are the fishing attractions at Wapiki and several adjoining small ponds. The lake lies at 4700 feet and is 10 acres. It is on E. edge of the Indian Heaven group of lakes, and is reached by taking FS trail 34 from road 24 about 0.5 miles NW of road 6020. It's a 4 mile hike to lake.

WHITE SALMON RIVER. (Upper). Heading on the W. slope of Mt. Adams, the White Salmon flows W. and S. into Klickitat County 3 miles N. of Trout Lake, continuing to Columbia River at Underwood. Planted with both summer and winter steelhead. FS road 23 from Trout Lake leads NW about 13 miles along upper river upstream to Swampy Meadows, offering easy access at many points. Fish species include rainbow and eastern brook. The Skamania portion of White Salmon offers best fishing during May, June and July.

WHITE SALMON RIVER. (Little). One of the best rainbow and eastern brook streams in the county for anglers willing to work for their fish. The Little White Salmon is a rocky, fast river which shows white water throughout most of its length. It

heads under Monte Cristo lookout station just E. of the Skamania-Klickitat County line and flows approximately 15 miles S. to its junction with Columbia River at Cook. A road parallels the Little White Salmon from its mouth to Monte Cristo. Fishermen can find seclusion and good fishing by exploring the river's steep canyon areas. Mid-June on into fall is best fishing. Watch for rattlesnakes and poison oak in lower stretches.

WILMA LAKE (Strawberry). Located 0.5 miles NE of Ghost Lake, Wilma covers 10 acres and lies at 5374 feet elevation. It holds eastern brook. (See Ghost Lake for route).

WIND RIVER. Spring or summer steelhead start grabbing during April in lower reaches of Wind, and furnish action into late November. In summer steelhead stack in canyon areas of the swift moving stream, and fly fishermen, particularly, work them over. The falls area may be reached by driving 1 mile E. of Carson, then turning left on Shipherd Fall's spur. A road follows Wind from its union with Columbia River near Carson upstream about 2 miles, with 2 FS campgrounds along this stretch. Upper reaches of the Wind have restricted fishing. The river receives steelhead plants.

WOODWARD CREEK. Woodward is a tributary of the Columbia, with its mouth located 0.4 miles W. of Beacon Rock on Hwy. 14. A road leads along W. bank upstream for approximately 2 miles. The stream holds steelhead.

WOODS LAKE. Located on the N. side of Bird Mt., Woods is an eastern brook and cutthroat lake of 13 acres. Elevation of lake is 5000 feet, with route via FS trail 108, 2 miles W. of Cultus Creek campground, 8 miles NW of Peterson guard station. Drainage to N. Fork Lewis.

ZIG ZAG LAKE. Zig Zag is a 2 acre pond situated at head of Canyon Creek at 3400 feet elevation. The lake holds eastern brook.

SKAMANIA COUNTY RESORTS

Northwestern Lake: Northwestern Lake Resort, White Salmon, WA 98672. 360-493-2802.

Columbia River: Skamania Lodge, Stevenson, WA. 1-800-221-7117.

SNOHOMISH

COUNTY

There are over 460 lakes listed for Snohomish County, the largest being Stevens. Of this number, 207 lie at or above 2500 feet elevation. About half of the county's 2112 square miles are mountainous, and highest point is Glacier Peak at 10,541 feet. Snohomish ranks 13th in relative size among the state's counties. Besides numerous lakes, major migratory fish streams including both forks of the Stillaguamish, Sauk, Skykomish and Snohomish Rivers provide winter, and summer steelheading plus salmon and sea-run cutthroat.

ARMSTRONG LAKE. Planted rainbow and cutthroat are the attraction in Armstrong, a 31 acre lake. Drainage is into Stillaguamish River via Armstrong and Harvey Creeks. Husky 'bows are often taken at spring opener in Armstrong. Coho are taken from mid-May. Bass are also present. The lake is reached by driving N. from Arlington on Hwy. 9, just 1 mile from Stillaguamish River bridge, then E. across R.R. tracks and up hill 0.5 mile, then N. again 0.5 miles to S. end of lake. There is a public access on S. shore.

ASHLAND LAKES. Lower Ashland covers 12.9 acres and the upper lake 7 acres. The eastern brook lakes are at 2700 and 2870 feet. Location is 5 miles SE from Verlot RS at head of Wilson Creek. Drainage to Pilchuck River.

BALLINGER LAKE. Ballinger contains bass, perch, black crappie, brown bullhead and rainbow, and receives plants of legal rainbow. Summer and fall are productive months for spiny rays. The lake is 103 acres and drains into McAleer Creek, then into Lake Washington. Hwy. 104 (205th St.) on the Snohomish-King County line runs adjacent to Ballinger's S. tip. Public access is from a park on the NE shore.

BANDANA LAKE. Rainbow stocked lake of 3 acres located 6.8 miles N. from Verlot on N. side of Meadow Mtn. Outlet is head of Meadow Creek.

BARCLAY LAKE. There are rainbow plus cutthroat in 11 acre Barclay, a brushy and swampy lake which lies at 2300 feet elevation. It drains into S. Fork of the Skykomish River, and is reached by leaving Stevens Pass Hwy. at Baring on FS road 6024 which follows Barclay Creek up stream. The road extends to within 1.5 miles of Barclay Lake. There are several campsites along shore.

BATH LAKE. Golden trout have been

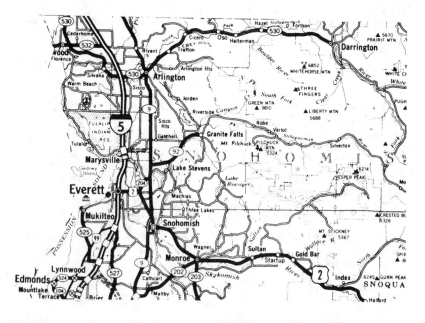

stocked in Bath, a 14.7 acre lake at 5950 feet elevation. It is the largest in a group of four lakes located 24.5 miles E. from Darrington and 2.5 miles NE from Sulpher Mtn. Drainage is to Suiattle River.

BEAR LAKE. Cutthroat have been stocked in this 19.8 acre lake situated at 2775 feet 2.8 miles SE from Verlot RS on E. side of Pilchuck Mtn. Drainage to S. Fork Stillaguamish River.

BEAVER PLANT LAKE. A 3.2 acre lake planted with rainbow and cutthroat. Location is about 6 miles SE from Verlot RS.

BECKLER RIVER. Upper stretches of the Beckler, which flows into Skykomish River's S. Fork at town of Skykomish on Stevens Pass Hwy. are in Snohomish County. Road from Skykomish leads N. for 14 miles along Beckler's entire length, linking with the Skykomish River's N. Fork road at Garland Mineral Springs. The Beckler contains rainbow and cutthroat and a few whitefish. Best fishing comes during June, July and August.

BEECHER LAKE. Beecher is a crescent shaped lake of 17 acres located 0.5 miles E. of Cathcart on the Connelley road in an old river channel. The lake hosts bass, cutthroat, pumpkinseed, crappie and catfish. It drains into Snohomish River 4 miles S. of town of Snohomish.

BEVIS LAKE. (Beaver). Bevis is a bass and eastern brook lake of 6 acres. It is reached by driving N. from Monroe up Wood Creek on Wood Creek road for 7.5 miles, then E. for 1.5 miles to Bevis. Lake is on Boy Scout property.

BITTER LAKES. (Tom, Dick and Harry). Trio of small lakes stocked with eastern brook. Location is 4 miles NE of Index on NW end of Jumpoff Ridge. They drain to N. Fork Skykomish watershed.

BLACKMANS LAKE. Located 1 mile N. of Snohomish on the Hill road, Blackmans covers 60 acres. Access from 13th street. Put and take for legal trout, but heavily infested with stunted sunfish, perch and carp. Handicapped fishing docks.

BLANCA LAKE. Rainbow and cutthroat in the 12 inch class are available in Blanca after mid-July. The lake is situated at 3975 feet and covers 179 acres. A marked trail leaves the N. Fork Skykomish River road 2.5 miles NE of Garland Hot Springs, and leads 3.5 steep miles to lake. Glacier fed and often off color.

BLUE LAKES. A pair of lakes nestled under the Cascade Crest at 5600 and 5700 feet, the Blue duo are 22 and 3 acres in size. They hold cutthroat. Route to lakes is 2.5 miles E. by trail from end of N. Fork Sauk River road, where Sloan Creek FS campground is located, then S. and E. another 9.5 miles. The trail continues 2 miles past lakes to meet Cascade Crest trail.

BOARDMAN LAKE. This 49 acre lake sheds ice early. It lies at 2981 feet 6 crow miles from Verlot RS. It holds rainbow and eastern brook. Route is E. of Verlot RS on Mt. Loop Hwy. 4.6 miles, then S. on road 4020, 4 miles to **EVAN LAKE** trailhead at 2750 feet. **EVAN** has brookies, cutthroat and rainbow, and covers 12 acres. It is planted annually with rainbow fry by Snohomish Sportsmen's club. Trail continues S. about 1 mile to Boardman.

BOSWORTH LAKE. Most action in Bosworth is from spring planted rainbow, although some cutthroat are also present in the 95 acre lake. It contains bass and some large trout. There is a public access on NE shore. The Robe-Menzel road from Granite Falls' city limits leads S. for 2.5 miles, then SW 0.5 miles on Utley road to lake.

Snohomish County

BOARDMAN LAKE sheds ice early.

BOULDER CREEK. Upper reaches of Boulder Creek provide fair to good rainbow fishing from July into fall. There are a few cutthroat and Dolly Varden in the creek which flows into N. Fork Stillaguamish 1 mile N. of Hazel on Hwy. 530. A road 2 miles N. of Hazel heads S. up French Creek, passing French Creek FS campground, then swinging W. to Boulder Falls, a total distance of about 4 miles. Trail up Boulder continues 3 miles to Boulder Ford camp.

BRYANT LAKE. Bryant is a 20 acre spiny ray lake holding bass, crappie and planted cutthroat. It lies adjacent to E. side of Hwy. 9, approximately 3 miles NW of Arlington.

BUCK CREEK. After snow run-off in mid summer, Buck Creek delivers fair rainbow angling. It is a tributary of the Suiattle River, entering that stream approximately 13 miles from its junction with Sauk River. There is a FS campground at mouth of Buck. FS road 26 extends 1 mile upstream, with way trail continuing another mile.

CANYON CREEK. Best noted as a summer steelhead stream, Canyon also carries winter steelhead. The large, white water stream joins S. Fork Stillaguamish 1 mile N. of Granite Falls. Top summer steelheading comes from July into fall. Access is difficult due to summer homes,

real estate developments and timber company holdings along lower river. Road from Granite Falls leads N. to cross Stillaguamish, then follows Canyon Creek 2 miles E. The Canyon Creek road leads N. from Mountain Loop Hwy. about 6 miles NE of Granite Falls. Clear cutting in headwaters has damaged this watershed and diminished summer steelhead fishing.

CANYON LAKE. Canyon has been planted with cutthroat and brook trout fry by the Snohomish Sportsmens' Club. It lies at 2700 feet elevation and covers 5 acres. It is reached by driving E. from Granite Falls on the Mountain Loop Hwy. 7 miles to FS road 41, then 2 miles to FS road 4110, then to FS road 4111 for 6 more miles to lake. Road is out last 3 miles. Drainage is into Wiley Creek.

CASSIDY LAKE. Variety of fish including coho, perch, crappie, pumpkinseed, brown bullhead, rainbow, and bass are present in Cassidy, a 125 acre lake with marshy shore lines. It receives rainbow and cutthroat plants and drains via Catherine Creek to Pilchuck River. July through October are best fishing months. The lake is reached by taking Cassidy road E. of Marysville for 3 miles to W. side of lake. Public access site on W. shore.

CAVANAUGH LAKE. (Little). There are

rainbow in Little Cavanaugh. It varies in size from 4 to 8 acres, and lies at 1500 feet elevation 5 miles S. of Goldbar. Nearby beaver ponds hold eastern brook. Drive E. on Hwy. 2 beyond Goldbar 6.3 miles to **NO NAME CREEK**, then right for 5.2 miles on gravel road to small road on right. Follow this road about 0.7 miles, then turn left to lake.

CEDAR PONDS. Eastern brook are present in Cedar, a brushy 9 acre private pond. Location is near **TOMTIT** and **DAGGER LAKES**.

CHAIN LAKE. There is a public access on Chain Lake's SW shore. The lake is 23 acres and contains planted rainbow, pumpkinseed and crappie. Drainage is to Snohomish River via French Creek. Head N. from Monroe on Lewis street, continuing N. for 3 miles on Chain Lake road to S. shore of lake.

CHAPLAIN LAKE. (Reservoir). A natural lake raised by dam and fed by Sultan River diversion. Eastern brook and cutthroat planted. It covers 443.7 acres and is located 5.8 miles N. from Sultan. City of Everett water supply.

CICERO POND. Cicero is a rainbow planted pond of 4 acres which lies adjacent to Mountain Loop Hwy. 0.5 miles E. of community of Cicero. It also contains catfish. The pond is reached by walking R.R. tracks 0.4 miles E. from Cicero.

CLEAR CREEK. There are rainbow, cutthroat, Dolly Varden and a few eastern brook in Clear Creek, a tributary of Sauk River. It joins the Sauk from the S. about 2 miles S. of Darrington. Clear Creek FS campground is situated at mouth, and a road leads upstream for 5.5 miles. Trail heads 0.5 miles downhill to Copper Creek shelter. **COPPER CREEK** produces during July and August. Trail up Clear Creek to Deer Creek Pass is not maintained, as a road now leads to the pass. Best fishing in Clear Creek is in July and August.

COAL LAKE. A road heads N. for 4 miles from the Mountain Loop Hwy. just beyond Big Four picnic area, 3.5 miles E. of Silverton, to Coal Lake. Coal Lake has brookies and cutthroat and lies at 3420 feet elevation. It covers 6 acres. The trail continues N. for 0.5 miles to **PASS LAKE** at 3700 feet. This lake is 2.5 acres and has

had cutthroat and rainbow plants. Cutthroat to 9 pounds have been taken here. There are campsites at Pass. The trail forks left 1.5 miles to **INDEPENDENCE LAKE** at 3700 feet. This lake has cutthroat and cutthroat.

COCHRAN LAKE. Cochran is a 33.6 acre rainbow planted lake located 5.5 miles NE of Monroe. Public access area on N. shore. Route is NE from Monroe up Woods Creek road 6 miles to within a short distance of lake's SE tip. It drains to Woods Creek.

CONEY LAKE. A 5 acre rainbow lake at 5000 feet 1.4 miles NE from Curry Gap. Drainage is to N. Fork Sauk River.

CONNER LAKE. Largemouth bass and pumpkinseed inhabit Conner, a 8.9 acre lake 1 mile E. from Hartford. It drains to Pilchuck River.

COWBELL LAKE. Rainbow planted lake of 3.4 acres at 3420 feet. Location is 1000 feet NW from upper **BOARDMAN LAKE**.

CRABAPPLE LAKE. A rainbow planted deep lake of 36 acres, Crabapple often holds carry-over 'bows at spring opener. Pumpkinseed present. It has a public access on N. side. Route to lake is N. on Hwy. 1-5 from Marysville for 6 miles, then W. 5.5 miles to Wenberg State Park entrance on E. side of **LAKE GOODWIN** where a road leads E. for 0.5 miles to Crabapple from Lake Goodwin road. Watch for signs.

CRESCENT LAKE. Crappie, catfish, perch and a few cutthroat are present in Crescent, a 9 acre brushy slough which lies S. of Monroe. The lake drains into Snoqualmie River, just above river's confluence with Skykomish. Route is S. from Monroe on Hwy. 203 for 3.5 miles to E. shore.

CUTTHROAT LAKES. Group of 7 small lakes planted with cutthroat. Elevation is 4300 feet. Location is on NE side of Bald Mt. summit. They drain to S. Fork Stillaguamish.

DAN CREEK. Rated fair for rainbow and planted cutthroat. Dan Creek enters Sauk River 2 miles NE of Darrington. Road NW from town crosses Sauk and continues 1.5 miles to point where a spur road leads SE up stream for about 4 miles. The creek is best during July and August.

DEVILS LAKE. (Lost). There is a public access area on SW shore of Devils, a 13 acre cutthroat and rainbow lake located E. of Maltby. Drainage is into Snoqualmie River via Ricci Creek. The lake yields best fishing early in season. It is reached by heading E. from Maltby 1.5 miles on Hwy. 202 to Echo Lake road, then S. on Echo Lake road for 1.5 miles to Lost Lake road, then E. for 0.7 miles to lake.

DIAMOND LAKE. Rainbow have been stocked in Diamonds's 9.6 acres. It is located at 5250 feet about 0.8 miles SE from Meadow Mt. Drainage is to Suiattle River.

DOLLAR LAKES. Rainbow planted lakes of 6 and 2 acres at 3950 and 3900 feet. Location is 2.8 miles N. from Index and 1 miles SE from E. end of Lake Isabel. Wallace River drainage.

DOWNEY LAKE. Cutthroat are present in Downey's 13 acres at 5500 feet elevation. Location is 20 miles E. from Darrington. Drainage is to Downey Creek and Suiattle River.

DUFFY CREEK. Summer cutthroat fishing is rated "fair" in Duffy, a tributary of Skykomish River. It is reached by driving across Skykomish River at Sultan to S. side of river, then 7 miles E. on Mann road to creek.

DUFFY LAKES. Rainbow lakes of 2.5 and 3.5 acres at 3000 and 3180 feet 4 miles S. from Gold Bar in headwaters of Duffy Creek. They drain to Skykomish River.

CANYON CREEK gets a workout by Jim Smith.

EBEY LAKE. (Little). Planted with cutthroat, Ebey covers 10 acres and is located on Ebey Hill. Outlet is Hell Creek which drains into Stillaguamish River's N. Fork. Boats may be launched on N. side of lake which is reached by driving 4 miles N. on Hwy. 503 to Trafton, then turning SE about 5 miles, then W. for 1.5 miles up hill to lake shore.

ECHO LAKE. (Eatons). Echo is a 17 acre lake which contains rainbow. There is a public access on lake's E. shore. Echo is located 1 mile S. of **DEVILS LAKE** and 3 miles SE of Maltby. It is 50 feet deep and often hosts carry-over 'bows. Drive 1 mile NE from Maltby on Hwy. 202, then 1 mile E., then 2 miles S. on Echo Lake road which encircles lake.

ECHO LAKE. Located 9 miles N. of Sultan at 1670 feet, this Echo is 25 acres and contains rainbow and cutthroat. Outlet has a 120 foot falls and empties into Pilchuck River. Best reached by the Echo Lake truck trail, which may be gated, from old Monroe log camp.

EMERALD LAKE. (Meadow). An 11 acre lake rainbow lake at 5150 feet. Location is 17 miles E. from Darrington on E. side of Meadow Mtn. Falls tumble 70 feet at outlet. Drainage to Lime Creek to Suiattle River.

EVAN LAKE. a 12.8 acre lake containing rainbow. Elevation is 2750 feet and location is 6 miles SE from Verlot RS and 1200 feet N. from Boardman Lake. Drainage to Boardman Creek and S. Fork Stillaguamish River.

FLOWING LAKE. Flowing is a 135 acre lake which is planted with rainbow and contains bass. It is fed by Storm Lake which lies 800 feet W. There is a public access on E. shore, and a resort. Flowing is reached by driving E. from Snohomish on 68th St. SE then on Three Lakes road for 4.5 miles to Flowing Lake road, then E. and N. 1 mile to lake on road between Flowing and Storm Lakes.

FONTAL LAKE. There are planted eastern brook in Fontal's 60 acres in addition to rainbow. The lake has a public access area on SE side. Route is Hwy. 203 for 3 miles S. of Monroe, then E. and S. on High Rock road for approximately 2 miles to fork. High Rock road continues NE from this

DEVIL'S LAKE is also known as Lost Lake.

point 7.5 miles to SW side of **HANNAN LAKE** and another 0.5 miles to E. tip of Fontal.

FORTSON MILL POND. A rainbow planted pond of 2 acres located 9.5 miles E. from Oso at Fortson. Drainage to N. Fork Stillaguamish.

FRENCH CREEK. French provides fair rainbow angling during summer months. The creek enters Stillaguamish River's N. Fork 2 miles E. of Hazel on Hwy. 530. A road leads upstream 1 mile to French Creek FS campground and continues upstream approximately 5 miles.

GISSBERG PONDS. (Smokey Point Ponds). Two 5 acre ponds created by mineral extraction located in Gissberg County Park just W. of I-5 and S. of Smokey Point Inn. Stocked with legal rainbow and channel catfish, these ponds also produce well for spiny rays including pumpkinseed and perch. The ponds drain into Quilceda Creek and lower Snohomish River.

GOAT LAKE. A 64 acre lake situated 4 miles E. from Barlow Pass. It contains both eastern brook and rainbow. Outlet is Elliott Creek. Elevation is 3154 feet. Route to Goat is on Mt. Loop Hwy. to Barlow Pass, then N. about 3 miles, then SE 1 mile to Elliott Creek trailhead. Trail 647 leads 4.8 miles to lake.

GOBLIN CREEK. Upper Goblin Creek provides fair rainbow and cutthroat fishing in summer months. The creek flows into N. Fork of Skykomish. Best route to Goblin is

by driving up the Skykomish River's N. Fork road from Index on Hwy. 2 for 3 miles past Garland Hot Springs to where the stream enters the Sky.

GOODWIN LAKE. This 547 acre lake has been stocked with cutthroat, and rainbow. The 'bows come on early as do the cutthroat. Large and smallmouth bass, black crappie, yellow perch and pumpkinseed are also present. Public access is through Wenberg State Park on lake's E. shore, and there are resorts on the lake. The park has a boat launch site and camping facilities. Goodwin is reached by driving N. from Everett on Hwy. I-5 about 9 miles to Smokey Point, then W. on Lake Goodwin road 5 miles to N. end of lake which is circled by a road.

HALCYON LAKE. Cutthroat planted lake of 5.3 acres located 3.4 miles S. from Gold Bar. Drainage to Skykomish River.

HALL LAKE. A 6.1 acre lake located 1 mile S. from Lynnwood. It contains largemouth bass and drains via Hall Creek to **LAKE BALLINGER.**

GREIDER LAKES. Lower Greider is 8.5 acres at 2900 feet and has received rainbow plants. Upper Greider covers 58.4 acres It lies at 2930 feet 8.5 miles NE from Goldbar. The lakes drain to Sultan River.

GULCH LAKES. Trio of small lakes at 3600 feet 9.5 miles N. from Index on E. side of Hard Pass. They have had rainbow plants. Drainage is to N. Fork Skykomish River.

HANNAN LAKE. Hannan is located 5 miles SE of Monroe. The lake is 48 acres and is planted with rainbow and eastern brook. It often holds husky hold-over 'bows at season's opener. Route to Hannan is Hwy. 203 for 3 miles S. of Monroe, then E. and S. on High Rock road for about 2 miles to fork, then NE for 7.5 miles to SW shore. Road continues 0.5 miles to Fontal. Church owned. Public access on Hannan's W. shore.

HANSON LAKE. (McAllester). There are rainbow, cutthroat and eastern brook in 10 acre Hanson Lake. Planted with brook fry by Snohomish Sportsmens' Club. The lake lies 5.5 miles SE of Granite Falls on Scotty road at 1430 feet elevation. It is shallow and ordinarily produces best early in season.

HEATHER LAKE. Cutthroat planted lake of 17.5 acres at 2450 feet. Location is 8.5 miles E. from Granite Falls on NW side of Pilchuck Mt.

HELENA LAKE. Golden trout have been stocked in this 27.5 acre lake. It lies at 3050 feet 8 miles S. from Darrington at head of Helens Creek. Drainage to Sauk River.

HEMPLE LAKE. A 7 acre rainbow lake at 3150 feet located 10 miles E. from Granite Falls. It drains to S. Fork Stillaguamish River.

HOWARD LAKE. This 27 acre lake has both planted cutthroat rainbow, along with bass. The lake usually starts slow, picking up tempo later in the season. Location of Howard is 1.4 miles W. of N. end of **GOODWIN LAKE** adjacent to S. side of Lake Goodwin road, via 65th Drive.

HUGHES LAKE. There are cutthroat plus eastern brook and bass in Hughes, a 20 acre lake used by Boy Scouts. It is located 8 miles N. of Monroe on Woods Creek road, then 0.5 miles NE to lake.

INDEPENDENCE LAKE. A 5.5 acre deep lake at 3700 feet which has received rainbow plants. Located about 5 miles NE from Silverton in headwaters of Coal Creek. It drains to S. Fork Stillaguamish River.

ISABEL LAKE. Eastern brook, rainbow, silvers, cutthroat and a few large mackinaw inhabit Isabel. It lies at 2842 feet elevation 4.5 miles E. of Gold Bar and has a maximum depth of 201 feet. Isabel is reached by driving E. from Gold Bar 4.5 miles, passing Camp Huston, to end of road at a mining claim. A trail continues 0.8 miles N. to lake.

JANUS LAKE. Located near Cascade Crest 6 miles N. of Stevens Pass, Janus is 29 acres. It lies at 4220 feet elevation. There are cutthroat in the lake. Route is E. from Stevens Pass on Hwy. 2 for 4.5 miles to Smith Brook road. Drive up Smith Brook road 2 miles to Janus Lake trail, then 3.7 miles hike to lake.

JOAN LAKE. A 3.5 acre lake that has received Atlantic salmon plants. The lake is located at 5100 feet 6 miles NW from Stevens Pass. It drains to Rapid River.

JULIA LAKE. An 8 acre cutthroat and

eastern brook pond, Julia lies 5 miles SE of Granite Falls on Scotty road, then S. 0.5 miles to N. end of lake on a rough road. Timber clear cuts have depreciated fishing.

KELCEMA LAKE. A 23.2 acre lake planted with cutthroat. Elevation is 3282 feet and location is 2.8 miles SW from Silverton at head of Deer Creek. Drainage to S. Fork Stillaguamish.

KELLOGG LAKE. Contains largemouth bass, black crappie, yellow perch, brookies, cutthroat and bullfrogs. It is a 20 acre lake which drains into Bear Creek and then into Wallace River. Route is 3 miles NE of Sultan on Sultan Basin road, then 1 mile E. on Kellogg Lake road to S. shore. Best fishing is in April and October.

KETCHUM LAKE. Ketchum is a 20 acre lake situated 3 miles N. of Stanwood. Fish species include planted rainbow, bluegill, largemouth bass and pumpkinseed plus a few cutthroat. Take Hwy. 530 N. 2.5 miles from Stanwood then turn E. on Ketchum Lake road for 0.4 miles to N. end of lake. Small boats may be launched from N. shore.

KI LAKE. Plants of rainbow and cutthroat make Ki an excellent early prospect. Largemouth bass and yellow perch are also present. The lake is located 8 miles NW of Marysville and covers 97 acres. Public access is from Lake Goodwin road on N. shore. Drive N. from Marysville on Hwy. 1-5 to Lake Goodwin road, then W. for 4 miles.

KING LAKE. An eastern brook and cutthroat planted lake of 9 acres which also holds rainbow. King lies SE of Arlington. Best fishing comes during April and May. Route is E. and S. of Arlington on Homestead and Jordan roads for 9 miles, passing Jordan, then E. and N. about 1 mile on rough road. Difficult access. Drainage is to Jordan creek.

KING LAKE. King is a cutthroat lake. It is 12 acres and is located 2 miles W. of **HANNON LAKE**, draining into **MARGARET LAKE**. Route is S. from Monroe 3 miles on Hwy. 203, then E. and S. on Highrock road for 1 mile, then E. for 2.5 miles, then N. 1 mile to lake.

KLEMENTS MILL POND. There are largemouth bass, rainbow and limited numbers

HANSON LAKE delivers early in season.

of cutthroat in Klements, a 3 acre pond. Route is 0.5 miles N. of Granite Falls on Mountain Loop Hwy., then NE for 0.5 miles to lake on NW slope of Iron Mt.

KROOZE LAKE. A 2 acre pond which has cutthroat, Krooze is located 3.5 miles NE of Arlington and drains into Stillaguamish River's N. Fork. The lake is reached by driving 3 miles out of Arlington on Darrington Hwy. Pond may be seen on the W. side of road. Fishing is poor.

LIME LAKE. Golden trout have been stocked in this deep 10.9 acre lake at 5550 feet. Location is 6 miles NW from Glacier Peak on Lime Ridge. Drainage to Suiattle River.

LOMA LAKE. There is a public access on Loma's NE shore. The lake contains planted rainbow and cutthroat, plus pump-kinseed and produces best in April and May. Route is N. from Marysville on Hwy. 1-5 for 4 miles, then W. at Stimson Crossing on 140th street NW for 3 miles, then 0.5 miles N. to Loma on Lake Drive which circles the 21 acre lake.

LOST LAKE. Cutthroat and rainbow inhabit Lost's 18 acres. Best angling months are April and May. Drainage is to Woods Creek. Lost lake is reached by driving N. from Monroe on Woods Creek road for 7

miles then walking E. on road which is closed to vehicles by City of Everett. Planted annually by Snohomish Sportsmens' Club.

MARTHA LAKE. (Alderwood Manor). Hold-over rainbow are not uncommon in Martha Lake which has a maximum depth of 48 feet. Plants of 'bows aid the 59 acre lake which has a small public access on its E. shore. The lake is reached by driving N. from Alderwood Manor on Hwy. 1-5 for 2 miles to 164th St. SW, then E. about 1.5 miles to S. end of lake. There are resort facilities.

MARTHA LAKE. (Warm Beach). Cutthroat and rainbow are available in Martha Lake in Warm Beach area. There is a public access on NW side of the 58 acre lake, plus a resort. Route to Martha is N. from Everett on Hwy. 1-5 for 9 miles to Smokey Point Crossing, then W. on Lake Goodwin and Warm Beach road for 8 miles to S. shore of lake. The lake gets regular plants.

MARTHA LAKE. (Little). This Martha is located 3.4 miles E. from Marysville and covers 13.4 acres. It contains largemouth bass, yellow perch and brown bullhead.

MAY CREEK. "Fair" is the rating given May Creek for spring rainbow angling. The creek flows into Wallace River about 1.5 miles E. of Gold Bar.

SPADA LAKE boat launch area.

MEADOW LAKE. A mountain lake of 9 acres situated at 4500 feet elevation in headwaters of Meadow Creek, Meadow holds rainbow and cutthroat in the 11 inch range, with a few larger fish. Route is SE from Darrington on Mountain Loop Hwy., 10 miles to mouth of Whitechuck River, then E. for 5.5 miles to Meadow Mt. road, then drive 7 miles to Meadow Mt. road, and hike 4 miles to lake. **CRYSTAL LAKE** lies 1 mile N. It is 21 acres and contains rainbow and cutthroat. Best way is to drive 1.5 miles to end of Crystal Creek road which branches from Meadow Mt. road, then strike trail for 1 mile E. to lake. Trail is at upper NE corner of cutting unit.

MEADOW LAKE. A private 14 acre lake which contains rainbow and cutthroat, 3 miles N. of Monroe.

MENZEL LAKES. Private lakes of 13 and 3 acres located SE of Granite Falls. Three beaver ponds above the lakes are planted annually with cutthroat fry by Snohomish Sportsmens' Club.

METAN LAKE. A cutthroat planted lake of 3.5 acres. Location is 12.5 miles SE from Darrington on SW side of Pugh Mt. at 2800 feet. Drainage to Sauk River.

MONTE CRISTO LAKE. S. Fork of the Sauk River feeds and drains the 14 acre lake. It holds rainbow, cutthroat and eastern brook and yields best fishing from July into fall. There are several FS campgrounds in the vicinity. The lake lies adjacent to the Mountain Loop Hwy. 19 miles SE of Darrington.

NORTH LAKE. Cutthroat have been stocked in North's 10.6 deep acres. It lies 8.8 miles SE from Darrington at head of North Falls Creek. Drainage is to Sauk River.

OLSON LAKE. Olson is rated "fair" for crappie and cutthroat during summer months. It is a 3 acre pond situated 3 miles SE of Arlington on W. side of Service road where the power line crosses the road.

PANTHER LAKE. A 48 acre lake holding stocked rainbow plus a few cutthroat and largemouth bass, black crappie, pumpkinseed and brown bullhead. Panther is located at former community of Three Lakes. There is a public access on lake's W. shore. Take 68th St. SE from Snohomish E. for about 6 miles, then turn N. on Panther lake road 1.5 miles.

PASS LAKE. A 2.4 acre lake at 3700 feet. Rainbow planted. Located 3.8 miles NE from Silverton at head of Coal Creek. Drainage is to S. Fork Stillaguamish River.

PEACH LAKE. Cutthroat have been stocked in this 17 acre lake at 4800 feet. It is located about 10 miles N. from Stevens Pass and drains to Beckler River.

PEEK-A-BOO LAKE. Rainbow planted lake of 22.4 acres. It lies 10 miles SE from Darrington at head of Peek-A-Boo Creek. Drainage to Sauk River.

PICNIC POINT POND. A 4 acre pond located 0.4 miles N. from Picnic Point adjacent to R.R. tracks and Puget Sound. Stocked with rainbow. Reached by hiking N. up R.R. tracks from Picnic Point.

PILCHUCK CREEK. Tributary to Stillaguamish River, entering river 0.5 miles W. of point the creek is crossed by Hwy. 1-5. Sea-run cutthroat are taken in lower reaches of Pilchuck in spring and fall, while steelhead are available from December through February. The medium-size creek clears and drops rapidly after high water periods and produces steelhead when larger streams are out of shape. Upper portions carry small cutthroat and rainbow. The Norman road offers access at mouth. The Stanwood-Bryant road crosses Pilchuck 1.5 miles N. of the Hwy. 1-5 bridge, and Hwy. 9 bridges stream about 4.5 miles N. of Bryant.

PILCHUCK RIVER. The Pilchuck heads N. of Sultan under Bald Mt. and flows W. and S. for approximately 30 miles to enter Snohomish River at E. limits of town of Snohomish. December through February is steelheading period. Other species of fish in the rain-fed stream include cutthroat and salmon. The river may be waded at riffles, and is paralleled along its lower stretches by the Machias road leading upstream N. from Snohomish through Machias. The Robe-Menzel road leads S. from Granite Falls, following river for about 4 miles. Upper reaches of Pilchuck are reached by driving SE from Granite Falls on Anderson road for 4 miles, then E. for about 6 miles. This road swings S. to town of Sultan.

PINACLE LAKE. Cutthroat and eastern brook have been planted in this 6.5 acre lake which lies at 3820 feet. Location is 10 miles E. from Granite Falls on E. side of Pilchuck Mt. It drains to S. Fork Stillaguamish River.

POWERLINE POND. A 2 acre pond that has received plants of rainbow, cutthroat and eastern brook. Location is 5.4 miles N. from Bothell on power line. It drains to North Creek.

PROCTOR CREEK. Limited rainbow fishing is provided in Proctor, a tributary of Skykomish River. The creek may be reached by driving 1 mile from Gold Bar to bridge crossing stream.

RAPID RIVER. The Rapid joins Beckler River 9 miles N. of town of Skykomish. A road from Skykomish leads upstream to Rapid's mouth, then turns E. for 6.5 miles. A trail continues along stream for approximately 2 miles before heading N. up Meadow Creek. There are rainbow in the river which produces in May, July, August, September and October. FS road 6530 extends up river to a point about 1 mile beyond Rapid River's N. Fork.

RILEY LAKE. Plants of rainbow and cutthroat boost Riley, a 30 acre lake which drains into Jim Creek. Riley has a public access on its SW end. It is reached by leaving Hwy. 530 at Trafton about 4 miles NE of Arlington and driving 6 miles E. on Trafton road, then 2 miles N. on Riley Lake road to S. end of lake which has a peat bog shoreline. It drains to N. Fork Stillaguamish.

ROESIGER LAKE. Roesiger is planted with rainbow and also holds bass, crappie, perch and brown bullhead. The 352 acre lake is 115 feet at deepest point and offers good fishing through the season. It has a county park plus an access area on the extreme S. shore. The lake is reached by driving N. from Monroe up Woods creek road for 10 miles to S. tip of lake. Roads flank both W. and E. shores.

ROUND LAKE. A snow fed lake of 12 acres at 5100 feet 16.5 miles SE from Darrington. Has rainbow planted. Drainage to Whitechuck River.

RUGGS LAKE. An 11 acre private lake located S. of Everett, Ruggs contains rainbow, cutthroat, brown bullhead and other spiny rays. It is fed by Silver lake which lies 1 mile NW. There is no public access. The Ruggs Lake loop road flanks N. shore.

SAUK RIVER. Upper section of Sauk, a major tributary of the Skagit, is in Snohomish County and provides winter and summer steelheading, plus cutthroat, Dolly Varden and whitefish angling. The Whitechuck joins Sauk from the E. about 9 miles SE of Darrington, often dumping cloudy water, but the stream usually is clear above this point. The N. and S. Forks join 15 miles SE of Darrington. Road leads up N. Fork for 7 miles to Sloan Creek campground. A good trail leads up N. Fork 5 miles to Mackinaw camp. The trail continues to join Cascade Crest trail. From Sloan Creek campground the road crosses N. Fork Sauk and continues 6 miles up Sloan Creek. The S. Fork road heads SE for about 10 miles to Monte Cristo where there is a campground under Poodle Dog Pass. Best fishing period for upper river is from June through October.

SCRABBLE LAKE. A 3 acre rainbow planted lake at 5000 feet on the W. side of Scrabble Mtn. It drains to Rapid River.

SCRIBER LAKE. Largemouth bass and yellow perch are present in this 3.4 acre lake. It is situated 2000 feet E. from Lynnwood. Drainage to Sammamish River.

SERENE LAKE. April and May are top months for Serene Lake's rainbow and cutthroat. The lake is located 3 miles N. of Lynnwood adjacent to W. side of Hwy. 99. There is a public access site on W. shore. Take Shelby road W. from Hwy. 99 to 43rd Ave. W., then N. to access.

SHOECRAFT LAKE. Shoecraft lies 600 feet SW of **GOODWIN LAKE**and is linked by a narrow canal. It covers 137 acres, is rainbow planted and also holds large and smallmouth bass, black crappie, yellow perch, pumpkinseed and brown bullhead. An access area is located on SW shore off 43rd Ave. W.

SILVER CREEK. Silver joins the Skykomish River's N. Fork 8 miles NE of Index. It furnishes fair to good fishing for rainbow from June on. A rough road leads up creek approximately 5 miles, with a non-maintained trail continuing NE about 3 miles to **SILVER LAKE** at 4200 feet elevation. The lake has been planted with cutthroat.

SILVER LAKE. A 102 acre rainbow and kokanee lake, Silver is situated 5.5 miles S. of Everett adjacent to Everett-Bothell Hwy. The lake has a resort and public access is gained from park on W. shore.

SKYKOMISH RIVER. (Main). The main Skykomish is a major winter steelhead river, usually ranking among the state's top 10 producers. It yields the big sea-run rainbow from December into April. Other species include sea-run cutthroat, whitefish, Dolly Varden, summer steelhead and salmon. The Sky flows approximately 25 miles from junction of N. and S. Forks at Index to point it joins Snoqualmie River to form the Snohomish River 3.5 miles SW of Monroe where Hwy. 202 bridges the Snohomish. The river is followed by Hwy. 2 for its entire length.

SKYKOMISH RIVER. (North Fork). The S. Fork joins N. Fork at Index. A road runs upstream from that town for about 18 miles, affording easy access. Best fishing comes during summer into fall for small rainbow. Summer steelhead are available from June into fall months.

SKYKOMISH RIVER. (South Fork). This branch of the Sky is approximately 13 miles in length, and is paralleled all the way by Stevens Pass Hwy. to town of Skykomish. The Beckler and Tye Rivers come together at this point. Only 3 or 4 miles of the S. Fork are in Snohomish County. (See King County).

SMELLING LAKE. Smelling Lake is unusual in that it measures 107 feet deep, yet covers only 7 surface acres. It holds cutthroat and brookies, with April, May and October best fishing months. Drainage is into Worthy Creek. Smelling is located 4.5 miles SE of Granite Falls on Scotty road and 1700 feet S. of Julia Lake.

SNOHOMISH RIVER. Formed by union of Skykomish and Snoqualmie Rivers 3 miles SW of Monroe, the Snohomish flows NW to enter Port Gardner Bay at Everett. The slow moving river divides into Union, Ebey and Steamboat Sloughs at its mouth and these open-year-around waters provide good sea-run cutthroat from August into November. There are winter and summer steelhead, Dolly Varden, coho, chinook and pink salmon in the Snohomish. It is most easily fished by boat, and there are public boat launch areas at town of Snohomish, upstream at Thomas eddy, and in the sloughs near its mouth. There are bridges at Everett, at town of Snohomish and at confluence of Skykomish and Snoqualmie Rivers.

SNOWSLIDE LAKE. (Slahal). Rainbow have been stocked in this 10 acre lake which lies at 4300 feet 5 miles N. from Index on Ragged Ridge. It drains to N. Fork Skykomish River.

SOUTH LAKE. A 13.2 rainbow planted lake at 4200 feet. Location is 5.8 miles N. of Barlow Pass on N. side of Stillaguamish Peak. It drains to Sauk River.

SPADA LAKE. A 760 acre lake formed by a dam on Sultan River in Sultan Basin. The reservoir is used by City of Everett for water storage. It is reached by driving E. from Sultan .05 miles on Hwy. 2, then turning left for 14 miles to lake. Take right fork of road 5.5 miles around lake and turn left 1 mile to boat launch site maintained by FS. The lake is stocked annually with rainbow, and also holds cutthroat. Spada is a good fly fishing lake. Fishermen are requested to observe all posted rules.

SQUIRE CREEK. Squire is a tributary of Stillaguamish River's N. Fork, entering river 2.5 miles W. of Darrington. There is a county park 0.8 miles upstream from its mouth. The creek contains rainbow, cutthroat and Dolly Varden. Top fishing comes in May and June. Road from center of Darrington heads W. and S. about 2 miles to hit Squire at Buckeye Creek. The road leads 6.5 miles up Squire. A trail continues upstream about 5 miles and through Squire Creek Pass, leading down Eight Mile Creek to Clear Creek.

STEVENS LAKE. There is a public access on the E. shore of Stevens, a 1021 acre lake situated 5.5 miles E. of Everett. There are kokanee, large and smallmouth bass, black crappie, yellow perch, 'bows and cutthroat in the lake which is 160 feet deep. It drains into Pilchuck River and is planted with kokanee and cutthroat. Good fall fishing for cutthroat, but the lake is best known for kokanee to 2 pounds which are caught from late June through early August. Some lunker bass over 5 pounds have been taken from Stevens. Route is 6 miles N. of Snohomish on Hwy. 9, then E. for 0.5 miles to W. side of the lake. Roads circle lake. In addition to the F&W department access, in community of Lake Stevens, there is a boat launch site at a county park on lake's SW shore.

STICKNEY LAKE. A 26 acre lake containing rainbow, perch, bass and brown bullhead. Stickney lies 4.5 miles NE of Lynnwood and .05 miles E. of Hwy. 99. There is a public access on lake's E. shore. It drains via Swamp Creek into Lake Washington. Route is E. from Hwy. 99 on N. Manor Way, S. on Admiralty Way, then N. on 20th Place W. to lake.

STILLAGUAMISH RIVER. (Main). The main stem of the Stilly produces sea-run cutthroat, summer and winter steelhead, coho and chinook, plus pink salmon in odd-numbered years. The N. and S. Forks join at Arlington, and the main river flows about 16 miles W. to Puget Sound at Stanwood. Hwy. 530 between Arlington and

SUNSET FALLS on So. Fork Skykomish River.

Stanwood offers access. This stretch of river is often cloudy, but is relatively under-fished.

STILLAGUAMISH RIVER. (South Fork). The S. Fork carries summer and winter steelhead, sea-run cutthroat and coho, chinook and pink salmon. The river above Granite Falls is planted with legal rainbow from mid-June on at intervals. Lower stretches of river are often dirty due to clay slides, but the upper river is usually clear. The Stehr road leads SE from Arlington along river's W. bank to Granite Falls, while Homestead and Jordan roads parallel E. side. The highway E. from Granite Falls closely follows S. Fork upstream for approximately 25 miles to its headwaters near Barlow Pass. There are 14 FS campgrounds adjacent to river along this stretch.

STILLAGUAMISH RIVER. (North Fork). The Stilly's N. Fork is rated one of the better summer steelhead streams in W. Washington. It is restricted to fly fishing only during summer fishing season. During winter steelheading the river produces well. Lower third of this fork is also plagued by clay slides. It carries good numbers of sea-run cutthroat from mid-summer into fall. The river has been planted with chinook salmon. Hwy. 530 follows the stream E. from Arlington to Darrington. Another road leads N. from Darrington ranger station N. for 7 miles to Stilly's headwaters.

STONE LAKE. Rainbow are present in this 1.5 acre lake which is located 1800 feet S. from Eagle Lake at 3800 feet. It drains to S. Fork Skykomish River.

STORM LAKE. A rainbow planted lake of 78 acres, Storm provides best angling during April, May and June and offers a public access on its W. shore. Route to lake is E. from Snohomish on 68th St. SE and Three Lakes road, and 1 mile NE on a road running between Flowing and Storm Lakes.

SULTAN RIVER. The Sultan is a major tributary of the Skykomish River, entering that river at town of Sultan where there is a boat launch site. City of Everett has dammed the Sultan about 12 miles from its mouth. There are limited numbers of winter steelhead in the lower stretch which flows through a steep canyon. The Reiner and Pipeline roads follow river's W. side, while Sultan Basin road leads up E. side for approximately 14 miles to mouth of **WILLIAMSON CREEK**, and then contin-

ues another 7 miles to road end near Sheep Gap Mtn. There is fair to good fishing for rainbow and cutthroat in upper river. A rough road heads N. up Williamson Creek for 5 miles.

SUNDAY LAKE. Spiny rays including largemouth bass, black crappie, yellow perch and pumpkinseed plus rainbow provide fishing action in Sunday's 39 acres. The lake is located 5 miles E. of Stanwood and drains into lower Stillaguamish River. The lake is reached by driving E. from Stanwood for 3 miles on Stanwood-Bryant road, then SE for 1 mile to lake on Sunday Lake road.

SUNSET LAKE. Golden trout are the attraction in Sunset's 34.4 acres. The lake lies at 4100 feet 7 miles E. from Index on N. side of Burley Mtn. It drains to N. Fork Skykomish River.

SWARTZ LAKE. (Waite's Mill Pond). There are cutthroat and spiny rays in Swartz which is situated 1.5 miles SE of Granite Falls. The lake covers 17 acres and drains into Milard Lake.

THOMAS LAKE. A boggy-shored lake of 7 acres, Thomas lies 7.5 miles N. of Bothell and 2 miles SE of **SILVER LAKE** on York road. It holds cutthroat and spiny rays including bass and yellow perch.

TOMTIT LAKE. Largemouth bass are the attraction in Tomtit, a lake of 27.9 acres located 3 miles S. from Sultan. Drainage to Skykomish River.

TROUT LAKE. (Mud). Formerly used for rearing steelhead, this 19 acre lake is a natural producer of cutthroat trout, with best fishing in the summer months. Drive N. and E. from the bridge across the S. Fork Stillaguamish near Granite Falls 3 miles to the Scott Paper company road, then N. 2.5 miles across Canyon Creek to the river. Take left fork in road after crossing Canyon Creek.

TWENTY TWO LAKE. Rainbow plants are made regularly in Twenty Two. The lake covers 44 acres and drains into Stillaguamish River's S. Fork via Twenty Two Creek. It is reached by driving E. of Granite Falls for 12 miles (1.5 miles E. of Verlot RS) then heading S. up Twenty Two Creek 2 miles to lake. Elevation is 2460 feet.

TWIN LAKES. Plants of cutthroat and rainbow are made in Twin Lakes which cover 32 (Lower Twin) and 34 (Upper Twin) acres. There are also, eastern brook and a few steelhead in lakes. They drain into Cub Creek, then into Jim Creek, and are located on a U.S.N. reservation. Limited access. Route is E. from Hwy. 530 at Trafton for 7 miles, then S. another 2 miles to check in point at Navy radio station. There is a boat launch site on upper lake.

TWIN LAKES. The Twins lie at 4700 and 4800 feet elevation 3 miles S. of Monte Cristo. Lower Twin is 24 acres; Upper Twin, 69 acres. The lakes contain rainbow, cutthroat and a few eastern brook. Drainage from upper to lower Twin is over a 75 foot falls into Troublesome Creek. Road up Silver Creek, which leaves N. Fork of the Skykomish road at Galena, leads N. about 5 miles to within 2 miles of W. side of the lake. Access also over Poodle Dog Pass via a 4.5 mile trail.

WAGNER LAKE. There are rainbow in Wagner, a 20 acre lake located 2.5 miles NE of Monroe. Take Wood Creek road NE of Monroe for 1.5 miles, then turn N. for 1 mile on Wagner road past Wagner community club, then right 100 yards to lake. Public access.

WALLACE LAKE. (Walton). There are cutthroat plus eastern brook in Wallace. The lake is 100 feet deep at deepest point and covers 55 acres. It drains into N. Fork of Wallace River. The Wallace Lake road leads N. from Gold Bar for about 6 miles to lake shore. Elevation is 1844 feet.

WALLACE RIVER. There is fair winter steelheading and whitefish angling in lower stretches of the Wallace which enters Skykomish River 1.5 miles E. of Sultan. The river flows under Hwy. 2 at E. outskirts for Startup and trails lead upstream along both banks for a short distance. The Wallace Lake road crosses N. Fork just below lake. Road from Gold Bar runs up E. side of the river, touching the stream near falls on the S. Fork.

WEDEN LAKE. Rainbow are the attraction in Weden's 5.5 acres at 4400 feet. Location is 3.5 miles S. from Barlow Pass. Drainage is to S. Fork Sauk River.

WHITECHUCK RIVER. Only limited fishing is available in the Whitechuck because of milky water, but the stream usually clears in fall. It contains Dolly Varden, steelhead, salmon, cutthroat and rainbow, and flows into Sauk River 9 miles SE of Darrington on Mountain Loop Hwy. A road follows Whitechuck E. for 10 miles providing easy access. Trail continues upstream for another 10 miles or so to headwaters.

WINTERS LAKE. A 11.2 acre lake containing largemouth bass. Location is 3 miles NE from Sultan. It drains to Bear Creek.

WOODS CREEK. Dolly Varden and cutthroat, along with a few winter steelhead, are found in the Skykomish River tributary. The Florence and Lower Woods Creek roads follow the lower portion of stream E. and N. from Monroe, with Woods Creek road paralleling middle stretches providing easy access.

SNOHOMISH COUNTY RESORTS

Goodwin Lake: Lake Goodwin Resort, E. Stanwood, WA 98292. 360-652-8169. Art Leonard's Resort, E. Stanwood, WA 98292. 360-659-5124. Cedar Grove, E. Stanwood, WA 98292.

Martha Lake: Lake Martha Resort. (Alderwood Manor) Lynnwood, WA 98036. 360-743-6207. Marion's Lake Martha Resort. (Warm Beach) 8105 Lakewood Rd., Stanwood, WA 98292. 360-652-8412.

Silver Lake: Silver Beach Resort, Everett, WA 98201.

Check the regulations

All fishermen should obtain free sport fishing regulations at sport shops. Look before you fish—all sections of all streams do not open at the same time for all species of fish. It is the individual's responsibility to check pamphlets to be certain that he is fishing in a legal manner before he wets a line.

Did you know?

The mayfly, of which there are more than 550 species in North America, spends all but a few days of its life underwater.

SPOKANE

COUNTY

Most of Spokane County is rolling prairie-type land, but there are mountainous areas in the NE and E. parts of the 1777 square mile county. Highest point is Mt. Spokane at 5878 feet. There are nearly 500 lakes listed for Spokane, all lowland, and the county provides some of the state's best fishing for quality trout. The Little Spokane River drains NE part of the county, the Spokane River the E. and central portions, with the SW part draining into Palouse River system. Spokane ranks 21st in size among Washington's 39 counties.

AMBER LAKE. (Calvert). Plants of rainbow, plus hold-over 'bows, make Amber an excellent prospect. Planted cutthroat afford good May fly fishing. The lake is 117 acres and is located 11 miles SW of Cheney on Mullinex road at community of Amber. Amber produces best in April and May.

Spokane County

BADGER LAKE. This 244 acre lake is stocked with rainbow plus plants of cutthroat. Bass present. Resorts and a public access are located on Badger. Best fishing period is April, May and September. Route is 12 miles S. of Cheney on Cheney-Plaza road. The May fly hatch in mid-May generates excellent dry fly fishing.

BAILEY LAKE. A 16 acre private lake with marshy shores, Bailey is located 5 miles NE of Deer Park. It holds rainbow, but is not stocked. Outlet is Bear Creek.

BEAR LAKE. (Kuester). Rainbow and spiny rays, including large and smallmouth bass, black crappie, yellow perch and pumpkinseed are available in this 33.8 acre lake situated 6 miles SE from Deer Park. Little Spokane River drainage.

BLANCHARD CREEK. An eastern brook stream which provides good fishing all season. It flows into Idaho and is reached by driving E. from Elk.

BONNIE LAKE. Bonnie is a 4.5 miles long enlargement of Rock Creek and covers 366 acres. About 82 acres are in Whitman County. The lake hosts bass, crappie, perch, sunfish and catfish. The S. portion of Bonnie is bordered by sheer rock cliffs up to 300 feet high. Route is S. and E. from Cheney 15 miles on Cheney-Plaza road, then S. about 1.5 miles on private road. Boats may be launched from N. end. Poor fishing except for years of low run-off when lake is clear of silt.

CHAPMAN LAKE. A rainbow and small and largemouth bass lake, Chapman also provides consistently good kokanee fishing. It is a "S" shaped lake of 146 acres. In addition to bass, there are perch and crappie in Chapman, which has resort facilities. Drive 9 miles S. of Cheney on Cheney-Plaza road, then turn E. for 1 mile to S. tip of lake. Bass fishing usually is good through summer.

CLEAR LAKE. Located 2 miles S. of town of Medical Lake, Clear contains brown trout, lake trout and rainbow and also has largemouth bass and brown bullhead. It is nearly 3 miles long and covers 375 acres. Public access is at S. end, and there are resorts.

COOKS LAKE. (Wandermere). Artificial lake of 11.4 acres 2.1 miles NW from Mead. Varies in size. Has been rainbow planted. Drains N. to Little Spokane River.

DOWNS LAKE. A 423 acre lake with extensive marshy shorelines. About 30 acres of Downs are in Lincoln county. The lake receives periodic rainbow and brown trout plants and also contains largemouth bass, pumpkinseed, yellow perch and brown bullhead. Downs is reached by driving SW from community of Amber for 7 miles on Harris and Falk roads to NE end of lake at Rodna. There is a resort on lake where small boats may be launched.

ELOIKA LAKE. Considered one of the state's better spiny ray lakes, Eloika offers a wide variety of fish including largemouth bass, crappie, bullhead catfish, perch and pumpkinseed. It is open year around. Peak fishing is during summer months. The lake

AMBER LAKE is an April and May producer. (T.O.P. Photo)

covers 659 acres. It has several resorts and private boats may be launched at resorts. Route is 7 miles N. of Chaytaroy on Newport highway, then NW for 1 mile on Eloika Lake road. Public access S. of Grays Landing.

FISH LAKE. Carry-over eastern brook make this lake an excellent prospect, particularly in spring and fall. It also contains brown trout. Elevation of Fish is 2171 feet. It covers 47 acres. Private boats may be launched at a county park. The lake is reached by driving 2.5 miles NE of Cheney on Cheney-Spokane highway.

HOG CANYON LAKE. (Deep). Most of Hog Canyon Lake's 53 acres are shallow, and planted rainbow find the necessary food to attain excellent growth. The lake is located 13 miles SW of Cheney and is reached by driving SW from Spokane on freeway to Fishtrap exit. Road to lake leads off old U.S. 10 Hwy. just S. of milepost 69. Cross R.R. tracks and drive dirt road to lake. Public access on S. end.

HORSESHOE LAKE. A 68 acre marshy lake (little open water) located 10 miles W. of Nine Mile Falls. Horseshoe gets rainbow and eastern brook plants, contains brown bullhead and is reported to hold walleyes. It is reached by driving S. from Nine Mile Falls to state park, then W. on 7-Mile and Coulee-Hite roads 11 miles and then 1.5 miles N. on McLaughlin road to lake. Boats may be launched at lake shore.

LIBERTY LAKE. Heavily fished, Liberty gives a good account of itself and can be productive early in the season. The 711 acre lake is stocked with rainbow and brown trout. There are largemouth bass, bluegill, yellow perch, pumpkinseed and brown bullhead in the lake. It has a public access. Liberty is located 15 miles E. of Spokane on Hwy. 10 to Liberty Lake road, then S. 1.5 miles to lake.

LITTLE SPOKANE RIVER. Heading in Pend Oreille County, the river enters Spokane County at Camden and meanders approximately 30 miles SW to join Spokane River at Old Fort Spokane on Stevens County line. Roads follow stream for its entire length, but access is tough in spots because of posted land. Little Spokane contains eastern brook, brown trout, rainbow and rough fish.

LONG LAKE. A 5020 acre reservoir, also called Spokane Lake, created by a dam on Spokane River 23 miles NW of Spokane. The reservoir extends 24 miles. Half the acreage is in Spokane County with most of remainder in Stevens. Fish species include perch, crappie, walleye, largemouth bass, bullhead catfish and a few northern pike. Planted with brown trout, lake trout and rainbow. Prime fishing periods are spring and fall. Several resorts are located along the lake. DNR camp and boat launch sites 3 miles E. of Long Lake Dam. Road from Nine Mile Falls parallels S. bank.

MASON LAKE. Spiny rays including bass, perch, crappie and catfish inhabit this 52 acre lake located W. of Amber. Route is 2 miles SW of Amber on Harris road, then N. for 1 mile on Ladd road which runs close to E. shore. Private lake, but permission to fish may be obtained.

MEDICAL LAKE. A 148.9 acre lake adjacent to W. side of town of Medical Lake. It has received plants of brown trout. Largmouth bass present. Public access and boat ramp.

MUD CREEK. Small eastern brook are taken from this Dragoon Creek tributary. Best fishing usually comes in summer. It is located E. of Dennison near Deer Park.

NEWMAN LAKE. Plants of rainbow, tiger musky and brown trout have been made in Newman, a 1190 acre lake located 14 miles E. of Spokane on Hwy. 290, then 3 miles N. on Starr road to lake's E. shore. The lake yields big bass, smallmouth bass, perch, crappie, bluegill and pumpkinseed. There is a resort on Newman and a public access site is situated on E. shore.

NORTH SILVER. A shallow, 87 acre rainbow lake located 1.1 mile E. of town of Medical Lake. The lake's rich waters produces large trout. Easy access. It is divided from Silver Lake by a road fill.

WEST MEDICAL LAKE produces large rainbow.

OPENING DAY ACTIVITY at Fishtrap Lake. (T.O.P. Press)

OTTER CREEK. A tributary of Little Spokane River, Otter Creek holds small eastern brook. It is rated best during spring and summer.

QUEEN LUCAS LAKE. Yellow perch are present in this 36.8 acre lake situated 5 miles NE from Cheney adjacent to railroad tracks. Drainage to Spokane River.

RING LAKE. A rainbow lake of 23 acres which lies 1 mile SE of town of Medical Lake. Private lake.

SILVER LAKE. This 559 acre lake is located 1 mile E. of town of Medical Lake and a county road crosses N. end of lake. Resorts, plus a public access on N. shore, service anglers. Excellent rainbow fishing. Silver also holds brown trout and bass.

SPOKANE LAKE. See Long Lake.

SPOKANE RIVER. This large river enters Spokane County from Idaho and flows through city of Spokane, then swings NW into head of **SPOKANE LAKE** (Long Lake) near Nine Mile Falls. Fish species include rainbow, eastern brook and brown trout. Most productive fishing stretch is from Idaho line to Spokane. Spokane River does best for fishermen during spring and summer.

WEST MEDICAL LAKE. An outstanding rainbow lake that puts out large numbers of quality rainbow. The lake covers 235 acres and is located 1 mile W. of town of Medical Lake. Carry-over trout of 13-17 inches are common. West Medical has a resort plus a public access site on W. shore.

WILLIAMS LAKE. Another excellent rainbow lake that yields big 'bows, plus cutthroat. Williams is 319 acres. It lies about 12 miles SW of Cheney via Mullinix road to W. shore. The public boat launch area is on NW shore, and there are also resort facilities.

SPOKANE COUNTY RESORTS

Amber Lake: Decker's Resort, Cheney, WA 99004. 509-235-2251.

Badger Lake: Badger Lake Resort, Cheney, WA 99004. 509-235-2331.

Chapman Lake: Dybdall's, Cheney, WA 99004. 509-523-2221.

Clear Lake: Barber's, Cheney, WA 99004. 509-299-3830. Rainbow Cove, Medical Lake, WA 99022. 509-299-3717.

Downs Lake: Down's Lake Resort, Amber, WA 99004. 509-234-2314.

Elolka Lake: Jerry's Landing, Elk, WA 99009. 509-292-2337. Water's Edge Resort, Elk, WA 99009. 509-292-2111.

Fish Lake: Myers Park, Cheny, WA 99004. 509-235-2391.

Long Lake: Willow Bay Resort, Nine Mile Falls, WA 99021. 509-276-2350. Forshee's Resort, 509-276-8568.

Newman Lake: Osborn's Cherokee Landing, Newman Lake, WA 99025. 509-226-3843.

Silver Lake: Picnic Pines, Medical Lake WA 99022. 509-299-3223. Bernie's Last Resort, Medical Lake, WA 99022. 509-299-7273.

West Medical Lake: W. Medical Boathouse, Medical Lake, WA 99022. 509-299-3921.

Williams Lake: William's Lake Resort. Cheney, WA 99004. 1-800-274-1540. Bunker's Resort, Cheney, WA 99004. 509-235-5212.

Stevens County

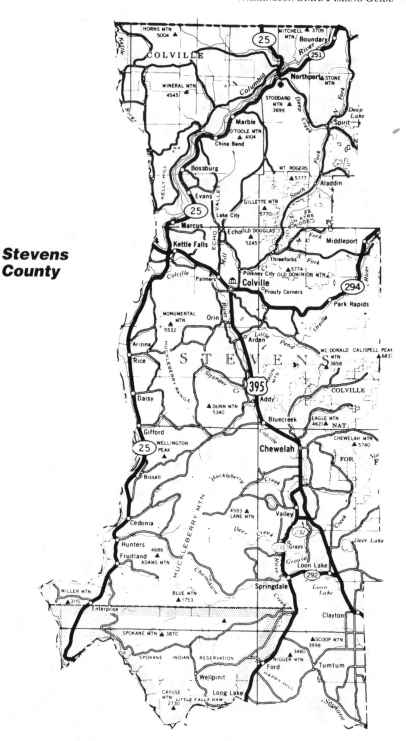

STEVENS
COUNTY

Stevens County covers 2551 square miles and ranks 5th in size in the state. There are over 300 lakes listed for the county with more than 100 of these located at or above 2500 feet elevation. Abercrombie Mt. at 7308 feet is the highest point. Most of Stevens is drained by the Colville River system into Columbia River. Canada borders the county on the N. The giant Franklin D. Roosevelt Lake on Stevens' W. side separates it from Ferry County. Loon, Deer and Waitts Lakes are the county's largest lakes, other than FDR, with most of remainder small.

BAYLEY LAKE. (Cliff). A marshy lake that varies in size from about 18 to 72 acres. Bailey is located 4.8 miles NE from Deer Park. It holds large eastern brook and planted rainbow. Route is N. and E. from Chewelah up N. Fork of Chewelah Creek about 5 miles, then up Bayley Creek to lake. **POTTER POND**, covering about 2.5 acres, is situated just N. of Bayley lake on W. side of Bayley Creek. It contains eastern brook and rainbow.

BENJAMIN LAKE. A 12.7 acre lake on Spokane Indian resevation 2 miles SW from Wellpinit. Has been planted with rainbow in past years. Drainage to Spokane River.

BIG SHEEP CREEK. Excellent fishing for rainbow and eastern brook to 14 inches is offered in upper reaches of Big Sheep. It enters Stevens County from B.C. about 1.5 miles NE of Lead Pencil Mtn. and flows SE 10 miles to Columbia about 2 miles N. of Northport. Top portion of creek has deep pools, is brushy and holds eastern brook, while lower stretches show white water and rainbow. Route is N. across the Columbia River at Northport on Hwy. 25, for .05 miles, then NW on road that follows Big Sheep to Canadian border. Sheep Creek campground is located 7 miles upstream from Hwy. 25. Road near campground leads W. up American Fork of Big Sheep Creek.

BLACK LAKE. A beautiful, secluded rainbow and eastern brook lake of 70 acres,

Black lies at 3700 feet elevation and receives limited fishing pressure. Brookies are in the 8-12 inch class. Black is reached by driving E. from Colville 15 miles on Hwy. 294, then N. up Gap Creek 1.5 miles to E. shore of lake where there is a resort. The road continues W. for 1 mile from N. end of Black to **TWIN LAKE** (formerly Spruce and Cedar Lakes, but joined by a FS dam). There are FS campgrounds on lake. It holds cutthroat.

BROWN'S LAKE. A 17 acre private lake located SW of Chewelah, Brown's drains into the Colville River via Huckleberry Creek.

CEDAR LAKE. This lake lies 4 miles inside U.S.-B.C. border and 1 mile N. of Leadpoint at 2135 feet. Plants of rainbow boost the 51 acre lake which has a public access. It has had brown trout plants. Cedar is reached by driving E. for 1.5 miles from Hwy. 251 about 0.4 miles before crossing the B.C. border, then turning S. up Cedar Creek 4 miles to lake. Most fishing action comes during May, June and July.

CHAMOKANE CREEK. Rated "fair" for rainbow with some brown trout, Chamokane drains into Spokane River. Top fishing is from May to September. The creek is reached by paved road from Reardan to Ford.

CHEWELAH CREEK. Enters Colville River at town of Chewelah, with the N. and S. Forks joining at outskirts of town. Roads

BLACK LAKE offers secluded angling.

LITTLE PEND ORIELLE lakes provide cutthroat.

follow both branches upstream to headwater regions. There are rainbow and eastern brook in Chewelah, with top fishing during May and June.

CLARK LAKE. (Bissel, Charles). This 24 acre private lake is situated at 1800 feet. Location is 8 miles N. from Hunters.

COFFIN LAKE. (Devils). A 20 acre private lake located 2.7 miles NE of Kettle Falls. Contains several species of trout plus kokanee and spiny rays. Elevation is 2280 feet. Rough boat launch site.

COLVILLE RIVER. The river heads S. of Waitts Lake and flows NE to enter FDR Lake 2 miles S. of Kettle Falls. Hwy 395 parallels river for approximately 35 miles through Colville. Fish species in river include rainbow and German brown trout. Top fishing section is from Chewelah to mouth from June through October. The river contains some large fish.

COTTONWOOD CREEK. Both eastern brook and rainbow are found in this stream. It offers best fishing in summer months. The creek is reached by driving E. from Chewelah.

DEEP LAKE. Early season and fall is best for Deep's cutthroat and eastern brook. The lake has a public access and resort facilities. It is reached by driving 9 miles SE from Northport to Spirit, then 2 miles NE to lake. Elevation of Deep is 2025 feet, and it covers 210 acres.

DEER LAKE. There is a great variety of fish in this large (1163 acre) and deep (maximum 75 feet) lake, including rainbow, kokanee, eastern brook, large and smallmouth bass, perch, crappie, pumpkinseed, catfish and lake trout. Planted with rainbow regularly and offers fair fishing throughout most of the season. There are several resorts offering full facilities plus public access area. Deer is reached by driving 3 miles N. of community of Loon Lake on Hwy. 395, then 1.5 miles E. to lake.

DOUGLAS LAKE. A 4 acre pond situated N. of Colville. Drainage is into Mill Creek. A road heads N. from Hwy. 294 about .05 miles from Colville's E. limits for 3.5 miles to within a short distance of Douglas. Seldom stocked because of winter kills.

ELBOW LAKE (Crown). Eastern brook are available in Elbow. It is 14 acres and lies at 2775 feet in headwaters of Crown Creek's W. Fork. Route is across Columbia on Hwy. 25 N. from Northport .05 miles, then N. and W. up Big Sheep Creek, turning W. up American Fork of Big Sheep to shore of lake. Total distance is approximately 12 miles. This road continues W. another 9 miles to **PIERRE LAKE**.

FRANKLIN D. ROOSEVELT LAKE. This is the largest lake in the state, 79,000 acres, and was created by Grand Coulee Dam on Columbia River 28 miles NE of Coulee City. The reservoir stretches 151 miles to B.C. border through a relatively remote and mountainous region. FDR Lake contains what is probably the widest variety of freshwater fish to be found in the state in one lake. Species include cutthroat, rainbow, eastern brook, Dolly Varden, Rocky Mountain whitefish, lake whitefish, kokanee, Kamloops, sturgeon, large and smallmouth bass, crappie, perch, sunfish, walleyes, carp, suckers, tench, shiners, chub, etc. Best fishing is at mouths of countless inlets along both shores of huge reservoir. The 660 miles of lake shore and 35 recreational areas in Coulee Dam RA administrated by national park service. All recreational areas may be reached by boat. Facilities include campgrounds, boat launch sites and dock. Reception center for the recreational areas is at the W. end of Coulee Dam where maps are available.

HATCH LAKE. Located SE of Colville, Hatch holds rainbow and is 34 acres. Public access. Elevation of the lake is 2141 feet. **LITTLE HATCH LAKE** is a private lake which covers 14 acres. It lies 500 feet W. of Hatch. It contains eastern brook. To reach the lakes, drive E. from Colville for 5 miles on Hwy. 294, then turn S. for 1 mile on county road which runs between the lakes.

HUNTERS CREEK. Heading on W. slope of Huckleberry Mtn., the creek flows W. for 11 miles to join **FDR LAKE** 1.5 miles W. of community of Hunters. The creek holds rainbow and is best in summer months. Road from Hunters on Hwy. 25 leads upstream for 5 miles, then on up S. Fork for about another 8 miles.

JUMPOFF JOE LAKE. A producer of planted rainbow, brown trout plus eastern brook. Largemouth bass, bluegill, pumpkinseed and yellow perch present. Jumpoff Joe lies in a timbered region at 2031 feet elevation. There is a resort in addition to a public access on lake. Route is 7.5 miles S. of Chewelah on Hwy. 395, then W. and S. for 1.5 miles to the lake's E. shore.

KEOUGH LAKES: Two lakes of 13.6 and 4.8 acres, separated by a narrow strip of land, which have received eastern brook and rainbow plants. Lakes are surrounded by marshy area. Location is 4.5 miles SE from Colville with drainage to Prouty Creek to Little Pend Oreille River.

KETTLE RIVER. The stream forms boundary between Stevens and Ferry Counties. It enters U.S. at Laurier and flows S. approximately 25 miles to join **FDR LAKE** 3 miles S. of Boyds in Ferry County. Stevens County roads follow river for about 12 miles, but easiest access is from Hwy. 395 in Ferry County, as the highway parallels entire length on W. bank. Fish present include rainbow, brown trout and whitefish. Best fishing in summer and fall. Whitefish best in winter.

LITTLE PEND OREILLE LAKES. A series of lakes which lie adjacent to Hwy. 20 about 23 miles E. and N. of Colville. Lakes include Sherry (26 acres), the lowest in the chain, then Gillette (48 acres), Thomas (163 acres), Heritage, (71 acres), all in Stevens County. Leo and Frater, the two top lakes, are in Pend Oreille County. All lakes have received plants of cutthroat, and they deliver good, but somewhat spotty, fishing. Fall is often an excellent time for fly fishermen. There are resorts on Gillette, Heritage, and Thomas, and FS camp-

LAKE ROOSEVELT delivers large rainbow as Terry Sheely can testify.

grounds at Gillette, Thomas and Leo Lakes. FS boat launch sites are located on Leo and Gillette Lakes. Elevation of lakes is 3160 feet.

LITTLE PEND OREILLE RIVER. A stream of approximately 25 miles in length that drains the string of Little Pend Oreille Lakes. It flows into Colville River at Arden, 6 miles S. of Colville on Hwy. 395. Eastern brook and rainbow furnish fair to good angling from May through September. Lower section, which holds browns, may be fished by heading E. on a county road upstream from Arden. Hwy. 294 from Colville E. and N. to Middleport touches and follows upper 10 miles of stream to source.

LONG LAKE. A 14 acre lake located 8 miles SE from Colville. Has received brown trout and smallmouth bass plants. No defined inlet or outlet.

LOON LAKE. Plants of rainbow, lake trout and eastern brook join populations of small and largemouth bass, perch, crappie, pumpkinseed and brown bullhead and kokanee in Loon to provide excellent fishing throughout the season in the 1119 acre lake. Loon usually delivers kokanee, starting in May. Several resorts and a public access are located on lake which lies at 2381 feet elevation 28 miles N. of Spokane via Hwy. 395 which runs along lake's E. shore.

McCOY LAKE. The 36 acre lake holds brookies, and is controlled by the Spokane Indian tribe. It is located at 1644 feet elevation. Road from Fruitland on Hwy. 25 leads S. about 8 miles to lake, passing Newbell and Mudgett Lakes enroute.

McDOWELL LAKE. Rainbow planted lake of 33 acres at 2325 feet located 11.5 miles SE from Coville in a marshy area. Lake drains to Little Pend Oreille River.

MILL CREEK. A tributary of Colville River, joining that stream 2 miles NW of Colville. Mill provides fair to good fishing for rainbow and eastern brook. Road leads N. and NE from E. limits of Colville to meet and follow creek. The S., Middle and N. Forks of Mill Creek come together at Three Forks, approximately 8 miles upstream from Colville. The road up S. Fork continues over ridge to drop into **LITTLE PEND OREILLE LAKES** group on Hwy. 294, a distance of about 10 miles.

MUDGETT LAKE. There is a public access on Mudgett, a 32 acre lake located 2 plus miles S. of Fruitland and adjacent to the W. side of old highway leading S. from Fruitland. The lake carries planted rainbow.

PHELAN LAKE. An eastern brook lake of 18 acres, Phelan lies at 2375 feet elevation It drains via Bruce Creek into Colville River. Route is SE from Bossburg on Hwy. 25 about 5 miles, then N. up Bruce Creek 6 miles to lake. Tough access.

PHILLIPS LAKE. A 1.3 acre eastern brook and rainbow pond located 2 miles SE from Bailey Lake. It drains to Colville River.

PEPOON LAKE. Eastern brook and rain-

STARVATION LAKE is good fly fishing water.

bow have been stocked in this 11 acre lake. Location is 5.5 miles W. from Northport in headwaters of Rattlesnake Creek at 2450 feet. Drainage to **FDR LAKE**.

PIERRE LAKE. Cutthroat to 5 pounds have been taken in this beautiful lake of 106 acres, but most are 8-14 inches. It also produces a few sizeable eastern brook, kokanee, brown bullhead, black crappie and largemouth bass. Plants of eastern brook, rainbow and cutthroat aid lake. It lies at 2012 feet elevation in the headwaters of Toulou Creek. Road leaves Hwy. 395 at Barstow, crosses the Kettle and heads N. 9 miles to lake, passing **LITTLE PIERRE LAKE** enroute. There is a FS campground on Big Pierre. Drainage to Kettle River.

POTTER LAKE. Rainbow inhabit Potter's 3.9 acres. Location is 3.5 miles N. from Colville at 2420 feet. Drainage to Colville River.

RIGHLY LAKE. A 6.8 acre marshy lake at 2531 feet 2.5 miles W. from Echo on Echo Mtn. Planted with rainbow, it drains to **FDR LAKE**.

ROCKY LAKE. The lake covers 20 acres and holds planted rainbow. DNR camp and launch sites. Route to lake is S. for 3.5 miles on county road at SE city limits of Colville.

SHEEP CREEK. A rainbow planted stream tributary to Colville River, joining that river about 5 miles S. of Valley. Hwy. 231 and 292 S. from Colville River Junction provide access at various points.

SUMMIT LAKE. Eastern brook lake of 6.9 acres at 2600 feet 7.4 miles NE from Orient. It lies 2.7 miles S. from U.S.—B.C. border. Drainage to Kettle River.

TWIN LAKES. (Spruce). The Twins cover 26.8 acres and are located 12 miles E. from Colville. The cutthroat planted lakes drain to Little Pend Oreille River.

TURTLE LAKES. Lakes of 8.9 and 1.7 acres on Spokane Indian reservation located 4.5 miles NW from Wellpinit on Wellipinit-Hunters road. Have been rainbow planted in past years.

STARVATION LAKE. Rainbow are the attraction in this 28 acre lake. It is located 9 miles E. of Colville on Hwy. 294, then S. .05 miles to lake. There is a public access on lake. Elevation is 2375 feet. Top fly fishing.

WAITTS LAKE. Waitts is a rich 455 acre lake where trout attain excellent growth, with fish of 3 to 5 pounds not uncommon. Good perch and largemouth bass fishing. It has been stocked with brown trout and rainbow. There are several resorts and a public access on lake. It is reached by driving 4 miles W. from community of Valley located on Hwy. 395.

WILLIAMS LAKE. Plants of rainbow are made in Williams. The lake is 38 acres and lies at 1980 feet elevation 16.5 miles N. of Colville. Route is 4 miles N. up FDR Lake, then looping S. on a county road 3 miles to NE shore.

STEVENS COUNTY RESORTS

Black Lake: Carney's, Colville, WA 99114. 509-684-2093.

Deep Lake: Wilderness West Resort, Colville, WA 99114. 509-732-4263. Deep Lake Resort, Aladdin Star Rt., Colville, WA 99114. 509-732-4202.

Deer Lake: Pearl-Ray Beach, Loon Lake, WA 99148. 509-233-2166. Sunrise Point Resort, Loon Lake, WA 99148. 509-233-2342. Styman's Resort, Loon Lake, WA 99148. 509-233-2233. Haney's Resort, Loon Lake, WA 99148. 233-2370.

Jump Off Joe Lake: Jump Off Joe Resort, Valley, WA 99181. 509-937-2133.

Little Pend Orellle Lakes: Beaver Lodge, (Gillette Lake), Colville, WA 99114. 684-4995. Lake Thomas Resort, Colville, WA 99114. 509-684-4817. Heritage Lake Resort, Colville, WA 99114. 509-684-2751.

Loon Lake: Granite Point Park, Loon Lake, WA 99148. 2509-33-2100. Robbin's Cottages, Loon Lake, WA 99148. 509-233-2130. Shore Acres Resort, Loon Lake, WA 99148. 2509-33-2474.

Waitts Lake: Silver Beach Resort, Valley, WA 99181. 509-937-2811. Waitts Lake Resort, Valley, WA 99181. 509-937-2400. Winona Beach Resort, Valley, WA 99181. 509-937-2231.

THURSTON

COUNTY

All of Thurston county's 100-odd lakes are classified as lowland lakes, being below 2500 feet elevation. Thurston covers 761 square miles and is the 32nd largest county in the state. Highest point is about 3000 feet. The county is drained by the Nisqually River, which forms boundary with Pierce County, and by the Deschutes, Skookumchuck and Black Rivers. The Deschutes is a good cutthroat and rainbow stream, while the Nisqually and the Skookumchuck carry winter steelhead, sea-run cutthroat and salmon. Nisqually also has summer steelhead. Black River produces sea-run cutthroat and bass.

ALDER LAKE. (See Pierce County).

BALD HILLS LAKE. Species of fish in this 45 acre lake include bass, perch and catfish. It is located 11.5 miles SE of Yelm and 1 mile E. of Clear Lake. Park and boat launch site at S. end of lake. Head from Yelm through Four Corners and continue 2 miles to fork. Take left fork for about 3 miles, then S. at forks for 3 miles past **CLEAR LAKE** and watch for signs.

BARNES LAKE. A 14 acre lake located 3 miles S. of Olympia. It contains large-

mouth bass and drains to Percival Creek.

BASS LAKE. Yellow perch and largemouth bass are found in this 6.6 acre lake in Bald Hills region. Nisqually River drainage.

BIGELOW LAKE. Yellow perch and largemouth bass are available in this 13.8 acre lake located 2 miles NE from Olympia. It drains to Budd Inlet.

BLACK LAKE. There is good spiny ray fishing in Black, including largemouth bass, black crappie, pumpkinseed, yellow perch and brown bullhead. It is a 576 acre lake which lies 4 miles SW of Olympia. Other species of fish include cutthroat and rainbow. There are resort facilities and a public access which is located on SE shore. Black drains out of both ends, with N. outlet dropping into Capitol Lake via Black Lake Ditch and Percival Creeks, and S. outlet flowing into Black River. Route to lake is W. 0.5 miles on Hwy. 101 from the Tumwater Junction on Hwy. 1-5, and then S. 1.5 miles to N. end of lake on Black Lake Blvd.

BLACK LAKE DITCH CREEK. A cutthroat planted stream flowing out of N. end of Black Lake and joining Percival Creek before entering Capitol Lake.

BLACK RIVER. Another outlet of Black Lake, this one flows SW about 20 miles to enter Chehalis River E. of Oakville. The upper 5 miles of river is swampy. Hwy. 801 from Little Rock follows river downstream for several miles. Boating is most effective

Thurston County

TOM SENN poised to teeter back on a Deep Lake trout.

way to fish the brushy, slow-moving river. May and June and again in fall are good periods for native sea-run cutthroat and rainbow, while bass take during summer months. There is some fall sea-run cutthroat action. Boats may be launched downstream from Littlerock and at the Rochester-Oakville Hwy. 12 bridge crossing.

CAPITOL LAKE. A 306 acre lake located in city of Olympia formed by a dam at mouth of Deschutes River. Contains steelhead, sea-run cutthroat and jack and adult salmon in fall months, as well as some rainbow and spiny rays. Easy access.

CHAMBERS LAKE. Open year around. Chambers offers cutthroat, bass, perch. crappie and catfish. The 72 acre lake has a public access on NW shore. It is situated 3 miles SE of Olympia. County road leads 1 mile S. from Hwy. 510 at Lacey to lake. **LITTLE CHAMBERS LAKE**, 49 acres, is the E. segment of Chambers. Fish species include largemouth bass and yellow perch.

CLEAR LAKE. (Bald Hills). A popular and productive rainbow lake with some eastern brook and brown trout. The lake covers 173 acres and is located SE of Yelm. Route is SW from Yelm through Four Corners and Smith Prairie 11 miles to SW tip of lake. Resort facilities and a F&W department public access area on lake.

COOPERS POTHOLE. Located 700 feet E. from Lake St. Clair, this 4.9 acre pond has largemouth bass.

DEEP LAKE. (Deep Drake). Planted rainbow furnish good fishing from April into July at Deep, a 66 acre lake located 9.5 miles S. of Olympia on Hwy. 185, then a short distance E. to lake. Watch for signs at Hwy. 121 turnoff. Spiny rays present include largemouth bass and bluegill. Millersylvania state park on lake's shore offers campsites, boat launch area and trailer hook-ups. There is a resort.

DESCHUTES RIVER. Headwaters of Deschutes are in Lewis Country, and the river flows approximately 35 miles NW across Thurston County to enter Olympia's Capitol Lake at head of Budd Inlet. May and June are best fishing months for this popular stream. There are a few steelhead and salmon, and the stream receives plants of sea-run cutthroat. The Deschutes is crossed by roads at numerous points, and a road SE from Olympia's airport roughly parallels river to Hwy. 507 about 2 miles SW of Rainier. County and logging roads continue SE up river into Lewis County. There is a Weyerhaeuser day park on the river 3 miles E. of Tenino on Hwy. 507.

EATON CREEK. A trout stream that gets

a "fair" rating in May and June. Eaton is a tributary of **ST CLAIR LAKE** and is reached by driving E. of Tumwater up Evergreen Valley road.

ELBOW LAKE. Spiny rays including bass, crappie, perch and catfish are the attraction in this 36 acre lake. It is situated 3500 feet NE of Clear Lake and has a state park and boat launch site at its NW end. See **CLEAR LAKE** for route.

FIFTEEN LAKE. Largemouth bass are found in this 4.2 acre lake. It is situated 1.5 miles SE from Rainier. Drainage to Deschutes River.

GEHRKE LAKE. Located 1.4 miles E. from Rainier. Contains largemouth bass. It drains to Deschutes River and covers 8 acres.

GRASS LAKE. A marshy lake of 120 acres which contains largemouth bass, yellow perch, black crappie and brown bullhead. Location is 2 miles W. from Olympia. It drains to Budd Inlet.

HEWITT LAKE. A 26 acre lake which lies in a deep bowl 2 miles SE of Tumwater. The lake holds rainbow and spiny rays, including bass and perch. Private residences ring lake, making access difficult.

HICKS LAKE. Planted with rainbow, cutthroat and brown trout, the lake covers 171 acres and has a public access. There are rock bass, largemouth bass, pumpkinseed, warmouth and yellow perch in the lake. It is located about 2 miles E. of Lacey on Hwy. 510, then S. for 1.5 miles to lake. Drainage is to **PATTERSON LAKE.**

KENNEDY CREEK. Heading on W. slope of Rocky Candy Mtn., Kennedy flows NW past the W. tip of **SUMMIT LAKE** to enter Mason County at Kennedy Falls. The creek provides fair cutthroat and steelhead fishing. Hwy. 101 crosses the creek and a road follows it for about 2 miles.

LAWRENCE LAKE. One of the county's top rainbow lakes, Lawrence is stocked with rainbow and brown trout. It covers 339 acres and drains into Deschutes River. The lake has a public access area, and provides good fishing from April into July. It is situated 6 miles S. of Yelm and 6 miles SE of Rainier. Road from Yelm leads E. to Four Corners. Turn right on Vail Loop road and follow signs to lake.

NISQUALLY RIVER reluctantly gave up this steelhead for Stan Jones.

LOIS LAKE. A 2.5 acre lake which receives rainbow plants. Location is N. from Lacey on N. side of Hwy. 99. Drainage to Henderson Inlet.

LONG LAKE. Actually 2 lakes joined by a narrow neck, Long encompasses 311 acres and lies 5.5 miles E. of Olympia. It is about 2 miles long. Fish species include brown trout, eastern brook, rainbow, largemouth bass, rock bass, black crappie, warmouth, pumpkinseed and yellow perch. Public access. Long is reached by turning S. from Hwy. 510 about 1.5 miles E. of Lacey, passing **HICKS LAKE** to W. shore of Long.

McINTOSH LAKE. A narrow, 1.4 mile long lake of 116 acres which lies adjacent to the N. side of Hwy. 507 about 3 miles E. of Tenino. McIntosh is planted with rainbow and produces trout of excellent quality. There is a public access on N. shore. April and May provide best fishing.

McLAIN'S CREEK. A small creek of approximately 4 miles in length which heads W. of Black Lake and flows N. into end of Mud Bay 3 miles W. of Olympia. A road leads S. from Hwy. 8 up creek. McLain's produces sea-run cutthroat in spring and fall.

MUNN LAKE. A rainbow planted lake of 29.8 acres located 4 miles S. from Olympia, Drainage to Deschutes River. Bluegill and largemouth bass are present.

OFFUT LAKE. There are some husky rainbow in this 192 acre lake. It is planted regularly with legal 'bows. There are perch, brown bullhead and largemouth bass in Offut which has both resort and public access facilities. The lake is reached by driving 3 miles S. of Olympia airport on Tumwater Tenino road, then turning 1 mile E. on Waldrick road to lake shore.

PATTERSON LAKE. In addition to spiny rays, Patterson holds some lunker rainbow. It is planted with brown trout and rainbow. There are also perch, crappie, rock bass, bluegill and largemouth bass in the 257 acre lake. Patterson has a public access. and is located 6 miles SE from Olympia. Route to the lake is Hwy. 510 to Lacey, then 3 miles SE to lake from center of town.

PURCIVAL CREEK. A tributary of Capitol Lake which holds rainbow, sea-run cutthroat and steelhead. **PURCIVAL LAKE,** 22 acres, is located at creek's mouth and connects with Capitol Lake. It is used as a salmon raising pond. Leave Hwy. 101 a short distance W. of Olympia on Mottman road and drive S. for .05 miles to creek. Stream may also be fished upstream from mouth.

REICHEL LAKE. Largemouth bass are in this 9 acre lake which is situated 3.4 miles E. from Vail. Drainage to Deschutes River.

SCOTT LAKE. Planted cutthroat, perch, largemouth bass and brown bullhead are found in Scott. It covers 67 acres and lies 9 miles S. of Olympia. Turn E. from Hwy. 1-5 about 6 miles S. of Tumwater and drive approximately 1 mile to lake shore. Access is limited.

SIMMONS LAKE. (Ken). The lake covers 24.6 acres and contains largemouth bass and yellow perch. Location is 2 miles W. from Olympia in marshy area. It drains to Budd Inlet.

SKOOKUMCHUCK RIVER. Headwaters of the river are on W. slope of Porcupine Ridge in SE Thurston County. The river flows W. and S. for about 20 miles before entering Lewis County near Bucoda. Upper reaches deliver cutthroat from May into July, with some late winter steelhead taken in late March and even at stream opening in May. Hwy. 507 runs S. from Tenino 2 miles to Prairie and then a county road leads E. to follow Skookumchuck upstream, while Hwy. 507 continues S. down-

UPPER SKOOKUMCHUCK River is cutthroat water.

stream. The river gets plants of steelhead and sea-run cutthroat. It is a Chehalis River tributary, entering that river at Centralia. Dam on upper river forms a large lake with no access.

SMITH LAKE. A 17.7 acre lake containing yellow perch and largemouth bass. Location is 4 miles SE from Olympia with drainage to Deschutes River.

SOUTHWICK LAKE. This 37.1 acre lake has been planted with cutthroat and also hosts largemouth bass and brown bullhead. Location is 5 miles SE from Olympia and 3300 feet from N. end of Patterson Lake to which it drains.

SPRINGER LAKE. Brown bullhead and largemouth bass are present in Springer's 5.5 acres. It is located 2.5 miles W. from Offutt Lake and drains to Deschutes River.

TRAILS END LAKE. Channel catfish have been stocked in this 12.8 acre lake. Location is 4 miles S. from Olympia and 600 feet S. of **MUNN LAKE**. It drains to Dechutes River.

ST. CLAIR LAKE. This 245 acre lake is a maze of countless inlets. It is deep in spots, up to 110 feet, and is reported to contain a few mackinaw along with planted rainbow and kokanee. Other species of fish include cutthroat, rock bass, largemouth bass, white crappie, pumpkinseed, warmouth and yellow perch. Some large rainbow are taken each year. There are 2 public access areas on St. Clair. Hwy. 510 runs close to N. tip of lake 7 miles E. of Lacey.

SUMMIT LAKE. Contains some large rainbow and cutthroat plus kokanee of moderate size and largemouth bass, yellow perch and brown bullhead. The lake is 110 feet deep in places, and covers 522 acres. It usually provides good fishing later in the season. There is a public boat launch site on SW shore of lake. Turn NW from Hwy. 8 about 11 miles W. of Tumwater Junction, and drive 1.5 miles to lake which is circled by a county road. Turnoff from highway is signed.

SUSAN LAKE. A 3.5 acre lake located 700 feet from N. end of **MUNN LAKE**. It holds largemouth bass.

TROSPER LAKE. Cutthroat have been stocked in this 17 acre lake. Largemouth

bass, yellow perch and brown bullhead are also present. Trosper is located 3.5 miles S. from Olympia. Drainage to Budd Inlet.

WADDLE CREEK. Cutthroat are present in Waddle during May and June. The creek flows into Black River near town of Little Rock on Hwy. 121. A county road from Little Rock leads NW up creek for about 5 miles.

WARD LAKE. There is a public access on Ward. It contains 'bows, largemouth bass and kokanee, with best fishing periods in April, May and June. Kokanee are most cooperative from mid-May on. The lake is 67 acres and is located S. of Olympia in a deep depression. Road from Tumwater SE to Rainier passes within .04 miles of lake about 1.5 miles E. of Tumwater. A county road skirts W. shore.

THURSTON COUNTY RESORTS

Black Lake: Salmon Shores RV Park, Olympia, WA 98501. 360-357-8618. Black Lake RV Park, Olympia, WA 98501. 360-357-6775. Columbus Park, Olympia, WA 98501. 360-786-9460.

Clear Lake: Clear Lake Resort, Yelm, WA 98597. 360-894-2543.

Deep Lake: Deep Lake Resort, Rt. 4, Box 259, Olympia, WA 98502. 360-352-7388.

Harts Lake: Harts Lake Resort, Yelm, WA 98597. 360-458-7093.

Offut Lake: Offut Lake Resort, Tenino, WA 98589. 360-264-3438.

Basic rules of back country travel

 Never go alone. Travel only in daylight. Know how and use map and compass. Keep close together. Leave a trip schedule. Wear adequate clothing. Know your area boundaries and weather forecast. Carry emergency overnight gear.

Did you know?

The dragonfly nymph, as an underwater insect, has been known to eat mosquito wrigglers at the rate of 20 per minute.

WAHKIAKUM

COUNTY

Lake fishing in Wahkiakum County is minimal. One lake, unnamed, of a single acre is the only water listed for this 269 square mile county. Wahkiakum ranks 37th in size in the state. Highest point is 2673 feet. The Southwest Washington County adjoins the lower Columbia River on its S. side, with Cowlitz County to the E., and Pacific County to the W. and most of the N. border. Besides the Columbia, the Elochoman and Grays Rivers provide most fishing action. All these streams carry steelhead, salmon and sea-run cutthroat.

BROOKS SLOUGH. Approximately 2 miles long, Brooks Slough is fed by Alger and Risk Creeks and is adjacent to the S. side of Hwy. 4. Mouth of slough is at town of Skamokawa where Skamokawa Creek joins it from the N. at the Columbia River. Brooks is bridged at its mouth and the county road doubles back to parallel slough's S. bank. Brooks offers largemouth bass, perch, crappie and bluegill fishing during summer months. The slough may be fished from shore. Boat launch and fishing areas adjacent to Hwy. 4 about 1 mile E. of Skamokawa.

COLUMBIA RIVER BARS. The most

ELOCHOMAN RIVER is a fine steelhead producer.

popular bars (river) in the county are located at Sunny Sands on Puget Island, and County Line Bar between Cowlitz and Wahkiakum Counties. June and July are best steelheading months, while jack salmon fishing perks during May and September. Silver and chinook salmon are taken in July, August and September, while cutthroat provide action from July to October. Boats may be launched into Columbia River at Abernathy Creek, Weyerhaeuser Bar and at mouth of Brooks

Wahkiakum County

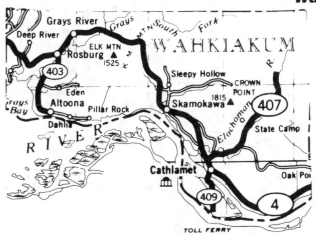

COLUMBIA RIVER bar fishing is a casual affair.

Slough. Ilwaco, at mouth of Columbia River, is base for sturgeon and salmon charters working the lower river.

DEEP RIVER. The river enters Grays Bay at mouth of Columbia River 16 miles W. of Skamokawa on Hwy. 4. A county road leads upstream from highway, 3.5 miles and then into Pacific County. Deep River was named for its considerable depth. It may be boated for 3 or more miles upstream from its mouth. The lower 5 miles is a deep tidal slough. Crappie, bass, catfish, cutthroat and perch are principal fish in the short-run river of approximately 8 miles with salmon and steelhead available in limited numbers.

ELOCHOMAN RIVER. An excellent winter steelhead stream which receives plants. It turns out steelhead from December into March. The river heads in Cowlitz County and flows SW about 15 miles in Wahkiakum County before joining Columbia River 2 miles NW of Cathlamet. Hwy. 407 closely parallels Elochoman for approximately 10 miles upstream from its mouth. Sea-run cutthroat and salmon are found in the river during fall months. The Elochoman receives cutthroat plants, and is good for cutts in October and November.

GRAYS RIVER. Another Columbia River

tributary that produces good to excellent steelhead angling. It receives plants of winter steelhead and comes on in December and in January, and then again with a surge of bright fish in March. Hwy. 4 touches the river at community of Grays River. Hwy. 403 leaves Hwy. 4 about 3 miles from river's mouth to lead SW down Gray's E. bank. Cutthroat and salmon are taken in lower reaches in fall months, and during some years smelt enter stream in the spring. Boat launch site at Rosburg Grange.

SKAMOKAWA CREEK. The creek is crossed at its mouth by Hwy. 4 at community of Skamokawa 8 miles NW of Cathlamet. A county road follows creek upstream for 4 miles. Lower reaches of Skamokawa provide crappie and bass, while upper stretches produce limited numbers of winter steelhead plus fall cutthroat. Best steelhead and cutthroat fishing is from mouth to forks. Tributaries include Wilson, Pollard and Falk Creeks.

Did you know?

The "walking catfish," a native of Southeast Asia, can remain dormant in summer, hibernate in winter and walk over land.

Walla Walla

COUNTY

There are no natural lakes in Walla Walla County. Most fishing opportunities come in the Snake, Touchet and Walla Walla Rivers. The county covers 1299 square miles and is the 26th largest in the state. Highest point is Lewis Peak at 4880 feet. Walla Walla County is bordered on the NW and N. by the Snake River and Franklin County, and on the E. by Columbia County. The W. border is the Columbia river and Benton county, and the S. portion looks into Oregon.

BURBANK SLOUGH. A 700 acre elbow shaped slough formed by backwaters of McNary Dam located near Burbank. It contains largemouth bass and bluegill.

CASEY POND. A 60 acre lake on McNary W.R.A. 4.5 miles SE of Burbank. It carries both large and smallmouth bass plus crappie, perch, sunfish and bullhead catfish.

COPPEI CREEK. Native and stocked rainbow provide action early in season. The stream heads in the Blue Mtns. and flows NW about 14 miles to enter Touchet River at Waitsburg. Hwy. 12 follows Coppei 3 miles S. from Waitsburg, then a county road parallels creek another 9 miles SE to its headwaters.

CURLEW POND. Located on McNary game range about 5.4 miles SE from Burbank. Fish species include largemouth bass and bluegill. Drainage to **WALLULA LAKE**.

DRY CREEK. Another good early season producer of planted and native rainbow. The creek joins Walla Walla River 4 miles E. of Touchet. A county road leads from Hwy. 12 at the mouth NE upstream for approximately 16 miles to cross Hwy. 12 at Dixie and continues another 5 miles to headwaters in the Blue Mtns.

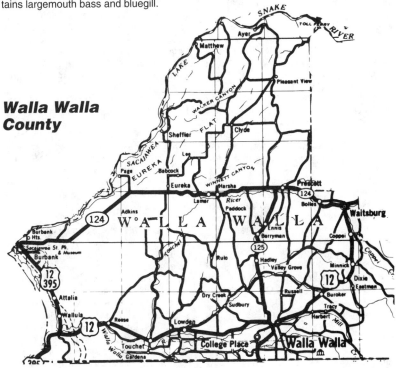

Walla Walla County

FISH HOOK POND. Formed by seepage from Ice Harbor Pool, the pond is about 2 acres and contains rainbow. It is situated E. of Burbank between Fish Hook Park and Ice Harbor Dam on S. side of R.R. tracks.

GARRISON CREEK. Rainbow and eastern brook are taken from Garrison, with May the best fishing month. The creek flows into Walla Walla River. Access is a problem as the stream, a diversion of Mill Creek, runs through backyards, etc. It is primarily a kid's fishing creek.

McNARY POOL. (Lake Wallula). Fluctuations in water levels influence fishing in these waters. Normally from spring on spiny rays including large and smallmouth bass, crappie, perch, sunfish and bullhead catfish are taken in good numbers. Best fishing areas are pumping plant above Hwy. 12 bridge on Snake River, Casey Pond-Burbank area, and Walla Walla River estuary. Boats may be launched at S. end of Hwy. 12 bridge on Snake River, at Casey Pond, "2 Rivers Area", and at mouth of Walla Walla River. McNary Pool is the name given water backed up by McNary Dam on Columbia River. It extends from dam at Umatilla, Oregon to Richland, Washington.

MILL CREEK. Heading high in the Blue Mtns. in Columbia County, Mill Creek loops SW into Oregon, then NW again into Walla Walla County. It enters Walla Walla River 3 miles W. of College Place. Roads follow stream for virtually its entire length. Upper stretches are reached by leaving Hwy. 12 at Eastgate scale house and driving E. and S. 13 miles into Oregon where the road ends. Upper portions of the creek are in the City of Walla Walla's watershed and are closed to entry except by permit. A trail continues upstream. Mill Creek is good throughout season except during spring months when it is often out of shape from excessive snow melt. Plants of legal rainbow help Mill Creek, and there are also Dolly Varden, native rainbow, whitefish and summer steelhead.

MILL CREEK RESERVOIR. An artificial lake of 52 acres created by a U.S. Corps of Engineers' dam on Mill Creek approximately 3 miles W. of Walla Walla. Rainbow planted. Deepening of reservoir has enhanced both rainbow and warm water species fishing.

MUD CREEK. Rated "poor" the rainbow

TOUCHET RIVER is a Walla Walla River tributary.

stream flows into Walla Walla River. Some angling is available from mouth upstream.

QUARRY LAKE. A 9 acre rainbow pond situated on the McNary W.R.A. It has a public access area and gets the nod for good May and June angling. The game range is reached by driving 5 miles SE of Burbank on Hwy. 12. Current fishing conditions may be obtained from recreation headquarters located in Burbank. Turn right to lake at public access sign.

SACAJAWEA LAKE. A 32 mile long reservoir on Snake River formed by Ice Harbor Dam. Half of pool acreage is in Franklin County. Contains a wide variety of fish including large and smallmouth bass, black crappie, white crappie, bluegill, yellow perch and channel catfish.

SNAKE RIVER. A major river which forms the N. and W. boundary of Walla Walla County. It joins Columbia at Burbank, across Snake from Pasco. Ice Harbor Dam blocks river 8 miles upstream from Lake Sacajawea on Snake River and forms Lake Sacajawea which extends 32 miles upstream to base of Lower Monumental Dam. Species of fish found in Snake include summer steelhead, spring and fall chinook, channel catfish, crappie, perch, sunfish, bullhead catfish, large and smallmouth bass and sturgeon. Best fishing period for the various species is as follows: Steelhead, August to end of October; chinook, April through September; channel catfish, March to October; sturgeon, March through September; largemouth bass, May through September; smallmouth bass, March through October. Top fishing areas on Snake include down stream from Ice Harbor Dam to mouth for all species. Steelheading is best at Ayer, Field's Gulch and Lyon's Ferry, Page, Levey, "25 mile", Walker's Pit, Burr Canyon and most inlets on Ice Harbor Reservoir are best for all species of spiny rays. Good smallmouth bass fishing at Burbank Heights, pumping plant, Ayer, Field's Gulch and Lyon's Ferry. Boats may be launched at Burbank, immediately above Ice Harbor Dam, Page, Walker Pit, Ayer and Lyon's Ferry.

SPRING CREEK. May and June are best for rainbow in this Walla Walla River tributary. Route to creek is W. from Walla Walla to Lowden, turning left about 1 mile E. of Lowden and continuing to point road crosses creek. Fishing is marginal.

TOUCHET RIVER. German brown trout are present in this beautiful stream. Besides the browns, which are most plentiful in vicinity of Waitsburg, the river holds stocked rainbow, steelhead and Dolly Varden, plus a few whitefish. Top fishing period is May through October. The 'bows are planted above town of Dayton. The Touchet flows W. from Dayton in Columbia County, entering Walla Walla County at Waitsburg, then turns S. to join Walla Walla River at town of Touchet. Good roads follow stream in the county, providing convenient access.

WALLA WALLA RIVER. A medium-size stream which heads in Oregon and flows NW into Walla Walla County 3 miles S. of College Place, and then W. to **WALLULA LAK**E adjacent to the Columbia River at Wallula Junction. It has spiny rays and steelhead. Bass fishing is good in lower reaches during March. Channel catfish from 10" to 20 pounds are taken during late spring. There is steelheading from December into March.

YELLOW HAWK CREEK. Planted with rainbow, Yellow Hawk is a diversion of Mill Creek which branches from that stream 2 miles E. of Walla Walla and flows SW 10

miles to its junction with the Walla Walla River. Access is difficult in some stretches. It offers best angling in April, May and June.

Several small ponds in Walla Walla County get regular plants of rainbow. They include Bennington, College Place and Jefferson Park.

In strange lakes, locate fish by trolling

Trolling is the most effective way to locate concentrations of fish in strange lakes. (If you don't have a state of the art fish finder, that is). By fishing mouths of creeks, coves, spring areas, near weed beds or other fishy looking spots, anglers can find the fish, then devote attention to the hot spot, either by continuing to troll, or by anchoring for a still fishing session.

Almost any light rod may be adopted to trolling. Fly rods in seven or eight foot lengths or spin rods work fine. Mimimum of 100 yards of of six or eight pound test monofilment line should be spooled on fly, casting or spin reels. This weight line is best for light lures, flies or trolls, but heavier line might be necessary if bulky gang trolls are used.

Recommended essentials for back country travel

Lug soled boots for firm footing; easy on-easy off clothing suitable for wind, rain or cold; a rucksack or belt pack to carry the equipment necessary to sustain life: waterproofed matches; candle or fire starter; extra food, extra clothes; first aid kit; compass and topographical map; knife; 20' light rope; folding saw; flashlight; and a light plastic tarp for emergency shelter. The essentials, if properly chosen, will weigh very little.

Did you know?

The pocket gopher spends most of its life in the dark, but needs no light since it has an excellent sounding system. Its whiskers and tail serve as sensitive feelers to keep it from bumping into underground walls.

WHATCOM
COUNTY

The north border of Whatcom County is adjacent to British Columbia. The 2180 square mile county is 11th in relative size in the state and contains approximately 240 lakes. Of this number, about 150 are situated above 2500 feet elevation. The Nooksack and Skagit River systems drain most of the county. There are two large reservoirs on the upper Skagit River— Diablo and Ross—which provide good to excellent trout fishing, particularly in late summer and fall.

ANN LAKE. Eastern brook and rainbow inhabit this high mountain lake (4700 feet elevation) of 6 acres. Leave Mt. Baker Hwy. at Austin Pass and hike 4 miles on Ann Lake trail to lake. Cutts planted.

ATHEARNS PONDS. A series of "permanent" beaver ponds holding eastern brook. The ponds are located adjacent to Nooksack River's S. Fork about 4 miles SE of Saxon, and cover about 5 acres.

BACON CREEK. Heading in Green and Berdeen Lakes, Bacon flows S. into Skagit County and into Skagit River at Bacon Creek siding 5 miles NE of Marblemount. A road extends upstream for about 5 miles, with a rough trail continuing upstream. A few summer steelhead are taken from Bacon, along with cutthroat, rainbow and the odd Dolly Varden.

BAGLEY LAKES. A pair of lakes of 9 and 11 acres which lie at 4200 feet within 1000 to 4000 feet SW of Mt. Baker Lodge. The lakes hold eastern brook and cutthroat. Austin Pass picnic area is located just above the lakes.

BAKER LAKE. An artificial lake of 5000 acres (10 miles long) formed by a Puget Sound Power & Light Co. dam on the Baker River. The lake hosts a variety of fish including rainbow, kokanee, cutthroat, whitefish and Dolly Varden. There is a resort on the lake's NW shore, plus Horseshoe, Cove, Panorama Point and Maple Grove Creek FS campgrounds. A PSP&L campground and boat launch site is located at S. end. Several spur roads, 6 or more, run down to lake's shore from W. side road which parallels entire lake. Route is N. from Concrete 17 miles to lower end of Baker. Best fishing in the big lake comes during May, June, September and October. The dam has eliminated bulk of the river's steelhead run.

BAKER RIVER. (Upper). The river heads on W. slope of Mt. Challenger, flowing SW about 12 miles to enter upper end of **BAKER LAKE.** A road extends 1 mile from the NE end of lake and a trail continues upstream 5 miles. During late summer and early fall months the upper river provides fly-fishing for rainbow.

BARRETT CREEK. A short-run creek, less than 1 mile in length, that drains **BARRETT LAKE** into Nooksack River 1 mile SE of Ferndale. There is spring and fall cutthroat fishing in the creek.

BARRETT LAKE. Cutthroat are present in this 40 acre lake, along with largemouth bass. It is situated 1 mile E. of Ferndale, with a road leading to lake. Inlets are Tenmile and Deer Creeks. May is top month.

BERTRAND CREEK. May and June are best months for Bertrand's rainbow and cutthroat. The creek is reached by driving SW from Lynden down N. bank of the Nooksack River 4 miles where Bertrand enters Nooksack.

BLUE LAKE. A 13 acre lake situated 7 miles N. of Concrete at 4000 feet elevation. Blue holds cutthroat, eastern brook, brown trout and rainbow, and drains via Bear Creek into **SHANNON LAKE**. Drive N. from Concrete 7 miles to diversion dam on Rocky Creek, then W. for 7 miles to Blue Lake road, then S. for 4 miles to Blue Lake—Dock Butte trail, then 1 mile hike to lake.

BLUM LAKES. Group of 4 lakes located 18.5 miles NE from Concrete, ranging from 1.5 to 145 acres. Stocked with rainbow. Drainage to Baker River. Elevations from 4950 to 5900 feet.

CAIN LAKE. April, May and June are best months for Cain's planted rainbow, plus cutthroat, kokanee, largemouth bass and yellow perch. The lake has a public access on its SW shore and is reached by road 2 miles S. of the SW tip of **WHATCOM LAKE** at South Bay.

CALIFORNIA CREEK. Sea-run cutthroat furnish fair fishing during spring and fall in this creek. It is 6 miles long and flows into Drayton Harbor at Blaine. Hwy. 5 parallels the stream's E. bank and several county roads cross it. Best fishing is in stretch near its mouth.

CAMP CREEK BEAVER PONDS. These shallow ponds are reported barren. They are located near Skookum Creek which joins Nooksack's S. Fork near Saxon.

CANYON CREEK. A tributary of Nooksack River which holds Dolly Varden, eastern brook and rainbow, offering best fishing after snow run-off from mid-June into fall. Canyon Creek road leaves Mt. Baker Hwy. just beyond Douglas Fir campground and parallels Canyon Creek from about the 4 mile point to the 13 mile point. Road forks at 14 mile point. Left fork leads to **DAMFINO LAKES** trail. No fish reported. From end of right fork it is possible to travel cross-country uphill to **BEARPAW MT.LAKES**. (Church Lakes). They are at 4450 and 5150 feet and have had cutthroat plants.

CANYON LAKE. Rated "good" for cutthroat in May and June. The lake covers 45 acres and is situated at 2250 feet elevation. Road from Deming leads NE along Nooksack River's Middle Fork on N. side for 4 miles to Canyon Creek, then E. up creek to within 1 mile of lake. A trail continues to Canyon Lake.

CEDAR LAKE. A cutthroat-planted, 4 acre lake situated on NE slope of Chuckanut Mtn. Road from S. Bellingham through Chuckanut Village leads to a trail to lake. Most productive period at Cedar is April and May.

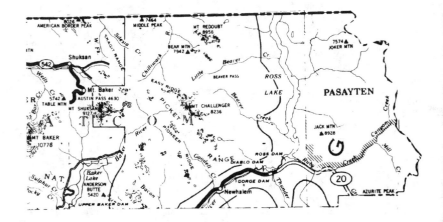

NORTH END of Baker Lake at Baker Lake Resort.

CHAIN LAKES. (Galena). Four small lakes which lie 2 miles W. of Mt. Baker Lodge at 4800 feet elevation. The lakes are Arbuthnot (5 acres), Hayes (13 acres), Mazama (1 acre), and Iceberg (36 acres). Most contain rainbow and eastern brook. Trail takes off at end of Mt. Baker Hwy. at Artist Point and continues 2 miles to lakes. They offer best fishing in late summer and fall. Drainage is to N. Fork Nooksack River.

CLEARWATER CREEK. Months of July, August and September are best for this mountain stream which flows into Nooksack River's Middle Fork 7 miles S. of community of Kulshan located 3 miles E. of Deming. Rainbow and cutthroat are present in creek. A road leads about 2.5 miles NE up Clearwater from the Nooksack (Middle Fork) road.

COPPER LAKE. Rainbow stocked lake of 8 acres situated 11.4 miles E. from Shuksan and 1.8 miles SE from Copper Mtn. at 5250 feet. Drainage to Chilliwack River.

DAKOTA CREEK. A small stream, 9 miles in length, which heads SE of Blaine and flows NW into Drayton Harbor. Hwy. 5 crosses Dakota at its mouth and county roads provide easy access upstream.

Spring and fall are top periods for the creek's sea-run cutthroat. There are a few steelhead taken in December, January and February.

DIABLO LAKE. Formed by a City of Seattle dam on upper Skagit River, Diablo is 4.5 miles long and covers 910 acres. It extends to foot of Ross Lake Dam. The big reservoir starts yielding rainbow, Dolly Varden and cutthroat in April, with excellent fishing in the fall. It is planted with rainbow. Tributaries include Riprap, Sourdough, Happy, Thunder and Colonial Creeks, plus the Skagit River. Boats may be launched near mouth of Colonial Creek where a bridge spans Thunder Arm, the S. inlet of Diablo. A national park campground is located near this point. Highway up Skagit River continues past Newhalem 7 miles, then crosses **GORGE LAKE** and heads SE on North Cascades Hwy. then continues E. over Cascade Crest and drops into Okanogan County.

DIOBSUD LAKES. Three rainbow lakes of 2, 2.5 and 3.5 acres 9.5 miles NW from Marblemount in headwaters of Diobsud Creek. Elevations are 4075 to 4490 feet. They drain to Skagit River.

ELBOW LAKE. A 5 acre lake at 3400 feet

elevation located 6.5 miles SW of summit of Mt. Baker on Sister Divide. There are cutthroat and rainbow in lake. Route is up Baker River road to Rocky Creek road, and up this road to its end on Nooksack's S. Fork. Logging road extends within .05 miles of lake. **DOREEN LAKE** is situated 400 feet S. of Elbow. It holds rainbow. **WISMAN LAKE** lies at 4250 feet and 1 mile W. of Elbow. It covers 18 acres and contains eastern brook, rainbow and cutthroat.

FAZON LAKE (Treecies). A 32 acre lake located in a boggy area 1.5 miles NW of Goshen. Public access on S. shore. Fish species include rainbow, bluegill, large-mouth bass and channel catfish. Road from Goshen leads to S. shore of lake.

FERGUSON PONDS. There are about 10 acres included in this group of ponds situated near Saxon Bridge on the S. Fork of Nooksack River. The ponds hold both cut-throat and rainbow.

FISHTRAP CREEK. Rated "fair" for rainbow in May, with cutthroat best in fall months. The stream flows through town of Lynden, entering Nooksack about 3.5 miles SW of town. Several roads cross the creek providing easy access.

FOUNTAIN LAKE. A 14 acre lake located 3 miles SE of Lynden with drainage to Nooksack River. Route is S. from Lynden 2 miles, then 1 mile E. to lake which contains catfish and bass. Best fishing comes in mid-summer.

FRAGRANCE LAKE. (Lost, Gates). The 6 acre lake lies on W. side of Chuckanut Mtn. It is stocked with cutthroat and is located in Larrabee State Park. Top angling is during April and May. Road up the mountain passes within 0.4 miles of lake. There is a good trail. **LOST LAKE**, a 12 acre rainbow lake lies 2400 feet E. of Fragrance Lake. Road past Fragrance leads to lake.

GOAT LAKE. (Mud). Cutthroat are present in this 4 acre pond which lies 1 mile from W. end of Samish Lake. Drainage is to Samish River. Access to lake is by logging road near Luther wood camp.

GOODELL CREEK. July and August are premium fishing months for this stream's cutthroat, eastern brook and rainbow. It joins Skagit River at Newhalem. A road leads N. up creek for 2.5 miles along E. bank. Goodell Creek campground is located at creek's mouth.

GORGE LAKE. An impoundment on upper Skagit River formed by Gorge Dam. It is about 4 miles long and is paralleled by highway to foot of Diablo Dam. The North Cascades Hwy. bridges Gorge. Fish species include rainbow and Dolly Varden. Boats may be launched near head of reservoir near town of Diablo.

GRANITE CREEK. The Cascade Crest trail follows Granite Creek from its source near Rainy Pass in Skagit County. The North Cascades Hwy. parallels Granite Creek from its mouth nearly to its source. Late summer and fall fishing is best for Granite's rainbow and cutthroat.

GREEN LAKE. An 80 acre lake located at 4300 feet elevation 11.5 miles N. of Marblemount. It has both cutthroat and rainbow. Best route is up Noisy Creek from Baker Lake to trail end, then cross county 7 miles. In North Cascades Nat. Park.

GREEN LAKE. (McLeod). Perch and brown bullhead are present in this 19 acre lake which is situated 4 miles SE of Lynden. May and June are fishiest months. Highway runs along lake's N. shore.

HIGHWOOD LAKE. A 2 acre rainbow pond located 1500 feet E. from Mt. Baker Lodge

DIABLO DAM on Skagit River forms Diablo Lake.

at 4100 feet. Drainage to N. Fork Nooksack River.

HOZOMEEN LAKE. An excellent eastern brook lake of 111 acres at 2800 feet elevation. Location is about 3 miles E. of head of Ross Lake. Trail from Hozomeen Camp leads approximately 4 miles to lake. (See Ross lake for route).

HUTCHINSON CREEK. Plants of rainbow boost this tributary to Nooksack River's S. Fork. It hits the river 1 mile SE of Acme. Road from Hwy. 9 at Acme meets and follows Hutchinson Creek for 2 miles about 2 miles E. of Acme. May and June are most productive months for stream's eastern brook and 'bows.

JERRY LAKE: Lower lake, number one in group of four Jerry Lakes, covers 30 acres and lies at 5900 feet. It has been planted with rainbow. Location is 7 miles E. from Ross Dam and 1.5 miles N. from Crater Mtn. Drainage to Ross Lake.

JOHNSON CREEK. Heading in B.C. Johnson flows S. through Clearbrook and enters Nooksack River near Everson. It receives rainbow plants.

JOHNSON CREEK. This Sumas River tributary usually starts producing well at season opener in May. It contains cutthroat, eastern brook and rainbow with lower 2 miles the best fishing.

JORGENSON LAKE. A 12 acre lake in marshy area 6 miles SE from Deming. It holds brown bullhead. Drainage to N. Fork Nooksack River.

JUDSON LAKE. (Boundary). A 112 acre lake which holds largemouth bass and black crappie located on the U.S.-Canada border 8 miles NE from Lynden. Sumas River drainage.

KENDALL LAKE. Cutthroat and eastern brook are the attraction in Kendall. It drains via Kendall Creek to Nooksack's N. Fork, and is 12 acres. Location is 1.4 miles N. of Kendall. It dries up occasionally.

LITTLE CANYON CREEK. Outlet of Canyon Lake which flows 3.5 miles W. to join Middle Fork of Nooksack at Kulshan. The creek holds Dolly Varden and cutthroat. A road parallels Canyon Creek from Kulshan about 2 miles upstream.

LOST LAKE. A spiny ray lake of 3 acres which lies 0.4 miles NW of Bellingham airport in a marshy area. Poor fishing.

MAIDEN LAKE. Rainbow are present in this 17 acre lake at 3900 feet elevation. Location is 18.7 miles N. from Concrete with drainage to **BAKER LAKE.**

MARTEN LAKE. Cutthroat have been reported in Marten, a 5 acre lake located 24 miles N. of Concrete at 3650 feet elevation. Road from Boulder Creek campground on W. shore of **BAKER LAKE**e leads N. for 5 miles. Then it's cross country 1.5 miles NW to the lake.

MIRROR LAKE. This 14 acre rainbow lake produces best in spring months. It is situated 0.5 miles NW of Wickersham and gets regular plants. Drainage is into **WHATCOM LAKE.** Best in April and May.

MOSQUITO LAKE. Channel catfish and brown bullhead are found in this 7 acre lake. It is located 5.7 miles SE from Deming. Drainage to N. Fork Nooksack River.

MUD LAKE. Small pond holding black crappie, yellow perch and brown bullhead. It lies .08 miles SE from Deming and drains to Nooksack River.

NOISY CREEK. July and August are the months to fish this stream's cutthroat and rainbow. It is a tributary to **BAKER LAKE** and is reached by driving to head of lake and crossing lake by boat.

NOOKSACK RIVER. (Main River). The North, Middle and South Forks of the Nooksack come together about 1 mile SE of Deming to form the main river. It flows NW 15 miles to Lynden, then SW another 15 miles to enter Bellingham Bay near Marietta. Roads follow river within striking range along its 30 mile length. There are steelhead and rainbow in main river, but Indian netting at the mouth has severely curtailed sport steelhead fishing. Early summer through fall months are fair to good for sea-run cutthroat and some Dolly Varden. A few salmon are taken at this time. The Nooksack is snow-fed and is often milky in spring and periods of hot weather. Long finned smelt enter the lower river with best dipping in November and December below Ferndale.

NOOKSACK RIVER. (North Fork). Late

VENCE MALERNEE tries the Nooksack River.

summer is best fishing because of clouded water earlier in year. This fork heads under glaciers on Mt. Shuksan's N. flank. It is closely followed by Hwy. 542 which leads to Mt. Baker N. and E. of Deming for over 25 miles. Falls at mouth of Wells Creek, 6.5 miles E. of Glacier, block migratory fish. Upper reaches contain rainbow, eastern brook, Dolly Varden and a few cutthroat.

NOOKSACK RIVER. (Middle Fork). This stream flows 20 miles W. and N. from S. side of Mt. Baker to join N. Fork 3 miles E. of Deming. Route is N. from Mt. Baker Hwy. on Mosquito Lake road at Welcome to junction of road 38 at Porter Creek. There are rainbow, Dolly Varden, cutthroat, salmon and steelhead in the river with best fishing in fall months.

NOOKSACK RIVER. (South Fork). The S. Fork enters main river 1 mile SE of Deming. It produces steelhead in winter, and cutthroat and rainbow in summer and fall. Hwy. 542 heads S. along stream for 6 miles, offering easy access. Upper stretch of S. Fork is in Skagit County and is reached by road NE from Hamilton Junction, about 16 miles up Jones Creek to Soundview logging camp, then E. up the stream. (See Skagit county).

PADDEN LAKE. A 152 acre lake located on S. outskirts of Bellingham. Old Hwy. 99 runs along the lake's E. shore. Padden contains kokanee. 'bows and a few cutthroat. Bellingham city park on lake. Padden Creek drains lake into Bellingham Bay.

PINE LAKE. A 6 acre lake which lies at 1570 feet elevation 5 miles S. of Bellingham and 800 feet SE from Cedar Lake. The lake contains eastern brook, cutthroat and rainbow. April, May and June are months to work Pine.

RACEHORSE CREEK. Limited cutthroat fishing is available in this tributary of the Nooksack River's N. Fork, which enters that stream from the E. about 6 miles NE of Deming. A road from Kulshan leads 3 miles up N. Fork to mouth of Racehorse, then E. for 1 mile upstream.

ROCKY CREEK. Baker Lake Hwy. crosses Rocky Creek 10 miles N. of Concrete. Road to W. parallels creek for about 6 miles. Road E. to **SHANNON LAKE** is rough. Late summer fishing is best for the stream's rainbow and cutthroat.

ROSS LAKE. An artificial reservoir of

11,678 acres stretching nearly 24 miles N. from Ross Dam on the Skagit River into British Columbia. Ross usually opens end of June and produces well at opener, slowing in mid-summer, and then comes on strong in fall. The lake holds large rainbow and large Dolly Varden, plus cutthroat, eastern brook and cutthroat. It is strictly a boat fishing show. Mouths of numerous inlets, including Pierce, Big Beaver, Skymo, Noname, Arctic, Little Beaver, Silver, Howlett, Hozomeen, Lightning, Dry, Devils, May Roland and Ruby Creeks are top fishing spots. Some of these tributaries are closed near mouths. Road to the lake from Canada leaves the highway 1.5 miles W. of Hope, B.C., and heads S. along Silver Creek about 40 miles to head of Ross Lake on B.C.-U.S. border at Hozomeen guard station. The road ends about 2 miles inside U.S. line, passing Hozomeen campground where small boats may be launched. Route from Whatcom County is up Hwy. 20 past Newhalem 7 miles, then across Gorge Lake bridge on North Cascades Hwy. to Milepost 134 where a trail leads 0.5 miles to lake and a phone connected with the resort. The highway also affords access to the lake at mouth of Ruby Creek near Panther Creek turnoff. A trail from this point leads .05 miles to Ross

Lake's S. tip, elevation 1600 feet. There are resort facilities including rental boats and cabins here. Campgrounds staggered along the lake's shore at mouths of Roland, May, Lightning and Little Beaver Creeks, plus unimproved campsites at other points. Trails from lake lead up Ruby, Big Beaver, Lightning, Little Beaver, Silver and Hozomeen Creeks. These streams, in legal fishing areas, provide good rainbow angling.

SAMISH LAKE. Not much fishing action in this 814 acre lake until kokanee start hitting in May. With warming water, the lake's spiny rays, largemouth bass and black crappie, cooperate. Samish also holds rainbow and some large cutthroat. Fall fishing is often excellent. There are resorts and a public access on the lake which is located 6.5 miles SE of Bellingham. Hwy. 1-5 parallels Samish Lake's E. shore.

SAMISH RIVER. (See Skagit county).

SHUKSAN LAKE. A 28 acre lake situated at 3700 feet elevation at head of Lake Creek. Road from Concrete leads 24 miles N. and E. up W. side of **BAKER LAKE** to Shannon Creek campground. Take FS road 1160 to end, then head N. cross coun-

ROSS LAKE backs up into British Columbia.

try 2 miles to lake which holds small eastern brook.

SILVER LAKE. (Fish). A good producer of rainbow in the 8-10 inch range, with some cutthroat to 18 inches. The lake covers 173 acres and is located 3 miles N. of Maple Falls at head of Maple Creek.. It has a public access and a county park. Best fishing at Silver comes early and again in the fall. Road from Maple Falls leads N. to lake shore.

SKAGIT RIVER. (Upper). Only 10 miles of the Skagit River is in Whatcom County with the 4.5 mile long **GORGE LAKE** included in this stretch. The Skagit heads in Canada and is blocked by Ross and Diablo Dams, plus Gorge Dam, with lakes behind each dam. A good road from Marblemount in Skagit County follows river upstream along its W. bank to base of Diablo Dam. Species of fish in the Whatcom section of the big river include rainbow, Dolly Varden, cutthroat, steelhead, salmon and whitefish. Productive fishing period is from May to October.

SKOOKUM CREEK. A tributary of Nooksack River's S. Fork rated fair for cutthroat and eastern brook in May and June. Skookum enters S. Fork 3 miles SE of Saxon. A road from Saxon bridge across Nooksack leads up Skookum Creek NE about 2.5 miles.

SQUALICUM LAKE. Cutthroat are present in this 33 acre lake which is located NE of Bellingham. Route is 6.5 miles on Mt. Baker Hwy. then S. .04 miles to lake. The lake drains into Squalicum Creek. Walk-in access from N. side.

SUMAS RIVER. Heading on W. slope of Sumas Mtn., the river flows N. through Nooksack and Sumas into British Columbia. Cutthroat are taken in May and June and again in fall. Plants of rainbow make the river a fine prospect at opening. Roads provide easy access along much of the rain-fed stream.

SWIFT CREEK. July and August are best fishing months for this stream's cutthroat and rainbow. Most productive secion is lower 2 miles. Swift Creek is a tributary to Baker River and is reached by driving up Baker Lake road.

TENNANT LAKE. A marshy lake of 43

GOLDEN TROUT have been stocked in Middle Thornton Lake

acres located 1 mile SE from Ferndale. It contains largemouth bass. Drainage to Bellingham Bay.

TENMILE CREEK. The small stream heads in a swampy region between Goshen and Wahl and flows W. about 10 miles to enter **BARRETT LAKE** and then out of the lake into Nooksack River 1 mile NE of Ferndale. Early season cutthroat fishing is often good. County roads grid the area the creek passes through so access is not difficult, although creek is brushy.

TERRELL LAKE. Located on the lake Terrell W.R.A. Take Ferndale exit from 1-5, drive 3.3 miles past Ferndale to Lake Terrell road. The lake's acreage varies from 400 to 500 acres. There is a public access. The lake holds brown bullhead, perch, largemouth bass, and cutthroat. Best fishing is during April, May, June and September. It drains into Terrell Creek.

THORNTON LAKES. Golden trout have been stocked in (Middle) Thornton lake which covers 11 acres and lies at 4680 feet. Location is 3.8 miles W. from Newhalem. All three Thornton Lakes drain to Skagit River.

THUNDER CREEK. A tributary of Diablo Lake which joins S. tip of the lake's Thunder Arm. The creek holds rainbow, Dolly Varden and cutthroat, and provides fishing from May to October. Route is via the North Cascade Hwy. which crosses the

Skagit E. of Gorge Dam and continues E. and S. to bridge Thunder Arm. Trail continues 1 mile SE to mouth of Thunder Creek and then upstream 4 miles to Middle Cabin shelter in Skagit County.

THUNDER LAKE. An 8 acre lake which lies adjacent to the North Cascade Hwy., .05 miles NW of the Thunder Arm bridge across Diablo Lake. The lake holds cutthroat.

TOAD LAKE. (Emerald). A rainbow lake of 30 acres that usually holds up from opening day into July. There is a public access on Toad. Route is N. from N. end of Lake Whatcom 1 mile on Toad Lake road to the SW tip of lake.

TOMYHOI LAKE. An 82 acre eastern brook lake which lies .05 miles inside U.S.-B.C. border at 3700 feet elevation. Drainage is N. into Canada's Chilliwack River. Tomyhoi offers best fishing from mid-July into fall. It is reached by turning N. at Shuksan on Mt. Baker Hwy. and driving N. up Swamp Creek about 3 miles where trail to Tomyhoi leaves road and heads N. over Gold Run Pass 4 miles to lake.

WANLICK CREEK. Rated good for cutthroat and rainbow in July and August. The creek is a tributary to Nooksack River's S. Fork. Route is up Baker Lake road to Rocky Creek bridge, then W. on Loomis-Nooksack road for about 10 miles.

WELLS CREEK. This small glacial stream offers good eastern brook fishing when cool weather slows snow melt. It joins Nooksack River's N. Fork 6 miles E. of Glacier just below Nooksack River Falls.

WHATCOM CREEK. Outlet of Whatcom Lake which flows from N. end of lake through Bellingham to Bellingham Bay. The creek carries rainbow and cutthroat and delivers best fishing in the spring. Some winter steelhead. It is planted.

WHATCOM LAKE. A lake of over 500 acres located at eastern city limits of Bellingham. Whatcom contains lunker cutthroat plus large numbers of kokanee. There are also rainbow, large and smallmouth bass and yellow perch in the lake, and a few mackinaw are reported to be present in its deep (340 feet) waters. Best fishing time for cutts is May to October, while kokanee fishing is good in May, June,

September and October. A public access area is situated on the lake's S. shore, and several resorts and city park offer full facilities. Lake waters are used by Bellingham for domestic purposes.

WISER LAKE. Hwy. 539 splits this 123 acre, spiny ray lake. It is located 8 miles N. of Bellingham. In addition to largemouth bass, perch and brown bullhead, Wiser holds a few rainbow, cutthroat and crappie. May and June are most productive months for anglers. There is a public access on N. shore. Drainage is via Wiser Lake Creek into Nooksack River.

WHATCOM COUNTY RESORTS

Baker Lake: Baker Lake Resort, Box 450, Concrete. WA 98237. 360-853-8325.

Ross Lake: Ross Lake Resort, Rockport, WA 98283. 360-386-4437.

Whatcom Lake: Sudden Valley Resort, Bellingham, WA 98225. 360-34-6430.

Take care of boots and waders like this

Fisherman who are concerned about care of their hip boots or waders, might well pay heed to the suggestions of manufacturers. The experts say:

1. Be sure you have a proper fit. Pull your waders up tightly with elastic suspenders. This will avoid snagging and chaffing.

2. After use always hang boot and waders inside out to dry. Never leave rubberized garments in your car trunk or on the floor of your car. Direct sun and intense heat are extremely harmful to rubber coatings.

3. To store boots and waders between seasons place them in air tight plastic bags, making positive they are completely dry. Never store in extreme cold or heat.

Did you know?

A n individual female of some dragonfly species lays up to 100,000 eggs, and there are 412 species in North America.

Whitman

COUNTY

Ten of Whitman County's 140 odd lakes lie above 2500 feet. The county covers 2179 square miles and is the 12th largest in the state. Despite the number of lakes in Whitman, there is little lake fishing. Most of the lakes are small and many are dry during summer. Rock Lake is the exception. Highest point in the county is Tekoa Mountain at 4006 feet. The Snake River, which forms the S. border of Whitman, and the Palouse River provide most of the county's stream fishing.

ALKALI FLAT CREEK. A small rainbow stream which offers limited angling in April and May. It enters the Snake River at Riparia, and roads follow the creek NE upstream for about 35 miles.

COTTONWOOD CREEK. The creek heads S. of Steptoe Butte and flows W. to join Rock Creek SW of Ewan. It has a few rainbow.

LOWER GRANITE DAM RESERVOIR. A 9000 acre reservoir formed by Lower Granite Dam on Snake River. The pool is 39 miles long. Large variety of fish including large and smallmouth bass, black crappie, white crappie, bluegill, yellow perch and channel catfish.

MILLER LAKE. This 25 acre lake is located 3.5 miles N. of Ewan at the N. end of Rock Lake. Road from Ewan leads to the lake shore. No plants.

NIGGER CREEK. The creek flows from Spokane county S. into Whitman, entering the N. tip of Rock Lake. It contains a few rainbow.

PALOUSE RIVER. (Lower). The river forms boundary between SW Whitman County and Franklin and Adams Counties,

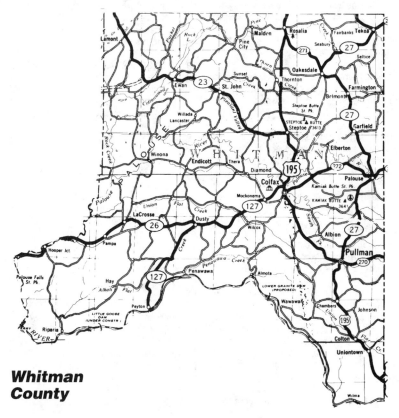

Whitman County

ROCK LAKE is an enlargement of Rock Creek. (Charlie Powell Photo)

then swings E. and S. to Colfax where the N. and S. Forks come together. Best period is during summer months. Some channel catfish and smallmouth bass are taken below Palouse Falls.

PAMPA POND. (LaCrosse). A 3 acre pond which is planted with rainbow. It is located 4 miles W. of LaCrosse between the R.R. track and highway.

PENAWAWA CREEK. Rated "fair" for rainbow in May. The creek is a tributary of Snake River, with mouth at Penawawa, 10 miles W. of Almota. It is reached and fished by driving up Penawawa Canyon where the road follows the creek. Limited fishing.

ROCK LAKE. Primarily a spiny ray lake—largemouth bass and black crappie—with planted rainbow and German browns. Rock covers 2147 acres and is located 1 mile N. of Ewan. There is public access area at S. end. Rock Lake is an enlargement of Rock Creek and stretches nearly 8 miles. Towering basalt cliffs hem the lake. Best fishing time is May and June, and again in September and October. Water conditions vary due to run-off from farms in area. Lake is subject to muddy conditions.

SILVER CREEK. A limited producer of rain-

bow, Silver flows into Palouse River's N. Fork at Elberton. It heads in Idaho 10 miles NE of Elberton, and roads from that community provide easy access.

UNION CREEK. A tributary of Palouse River entering that stream 5 miles W. of LaCrosse. May and June are the best months for Union Creek's rainbow. Roads parallel stream for most of its length.

WILLOW CREEK. Heading approximately 8 miles E. of LaCrosse, Willow flows W. 17 miles to its junction with Palouse River on Whitman-Adams County line. It hosts a few rainbow. Several small Whitman County ponds receive regular rainbow plants. They include Garfield, Gilerest and Alkali. Riparia Pond has been stocked with brown trout in addition to rainbow.

Who needs a scale?

If your wife won't allow you to weigh your big steelhead on the baby's scales, don't argue about it—just reach for a yardstick.

Figure four pounds for the first 24 inches, then one pound per inch after that. This is pretty accurate up to 30 inches for a winter steelhead.

YAKIMA

COUNTY

Bordered by the Cascade Mountains on the W., Yakima County covers 4286 square miles and is the 2nd largest county In the state. It contains over 300 lakes, with about 180 of them over 2500 feet el-

evation. Highest point in the county is Mt. Adams at 12,307 feet. Yakima County is drained by the Yakima, Tieton, Naches and Klickitat Rivers. Permanent water courses are stocked each summer with trout and provides some fine fishing. Mountain lakes in the county often are excellent for trout from mid-summer into fall. Irrigation reservoirs support kokanee, ling and trout, but are subject to periodic draw-downs. Whitefish are found in most water courses and some reservoirs.

AHTANUM CREEK. Fair fishing in both N. and S. Forks for 8-9 inch rainbow in May and June. Small cutthroat in top sections. Turn W. at Union Gap on lower Ahtanum road which follows creek. Campground and cabins at Soda Springs about 35 miles upstream from Union Gap. **FOUNDATION**

Yakima County

CREEK joins Ahtanum near Soda Springs and provides angling for small cutthroat.

AMERICAN RIVER. Furnishes fair fishing during mid-summer months for cutthroat, eastern brook and whitefish. The American joins Bumping River at the Bumping Lake road on the Naches Hwy. 32 miles NW of Naches. Cabins and camping sites located along river. American River drains **DEWEY LAKES** which are reached by Cascade Crest trail 2 miles S. of Chinook Pass. The lakes contain eastern brook.

ART LAKE. A rainbow lake of 2.1 acres situated at 5230 feet 4.7 miles NE from White Pass. Drainage is to Rimrock Lake.

ASPEN LAKE. An urban artificial pond created along Naches River drainage near 16th Ave. in Yakima. Contains pumpkinseed, largemoth bass and channel catfish.

BACHELOR CREEK. Located S. of Yakima city limits along lower Antanum road near airport. Holds rainbow and is best in April and May.

BARTON CREEK BEAVER PONDS. Se-

ries of ponds situated near E. end of Bumping Lake which provide August and September fishing for both rainbow and eastern brook depending upon water levels.

BASIN LAKE. Cutthroat have been stocked in this 4.6 acre lake which lies at head of N. Fork Union Creek at 5820 feet 6.7 miles NE from Chinook Pass. It drains to American River.

BEAR LAKE. Located at head of Oak Creek and accessible by car in late May. Produces rainbow of 8-10 inches and eastern brook with early summer months best. Lynne Lake adjoins Bear.

BENCH LAKE. An 18.4 acre lake at 4850 feet hosting rainbow and eastern brook and located 11.2 miles NW from Glenwood and 5.2 miles SE from Mt. Adams summit. Campsites on lake. Best access is from Trout Lake heading N. on Hwy. 141 then follow Bird Creek Meadow signs or check with Mt. Adams ranger station in Trout Lake for map and directions. Lake not accessible until late July or early August because of snow. Drainage to Klickitat River.

BERGLUND LAKE. A 14 acre lake containing largemouth bass, black crappie and pumpkinseed along with a few rainbow. Located within city limits of Yakima at confluence of Yakima and Naches Rivers. Questionable access.

BIRD LAKE. Rainbow and eastern brook are present in this 6 acre lake at 5575 feet located 11 miles NW from Glendale and 4.8 miles SE from Mt. Adams summit. See Bench Lake for route. Drainage to Klickitat River.

BLANKENSHIP LAKES. Group of 3 lakes at 5230 feet in Mosquito Valley about 6.4 miles NE from White Pass. The cutthroat lakes range in size from 4.1 to 9.6 acres. They drain to Rimrock Lake.

BLUE LAKE. Rainbow are the attraction in this 3.5 acre lake at 6200 feet. It is located 7.8 miles SW from Tieton Dam on Rimrock Lake and 2000 feet SW from Blue Slide lookout. Drainage to S. Fork Tieton River.

BRIDGEMAN POND. Black crappie and brown bullhead are present in this 6 acre pond on Sunnyside Game Range 2.5 miles N. from Mabton.

AMERICAN RIVER campground.

BYRON PONDS. Two ponds totaling 50 acres on Sunnyside Game Range. They hold largemouth bass and pumpkinseed. Drainage to Yakima River.

BUMPING LAKE. A 1310 acre lake formed by dam on Bumping River. Impounded water is used for irrigation, and lake is sometimes pulled down to about 600 acres. Leave Naches Hwy. at American River junction and follow Bumping River for 12 miles. Lake is at 3426 foot elevation and usually cannot be reached until mid-May. Kokanee in 7-9 inch range start hitting around June 1 and rainbow of 8-11 inches are taken from mid-June through fall. Also produces occasional native cutthroat, Dolly Varden and whitefish. Public access and developed campsites along E. end of the lake. Rental boats available.

BUMPING RIVER. Feeds Bumping Lake and then continues about 14 miles to join American River at American Forks on Naches Hwy. Good road parallels the river to Bumping Lake. Developed FS campground at American Forks, Cedar Springs, Soda Springs and Cougar Flat along road to lake. Heavily fished for 8-9 inch planted rainbow in late June and July.

CLEAR CREEK. Outlet of Dog and Leach Lakes that feeds Clear Lake. Take road S. at W. end of Rimrock Lake from White Pass Hwy. to N. end of Clear Lake where a road follows the creek for 2 miles. Eastern brook in adjoining beaver ponds. Four developed FS campgrounds adjacent to Clear Lake.

CLEAR LAKE. Public boat launch site on E. shore of this popular lake located 1 mile W. of Rimrock Lake. Contains rainbow in the 8-12 inch bracket. Developed campground. Clear is a 265 acre irrigation reservoir formed by dam on the N. Fork of Tieton River. Elevation is 3615 feet and location is 5.7 miles east of White Pass. Lake has been restored and stablilized, although vulnerable to drainage for irrigation purposes.

CONRAD LAKES: (Long Creek Lakes). Two small cutthroat stocked ponds of 1 and 1.2 acres situated at 5290 feet 8.5 miles S. from Clear Lake dam. They drain to S. Fork Tieton River.

COUGAR LAKES. Situated at head of Cougar Creek. Drive up E. side of Bumping Lake, holding right to end of road. Trail crosses upper Bumping River near junction of Cougar Creek and continues past **SWAMP LAKE** (3 miles) another 2 miles. It hosts rainbow and eastern brook. **LITTLE COUGAR** is 13 acres. **SWAMP LAKE** also holds rainbow and brookies.

COWICHE CREEK. Road from Cowiche follows creek for 15 miles. Produces rainbow and cutthroat. Early season fishing best.

CRAMER LAKE. Strike trail No. 1106 on SW shore of Dog Lake at Dog Lake campground 2 miles E. of White Pass and continue approximately 3.2 miles to lake. Planted with rainbow. Cramer is 19 acres and is located at 5025 feet elevation. One-half mile NW is **DUMBBELL LAKE** which is in Lewis County. There are a large number of small lakes in this area. Many of them contain rainbow or cutthroat.

DEVILS WASHBASIN LAKE. A cutthroat lake of 1.9 acres located at 6268 feet 8.2 miles S. from White Pass. It drains to N. Fork Tieton River.

DOG LAKE. Located a short 2 miles E. of White Pass summit on N. side of highway. Fair for 7-10 inch rainbow and brookies by early June. Improved FS campground. Lake is 60 acres and lies at 4207 feet elevation. About 1000 feet downstream from outlet is a 100 foot sheer-drop falls.

ELTON LAKE. (North and South). A 14 acre lake located E. of 1-82, 6 miles N. of Yakima. Rainbow, brown bullhead, perch, whitefish and largemouth bass present. Public access. No public access to South Eaton Lake.

FENNER LAKE. A cutthroat lake of 3.1 acre at 5460 feet located about 3 miles SW from Raven Roost lookout. It drains to Naches River.

FISH LAKE. A 10 acre lake situated just E. of Carlton Pass. Elevation is 4114 feet. Approximately a 7 mile hike from end of road at SW end of Bumping Lake up Bumping River. Contains brookies. **CRAG LAKES** lie about 1 mile N. of Fish.

FREEWAY LAKE. (Rotary). A 23 acre rainbow and brown trout lake best in spring and fall. It also contains largemouth bass and pumpkinseed. Located 1 mile N. of city of Yakima. Hike of .04 miles from public parking area.

FLATIRON LAKE. Rainbow inhabit this 7 acre lake located 1.6 miles SW from Little Bald Mtn. lookout at 5700 feet. It drains to Bumping Lake.

GIFFIN LAKE: A 104.8 acre lake located on Sunnyside Game Range 2.8 miles NW from Mabton. It has received rainbow

BENCH LAKE, at 4850 feet, holds rainbow and brook trout. (Harold E. Dexter Photo)

plants and also holds largemouth bass, black crappie, pumpkinseed and brown bullhead. Drainage to Yakima River.

GREEN LAKE. Situated at 5900 feet elevation, this 4.5 acre rainbow lake lies 7.4 miles S. from Tieton Dam at Rimrock Lake and 1.4 miles E. from Blue Slide lookout. Drainage to Yakima River.

GRAHAM-MORRIS POND. Gravel pits near Toppenish containing largemouth bass, bluegill, yellow perch, pumpkinseed and black crappie.

GRANGER LAKE. Small pond at town of Granger containing rainbow, bass, bluegill and catfish.

HELL LAKE. Cutthroat are available in this 3.4 acre lake at 5414 feet elevation 1.4 miles SE from White Pass. Drainage to N. Fork Tieton River.

HORSESHOE POND. Largemouth bass, black crappie and yellow perch are found in Horseshoe's 59 acres. Location is about 4 miles NW from Mabton adjacent to N. side of Yakima River.

I-82 PONDS. Seven small man-made ponds located along highway between Union Gap and Zillah. Ponds 1 (15 acres) and 2 (25.5 acres), located between Wellis and Donald roads support largemouth bass, yellow perch and pumpkinseed. Pond 2 stocked with rainbow. Pond 3 (19 acres) situated E. of Donald road holds bluegill, largemouth bass, yellow perch and pumpkinseed. To the E., Ponds 4 (29.5 acres) and 5 (27 acres) have largemouth bass, black crappie, bluegill and brown bullhead. Pond 4 has been stocked with walleye and brown trout and Pond 5 with largemouth bass, black crappie, bluegill, pumpkinseed and brown bullhead. Pond 6, on Buena Loop road, has been planted with rainbow, largemouth bass and brown bullhead. Pond 7 (8 acres) located E. of Buena has largemouth bass, black crappie and pumpkinseed. Walk-in to all ponds except Pond 7. No power boats allowed.

KLICKITAT RIVER. Upper section of this river in Klickitat Meadow produces rainbow and cutthroat in July, August and September. Located on Yakima Indian reservation. Reached by driving W. past Ahtanum ranger station to Klickitat Meadows road. Indian license required.

KRAMER PONDS. Series of small ponds situated S. of Zillah and N. of Yakima river. Holds warm water species. No public access.

LEECH LAKE. This 40 acre lake lies at the summit of White Pass on the Cascade Crest. Contains eastern brook of 7-10 inches with some larger. Developed campground. Small boats may be launched.

LILY LAKE. Cutthroat are present in Lily's 5.3 acres situated at 3860 feet 3.4 miles SW from Bumping Lake Dam. It drains to Bumping Lake.

LITTLE NACHES RIVER. Drive N. from Naches highway at Little Naches FS camp 29 miles NW of town of Naches. Road follows river 14 miles to road end above junction of middle and north forks. Numerous campsites. Rainbow in 8-9 inch range taken after mid-June, and small cutthroat furnish action in higher reaches. Road to Huckleberry campground and Raven Roost along Sand Ridge takes off W. from Little Naches road about 2 miles N. of Kaner Flat campground. Last mile of road closed to vehicles. Tough 3.5 miles from end of this road to **CROW CREEK LAKE** which has been planted with cutthroat. Lake is silting, but produces fish to 14 inches. Several "hidden" lakes in the immediate vicinity include Sheepherder, Janet, Rae and Anna. All support cutthroat.

LONG JOHN LAKE: A cutthroat lake of 4.8 acres located in Cowlitz Pass area 4.2 miles N. from White Pass. The narrow, 1200 feet long lake, drains to Tieton River.

LOST LAKE. Road crosses Tieton River just W. of Hause Creek campground on White Pass Hwy. and then the paved road continues .05 miles to FS road 1402, then turns E. to lake. Lake is at 3675 feet and is 9 acres. Holds rainbow to 12 inches. Small boats may be launched. Road continues S. 3 miles to Pickle Prairie trail No. 1125 which turns E. .04 miles to LONG LAKE, an 8 acre lake at 4350 feet elevation containing eastern brook.

MAL LAKE. A 4 acre lake at 5100 feet containing eastern brook. It lies 11.3 miles SW from Naches RS. Drainage is to Naches River.

McDANIELS LAKE. A 10 acre rainbow lake in marshy area at 3550 feet. Location

BYRON PONDS on Sunnyside Game Range.

is 8 miles SW from Naches ranger station with drainage into Naches River.

MILK CREEK. A small stream located 28 miles W. of Naches on Chinook Pass Hwy. Fair in July and August for cutthroat and eastern brook. Milk Lake feeds the creek.

MORGAN LAKE. A shallow, 24 acre pond located on the Sunnyside W.R.A. 2.5 miles N. of Mabton. Holds largemouth bass and pumpkinseed. GRIFFIN LAKE, .05 miles farther W. on the recreation area, is rainbow planted and also holds small perch and bass. Best in spring.

MYRON LAKE. A small rainbow-planted lake situated W. of Yakima off Fruitvale Blvd. Public access.

MUD LAKE. Rainbow and brook trout have been stocked in Mud's 4 acres situated at 2500 feet elevation on S. side of Cleman Mtn. and 7.4 miles NW from Naches. It drains to Naches River.

NACHES RIVER. Joins Yakima River 3 miles W. of Yakima. Over 40 miles of river upstream from this point is paralleled by the Naches Hwy. offering easy access at many points. The river holds rainbow, cutthroat and whitefish. Rainbow best in August, whitefish in winter.

NILE CREEK. A tributary of Naches which enters the river about 32 miles NW of Yakima. Road follows N. side of creek for 3 miles, then along N. Fork of Nile for about 15 miles past Little Bald Mtn. and Clover Springs near headwaters of Nile. Yields rainbow in lower reaches and cutthroat higher up. May, June and July are best months.

OTTER LAKE. Cutthroat have been planted in Otter which covers 7.2 acres. It is located 4 miles NE of White Pass at 5030 feet. It drains to Tieton River watershed.

PEAR AND APPLE LAKES. Source of Indian Creek. Take Indian Creek road at W. end of Rimrock Lake from White Pass highway for approximately 3 miles, then strike trail #1105 about 5 miles to Pear. Trail #1148 leads to Apple. The lakes may also be reached via trail #1105 from Deep Creek road S. of Bumping Lake. The lakes lie side-by-side. Pear is 20 acres while Apple is 9 acres. Elevation is 5060 feet. Both lakes hold eastern brook. Excellent campsites which are often used by elk hunters in November.

PLACER LAKE. Artificial lake of 4.7 acres at 5380 feet at site of former mining claim. It hosts cutthroat and lies at head of Morse Creek 2.7 miles NE from Chinook Pass.

RATTLESNAKE CREEK. Enters Naches River 30 miles W. of Yakima. Good road leaves Naches Hwy. 2.5 miles E. of Nile and follows Rattlesnake Creek on S. side for about 10 miles before crossing it again. Road turns S. 1 mile from mouth of Rattlesnake to parallel Little Rattlesnake Creek. Both Big and Little Rattlesnake rated fair for 8-10 inch rainbow in June and July. Upper walk-in sections hold native cutthroat.

RIMROCK LAKE. A 2530 acre reservoir 12.5 miles E. of White Pass summit created by a dam on Tieton River. Numerous camping sites. Boat launch areas on N. side off Hwy. 12 and at E. end of lake. Delivers kokanee fishing from mid-May through fall months. Holds some rainbow to 15 inches plus Dolly Varden and whitefish. Elevation is 2918 feet. Resorts on lake. Reservoir highly vulnerable to irrigation demand and has no conservation pool to prevent total drainage which periodically destroys kokanee populations.

ROOT LAKE. A 5.1 acre rainbow lake at 5300 feet on N. side of Miners Ridge lookout 8.3 miles SE from Chinook Pass. Drainage to Bumping River.

SATUS CREEK. Located on Yakima Indian reservation S. of Toppenish. Hwy. 97 from Toppenish to Goldendale follows creek for several miles. Closed to non-Indian fishing.

SANDSTONE LAKE. Cutthroat are present in this 3 acre lake at 3800 feet. It lies 2.2 miles S. from mouth of Bumping River and drains to that river.

SHEEPHERDER LAKE. A cutthroat lake of 3.3 acres situated at 4931 feet ll miles NE from Chinook Pass. It drains to Naches River.

SNOWPLOW LAKE. Rainbow are present in this 6 acre lake at 4500 foot elevation. It is located 8 miles SE from Mt. Adams and 1.2 miles SE from Snowplow Mtn. Drainage to Klickitat River.

SURPRISE LAKE. Road No. 133 follows S. Fork of Tieton from E. end of Rimrock Lake about 12 miles past Grey Creek campground to end of road. Trail No. 1120 continues through Conrad Meadows about 5 miles to the 14 acre lake. Contains cutthroat of 8-10 inches. Elevation is 5300 feet. Surprise is located at base of Goat Rocks. There are campsites.

SWAMP LAKE. Reached via Cougar Lake trail at head of Bumping Lake. Take right hand fork of trail near Cougar Creek 4 miles to Swamp Lake. Elevation is 4797 feet and the lake covers 51 acres. Excellent fly fishing for rainbow from open NW shoreline. Some eastern brook present. Camping sites on lake shore. Trail continues past Swamp to Cougar Lake. No trail to **CEDAR LAKES** located N. of this point. Cutthroat in Cedar.

TIETON RIVER. The White Pass Hwy. follows Tieton River from its source at Rimrock Lake to its junction with Naches River about 20 miles NW of Yakima. Another road runs along S. shore of Rimrock, heading S. up Tieton's S. Fork past Gray Creek campground at end of road near Conrad Meadows. Trail continues upstream to source at Surprise Lake. The S. Fork has small 'bows and cutthroat. Road 134 up Tieton's N. Fork takes off from W. end of Clear Lake. Fly fishing in clear waters of the N. Fork for cutthroat and rainbow. The main Tieton holds stocked rainbow after snow run-off. Plants of rainbow are staggered through season. Whitefish are plentiful. Many pleasant campsites are located along the river. The Tieton below Rimrock is subject to high flows and "no flows" because of irrigation needs.

TUMAC LAKE. (Hill). A rainbow planted lake of 5.8 acres located at 5110 feet elevation 4.6 miles NE from White Pass and 1 mile S. from Tumac Mtn. lookout. Drainage is to Rimrock Lake.

WILDCAT CREEK and **OAK CREEK**S: They enter lower Tieton River and furnish fair fishing for small rainbow and cutthroat. Oak also has eastern brook. There are a wide range of accommodations available along Rimrock Lake including several FS campgrounds. Road No. 144 parallels Wildcat Creek, and road No. 140 follows Oak Creek.

TWIN SISTERS LAKE. Road past Bumping Lake up Deep Creek ends about 2 miles from lakes. Trail takes off from end of road. Elevation is 5150 feet, with Big Twin Sister Lake covering 104 acres and Little Twin Sister 31 acres. Both lakes contain eastern brook. There are good campsites around both lakes. Trail continues W. about

DAVE FLORY scored in canyon stretch of Yakima River.

2 miles to strike Cascade Crest trail. A cluster of small lakes are located within 4 miles of Twin Sister including **PILLAR**, **LONG JOHN**, **DANCING**, **OTTER**, **SHELLROCK** and **DUMBELL**. These lakes hold rainbow and cutthroat. They sometimes winter-kill.

WENAS LAKE. A 61 acre reservoir in the Wenas Valley created by damming of Wenas Creek. May be reached by road from either Ellensburg or Selah. Wenas is stocked with rainbow and brown trout, and usually produces best early in season and then again in fall. Brown trout to 13 pounds have been caught here. Public access on lake plus a resort.

WIDE HOLLOW CREEK. Brown trout and cutthroat have been stocked in this Yakima River tributary joining that river S. of Union Gap. The creek skirts SW border of City of Yakima where it is polluted and developed. The Cottonwood Canyon road follows creek W. of Yakima.

YAKIMA RIVER. One of best streams in the state for large trout. (See listing also under Kittitas and Benton counties). Paralleled by highway from Lake Keechelus to mouth. Large rainbow are caught in canyon stretches, and there is excellent whitefish angling during winter months. Smallmouth bass and channel catfish are caught in lower reaches. Best trout fishing in

Yakima county section is between Roza Dam and Selah. Boat launch sites on Yakima at town of Sawyer, at Roza and at mouth of Squaw Creek. Fishing in the Yakima below Wapato diversion subject to low and polluted flows. Users of "bottom" fish are warned of persistent presence of DDT in flesh by health officials.

YAKIMA COUNTY RESORTS

Naches River: Whistlin' Jack Lodge, 1–800–827–2299.

Rimrock Lake: Rimrock Lake Resort, 509-547-9783; Silver Beach Resort, Star Rt., Box 212; Squaw Rock Resort, 509-658-2926, 15690 Hwy. 410. All Naches, WA 98937.

Wenas Lake: Wenas Lake Resort, Selah, WA 98942. 509-697-7870.

Yakima River: Yakima KOA, 509-248-5882.

Did you know?

The skunk's artillery is capable of hitting its target at ranges of five to ten feet and can be discharged five or six times in rapid succession.

NORTH CASCADES

NATIONAL

PARK

There are four distinct units in the North Cascades group covering 1,053 square miles of some of the most magnificent mountain territory in the United States. There are the north and south units of North Cascade National Park itself, and also the Ross Lake and Lake Chelan National Recreation Areas. The park and recreation areas were created by an act of Congress in 1968. Washington State fishing licenses are required in North Cascades National Park as well as in the recreation areas. Hunting is permitted in season in the recreation areas only for state licensed hunters.

There are approximately 360 miles of hiking and horse trails throughout the four units. Permits are required for all back-county camping, and they may be obtained at any park service office or ranger station. Headquarters for the North Cascades group is in Sedro Woolley, Wash. The North Cascades Highway cuts through the heart of the park and recreation units, crossing the Cascades Crest trail at the 4680 foot Rainy Pass. It links Newhalem on the west side of the Cascades Mountains with Winthrop on the east slope. Following is a list of lakes and streams which are wholly or partially within North Cascades National Park, Ross Lake National Recreation Area or Lake Chelan National Recreation Area. See county listings for additional information.

NORTH UNIT N.C.N.P.

BACON CREEK. Upper stretches are in the park, most of which are rather inaccessible. It is reached by heading N. from Hwy. 20 on a gravel road 5.5 miles NE of Marblemount. Fish species include cutthroat, rainbow, Dolly Varden and steelhead. Cutthroat are found in stream below Berdeen Lake.

BAKER RIVER. Lower portions above Baker Lake accessible by trail from top of lake. Rainbow, cutthroat and Dolly Varden.

BERDEEN LAKE. A remote lake of 127 acres situated at 5,000 feet elevation, and draining into Bacon Creek. It lies 12.5 air miles N. of Marblemount and holds small numbers of Montana black spot cutthroat. A smaller, unnamed lake lies below. It contains cutthroat.

CHILLIWACK RIVER. (Lower). Reached by trail from head of Chilliwack Lake in B.C., or from Hannegan Pass. Fish species include whitefish, Dolly Varden, cutthroat and kokanee, which spawn in August. **LITTLE CHILLIWACK RIVER** enters the main river from the west near the border. It holds cutthroat and dollies. No trails.

COPPER LAKE. Cutthroat and rainbow inhabit Copper's 8 acres. The lake is at 5250 feet and is reached by trail over Hannegan Pass from FS Hannegan campground. Drainage to Chilliwack River. Campsite at lake.

GOODELL CREEK. Lower reaches in Ross Lake NRA reached by rough road heading NW for 1 mile at S. outskirts of Newhalem. Upper portion of stream is in N.C.N.P. Fish include rainbow, steelhead and Dolly Varden.

GREEN LAKE. An 80 acre lake at 4300 feet situated 11.5 miles N. of Marblemount. No trail to the rainbow and cutthroat lake which drains into Bacon Creek.

NOOKSACK RIVER. (North Fork). Source is several glaciers in the Nooksack Cirque. Sparse numbers of rainbow and cutthroat.

THORNTON LAKE. (Lower). Cutthroat and golden trout are found in this 56 acre lake at 4450 feet elevation. Periodic stocking. Route is SW from Hwy. 20 on a dirt road which takes off about 3 miles SW of Newhalem for 4 miles where a trail leads 5 miles to lake.

SOUTH UNIT N.C.N.P.

CASCADE RIVER. (North Fork). Paralleled by gravel road to Cascade Pass. Produces small rainbow.

DAGGER LAKE. Drainage of this 10.5 acre lake is to Stehekin River. It is reached by trail over Twisp Pass from the Stehekin

IMAGE LAKE with Glacier Peak in background. (U.S. Nat. Park Photo)

road or the Bridge Creek trail from Rainy Pass. It holds cutthroat.

HIDDEN LAKE. Rainbow and small golden trout are found in this 55 acre lake which lies at 6000 feet 12 miles E. of Marblemount. Partial access by trail up Sibley Creek from Cascade River road.

MONOGRAM LAKE. Trail to this 28 acre lake leaves Cascade River road about 7 miles from Marblemount. There are cutthroat and rainbow in the lake which is at 4850 feet. Camp at outlet which drains into Cascade River.

TRAPPER LAKE. A remote lake of 147 acres at 4165 feet located in upper Stehekin River drainage. Contains cutthroat. Access via way trails from W. side of Cascade Pass and from Stehekin road near Cottonwood.

ROSS LAKE N.R.A.

DIABLO LAKE. Hwy. 20 offers access to this 910 acre impoundment of the Skagit River at Colonial Creek. Boat launch site at Colonial Creek. Rainbow, Dolly Varden and cutthroat are available.

GORGE LAKE. Covering 210 acres, Gorge holds rainbow and Dolly Varden. Access from Hwy. 20, with a boat launch at town of Diablo.

HOZOMEEN LAKE. A trail of 3.5 miles from Hozomeen area at head of Ross Lake leads to this 111 acre lake at 2800 feet elevation. It contains eastern brook. **ROSS LAKE**. Naturally spawning rainbow, cutthroat, Dolly Varden and eastern brook offer good fishing in this Skagit River impoundment of 11,678 acres. Main access, campground and boat launch is at N. end reached through B.C. Trail access at S. end of lake. Ross Lake Resort with cabins and boat rentals at S. end. (Phone 360-386-4437).

SKAGIT RIVER. The 10 mile stretch of free-flowing river in the recreation area contains steelhead, salmon, rainbow, cutthroat, Dolly Varden and whitefish. Hwy. 20 parallels this section.

WILLOW LAKE. A 27 acre lake at 2900 feet located 1.4 miles SE of Hozomeen Lake. Contains rainbow and cutthroat.

LAKE CHELAN N.R.A.

BOULDER CREEK. Reached by a short trail upstream from Stehekin road. Cutthroat and rainbow are present.

BRIDGE CREEK. Paralleled by trail from Stehekin road to Twisp and Rainy Passes. Primarily a cutthroat stream.

CHELAN LAKE. Road access at Chelan, Manson and other areas at foot of lake. Fish species include rainbow, kokanee, cutthroat, ling and chinook salmon.

COMPANY CREEK. A Stehekin River tributary reached from the Company Creek road and a trail paralleling lower reaches. Most of stream is in Glacier Peak Wilderness. Cutthroat, rainbow and brook trout available.

COON LAKE. Reached by short hike on trail from High Bridge on Stehekin road, the 9 acre lake is situated at 2172 feet elevation. Holds cutthroat with some brooks in outlet stream. No camping on lake.

McALESTER LAKE. This 15 acre lake may be reached by trail from Rainy Pass, Twisp River road over South Creek Pass, or from Stehekin road up Rainbow Creek. It lies at 5500 feet and hosts an abundant number of small cutthroat. Campsites at lake.

RAINBOW CREEK. Access to lower sections from Stehekin road and trail. Rainbow and cutthroat plus kokanee in fall at confluence with Stehekin River.

STEHEKIN RIVER. Easy access from the paralleling Stehekin road. Contains rainbow and cutthroat, with cutthroat only above High Bridge.

TRIPLET LAKES. Two lakes of 3 and 4 acres at 6100 feet elevation S. of War Creek Pass in Four Mile Creek drainage. It's a 1 mile cross-country hike from the Summit trail. They hold cutthroat. Drainage is to Lake Chelan.

NOOKSACK RIVER'S North Fork in Lake Chelan National Recreation Area. (U.S. Park Service Photo)

OLYMPIC

NATIONAL PARK

*There are nearly 1400 square miles in Olympic National Park which covers a large portion of Washington's Olympic Peninsula. Few roads reach deep into the park, with the exception of the spectacular Hurricane Ridge road from Port Angeles which climbs to near the 5000 foot mark on the N. border of the park. Best hiking and fishing time is from mid-summer into fall since most of the park's prime fishing lakes are above 3500 feet elevation. Portions of the Queets, Hoh, Quinault, Duckabush and Dosewallips Rivers are within the park's boundaries. The upper Elwha River provides good to excellent stream fishing with flies. The park service no longer stocks fish in any of the park's waters. No fishing licenses are required in Olympic National Park, but salmon and steelhead punch cards are required as they are in other state waters. Official park fishing regulations are available from park headquarters at 600 E. Park Ave., Port Angeles, WA 98362 or by phoning 360/452-4501. Because of many new regulations on park fishing waters it is important that fishermen read these regulations before making trips. Park shelters are being phased out, and there are more open fire restrictions. Check these points with park headquarters in Port Angeles before trips. No open fires are permitted at lakes with *. Camp stoves are permitted.*

Here are the principal lakes and streams within the park:

ANGELES LAKE.* Easily reached by good trail 3.5 miles above Heart 'O The Hills campground 6 miles S. of Pt. Angeles. Located at 4196 feet, the 19 acre lake is one of the largest alpine lakes in park. Steep cliffs on three sides make fishing difficult. Big population of eastern brook. Usually ice free in June.

BARNES CREEK. Major inlet of Lake Crescent, and principal spawning stream for the lake's cutthroat. Trail to Marymere

Falls and/or to Mt. Storm King parallels Barnes, then trail continues upstream to vicinity of Happy Lake. Some eastern brook high. Best bet is the canyon stretch below Mt. Storm King for larger cutthroat.

BIG CREEK. Enters N. side of Quinault River about 4.5 miles above Lake Quinault. Holds eastern brook, Dolly Varden, cutthroat, steelhead and some sockeye and silver salmon in lower reaches. Middle stretch is underground except in rainy weather.

BLACKWOOD LAKE. A small, beautiful lake located at 3000 feet at base of the ridge separating the Sol Duc and Bogachiel drainages. Take Mink Lake trail from Sol Duc Hot Springs to divide, go W. for 0.5 miles on trail then drop .08 miles down steep terrain to lake. Has large numbers of eastern brook.

BOGACHIEL LAKE. A 2 acre, shallow lake situated 1 mile SW of Deer Lake at head of S. Fork Bogachiel River. Accessible from the Deer Lake-Mink Lake trail on poorly defined trail. Sharp drop of 0.4 miles to lake. Holds moderate number of eastern brook in 7 to 9 inch range. E. and S. shores best.

BOGACHIEL RIVER. Heads in two forks S. and W. of Seven Lakes Basin. Trail follows main river and N. Fork. Holds both summer and winter steelhead, rainbow, cutthroat, Rocky Mountain whitefish, Dolly Varden and a few eastern brook. Adult silver salmon and jack salmon run high in the river. A rough trail from Bogachiel RS over Indian Pass leads to upper Calawah River. Bogachiel flows W. of Forks, and then into Quilayute River.

BOULDER CREEK. Flows into Lake Mills on the Elwha River from the W. May be reached by trail along W. side of Lake Mills, 2 miles from boat launch site. Has rainbow and eastern brook. Upper sections of Boulder Creek reached by Olympic Hot Springs road. Public campground at end of road.

BOULDER LAKE. A 3.5 mile hike from Boulder Creek campground on excellent trail. Many good campsites. Elevation of lake is 4450. Contains eastern brook in 8-10 inch range with some larger. W. shore inlet area best fishing. Beautiful lake and setting.

BUCKING HORSE CREEK. Enters Elwha River about 23 miles upstream from Whiskey Bend. Elwha trail crosses creek. Holds rainbow, Dolly Varden, eastern brook and some cutthroat.

BUNCH LAKE. A 10 acre lake at 3,000 feet located at head of Bunch Creek. Reached from E. Fork of Quinault road by rough, cross-country travel. Reported to contain rainbow.

CALAWAH RIVER. South Fork. Tough going on the Indian Pass trail striking north from Bogachiel RS over Indian Pass. Some excellent fishing, but rough country. Rainbow, cutthroat and Dolly Varden.

CAMERON CREEK. A Graywolf River tributary. Trail leads from Deer park 4.5 miles to Three Forks. Also reached by trail from Slab Camp. Contains rainbow, Dolly Varden and cutthroat.

CAT CREEK. Feeds into S. end of Lake Mills. A good sized stream that produces rainbow and Dolly Varden. Easiest access is by boat.

CEDAR LAKE. An alpine lake of 21 acres lying at 5,500 feet. Fine fishing for rainbow in the 10-14 inch bracket. Leave Graywolf trail at Falls shelter and head S. for 3 miles over meadows and through forest on indistinct trail. Excellent campsites along open shoreline.

CONSTANCE LAKE.* Reached by steep, difficult trail of 2 miles from Dosewallips River road. Elevation is 4750 feet, and lake is surrounded by rock cliffs on three sides. Fair campsites on S. shore. Holds rainbow and eastern brook. Mountain goats often seen from the lake.

LAKE CRESCENT. The second largest lake in the park, Crescent covers 4700 acres and is about 9 miles long by 1 mile wide. The lake is noted for Beardslee (rainbow) and Crescenti (cutthroat) trout, although it is questionable whether pure strains of these fish remain. Crescent has received eastern brook, cutthroat, steelhead, silver trout and many strains of rainbow over the years. Trout to 10 pounds are taken in this lake. Resorts and public campgrounds around the lake offer a vari-

MORGENROTH and NO NAME LAKES are in the Seven Lakes Basin. (Olympic Nat. Park Photo)

ety of accommodations including trailer space.

DEER LAKES.* A pair of small lakes of 8 and 1 acres situated at 3525 feet and reached by good trail 4 miles from the Sol Duc Falls parking area. Two shelters on E. shore of the larger lake. Both eastern brook and rainbow found in good numbers. Wooded shorelines.

DOSEWALLIPS RIVER. An excellent trail follows the Dosewallips from the end of the road to the headwaters at Dose Meadows below Hayden Pass. The trail branches 1.5 miles upstream from the trailhead. One branch follows West Fork 9 miles to Anderson Pass. The other trail climbs through virgin timber about 9 miles before entering alpine meadows above Camp Marion. West Fork holds rainbow, while the main branch of the Dosewallips has rainbow and eastern brook plus a few Yellowstone cutthroat trout in the steep-walled canyon stretches near Camp Marion. Steelhead and salmon are found in lower reaches, and some mountain whitefish are taken. The Dosewallips flows into Hood Canal.

DUCKABUSH RIVER. There are approximately 13 miles of fishable water inside the park along the Duckabush. The river heads at O'Neil Pass and is fed by Hart, Marmot and LaCrosse Lakes. Road up N. side of Duckabush from Hood Canal ends about 5 miles from park boundary. Rainbow are primary fish in this brushy stream, although salmon and steelhead are found in lower portions. Trail follows river all the way to headwaters.

EAGLE LAKES. Three small lakes on N. slope of Aurora Ridge above Lake Crescent at about 3,000 feet. Largest lake is 1.5 acres. Population of eastern brook to 13 inches. Aurora Ridge trail passes within 0.5 miles of Eagle. Easy way trail. Shoreline is brushy. Camp on high ground above lake to avoid mosquitos. **ELK LAKE.** A 6 acre lake at 2550 feet on Glacier Creek which feeds into the Hoh River. About 14.5 miles from end of Hoh River road on excellent trail that touches E. side of Elk on way to Mt. Olympus. Shelter and good campsites. Elk Lake holds eastern brook of 7-11 inches with some larger.

ELWHA RIVER. Considered one of finest fly fishing streams in the park. An excellent trail follows the river for 28 miles from parking area at Whiskey Bend which is 9 miles from U.S. 101 W. of Pt. Angeles. Grade along the river is moderate except for a drop in and out of Lillian River Canyon. Shelters are located along the Elwha at the 8.8, 11.5, 11.7, and 20.9 mile points. Major tributaries include Lillian, Long, Goldie and Hayes Rivers. They have fishermen's trails upstream and furnish good fishing. Rainbow and Dolly Varden furnish most of the action.

FLAPJACK LAKES.* Two lakes of 7 and 6 acres at head of Madeline Creek which drains into N. Fork of the Skokomish River. Trail leaves from Staircase and continues 7 miles to lakes. Good camping spots. Lakes are connected with a stream and hold rainbow and eastern brook trout. Lower lake produces largest fish. Brooks are 7-14 inches; rainbow measure 7 to 18 inches. Elevation of lakes is 3900 feet.

GLADYS LAKE.* The top lake in a series of three in Grand Valley. It covers about 6 acres and lies at 5,400 feet. Gladys hosts both rainbow and eastern brook, with the 'bows to 14 inches. The brookies are 7-8 inches. Good campsite. Inlet is best fishing spot.

GODKIN CREEK. Enters Elwha River about 10 miles above Elkhorn RS. Holds rainbow, eastern brook, Dolly Varden and a few cutthroat.

GRAND CREEK. Drains Grand, Gladys and Moose Lakes and joins Graywolf River at Three Forks shelter, 4.5 miles from end of road at Deer Park under Green Mtn. Grand Lake-Badger Valley trail follows upper Grand Creek for several miles. No trail access from Badger Valley to Three Forks area. Rainbow plus Dolly Varden in lower reaches.

GRAVES CREEK. A good sized tributary to Quinault River. Trail leaves road at mouth of stream and follows creek about 5 miles to Graves Creek Basin. Trail continues about 1.5 miles to and past Sundown Lake. Contains rainbow and Dolly Varden. Campground at mouth of creek.

GRAND LAKE.* (Etta). A 13 acre lake at 4700 feet elevation. An excellent trail leads 4 miles from end of Obstruction Point road. Contains eastern brook, with S. and SE shorelines best. Outlet stream sometimes produces.

QUEETS RIVER delivers both steelhead and salmon along with cutthroat trout.

GRAYWOLF RIVER. Major tributary of Dungeness River. Popular fishing spot where Grand and Cameron Creeks join the Graywolf below Green Mtn. Trail up Graywolf offers access to river at many places before climbing Graywolf Pass and dropping into Dosewallips drainage. Rainbow, Dolly Varden, steelhead, salmon and some eastern brook are present in the river. Leave Hwy. 101 at Sequim State Park and drive to Dungeness Forks, bearing W. 2 miles to end of road and start of trail. Also reached via Slab Camp road and trail to river.

HAPPY LAKE. A shallow lake at 4,500 feet altitude at head of Barnes Creek in basin between Crescent and Boulder Lakes drainages. Reached by good trail from Olympic Hot Springs road—about 5.5 miles. Hit Happy Ridge trail above Lookout Point. The alpine lake has good campsites along E. shore. Eastern brook in Happy to 14 inches. Some problem here with winter kill.

HAYES RIVER. Enters Elwha River 16.8 miles upstream from Whiskey Bend. Rough fishermen's trail follows the Hayes for a mile or so. Can offer top rainbow fishing.

HART LAKE.* A beautiful alpine lake at head of Duckabush River. Situated at 4800 feet in a glacial cirque basin, Hart covers 16 acres. Excellent campsites along the open shores. Reached by trail up Duckabush river 21 miles, or by 16 mile trail from end of Skokomish N. Fork road. Rainbow and eastern brook.

HOH LAKE.* A producer of rainbow and eastern brook, Hoh Lake lies at 4600 feet in the headwaters of the Hoh River. It covers 10 acres and is reached by a good trail of 9.5 miles via the Sol Duc River-Deer Lake route past the High Divide. Also ties into Hoh River trail. N. shore one of top fishing spots for larger trout.

HOH RIVER. Largest of all Olympic Peninsula rivers, the Hoh heads at the glaciers on Mt. Olympus and Mt. Tom. It carries glacial silt during summer months and is difficult to fish, but many varieties of fish are present despite the cloudy appearance. Winter and summer steelhead, chinook and silver salmon and jack salmon, sea-run cutthroat, Dolly Varden and whitefish all are found in the river. A hard-surfaced road leads 19 miles E. from Hwy. 101 to the Hoh RS and campground. A trail starts here and follows the river to Glacier Creek, then parallels this creek to Elk Lake and Glacier Meadow. A branch of the trail takes off 9.5 miles from end of the road to Hoh Lake, Bogachiel Park and Sol Duc Hot Springs.

IRELY LAKE. A log-filled, 10 acre lake situated at 550 feet adjacent to Big Creek, a tributary to the Quinault River. Trail takes off 1 mile short of end of N. Fork of Quinault road for 1 mile to lake. Carries rainbow, cutthroat and brook trout.

LA CROSSE LAKE. An alpine lake that lies at head of the Duckabush River at 4800 feet elevation. La Crosse covers 15 acres and is located 1 mile N. of Hart Lake. No fish reported.

LILLIAN RIVER. Tributary to Elwha River. Elwha trail crosses Lillian River 4.6 miles upstream from Whiskey Bend. Fishermen's trail follows bank of stream for several miles. Good fishing for rainbow and eastern brook.

LITTLE RIVER. Enters Elwha River at Hwy. 101 bridge above Lake Aldwell. Only upper stretch is in park. Fishing is poor.

LOST RIVER. Another Elwha River tributary which joins the Elwha about 1.5 miles above Elkhorn shelter, approximately 13 miles by trail from Whiskey Bend. Lost River is good sized and offers rainbow and Dolly Varden fishing.

MARGARET AND MARY LAKES. Situated at 3600 and 3550 feet respectively, the lakes are 6 and 3 acres and are positioned in the Low Divide separating Mt. Seattle and Mt. Christie. Drainage is to Elwha River. Mary Lake, although the smaller, furnishes fishing for eastern brook. Margaret is subject to winter kill and has no fish. The lakes lie about 16 miles by trail from end of Quinault's N. Fork road.

MARMOT LAKE.* Lies just below Hart Lake at 4,300 feet at head of Duckabush River. Trail 21 miles up Duckabush. Few if any trout.

MILLS LAKE. Formed by a dam on lower Elwha River, Mills is about 2.4 miles long by 0.4 miles wide and covers 451 acres. Contains rainbow, eastern brook, Dolly Varden and a few cutthroat. Public boat launch at lower W. end. Road to Whiskey Bend parallels E. side of lake. Good fish-

BEARDSLEE TROUT of 12.5 pounds was caught from Lake Crescent by Matt Warren on a Mack's Squid Plug. State record Beardlee of 15.4 pounds was taken from Crescent. (Mehler Tackle Photo)

ing where Elwha flows from sharp-walled canyon at upper end of lake, particularly in fall months. Rough campsites at this point most easily reached by boat.

MINK LAKE. A marshy lake of 10.5 acres located 2.5 miles by trail from Sol Duc Hot Springs. Elevation is 3080 feet. Brook trout in lake. Mosquito dope a must.

MOOSE LAKE.* A 7 acre lake in Grand Valley at head of Grand Creek. Lake is situated at 5,100 feet and holds eastern brook. Rough trail of 4.4 miles from Obstruction Point leads to Moose. Best fishing in deep water at inlet streams. Average fish are 9-10 inches.

PELTON CREEK. Upper Queets River tributary. Campsite at point where creek enters river. It contains Dolly Varden and rainbow.

P.J. LAKE. Located at N. base of Eagle Point and about .05 miles by rough trail from Waterhole picnic site on the Obstruction Point road. Eastern brook of 7-10 inches are found in the 2 acre lake. Elevation is 4700 feet. Top fishing spot is between the two inlets along SE shore.

QUEETS RIVER. Road from Hwy. 101 follows river 14 miles to campground at road end. The river may be reached at a number of spots along this road. It is necessary to wade the Queets to the N. side at end of road to hit trail up the river. Both summer and winter steelhead plus spring and fall chinook, cutthroat, Dolly Varden, whitefish and silver salmon offer variety in the Queets. Because of glacial silt and clay banks the river is often off color. Vicinity of Tshletshy Creek upstream about 7 miles by trail is good for summer steelhead from July through fall months.

QUINAULT RIVER. Road up S. side of main Quinault River above lake continues upstream past Graves Creek campground a total distance of about 22 miles from Hwy. 101. Best fishing is for summer steelhead commencing in late June and continuing into fall months. Stretch in the canyons above Graves Creek is best. Chinook salmon are found high, and Dolly Varden, whitefish and rainbow are also present. The Quinault flows from Enchanted Valley, and an easy, graded trail offers access to the river at many places. Campsites at Enchanted Valley.

QUINAULT RIVER. North Fork. Road up S. side of main Quinault River crosses bridge at forks and continues N. up the N. Fork. Total distance from Hwy. 101 is about 16 miles. Trail leads from this point 16 miles to Low Divide. The N. Fork holds rainbow, steelhead, salmon, Dolly Varden and whitefish.

REFLECTION LAKE. Situated at head of Big Creek, a branch of the Quinault's N. Fork. The lake is at 3500 feet and covers about 1 acre. Trail leaves N. Fork of Quinault road about 2.5 miles upstream from forks, passes N. shore of Irely Lake and continues about 5 miles to Reflection and Three Lakes where there is a campsite. Reflection lies 0.4 miles below the Skyline trail and is not visible from trail. Eastern brook in lake are plentiful and measure 7-10 inches. Campsites on W. shore.

ROYAL CREEK. This Dungeness River tributary enters the river about 10 miles

upstream from Dungeness Forks. It drains from Royal Basin and Royal Lake.

ROYAL LAKE.* Situated at head of Royal Creek, Royal Lake lies at an elevation of 5,100 feet and covers 2 acres. Contains eastern brook. Reached by trail up Dungeness River and then up Royal Creek.

RUSTLER CREEK. A major tributary to the N. Fork of the Quinault River that enters the river approximately 4 miles upstream from end of the N. Fork road. Rough fishermen's trail follows along creek about 2 miles. Holds rainbow, Dolly Varden and a few cutthroat.

SALMON RIVER. Heading in Jefferson County and flowing through the Quinault Indian reservation, Salmon enters the park and Queets River about 1.5 miles NE of Hwy. 101 on the Queets River road. The river has received winter steelhead plants.

SCOUT LAKE.* Situated NE of Mt. Stone with drainage into Duckabush River. Elevation is 4250 feet, and the lake covers 15 acres. Rough, poorly marked trail leads 2 miles from Upper Lena Lake, dropping over 600 feet in last 0.5 miles to lake. Rainbow to 18 inches in the lake. Campsite near inlet which forms One Too Many Creek.

SEVEN LAKES BASIN.* Group of lakes in upper Sol Duc River drainage at elevations ranging from 3,500 to about 5,000 feet. Lakes are located N. of Bogachiel Peak and hold eastern brook and rainbow. They include Soleduck, Morganroth, No Name, Long, Clear, Lake #8, Lunch and Round Lakes. Lunch and Round reached by trail from end of Sol Duc Hot Springs road. Rest of lakes accessible by way trails or cross country in open, sub-alpine region. Trail distance 8 miles.

SKOKOMISH RIVER. Portion of the N. Fork above Lake Cushman is in the park. Road leads to park campground at Staircase. Trail follows river upstream and drops into Duckabush River drainage. An occasional huge Dolly Varden is taken (when legal) from the river in canyon near point where it joins the lake. Rainbow furnish most action up the river.

SMITH LAKE. A 7 acre lake lying at 4000 feet at head of Hammer Creek which flows into the N. Fork of the Skokomish River.

Contains eastern brook. About a 6 mile hike from end of Skokomish River's N. Fork road. Last 0.5 mile is down steep way trail to lake.

SOL DUC RIVER. Upper stretches of this whitewater stream are in the park and are reached by leaving Hwy. 101 about 1.5 miles from W. end of Lake Crescent. Road continues for approximately 14 miles to campground and Sol Duc Hot Springs. Ranger station is located near end of road where current fishing and trail information is available. The Sol Duc carries both summer and winter steelhead, plus rainbow, salmon, Dolly Varden and a few eastern brook and cutthroat. Major trails from end of road branch out to many sections of the park.

SUNDOWN LAKE. Situated at 3900 feet at head of Graves Creek, a tributary of the Quinault. The 8 acre lake contains rainbow and is reached by hiking 8.5 miles up Graves Creek trail from Quinault River road.

TOM CREEK. Enters the N. Fork of the Hoh River 3 miles from end of road at Hoh RS. A trail heads S. about 1 mile following the rapid stream. Tom Creek holds rainbow, Dolly Varden and cutthroat.

TSHLETSHY CREEK. A major tributary of the Queets River about 7 miles upstream from end of road at Queets campground. Summer steelhead gather at mouth of the creek and in the Queets just below. Trail follows Tshletshy Creek to high Ridge and then drops into the Quinault drainage. The creek holds rainbow, Dolly Varden, steelhead and a few cutthroat.

UPPER LENA LAKE.* A 10 acre lake located at 4500 feet, and 2.5 miles W. of **LOWER LENA** (55 acres at 1800 feet elevation). Lakes drain into Hamma Hamma River. Reached by road following Hamma Hamma River to Lena Creek campground, then by trail N. 3.5 miles to **LOWER LENA** where a rough trail takes off for **UPPER LENA.** The **LENA** lakes contain rainbow. **MILK LAKE,** a small lake, is located 1.5 miles S. of **UPPER LENA.** It contains eastern brook.

WILDCAT LAKE. Located at head of Tumbling Creek which enters Dosewallips River from the S. about 1 mile from end of Dosewallips road. Elevation of lake is 4150

feet. Rough trail via Muscott way trail. When the trail enters meadows in Muscott Basin, head NE to the ridge and cross into Wildcat Lake Basin. Eastern brook are present.

OLYMPIC NATIONAL PARK RESORTS

Lake Crescent: Fairholm Resort, Star Rt., Box 15, Port Angeles, WA 98362. 360-828-3020. Lake Crescent Lodge, Star Rt., Box 11, Port Angeles, WA 98362. 360-928-3211. Log Cabin Resort, Rt. 1, Box 416, Port Angeles, WA 98362. 360-928-3325.

Sol Duc River: Sol Duc Hot Springs Resort. 360-327-3583.

Fish and game laws in ancient Rome

In the time of the Roman Empire, nearly 2000 years ago, fish and game regulations read as follows: I) Fish and wild animals in a state of nature belong to no one person; 2) Fish and wild animals become the property of the person who first "reduces them into possession;" 3) The sea and public rivers are not capable of individual ownership; and 4) No citizen can be prevented from fishing in the sea and such rivers by any person. In general, these are very similar to laws now in effect in Michigan and throughout much of the United States. No one person "owns" fish and game in a state of nature in Michigan, but under license and in the proper season, anyone who "reduces game or fish to possession" does then own such meat. Further our public lakes and rivers are available to the public and are not owned by individuals, and no legal hunter or fisherman may be prevented from hunting or fishing such waters.

Check the regulations

All fishermen should obtain free sport fishing regulations at sport shops. Look before you fish—all sections of all streams do not open at the same time for all species of fish. It is the individual's responsibility to check pamphlets to be certain that he is fishing in a legal manner before he wets a line.

MOUNT RAINIER

NATIONAL

PARK

Fishing in Mt. Rainier National Park requires leg work, since virtually all productive waters are far removed from roads. There are over 260 miles of trails within the park, however, which lead to or close to countless lakes and streams. Because of the elevation most lakes do not shed ice until late-June at the earliest, icing up again about mid-November. There are 384 permanent lakes and ponds and 470 rivers and streams in forest, sub-alpine and alpine environments. Park waters are open to fishing all year. No fishing license is required to fish Mount Rainier National Park waters. Limit is 12 fish and there is no minimum size restriction. Detailed information about fishing regulations and the park in general may be obtained by writing Mt. Rainier National Park, 909 First Ave., Seattle, WA 98104.

During periods of warm weather, increased glacier movement and melting causes most glacial streams to become too cloudy to fish. During cool summer periods, and in the spring and fall, the following glacial streams provide fair angling:

Nisqually, Tahoma, Puyallup (both N. and S. Forks), Carbon, N. and S. Forks of Mowich, W. Fork of White, Stevens and Frying Pan.

Ohanapecosh River, which is restricted to fly fishing only, is a clear running stream and may be fished most of the season. There are over 200 miles of clear water streams in the park. Most are small tributaries of glacial rivers, or are lake outlets.

A back country permit (no charge) is required for all overnight use in the back country of the park. In 1988 approximately

97% of the total park acreage was designated wilderness.

Here are the major lakes and streams in Mt. Rainier National Park:

ADELAIDE LAKE. An 8 acre lake at 4584 feet elevation lying N. of James and Ethel Lakes. Contains chunky rainbow. One of a group of 4 lakes. (See Marjorie and Oliver Lakes).

ALLEN LAKE. A 5 acre cutthroat and eastern brook lake which lies at 4596 feet. Fishing is often excellent, but the lake is difficult to reach. Route is via a very steep climb of 2.5 miles along an informal trail which leaves the W. side road 1.9 miles from the beginning of the road.

BEAR PARK LAKE. A cutthroat lake of 1.9 acres at 5400 feet. Difficult access across a divide E. of Palisades Lakes in White River drainage.

BENCH LAKE. An open lake of 7 acres which lies at 4600 feet in burned-off country 0.7 miles by trail from Stevens Canyon road. It hosts eastern brook, rainbow and cutthroat. **SNOW LAKE** is located a short distance above Bench at 4678 feet. It contains cutthroat and possibly a few eastern brook.

CHENUIS LAKE. No trail into this 3 acre cutthroat lake located at 5090 feet. Check route with ranger at Carbon River entrance.

CHINOOK CREEK. Heading in Tipsoo Lake on Chinook Pass highway, Chinook flows S. along E. side of the park to join the Ohanapecosh River. It is followed by the E. side park road for 2 miles S. from Cayuse Pass. Also accessible by road from Ohanapecosh. It holds eastern brook, cutthroat and rainbow and is restricted to fly fishing only.

CLOVER LAKE. An open lake of 7 acres reached by trail from Sunrise Point. No fish reported.

CRYSTAL LAKES. Two small cutthroat and rainbow lakes situated at 5830 feet elevation. The larger lake is 8 acres. Trail to Crystal Peak leaves Chinook Pass Hwy. at the state highway maintenance camp about 0.5 miles below junction of White River road. Branch trail to lakes forks left about 1.3 miles below lookout. The lakes

BENCH LAKE is located in upper west end of Stevens Canyon. (U.S. Park Service Photo)

are about 3 miles from the highway. Back country camps located near both lakes.

DEADWOOD LAKES. A pair of small lakes at 5300 feet elevation which are close to one another. The clear, shallow lakes contain cutthroat. Leave car 0.5 miles E. of Chinook Pass summit, and head N. through low saddle for 0.5 miles to the lakes.

ELEANOR LAKE. A 20 acre rainbow lake at 4960 feet elevation situated in open, alpine country. Route is Wonderland Trail from Sunrise Lodge in Yakima Park past Frozen Lake and Berkeley Park to Grand Park, then N. and E. through Grand Park to the lake. Total distance is 9.3 miles through beautiful, open parks. Campsites on lake.

GEORGE LAKE. There is a shelter and campsites on this beautiful 26 acre lake which lies at 4232 feet elevation. Drive to summit of Round Pass on the W. side road from Nisqually entrance. Marked trail takes off from Round Pass parking lot 0.8 miles

to the lake. George is heavily populated with sculpin.

GOLDEN LAKES. A group of small lakes situated at 4556 elevation. Only two of the lakes contain fish. The largest lake, which lies about 0.5 miles NW of the shelter cabin, and the smaller lake into which it drains, both offer good eastern brook angling. The lakes are reached via the Nisqually entrance then to the W. side road which is closed to vehicles beyond Fish Creek. Trail starts from the N. Puyallup bridge and continues 4.5 miles to the lakes, which lie at head of **RUSHING WATER CREEK**. Access also from Mowich trailhead near Mowich Lake.

GREEN LAKE. A cutthroat lake of 10 acres located at 3000 feet. It is reached by trail up Ranger Creek from the Carbon River road.

GREEN PARK LAKES. There are cutthroat in the largest lake which covers 11 acres. Elevation is 5400 feet. They are reached by leaving the Yakima Park road at Sunrise Point on the Hidden Lake trail, then NW cross-country.

HIDDEN LAKE. Eastern brook and rainbow are found in this 5 acre lake which lies at 5926 feet elevation. Route is via the Clover Lake trail, then continuing N. Hidden is located in a depression about 4 miles N. of Sunrise Point on the Yakima Park road.

HUCKLEBERRY CREEK. The stream heads a short distance N. of Sourdough Ridge and the upper stretches are reached by trail from Sunrise Lodge. Lower portions of Huckleberry may be fished by leaving the Chinook Pass highway 6 miles E. of Greenwater where logging roads follow the creek upstream toward the park. A trail continues from the road terminus into the park. The creek contains cutthroat with best fishing between mouth of Josephine Creek and park boundary.

KENWORTHY LAKE. An 8 acre rainbow lake situated N. and below Gobbler's Knob Lookout. Elevation is 4700 feet.

KOTSUCK CREEK. A cutthroat stream tributary to Chinook Creek. Take Deer Creek trail which leaves the highway 4 miles S. of Cayuse Pass, then follow Owyhigh Lake trail along the creek. Fly fishing only.

JAMES LAKE. Route to this 10 acre rainbow lake is through the Carbon River entrance to Ipsut Creek campground, then across the Carbon River on a foot bridge 1.3 miles above the campground. Trail takes off here, switch-backing steeply to Windy Gap, climbing 3000 feet. At the gap the trail drops 2500 feet to James at 4370 feet elevation. Total distance is 5.8 miles. No camping permitted. **ETHEL LAKE** is located about 0.4 miles NW of James and is connected by a rough trail. Ethel covers 21 acres and contains rainbow. Steep and brushy shore lines make fishing difficult. Elevation of Ethel is 4287 feet. **MARJORIE LAKE** lies at 4,555 feet between Adelaide and Oliver Lakes. An informal fishermen's trail starts slightly W. of the outlet of Ethel and leads about 0.8 miles to Marjorie. The lake is 11 acres and holds rainbow. **OLIVER LAKE** is 20 acres. Elevation is 4458 feet. There are rainbow in Oliver. The lake is located about 100 yards W. of Marjorie. **ADELAIDE LAKE** is situated over a small ridge about 0.7 of a mile NE of Oliver. It contains rainbow.

LOST LAKE. Eastern brook are found in this tiny (2 acre) lake which drains into Huckleberry Creek. Check with rangers at Sunset RS as the lake is really "lost" and is very difficult to locate.

LOUISE LAKE. Eastern brook are found in this 11 acre lake and they provide fair to good fishing. Elevation of Louise is 4592 feet. The lake is easily reached from Stevens Canyon road about 1.5 miles E. of junction with Longmire-Paradise road. It may be seen from the road.

MARSH LAKE. A beautifully situated cutthroat lake of 4 acres which lies at 3900 feet. The lake sometimes offers top angling. An informal trail takes off from across the road from Box Canyon picnic area to climb to Marsh. A 2 acre pond adjoins Marsh. Total trail distance from the road is about 1 mile.

MOWICH LAKE. May be reached by road in late July after snow has melted. The 100 acre lake contains eastern brook, rainbow, cutthroat and kokanee. Limited camping areas. Road up Meadow Creek leads to SW tip of the lake where there is a ranger station.

MOWICH RIVER. A Puyallup River tributary accessible via the Paul Peak trail from

MOWICH LAKE lies in the northwest corner of the park. (U.S. Park Service Photo)

OHANAPACOSH RIVER is a turbulent but productive trout stream.

Mowich road 1 mile inside the park boundary. When clear and low the large glacial river provides good cutthroat and rainbow fishing.

MYSTIC LAKE. An 8 acre cutthroat, rainbow and eastern brook lake which is reached by a trail of 7.6 miles from Ipsut Creek campground. Elevation is 5700 feet. The trail crosses Carbon River at foot of Carbon Glacier. The lake may also be reached by a 10 mile trail crossing the foot of Winthrop Glacier out of Yakima Park. There is a shelter on Mystic.

NISOUALLY RIVER. This large glacial stream is usually too cloudy to fish, but does contain eastern brook, cutthroat and rainbow. A road parallels the river from Nisqually Park entrance upstream to Nisqually Glacier bridge.

OHANAPECOSH RIVER. The E. side park road parallels river for several miles S. of Cayuse Pass on the E. side, while a trail follows the W. bank. This clear, beautiful stream contains cutthroat, eastern brook and rainbow and is restricted to fly fishing only. There is a campground at Ohanapecosh.

PALISADES LAKES. Two rainbow and eastern brook lakes of 3 and 5 acres which lie at 5500 and 5800 feet. They are reached

via a one mile trail beyond Hidden Lake. (See Hidden for route).

STEVENS CREEK. Fair fishing for rainbow and eastern brook is available in Stevens when it is clear enough to fish. The creek extends through Stevens Canyon E. of Paradise Park.

SUNRISE LAKE. A 4 acre lake located at 5800 feet elevation. No fish reported.

TAHOMA CREEK. Snow melt discolors this creek during warm weather, but good rainbow, eastern brook and cutthroat fishing is often available during early spring and fall. Tahoma is crossed by the Longmire road 1 mile inside the park entrance, and is paralleled upstream by the W. side highway to its junction with Fish Creek. Caution: Debris flows.

TATOOSH CREEK. Outlet to Reflection Lake, Tatoosh is a clear stream which holds eastern brook and often provides excellent fishing. It empties into Paradise River about 1.5 miles below Narada Falls.

TIPSOO LAKE. A rainbow lake lying near the summit of Chinook Pass at 5314 feet elevation. No fishing permitted because of the fragility of the lake shore ecosystem. An excellent view and photograph point of Mt. Rainier.

WHITE RIVER. (West Fork). The W. Fork logging road leaves the Chinook Pass Hwy. about 3 miles E. of Greenwater and follows the creek upstream for several miles to within 2 miles of the park boundary. There are cutthroat and rainbow in the swift glacial river which is too cloudy to fish during warm weather.

A eutrophy what?

Here's a new worry word for sportsmen:

Eutrophication, the excessive fertilization of algae and other aquatic plants with nutrients, principally phosphates, a common element found in municipal sewage, human waste, agricultural fertilizers and industrial discharges.

The most serious example of eutrophication in the U.S. is Lake Erie, where much of the oxygen had disappeared and aquatic plants are filling the lake.

Fishing Tips

Take A Youngster Fishing

This page is directed to non-fisher fathers and mothers who have a youngster who wants to go fishing. I suspect that the kids don't get to go, in many cases, because their dad or mom doesn't know what equipment is necessary, how to rig the gear, or where to go. Honest, dad and mom, it isn't that tough. You'll make yourself a hero by getting your boy or girl out on lake or stream and into some fish. And do you know something else? Even if you don't like fishing yourself, neither you nor your youngster will ever forget those beginning fishing experiences together.

Equipment is simple

Forget the fancy equipment, You can buy a small, open-face spinning reel loaded with six pound test monofilament line, plus a 6 or 7 foot light spinning rod for under $20. For the $20 you'll probably be able to include a dozen snelled (hooks with leaders tied to them) number 8 hooks, a dozen small snap swivels, some split sinkers and four or five small, round bobbers. That's it. You may want to buy a jar of salmon eggs, but common garden worms are as good or better bait.

Practice a bit

Before making the trip, string the line through the rod guides and tie a rubber eraser or small weight to the end. Then go outside and let the youngster try casting. Spinning reels are simple. A 6-year-old can learn to cast reasonably well in 15 minutes. Now, where to go? Look in your county listings for lakes that contain spiny ray fish, or the story on pages 255-256 that list all waters in the state which hold spiny rays. It is not necessary to get up early for perch, crappie, sunfish or catfish, the type fish your boy or girl is going to catch. Late afternoon into evening hours on a sunny day in mid-summer is a good fishing time.

JORDON PROBASCO started fishing at an early age with dad Steve and is still going strong.

Fish from shore

You may fish from a boat, but with a little guy along I prefer to fish from shore. They get wiggly sometimes. If there is a resort on the lake, ask the resort operator where the best spiny ray fishing areas are. If this isn't possible, walk around the lake until you find a place where there are logs, lily pads or brush in the water. String line through the rod guides and tie a swivel to the end. Snap the swivel to one hole in the bobber. Attach another snap swivel to the other hole in the bobber and tie the leader to the swivel. Let your youngster select his worm and hook it in several places, permitting the ends to squirm. Then direct him to cast as close to the logs or other cover as he can. (If you need help on proper fishing knots, see charts elsewhere in this book).

Keep moving

If the bobber doesn't start dancing in 10 to 15 minutes, try another spot. When you locate fish and they start attacking the worm, try to keep the youngster from setting the hook until the bobber goes completely under the water. Your youngster will want to keep those first few fish, but after several trips and when fishing is particularly good, suggest that he return some fish to the water so he or some other fisherman might catch them again. You might want to take a pail along, fill it with lake water and place fish in it. Then, when you are ready to go home, the youngster can select a few "choice" fish and have the pleasure of releasing the rest. Kids started out this way are not likely to turn into game hogs when they get older. It really IS that simple, dad and mom. If you have any specific questions, call or write me and I'll try to help.

Stan Jones

Steelhead Secrets

Winter steelheading in Washington is a four month show, with first appreciable number of fish appearing in December. Successive runs of steelhead enter rivers into March and even into April. Fishermen can determine what particular time fresh, clean steelhead will be stacking in lower reaches of rivers by directing close attention to river levels during the December-March period. It's a sure bet that every flush of water brings new fish into major steelhead streams.

Wait for water drop

Steelhead don't do much traveling when rivers are at flood stage. After the water receeds, they will be on the move. During this period fish will be located throughout lower stretches of the river, and not always in drifts. Using the rule of thumb that "the higher the water, the lower in the pool steelhead will hold," tail-outs or fans of pools should be systematically fished. Fish in front of, in back of, and on both sides of every rock or stump that elbows the current. Fish at your feet. Steelhead won't fight high velocity currents when there are easier routes. Wait two to four days after rivers first start dropping. By then steelhead will have found holding riffles and pools, and rather than hitting the odd fish you can work on clusters. This is the time they gang.

Fish need cover

Cover is the only defense steelhead have. If you can see bottom in the fishy portion of the drift, forget it. Almost with exception, good holding water must have rocks, logs, over-hanging branches or depth. Besides protection, rocks and logs provide "soft"

JACK EPLEY with husky Sol Duc River steelhead.

water where steelhead may hold against the current with little or no effort. Current boils and threads indicate rugged bottom that means cover—and fish.

Set alarm early

Productive drifts are those located either just above or below rough stretches of rapids. Watch for first good slicks upstream or downstream from long, flat sections or river where cover is at minimum. These particular spots are excellent prospects for early morning trips since steelhead wait for cover for darkness to pass water in which they are vulnerable. They'll often take the first bait or lure offered. Steelhead also school in first holding water below falls or rough rapids. Upstream movement is done primarily at night and is governed by amount of water coming over falls or other barrier. Fish below the falls during low water periods, and in first few good drifts above this point following a raise in water. Mouths of feeder streams should not be over looked. When the main river is dirty the clear-dark line caused by clean water spilled by the creek should be worked. Sometimes it is the feeder stream dumping mud which offers cover for steelhead in the main river.

River aids fishing

Besides bringing new steelhead in from saltwater, rain-caused raises increase water temperatures of rivers which improve fishing, since fish tend to be sluggish when river water registers in the chilly 30's. Save the rising barometer theory for other fish. That's not the way it works for winter steelhead which live in snow-fed rivers. They react to the warmth brought by rain water by hitting more freely.

Although fishermen may locate the lay holes for steelhead by busting brush, it is much easier to drift the river in a boat. Boating should be done with great caution. Every steelhead season fishermen are drowned in boating mishaps. It is wise to locate five or six top holding drifts in a ten mile section of river. First location would probably be near tide water. Since steelhead must undergo biological changes in moving from salt to fresh water, they follow several high tides into lower holes before committing themselves to the river. Find the last good riffle that is touched by tidal waters and work the drift thoroughly.

Don't dally

Each of the pre-located drifts should be fished in order. An hour of hard fishing at each location should be maximum time spent unless fish are hit. Most novice steelhead fishermen expend far too much time on one drift before moving on. The time to carefully comb every possible section of

PRIME BUCK steelhead from Olympic Peninsula's Hoh River.

the drift is after steelhead have been located. Characteristically, steelhead that haven't been spooked will bite the first time lure or bait is properly presented if they want to hit. Once a fisherman is satisfied that he has worked the key water at correct depth and speed, it's time to move on.

Not much time

Rivers will not remain in top condition for more than a week at most. Four days is more realistic. Steelheading will be good when water levels and color are right and beginners and semi-skilled fishermen will score along with the pros during this period. The situation gets a bit tough when rivers drop and clear. Even though steelhead are there, they aren't too cooperative. Water temperatures drop as rain water runs off, and it is necessary to place bait or lure close to steelhead as they become less active. Clear water means spooky fish.

The rule that steelhead will be found where there is cover still applies. The long, deep drifts that held fish when water levels were up become clear. Now the situation is reversed, and it's "the lower the water the higher in the pool" rule to follow. It is helpful to use longer, lighter leaders, smaller lead and lures, and to cover white water in order to take fish.

Lay it there

Precision casting is imperative. Up-stream casts are particularly effective during low water periods. This technique will exact a heavy toll of terminal tackle but steelheaders who hook fish in this manner don't complain.

Work back side

An effective method of connecting with steelhead when rivers are low is to fish the back side of the creek. This appears obvious, but it is surprising how fisherman after fisherman will approach a drift, plant his boots in the tracks of the man who just left a drift and cast repeatedly to the same spot that has been pounded all day. First angler through may hook a fish, but after the drift has been beat for hours the fish will lay tight against the far bank in snags or rocks, or in undercuts of the bank.

All but the largest steelhead streams may be waded during low water. A steelheader

HOH RIVER beauty beached by Lee Meyers.

wearing chest-high waders can usually make it at tail of pools. Crossing to the back side of the heavily worked drift will put you right on top of fish.

Fishing equipment

A standard winter steelhead rod is 8 to 8 1/2 feet long. It's gutty in the butt section so that heavy hooks may be set in a steelhead's tough mouth, but the last 12 to 18 inches of the tip section is sensitive. This aids anglers in detecting the light pickup of steelhead. Handle of the rod back of the reel seat extends approximately the length of the angler's forearm to provide needed support. Heavy-duty spin reels or level wind reels are standard, with minimum of 150 yards of 12 to 15 pound test mono line usually required. Use lower test line than your main line for leaders so that hang-ups will not result in excessive main line loss.

Mix'em up

Chioce of lures or bait is governed by water conditions, lateness of season and by individual preference. Experienced steelheaders may stick with a favored style spoon, bobber, fly or bait through high water and low, but their success in hooking fish is because they are getting it in front of fish consistently. Less skilled steelheaders would do well to mix their offerings. Night crawlers or eggs are natural baits. They should be presented first. After systematically sweeping every bit of good looking water, take it from the top again using a spoon or spinner. No action? Tie the bait leader back on and follow the hardware with bait.

Toward end of the winter steelhead season as fish approach maturity they hit spoons, plugs and brightly painted bobbers. Buck steelhead, particularly, chase spoons and plugs during late season.

Mark the hot spots

Year after year fish will come to the same holding drift. A rock ledge, stump, root or brush that hangs into the river to provide cover for steelhead will harbor them repeatedly. When fish are caught in such a spot, others will move in. As fishermen take time to examine and understand why the big sea-run rainbows act as they do under varying water conditions, they will hook steelhead consistently.

Summer Steelhead

There are more Washington streams carrying summer run steelhead than most anglers realize, and steelheaders with the pioneering spirit can help themselves to some top sport if they want to explore. Approximately 100 of the state's rivers and creeks host this fish, the finest of all in the opinion of many experts.

Summer run steelhead move in from the ocean during June, July, August and September, but may enter home rivers as early as February. Even though the fish come in early, they spawn about the same time as do winter steelhead. Peak spawning time is March and April. The summer steelhead live in deep pools while waiting for eggs and sperm to mature. They do little feeding after leaving the ocean, relying on fats stored in their bodies. Thus, an early summer or "springer" steelhead taken in March or April, particularly, is loaded with energy and is a rough fish to control.

SKYKOMISH RIVER produced summer steelhead for Oliver Van Den Berg.

The Columbia River and tributaries, produce many of the state's summer steelhead, although approximately 20 major river systems in W. Washington now carry them. Average yearly catch has been over 50,000 fish. The total is climbing each year with more summer steelhead plants made annually.

Use lighter gear

Because of lower, clearer water during summer months in many rivers, lighter terminal tackle is used, and leaders are lengthened. Summer steelhead are often found in fast, white water during the day or when fished hard, as the deep pools may not afford enough cover. Single eggs work well, along with small egg clusters, spinners and spoons. Sand shrimp are also an effective bait. The fish spook easily.

Following are among Washington best summer steelhead streams listed by months in order of their productivity:

BOGACHIEL, June, July. **CANYON CREEK**, June. **COLUMBIA**, July, Aug., Sept., Oct. **CASCADE**, May, June. **CEDAR**, July. **CLEARWATER**, July. **COWLITZ**, July, June. **DUNGENESS**, June, July. **ELWHA**, July, June, Oct. **GREEN** (King Co.), Sept., June, July, Oct. **HOH**, Sept., Oct., July. **KALAMA**, June,

July, May. **KLICKITAT**, Sept., Oct., July, Aug. **LEWIS**, June, July, May. **NORTH FORK LEWIS**, Sept. **EAST FORK LEWIS**, June, July, May. METHOW, Oct., Feb., March. **NACHES**, Oct. **NISQUALLY**, Aug., July. **NOOKSACK**, July. **QUEETS**, Aug., July, Sept. **ROCK CREEK** (Clark Co.), Sept. Oct. **ROCK CREEK** (Skamania Co.), July. **SAUK**, July, Sept. **SKAGIT**, June, May. **SKYKOMISH**, June, July. **NORTH FORK SKYKOMISH**, Aug. July. **SOUTH FORK SKYKOMISH**, June. **SNAKE**, Oct. **SNOHOMISH**, June. **SNOQUALMIE**, June, July. **SOL DUC**, June. **STILLAGUAMISH**, Oct., June. **NORTH FORK STILLAGUAMISH**, June. **TOKUL CREEK**, July, Aug. **TOLT**, Aug., June. **WASHOUGAL**, June, May, July. **LITTLE WASHOUGAL**, June, May. **WENATCHEE**, Oct., Sept., Nov. **BIG WHITE SALMON**, Aug., Sept., July. **LITTLE WHITE SALMON**, Sept., July, Aug. WIND, June, July, Sept., Aug. **WYNOOCHEEE**, Aug., July. **YAKIMA**, Feb., March, April

Note—Often only a few fish will separate a "best" month from a preceeding or following month. Although punch card returns indicate the above months are most fruitful for summer runs, summer steelhead are in rivers during other months.

Bang The Bottom
To Catch Steelhead

One of the tough features of winter steelhead fishing is that the big, ocean run rainbows lie close to the bottoms of rivers. Tough, because fishermen have to get bait or lures down where the fish live and where the rocks and snags are. This bottom fishing in the steelhead zone takes a heavy toll of terminal gear. At least some of the frustration, loss of gear and time might be avoided by paying more attention to sinker hookups.

Break-away hookup

Many steelheaders use break-away lead hookups exclusively, figuring to give up some lead to save a bobber or spoon. Standard hookup involves a small barrel swivel tied with a jam knot to the end of the line. The leader goes on the other end of the swivel, then a lighter piece of leader material, about three or four inches long, is tied to one of the swivel's (Incidently—small swivels should be used since large swivels are a source of hangup as they jam between rocks.)

A common practice is to allow three or four inches of leader material to extend after tying a jam knot. Hollow core pencil lead, large "cannonball" buck shot or grooved or slotted pencil lead are clamped on the dropper line in both cases. The advantage of the lighter dropper line is that even though the lead won't slip off in some cases when hung up, the light line will break leaving the terminal gear with the fishermen. A disadvantage is that it takes more time.

The trick to clamp on type sinkers is to put them on tight enough so that they won't sail out across the river and into the alders on a cast, but loose enough to slide off when they jam under a grabby rock.

Three-way swivels with surgical tubing tied with dental floss to the hanging arm of the swivel is another method. Pencil lead is inserted in the tubing. This method probably results in more hang ups than the others.

Surgical tubing

A simplified technique of sinkering consists of cutting surgical tubing into two inch pieces, then bending the tubing near one end and cutting a notch with scissors. The main line, just above the swivel, is doubled, pushed down through the notch in the tubing, then brought outside the tubing. This provides a snubber effect. Pencil lead is inserted.

Another simple sinker system involves slipping a two inch piece of surgical tubing on the main line above the swivel, then jamming pencil lead into the tubing so that it is parallel to the line. A disadvantage of this system is that your line is more subject to abrasion from the bottom.

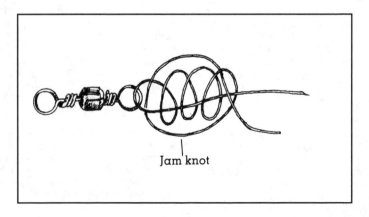

Jam knot

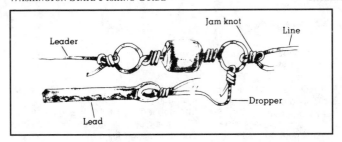

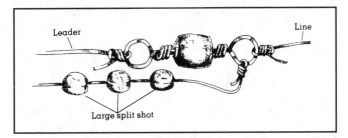

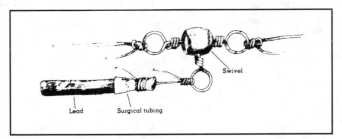

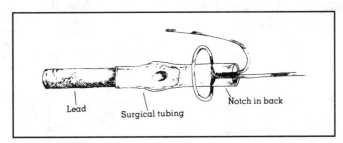

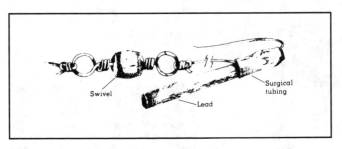

Float Fishing

Canadian steelheaders first developed an effective system of float fishing that has evoked interest among their state-side counterparts. The technique involves using a large, color-topped cork float which holds bait off sticky river bottoms.

Advantages of float fishing for steelhead, in addition to the obvious off-the bottom factor, include the ability to extend a drift. By spilling line, anglers are able to keep their float, and the bait under it, working downstream along a fishy looking current thread. When the float reaches a particularly good looking pocket, the float may be "stalled" by lifting the rod tip, thus keeping the bait in the hot spot for those important few more seconds.

Float fishing comes into its own in slow, "soft" water and close to shore. Even though the water is ruffled by wind or current, the brightly colored float may be easily seen and provides an instant signal to a steelhead strike. With conventional steel-

LONG DRIFTS in soft water may be made by using floats, extending the time baits are presented. Another plus is that there is less chance of spooking fish under clear water conditions.

head gear, the bait or lure would be hung up on bottom in this type of water.

Another plus is that slower water may be thoroughly worked without the hang ups that happen with even the lightest lead when using the bottom-banging technique. The float allows fishermen to keep close track of their bait, since there is little line belly in the short piece of leader between the float and hooks. It also is a visual aid to strikes. When a steelhead takes the bait, the float will go under the surface of the water either partially or all the way. This should tend to make a steelhead fisherman a bit suspicious .

Long rods, level wind reels

Most float anglers use long rods and are able to cast longer distances than is possible with more conventional steelhead gear. The long rods also enable fishermen to keep more line out of the water, cutting down on the amount of drag-producing belly in the line. This makes it easier to ram the hooks home past the barbs on strikes...a straight line is the shortest distance between the angler and the fish and results in more fish on the beach.

Long rods, from 10 1/2 to 13 feet, are used because the floats are fixed on the line and sufficient leader must be tied below them to reach close to the bottom. Thus, when fishing water that is around ten feet in depth, about nine feet of leader, lead and bait dangles under the float which is reeled in close to the rod's tip.

Level wind reels loaded with 15 pound test line are standard for float fishing although some use Canadians use Silex single-action fly reels. These reels will hold around 300 yards of 15 pound test line which compensates in part for the fact that they do not have drags. Most steelheaders prefer level wind reels.

How to hookup the float

Floats are made of cork and are three to five inches long. Bright red paint is applied to the top fourth of the float to aid visibility. Some fishermen carve their own floats out of cork, drilling a hole down the length through the center. Plastic straws are applied with glue then inserted in the holes so that the line does not bear on the cork. Small pointed sticks are wedged into the top hole of the float to hold it in the desired position. Floats are constantly being readjusted as different depths of water are fished.

The line extends from the bottom of the float about two feet, depending upon the depth of water being fished, and a barrel swivel is tied on with a jam knot. A leader of around three feet is tied to the other end of the swivel, and two 1/0 or 2/0 hooks are tied one above the other.   Split shot, spaced at intervals down the leader, is used by some anglers. Others use a piece of pencil lead with one of the surgical tubing hook-ups tied to the swivel. Split shot will probably hold the bait closer to the bottom, although there is the danger of the leader being weakened when the shot is squeezed on.

Use shrimp or eggs for bait

Ghost shrimp, fished live, are a popular bait. The bait is sold at sport shops, but many anglers dig their own on saltwater beaches. Sand-mud combination seems to be best digging grounds for ghost shrimp. A hole is dug in a likely spot, then the digger waits for a few minutes. The shrimp live in lateral channels. When water drains into the hole from the channels they flush more ghost shrimp into the hole.

Fishermen who don't have a clam shovel, or haven't a handy saltwater beach, may use fresh or frozen prawns or salmon or steelhead eggs.

The two hook terminal set-up is particularly suited when using live ghost shrimp. The shrimp is lightly hooked with one hook near its head, then very light wire is wrapped around the shrimp's body and the bottom hook. (As to the wrapping wire, some anglers swear by the light wire on the outside of a bottle of Haig Pinch Scotch. Others swear by the Scotch).

Another technique has been developed which permits the use of shorter rods for float fishing. Rather than using the wooden peg to anchor the float on the line, a nonbulky stop is applied to the line where the float is to end. The stop, which is either a nail knot or a piece of small diameter rubber tubing, may be reeled through the

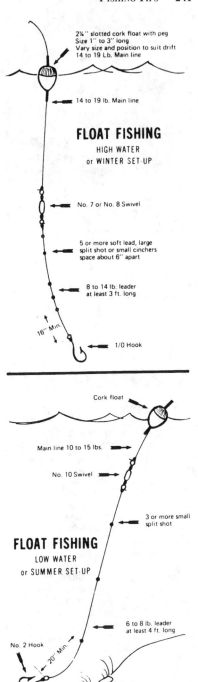

2¼" slotted cork float with peg
Size 1" to 3" long
Vary size and position to suit drift
14 to 19 Lb. Main line

14 to 19 lb. Main line

FLOAT FISHING
HIGH WATER
or WINTER SET-UP

No. 7 or No. 8 Swivel

5 or more soft lead, large split shot or small cinchers space about 6" apart

8 to 14 lb. leader at least 3 ft. long

16" Min.

1/0 Hook

Cork float

Main line 10 to 15 lbs.

No. 10 Swivel

3 or more small split shot

FLOAT FISHING
LOW WATER
or SUMMER SET-UP

6 to 8 lb. leader at least 4 ft. long

No. 2 Hook

20" Min.

RELATIVE SIZE of ghost shrimp is shown alongside a hand-carved, four-inch cork float. The shrimp are delicate and must be hooked lightly with the top hook while being wired or tied to the bottom hook in order to keep them in a wiggly state.

guides, enabling the leader swivel to come to the rod's tip. After the cast is made, the float slips up the line to the stop. Bearing beads on either end of the float help it slide smoothly. The stops are applied so that they may be adjusted.

Steelheaders have adapted the float technique for particular stretches of water that are almost impossible to fish using standard techniques.

Did you know?

German carp average from 10 to 15 pounds in weight and some have been caught in the 20-pound class.

Five million eggs insure the survival of but two mature cod fish.

River Run Salmon

River fishing for salmon is gaining popularity in Washington state as more anglers learn that these fish provide tremendous sport. The state F&W has gained valuable information from punch card returns and has liberalized seasons and limits. Approximately 50 Washington rivers carry significant numbers of salmon and are open to sport fishing. These rivers are listed along with seasons, limits, etc., in the official Washington F&W department sport fishing regulations available free at sport shops and boathouses.

Species of salmon furnishing most fresh water action include fall and spring chinook (king), silvers and humpies (pinks). The humpies run only in odd numbered years in state rivers, (except for even year runs in the Hoh, Dosewallips and Duckabush Rivers) while chinook and silvers make annual runs. Probably most fresh water action from salmon is provided by jack chinook and jack silvers. Jacks are 2-year-old salmon always males, which mature early and return to native streams. They are capable of spawning and often are present in large numbers.

Occasionally stream fishermen will catch chum and sockeye salmon, the other two species of salmon commonly found in Washington rivers. These salmon do not often hit lures or bait even when present in large numbers, although fisheries are developing for both species as anglers experiment with baits.

Differences in weight of the various species of jack and adult salmon may be better understood by noting the following brief biological sketches:

COHO (SILVER) SALMON. Mature in 3 years. Young silvers live in parent rivers about 18 months before migrating to the saltchuck. They spend 18 months in the ocean before making spawning runs at 3 to 30 pounds. Silvers of 14 to 20 pounds are not uncommon. Puget Sound resident silvers are smaller, with adults in the 3 to 6 pound bracket. Silvers enter rivers from July to January and spawn mainly during November and December.

SILVER JACK SALMON. Mature in 2

years. They spend same amount of time in home rivers as do other silvers, but live in the ocean only 4 to 5 months. Weights vary from .05 to 3.5 pounds. Silver jacks enter rivers from September to November.

FALL CHINOOK SALMON. Mature in 3 to 5 years. They spend about 90 days in freshwater before going to sea where they stay until they approach maturity. There is great variance in spawning weights, but most fish are 10 to 35 pounds. In large river systems chinook in the 30 and 40 pound class are not uncommon. Fall chinook enter rivers in August and September and spawn principally during October and November.

CHINOOK JACK SALMON. Mature in 2 years. They live in native river for 90 days, then go to sea until nearly mature. They weigh from 2 to 8 pounds when entering rivers during August and September. Some are heavier.

SPRING CHINOOK. Mature in 4 to 5 years. The springs live in home rivers for about 18 months before migrating to sea where they stay until the spring of their final year. Most weigh from 12 to 30 pounds at spawning. Spring chinook enter rivers from February through May and spawn principally during September.

HUMPY SALMON.(Pink). Mature in 2 years. Fry head for saltwater immediately after wriggling out of the gravel. They spend about 18 months in the ocean. Adults commonly weigh 4 to 8 pounds with some heavier. They spawn in odd-numbered years in Washington, except for even year runs in the Hoh, Duckabush and Dosewallips rivers, entering rivers from July through September. Most pinks spawn during October.

CHUM SALMON. Mature in 3 to 5 years. They stay in home rivers for about the same period as pinks and live in saltwater for most of their remaining life. Average spawning weight is about 10 pounds, and spawning occurs from September to December. They are caught by sport fishermen in some areas.

SOCKEYE SALMON. Mature in 3 to 5 years. Sockeyes leave native streams after hatching, dropping into lakes in the river system where they live for about a year. They live in saltwater until nearly mature. Average spawning weight is 4 to 7 pounds. Sockeyes enter rivers from May to September and spawn in October and November. It is unusual for sockeyes to be taken by river fishermen, although some are caught by trolling when the mature fish are milling in lakes.

All Pacific coast salmon, including jacks, die after spawning.

Locating salmon

Salmon are found in a bit different type water than steelhead. They usually favor slower and deeper runs. Silver and humpy salmon, particularly, are often active and do considerable rolling and jumping in rivers when stacked in holes. Some fishermen locate rolling fish before settling down to serious fishing.

Here are some hints which should help:

COHO (SILVER) SALMON. (Adult). Fish the deep, slack water which contains cover such as logs, rocks, over-hanging brush or under-cut banks. This is the type water that holds sea-run cutthroat. Watch for rolling fish and pitch golf tee spinners, large spinners, winged bobbers or colorful wobbling spoons. Silvers will sometimes pick

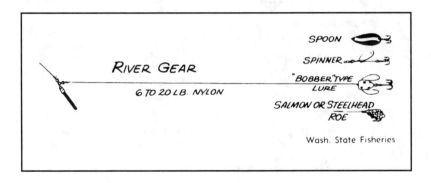

up egg and yarn offerings. Medium weight steelhead tackle is ideal.

CHINOOK SALMON. (Adult). These fish are found close to the heavy current line in deeper water. They should be fished deep and slow. Spring chinook may be found a bit higher in the pool than the riper fall chinook. Winged bobbers, large spinners, wobbling spoons and eggs and yarn will take them. In SW Washington rivers fresh prawns are used effectively. Because of the chance of hooking giant chinook, heavy steelhead gear is in order.

HUMPY SALMON. These salmon commonly gang in deep pools and are often very active. Tiny wobblers fished deep and slow, will entice them, as will small spinners.

JACK SALMON. (Chinook and Silvers). The jacks are found with adult salmon, and also frequent riffles. Cluster eggs are probably the most effective bait, but spinners and spoons will take them. Light spinning gear will handle jacks. The salmon provide great sport when taken with tackle geared to their size.

Here's where and when to catch them:

BOGACHIEL RIVER. Fall chinook, jack chinook, silvers, jack silvers. October best, September good.

CALAWAH RIVER. Fall chinook, jack chinook, silvers, jack silvers. October best, September good.

CAPITOL LAKE. (Olympia). Fall chinook, jack chinook, silvers, jack silvers. September best, October good.

CHEHALIS RIVER. Spring and fall chinook, jack chinook, silvers, jack silvers. August best for springs. Fall chinook best in October, with silvers and jacks taken in September, October, November and December. Good late silver fishing. Best fishing below mouth of Satsop River.

CLEARWATER RIVER. (Queets tributary). Silver and chinook jacks. Best in September. August and October good.

COLUMBIA RIVER. Fall and spring chinook, silvers. Chinook and silver jacks. Best spring chinook fishing in April. September best for fall chinook. October best

for silvers. Salmon are taken from March into November.

COPALIS RIVER. Silvers and silver jacks. October best, September good.

COWLITZ RIVER. Fall and spring chinook and jacks, silvers and silver jacks. Salmon available from April to October. April best for springs. October best for fall salmon.

DESCHUTES RIVER. Chinook jacks. Best in October.

DEWATTO CREEK. Silver jacks. October best.

DOSEWALLIPS RIVER. Silvers and jack silvers. Best in October. Good in September. A few spring chinook in mid summer. Humpies in lower river during both odd and even-years.

DRANO LAKE. (Mouth of Little White Salmon River). Fall Chinook and jacks. September best, October good.

DUCKABUSH RIVER. Silvers and jack silvers. Best in October, September good. Humpies in lower river odd and even years.

DUNGENESS RIVER. Chinook and silver jacks. October best. September and November good. Some spring chinook.

DUWAMISH RIVER. Chinook and silver jacks. October best, September and November good.

GREEN RIVER. Chinook and silver jacks. October best, September and November good .

HAMMA HAMMA RIVER. Silvers and silver jacks. October best, September good. Humpies in lower river.

HOH RIVER. Fall and spring chinook, chinook jacks, silvers and silver jacks. August best, May and November good.

HOQUIAM RIVER. Chinook jacks, silvers, silver jacks. October best, September and December good.

HUMPTULIPS RIVER. Fall chinook and jacks, silvers and silver jacks. October best, August and December good.

DAVE PERINE leans back on a hefty river-run salmon.

JOHN'S RIVER. Silvers and silver jacks. October best, September good.

KALAMA RIVER. Fall chinook and jacks, silvers and jack silvers. September best, August and October good.

LAKE SAMMAMISH. Fall Chinook and jacks, silvers and silver jacks. October best, September and November good.

LAKE WASHINGTON. Fall chinook and jacks, silvers and silver jacks. October best, September and November good. Sockeye from June through September. Fishing concentrated near mouths of Cedar and Sammamish Rivers.

LEWIS RIVER. Fall chinook and jacks, silvers and silver jacks. Best in Septem ber, good in August and October.

NASELLE RIVER. Fall chinook and jacks, silvers and silver jacks. Best in September, good in August and December.

NEMAH RIVER. Chinook and silver jacks. Best in September, good in August and November.

NISOUALLY RIVER. Jack, chinook and silvers. September best, August and November good.

NOOKSACK RIVER. Fall and spring chinook, chinook jacks, silvers and silver jacks, humpies. October best, May and November good.

NORTH RIVER. Fall chinook and jacks, silvers and silver jacks. Best in October, good in December.

PUYALLUP RIVER. Chinook and silver jacks. October best, November good.

QUEETS RIVER. Fall and spring chinook, chinook jacks, silvers and silver jacks. August best, May and October good.

QUILCENE RIVER. Jack chinook and silvers. October best. September, November good.

QUILLAYUTE RIVER. Fall and spring chinook and jacks, silvers and silver jacks. October best, August good.

QUINAULT RIVER. Spring and fall chinook, chinook jacks, silvers and silver jacks, sockeye. October best, June and November good.

SAMISH RIVER. Chinook and silver jacks. October best, September and November good.

SAMMAMISH RIVER. Jack chinook and jack silvers. October best, November good.

SATSOP RIVER. Chinook jacks, silvers and silver jacks. December best, August good .

SKAGIT RIVER. Spring and fall chinook, chinook jacks, silvers, silver jacks, humpies. September best on odd-numbered years because of big humpy runs. August best on even-numbered years. April and October good.

SKOKOMISH RIVER. Spring and fall chinooks. Chinook jacks, silvers, silver jacks, chum. September best for jacks, October good.

SKYKOMISH RIVER. Jack chinook and silvers. Best in October, good in September. **SNAKE RIVER**. Fall and spring chinook, jack chinook. July best, good in May and September.

SNOHOMISH RIVER. Fall chinook and chinook jacks, silvers and silver jacks. October best, August and November good.

SNOQUALMIE RIVER. Chinook and silver jacks. Best in October, good in September and November.

SOL DUC RIVER. Fall and spring chinook, chinook jacks, silvers, silver jacks. Best in October, good in September, November and May, June.

STILLAGUAMISH RIVER. Spring and fall chinook, chinook jacks, silvers and silver jacks, humpies. Best in September on odd-numbered years due to heavy humpy run. Best in October in even numbered years. July good.

TAHUYA RIVER. Silver jacks. Best in October, poor fishing.

TOLT RIVER. Silver jacks. Best in October.

TOUTLE RIVER. Fall chinook and jacks, silvers, silver jacks. September best, August and October fair.

TUCANNON RIVER. Spring chinook. Best above Marengo in June. May good.

UNION RIVER. Silver jacks. October best

WASHOUGAL RIVER. Silvers and silver jacks, fall chinook, chinook jacks. September best, October good.

WILLAPA RIVER. Fall chinook and jacks. Silvers and silver jacks. October best. August and November good.

WISHKAH RIVER. Chinook and silver jacks. October best, September and December good.

WYNOOCHE RIVER. Chinook jacks, silvers, silver jacks. December best, September good.

Note: It is essential that anglers read the official F&W regulations before fishing rivers since there are many seasonal and area closures. The regulations are free at sport shops and boathouses.

Fish surface for just planted 'Bows

Since a large number of lakes are planted with legal size rainbow just prior to season opener, fishermen would be wise to study habits of these hatchery reared fish. Experiments have shown that such fish, planted shortly before an opener, remain close to the surface. They are used to surface feed in shallow hatchery ponds and it takes some time for them to kick the habit.

Small spoons, trolled near the surface with little or no weight, will catch more recently liberated hatchery fish than any other method short of a DuPont spinner. The rainbow usually get the picture after a few weeks in their lake environment, depending somewhat on the pressure, and join larger, native trout closer to the bottom.

Single Egging

In waters where there are substantial plants of legal sized trout prior to the season's opening, it's no great deal to catch them. The fish are naive and not too particular as to what they hit. As the season progresses, however, trout become not only more wary, but scarcer and it is those fishermen who sharpen their techniques (and hooks) who come up with the fish.

Techniques from the Pros

Expert trout fishermen using eggs will choose a 7 to 8'1/2 foot fly or spinning rod with a very sensitive tip. They'll hang a single action fly reel or light spinning reel on the rod and load either one with six pound test monofilament. Lighter lines, particularly when using a fly rod, tend to slap and overlap the guides on casts.

Clarity of water will somewhat determine the weight of leaders, which may be as light as one pound test. Leaders of one to three pound test will handle most situations. Very small swivels should be used. Before tying the line to the swivel, a small egg-type leader is slipped on the line. This type sinker has a hole through it so that it will slide up and down the line, but will stop at the swivel.

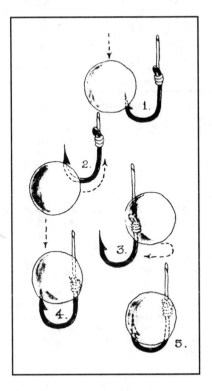

Hooks and hookups

Hook sizes for this type of fishing range from six to twelve. Even though they just came out of the box they should be sharpened with a fine stone so that the point is sharp enough to stick in a fingernail.

Salmon eggs are placed on the hook by inserting the point just under the skin of the egg, taking care to make as small an opening as possible. The egg is then worked up the shank and over the eye of the hook, rotated and then pushed back down over the point of the hook. The softest eggs will stay on since the bend of hook cradles the bottom of the egg, providing easy casts are made.

Line is stripped from the reel and laid in loose coils on the boat seat or bank. Then lob casts are made to insure that the egg will stay put. When the egg and sinker have settled to the bottom, slack line is

reeled in. Rods may be propped in the boat or off the shore, but the tip should be high. By watching the point where the line enters the water, and also the rod tip, anglers can tell when trout pick up the egg. With the center-bored, free-wheeling sinker, trout may pick up the egg, turn and head south without feeling much drag as the line feeds through the sinker which holds on the bottom. This is the time to set the hook.

The egg should not be left in one spot too long. If action is slow, reel in a few inches at a time. At the slightest hint of drag, reel in to clear any debris from the hook and egg, then pitch it out again.

Hook disgorgers are in order as trout are often hooked deep with this system. Because of the light leader involved, a net is required equipment.

Save The Eggs

Mention "fresh eggs" to a veteran steel-head or river salmon fisherman and you will immediately receive a large chunk of undivided and earnest attention. This is particularly true if the angler has gone through the trama caused by failure to beach a mature lady fish during the past few outings. Experienced egg-fishing anglers try to avoid baitless days by preserving every skein of eggs they acquire. And, while there are many methods of preserving eggs, the simple way is as effective as any.

Preserving the eggs

Separate layers of eggs in the skeins and rub powdered borax in thoroughly, then sprinkle and rub more borax over the outside of the skeins. Wrap each skein separately in absorbent paper towels, then in several layers of newspaper and place in refrigerator. When well wrapped, there is no smell. The maturity of the eggs regulate the number of days they are refrigerated in this first step. Tight skeins require only one day, while juicy eggs from fish caught near spawning time may need three to four days.

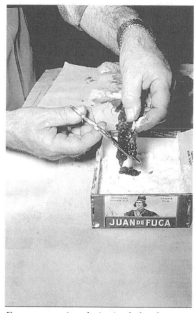

Eggs are cut into bait-sized chunks

After excess moisture has been absorbed by the paper towels and the eggs toughened by the borax, remove the skeins from the refrigerator. Large skeins should be cut laterally with scissors, then cut into bait-sized clusters over a pile or box of powdered borax. The baits are then rolled or shaken in the box until they are completely covered with borax. Generous amounts of borax should be used.

Sprinkle a little borax into a glass container such as a peanut butter jar, then add baits to the brim, topping them with more borax before tightly screwing the lid on. Eggs prepared in this manner may be stored in a refrigerator for two weeks. If they are not to be used within this period, they should be frozen. Frozen eggs fish well after up to a year of freezer life, but once thawed should be used within a week or so.

Making strawberry clusters

Since egg clusters are somewhat difficult to keep on a hook with repeated casts,

Thick egg skeins are scissored laterally.

some fishermen stretch their egg supply by making "strawberries." This calls for maline cloth (light net material used on women's hats and available at dry goods stores) to be cut into three or four inch squares. Bait-sized chunks of eggs are placed on the squares and the netting is pulled snug around the bait, gathered and tied at the top with red thread. Strawberry clusters may be frozen in glass jars, but waxed paper should be placed between layers for easy separation.

Rather than powdered borax, some anglers use Sodium Sulfite, Merck No. 5201, to preserve eggs. Too heavy application of this material will dry the eggs excessively, but baits correctly prepared will milk well in the water. They may be frozen like boraxed eggs.

Preparing single eggs

Should a fisherman find himself with a large supply of eggs, he may want to prepare some single eggs for trout fishing. Skeins of mature eggs are "singled" by light pressure over a screen large enough to permit single eggs to drop through.

Six cups of eggs are placed in six cups of

Baits are rolled in borax until moisture is gone.

cold water to which is added two table spoons of table salt, two tablespoons of borax, two tablespoons of benzoate of soda (pharmacies sell it) and vegetable dye. The project is brought to a slow, easy boil. Constant stirring and testing is required, with eggs tested with a pin every 30 seconds for firmness. When the outer skin is tough, but the interior soft, remove the eggs and place them in a container of cold water. The eggs are then drained and packed in eight ounce jars containing one ounce of glycerin. After jars are tightly sealed, rotate to coat all the eggs with the glycerin.

An old Indian on-the-creek technique is to strip loose eggs from a ripe female into a can and add a bit of water. Place the can over coals of a fire. When the eggs turn an opaque white they will stick on the hook, according to the legend. The word from the tribe is not to over cook them.

Tip for large fish

An effective method to locate the deep pockets on the bottom of lakes where lunker trout often lurk is as follows:

Tie a small swivel to the end of a mono line, then rig three feet of six to eight pound test line to the same end of the swivel. Tie a 1.4 ounce sinker to end of this dropper line. Lighter leader of 18 to 24 inches is then tied to the open end of the swivel and a small trolling spoon is attached.

With this trolling system the sinker is continuously searching for and bumping bottom, with the light spoon fluttering just above bottom. When contact with the bottom is lost, indicating a hole, additional line is quickly paid out until the sinker makes contact.

Did you know?

The Kangaroo rat, barely 2 inches high, has outsize legs, enormous feet and a tufted tail 3 times as long as itself. Using its tail as a rudder, it can make 90-degree turns in mid-flight.

Fishing Alpine Lakes

High lake fishermen start getting a bit itchy around the first part of June, eye balling the snow, still hanging on the slopes of the Cascades and Olympics, but realistically alpine lake angling doesn't really get rolling until the end of June or the first of July. By this time ice cover is gone or going from many lakes, and snow drifts no longer effectively block trails or cover blaze marks. As a rule-of-thumb, lakes with W. or S. exposures will shed the ice lid first. Sizeable streams running in and out of lakes hasten the ice-out time, also.

Early openers

By counties here are some of the high lakes which generally are open, or are partially so, earliest in the season: **KING COUNTY**: Calligan, Dorothy, Hancock. Big Pratt, Granite, Trout, Eagle and Little Eagle. **SNOHOMISH COUNTY**: Airplane, Goat, Isabel, Boardman, Upper Boardman, Ashlands and Island. **WHATCOM COUNTY**: Canyon. **LEWIS COUNTY**: Packwood, Newaukum, Glacier and Backbone. **COWLITZ COUNTY**: Merrill. **SKAMANIA COUNTY**: Goose. **KITTITAS COUNTY**: Menastash, Milk and Lost. **CHELAN COUNTY**: Eight-Mile, Colchuck, Domke, Stuart. **YAKIMA COUNTY**: Lost, Long, Dog and Leach.

Alpine lakes in Mt. Rainier, Olympic and North Cascades national parks usually do not offer good fishing until mid-July. September and early October are the best months to fish mountain lakes, but a wary eye must be kept on the weather.

Species of fish in Washington's mountain lakes include rainbow, cutthroat, eastern brook, Montana blackspot (a type of cutthroat), golden, mackinaw or lake trout, a few Atlantic salmon and grayling.

Grayling are found in Upper (Big) Granite lake in Skagit county. Recent grayling plants have been made in King's and Marshall Lakes in Pend Oreille County. Joan Lake in Snohomish County has received Atlantic salmon plants.

Golden trout locations

KING COUNTY. Crawford, Cougar, Edds, Little Hester, Ptarmigan, T'ahl. KITTITAS

Mosquito dope is a necessity for alpine lakes fishing, but the fish and scenery are worth the buzzing.

COUNTY. Glacier, Lemah, Ridge, Summit Chief, Three Queens. CHELAN COUNTY. Choral, Edna, Elsey, Enchanted, King, Rock. OKANOGAN COUNTY. Scheelite. SKAGIT COUNTY. Cyclone, Enjar. SNOHOMISH COUNTY. Bath, Helena, Lime, Sunset. WHATCOM COUNTY. Thornton. NORTH CASCADE NATIONAL PARK. Hidden, Thornton.

Mackinaw lakes

High lakes holding mackinaw include Isabel (Snohomish) and Eight Mile (Chelan). There are also "macks," or lake trout, in such lowland lakes as Deer and Loon in Stevens county; Cle Elum in Kittitas county; and Bonaparte in Okanogan.

In past years there have been plants of mackinaw in Deep (King), Clear (Pierce), Sammamish, Hewitt, St. Clair, Offut, Wallace, Whatcom, Quinault, Pine (King), Keechelus, Kachess, Crescent, Steilacoom, Badger, Chapman, Bear (King), and Black Diamond. Some of these lakes have since been rehabilitated with no signs of large lake trout, although there are periodic reports of the big fish being taken in Sammamish and other large lakes.

For high lake fishing, spinning gear with plastic bubbles to which are attached a length of light leader and bait or flies, is highly effective. Fly fishermen score with both wet and dry flies. Trolling works on those lakes which have rafts.

Tiger Muskies
A "New" Trophy Fish

Washington sport fishermen have another real trophy fish to pursue with increasing numbers of tiger muskies in a few state lakes. The fish is a hybrid cross produced when a male northern pike fertilizes the eggs of a female muskellunge. The fish grow to over 50 pounds, with present world record of 51 pounds from a Wisconsin lake. The hybrid is very much like the true muskellunge in size and appearance and is prized equally. It differs in side markings with the tiger musky having wavering tiger stripes. The flesh is white and flaky and is said to be of comparable in quality to that of the muskellunge.

They were introduced to Mayfield Lake on Cowlitz River in 1988 with eggs furnished by Minnesota's game department. The fast growing fish have already exceeded 28 pounds in Mayfield. The fish grew 12 to 18.5 pounds in four years. Tiger musky plants were also made in Spokane County's Newman Lake in 1992 where some should be over 36 inches, the mimimum legal length.

Other state waters under consideration for tiger musky plants include Merwin Reservoir on Cowlitz County's Lewis River, and Curlew Lake in Ferry County. Plans call for additional plants from eggs reared at Cowlitz and Mossyrock hatcheries.

The fish were introduced to state waters through efforts of F&W Dept. biologist Jack Tipping who saw them as a means of controlling Mayfield's huge squawfish and sucker population as well as providing a new trophy fishery. Subsequent testing revealed a substantial reduction in these scrap fish. Because of this welcomed development, rainbow trout are once again being planted in Mayfield from Mossyrock hatchery.

Since tiger muskies are sterile and cannot reproduce they just keep growing while depleting squawfish and sucker populations which target on trout and juvenile coho salmon which are found in Mayfield.

Although anglers may keep "tigers" (see offical F&W regulations) most sportsmen release the fish so that they can continue reducing scrap fish numbers.

Best fishing periods appear to be afternoons and evenings on warm summer days, fishing near weed beds. Steel leaders are a must for these fish because of their sharp teeth. Big lures such as bucktail spinners are commonly used.

TIGER MUSKY of 14 pounds is displayed here by Jack Tipping. The fish, which was released, measured 37 inches. (Photo by J. Pierce)

Kokanee Come On in May

Fishermen are treated to another "season" in early May each year when kokanee or silver trout (land locked sockeye salmon) start changing their preference in food from plankton to insects and other more meaty foods. Up to the time the kokanee are about 6 inches they strain feed through their gill rakers and are difficult to take with bait.

The kokanee are either 3 or 4 years of age when they start entering the sport catch, and range from 7 or 8 inches to over 3 pounds depending upon the race and availability of food in the particular lake. While May and June are generally the peak months for these fish, deeper lakes sometimes provide good fishing beyond this time.

Some Silver Salmon

Most of the "silver trout" planted are sockeye salmon, but there are a limited number of lakes in Washington which have been planted with silver salmon. While not so numerous as the sockeye, the lake variety of silver salmon go on solid foods early in life, rather than depending upon plankton. They are 2 and 3 year fish when taken by hook and line. They range in size from 6 to 16 inches, with 9 to 12 inches average. Silver salmon do not peak in terms of best fishing period, but provide action from the spring opener into summer. They take

KOKANEE catch from Rimrock Lake.

worms and eggs and other bait similar to rainbow. The following "how-to" refers to the sockeye version of "silver trout."

Use soft rods

Very soft actioned rods are necessary for successful kokanee still fishing. Long fly rods with sensitive tips are ideal. Any type reel may be used with 6 or 8 pound test monofiliment line. It is important to use about 3 feet of 2 pound test leader. Either size 10 or 12 single egg hooks are OK. A small split shot is clamped about a foot above the hook. Single eggs, maggots, uncased caddis larvae (periwinkles), worms and eggs are used for bait.

Fishing should start about 6 inches above the bottom, with the bait being inched up a few inches at a time to about 6 feet from bottom. If there is no action, the bait should be lowered to the bottom and inched in again.

In some deep lakes the kokanee are found in up to 70 feet of water at or just below the developing thermocline which usually rises as the season progresses. Fish finders are useful in locating schools.

They bite light

Kokanee are very dainty nibblers, so the rod tip must be watched very carefully. It is best to set the hook on the first nibble. Since with this technique fishing is often done in deep water, fishermen will have to set very hard to offset the belly and stretch of the line and the limber-actioned rod. Many anglers prop their rod in the boat and concentrate on the tip for the strike signal.

A trick some fishermen use in Rimrock Lake in Yakima County is to tip a fluorescent whitefish fly with either goldenrod or fly maggots. Usually early morning hours are most productive for kokanee.

Trolling works, too

For fishermen who prefer to keep moving, trolling is effective. Small gang trolls followed by a leader of about 12 inches with 2 single hooks, sizes 4, 6 or 8, baited with worms and single eggs, take a lot of fish. Some anglers prefer using leaded line and small spoons to get away from the drag of gang trolls. Technique is to insert a barbed eye into the end of the leaded

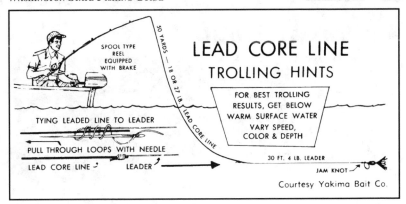

SPOOL TYPE
REEL
EQUIPPED
WITH BRAKE

50 YARDS — 18 OR 27 LB. LEAD CORE LINE

LEAD CORE LINE
TROLLING HINTS

FOR BEST TROLLING
RESULTS, GET BELOW
WARM SURFACE WATER
VARY SPEED,
COLOR & DEPTH

TYING LEADED LINE TO LEADER

PULL THROUGH LOOPS WITH NEEDLE

LEAD CORE LINE   LEADER

30 FT. 4 LB. LEADER

JAM KNOT

Courtesy Yakima Bait Co.

line, then attach 25 feet of 6 pound test mono line. A small spoon is tied to the end of the leader. Leaded line comes color-coded so that fishermen may determine exactly how much line is out. The color changes every 25 or 50 feet. Because of the bulk of leaded line, large casting or trolling reels are used. A technique which is growing in popularity and which works well, involves a lead line or mono with salmon trolling weight (banana) followed by 4-6 feet of leader and a small dodger (4 1/2" long). To this is tied a 20-30 inch leader with either a very small wing bobber or a kokanee wobbler spoon.

Vary speed and depth

Whether trolling with mono line and gang troll, or with leaded line, fishing should start shallow with more line gradually played out until the correct or fishy depth is discovered. Frequent lazy "S" turns and changes in trolling speed often coax kokanee to hit.

Best kokanee lakes

The state's top kokanee lakes by counties are as follows:

KING COUNTY. Sammamish, Washington and Sawyer. (May through July best).

SNOHOMISH COUNTY. Stevens, Goodwin, Armstrong. (May through July).

KITSAP COUNTY. Wildcat, Tiger, Mission. (May through July best).

PIERCE COUNTY. American, Alder, Clear, Tapps. (May through July best, fall often excellent).

THURSTON COUNTY. Summit, St. Clair.

(May through July best, fall sometimes good).

SKAGIT COUNTY. Cavanaugh, Baker, Shannon. (May through July. Shannon best in October).

WHATCOM COUNTY. Samish, Whatcom. (May through July best).

ISLAND COUNTY. Cascade, Mountain. (May through July best).

CLARK and **COWLITZ COUNTIES.** Yale, Merwin reservoirs, (Mid-summer and fall best).

CLALLAM COUNTY. Pleasant, Sutherland, Ozette. (Mid-summer best).

KITTITAS COUNTY. Kachess, Keechelus, Cle Elum and Cooper. (June, July best).

THURSTON COUNTY. Summit. (May through JULY best, fall sometimes good).

GRANT COUNTY. Banks, LongLake, Billy Clapp. (Late spring, summer best).

SPOKANE COUNTY. Chapman, (April, May and June).

STEVENS COUNTY. Loon, Deer, (June, July best).

PEND OREILLE COUNTY. Bead, Davis, Horseshoe. (April and May best).

LINCOLN, STEVENS, FERRY COUNTIES. Lake Roosevelt. (Late summer)

YAKIMA COUNTY. Bumping, Rimrock.

Cutthroat Trout

A cutthroat's early life is very similar to that of steelhead. They remain in home streams for two summers before going to sea on a spring freshet at about 20 months of age. Cutts do not roam far from land as steelhead do. They work along beaches near mouths of streams. Most sea-run cutthroat will return to home streams. The first return is usually a fall feeding run, with only about 10 out of 100 females spawning at this time.

Peak in fall

Cutthroat enter rivers from the saltchuck every month of the year, but usually do not appear in large numbers until July or August. They increase from this time with peak in late September and October. Most spawn by early April, but ripe fish have been caught from January into June.

Eastern Washington cutthroat vary in appearance from coastal cutts, being chunkier and more colorful. They have fewer black spots.

Fish shallow

Sea-run cutthroat are taken in salt water by trolling or by casting small spoons from the beach over a rocky bottom near mouths of streams. If using a boat, fishermen should keep the bottom in sight on the beach side. The cutts also bang small herring.

Since cutthroat often dine on small fish such as bullheads, sand lance, smelt, herring and occasionally salmon fry, streamer flies are highly effective. In streams the fish prefer slow, snaggy stretches or pools overhung with brush. Spinner and worm fishing is a standby for both sea run and native cutthroat. Crawfish tails, sucker meat or prawns work great for late evening or night fishing.

Locate beaver ponds

Some of the finest trout fishing available in W. Washington is for cutthroat in beaver ponds. Even the smallest stream may have beaver ponds along its length. Fishermen should look for fresh beaver signs, then explore. Patches of dead trees may signal a permanent type pond, since water kills trees after a period. If a beaver pond holds water in late September, the driest month

FINE CATCH of cutthroat trout.

of the year, it is a good prospect. Most major beaver pond systems in W. Washington have been planted with cutthroat and some eastern brook.

Good fishing areas

Among the better salt water areas for cutthroat are Hood Canal, Port Gardner, Port Susan, Mukilteo shoreline, beaches along Camano, Whidbey, Bainbridge and Vashon islands.

Top rivers for sea-run cutthroat include Cowlitz, Columbia River bars, North, Satsop, Skokomish, Stillaguamish, Samish, and Skagit. Fly fishermen watch for early hatches of flying ants, then reach for their tackle.

Sometimes cutthroat just in from salt water do not carry the red slash marks on the underside of the lower jaw which give the fish its name. Cutthroat have teeth on the back of the tongue, and rainbow do not, which is an easy way to determine whether the fish is a 'cutt of a 'bow.

Did you know?

The burrowing owl is the only member of its clan that lives underground. It usually moves into subterranean homes built by prairie dogs, badgers, skunks, foxes and other animals.

The Spiny Ray Lakes

Although much of the emphasis in Washington fishing is on trout, salmon and steelhead, the state offers tremendous spiny ray fishing. The variety of fish available is wide and there are good fishing waters in nearly every county.

One of the plusses for spiny rays (so named because of the stiff points on the tips of dorsal and other fins) is that they start providing good fishing when trout action is tapering off in many lakes. Early summer through early fall are most productive bass, perch, crappie, bluegill and catfish fishing periods in most sections of the state, although there is some ice fishing for these species. (See ice fishing story).

Here are the state's spiny ray (warm water fish) lakes and streams by counties. (See individual county listings for fish species and locations).

ADAMS COUNTY: Black (upper), Butte, Cow, Deadman, Finnel, Green, Hallin, Linda, Royal, Sprague.

BENTON COUNTY: Mitchell Pond, Mound Pond, Palmer Pond, Switch Pond, Yellepit Pond, below Prosser Dam, Umatilla, Wallula.

CHELAN COUNTY: Antilon, Dry (Grass), Entiat, Fish, Meadow, Pateros, Rock Island Pool, Three Lakes Reservoir, Wapato.

CLALLAM COUNTY: Beaver.

CLARK COUNTY: Campbell, Canvasback, Carty, Curtis, Green, Hathaway, Lacamas, Lancaster, Long, Mud, Post Office, Round, Vancouver, Widgeon.

COLUMBIA COUNTY: Bryan (Little Goose).

COWLITZ COUNTY: Horseshoe, Kress, Sacajawea, Silver.

DOUGLAS COUNTY: Rufus Woods.

FERRY COUNTY: Curlew, Roberta.

FRANKLIN COUNTY: Clark Pond, Dalton, Emma, Herbert G. West, Kahlotus, Mesa, Scootney, Worth.

GRANT COUNTY: Alkali, Ancient, Banks, Stratford, Crater, Crescent, Crescent Bay, Evergreen, Flat, Frenchman Hills, Goose, Long, Mallard, Moses, Potholes, Priest Rapids, Roosevelt, Sand, Soda, Stan Coffin, Thompson, Trail, Wanapum, Williams, Willow, Winchester.

GRAYS HARBOR COUNTY: Duck.

ISLAND COUNTY: Cranberry, Deer, Pondilla.

JEFFERSON COUNTY: Crocker, Gibbs, Leland, Ludlow, Sandy Shore, Upper Twin.

KING COUNTY: Angle, Beaver, Bitter, Boren, Desire, Doloff, Fenwick, Green, Haller, Horseshoe Slough, Janicke Slough, Killarney, Larsen, Leota, Meadowbrook, Meridian, Phantom, Pine, Reid Slough, Round, Rutherford Slough, Sammamish, Sawyer, Shadow, Sikes, Spring, Star, Steel, Stickney Slough, Tradition, Twelve, Union, Walker, Washington, Wittenmeyer.

KITSAP COUNTY: Fairview, Flora, Horseshoe, Island, Kitsap, Koeneman, Long, Ludvick, Mission, Panther, Square, Tahuya, Wildcat, Wye.

ERIC SMITH took this 8.75 pound largemouth bass from Bonnie Lake in Spokane County.

KITTITAS COUNTY: Fio Rito, McCabe Pond, Sorensen Pond, Woodhouse Ponds.

KLICKITAT COUNTY: Chamberlain, Locke, Rowland.

LEWIS COUNTY: Airport, Carlisle, Davis, Mayfield, Riffe, Swofford.

LINCOLN COUNTY: Coffee Pot, H, Icehouse, Tanwax, Wall, Wederspahn.

MASON COUNTY: Blacksmith, Camp Pond, Collins, Cushman, Forbes, Hanks, Isabella, Island, Jiggs, Limerick, Lost, Mason, Nahwatzel, Simpson, Spencer, Stump, Tee, Trails End, West.

OKANOGAN COUNTY: Bonner, Buck, Duck, Indian Dan, Osoyoos, Palmer, Whitestone, Washburn.

PACIFIC COUNTY: Black, Breaker, Clam, Cranberry, Deer, Freshwater, Gile, Island, Litschke, Loomis, Lost, Skating, Tape, Tinker.

PEND OREILLE COUNTY: Boundary Reservoir, Box Canyon Reservoir, Davis, Chain.

PIERCE COUNTY: American, Bonney, Chambers, Florence, Forest, Harts, Little Harts, Kapowsin, Louise, Ohop, Rapjohn, Silver, Spanaway, Steilacoom, Tanwax, Tule, Wapato, Whitman.

SAN JUAN COUNTY: Egg, Hummel, Killebrew, Sportsman.

SKAGIT COUNTY: Beaver, Big, Campbell, Cannery, Caskey, Clear, Cranberry, McMurray, Minkler, Mud, Whistle.

SKAMANIA COUNTY: Ashes, Bass, Franz, Grant.

SNOHOMISH COUNTY: Ballinger, Beecher, Bosworth, Bryant, Cassisy, Chain, Connor, Crabapple, Crescent, Flowing, Gissberg Ponds, Goodwin, Hall, Kellogg, Ketchum, Ki, Loma, Little Martha, Roesiger, Ruggs, Scriber, Shoecraft, Stevens, Stickney, Sunday, Thomas, Tomtit, Winters.

SPOKANE COUNTY: Bear, Chapman, Clear, Downs, Eloika, Horseshoe, Liberty, Long, Medical, Newman, Queen Lucas.

WHITE STURGEON of 763 pounds was captured in 1935 in the McGowan fish wheel one-half mile below Cascade Locks in Columbia River. (A. Pierce Photo)

STEVENS COUNTY: Deer, Jump-Off-Joe, Loon, Pierre, Waitts.

THURSTON COUNTY: Alder, Bald Hill, Barnes, Bass, Bigelow, Black, Chambers, Coopers Potholes, Deep, Elbow, Fifteen, Gehrke, Grass, Hewitt, Hicks, Long, Munn, Offut, Patterson, Pitman, Reichel, Scott, Simmons, Smith, St. Clair, Summit, Susan, Trosper, Ward.

WALLA WALLA COUNTY: Burbank Slough, Casey Pond, Curlew Pond, Sacajawea.

WHATCOM COUNTY: Barrett, Cain, Fazon, Green, Jorgenson, Judson, Mosquito, Mud, Samish, Tennant, Terrell, Weiser, Whatcom.

WHITMAN COUNTY: Lower Granite, Rock.

YAKIMA COUNTY: Berglund, Bridgeman Pond, Byron Pond, Giffin, Granger Pond, Horseshoe Pond, I-82 Ponds, Morgan Pond, Rotary, Yakima River.

Sturgeon Are Ancient Fish

Both white and green sturgeon are taken by sport fishermen in Washington waters. The Columbia and Snake rivers provide most of the fish, although such rivers as the Chehalis, Naselle and Willapa, in their tidewater reaches, yield the fish. White sturgeon are found in the Columbia, Snake, Chehalis, Naselle and Willapa rivers, with the greens, which apparently prefer saltwater over fresh, taken in Grays and Willapa Rivers.

Whites are big

The whites are larger—up to 20 feet and 1800 pounds—and are considered better eating than the greens, which may reach 7 feet and 350 pounds. It is thought that the whites live part of their lives in the sea, ascending rivers to spawn. Some are land-locked in the upper Columbia and Snake Rivers because of numerous dams.

Sturgeon are bottom feeders in fresh water, eating mollusks and crustaceans, along with smelt, lampreys, trout and salmon smolts. The fish, which are representatives of an ancient group of fish, has a skeleton made up of cartilage. They grow very slowly, and probably do not reach spawning age until about 6 feet long, in the case of whites.

Taken all year

Sturgeon may be caught on a year around basis, but usually the best period is from late fall through early spring. Tackle must be stout—60 pound test line is common for bank fishermen, with 10 or 12 ounces of lead. Smelt or herring are used for bait. Fishing is done in deep holes, with the bait left to "soak" until a sturgeon picks it off the bottom. Ghost shrimp, in addition to smelt or herring, are used in tidal areas.

MODERN SPORT sturgeon terminal gear.

DENNIS CLAY, left, with a Snake River sturgeon. Skipper Dan Fleshman of Beamer's Hell's Canyon Tours helps with the release of the five footer.

Ice Fishing

By FRED L. PETERSON, The Outdoor Press

Ice fishing in Washington doesn't necessarily mean going on the ice, drilling a hole and fishing with bait or jigs.

Many winters popular fishing spots barely freeze over, or leave big areas of open water. This gives the angler with a car topper the chance to break through thin shore ice, or cast from the bank. But some winters bring 6 inches of ice early in-November and it lasts until late March.

So when thinking about "ice fishing," keep your mind open, especially if you read there is open water. Go and fish from the bank in any open water strips.

Technically, one doesn't go "ice fishing," any more than he does "catfishing." We never fish for cats or ice. We angle through the ice and fish for catfish.

Lures and methods

If fishing through the ice, you'll find techniques have broadened in the past couple of years. Once about all anyone did was "plunk" (still-fish) bait, sometimes off a bobber. This still works, of course.

In recent winters anglers have developed skills in jigging through the ice, too. Most any small (1/8 ounce) jig will work, especially if touched up with a piece of worm or perch eye.

Others jig with spoons such as the Swedish pimple, Teazer or midget spinners. I've even "jigged" with big wet flies, tied with an under-body or lead wire to make then sink quickly. Deep purple is my favorite winter spoon and fly color.

One does not need a special rod for fishing through the ice. Anything from a 9 foot fly rod to a 5 foot bass casting rod will do. However, we are learning that short rods make fishing more convenient because one is able to sit closer to the hole in the ice.

If using a bobber, there's not much need for a rod with a sensitive tip. A broom stick will do. But without a bobber, a rod with a

ICE FISHING in Alkali Lake, Grant County

very sensitive tip is a great help, which means one of graphite.

Bobbers come in all sizes, shapes and weights. Most ice anglers like quill or vertical type bobbers — those in which the "stick" is suspended vertically. these give a tip-off to the bite better than round bobbers. My winter tackle box is filled with round bobbers, and they work, too, so go ahead and use a round bobber if that is all you have at hand.

Bait for winter fish is usually worms, salmon eggs, corn or maggots. Perch eyes work beautifully, as do strips of perch meat, cut into angle-worm configuration. Don't forget the maggots and meal grubs.

Easiest way to get a perch eye is not to dig it out with the point of a knife but "pop" it out with the bent end of a large paper clip.

Ice drilling techniques

Twenty years ago most used axes to chop holes in the ice. It was hard work, messy and often wet. It left the hole full of big ice chunks and chips.

Now ice augers are the tool of most fishermen. Popular sizes are 4, 6 and 8 inch. Unless fishing for northern pike, 8 inch generally proves bigger than necessary. The bigger the bit, the more work it takes to drill a hole.

I never cared for 4 inch drills, but many do. Six inches is my favorite size. When buying an ice auger, check with the dealer to see if the auger can be sharpened. Some have replaceable bits. Other bits are an integral part of the drill.

First-timers are always surprised to learn ice can dull an auger in a dozen drillings. Make sure yours can be sharpened and find out, positively, who does it, before you buy a particular style.

Other than the auger bits, the main variable is the handle. Some fold for easier carrying. Some have a straight handle across the top. Others have an off-set in the handle, like a carpenter's bit and brace. I find off-set handles faster, but more difficult to use if the ice is very hard and thick.

Lastly one can purchase a power ice auger, run by a little two-stroke gas engine. They can drill through a foot of ice per sec-

ond. They can also cost several hundred dollars. Hand augers run $35-60.

One also needs an ice skimmer, to fish out chips of ice and keep the hole open on very cold days. A kitchen strainer works, but regular ice skimmers sold in sports shop are inexpensive and better.

Packing equipment

Getting equipment out on the ice still has no better solution than pulling it in a kid's plastic sled—unless it's on a snowmobile. Snowmobiles are very popular with ice anglers, especially those who have cabins on lakes open to fishing through the ice.

A good trick is to put most of one's gear in 5 gallon plastic buckets, the kind laundry soap is sold in. Two of these can carry a lot of gear and keep it stowed neatly.

Once out on the ice, take a 5 gallon bucket and turn it over and use it for a seat or rod prop. Folding camp stools are also handy if you get tired of standing.

Some days can be bitterly cold and a propane heater is just the ticket to thaw frozen reels, lines and warm one's hands.

Reels and line important

Closed face spinning reels are not a good choice for winter fishing because they trap water inside and it can freeze. Regular spinning reels probably work best. Fly reels and level wind casting reels are also good choices.

One can also purchase very large diameter ice fishing reels, usually sold as a package with ice fishing rods.

Only one line I know of is especially made for fishing through the ice, and that is by Berkley, called "Ice" or "Cold Weather" line. It tends to stay more flexible when cold than other lines.

Fish finders help, too

I seldom go ice fishing without a fish finder. Many sonars have battery pack adapters. The trick is to keep the batteries warm as they lose power almost down to zero if left out the cold very long. Your propane heater quickly warms them, however.

The reason sonar is helpful is it lets you locate fish without the chore of drilling so many holes. If placed on the ice and dampened with a little anti-freeze, or water, it can "shoot through" a foot of clear ice and still show schools of fish below.

We all know perch, crappie and blue gills are schooling fish. If you find one fish, others are near by. A school of perch can stay in an area for several hours, or move off after a few minutes.

There's no sense in waiting at a hole the school has left in hopes it will come back. Best tactic is to scout in every widening circles until the school is re-located, drill new holes and fish.

Sonar is helpful in locating the proper depth of the school, too. Not all perch hang right on the bottom. One day I spent an hour without a bite fishing a few inches off the bottom because at first I caught three in rapid succession. A check with the sonar showed the perch had moved from 30 feet deep to 15 feet deep. When I came up to that level I got bites again.

Other important considerations

How thick should ice be to fish safely? I say 4 inches of hard, clear ice. Others tread on 2 inches. Not this old-timer. Carry a boat seat cushion tied to at least 50 feet of rope so if someone goes through the ice it's possible to heave him a line. I like life lines 100 feet long, just for an extra length of safety. None of this human-chain stuff for experienced, chicken-hearted anglers.

Something warm to drink (coffee, tea, hot chocolate) helps to ward off the chills, but I have found hot soup much better. A thermos of hot tomato soup really warms the inner boilers for hours, at least mine.

You won't fish on the ice too many times before you discover waterproof footwear is a must. This usually means shoe-pacs or rubber boots. Moon boots are a good choice, too. Regular leather hunting boots are the pits on the ice.

Ice can be slippery, especially if wet. Little strap-on traction chains are a blessing and should be carried, just in case. I can testify a fall on the ice can result in a broken arm, which limits your fishing for about six weeks.

The nicest days to fishing through the ice are those sunny ones without wind. It gets surprisingly warm.

On some lakes, such as Waitts in Stevens county and Bead in Pend Oreille county, a lot of ice fishing is done at night. Take a Coleman lantern both for light and heat.

Snow cover on the ice seems to help the bite. Many feel the fish can see one through clear ice. Generally I've found this true. Feel free to make a liar of me.

A Really Secret Way To Barbecue Fish

So you caught a steelhead or salmon and have proudly flopped the fish on your kitchen's clean drain board. While there are scales all over the sink, why not put the knife to the fish and prepare if for a barbecue?

Prepare the fish

Sharpen the knife and make a cut along the gill cover as deep as the backbone, then carefully work the blade of a limber fillet knife along the backbone. Turn the fish over and do the other side. You should come up with a slab of meat from both sides with most of the bones remaining on the carcass of the fish.

If the barbecue event is a week or more away, break out a cake pan and place the fillets therein. Then fill the pan with water, covering all the fish. After the fish is frozen, pull the pan out of the freezer and give it a sharp rap. Presto, you now have a cake of ice enclosing the fish which may be easily stacked in the freezer.

PLACE FISH flesh side down for quick searing.

Remove the fish from the freezer the night before B-Day and lay in a supply of heavy duty aluminum foil and charcoal briquettes. Fire up the barbecue unit well in advance, making sure that coals cover the entire bottom of the rig. Now comes the secret part.

Secret sauce

The barbecue sauce made in advance like this:

One and one-half pound of margarine, 1 cup water, 1 1/2 cup tomato juice, 1/3 T. dry mustard, 3/4 T. salt, 3/4 T. sugar, 3/4 T. chili powder, 1/2 T. Worcestershire sauce, 1.2 T. Tabasco, 3/4 T. black pepper, 1 T. paprika, 1/4 cup vinegar, 1 grated onion, 1 clove garlic. Combine all ingredients and simmer for 30 minutes. Make a double or triple batch if desired and freeze the excess. The sauce freezes well.

This is Cowboy Sauce per Mrs. Herb Angle of Shelton, Wash.

Cooking method

Make an aluminum foil dish the same size as the top of your barbecue unit, forming a lip of an inch or more all around so that all juices will be retained. Then cut the fish into serving pieces.

Grease the grill then place the fish fillets flesh side down on the grill close to the coals. The idea is to achieve a quick sear job.

When those chunks of fish have browned nicely, use a flapjack turner and place them, flesh side up, in the foil pan you've fashioned. Then raise the grill away from the coals and place the pan back over the fire. The fillets should have cracks from the fast searing. Baste the Cowboy Sauce over the fish and into the cracks. Keep spooning. You can't get enough of this sauce over and into the fish. With the cracks in the fillets it is easy to determine when the fish is done. Don't overcook it.

If you have plenty of fish, not much more food will be needed for an outstanding meal, but you might also serve garlic bread, corn on the cob, fruit or tossed salad.

Enjoy!

Lakes of Washington

A

LAKE	COUNTY	ACRES	DRAINAGE	ELEV.	LOCATION
ABERDEEN	Grays Hbr	64	Chehalis R	22	6.5 mi W Montesano
ABERNATHY	Okanogan	4	Methow R	6300	1.5 mi SE Lamont Lk
ABIEL	King	1.5	Nf Cedar R	430	.05 mi SE Annette Lk
ACKER	Skamania	1.5	Nf Lewis R	4650	.03 mi S Bear Lk
ADELAIDE	Pierce	6.8	Wf White R	4584	9 mi N Mt Rainier
ADS	Okanogan	5	Kettle R	3650	1 mi SE Fields Lk
AENEAS	Okanogan	61	Okanogan R	1350	4 mi SW Tonasket
AFRICAN	Skamania	21	Green R	4653	5 mi N Spirit Lk outlet
AGNES	Chelan	7	Stehekin R	6364	8.5 mi SW High Bridge G.S.
AIRPLANE	Chelan	10	White R	5350	32 mi NW Leavenworth
AIRPLANE	Snohomish	2	Skykomish R	3050	3.5 mi SW Gold Bar
AIRPLANE	Snohomish	2.5	Suiattle R	3600	7.5 mi E Darrington
AIRPORT	Lewis	4	Chehalis R	175	2.5 mi S Centralia
AIRPORT PD	Whatcom	2	Bellingham Bay	145	Bellingham Airport
AIRVIEW	Okanogan	5	Chewack R	6200	31.5 mi N Winthrop
ALASKA	Kittitas	35	Yakima R	4230	4 mi NE Snoqualmie Pass
ALBERT	King	1.5	Green R	3100	1.7 mi E Goat Mtn
ALDEN	Okanogan	12	Kettle R	3900	5 mi NW Chesaw
ALDER RES	Pierce	3931	Nisqually R	1207	5 mi S Eatonville
ALDERMAN	Spokane	11	Crab Cr	2360	9 mi W Cheney
ALDRICH	Mason	9	Hood Canal	520	1.5 mi S DeWatto
ALDWELL RES	Clallam	204	Elwha R	321	6 mi W Port Angeles
ALEXANDER	Kitsap	19.5	Sinclair Inlet	238	4 mi SW Bremerton
ALICE	Chelan	4	Wenatchee R	6500	12 mi NW Leavenworth
ALICE	King	33	Raging R	875	2.5 mi S Fall City
ALKALI	Grant	308	Lenore Lk	1085	9 mi N Soap Lake
ALKALI	Spokane	96	Palouse R	2270	9.5 mi SW Cheney
ALLEN	Pierce	5	Nisqually R	4596	4 mi W Longmire
AL'S	King	4.5	Ef Foss R	4600	W Necklace Valley
ALSOP SLOUGH	Chelan	10	White R	1975	6.5 mi NW Lk Wenatchee
ALTA	Okanogan	187	Columbia R	1163	2 mi SW Pateros
AMERICAN	Pierce	235	Puget Sound	1125	8 mi SW Tacoma
AMERICAN	Yakima	3.5	Sf American R	5260	2700' NW Little Cougar Lk
AMES	King	80	Snoqualmie R	240	2 mi W Carnation
AMES POTHOLE	King	1	Snoqualmie R	306	2100' NW Ames Lk
AMES	Lincoln	29	Palouse R	2190	7 mi NE Sprague
AMY	Okanogan	3.5	Okanogan R	1900	3 mi NW Riverside
ANDERSON	Jefferson	59	Pt Townsend Bay	250	.5 mi W Chimacum
ANDERSON	King	2	Taylor R	4500	1.4 mi NE Marten Lk
ANDERSON	Lewis	8	Nisqually R	3900	4.5 mi S Ashford
ANDERSON	Pend Oreille	15	Pend Oreille R	2550	7 mi SE Ione
ANDERSON	Whatcom	2.5	Fraser R	500	5 mi NW Kendall
ANDERSON LKS (4)	Whatcom	1-4	Baker R	5000	1 mi NW Mt Watson
ANDREW	Okanogan	10	Okanogan R	2292	2.5 mi S Conconally
ANGELES	Clallam	20	Juan De Fuca	4196	8 mi S Port Angeles
ANGELINE	King	198	Wf Foss R	5100	9.5 mi S Skykomish
ANGELINE	Snohomish	4	Sauk R	3270	3 mi E Darrington
ANGLE	King	102	Green R	370	12 mi S Seattle
ANN	Kittitas	3	Cle Elum R	6156	19 mi N Cle Elum
ANN	Whatcom	6	Baker R	4700	2 mi W Mt Shuksan
ANNA	Yakima	3	Naches R	4800	1900' N Crow Cr Lk
ANNETTE	King	18	Sf Snoq R	3620	5.5 mi SW Snoq Pass
ANSALDO	Stevens	15	Columbia R	3050	6.25 mi W Northport
ANTILON	Chelan	96	Lk Chelan	2327	10.5 mi NW Chelan
APEX	Ferry	3	FDR Lk	2020	4 mi S Inchelium
APPLE	Yakima	9	Tieton R	5060	7.5 mi NE White Pass
ARBUTHNOT	Whatcom	5	Nk Nooksack R	4800	2 mi W Mt Baker Lodge
ARMSTRONG	Columbia	1	Tucannon R	2400	4 mi S Tac Game Range
ARMSTRONG	Mason	4	Hood Canal	650	3 mi NE Eldon
ARMSTRONG	Snohomish	31	Stilly R	135	2.5 mi N Arlington

LAKE	COUNTY	ACRES	DRAINAGE	ELEV.	LOCATION
ARROW	King	5	Puget Sound	265	2.5 mi S Burien
ARROWHEAD	Skagit	15	Cascade R	4500	9.5 mi SE Marblemount
ASHLAND LKS (2)	Snohomish	7-13	Pilchuck R	2870	5 mi SE Verlot R.S.
ATHEARNS PD	Whatcom	5 Sf	Nooksack R	450	4 mi SE Saxon
ART	Yakima	2	Tieton R	5230	1400' W Hill Lk
ARTESIAN	Grant	32	Crab Cr	1236	4.5 mi E Gloyd
ASOTIN DAM RES	Asotin	3900	Snake R	842	Town of Asotin
ATKINS	Douglas	140	Jameson Lk	2370	5.5 mi SW St Andrews
AGUSTA	Chelan	26	Wenatchee R	6750	9 ml NW Leavenworth
AUSTIN PASS	Whatcom	1	Nf Nooksack R	4950	1300' N Austin Pass
AUVIL PD	Island	1	Puget Sound	200	S portion Whidbey 191
AVALANCHE	King	3	Mf Snoq R	3780	2600 SW Burnt Boot Lk
AZURE	Whatcom	89	Skagit R	4200	6.5 mi N Newhalem
AZURITE	King	44	Wf Foss R	5100	9.4 mi S Skykomish

B

LAKE	COUNTY	ACRES	DRAINAGE	ELEV.	LOCATION
B & W	Skamania	1.5	Columbia R	950	RB 5 mi W No Bonneville
BABCOCK RIDGE	Grant	20	Columbia R	1258	3.5 mi W Quincey
BACKBONE	Lewis	3.5	Cowlitz R	2050	6 mi NE Packwood
BADGER	Spokane	244	Palouse R	2180	8.5 mi S Cheney
BADGER	Skamania	2.5	Muddy R	5000	10.5 mi E Spirit Lk inlet
BAGLEY LKS (2)	Whatcom	9-11	Nf Nooksack R	4200	1000' SW Mt Baker Lodge
BAILEY	Spokane	15	L Spokane R	1900	5 mi NE Deer Park
BAILIE PD	Franklin	23	Columbia R	900	1 mi N Mesa
BAKER	Pend Oreille	3.6	Pend Oreille R	2350	11 mi W Newport
BALCH	Klickitat	3	Columbia	600	2 mi NW Lyle
BALD	Skagit	2.5	Skagit R	3750	8.5 mi E Concrete
BALD	Whatcom	2.5	Nf Nooksack R	4400	6 mi N Glacier
BALD EAGLE	King	4	Wf Foss	4500	8 mi SE Skykomish
BALD HILL	Thurston	45	Nisqually R	633	11.5 mi SE Yelm
BALD MTN PD	Skagit	1.5	Stilly R	1050	2 mi NW Cavanaugh Lk
BALLINGER	Snohomish	103	Lk Washington	278	3 mi SE Edmonds
BALLINGER	Spokane	64	Palouse R	2300	5.5 mi SW Cheney
BANDANA	Snohomish	3	Sf Stilly R	3235	7 mi N Verlot
BANDYS	Lincoln	6	Crab Cr	2150	1.5 mi NW Wilbur
BANKS (RES)	Grant	24900	Main Canal	1560	1.6 mi SW Grand Coulee Dan
BANNOCK LKS (3)	Chelan	7-11	Stehekin R	5900	10.5 mi SW High Bridge G.S
BARLCAY	Snohomish	11	Sf Skykom R	2300	3 mi NE Baring
BARING BV PDS	Snohomish	2	Sf Skykom R	850	1 mi NW Baring
BARRINGS	Lincoln	5	Crab Cr	2250	7 mi S Creston
BARKER CANYON	Douglas	12	Banks Lk	1800	4.5 mi S 4 Corners
BARLOW GRAVEL PIT	Pierce	3	Puget Sound	250	2700' E Clover Pk H.S.
BARNES	Thurston	14	Budd Inlet	150	3 mi S Olympia
BARNETT	Pierce	1	White R	2900	2 mi S Silver Cr R.S.
BARNSLEY	Okanogan	9.5	Methow R	1950	1 mi SW Winthrop
BARRETT	Whatcom	40	Nooksack R	20	1 mi E Ferndale
BASALT	Adams	5	Potholes Canal	970	5 mi N Othello
BASIN	King	7	Tye R	5500	8 mi S Scenic
BASIN	Skagit	2.5	Cascade R	4200	8 mi S Marblemount
BASS	King	24	Green R	665	3.5 mi N Enumclaw
BASS	Thurston	7	Nisqually R	500	1900' E Elbow Lk
BATEMAN PD	Yakima	3	Yakima R	990	.05 mi NW Birchfield
BATH	Snohomish	15	Suiattle R	5950	25 mi E Darrington
BATHTUB LKS (8)	Snohomish	10	Pilchuck R	4800	Pilchuck Mtn
BATHTUB	Mason	2	Oakland Bay	350	6 mi N Shelton
BATTALION	Chelan	6.4	Stehekin R	5234	3.5 mi SE High Bridge G.S.
BATTLEGROUND	Clark	28	Columbia R	504	12 mi NE Vancouver
BATT SLOUGHS (2)	Snohomish	3-5	Snohomish R	15	1.5 mi S Snohomish
BAY	Pierce	130	Carr Inlet	27	2 mi S Home
BAYLEY BV PDS (3)	Stevens	3	Colville R	2400	2 mi S Baley Lk
BEACH	Clallam	7	Juan de Fuca	10	Angeles Point
BEALL PDS (3)	Clark	1	Columbia R	280	6 mi N Camas
BEAD	Pend Oreille	720	Pend Oreille R	2850	8 mi NW Newport
BEAR	Chelan	1	Entiat R	6800	21 mi NW Entiat
BEAR	King	49	Taylor R	3670	19 mi NE North Bend
BEAR LKS (3)	King	5	Nf Snoq R	4850	7 mi S Skykomish
BEAR	Kitsap	12	Case Inlet	400	4 mi E Belfair
BEAR	Skagit	2.5	Cascade R	3900	8.5 mi SE Marblemount
BEAR	Skagit	4	Sf Nooksack R	3550	1 mi SW Three Lakes
BEAR	Skamania	11	Muddy R	1700	6 mi E Mt St Helens
BEAR	Whatcom	23	Chilliwack R	5800	1 mi SW Mt Redoubt
BEAR CREEK RES	Skagit	0.2	Baker R	912	5.5 mi N Concrete
BEAR PARK	Pierce	4	White R	5405	11 mi NE Mt Rainier
BEAUSITE	Jefferson	17	Ft Townsend Bay	430	3 mi SW Chimacum
BEAUTY	Jefferson	3	Queets R	4700	Hwtrs Heehaw Cr

LAKE	COUNTY	ACRES	DRAINAGE	ELEV.	LOCATION
BEAVER	Clallam	36	Sol Duc R	550	3 mi NE Sappho
BEAVER	Columbia	2	Tucannon R	2375	4 mi S G.D. Hdq
BEAVER LKS (3)	King	62	Sammamish R	406	4 mi N Issaquah
BEAVER	Kittitas	1	Yakima R	3450	1 mi SW Snoq Pass
BEAVER	Lewis	7	Cowlitz R	4500	7 mi E Packwood
BEAVER	Skagit	74	Skagit R	30	1 mi SE Clear Lk
BEAVER	Skamania	3	Columbia R	550	4 mi E Carson
BEAVER PUSS LKS (4)	Kittitas	2	Kachess R	5300	E side Rampart Ridge
BEBE PDS (2)	Cowlitz	2-3	Cowlitz R	560	6 mi NW Castle Rock
BEDAL	Snohomish	3	Nf Sauk R	3500	5.5 mi NE Barlow Pass
BEDARD	Okanogan	13	Columbia R	2460	11 mi NE Bridgeport
BEE	Skagit	10	Suiattle R	4600	10 mi S Marblemount
BEEHIVE RES	Chelan	12	Columbia R	4150	8 mi S Wenatchee
BEECHER	Snohomish	16	Snohomish R	13	.05 mi E Cathcart
BEN LKS (3)	Jefferson	2	Quinault R	4600	1 mi SW Mt Steel
BENCH	King	2.5	Nf Snoq R	4180	17 mi NE North Bend
BENCH	Lewis	3	Ohanapecosh R	5200	6 mi N White Pass
BENCH	Lewis	6	Cowlitz R	4600	5.5 mi E Longmire
BENCH	Skagit	49	Suiattle R	5200	22 mi NE Darrington
BENGSTON	King	4	Nf Tolt R	2600	7 mi S Startup
BENNETTSEN	Mason	25	Tahuya R	381	6 mi W Belfair
BENSON	Stevens	12	Colville R	2750	7 mi E Valley
BERDEEN	Whatcom	127	Skagit R	5000	12 mi N Marblemount
BERGEAU	Lincoln	31	Crab Cr	2100	11 mi SE Wilbur
BERGSTROM	Adams	36	Crab Cr	750	2700' S Royal Lk
BERRY LKS (2)	Kitsap	3	Sinclair Inlet	200	2 mi SW Pt Orchard
BERTHA	King	2	Beckler R	4400	W side Mt Fernow
BERTHA MAY LKS (2)	Lewis	6-30	Nisqually R	3700	7 mi SE National
BESTS	Skagit	15	Skagit Bay	390	Fidalgo Island
BEVIS	Snohomish	6	Skykomish R	540	8.4 mi NE Monroe
BIDDLE	Clark	1	Columbia R	45	6.5 mi E Vancouver
BIG	Kittitas	4	Teanaway R	2380	2.5 mi E Teanaway Jct
BIG	Skagit	545	Skagit R	81	5 mi SE Mt Vernon
BIG BEEF PDS	Kitsap	5	Hood Canal	500	.05 mi E Hintzville
BIG FOUR	Columbia	5	Tucannon R	2525	Mouth Big 4 Canyon
BIGELOW	Thurston	14	Budd Inlet	151	2 mi NE Olympia
BIG GRANITE	Skagit	144	Cascade R	5000	7 mi SE Marblemount
BIG HANKS	Mason	27	Oakland Bay	400	8 mi NW Shelton
BIG HEART	King	191	Wf Foss R	5100	9 mi S Skykomish
BIG HIDDEN	Okanogan	71	Ef Pasayten R	4300	34 mi NW Winthrop
BIG JIM MTN LKS (2)	Chelan	4-5	Wenatchee R	6850	9 mi NW Leavenworth
BIG JOES	Clallam	15	Wf Dickey R	152	10 mi NW Forks
BIG MACK	Okanogan	9	Okanogan R	4000	7.5 mi SE Oroville
BIG SNOW	King	15	Mf Snoq R	5000	8.5 mi N Snoq Pass
BIG SWAMP	Spokane	11	Palouse R	2340	1.1 E Medical Lake
BIG TWIN SISTER	Yakima	104.5	Bumping R	5152	7 mi N White Pass
BILL	Lewis	4	Ohanapecosh R	5000	5.5 mi N White Pass
BINFORD RES	Clark	3	Ef Lewis R	600	2.5 mi NE La Center
BIRD	Yakima	4	Klickitat R	5575	11 mi NW Glenwood
BITTER	King	19	Puget Sound	440	In Seattle
BITTER LKS (3)	Snohomish	3	Nf Skykomish R	3500	4 mi NE Index
BIVIN	Lewis	3	Cowlitz R	980	4.5 mi SW Packwood
BLACK LKS (2)	Adams	14-25	Columbia R	790	8 mi NW Othello
BLACK	King	26	Snoqualmie R	1213	9.5 mi NE Snoqualmie
BLACK	Stevens	70	L Pend Oreille	3701	12 mi E Colville
BLACK	Okanogan	66	Chewack R	4000	24 mi N Winthrop
BLACK LKS (10)	Okanogan	26	Columbia R	2450	9 mi NE Bridgeport
BLACK	Thurston	576	Chehalis R	127	4 mi SW Olympia
BLACK DIAMOND	King	9	Green R	540	1 mi SW Blk Diamond
BLACK DIAMOND	Okanogan	2.5	Okanogan R	2400	2 mi SE Oroville
BLACK & WHITE LKS (3)	Mason	3	Skykomish R	4500	5 mi N Hd Lk Cushman
BLACKMAN'S	Snohomish	60	Snohomish R	140	1 mi N Snohomish
BLACK PINE	Okanogan	19	Twisp R	3900	8 mi SW Twisp
BLACKSMITH	Mason	18	Tahuya R	422	5.5 mi NW Belfair
BLACKWOOD	Clallam	16	Sol Duc R	3000	3 mi SW Sol Duc Hot S
BLAIR RES	Benton	7	Columbia R	445	3 mi S Kennewick
BLAKES PD	Clallam	1	Juan de Fuca	120	1 mi E Sequim
BLALOCK	Walla Walla	6	Walla Walla R	750	4 mi W Walla Walla
BLANCA	Snohomish	179	Nf Skykomish R	4064	7 mi SE Barlow Pass
BLANKENSHIP PTHLS	Yakima	7	Tieton R	5250	6.5 mi NE White Pass
BLANKENSHIP LKS (3)	Yakima	12	Tieton R	5230	6.5 mi NE White Pass
BLAZER	King	6	Pratt R	4060	12 mi SE North Bend
BLETHEN LKS (2)	King	3-8	Taylor R	3198	10 mi NE North Bend
BLUE	Columbia	3	Tucannon R	2150	Tucannon
BLUE	Cowlitz	8	Sf Toutle R	3294	29.5 mi NE Woodland
BLUE	Grant	536	Lenore Lk	1093	11 mi N Soap Lk

LAKE	COUNTY	ACRES	DRAINAGE	ELEV.	LOCATION
BLUE	Lewis	128	Cispus R	4050	15.5 mi SE Randle
BLUE	Lewis	6	Cowlitz R	4550	5.2 mi W Ohanap H.S.
BLUE	Okanogan	186	Similkameen R	1686	9 mi S Loomis
BLUE	Pend Oreille	6.5	L Spokane R	2000	8.5 mi NW Elk
BLUE	Skamania	12	Salmon R	4640	18 mi N Carson
BLUE	Skamania	16	Nf Lewis R	4300	21 mi S Randle
BLUE	Snohomish	22	Nf Sauk R	5600	9 mi S Glacier Peak
BLUE	Whatcom	13	Baker R	4000	7 mi N Concrete
BLUE	Yakima	3.5	Sf Tieton R	6200	8 mi SW Tieton
BLUE GULCH RES	Stevens	1.5	Columbia R	1400	Blue Gulch
BLUFF	Grant	11	Grand Coulee	1445	Lower Grand Coulee
BLUFF	Lewis	8	Cowlitz R	3900	7 mi NE Packwood
BLUFF	Skagit	21	Suiattle R	4000	11 mi S Marblemount
BLUFF	Skamania	5	Columbia R	2250	6 mi W No Bonneville
BLUFF	Yakima	3	Klickitat R	5800	10.5 mi NW Glenwood
BLUM LKS (4)	Whatcom	2-14	Baker R	5800	18 mi NE Concrete
BLYTHE	Grant	30	Crab Cr	915	10.5 mi NW Othello
BOARDMAN LKS (3)	Snohomish	10-49	Pilchuck R	3420	8 mi SE Verlot Res
BOGACHIEL	Clallam	1.5	Bogachiel R	3525	3 mi SE Sol Duc H.S.
BOILING	Chelan	8	Lk Chelan	6900	30 mi NW Chelan
BOISE-CASCADE MILL P	Yakima	1	Naches R	1450	3500' S Naches
BONAPARTE	Okanogan	159	Okanogan R	3554	18 mi NE Tonasket
BONE	King	1	Green R	4300	6 mi SW Lester
BONER	King	3	Skykomish R	4500	3 mi SW Grotto
BONNEY	Pierce	17	Puyallup R	605	2.5 mi SE Sumner
BONNIE	Whit/Spo	366	Rock Cr	1790	9 mi NW Rosalia
BOOHER	Okanogan	25	Okanogan R	967	4 mi NW Riverside
BOOMERANG	King	1	Nf Snoq R	3215	10.5 NE North Bend
BOOT	Skamania	16	Green R	4550	4.5 mi N Spirit Lk
BOREN	King	15	Lk Washington	300	4 mi N Renton
BORGEAU	Ferry	22	Columbia R	1900	4.5 mi S Inchelium
BORST	Lewis	5	Skookumchuck R	175	Ft Borst Park
BOSWORTH	Snohomish	96	Pilchuck R	563	2 mi S Granite Falls
BOTTOMLESS	Skagit	4	Samish R	200	2 mi N Sedro Woolley
BOUCK	Whatcom	14	Skagit R	4000	3 mi E Newhalem
BOULDER	Skagit	55	Suiattle R	5000	13 mi NE Darrington
BOULDER	Snohomish	22	Sultan R	3750	8 mi N Index
BOUNDARY	King	8	Skykomish R	2310	11 mi NE Carnation
BOUNDARY LKS (2)	Mason	3-4	Sf Skok R	500	12 mi NW Shelton
BOUNDARY RES	Pend Oreille	1600	Pend Oreille R	1990	9 mi N Metaline Falls
BOUNDARY	Yakima	10	Naches R	3300	9 mi S Naches R.S.
BOW	King	13	Puget Sound	340	Opp Sea Tac
BOWERS PD	Snohomish	6	Sf Stilly	940	5 mi NE Granite Falls
BOWMAN	Pierce	2.5	Nisqually	300	Ft. Lewis Res
BOWMAN	Pierce	11	Stuck R	470	4.5 mi SE Auburn
BOWSER	Snohomish	3	Nf Sauk R	4300	9 mi S Barlow Pass
BOX CANYON	Kittitas	2	Kachess R	4500	4 mi E Snoq Pass
BOX MTN LKS (3)	Snohomish	2-24	Suiattle R	5000	19 mi E Darrington
BOYD	Snohomish	13	Pilchuck R	500	2 mi SE Granite Falls
BOYLE	King	24	Snoqualmie R	1040	6 mi NE Snoqualmie
BOYLES	Pierce	3	Puget Sound	230	2 mi SE Steilacoom
BRADER	Skamania	3	Wind R	4600	20 mi N Carson
BRANDENBURG MARSH	Pierce	35	Nisqually R	300	.04 mi NW Roy
BRANDMEIRS BOG	Snohomish	1	Snoqualmie R	1500	9.7 mi NE Carnation
BREAKER	Pacific	20	Pacific	20	1.5 mi N Long Beach
BREWSTER	King	3	Sf Snoq R	1030	3 mi S North Bend
BRIDGEMAN PD	Yakima	6	Yakima R	655	2.5 mi N Mabton
BRIDGES	King	34	Snoqualmie R	1045	6 mi NE Snoqualmie
BRIGGS PD	San Juan	29	Westcott Bay	231	1 mi SE Roche Hbr
BRIGHAM	Chelan	4	Wenatchee R	6500	13 mi NW Leavenworth
BRISCOE	Pacific	11	Pacific Ocean	20	2 mi N Long Beach
BRITT SLOUGH	Skagit	21	Skagit R	15	1 mi SW Mt Vernon
BROKEN ROCK LKS(2)	Grant	20-40	Crab Cr	1251	7.5 mi SW Wilson Cr
BRONSON PD	Snohomish	5.5	Sultan R	710	3 mi NE Sultan
BROWNIE	Pend Oreille	11	P. Oreille R	2350	7 mi N Cusick
BROWNS	Lincoln	42	Crab Cr	167	57 mi NW Odessa
BROWNS	Pend Oreille	88	P. Oreille R	3450	8.5 mi NE Cusick
BROWNS	Stevens	17	Colville R	2025	5 mi SW Chewalah
BRYANT	Lewis	2	Cowlitz R	1720	5 mi E Winston
BRYANT	Snohomish	20	Stilly R	146	3 mi NW Arlington
BUCK	Douglas	12	Columbia R	2300	5 mi SW Del Rio
BUCK	King	13	Mf Snoq R	3150	9 mi E North Bend
BUCK	Kitsap	20	Puget Sound	140	1 mi SW Hansville
BUCK	Okanogan	15	Chewack R	3247	9 mi N Winthrop
BUCK	Yakima	2	Bumping R	4660	9 mi S Chinook Pass
BUCK	Yakima	1.5	Naches R	4800	1.5 mi SE Nelson Butte

LAKE	COUNTY	ACRES	DRAINAGE	ELEV.	LOCATION
BUCK & DOE LKS (2)	Stevens	1-1	Colville R	2950	9 mi W Chewelah
BUCKHORN	Jefferson	1	Dunqeness R	5150	11 mi W Quilcene
BUCKHORN	King	1	Nf Tolt R	1450	4 mi N Carnation
BUESCH	Lewis	10	Ohanapecosh R	5175	4 mi N White Pass
BUFFALO	Okanogan	542	Columbia R	2042	7 mi SE Nespelem
BUGGER	Okanogan	3	Twisp R	5200	22 mi W Twisp
BULLER	Skagit	2	Cascade R	3500	5 mi E Marblemount
BULLFROG PD	King	3	Skykomish R	800	2 mi SE Baring
BUMPING	Yakima	1310	Bumping R	3426	10 mi Chinook Pass
BUNCH	Grays Hbr	16	Quinault R	3000	7 mi E Quinault Lk
BUNCHGRASS	Pend Oreille	18	P.Oreille R	4950	11 mi SE Ione
BURBANK SLOUGH	Walla Walla	700	Columbia R	341	At Burbank
BURDEN	Okanogan	2.5	Okanogan R	1820	6 mi SW Tonasket
BURKE	Grant	73	Columbia R	1193	7.5 mi S Quincey
BUSHMAN	Thurston	40	Deschutes R	255	1 mi NE Offut Lk
BUSCH PD	Whitman	1	Palouse R	2720	1 mi SE Colton
BUTCH EVANS SLOUGH	King	4	Mf Snoq R	860	1.5 mi SW Pratt R Mouth
BUTLERS PD	Skamania	1.5	Columbia R	150	1 mi N No Bonneville
BUTTE LKS (3)	Adams	30	Crab Cr	B00	7 mi NW Othello
BUZZARD	Okanogan	16	Okanogan R	3380	7 mi NW Okanogan
BYERS PD	Clallam	1	Sequim Bay	680	9 mi SW Port Angeles
BYRNE	Snohomish	51	Whitechuck R	5550	20 mi SE Darrington
BYRON PDS (2)	Yakima	50	Yakima R	700	4.5 mi S Grandview
BONNEVILLE POOL	Skamania	20200	Columbia R	72	36 mi E Vancouver

C

LAKE	COUNTY	ACRES	DRAINAGE	ELEV.	LOCATION
CABIN	Grant	4	Columbia R	1250	5 mi SW George
CABIN	KIttitas	5	Teenaway R	2400	2.5 mi E Teenaway Jct
CAD	King	1	Pratt R	4320	2 mi NW Snoq Pass
CADET	Snohomish	2	Nfk Sauk R	5500	5 mi E Barlow Pass
CADY	Mason	15	Hood Canal	450	2 mi SE DeWatto
CAIN	Whatcom	72	Samish R	391	9.5 mi SE Bellingham
CALDWELL	Pend Oreille	15	Pend Oreille R	2560	7.5 mi SE Ione
CALICHE LKS (2)	Grant	10-17	Columbia R	1300	5.5 mi SW George
CALISPELL	Pend Orellle	1031	Callspell R	2028	2 mi SW Usk
CALLIGAN	King	361	Nf Snoq R	2222	9 mi E North Bend
CAMILLE	Ferry	19	Columbia R	1958	2.5 mi W Inchelium
CAMP	Franklin	19	Columbia R	870	5.5 mi N Mesa
CAMP	Skagit	3	Bellingham Bay	1150	Cypress Island
CAMP PD	Mason	6	Tahuya R	350	4 mi NW Belfair
CAMP 1 POND	Pierce	1	Puyallup R	600	E side Kapowsin Lk
CAMP 3 POND	Skagit	2	Skagit R	500	2.5 mi NW Hamilton
CAMP 7 POND	Pacific	4	Willapa R	275	10 mi SE Raymond
CAMPBELL	Adams	115	Pothole Canal	975	5 mi N Othello
CAMPBELL	Clark	247	Columbia R	10	2.5 mi S Ridgefield
CAMPBELL	Pierce	3.5	White R	5500	3 mi NE Chin Pass
CAMPBELL	Skagit	410	Skagit Bay	43	5 mi S Anacortes
CAMPBELL	Spokane	33	Palouse R	2300	4.5 mi SW Cheney
CAMP ROBBER	King	4-5	Ef Miller R	4200	8 mi SE Skykomish
CANAAN	Chelan	2.5	Wenatchee R	5500	8.5 mi NE Stevens Pass
CANAL	Grant	76	Crab Cr	986	6.5 mi N Othello
CANNERY	Skagit	18	Guemes Ch	6	Shannon Pt
CANVASBACK	Clark	167	Columbia R	10	Bachelor Island
CANYON	Snohomish	21	Suiattle R	21	11 mi NE Glacier Pk
CANYON	Whatcom	2	Nf Nooksack R	4775	5 mi NW Shuksan
CAPITOL	Thurston	306	Budd Inlet	0	Olympia
CAREYS	Skagit	4	Skagit R	100	1 mi NE Hamilton
CARLISLE LKS(5)	Grays Hbr	1-4	Copalis R	85	2 mi N Copalis Cross
CARLISLE	Lewis	20	Sf Newaukum R	500	Onalaska
CARLSON PD	Mason	1	Hood Canal	200	1 mi S Union
CARNEY	Pierce/Kit	39	Case Inlet	350	4 mi N Vaughn
CAROLE	King	11	Taylor R	3700	.07 mi W Nordrum Lk
CAROLINE LKS (2)	Chelan	4-8	Wenatchee	5400	10 mi SW Leavenworth
CAROLINE	King	60	Mf Snoq R	4740	6 mi NW Snoq Pass
CARP	Island	7	Saratoga Pass	410	Camano Island
CARP	Klickitat	22	Lk Klickitat	2450	7 mi W Goldendale
CARP	Lincoln	5	Spokane	1900	11 mi N Davenport
CARP	Pierce	11	Puget Sound	240	2 mi SE Steilacoom
CARPENTER	Kitsap	3-5	Puget Sound	30	1 mi W Kingston
CARPENTERS	Skamania	4	Columbia R	630	2 mi NW No Bonneville
CARRIE	Chelan	15	Wenatchee R	5100	11.7 mi N Salmon la Sac
CARTER	Chelan	2	Wenatchee R	6400	1 mi SW Lk Agusta
CARTER	KItsap	1	Dyes Inlet	230	3.4 mi NW Bremerton
CARTER	Pierce	6	Puget Sound	280	McChord AFB
CARTY	Clark	42	Columbia R	10	Ridgefield

LAKE	COUNTY	ACRES	DRAINAGE	ELEV.	LOCATION
CASCADE	Grant	3	Columbia R	1090	500' N Crystal Lk
CASCADE	San Juan	172	East Sound	346	Morton State Park
CASCADE MILL PD	Yakima	33	Yakima R	1060	NE Yakima
CASEY PD	Walla Walla	60	Lk Wallula	340	4.5 mi SE Burbank
CASTOR	Okanogan	18	Okanogan R	1950	4 mi NW Riverside
CASSIDY	Snohomish	125	Pilchuck R	319	3.5 mi E Marysville
CAT	Clallam	7	Pt Discovery	329	3 mi N Blyn
CAT	Thurston	3	Nisqually R	450	4 mi NW Yelm
CATFISH	Mason	7	Ef Satsop R	460	1000' SE Nahwatzel Lk
CATFISH	Mason	7	North Bay	70	1.5 mi S Allyn
CATHERINE CECILLE	Okanogan	10	San Poil R	2580	SE end Aeneas Valley
CATTAIL	Grant	18	Crab Cr	945	8.5 mi N Othello
CATTAIL	Skamania	5	ColumbiaR	100	1 mi NW No Bonneville
CAVANAUGH	Skagit	844	Stilly R	1008	10 mi NE Arlington
CAYUSE	Okanogan	11	Okanogan R	1840	5 mi NW Tonasket
CECILIA	Snohomish	1.5	Wallace R	3450	5 mi N Gold Bar
CECIL'S	King	8	Ef Miller R	4400	8.5 mi SE Skykomish
CEDAR	Pierce	36	White R	4200	11 mi SE Enumclaw
CEDAR PD	Snohomish	9	Skykomish R	700	4 mi S Sultan
CEDAR	Stevens	51	P Oreille R	2135	2 mi N Leadpoint
CEDAR	Whatcom	4	Chuckanut Bay	1530	5 mi S Bellingham
CEDAR—LOWER	Yakima	3	Bumping Lk	4750	5 mi SE Chin Pass
CEDAR—UPPER	Yakima	8	Bumping Lk	4750	5 mi SE Chin Pass
CELERY MEADOW	Pierce	1	White R	4700	1800' S Cedar Lk
CELILORES	Klickitat	11200	Columbia R	160	20 mi SW Goldendale
CEMENT	King	2.5	Sf Skykomish R	4000	3 mi SW Grotto
CHAIN LKS (3)	Chelan	5-8	Wenatchee R	5700	5 mi SE Stevens Pass
CHAIN LKS (6)	King	3.5	Mf Snoq R	5700	W side LaBohn Gap
CHAIN LKS(4)	Lewis	1-4	Ohanapecosh R	5000	7 mi N White Pass
CHAIN	Pend Oreille	78	Spokane R	1950	3.5 mi NE Elk
CHAINOFLAKES(10)	Skamania	30	Cispus R	4300	24 mi SE Randle
CHAIN	Snohomish	23	Snohomish R	390	3 mi N Monroe
CHAIN LKS (4)	Snohomish	2	Nf Stilly R	900	7 mi N Granite Falls
CHAMBERLAIN	Klickitat	81	Columbia R	72	.05 mi W Lyle
CHAMBERS	Lewis	14.5	Cispus R	4525	11 mi SE Packwood
CHAMBERS	Pierce	80	Nisqually R	315	1 mi NE Roy
CHAMBERS LKS (2)	Thurston	49-73	Dechutes R	194	3 mi SE Olympia
CHAPLAIN	Snohomish	444	Sultan R	640	6 mi N Sultan
CHAPMAN	Spokane	146	Palouse R	2154	8 mi S Cheney
CHARLES	Chelan	.11.5	Wenatchee R	6900	13.5 mi NW Leavenworth
CHARLEY—UPPER	Asotin	5	Snake R	2600	16 mi W Asotin
CHARLEY—LOWER	Asotin	6	Snake R	2300	16 mi W Asotin
CHARLEY POND	Yakima	8.5	Yakima R	800	2 mi SE Harrah
CHARLOTTE	Franklin	20	Snake R	440	2 mi NE Ice Hbr Dam
CHARLIA LKS (2)	Jefferson	3-9	Big Quilcene R	5500	12 mi W Quilcene
CHARLIE LKS (4)	King	2-4	Ef Miller R	4000	9 mi Skykomish
CHARLIE BROWN	King	2	Taylor R	4700	16 mi E North Bend
CHASE	Island	5	Holmes Hbr	200	Whidbey Isl
CHASE	Snohomish	1	Lk Ballinger	400	1 mi NW Lk Ballinger
CHAVAL	Skagit	11	Suiattle R	4900	14 mi SE Marblemount
CHENAMUS	Skamania	4	Nf Lewis R	4150	22 mi N Carson
CHENUIS LKS (3)	Pierce	2-4	Carbon R	5000	Chenuis Mtn
CHERRY	King	3	Snoqualmie R	970	6 mi NW Lk Joy
CHESTER MORSE RES	King	1682	Cedar R	1555	7 mi SE North Bend
CHETWOOT	King	111	Wf Foss R	5200	11 mi S Skykomish
CHINA GARDENS DAM R	Asotin	1300	Snake R	910	26 mi S Clarkston
CHITWOOD LKS (2)	Snohomish	1-5	Sf Stilly R	700	4 mi E Granite Falls
CHIWAUKUM	Chelan	67	Wenatchee R	4950	14 mi NW Leavenworth
CHIWAUKUM BV PDS	Chelan	10	Wenatchee R	3500	Below Chiwaukum Lk
CHOPAKA	Okanogan	149	Simlihekum R	2921	6 mi N Loomis
CHORAL	Chelan	1.5	Entiat R	7200	35 mi NW Entiat
CHRISTINE	Pierce	4.5	Nisqually R	4700	6 mi E National
CHRISTMAS	King	8	Sf Snoq R	960	1 mi NE Cedar Falls
CHUCKANUT	Whatcom	2.5	Chuckanut Bay	130	.05 mi NE Chuckanut Vill
CHUKAR	Grant	30	Crab Cr	908	11 mi NW Othello
CHURCH	Whatcom	4	Nf Nooksack R	5150	6 mi NE Glacier
CICERO PD	Snohomish	4	Nf Stilly R	100	.05 mi E Cicero
CINDER	King	7	Lk Sawyer	680	1.5 mi N Blk Diamond
CIRCLE	Kittitas	49	Waptus R	6100	11 mi N Salmon La Sac
CIRQUE	Yakima	7	Tieton R	5650	13 mi SE White Pass
CITY	Jefferson	16	Big Quilcene R	600	1 mi E Discovery Jct
CLARA	Chelan	2	Columbia R	5500	1.5 mi NE Mission Pk
CLARK PD	Franklin	49	Columbia R	758	5 mi SW Mesa
CLARK	Stevens	24	Columbia R	1900	8 mi N Hunters
CLARKSTONE RES	Asotin	4	Snake R	1025	Clarkston Heights
CLAM	Pacific	10	Willapa Bay	20	3 mi N Long Beach

LAKE	COUNTY	ACRES	DRAINAGE	ELEV.	LOCATION
CLARICE	King	41	Tye R	4500	6 mi S Scenic
CLARK RES	Clark	1.5	Columbia R	380	3 mi N Camas
CLAYWOOD	Jefferson	10	Dosewallips R	6100	22 mi S Pt Angeles
CLEAR	Chelan	5	Columbia R	3000	9 mi S Wenatchee
CLEAR	Clallam	6	Sol Duc R	4225	5 mi SE Sol Duc H Spr
CLEAR	Mason	11	Oakland Bay	350	5 mi NW Shelton
CLEAR	Pacific	11	Pacific Ocean	25	1.5 mi N Long Beach
CLEAR	Pierce	155	Nisqually R	772	4 mi N Eatonville
CLEAR	Skagit	223	Skagit R	30	at Clear Lk Vill
CLEAR	Skagit	19	Baker R	4075	8 mi NE Concrete
CLEAR	Skamania	13	Nf Lewis R	4800	2 mi SW Cultus G.S.
CLEAR	Snohomish	2	Sauk R	2240	4 mi NW Silverton
CLEAR	Spokane	7	Palouse R	2190	9 mi NE Sprague
CLEAR	Spokane	375	Crab Cr	2342	2 mi S Medical Lk
CLEAR	Thurston	173	Nisqually R	518	10 mi SE Yelm
CLEAR	Whitman	4	Palouse R	1301	2 mi S Hooper
CLEAR	Yakima	265	Nf Tieton R	3615	6 mi E White Pass
CLE ELUM PDS (2)	Kittitas	5-15	Yakima R	1950	1 mi SW Cle Elum
CLE ELUM RES	Kittitas	4810	Yakima R	2223	7 mi NW Cle Elum
CLEMENTS	Okanogan	3	Okanogan R	1250	3 mi N Omak
CLEVELAND	King	2.5	Miller R	4300	3.4 mi SW Skykomish
CLIFF	Grant	2	Dusty Lk	1060	6.5 mi SW Quincy
CLIFF	Skagit	5	Suiattle R	4800	12 mi S Marblemount
CLOUDY	King	6	Ef Foss R	4800	10 mi SE Skykomish
CLOVER CR PDS	Pierce	1	Puget Sound	300	McChord AFB
CLOVER	Pierce	9	White R	5728	White R Park
COAL	Snohomish	6	Sf Stilly R	3420	3.5 mi SE Silverton
COCHRAN	Snohomish	34	Skykomish R	425	5.5 mi NE Monroe
CODY	Ferry	6	San Poil R	3500	22 mi S Republic
COFFEE POT	Lincoln	317	Crab Cr	1850	12 mi NE Odessa
COFFIN	Stevens	20	L Pend Ore R	3150	16 mi E Colville
COLCHUCK	Chelan	88	Wenatchee R	5570	10.5 mi S Leavenworth
COLLINS	Mason	4	Tahuya R	410	8 mi W Belfair
COMCOMLY	Skamania	5	W Salmon R	4500	10 mi W Mt Adams G.S.
CONCONULLY RES	Okanogan	450	Okanogan R	2287	at Conconully
CONEY	Chelan	18	Wenatchee R	7400	9 mi SW Leavenworth
CONEY	King	21	Wf Miller R	5300	on Lennox Mtn
CONEY PTHLS (3)	King	1	Wf Miller R	5250	SE side Coney Lk
CONEY	Snohomish	5	Nf Sauk R	5000	1.5 mi E Curry Gap
CONGER PDS (2)	Pend Orielle	3-5	Pend Oreille R	2800	5 mi NW Cusick
CONKLIN	Pend Oreille	8	Pend Oreille R	2100	5 mi SE Usk
CONNIE	Jefferson	7	Sf Quinault R	4200	12 mi E Lk Quinault
CONNOR	Snohomish	9	Pilchuck R	190	1 mi E Hartford
CONRAD LKS (2)	Yakima	1-1	Sf Tieton R	5293	8.5 mi S Clear Lk Dam
CONRADI PD	Cowlitz	12	Cowlitz R	275	5 mi SE Toledo
CONSTANCE	Jefferson	11	Dosewallips R	4750	13.5 mi SW Quilcene
COOK CR PDS	Grays Hbr	25	Ef Satsop R	100	5 mi N Elma
COOKS	Pend Oreille	11	Pend Oreille R	3075	5 mi NE Usk
COON	Chelan	9	Stehekin R	2172	1 mi N High Bridge G.S.
COONEY	Okanogan	8	Methow R	7300	16 mi W Methow
COOPERS PTHL	Thurston	5	Nisqually R	79	700' E Lk St Clair
COOPER	Kittitas	120	CleElum R	2788	3.5 mi NW Salmon la Sac
COOT	Grant	4	Crab Cr	940	6.5 mi N Othello
COPLAY	Pierce	20	Carbon R	4100	13 mi SE Enumclaw
COPPER LKS (2)	Ferry	1-4	San Poil R	3040	3.5 mi SW Republic
COPPER	King	148	Wf Foss R	4000	7 mi S Skykomish
COPPER	Snohomish	2	Sauk R	3300	6 mi NE Verlot R.S.
COPPER	Whatcom	8	Chilliwack R	5250	11.5 mi E Shuksan
COPPER GLANCE	Okanogan	4	Chewack R	6100	20 mi NW Winthrop
CORA	Lewis	28	Nisqually R	3900	9 mi SE National
CORNWALL	Stevens	4	Columbia R	2930	7 mi NE Hunters
CORRAL	Grant	80	Crab Cr	921	11 mi NW Othello
CORRAL	Okanogan	21	Ashnola R	7200	33 mi N Winthrop
CORRAL	Yakima	6	Klickitat R	5800	12 mi S White Pass
COSSALMAN	Spokane	41	Palouse R	2300	3.5 mi S Cheney
COTTAGE	King	63	Sammamish R	231	4 mi E Woodinville
COTTONWOOD	Kittitas	8	Yakima R	3900	5.5 mi S Snoq Pass
COTTONWOOD—UPPER	Kittitas	1.5	Yakima R	4040	6 mi S Snoq Pass
COUGAR—LITTLE	King	9.5	Nf Snoq R	4117	15 mi NE North Bend
COUGAR—BIG	King	20	Nf Snoq R	4123	14 mi NE North Bend
COUGAR	Okanogan	9	Methow R	3400	4 mi E Winthrop
COUGAR	Okanogan	21	Lost R	4200	31 mi NW Winthrop
COUGAR	Snohomish	4	Nf Sauk R	5000	17.5 mi SE Darrington
COUGAR—BIG	Yakima	82	Bumping R	5015	5 mi SE Chinook Pass
COUGAR—LITTLE	Yakima	13	Bumping R	5020	adj Big Cougar Lk
COULEE	Grant	10	Crab Cr	1500	adj Coulee City

LAKE	COUNTY	ACRES	DRAINAGE	ELEV.	LOCATION
COUNCIL	Skamania	48	Cispus R	4200	25 mi SE Randle
COUNDLY	Pierce	16	Carbon R	4150	14 mi SE Enumclaw
COUNTRY LINE PD	Skagit	4	Nf Stilly R	2000	3.5 mi NW Oso
COW	Adams	226	Palouse R	1749	10 mi E Ritzville
COWBELL	Snohomish	3.5	Pilchuck R	3420	7 mi SE Verlot
COWEMAN	Cowlitz	7	Coweman R	2750	22 mi E Kelso
COX	Okanogan	11	Nespelem R	2590	5 mi NE Nespelem
COX PD	Whatcom	1.5	Whatcom Cr	480	.05 mi NW Silver Beach
COYOTE	Adams	10	Crab Cr	815	5.5 mi NW Othello
COYOTE	Lewis	4	Cowlitz R	5100	5 mi SW White Pass
CRABAPPLE	Snohomish	36	Lk Goodwin	415	7.5 mi NW Marysville
CRADLE	Chelan	9	Wenatchee R	6050	16 mi W Leavenworth
CRAG—UPPER	Yakima	5	Bumping R	5020	8 mi S Chinook Pass
GRAIG LKS (3)	Snohomish	6-11	Nf Stllly R	4400	6 mi SW Darrington
CRAMER	Yakima	19	Tieton R	5025	3 mi NE White Pass
CRANBERRY	Island	2	Saratoga Pass	245	Camono Island
CRANBERRY	Island	128	Rosario St	20	Deception Pass Prk
CRANBERRY SL	King	1	Lk Sawyer	550	2 mi N Blk Diamond
CRANBERRY	Pacific	18	Willapa Bay	20	3.5 mi N Long Beach
CRANBERRY	Pierce	26	Nisqually R	644	5 mi NW Eatonville
CRANBERRY	Skagit	8	Samish R	300	4 mi N Sedro Woolley
CRANE	Skamania	1	Lewis R	1750	6 mi E Mt St Helens
CRATER	Grant	25	Columbia R	1230	4 mi W Quincey
CRATER	Skagit	63	Suiattle R	4800	13.5 mi E Marblemount
CRAWFISH	Okanogan	80	Sf San Poil R	4475	15 mi NE Omak
CRAWFORD	King	20	Mf Snoq R	5350	11 mi S Skykomish
CREAM	Jefferson	3	Hoh R	4250	2 mi NW Mt Ferry
CRESCENT	Chelan	2.5	Wenatchee R	5500	8 mi NE Stevens Pass
CRESCENT	Grant	40	Columbia R	994	8 mi N Othello
CRESCENT	Pend Oreille	22	Pend Oreille R	2500	9 mi N Metaline Falls
CRESCENT	Pierce	47	Gig Harbor	166	3.5 mi N Gig Harbor
CRESCENT	Skamania	1.5	Columbia R	780	3 mi SW Stevenson
CRESCENT	Snohomish	9	Snoqualmie R	25	3.5 mi S Monroe
CRESCENT BAY	Grant	70	Columbia R	1290	Grand Coulee
CROCKER	Jefferson	65	Discovery Bay	190	3.5 mi S Pt Discovery Bay
CROSBY	King	1.5	Sf Skykomish R	4500	3.5 mi SW Grotto
CROW	Okanogan	5	Ashnola R	6800	33 mi N Winthrop
CROWFOOT	Okanogan	7	Okanogan R	2420	11 mi SE Malott
CRYSTAL	Chelan	6	Wenatchee R	7020	11 mi SW Leavenworth
CRYSTAL	Grant	1.5	Columbia R	1160	8 mi SW Quincey
CRYSTAL	King	6.5	Pratt R	4740	3 mi W Snoq Pass
CRYSTAL LKS (2)	King	1-3	Sf Skykomish R	3100	5.5 mi S Skykomish
CRYSTAL	Okanogan	3	Chewack R	6850	25 mi N Winthrop
CRYSTAL	Pierce	9	White R	5830	2.5 mi W Chinook Pass
CRYSTAL	Snohomish	21	White Chuck R	4800	14 mi SE Darrington
CUB	Chelan	28	Lk Chelan	5300	17.5 mi SW Twisp
CUB	Skagit	11	Suiattle R	5400	24.5 mi NE Darrington
CUITIN	Chelan	6	Wenatchee R	5850	8 mi S Stevens Pass
CUMMINGS	Snohomish	2	Pt Susan	375	8 mi NW Marysville
CUP	Chelan	8	Wenatchee R	6400	9 mi E Stevens Pass
CUP	Snohomish	11	Rapid R	4600	6 mi N Stevens Pass
CURL	Columbia	3	Tucannon R	2550	10 mi S Pomeroy
CURLEW	Ferry	870	Columbia R	2333	5 mi NE Republic
CURLEW PD	Walla Walla	35	L Wallula R	340	5 mi SE Burbank
CURTIS	Skamania	2.5	Muddy R	3610	3 mi fm Spirit Lk Inlet
CUSHMAN	Mason	4003	Hood Canal	735	4 mi NW Hoodsport
CUSHMAN PDS	Mason	5	Lk Cushman	800	NE side Lk Cushman
CUTTHROAT	Okanogan	9	Methow R	4935	23 mi W Winthrop
CYCLONE	Skagit	56	Cascade R	5300	11 mi SE Marblemount

D

D" (DEE)	Chelan	10	Chiwawa R	6400	1 mi N fm W end Schaefer Lk
DAGGER	Chelan	11	Stehekin R	5500	.05 mi W Twisp Pass
DAGGER	Snohomish	28	Skykomish R	662	4.5 mi SE Sultan
DAHLBERG PDS	Snohomish	1-3	Stilly R	1560	3.8 mi N Granite Falls
DAILEY	Stevens	5	Pend Oreilie R	2300	3.4 mi E Arden
DALLES LKS (2)	Pierce	1-2.5	White R	4550	7 mi SE Greenwater
DALTON	Franklin	30	Snake R	440	6.2 mi N Ringold
DAMFINO (2)	Whatcom	1.5	Chilliwack R	4500	8 mi NE Glacier
DAMON	Grays Hbr	16	Humptulips R	40	2 mi NE Copalis Crossing
DANCING LADY	Yakima	7	Tieton R	4980	.07 mi NE White Pass
DARLENE	Skamania	2	Wind R	4250	.08 mi SW Gifford Peak
DAVIS	Ferry	17	Kettle R	4550	4 mi SW Barstow
DAVIS	Lewis	18	Tilton R	940	1.4 mi SE Morton
DAVIS	Okanogan	39	Methow R	2350	4 mi SE Winthrop

LAKE	COUNTY	ACRES	DRAINAGE	ELEV.	LOCATION
DAVIS	Okanogan	5	Okanogan R	3450	10 mi SE Tonasket
DAVIS	Pend Oreille	146	Pend Oreille R	2150	6 mi S Usk
DAVIS SL	Skagit	7	Skagit R	120	1.4 mi E Hamilton
DAWN	Clallam	8	Pt Angeles Bay	1800	5.4 mi S Port Angeles
DEAD	Clark	16	Washougal R	180	1 mi N Camas
DEADHEAD	Kittitas	11	Waptus R	5300	9 mi N Salmon La Sac
DEADMANS	Skamania	34	Green R	4330	8.8 mi S Kosmos
DEADWOOD—LOWER	Pierce	7	White R	5250	1.4 mi N Chinook Pass
DEADWOOD—UPPER	Pierce	6	White R	5255	1 mi N Chinook Pass
DECEPTION LKS (3)	King	3-12.5	Tye R	5100	5.5 mi S Scenic
DECEPTION LKS (2)	Pend Oreille	3-4	Pend Oreille R	3100	4 mi E Ione
DEEP	Franklin	10	Palouse R	980	5 mi SE Washtucna
DEEP	Grant	140	Grand Coulee	1231	5 mi SW Coulee City
DEEP	King	39	Green R	770	.08 mi SW Cumberland
DEEP	Kitsap	3	Sinclair Inlet	190	3.5 mi S Pt Orchard
DEEP	Kittitas	53	Waptus R	4450	9.7 mi N Salmon La Sac
DEEP	Okanogan	5	Okanogan R	2150	2 mi SE L Soap Lk
DEEP	Skamania	6	White Salmon R	4950	1.4 mi SW Cultus Cr G.S.
DEEP	Skamania	3	Cispus R	3963	9 mi SE Kosmos
DEEP	Stevens	198	Columbia R	2025	9 mi SE Northport
DEEP	Thurston	66	Black R	198	9.5 mi S Olympia
DEEPWATER	Mason	11	Oakland Bay	240	7.3 mi NE Shelton
DEER LKS (2)	Clallam	1-8	Soleduck R	3525	3.4 mi SE Sol Duc H.S.
DEER	Columbia	2	Tucannon R	2250	10 mi S Pomeroy G.D.R. Hq
DEER	Island	82	Posession Snd	352	1 mi W Clinton
DEER	King	46	Taylor R	3630	18.5 mi NE North Bend
DEER	Kittitas	53	Waptus R	4450	9.7 mi N Salmon la Sac
DEEP	Okanogan	5	Okanogan R	2150	2.2 mi SE Soap Lk
DEER	Mason	12	Pickering Pass	190	10.8 mi NE Shelton
DEER	Pacific	8	Pacific Ocean	25	2 mi N Long Beach
DEER	Skamania	5.5	Nf Lewis R	4800	2.4 mi SW Cultus Cr G.S.
DEER	Skamania	2.5	Green R	2880	6.5 mi N Spirit Lk Outlet
DEER	Stevens	1163	Colville R	2482	32 mi N Spokane
DEER	Yakima	12	Tieton R	5206	1.3 NW White Pass
DEER MEADOW	Mason	3	Nf Skokomish R	720	.08 mi SW Cushman Lk Dam
DEER SPRINGS	Lincoln	60	Crab Cr	1800	11 mi NE Odessa
DEER SPRINGS	Pend Oreille	2	Pend Oreille R	3000	10 mi N Cusick
DE HART	Stevens	2	L Pend Ore R	1650	4.8 mi E Colville
DELANTY	Jefferson	13	Pt Townsend Bay	505	1.4 mi SE head Discovery Bay
DELTA	King	47	Wf Foss R	3500	8.4 mi S Skykomish
DEMPSEY MTN PDS	Skagit	4	Grandy Cr	450	5 mi E Hamilton
DENNY	King	14	Sf Stilly R	43i30	2.5 mi W Snoq Pass
DERPICK	King	37	Mf Snoq R	3686	6.4 mi NW Snoq Pass
DERRY	King	6	Sf Snoq R	744	4.5 mi SE North Bend
DESIRE	King	72	Cedar R	500	5 mi SE Renton
DEVEREAUX	Mason	100	Hood Canal	215	1.5 mi NW Allyn
DEVIL	Chelan	1	Entiat R	6000	24 mi N Leavenworth
DEVILS	Jefferson	12	Quilcene Bay	844	2 mi S Quilcene
DEVILS	Skagit	31	Skagit R	826	5.8 mi SE Mt Vernon
DEVILS	Snohomish	2.5	Sf Stilly R	3820	2 mi W Pass Lk
DEVILS SLIDE	Kittitas	1.5	Naches R	4700	4 mi SW Cliffdell
DEVILSWASH BASIN	Yakima	2	Nf Tieton R	6268	8.2 mi W White Pass
DEWEY—LOWER	Yakima	51	American R	5112	1.7 mi SE Chinook Pass
DEWEY—UPPER	Yakima	8	American R	5140	1.5 mi SE Chinook Pass
DIABLO RES	Whatcom	910	Skagit R	1205	6 mi NE Newhalem
DIAMOND	Kittitas	5	Waptus R	4950	4 mi NW Salmon La Sac
DIAMOND	Pend Oreille	745.5	Wbr L Spokane R	2360	7 mi SW Newport
DIAMOND	Snohomish	10	Suiattle R	5250	.08 mi SE Meadow Mtn
DIAMOND	Yakima	18	Klickitat R	5750	13.5 mi SE White Pass
DIAMOND MTN	Jefferson	10	Dosewallips R	5575	E Side Diamond Mtn
DIBBLE	Okanogan	5	Methow R	1900	3.4 mi S Winthrop
DICKEY	Clallam	527	Wf Dickey R	193	12 mi NW Forks
DIKE 1	Grant	6	Columbia R	997	9 mi N Othello
DILLY	Jefferson	10	Queets R	2350	3 mi SE Spruce B Shelter
DIOSBUD LKS (3)	Whatcom	2-3.5	Skagit R	4075-4490	9.5 mi NW Marblemount
DIVIDE	Kittitas	2	Keechelus Lk	3870	2 mi S Snoq Pass
DIXIE	Skagit	4	Skagit R	3500	9 mi SE Sedro Woolley
DIXONS PD	Lincoln	4	Palouse R	1900	5.5 mi E Sprague
DOC MENIGS PD	Kittitas	9	Yakima R	1455	3.3 mi SE Ellensburg
DOELLE LKS (2)	Chelan	4-8	Wenatchee R	6200	5.4 mi E Stevens Pass
DOG	Yakima	61	Nf Tieton R	4207	2 mi NE White Pass
DOLE LKS (3)	Chelan	3-7	Lk Chelan	6150-6550	6.7 mi W Lucerne
DOLLAR LKS (2)	Snohomish	2-6	Wallace R	3900-3950	2.8 mi N Index
DOLLOFF	King	21	Green R	400	3 mi NW Auburn
DOMKE	Chelan	272	Lk Chelan	2192	35 mi NW Chelan
DON	Mason	17	Hood Canal	520	1.5 mi S Dewatto

LAKE	COUNTY	ACRES	DRAINAGE	ELEV.	LOCATION
DONALD	Chelan	12	Wenatchee R	5800	14.4 mi NW Leavenworth
DOREEN	Whatcom	1	Sf Nooksack R	3380	6.5 mi SW Mt Baker summit
DOROTHY	King	290	Ef Miller R	3052	7.8 mi S Skykomish
DOSSER	Spokane	9.5	Spokane R	2075	4 mi SE Greenacres
DOUBTFUL	Chelan	30	Lk Chelan	5385	66 mi NW Chelan
DOUGLAS	Stevens	3	Colville R	2500	4.4 mi N Colville
DOW	Snohomish	3.5	Rapid R	4800	4 mi N Stevens Pass
DOWNEY	Snohomish	13	Suiattle R	5500	20 mi E Darrington
DOWNS	Spokane	423	Palouse R	1958	7 mi E Sprague
DRAGON	Jefferson	9	Hoh R	3350	7 mi W Mt Olympus
DRAGOON	Spokane	22	L Spokane R	2080	.04 mi NW Deer Park
DRANO	Skamania	220	Columbia R	72	7 mi W White Salmon
DRAPERS	Lincoln	34	Crab Cr	1900	11 mi S Wilbur
DREAM	King	35	TaylorR	3800	17.5 mi NE North Bend
DREDGE PDS	Cowlitz	4	Sf Toutle R	500	.05 mi E Toutle
DRUNKEN CHARLIE	King	3	Mf Tolt R	1380	4 mi NE Carnation
DRY	Chelan	1.5	Lk Chelan	7000	15 mi SW Twisp
DRY BED—UPPER	Mason	4.5	Satsop R	1250	900' NE Lower Dry Bed Lk
DRYBED—LOWER	Mason	7	Satsop R	1150	15 mi NW Shelton
DRY POND	Mason	2	Tahuya R	400	2.5 mi NE Tahuya
DUCK	Lewis	14	L Nisqually R	3715	7.5 mi N Morton
DUCK	Okanogan	29	Okanogan R	1241	3 mi N Omak
DUFFEY LKS (2)	Snohomish	2.5-3.5	Skykomish R	3000-3180	4 mi S Gold Bar
DUFFY	Okanogan	9	Twisp R	6500	1 mi N Oval Peak
DUFFYS	Lincoln	2.5	Crab Cr	0	8 mi S Almira
DULEY	Douglas	9	Columbia R	2240	12 mi E Bridgeport
DULEY	Okanogan	53	Columbia R	2430	14 mi S Okanogan
DUMBBELL	Lewis	42	Ohanapecosh R	5200	3.8 mi N White Pass
DUNBAR	Spokane	2.5	L Spokane R	2100	3.7 mi NE Elk
DUNLAP PD	Thurston	2	Chehalis R	220	4.8 mi N Bucoda
DUSTY	Grant	30	Columbia R	888	7 mi SW Quincey

E

LAKE	COUNTY	ACRES	DRAINAGE	ELEV.	LOCATION
EAGLE LKS (3)	Clallam	0.5-1.5	Lyre R	2625-3075	1.5 mi W end Lk Crescent
EAGLE	King	53	Nf Green R	2230	8 mi E Kanasket
EAGLE	Snohomish	20	Beckler R	3750	3.5 mi NE Baring
EAGLE LKS (2)	Okanogan	9-15.5	Methow R	6400-7100	18 mi NW Methow
EAGLE SPRINGS	Lincoln	4	Crab Creek	1740	11.5 mi N Odessa
EARLE	Chelan	16.5	Wenatchee R	6600	8 mi SW Leavenworth
EAST	Pierce	4	Carbon R	4000	15 mi SE Enumclaw
EAST LKS (2)	Whatcom	2-7.5	Skagit R	5600-6100	1.8 mi NE Whatcom Pass
EAST BOARDMAN	Snohomish	25	Sf Stilly R	3370	7.5 mi SE Verlot
EASTER SUNDAY	Stevens	1	Kettle R	3275	10 mi SE Orient
ECHO	King	19	Raging R	910	2.4 mi SW Snoqualmie
ECHO	King	12	Lk Washington	393	6 mi N Seattle
ECHO	Pierce	61	White R	3819	29 mi SE Enumclaw
ECHO	Snohomish	17	Sammamish R	477	3 mi SE Maltby
ECHO	Snohomish	25	Pilchuck R	1670	9 mi N Sultan
ECHO LKS (5)	Stevens	0.6-3.8	Colville R	1870	8 mi N Colville
EDDS	King	26	Mf Snoq R	4300	4.5 mi NE Snoq Pass
EDGAR	Skagit	4	Shannon Lk	3250	9 mi E Concrete
EDNA	Chelan	3.5	Wenatchee R	6500	13 mi NW Leavenworth
EGG	San Juan	7	San Juan Ch	155	3.5 mi NW Friday Hbr
ELBOW	Douglas	25	Columbia R	2320	1800' S Del Rio G.H.
ELBOW	Ferry	51	Columbia R	2150	13.5 mi N Inchelium
ELBOW	King	6	Mf Snoq R	3900	6.5 mi NW Snoq Pass
ELBOW	Stevens	13.5	Columbia R	2775	9.5 mi W Northport
ELBOW	Thurston	36	Nisqually R	479	9.5 mi SE Yelm
ELBOW	Whatcom	5	Nooksack R	3400	6.5 mi SW Mt Baker summit
ELEANOR	Pierce	20	White R	4960	11 mi NE Mt Rainier summit
ELECTRON RES	Pierce	13	Puget Snd	1540	1 mi SE Electron
ELIZABETH	King	7	Sf Skykomish R	2865	8 mi NW Skykomish
ELIZABETH	Pierce	4	White R	5900	3.5 mi N Chinook Pass
ELK	Clallam	59	Ozette Lk	380	11 mi S Neah Bay
ELK	Grays Hbr	11	Quinault R	3000	6 mi E Quinault Lk
ELK	Jefferson	6	Upper Hoh R	2550	4 mi N Mt Olympus
ELK—LOWER	Mason	6	Hamma Hamma R	1050	1.5 mi S Hamma Hamma G.S.
ELK—UPPER	Mason	3	Hamma Hamma R	1200	1200' S Elk Lk
ELK	Skamania	13	Nf Lewis R	4700	2.5 mi SW Cultus Cr G.S.
ELK	Skamania	30,5	Green R	3978	6 mi NW Spirit Lk outlet
ELL	Okanogan	21	Wf San Poil R	2592	16 mi SE Tonasket
ELLEN	Ferry	78	Columbia R	2300	8.5 mi SE Sherman Cr Pass
ELTON LKS	Yakima	14	Yakima R	—	6 mi N Yakima
ELMER RES	Clark	4	Ef Lewis R	800	6.5 mi N La Center
ELOCHOMAN	Cowlitz	4 5	Ef Elochoman R	1650	12.5 mi NE Cathlamet

LAKE	COUNTY	ACRES	DRAINAGE	ELEV.	LOCATION
ELOIKA	Spokane	659	WB L Spokane	1920	4 mi W Elk SE, end
ELSEY	Chelan	16	Napeegua R	6200	18.5 mi NE Stevens Pass
EMBRO	King	9.5	Tye R	4200	2 mi N Scenic
EMERALD	King	4	Jade Lk	4725	10 mi SE Skykomish
EMERALD	Snohomish	11	Suiattle R	5150	17 mi E Darrington
EMERSON	Pierce	5	American Lk	260	1 mi SW Ponders Corner
EMMA	Franklin	20	Snake R	440	7 mi NE Ice Hbr Dam
EMPIRE LKS (3)	Ferry	0.6-4	Kettle R	3600	11 mi N Republic
ENCHANTMENT LKS(10)	Chelan	1-23	Wenatchee R	6875	10 mi SW Leavenworth
ENJAR	Skagit	12	Skagit R	4300	1.5 mi NW Snowking Mtn
ENTIAT (RES)	Chelan	9860	Columbia R	707	7.5 mi N Wenatchee
ERICKSON RES	Kitsap	2	Manzanita Bay	60	4.5 mi NW Winslow
ERICKSON	Mason	15	Dewatto R	475	4.8 mi NW Belfair
ERICKSON	Stevens	5.5	Colville R	2175	9.5 mi SE Colville
ERIE	Skagit	111	Skagit Bay	140	4 mi S Anacortes
ESCONDIDO	Kittitas	4	Cooper R	4630	10 mi NE Snoq Pass
ETHEL	Chelan	16	Wenatchee R	5400	9.8 mi E Stevens Pass
ETHEL	Pierce	31	Wf White R	4287	8.5 mi NW Mt Rainier summit
ETTA	Clallam	13	Greywolf R	477	16 mi S Port Angeles
EUNICE	Skamania	6.5	Wind R	4500	19.5 mi N Carson
EVANS	King	11	Foss R	3600	4 mi S Skykomish
EVANS	Okanogan	27	Okanogan R	1712	3 mi W Riverside
EVAN	Snohomish	13	Stilly R	2751	6 mi SE Verlot R.S.
EVELYN	King	2	Tye R	5200	7.5 mi S Scenic
EVERETT	Skagit	8	Sherman Lk	650	1 mi E Concrete
EVERGREEN RES	Grant	235	Columbia R	1185	7.5 mi SW Quincey

F

LAKE	COUNTY	ACRES	DRAINAGE	ELEV.	LOCATION
FAILOR (RES)	Grays Hbr	60	Humptulips R	117	9.4 mi N Hoquiam
FAIRVIEW	Kitsap	7	Case Inlet	380	6.7 mi SW Pt Orchard
FALLS	Skagit	60	Cascade R	4200	4.8 mi SE Marblemount
FAN	Pend Oreille	73	WBr L Spokane	1930	8.4 mi NE Deer Park
FANCHERS DAM RES	Okanogan	20	Okanogan R	3150	11.5 mi NE Tonasket
FARGHER PD	Clark	3	Ef Lewis R	700	3.5 mi W Amboy
FARLEY	Okanogan	14	Okanogan R	2350	6.5 mi SE Malott
FAWN	Cowlitz	24	Green R	3700	6 mi NW Spirit Lk outlet
FAWN	Okanogan	6	Chewack R	5500	29.5 mi N Winthrop
FAZON	Whatcom	32	Nooksack R	128	1.5 mi NW Goshen
FEEKS MARSH	Island	10	Puget Sound	100	3.4 mi W Clinton
FENNER	Yakima	3	Naches R	5460	1.5 mi NW Crow Lk
FENWICK	King	18	Green R	120	1 mi NE Star Lk
FERGUSON	Okanogan	9	Mf Pasayten R	6900	29 mi NW Winthrop
FERGUSON PDS	Whatcom	10	Sf Nooksack R		nr Saxon Bridge
FERN	Chelan	17	Nf Entiat R	6875	34 mi NW Entiat
FERRY	Ferry	19	San Poil R	3329	9.4 mi SW Republic
FIANDER	Thurston	15	Deschutes R	450	4 mi W Yelm
FIDDLE	Mason	1.5	Hood Canal	800	3 mi NE Lilliwaup
FIFTEEN	Thurston	4	Deschutes R	500	1.5 mi SE Rainier
FIGURE EIGHT	Okanogan	31	Okanogan R	2750	11 mi SE Okanogan
FINDLEY LKS (3)	King	1.7-22	Cedar R	3580-3710	14.5 mi E Kanasket
FINDLEY	Spokane	15	Palouse R	2290	2.4 mi S Cheney
FIO RITO	Kittitas	54	Yakima R	—	5 mi S Ellensburg
FIREWEED PDS (2)	Kittitas	0.9-1.5	Keechelus L	4055	7 mi S Snoq Pass
FIRST	King	2.5	White R	1100	3.4 mi E Enumclaw
FIRST HIDDEN	Okanogan	19	Lost R	4250	32.5 mi NW Winthrop
FIRST THOUGHT	Stevens	2	Kettle R	3500	3 mi NE Orient
FISH	Chelan	513	Wenatchee R	1850	16.4 mi N Leavenworth
FISH	King	16.5	Green R	720	1.5 mi SW Cumberland
FISH	Okanogan	102	Okanogan R	1798	4.5 mi NE Conconully
FISH	Spokane	47	Spokane R	2171	3 mi NE Cheney
FISH	Yakima	10	Tieton R	3400	2.5 mi S Tieton Dam
FISH	Yakima	11	Bumping R	4114	8.5 mi S Chinook Pass
FISHTRAP (RES)	Lincoln	196	Palouse R	1980	6.5 mi E Sprague
FISHER	King	65	Tye R	4850	7.8 mi SE Skykomish
FITCHENER SL	King	3	Nf Snoq R	1470	12.8 mi NE Snoq
FIVEMILE	King	38	Stuck R	400	4 mi SW Auburn
FLANDERS PD	Clallam	2	Pt Discovery Bay	200	2.5 mi NE Blyn
FLAPJACK LKS (2)	Mason	6-10	Nf Skok R	3900	4.3 mi N hd Lk Cushman
FLAT	Lincoln	20	Crab Creek	2150	11.5 mi SE Wilbur
FLAT	Lincoln	11	Crab Creek	2100	2.5 mi SW Govan
FLAT	Mason	2	Sf Skok R	1250	18 mi NW Shelton
FLAT IRON	Yakima	7	Bumping R	57W	1.5 mi SW Bald Mtn L.O.
FLORA	Chelan	11	Wenatchee R	5900	12.8 mi NW Leavenworth
FLORENCE	Lincoln	34	Crab Cr	2300	11 mi S Creston
FLOWING	Snohomish	135	Pilchuck R	526	6 mi N Monroe

LAKE	COUNTY	ACRES	DRAINAGE	ELEV.	LOCATION
FLUME CR BV PDS	Skagit	4	Sauk R	1000	4.7 mi S Rockport
FLY	Skagit	2	Cascade R	4000	7.4 mi SE Marblemount
FOGGY	Snohomish	19	Sf Sauk R	5000	3 mi S Barlow Pass
FOHN	King	1	Wf Foss R	5500	3000' SW Opal Lk
FONTAL	Snohomish	37	Skykomoish R	1081	4.5 mi SE Monroe
FORBES	King	7	Lk Washington	250	1.5 mi E Kirkland
FORDE	Okanogan	24	Similkameen R	1560	6 mi S Loomis
FOREST	Pierce	6	Puyallup R	520	3.3 mi S Orting
FOREST	Pierce	2~5	Greenwater R	3900	8 mi SE Greenwater
FOREST	Skamania	8	Green R	3900	5.8 mi NW Spirit Lk outlet
FORLORN LKS (12)	Skamania	1-20	White Salmon R	3700	19 mi N Stevenson
FORTSON MILL PD	Snohomish	2	Nf Stilly R	400	9.5 mi E Oso
FORTUNE PDS (2)	Snohomish	8-1	Nf Skyk R	4600-4700	10.5 mi NW StevensPass
FOUND	Skagit	71	Cascade R	4150	10.8 mi SE Marblemount
FOUNTAIN	Whatcom	14	Nooksack R	70	3 mi SE Lynden
FOUR POINT	Okanogan	16	Chewack R	7100	31 mi N Winthrop
FOURTH OF JULY	Adams	110	Palouse R	1900	2.2 mi S Sprague
FOURTH OF JULY	Snohomish	1	Beckler R	4350	7.5 mi E Index
FOX LKS (2)	Okanogan	4-8	Chewack R	6700	27.5 mi N Winthrop
FRAGRANCE	Whatcom	6.5	Chuckanut Bay	1025	6.5 mi S Bellingham
FRAILEY PDS	Skagit	1	Stilly R	1100	1.4 mi W Cavanaugh Lk
FRANCIS	King	19.5	Cedar R	470	2 mi N Maple Valley
FRANCIS	King	40	Wf Miller R	4200	6 mi SW Skykomish
FRANKLIN ROOSEVELT	Stevens	79000	Columbia R	1288	28 mi NE Coulee City
FRATER	Pend Orellle	11	L Pend Ore R	3200	6.5 mi S Ione
FRAZIER MARSH	King	98	Snoqualmie R	500	7.5 mi S Snoqualmie
FREDS	Okanogan	6	Mf Passayten R	6500	30.4 mi NW Winthrop
FREEWAY	Yakima	23	Yakima R	1070	N side Yakima
FREEZEOUT	Whatcom	9	Skagit R	5800	15 mi NE Ross Dam
FRENCH	Skamania	1.5	Columbia R	440	1.7 mi SW Stevenson
FRENCH CREEK PD	Snohomish	6	Nf Stilly R	900	1.5 mi S Hazel
FRENCH PTHLS/LOWER	Chelan	5	Wenatchee R	5375	11.5 mi N Salmon La Sac
FRENCH PTHLS/UPPER	Chelan	6	Wenatchee R	5875	1500' NW Lower Potholes
FRENCH JOHNS	Ferry	14	FDR Lk	1320	5 mi S Keller
FRESHWATER	Pacific	5	Willapa Bay	20	5 mi N Long Beach
FROG	Kittitas	1	Yakima R	3550	3 mi S Snoq Pass
FROG	Skamania	4	Columbia R	375	4 mi E Carson
FROG	Snohomish	1.5	Sauk R	950	3.4 mi S Darrington
FROSTY	Okanogan	3.5	Similkameen R	5400	22 mi NE Ross Dam
FRY	Okanogan	10	Okanogan R	1242	3.3 mi NW Omak
FRYE	Okanogan	4	Okanogan R		.05 mi NW Riverside
FRYING PAN	Lewis	23	Ohanapecosh R	4850	6.5 mi N White Pass
FURY	King	1	Snoqualmie R	1005	6.7 mi N North Bend

G

LAKE	COUNTY	ACRES	DRAINAGE	ELEV.	LOCATION
GADWELL	Grant	5	Crab Cr	950	8.5 mi N Othello
GALLAGHER HEAD	KIttitas	1.5	Nf Teanaway R	5595	17.5 mi N Cle Elum
GARBER	Stevens	1.5	Colville R	3000	8 mi W Valley
GARFIELD MTN/LOW	King	8	Taylor R	4000	15 mi E North Bend
GARFIELD MTN/UPPER	King	7	Taylor R	4500	1300' SE lower lk
GEE POINT	Skagit	4	Skagit R	4100	8.5 mi SW Concrete
GEHRKE	Thurston	8	Deschutes R	450	1 mi E Rainier
GENEVA	King	29	Commencement B	385	2.5 mi SW Auburn
GEORGE	Grant	5	Crab Cr	1200	0.8 mi NE George
GEORGE	Pierce	33	Nisqually R	4232	5 mi NW Longmire
GEORGE	Pierce	2	Greenwater R	5470	26 mi SE Enumclaw
GERTRUDE	Lewis	14	Cispus R	5750	20 mi SE Packwood
GHOST	Skamania	5	Muddy R	3767-	.04 mi SW Strawberry Lk
GIBBS	Jefferson	37	Pt Townsend Bay	340	7 mi NW Port Ludlow
GILBERT	Stevens	4	Kettle R	2200	5 mi NE Orient
GILE	Pacific	19	Willapa Bay	20	2.5 mi N Long Beach
GILLETTE	Skamania	3.5	Columbia R	300	1.5 mi N No Bonneville
GILLETTE	Stevens	48	L Pend Ore R	3160	17 mi NE Colville
GISSBERG PDS	Snohomish	5	Snohomish R	—	8 mi N Everett
GLACIER	Lewis	20	Cowlitz R	3000	5.5 mi SE Packwood
GLACIER	King	60	Tye R	4900	3.5 mi S Scenic
GLACIER	Kittitas	21	Cooper R	4750	6.4 mi NE Snoq Pass
GLADYS	Clallam	1	Greywolf R	5500	Hwtrs Grand Cr
GLASSES	Chelan	25	L Wenatchee R	4750	7 mi N Stevens Pass
GLORY	Okanogan	3.5	Ashnola R	6600	31 mi N Winthrop
GLUD PDS	Kitsap	1	Burke Bay	45	3.8 mi S Keyport
GOAT	King	19.5	Mf Snoq R	3600	17.4 mi NE North Bend
GOAT	Lewis	10	Cispus R	6900	9.4 mi SW White Pass
GOAT	Pierce	10	Nisqually R	4300	6.7 mi NE National
GOAT	Pierce	3	White R	5500	7.4 mi N Chinook Pass

LAKE	COUNTY	ACRES	DRAINAGE	ELEV.	LOCATION
GOAT	Snohomish	64	Sf Sauk R	3154	4 mi E Barlow Pass
GOAT MARSH #1	Cowlitz	13	Sf Toutle R	2910	4.4 mi N Merrill Lk
GOAT MARSH #2	Cowlitz	5	Sf Toutle R	2911	750' SE Lk #1
GOLD	King	56	Ef Miller R	5000	9 mi NE Snoq Pass
GOLD—UPPER	Okanogan	19	Wf San Poil R	2950	14 mi N Nespelem
GOLD—LOWER	Okanogan	11	Wf San Poil R	2945	1000' mi NE upper lk
GOLD BASIN PD	Snohomish	1	Sf Stilly R	1100	at Gold Basin
GOLDEN	King	8	Wf Foss R	5200	9.8 SW Skykomish
GOLDEN LKS (3)	Pierce	4-18	Mowich R	4450-4950	7 mi W Mt Rainier summi
GOLDENEYE	Grant	30	Crab Cr	930	10.8 mi N Othello
GOLNICK	Island	2.5	Skagit Bay	325	on Whidbey Island
GOODWIN	Snohomish	547	Tulalip Bay	324	7.5 mi NW Marysville
GOODWIN	Thurston	3	Nisqually R	415	3.4 mi S Yelm
GOOSE LKS (2)	Grant	50-112	Crab Cr	860	9.2 mi NW Othello
GOOSE	Lewis	8	L Nisqually R	2850	8 mi N Morton
GOOSE	Okanogan	181	Columbia R	1225	17 mi W Nespelem
GOOSE	Skamania	58	White Salmon R	3050	15 mi N Carson
GOOSE PD	Thurston	2	Henderson Inlet	170	5 mi E Olympia
GORDON	Skagit	2	Stilly R	3000	on N side Table Mtn
GOSS	Island	55	Holmes Hbr	130	3 mi W Langley
GOUGING	King	11	Wf Miller R	3400	7.4 mi SW Skykomish
GRACE LKS (3)	Chelan	1-7	Wenatchee R	64 6800	7.8 mi SE Stevens Pass
GRANDY	Skagit	56	Skagit R	809	3 mi NW Concrete
GRANITE LKS (2)	King	9-15	Mf Snoq R	2950-3060	8.8 mi SE North Bend
GRANITE	Lewis	29	Nisqually R	4163	7.5 mi SE National
GRANITE	Skagit	16.5	Nf Stilly R	3521	7 mi NE Oso
GRANITE LKS (4)	Skagit	5-144	Cascade R	4500	7 mi SE Marblemount
GRANITE PTHLS (20)	Skagit	1-8	Nf Stilly R	3400	7 mi NE Oso
GRANITE	Yakima	7	Bumping R	5035	1 mi E Miners Ridge L.O.
GRANITE FALLS RES	Snohomish	2	Pilchuck R	680	1 mi E Granite Falls
GRANITE MTN PTHLS (3)	Chelan	2-6	Wenatchee R	6100	SE side Trico Mtn
GRANT	Okanogan	22	Lost Cr	2598	7 mi NW Nespelem
GRANT	Pierce	1.5	Puget Sound	220	1 mi W Du Pont
GRASS	Chelan	3	Wenatchee R	3550	4.2 mi S Stevens Pass
GRASS	King	12	Green R	470	1.7 mi SE Covington
GRASS	Snohomish	2	Nf Rapid R	4700	10 mi N Stevens Pass
GRAVEL	King	9	Mf Snoq R	5100	3.5 mi NE Snoq Pass
GRAVEL PIT	King	1	Green R	655	3.5 mi NW Enumclaw
GREAT WESTERN	Okanogan	5	Nespelem R	2340	4.8 mi NW Nespelem
GREEN	Clark	127	Columbia R	10	8 mi NW Vancouver
GREEN	King	255	Puget Sound	170	In Seattle
GREEN LKS (2)	Okanogan	9-45	Okanogan R	1560	5.4 mi NW Omak
GREEN	Pierce	12	Carbon R	2950	10 mi NW Mt Rainier summit
GREEN	Whatcom	80	Skagit R	4300	11.5 mi N Marblemount
GREEN	Whatcom	19.5	Nooksack R	74	4 mi SE Lynden
GREEN	Yakima	4.5	Yakima R	5900	7.5 mi S Tieton Dam
GREENLEAF SL	Skamania	48	Columbia R	65	.05 mi W No Bonneville
GREEN MOUNTAIN	Skamania	4	Cispus R	4000	24 mi SE Randle
GREEN PARK	Pierce	12	White R	5400	4.5 mi NE Mt Rainier summit
GREEN RIDGE	King	15.5	Mf Snoq R	4200	2000' SW Rock Lk
GREEN VIEW	Chelan	40	Stehekin R	5455	SE side Goode Mtn
GREENWOOD	Lewis	7.5	Nisqually R	4450	9.8 mi SE National
GREIDER LKS (2)	Snohomish	8-58	Sultan R	2935	8.5 mi NE Gold Bar
GRIMES	Douglas	150	Columbia R	1800	8 mi SE Mansfield
GRISDALE PD	Grays Hbr	13	Wynooche R	450	5.4 mi S Camp Grisdale
GRIZZLY	Snohomish	1	Nf Rapid R	4800	9 mi E Granite Falls
GROTTO	King	4	Sf Sky R	3900	NE side Grotto Mtn
GULCH LKS (3)	Snohomish	2-4	Silver Cr	3600	10 mi NE Index
GUNN	Snohomish	6	Lewis Cr	4500	4 mi E Index
GUS'S	King	16	Ef Miller R	4600	10 mi NE Snoq Pass

H

LAKE	COUNTY	ACRES	DRAINAGE	ELEV.	LOCATION
"H"	Grant	7	Columbia R	1165	7 mi SW Quincey
"H"	Lincoln	26	Crab Cr	2200	6 mi S Wilbur
"H" RES NO 1	Chelan		Squilchuck Cr	4250	7.5 mi S Wenatchee
HAGER	Lewis	2	Cowlitz R	3000	2.5 mi SE Packwood
HAIGS	Clallam	5	Sol Duc R	4675	Hwtrs Sol Duc R
HALCYON	Snohomish	5	Skykomish R	3250	3 mi S Gold Bar
HALE LKS (3)	Spokane	10-24	Badger Lk	2300	6 mi S Cheney
HALFMOON	Adams	27	Crab Cr	820	6 mi SW Othello
HALFMOON	Okanogan	16	Lake Cr	6700	24 mi N Winthrop
HALFMOON	Pend Oreille	14	Pend Ore R	3250	6 mi NE Cusick
HALL	Snohomish	6	Lk Ballinger	340	1 mi S Lynnwood
HALLER	King	15	Thornton Cr	370	In Seattle
HALLIN	Adams	33	Palouse R	1760	11 mi E Ritzville

LAKE	COUNTY	ACRES	DRAINAGE	ELEV.	LOCATION
HAM	King	2	Green R	500	5 mi E Kent
HAMAR	Skagit	2	Skagit R	4310	2 mi SW Snowking Mtn
HAMILTON SL	Skagit	g	Skagit R	90	At Hamilton
HAMPTON—LOWER	Grant	19	Crab Cr	895	7 mi N Othello
HAMPTON—UPPER	Grant	53	Crab Cr	901	7 mi N Othello
HAMPTON SLGHS	Grant	12	Para Lk	875	7 mi N Othello
HANAFORD	Skamania	24	Green Lk	4090	6 mi NW Spirit Lk outlet
HANCOCK	Island	38	Admiralty Inlet	6	1 mi NW Greenbank
HANCOCK	King	236	Nf Snoq R	2172	7 mi NE North Bend
HANGING	Whatcom	74	Chilliwack R	4550	23 mi NE Mt Baker
HANKS LKS (2)	Mason	6-27	Goldsborough Cr	400	8 mi NW Shelton
HANNA	Snohomish	48	Snoqualmie R	1094	5.4 mi SE Monroe
HANS	King	24	Snoqualmie R	490	4.4 mi NE Fall City
HANSON	Snohomish	10	Pilchuck R	1430	5.5 mi SE Granite Falls
HAPPY	Clallam	2.5	Lk Crescent	4875	4.5 mi S Sutherland Lk
HARBOR	Okanogan	3	Okanogan R	3430	8.7 mi NE Tonasket
HARDSCRABBLE (2)	King	8-10	Mf Snoq R	4800	8 mi NE Snoq Pass
HARRY	Skagit	3	Nf Stilly R	3600	10.5 mi NW Darrington
HART	Chelan	11	Wenatchee R	5500	7.5 mi SW Leavenworth
HART	Chelan	33	Lk Chelan	3965	3.5 mi W Holden
HARTS SWAMP	King	7	Snoqualmie R	780	.07 mi NE Duvall
HARTS	Pierce	109	Nisqually R	349	7.4 mi SE Yelm
HASKEL SL	Snohomish	19	Skykomish R	40	.05 mi N Monroe
HATCH	Stevens	34	L Pend Ore R	2141	5.4 mi SE Colville
HATHAWAY	Clark	154	Columbia R	10	1.4 mi S Ridgefield
HATTEN	Lincoln	11	Crab Cr	2150	12.4 mi S Creston
HAUGENS PD	Snohomish	2	Skykomish R	600	4 mi SW Sultan
HAVEN	Mason	15	Sf Skok R	1016	10.8 mi NW Shelton
HAVEN	Mason	70.5	Tahuya R	366	7.4 mi SW Belfair
HAWKINS	Skagit	7	Nf Stilly R	3500	9.4 mi NE Oso
HAYES	Whatcom	13	Nf Nooksack R	4800	400' N Iceberg Lk
HAYES CR PDS	Adams	5	Crab Cr	750	6.5 mi NW Othello
HAZEL MILL PD	Snohomish	2 5	N Stilly R	320	In Hazel
HEART	Grant	26	Crab Cr	978	7.5 mi SW Warden
HEART	Lewis	4	Cowlitz R	5700	9 mi SE Packwood
HEART	Skagit	61	Fidalgo Bay	340	2.5 mi S Anacortes
HEART	Skagit	15	Sf Nooksack R	4050	9 mi N Hamilton
HEART	Skamania	5	Nf Toutle R	4645	4 mi N Spirit Lk
HEATER PD	Pend Oreille	6	Pend Ore R	2050	7 mi N Cusick
HEATHER	Chelan	90	L Wenatchee R	3890	8 mi N Stevens Pass
HEATHER	Okanogan	19	Similkameen R	5700	43 mi NW Winthrop
HEATHER	Skamania	4	Skykomish R	3600	6 mi E Gold Bar
HEATHER	Snohomish	17	Sf Stilly R	2450	8 mi E Granite Falls
HEIDE	Whatcom	1.5	Terrell Cr	20	2 mi S Birch Bay
HELEN	Pierce	5	Puyallup R	4000	7.5 mi NE National
HELENA	Kitsap	6	Case Inlet	390	5 mi E Belfair
HELENA	Snohomish	28	Sauk R	3050	8 mi S Darrington
HELL	Yakima	3.5	Nf Tieton R	5414	1.3 mi SE White Pass
HELLROARING	Yakima	2	Klickitat R	5300	12 mi NW Glenwood
HELMICKS PD	Lewis	1 5	Chehalis R	360	.05 mi N Pe Ell
HEMPLE	Snohomish	7	Sf Stilly R	3820	10 mi E Granite Falls
HENRY	Lewis	1 5	Ohanapecosh R	5150	5 mi N White Pass
HENSKIN LKS (2)	Pierce	2-3.5	White R	5500-5600	3.5 mi NE Chinook Pass
HERITAGE	Stevens	71	L Pend Ore R	3163	25 mi N Chewelah
HERMAN	Adams	35	Crab Cr	924	6 mi N Othello
HERON	Grant	7	Crab Cr	954	Adj O'Sullivan Dam
HERRON	Pierce	10	Case Inlet	182	1 mi S Herron
HESS	Okanogan	6	Okanogan R	1400	6 mi W Riverside
HESTER LKS (2)	King	67-9.5	Mf Snoq R	4050	5.8 mi NE Snoq Pass
HEWITT	Thurston	27	Deschutes R	125	2.5 mi S Olympia
HIBOX	Kittitas	3	Kachess R	4620	6 mi E Snoq Pass
HICKS	Thurston	171	Patterson Lk	158	5 mi E Olympia
HIDDEN	Chelan	10	Wenatchee R	2400	15 mi N Leavenworth
HIDDEN	Chelan	1.5	Columbia R	2000	7 mi NE Chelan
HIDDEN	Clallam	5	Sol Duc R	2625	2 mi SE Sol Duc H.S.
HIDDEN	Pierce	7	Sunrise Cr	5926	1 mi N Clover Lk
HIDDEN	Pierce	2.5	White R	4187	1 mi E Corral Pass
HIDDEN	Skagit	55	Nf Cascade R	6000	12 mi E Marblemount
HIDDEN LKS (3)	Skamania	3-10	White Salmon R	4100	1 mi E Cultus Cr G.S.
HIDDEN	Snohomish	2	Pilchuck R	1400	4.5 mi SE Granite Falls
HIGHWOOD	Whatcom	2	Nf Nooksack R	4100	1000 NE Mt Baker Ldg
HIIM RES	Clark	6	Ef Lewis R	180	1.5 mi S La Center
HILL	Yakima	6	Tieton R	5110	5 mi NE White Pass
HILLE	Pierce	3	Stuck R	475	4.5 mi NE Sumner
HILLMAN FISH PD	Mason	4	Ef Satsop R	380	9 mi W Shelton
HILLTOP	Grant	6	Columbia R	1300	5.5 mi SW George

LAKE	COUNTY	ACRES	DRAINAGE	ELEV.	LOCATION
HI-LOW	King	4	Mf Snoq R	4300	17 mi NE North Bend
HILT	Skagit	3	Sauk R	1300	4.8 mi SE Rockport
HILTON	Snohomish	3	Snohomish R	375	4.5 mi SE Everett
HINTER	King	5	Ef Miller R	4950	6.7 mi S Skykomish
HINTZVILLE PDS	Kitsap	3	Hood Canal	540	.04 mi S Hintzville
HIRSCH PD	Stevens	7.5	Colville R	2175	3.5 mi E Valley
HOBUCK	Clallam	7	Makaw Bay	150	2.5 mi SW Neah Bay
HOG	Spokane	53	Palouse R	2000	9.5 mi NE Sprague
HOFSTADS PTHL	Thurston	3	Nisqually R	21	6.8 mi NW Yelm
HOH	Clallam	19	Hoh R	4500	2700' SW Bogachiel Pk
HOLDEN	Chelan	19	Railroad Cr	5275	3 mi NW Holden
HOLM	King	19	Green R	400	5 mi E Auburn
HOLMSTEDT	Skamania	5	Panhandle Lk	5100	NE side Mt Whittier
HOLOMAN	King	6	Nf Tolt R	3650	5 mi SW Index
HOME	Jefferson	1.5	Dungeness R	5350	14 mi SW Quilcene
HONEY	King	9	Nf Snoq R	3233	13 mi NE North Bend
HONEY	Kitsap	1	Sinclair Inlet	240	2.5 mi SW Pt Orchard
HONOUR	Chelan	6.5	Wenatchee R	5100	14 mi NW Leavenworth
HOO HOO	Skamania	5	Nf Lewis R	1600	6 mi E Mt St Helens
HOOKNOSE	Stevens	2	Pend Ore R	5950	6.5 mi NW Metaline Falls
HOPE	Chelan	2 5	Icicle Cr	4400	3 mi S Stevens Pass
HOPKINS	Okanogan	9	Similkameen R	6400	42 mi SW Winthrop
HORSE	Douglas	12	Columbia R	2200	4 mi NE Sims Corner
HORSE	Skagit	10	Suiattle R	5000	19 mi NE Darrington
HORSESHOE	Adams	13	Palouse R	1670	1 mi NW McCall
HORSESHOE	Chelan	8	Wenatchee R	6275	13 mi SW Leavenworth
HORSESHOE	Jefferson	13	Pt Ludlow	320	4 mi SW Pt Ludlow
HORSESHOE	King	8	Green R	500	2 mi SW Blk Diamond
HORSESHOE	King	8.5	Mf Snoq R	4250	6 mi NW Snoq Pass
HORSESHOE	King	25	Dingford Cr	3500	17 mi E North Bend
HORSESHOE	King	19	Snoq R	50	1 mi N Carnation
HORSESHOE	Kitsap	40	Henderson Bay	270	9 mi S Pt Orchard
HORSESHOE	Lewis	4	Chehalis R	160	2 mi SW Centralia
HORSESHOE	Okanogan	59	Okanogan R	910	5 mi S Oroville
HORSESHOE	Pend Orellle	22	L Spokane R	2125	9 mi NW Elk
HORSESHOE	Pend Orellle	8	Pend Ore R	2150	5.3 mi SE Usk
HORSESHOE	Pierce	9	Ohop Cr	750	3 mi N Eatonville
HORSESHOE	Skamania	24	Cispus R	4150	24 mi SE Randle
HORSESHOE	Spokane	68	Spokane R	2449	9.5 mi W Nine Mi~e Falls
HORSESHOE	Stevens	23.5	Colville R	3050	4 mi NW Othello
HORSESHOE	Yakima	59	Yakima R	650	1.5 mi NW Mabton
HORSESHOE PD	Yakima	59	Yakima	650	4 mi NW Mabton
HORSETHIEF	Klickitat	92	Columbia R	160	2.5 mi NE The Dalles Dam
HOURGLASS	Grant	2	Crab Cr	940	8.8 mi N Othello
HOWARD HANSON RES	King		Green R	1206	6 mi SE Kanasket
HOWARD	Snohomish	3.5	Nf Skykomish R	4000	7 mi NE Index
HOWARD	Snohomish	27	Martha Lk	238	9 mi NW Marysville
HOWARD	Yakima	49	Wf Klickitat R	4887	17 mi S White Pass
HOWELL	Mason	10	Tahuya R	450	2600' S Collins Lk
HOZOMEEN	Whatcom	111	Ross Lk	2800	16 mi N Ross Dam
HUBBARD	Snohomish	6	Sf Stilly R	500	2 mi E Granite Falls
HUBBARD	Thurston	3	Nisqually R	300	6 mi W Yelm
HUFF	Pend Oreille	1	Priest Lk	3150	18.5 mi NE Ruby
HUGHES	Snohomish	20	Woods Cr	540	8 mi NE Monroe
HUGO	Lewis	1.5	Cowlitz R	4100	12 mi SE Packwood
HULL	King	6	Snoqualmie R	822	9 mi N Snoqualmie
HUMMMEL	San Juan	36	Lopez Sound	97	Lopez Island
HUNSINGER	Okanogan	2	Okanogan R	2540	4 mi NW Omak
HUNTER	Okanogan	5	Okanogan R	4050	8.5 mi W Tonasket
HUTCHINSON	Adams	50	Crab Cr	700	4 mi E Chewelah
HUTTULA	Grays Hbr	11	Chehalis R	20	3 mi SW Elma
HYAK	Kittitas	2	Yakima R	3500	2.4 mi S Snoq Pass
HYAS	Kittitas	124	Cle Elum R	3550	11 mi N Salmon La Sac
HYAS	Skagit	4	Suiattle R	4000	11 mi S Marblemount
HYDE	King	5.5	Green R	800	.05 mi W Cumberland

I

I-82	Yakima	8-25	Yakima R		S Union Gap on I-82
ICE LKS (2)	Chelan	21-54	Entiat R	68OU	37.5 mi N Leavenworth
ICE	King	2	Pratt R	4450	4.5 mi NW Snoq Pass
ICE	Lincoln	2	Crab Cr	2400	2 mi SE Creston
ICEBERG LKS (2)	Jefferson	1-2	Dosewallips R	6100	Hwtr Dosewallips R
ICEBERG	King	21	Mf Snoq R	4850	7.5 mi NE Snoq Pass
ICEBERG	Whatcom	37	Nf Nooksack R	4800	2 mi S Mt Baker Ldg
ICEHOUSE	Skamania	2.5	Columbia R	150	2.5 mi SW Stevenson

LAKE	COUNTY	ACRES	DRAINAGE	ELEV.	LOCATION
IDA	Chelan	16	Wenatchee R	7200	9.5 mi W Leavenworth
IDA	Snohomish	3	Sultan R	830	5 mi N Sultan
ILLABOT	Skagit	4	Skagit R	2550	8 mi SE Marblemount
ILSWOOT	King	48	Ef Ross R	4700	10 mi SE Skykomish
IMAGE	Snohomish	4	Suiattle R	6050	27 mi E Darrington
IMAN	Skamania	2.5	Columbia R	300	1 mi W Stevenson
IMBERT	Grant	15	East Low Canal	1190	2.5 mi SW Warden
INDEPENDENCE	Snohomish	5.5	Stilly R	3700	1 mi W Pass Lk
INDIAN DAN	Okanogan	14	Columbia R	1500	4 mi W Brewster
INDIGO	Snohomish	22	Suiattle R	4500	13 mi E Darrington
INGALLS	Chelan	17	Wenatchee R	6463	15 mi NW Blewett Pass
INKSTER LKS (2)	Lincoln	1-1	Spokane R	2430	12 mi N Davenport
INMAN	Thurston	25	Deschutes R	450	1 mi E Rainier
IONE MILL PD	Pend Orellle	37	Pend Orelle R	2050	At Ione
IPSOOT	Whatcom	9	Baker R	4500	13 mi N Marblemount
IRELY	Jefferson	4	Quinault R	550	9 mi NE Lk Quinault
ISABEL	Snohomish	176	Wallace R	2842	4 mi E Gold Bar
ISABELLA	King	12.5	Nf Snoq R	3510	11 mi NE North Bend
ISABELLA	Mason	208	Mill Cr	150	2.5 mi S Shelton
ISLAND	King	17	Sf Snoq R	4260	13 mi SE North Bend
ISLAND	Kitsap	43	Dyes Inlet	217	2 mi SW Keyport
ISLAND	Mason	109	Oakland Bay	230	2.5 mi S Shelton
ISLAND	Okanogan	9	Okanogan R	2350	11.5 mi S Okanogan
ISLAND	Pacific	59	Pacific Ocean	20	4 mi S Ocean Park
ISLAND	Snohomish	2.5	Pilchuck R	3500	10.5 mi SE Granite Falls
ISLAND	Yakima	1.5	Nf Tieton R	5240	.04 mi E S end Long John Lk
ITSWOOT	Skagit	33	Suiattle R	5100	24.5 mi E Darrington
IVANHOE	Kittitas	21	Waptus R	4700	1 mi NW Salmon La Sac

J

LAKE	COUNTY	ACRES	DRAINAGE	ELEV.	LOCATION
JACK	Chelan	1	Wenatchee R	6300	13.3 mi SW Leavenworth
JACKPOT	Lewis	5.5	Nf Cispus R	4450	9.8 mi S Packwood
JACKSON	Grant	13	Columbia R	450	.04 mi blw Priest Rapids Dam
JACKSON	Pierce	16	Carr Inlet	196	4 mi S Vaughn
JADE	King	28	Ef Foss R	5400	7 mi S Scenic
JADE	King	7	Ef Foss R	4650	10 mi SE Skykomish
JAKES	King	7	Tye R	5000	6.8 mi W Stevens Pass
JAMES	Pierce	19	Wf White R	4370	8 mi N Mt Rainier summit
JAMESON	Douglas	332	Columbia R	1800	Head Moses Coulee
JAMESON PTHL	Douglas	21	ColumbiaR	1800	Adj S end Jameson Lk
JANELLE	Lewis	7	Wf Tieton R	3300	7.4 mi N Morton
JANET	Yakima	4	Naches R	5032	2.5 mi SW Ravens Roost L.O.
JANICKE SL	King	10	Snoqualmie R	75	2 mi N Fall City
JANUS	Snohomish	29	Sf Rapid R	4220	5.8 mi N Stevens Pass
JAP	Snohomish	1.5	Sultan R	740	4.8 mi N Sunan
JACKSON LKS (3)	Chelan	1.5-7	Wenatchee R	5500	13.4 mi NW Leavenworth
JAY	Snohomish	5	Wallace Lk	1900	3.5 mi NW Gold Bar
JEFFERSON LKS (2)	Mason	3-10	Hamma Hamma R	1800	7 mi W Eldon
JERRY LKS (4)	Whatcom	2-35	Skagit R	5900	7 mi E Ross Dam
JESS	Lewis	8.5	Ohanapecosh R	5175	4.4 mi N White Pass
JEWEL	King	8.5	Ef Foss R	4400	9.3 mi SE Skykomish
JEWEL LKS (2)	King	1.5-2	Ef Foss R	4500	6.5 mi SE Skykomish
JIGGS	Mason	9	Tahuya R	380	1.5 mi NE Tahuya
JOAN	Snohomish	3.5	Rapid R	5100	6 mi NW Stevens Pass
JOE	Kittitas	30	Keechelus Lk	4624	4.8 mi NE Snoq Pass
JOHN SAM	Snohomish	15	Tulalip R	506	5 mi NW Marysville
JOHNS	Mason	8	Oakland Bay	240	3.5 mi NW Shelton
JOHNSON	Okanogan	58	Nespelem R	2180	7.3 mi NE Nespelem
JOHNSON	Spokane	'5	Palouse R	2260	12.4 mi S Cheney
JOHNSONS SWAMP	Snohomish	7	Snoqualmie R	1050	4 mi SE Monroe
JONES	King	22.5	Lk Sawyer	530	.05 mi S Blk Diamond
JORDAN LKS (2)	Skagit	59-65	Cascade R	4150	6.5 mi SE Marblemount
JORDAN PDS (3)	Snohomish	3	Sf Stilly R	1600	4.7 mi N Granite Falls
JOSEPHINE	Chelan	22	Wenatchee R	4550	2.3 mi SE Stevens Pass
JOSEPHINE	Pierce	72.5	Puget Sound	196	E side Anderson Island
JOSEPHINE LKS (2)	Skagit	2.5-3.5	Skagit R	2850	5 mi NE Hamilton
JOSEPHINE MTN PDS	Skagit	1	Skagit R	1100	3 mi NE Hamilton
JOY	King	105	Snoqualmie R	527	3.8 mi N Carnation
JUDITH POOL	Grant	1.5	Columbia R	1110	6.4 mi SW Quincey
JUDSON	Douglas	10	Columbia R	2240	9 mi NE Bridgeport
JUDY	King	10	Taylor R	3700	1500' W Nordrum Lk
JUG	Lewis	28	Ohanapecosh R	4550	6.4 mi N White Pass
JUG LKS (2)	Skagit	1-20	Skagit R	3800	10 mi S Marblemount
JULIA	Snohomish	7.5	Pilchuck R	950	4.3 mi SE Granite Falls
JULIUS	Chelan	13	Wenatchee R	4950	10 mi E Stevens Pass

LAKE	COUNTY	ACRES	DRAINAGE	ELEV.	LOCATION
JUMPOFF	Stevens	105	Colville R	2031	10 mi S Chewelah
JUNCTION	Skamania	8	Nf Lewis R	4750	3 mi SW Cultus Cr G.S.
JUNE	King	3.5	Ef Foss R	4800	7 mi SE Skykomish
JUNE	Skamania	2	Nf Lewis R	3118	3.5 mi S Mt St Helens
JUNGFRAU	Chelan	4 5	Wenatchee R	5450	20.5 mi W Leavenworth
JUPITER LKS (4)	Jefferson	0.5-6	Dosewallips R	3550	11 mi SW Quilcene

K

LAKE	COUNTY	ACRES	DRAINAGE	ELEV.	LOCATION
KACHESS	Kittitas	4540	Yakima R	2254	2.3 mi NW Easton
KAHLOTUS	Franklin	321	Columbia R	880	40 mi NE Pasco
KALEETAN	King	43	Pratt R	3850	4.5 mi NW Snoq Pass
KANIM	King	18	Nf Snoq R	4300	6.5 mi SW Skykomish
KAPOWSIN	Pierce	512	Puyallup R	600	Adj Kapowsin
KARNES	Jefferson	1	Bg Quilcene R	4600	9.8 mi SW Quilcene
KATHLEEN	King	38.5	Lk Washington	520	5.4 mi NW Maple Valley
KATRINE LKS (2)	King	24-51	Nf Snoq R	2885-4250	12.5 mi NE North Bend
KATY	Grant	8	Crab Cr	1030	7.8 mi W Warden
KEECHELUS	Kittitas	2560	Yakima R	2517	8 mi SE Snoq Pass
KEEFE	Whatcom	4	Nooksack R	25	3.8 mi NE Ferndale
KEENE	Mason	8	Skokomish R	380	2 mi S Union
KEEVIES	King	3.5	Green R	500	2 mi W Blk Diamond
KELCEMA	Snohomish	23	Sf Stilly R	3182	2.8 mi NW Silverton
KELLOGG	Snohomish	20	Wallace R	650	3.8 mi NE Sultan
KENDALL	Whatcom	12	Nf Nooksack R	490	1.3 mi N Kendall
KENDALL PEAK LKS 2	Kittitas	4-7	Keechelus R	4740	W side Kendall Peak
KENDALL PEAK—LOWER	Kittitas	2	Keechelus Lk	4380	1.8 mi E Snoq Pass
KENT	Mason	19	Oakland Bay	350	5 mi NW Shelton
KEPPLER	Spokane	9o	Palouse R	2290	3.5 mi SE Cheney
KETCHUM	Snohomish	20	Skagit Bay	190	3 mi N Stanwood
KETTLE	Yakima	1	American R	5645	8.4 mi E Chinook Pass
KETTLING	Chelan	10	Stehekin R	5500	9.5 mi N Lk Chelan
KI	Snohomish	97	Stilly R	414	7.8 mi NW Marysville
KIDNEY	Okanogan	13	Chewack R	7400	24 mi N Winthrop
KIDNEY	Skamania	12	Columbia R	140	1 mi N North Bonneville
KILLARNEY	King	31	Commencement B	385	3.5 mi SW Auburn
KINGS	King	3	Snoqualmie R	950	1 mi W Boyle Lk
KING	Snohomish	12	Snoqualmie R	1359	3.8 mi SE Monroe
KING	Snohomish	g	Sf Stilly R	460	6 mi SE Arlington
KIRK	Snohomish	1.5	Sauk R	630	.08 mi SW Darrington
KITSAP	Kitsap	238	Dyes Inlet	156	3 mi W Bremerton
KITTITAS GRAVEL PTS	Kittitas	4	Yakima R	1445	3.8 mi SE Ellensburg
KITTITAS PD	Kittitas	2	Yakima R	1660	5.5 mi E Ellensburg
KLAUS	King	62	Snoqualmie R	980	4.8 mi NE Snoqualmie
KLEMENTS MILL PD	Snohomish	3	Sf Stilly R	460	1.4 mi NE Granite Falls
KLONAQUA LKS (2)	Chelan	66-67	Wenatchee R	5450	19 mi W Leavenworth
KLONE LKS (3)	Grays Hbr	2-9	Wynooche R	3175	8.8 mi NE Grisdale
KNOX	Chelan	7	Wenatchee R	6300	10 mi SE Stevens Pass
KNUPPENBURG	Lewis	45	Cowlitz R	4200	1.5 mi SW White Pass
KOUCHEL PD	King	3	Cedar R	640	2.7 mi NE Ravensdale
KREGER	Pierce	42	Nisqually R	532	6 mi W Eatonville
KROEZE	Snohomish	1.5	Nf Stilly R	65	3.5 mi NE Arlington
KULLA KULLA	King	60	Pratt R	3765	11.5 mi SE North Bend
KWAD-DIS	Skamania	3.5	Wind R	4300	18.5 mi N Carson

L

LAKE	COUNTY	ACRES	DRAINAGE	ELEV.	LOCATION
"L"	Okanogan	'7	Omak Lk	2550	6.8 mi SE Okanogan
"L"	Okanogan	21	Wf San Poil R	2592	16.2 mi SE Tonasket
LA BARGE	Snohomish	3	Nf Stilly R	900	7 mi N Granite Falls
LACKAMAS	Clark	315	Washougal R	179	1 mi N Camas
LA CROSSE	Jefferson	3	Duckabush R	5050	2 mi SW Mt La Crosse
LAKE ANDREWS	Okanogan	4.5	Okanogan R	960	6.7 mi S Oroville
LAKE CITY LKS (4)	Stevens	2-7 5	Colville R	1879	2 mi N Echo
LAKE NO 8	Clallam	7	Morganroth Lk	4175	6 mi S Sol Duc H.S.
LAKE OF THE PINES	Okanogan	21	Pasayten R	5750	37.5 mi NW Winthrop
LAKE OF WOODS	Okanogan	2.5	Lost R	6200	25.5 mi NW Winthrop
LAKE OF THE WOODS	Pend Oreille	6.5	LSpokane R	2400	4 mi NE Camden
LAKE SAWYER SWAMP	King	9	Green R	500	1000' SE S end Lk Sawyer
LAKEVIEW PEAK	Cowlitz	3	Kalama R	2950	10.5 mi E Pigeon Springs
LAMONT	Okanogan	5	Methow R	7200	16 mi W Winthrop
LANGENDORFER	King	5.4	Tolt R	580	6 mi NE Stillwater
LANGLOIS	King	40	Tolt R	122	1.4 mi SE Carnation
LANHAM	Chelan	6	Wenatchee R	3900	3.3 mi E Stevens Pass
LARCH	Chelan	31	Wenatchee R	6150	8.5 mi E Stevens Pass
LARCH LKS (2)	Chelan	5-10	Entiat R	5650	32 mi N Leavenworth

LAKE	COUNTY	ACRES	DRAINAGE	ELEV.	LOCATION
LARCH	Skagit	9.5	Nf Stilly R	2300	5.4 mi N Oso
LARSEN	King	7	Lk Washington	260	3 mi E Bellevue
LARSON	Mason	2	Union R	280	1.4 mi W Belfair
LARSON	Mason	9	Hood Canal	400	3 mi E Dewatto
LARSON LKS (3)	Skamania	1-3	Columbia R	1950	5 mi SW Willard
LA RUSH	Skagit	3	Cascade R	3200	7.4 mi SE Marblemount
LAURA	Kittitas	4	Yakima R	4410	3.5 mi SE Snoq Pass
LAVA LKS (7)	Skamania	3.5	Columbia R	440	1.8 mi SW Stevenson
LAWRENCE	Thurston	339	Deschutes R	421	6 mi S Yelm
LEADER	Okanogan	159	Okanogan R	2273	4.5 mi W Okanogan
LEDBETTER	Pend Oreille	22.7	Pend Oreille R	2575	3.5 mi N Metaline Falls
LEE	Stevens	5	Colville R	2250	6.5 mi NW Colville
LEECH	Yakima	41	Tieton R	4412	In White Pass
LE FAY	King	7	Mf Snoq R	4300	7.5 mi NW Snoqualmie Pass
LEHRMANS PD	Okanogan	3	Okanogan R	950	.05 mi N Oroville
LELAND	Chelan	36	Wenatchee R	4600	19.8 mi W Leavenworth
LELAND	Jefferson	99	L Quilcene R	190	4.5 mi N Quilcene
LEIMI	Skamania	7	Nf Lewis R	5000	2.4 mi SW Cultus Cr G.S.
LEMNA	Grant	3	Crab Cr	950	8.5 mi N Othello
LENA	Grant	25	Grand Coulee	1500	S sd Dry Falls Dam
LENA—LOWER	Jefferson	55.5	Hamma Hamma R	1800	15 mi N Hoodsport
LENA—UPPER	Jefferson	26	Hamma Hamma R	4500	1800 S Upper Lena Lk
LENICE	Grant	100	Crab Cr	—	Crab Cr WRA
LENORE	Grant	1400	Crab Cr	—	4 mi N Soap Lake
LENNOX	King	~.9	Nf Snoq R	5000	17 mi NE North Bend
LENZ	Stevens	7	Colville R	2175	9 mi S Colville
LEO	Pend Oreille	39	L Pend Ore R	3190	7 mi SW Ione
LEOTA	King	10	Sammamish R	10	2 mi E Woodinville
LEWIS	Pierce	54	Nisqually R	350	3.5 mi NE Yelm
LIBBY	Okanogan	10	Methow R	7600	13 mi SW Twisp
LIBERTY	Spokane	714	Spokane R	2053	15 mi E Spokane
LICHTENWASSER	Chelan	23	Wenatchee R	4754	3.3 mi N Stevens Pass
LIDER	Kitsap	3	Union R	310	2.5 mi NE Belfair
LILA	Kittitas	3	Kachess R	5180	4.4 mi E Snoq Pass
LILLIAN	Jefferson	8	Elwha R	5800	17.5 mi S Port Angeles
LILLIAN	Kittitas	17	Yakima R	4800	3.8 mi SE Snoq Pass
LILLIWAUP SWAMP	Mason	225	Hood Canal	800	6 mi N Hoodsport
LILY	Chelan	15	Columbia R	3100	9 mi S Wenatchee
LILY	Jefferson	2.5	Queets R	3'50	.04 mi N Finley Park L.O.
LILY	Lewis	25	Cowlitz R	3750	3.8 mi W White Pass
LILY PD	Mason	9	Case Inlet	350	6.4 mi N Shelton
LILY	Skagit	2	Samish Bay	2000	2.4 mi N Blanchard
LILY	Skamania	8	Columbia R	1700	6.8 mi W Stevenson
LILY	Yakima	5	Bumping Lk	3860	3.4 mi SW Bumping Lk Dam
LINDBERG	Okanogan	3	Kettle R	4060	2.4 mi NE Molson
LITSCHKE	Pacific	5	Willapa Bay	25	4 mi N Long Beach
LITTLE	Snohomish	23	Nf Stilly R	1509	6.5 mi NE Arlington
LITTLE ASHES	Skamania	5	Columbia R	75	2 mi SW Stevenson
LITTLE BEAVER	Okanogan	6	Kettle R	2675	18.4 mi NW Republic
LITTLE BLUE	Skamania	1	Columbia R	390	2.8 mi SW Stevenson
LITTLE CALLIGAN	King	2	Nf Snoq R	2700	8 mi NE North Bend
LITTLE CAROLINE	Chelan	35	Wenatchee R	5900	10 mi SW Leavenworth
LITTLE CAVANAUGH	Snohomish	8	Skykomish R	1500	5 mi S Gold Bar
LITTLE CHETWOOT	King	1	Angeline Lk	5150	300' N Chetwoot Lk
LITTLE DEEP	Skamania	1.5	Columbia R	150	2.4 mi SW Stevenson
LITTLE DERRICK	King	2	Mf Snoq R	3650	500' NE Derrick Lk
LITTLE EAGLE	King	7	Nf Green R	2150	3900' NW Eagle Lk
LITTLE FISH	Chelan	3	L Wenatchee R	4850	12.4 mi N Stevens Pass
LITTLE FISH	Skamania	4.5	Nf Lewis R	3800	13.4 mi NW Mt Adams R.S.
LITTLE GEE	Skagit	1.5	Skagit R	4240	4750' SE Gee Pt
LITTLE GOOSE	Okanogan	9	Okanogan R	2740	6.7 mi SE Okanogan
LITTLE HART	Pierce	11	Nisqually R	350	3000' SE Harts Lk
LITTLE HEART	King	29	Wf Foss R	4250	7.5 mi S Skykomish
LITTLE HICKS	Thurston	2	Patterson Lk	158	800' S Hicks Lk
LITTLE HORSESHOE	Spokane	68	Spokane R	2440	9.6 mi W Nine Mile Falls
LITTLE ISLAND	Mason	3.5	Case Inlet	330	6.5 mi NE Shelton
LITTLE JOE	Kittitas	5	Cle Elum R	4690	3 mi SW Salmon La Sac
LITTLE KLONAQUA	Chelan	7	Wenatchee R	5450	1300' SE L Klonaqua Lk
LITTLE MASON	King	4	Sf Snoq R	4260	11.4 mi SE North Bend
LITTLE MYRTLE	King	4	Mf Snoq R	4400	9 mi N Snoq Pass
LITTLE PLUG	King	1	Tye R	5500	900' NE Spark Plug Lk
LITTLE PRATT	King	4	Pratt R	4080	2400' E Pratt Lk
LITTLE SI	King	2	Mf Snoq R	1080	1.4 mi NE North Bend
LITTLE SNOW	Lewis	2	Ohanapecosh R	4800	500' W Frying Pan Lk
LITTLE SPEARFISH	Klickitat	6	Columbia R	160	.05 mi NE The Dalles Dam
LITTLE TIFFANY	Okanogan	4	Chewack R	7400	4200' S Tiffany Lk

LAKE	COUNTY	ACRES	DRAINAGE	ELEV.	LOCATION
LIZARD	King	5	Green R	3540	On Cascade Crest
LIZARD	Skagit	2	Samish Bay	1862	2.4 mi N Blanchard
LOCH EILEEN	Chelan	25	Wenatchee R	5200	9.4 mi E Stevens Pass
LOCKE	Klickitat	20	Columbia R	80	3 mi E Bingen
LOCKET	King	56	Ef Foss R	4600	9.5 mi SE Skykomish
LODGE	King	9	Sf Snoq R	3125	1.4 mi SW Snoq Pass
LOIS	Thurston	2.5	Henderson Inlet	150	Adj N fm Lacey
LOMA	Snohomish	21	Tulalip Bay	465	6.5 mi NW Marysville
LONE	Island	17			2.5 mi SW Langley
LONE DUCK	Mason	3.5	Hood Canal	550	1.8 mi S Dewatto
LONELYVILLE	Spokane	23	Crab Cr	2420	3.5 mi SW twn Medical Lake
LONE PINE	Douglas	10	Columbia R	2200	9.5 mi NE Bridgeport
LONESOME	Pierce	11.5	Wf White R	4860	10.5 mi S Greenwater
LONG	Clallam	15	Soleduck R	3850	5 mi SE Sol Duc Hot Spr.
LONG	Clark	12		10	.05 mi NW Ridgefield
LONG	Ferry	14	Wf San Poil R	3250	11 mi S Republic
LONG	Franklin	2.5	Palouse R	1043	5.4 mi SE Washtucna
LONG (Billie Clapp)	Grant	25	Columbia R	2300	23.8 mi S town Grand Coulee
LONG	Kitsap	314	Yukon Hbr	118	3.5 mi SE Port Orchard
LONG	Lewis	6	Cowlitz R	4000	6.5 mi W Packwood
LONG	Okanogan	20	Columbia R	2650	12.5 mi SE Okanogan
LONG	Okanogan	17	Wf San Poil R	2600	15 mi SE Tonasket
LONG	Thurston	311	Henderson Inlet	153	5.5 mi E Olympia
LONG	Yakima	8	Tieton R	4350	3.5 mi SE Tleton Dam
LONG JOHN	Yakima	5	Tieton R	5140	4.4 mi N White Pass
LONGS	Thurston	10	Henderson Inlet	150	.05 mi E Lacey
LONG-BELL LOG PD	Cowlltz	132.5	Columbia R	10	SE portion Longview
LONG-BELL MILL PD	Lewis	10	Cowlitz R	700	2 mi E Winston
LOOKING GLASS	Skamania	1 5	Whlte Salmon R	5600	12 mi N Mt Adams R.S.
LOOKOUT	Snohomish	1 5	Suiattle R	5575	2300' N Sulphur Mtn summit
LOOMIS	Pacific	151	Paclfic Ocean	17	2.5 mi S Ocean Park
LOON	Stevens	1118.5	Colville R	2381	28 mi N Spokane
LOOP	King	36	Tolt R	550	2.8 mi E Carnatlon
LORRAINE	Chelan	4.5	Wenatchee R	5050	5.8 mi S Stevens Pass
LOST	Chelan	31	L Wenatchee R	4900	9 mi NE Stevens Pass
LOST	Chelan	4	Chiwawa R	5500	20 mi N Leavenworth
LOST	Clark	2	Nf Lewis R	1500	7.5 mi NE Yacolt
LOST	Jefferson	7	Hood Canal	350	2 mi SW Squamish Hbr
LOST	Kittitas	10	Yakima R	4820	20 mi W Ellensburg
LOST	Klttltas	145	Keechelus Lk	3089	6.5 mi S Snoq Pass
LOST	Lewis	21	Cowlltz R	5100	7.5 mi E Packwood
LOST	Mason	122	Oakland Bay	480	7.8 mi SW Shelton
LOST	Okanogan	47	Kettle R	3817	20 mi NE Tonasket
LOST	Pacific	14	Pacific Ocean	20	1.8 mi SE Klipsan Beach
LOST	Pend Oreille	22	W Br L Spokane	2125	9 mi NW Elk
LOST	Pend Orellle	6	Pend Oreille R	3150	5.5 mi N Ione
LOST	Pierce	1	White R	6050	1.5 mi NE Skyscraper Mtn
LOST	Pierce	26	Greenwater R	3985	27 mi SE Enumclaw
LOST	Skamania	8	Wind R	3760	2.5 mi W Gov Mineral Sp G.S.
LOST	Snohomish	9	Skykomlsh R	617	2.5 mi SE Sultan
LOST	Snohomish	18	Skykomish R	980	6 mi N Sultan
LOST	Snohomish	3	Sf Sauk R	2000	2 mi N Barlow Pass
LOST	Snohomish	3	Sf Stilly R	1650	4.4 mi N Granite Falls
LOST	Whatcom	3	Belllngham Bay	140	.04 mi NW Bellingham Airport
LOST	Whatcom	4	Sumas R	2850	3 mi W Kendall
LOST	Yakima	9	Tieton R	3675	3 mi SE Tieton Dam
LOST HAT	Lewis	3	Cowlitz R	4500	3.7 mi NE Packwood Lk outlet
LOST HORSE	Snohomish	3.5	Rapid R	4800	4 mi N Stevens Pass
LOUIS	Chelan	4	L Wenatchee R	4500	8 mi N Stevens Pass
LOUIS	Okanogan	27	Twisp R	5300	21 mi W Twisp
LOUISE	Lewis	17	Cowlitz R	4592	4.8 mi NE Longmire
LOUISE	Skagit	6	Sauk R	5000	8.8 mi S Marblemount
LOWER BEAR PAW MTN	Whatcom	6.5	Nf Nooksack R	4450	6.5 mi NE Glacier
LOWER CATHEDRAL	Okanogan	6	Similkameen R	6000	36 mi N Wlnthrop
LOWER CRYSTAL	Pierce	1.5	White R	5550	8.5 mi SW Quincey
LOWER FISHER	King	3.5	Tye R	4500	8 mi SE Skykomish
LOWER FLORENCE	Chelan	5	Wenatchee R	6000	13.3 mi NW Leavenworth
LUCERNE	King	16	Cedar R	530	4.5 mi NW Blk Diamond
LUDLOW	Jefferson	16	Port Ludlow Hbr	450	4.5 mi W Port Ludlow
LUDVICK	Kitsap	2	Dewatto R	440	2 mi S Holly
LUNA	Whatcom	17	Skagit R	4900	2 mi SE Mt Challenger
LUNCH	Clallam	7	Soleduck R	4475	3200' S Soleduck Lk
LUNKER	King	3.5	Taylor R	4300	800' SE Rock Lk
LYLE	Adams	22	Crab Cr	925	
LYLE	Pierce	9	Clearwater R	4150	4000' E Cedar Lk
LYMAN	Chelan	76	Lk Chelan	5887	48 mi NW Chelan

LAKE	COUNTY	ACRES	DRAINAGE	ELEV.	LOCATION
LYNN	King	6	Green R	3500	10 mi E Enumclaw
LYNNE	Yakima	1.5	Tieton R	4310	Just blw Bear Lk

M

LAKE	COUNTY	ACRES	DRAINAGE	ELEV.	LOCATION
MAD	Chelan	5	Entiat R	5950	23 mi N Leavenworth
MAIDEN	Whatcom	17	Baker R	3900	18.8 mi N Concrete
MAL	Yakima	4	Naches R	5100	11.3 mi SW Naches R.S.
MALACHITE	King	80	Wf Foss R	4200	7.4 mi S Skykomish
MALLARD	Grant	8	Crab Cr	980	10 mi N Othello
MALLARD	Pacific	5	Pacific Ocean	20	1.5 mi SE Klipsan Beach
MALO	Ferry	2	Kettle R	2300	10.5 mi NE Republic
MALONEY LKS (3)	King	1-1.5	Sf Skykomish R	4000	2.4 mi S Skykomish
MALONEY MEADOW	King	5.5	Sf Skykomish R	4150	3.4 mi S Skykomish
MALONEY	Pierce	5	Hale Passage	248	2 mi W Gig Harbor
MANASTASH	Kittitas	23.5	Yakima R	5000	19 mi W Ellensburg
MARCO POLO	Grant	10	Crab Cr	1025	8.3 mi N Othello
MARCUS	King	1		610	1.4 mi NE Ravensdale
MARGARET	Chelan	15	Wenatchee R	5500	8.2 mi SE Stevens Pass
MARGARET	King	44	Snoqualmie R	798	4.4 mi NE Duvall
MARGARET	Kittitas	4	Kachess R	4790	4.8 mi SE Snoq Pass
MARIE	King	10	Snoqualmie R	953	2 mi E Fall City
MARION	Chelan	1	Columbia R	5500	1.2 mi NE Mission Pk
MARJORIE	King	10	Wf White R	4555	Adj E end Oliver Lk
MARLENE	King	3	Ef Miller R	4500	8.4 mi S Skykomish
MARLOW	King	3	Green R	420	1.4 mi S Covington
MARMOT	King	135	Tye R	4900	6.7 mi S Scenic
MARPLE	Okanogan	3	Okanogan R	2550	14.8 mi SE Tonasket
MARSH LKS (2)	Lewis	2-4	Cowlitz R	3950	9.8 mi SW Chinook Pass
MARSHALL	Pend Oreille	189	Pend Oreille R	2750	5.5 mi N Newport
MARTEN	King	40	Taylor R	2959	14 mi NE North Bend
MARTEN	Skagit	10	Skagit R	4650	5 mi S Marblemount
MARTEN	Whatcom	5	Baker R	3650	16 mi N Concrete
MARTHA	Grant	12	Crab Cr	1200	.07 mi NE George
MARTHA	Snohomish	59	Sammamish R	450	2.5 mi NE Alderwood Manor
MARTHA	Snohomish	13	Pilchuck R	324	3.4 mi E Marysville
MARTHA	Snohomish	58	Port Susan	186	10.5 mi NW Marysville
MARTIN LKS (2)	Okanogan	5-9	Methow R	6800	16 mi W Methow
MARTINS	San Juan	21.5	East Sound	500	5.4 mi S East Sound
MARY	Chelan	3.5	Wenatchee R	5850	8.5 mi SE Stevens Pass
MARY	Jefferson	3	Elwha R	3550	.04 mi NE Low Divide shelter
MARY	King	3.5	Ef Foss R	s200	2500' W Upper Ptarmfgan Lk
MARY LEE	Pierce	1.5	Mashel R	4350	5.5 mi N Ashford
MARY SHELTON	Snohomish	12	Tulalip Bay	368	5.7 mi NW Marysville
MASON	King	33	Sf Snoq R	4180	12 mi SE North Bend
MASON	Mason	996	Case Inlet	194	8 mi SW Belfair
MASON	Spokane	2	Palouse R	2110	2.4 mi W Amber
MASSIE	Chelan	15	Chiwawa R	5950	39 mi N Leavenworth
MATHEWS	Kitsap	3	Sinclair Inlet	410	4300' S Square Lk
MATSUDA RES	King	1	Quartermaster H	300	1.5 mi S Vashon
33358	Stevens	4	Colville R	2450	2.5 mi N Colville
MAZAMA	Whatcom	1	Nf Nooksack R	4750	2 mi SW Mt Baker Ldg
McALESTER	Chelan	15	Stehekin R	5500	7.5 mi N Lk Chelan
McALLISTER SPRINGS	Thurston	3	Nisqually Reach	15	8.5 mi E Olympia
McBRIDE	Cowlitz	9	Kalama R	2700	28 mi NE Woodland
McCOY	Stevens	38	Spokane R	1644	7.3 mi S Fruitland
McDANIEL	Yakima	10	Naches R	3550	8 mi SW Naches R.S.
McDONALD	King	18	Sammamish Lk	560	6 mi E Renton
McDOWELL	Spokane	81	Palouse R	2300	4.7 mi S Cheney
McGINNIS	Okanogan	115	Columbia R	2375	9.5 mi SE Nespelem
McGOWAN PD	Pacific	2	Columbia R	25	7.4 mi SE Ilwaco
McINTOSH	Thurston	116	Deschutes R	336	4 mi E Tenino
McKINLEY	Lewis	3	Ef Tilton R	3200	7 mi NE Morton
McLEOD	King	13	Nf Snoq R	1006	5 mi N North Bend
McMANNAMAN	Adams	7	Crab Cr	830	6.2 mi NW Othello
McMURRAY	Skagit	161	Skagit R	225	9 mi NW Arlington
MEADOW	Chelan	36	Columbia R	875	1 mi SW Malaga
MEADOW	Grant	5	Grand Coulee	1160	Sun Lks State Park
MEADOW	Okanogan	24	Okanogan R	3550	1.5 mi S Bonaparte Lk
MEADOW	Okanogan	6.5	Chewack R	6400	26.5 mi N Winthrop
MEADOW	Skamania	2.5	Nf Lewis R	3900	2 mi W Mosquito Lk G.S.
MEADOW	Snohomish	20	Skykomish R	500	4 mi N Monroe
MEADOW	Snohomish	9	Suiattle R	4500	14.4 mi SE Darrington
MEADOW	Spokane	32	Spokane R	2371	.05 mi S twn Four Lakes
MEADOWBROOK SL	King	14	Snoqualmie R	400	1 mi E Snoqualmie
MEEKER LKS (2)	Pierce	4-6	White R	2780	26.5 mi E Enumclaw

LAKE	COUNTY	ACRES	DRAINAGE	ELEV.	LOCATION
MELAKWA LKS (2)	King	2-8	Pratt R	4490	3 mi NW Snoq Pass
MENZEL	Snohomish	13	Pilchuck R	470	3.8 mi SE Granite Falls
MERIDIAN	King	150	Green R	370	4 mi E Kent
MERLIN	King	6	Mf Snoq R	4200	2200' W Myrtle Lk
MERRILL	Cowlitz	344	Kalama R	1541	24 mi NE Woodland
MERRITT	Chelan	7	Wenatchee R	5000	2900' SE Lost Lk
MERRITT SL	Chelan	6	Wenatchee R	2100	12.3 mi E Stevens Pass
MERRY	Grant	—	Crab Cr		Crab Cr W.R.A.
MERWIN RES	Clark	4090	Nf Lewis R	239	9.8 mi NE Woodland
MESA	Chelan	4.5	Wenatchee R	6500	500' NE Earle Lk
MESA	Franklin	50	Columbia R	748	1 mi SW Mesa
META	Skamania	9	Muddy R	3580	1.7 mi E Spirit Lk Inlet
METAN	Snohomish	3.5	Sauk R	2800	12.5 mi SE Darrington
METCALF	King	6	Snoqualmie R	1010	6.8 mi N North Bend
METCALF SL	King	5	Snoqualmie R	1040	7.5 mi N North Bend
MICA	Snohomish	13	Suiattle R	5450	4.8 mi NW Glacier Pk
MICHAEL	Kittitas	18	Waptus R	5100	5 mi W Salmon la Sac
MIDDLE HIDDEN	Okanogan	19	Lost R	4300	33 mi NW Winthrop
MILDRED LKS (3)	Mason	6.5-38	Hamma Hamma R	3900	3.8 N Hd Lk Cushman
MILE LONG	Grant	75	Columbia R	996	6.9 mi N Othello
MILK	Jefferson	6	Hamma Hamma R	4800	1800' S Upper Lena Lk
MILK	Kittitas	3	Naches R	4700	4.4 mi NE Cliffdell
MILL PD	Mason	6	Case Inlet	15	1.5 mi S Allyn
MILL CREEK RES	Walla Walla	52		1205	3 mi E Walla Walla
MILLER MARSH	Mason	15	Hood Canal	650	6.8 mi NE Hoodsport
MILLER	Whitman	25	Palouse R	1865	3.3 mi N Ewan
MILLES	Okanogan	9	Twisp R	2150	3.5 mi NW Twisp
MILLS	Clallam	451	Elwha R	600	11 mi SW Port Angeles
MINERAL	Lewis	277	Nisqually R	1430	At Mineral
MINK	Clallam	11	Soleduck R	3080	1.5 mi S Sol Duc Hot Spr
MINKLER	Skagit	37	Skagit R	60	1.7 mi W Lyman
MINOTAUR	Chelan	24	L Wenatchee R	5575	7.5 mi NE Stevens Pass
MINT MARSH	Mason	10	Hood Canal	800	6 mi N Hoodsport
MIRROR	Chelan	27	Lk Chelan	5490	4 mi SW Lucerne
MIRROR	Grant	4.5	Park Lk	1097	Sun Lks State Park
MIRROR	King	19	Puget Sound	320	2 mi W Steel Lk
MIRROR	Kittitas	29	Keechelus Lk	4195	5.8 mi S Snoq Pass
MIRROR	Okanogan	7	Okanogan R	2840	8.4 mi SE Okanogan
MIRROR	Whatcom	14	Whatcom Lk	350	3200' NW Wickersham
MIRROR	Yakima	1.5	Klickitat R	5250	10.5 mi NW Glenwood
MISSION	Kitsap	88	Hood Canal	516	9 mi W Bremerton
MISSION PD	Kitsap	4	Union R	580	2000' SE Mission Lk
MITCHELL PD	Benton	4	Lk Wallula	340	13.5 mi SE Kennewick
MOCCASIN	Okanogan	33	Methow R	2193	3.9 mi S Winthrop
MOCCASIN	Okanogan	6.5	Kettle R	3600	2 mi NW Wauconda summit
MOIRA	King	5	Dorothy Lk	4600	8.5 mi S Skykomish
MOLSON	Okanogan	20	Kettle R	3675	1800' N Molson
MONEYSMITH	King	22	Green R	415	4.8 mi E Auburn
MONOGRAM	Skagit	28	Cascade R	4850	8 mi SE Marblemount
MONTE CRISTO	Snohomish	14	Sf Sauk R	1970	16 mi SE Darrington
MOOLOCK	King	45	Nf Snoq R	3903	7.3 mi NE North Bend
MOOSE	Clallam	9	Greywolf R	5100	16.5 mi S Port Angeles
MOOSE	Pacific	3	Willpa R	80	7 mi SE Raymond
MORAINE	Skagit	52	Diablo Lk	4500	2.4 mi SE Eldorado Peak
MORGAN	Adams	35	Crab Cr	821	5.8 mi NW Othello
MORGAN MARSH	Kitsap	95	Hood Canal	510	7 mi N Belfair
MORGAN PD	Yakima	25	Yakima R	650	2 mi N Mabton
MORGANROTH	Clallam	10	Soleduck R	4125	5.8 mi SE Sol Duc Hot Sprs
MORGE LKS (3)	Pierce	1.5-3	Mashel R	4400	4.4 mi NE National
MORROW	Mason	5	Ef Satsop R	400	1.5 mi SE Nahwatzel Lk
MORTON	King	66	Green R	500	4 mi W Blk Diamond
MOSES	Grant	6815	Crab Cr	1046	Adj City Moses Lk
MOSES MEADOWS PDS	Okanogan	1-2	Wf San Poil R	3500	19.5 mi E Omak
MOSLEY LKS (5)	Skamania	3.5	Columbia R	700	2 mi W Stevenson
MOSQUITO	King	2	Tye R	5300	3 mi NW Stevens Pass
MOSQUITO	Okanogan	6	Twisp R	5300	6.5 mi N Lk Chelan
MOSQUITO LKS (2)	Skamania	5-25	White Salmon R	3900	14 mi NW Trout Lk
MOSS	Lewis	3.5	Sf Newaukum R	3024	1000' SW Newaukum Lk
MOUND PD	Benton	35	Lk Wallula	340	14.5 mi SE Kennewick
MOUSE	Okanogan	4.5	Columbia R	1680	5.5 mi N Brewster
MOUSE	Skamania	9	Cispus R	4500	18.5 mi SE Randle
MOUNTAIN	San Juan	198	East Sound	914	4.4 mi SE East Sound
MOWICH	Pierce	123	No Mowich R	4929	7.5 mi NW Mt Rainier summit
MOWITCH	King	16	Nf Snoq R	3196	13 mi NE North Bend
MOXEE PD	Yakima	5	Yakima R	990	S side Moxee Hwy
MT ADAMS	Yakima	69	Wf Klickitat R	4500	16 mi N Glenwood

LAKE	COUNTY	ACRES	DRAINAGE	ELEV.	LOCATION
MT FERNOW PTHLS (5)	King	1-3	Beckler R	3900-4500	1 mi N Fernow Mtn
MT ROOSEVELT	King	4	Pratt R	4460	6.4 mi NW Snoq Pass
MUD	Clark	92	Lewis R	15	2.5 mi W La Center
MUD	King	24	Green R	750	1 mi NE Blk Diamond
MUD	King	16	Snoqualmie R	1270	10 mi NE Snoqualmie
MUD	King	12	Sf Skykomish R	2000	3.8 mi S Index
MUD	Lewis	7.5	Nf Cispus R	4850	3.8 mi E Blue Lk
MUD LKS (15)	Mason	20	Chehalis R	400	8 mi SW Shelton
MUD	Pierce	22	Puget Sound	230	1.5 mi E Stellacoom
MUD	Thurston	10	Black R	250	2.4 mi N Tenino
MUD	Whatcom	4.5	Samish R	940	1 mi W Samish Lk
MUD	Yakima	4	Naches R	2500	7.4 mi NW Naches
MUDGETT	Stevens	32	Columbia R	1900	2.3 mi S Fruitland
MULE	Pierce	2.5	Wf White R	4600	10 mi S Greenwater
MULHOLLAND MARSH	Kitsap	6.5	Tahuya R	550	2 mi SW Hintzville
MUNN	Thurston	30	Deschutes R	139	4 mi S Olympia
MURPHY	Douglas	9	Columbia R	2160	9.8 mi E Bridgeport
MURPHYLKS(2)	King	3.5-7	Tye R	4300-4500	1.8 mi S Scenic
MUSKEGON	Pend Orelile	7.5	Priest R	3450	16 mi SE Metalline Falls
MUTUAL	Thurston	2	Chehalls R	325	1.4 mi E Tenlno
MY	King	1	Pratt R	3930	3.4 mi NW Snoq Pass
MYRON	Yakima	—	Yaklma R	—	W of Yakima
MYRTLE	Chelan	19	Entiat R	3750	35 mi NW Entlat
MYRTLE	King	18	Mf Snoq R	3950	8.5 mi N Snoq Pass
MYRTLE	Skagit	B	Nf Stilly R	3550	6 mi NE Oso
MYRTLE	Snohomish	2	Sf Sauk R	2000	2.4 mi N Barlow Pass
MYSTIC	Pend Orellle	17	Pend Oreille R.	2975	6.3 mi E Usk
MYSTIC	Pierce	7	Wf White R	5700	4.4 mi N Mt Rainier summit

N

LAKE	COUNTY	ACRES	DRAINAGE	ELEV.	LOCATION
NADA	Chelan	9	Wenatchee R	5500	7.5 mi SW Leavenworth
NADEAU	King	19	Nf Snoq R	3722	7 mi NE North Bend
NAHWATZEL	Mason	269	Ef Satsop R	440	11 mi W Shelton
NANEUM	Kittitas	1.5	Yakima R	1655	4 mi E Ellensburg
NASELLE PD	Pacific	1	Naselle R	60	2.5 mi E Naselle
NASON	Thurston	6	Budd Inlet	155	2200' NW Bigelow Lk
NATIONAL MILL PD	Pierce	9	Nisqually R	1550	At National
NAZANNE	King	9.5	Wf Foss R	5000	8.5 mi SE Skykomish
NEELYS	Thurston	'0	Nisqually R	400	1.5 mi S Yelm
NEORI	Skagit	'3	Cascade R	4400	1300' W Found Lk
NETTLETON	Stevens	'	Columbia R	1950	3.5 mi N Rice
NEVES	Lincoln	25	Crab Cr	1665	6.3 mi N Odessa
NEWAUKUM	Lewis	'7	Sf Newaukum R	3000	13 mi NE Onalaska
NEWMAN	Spokane	1190	Spokane R	2124	16 mi NE Spokane
NIGGER	Adams	24	Palouse R	1438	3.6 mi S Benge
NIGGER SL	Mason	16	Hood Canal	400	2.4 mi N Tahuya
NIGGERHEAD PD	Lewls	6	Cispus R	2000	11.5 mi SE Randle
NIMUE	King	5	Mf Snoq R	4100	1000' SW Merlin Lk
NINE HOUR	King	6	Mf Snoq R	3931	4800' NE Rainy Lk
NISQUALLY	Pierce	98.5	Nisqually R	229	4.5 mi NW Roy
NO NAME	Pend Oreille	18	Pend Oreille R	2850	9 mi NW Newport
NO NAME	Whatcom	10	Ross Lk	3900	8.5 mi N Ross Dam
NORDRUM	King	60	S Br Taylor R	3800	16.5 mi NE North Bend
NORTH	King	55	Commencement B	390	3 mi W Auburn
NORTH	Okanogan	8	Twisp R	5800	19.5 mi W Winthrop
NORTH	Snohomish	11	Sauk R	4100	8.8 mi SE Darrington
NORTHRUP	Grant	3	Banks Lk	2100	2.9 mi S Electric Clty
NORTH SILVER	Spokane	—	Crab Creek	559	1.1 mi E turn Medical Lk
NORTH SKOOKUM	Pend Oreille	38.5	Pend Oreille R	3550	7.2 mi NE Cusick
NORTHSTAR	Okanogan	8.5	Nespelem R	4420	13.8 mi N Nespelem
NORTH TEAL	Grant	22	Crab Cr	954	6.4 mi N Othello
NORTH TWIN	Ferry	744	FDR Lk	2572	8 mi W Inchelium
NORTHWESTERN	Skamania	97	White Salmon R	301	2.7 mi N White Salmon
NORTH WINDMILL (2)	Grant	5-22	Crab Cr	1000	6.6 mi SW Warden
NUNNALLY	Grant	—	Crab Cr	—	Crab Cr W.R.A.

O

LAKE	COUNTY	ACRES	DRAINAGE	ELEV.	LOCATION
OAK	Mason	15	Hood Canal	190	3.8 mi NE Dwatto
OBSCURITY	Skamania	7	Green R	4337	5.4 mi NE Spirit Lk Inlet
ODENRIDER	Lincoln	9	Crab Cr	2050	1.4 mi SW Govan
OFFUTT	Thurston	192	Deschutes R	236	9 mi S Olympia
OHOP CREEK PDS	Pierce	2-2.5	Puyallup R	1900	7.5 mi SE Kapowsin
OHOP	Pierce	236	Nisqually R	524	1.5 mi N Eatonvllle
OLALLIE	King	13	Sf Snoq R	3780	4.5 mi W Snoq Pass

LAKE	COUNTY	ACRES	DRAINAGE	ELEV.	LOCATION
OLALLIE	Skamania	16	Cispus R	4250	23.5 mi SE Randle
OLD CLE ELUM H PD	Kittitas	2	Yakima R	2080	4.2 mi SE Easton
OLD COLUMBIA MILL PD	Clark	2	Lk Merwin	1450	3.5 mi N Amboy
OLD MILL PD	Pacific	2	Willapa R	20	1.4 mi W South Bend
OLIVER	Pierce	20	Wf White R	4558	8.8 mi N Mt Ralnier summlt
OLNEY	Yakima	9	Yakima R	1810	7 mi S White Swan
OLSON	Skagit	4	Skagit R	4050	3 mi NW Marblemount R.S.
OMAK	Okanogan	3244		950	7 mi SE Omak
OMALLEY	Pierce	1	White R	2900	0.5 mi W Norse Peak
ONE	Yakima	2	U Bumpinq R	5050	7 mi SE Chinook Pass
ONE ACRE	Snohomish	1.5	Wallace R	4150	.08 mi SE Stickney Lk
ONEIL	Pacific	~0	Columbia R	25	1.8 mi SW Ilwaco
OPAL	King	3	Ef Foss R	4750	11 mi SE Skykomish
ORR'S PD	Island	1	Possession Snd	200	On Whidbey Island
ORTING	Pierce	4	Carbon R	738	1.8 mi NE Orting
OSBORNE LKS (2)	Mason	2-4	Hood Canal	750	6 mi N Hoodsport
OSOYOOS	Okanogan	2038	Columbia R	9"	1 mi N Oroville
OTTER	King	183	Wf Foss R	4400	9.3 mi S Skykomish
OTTER	Yakima	7	Tieton R	5030	3.5 mi NE White Pass
OVAL LKS (3)	Okanogan	8-21	Twisp R	6200	16.5 mi SW Twisp
OVERCOAT	King	14	Mf Snoq R	5900	8.4 mi NE Snoq Pass
OWENS PDS (3)	Pacific	6	Willapa R	60	5 mi E Raymond
OWL	Adams	21	Crab Cr	825	2.5 mi NW Othello
OZETTE	Clallam	7787	Ozette R	29	15 mi S Neah Bay

P

LAKE	COUNTY	ACRES	DRAINAGE	ELEV.	LOCATION
P.J.	Clallam	2.5	Juan de Fuca	4700	10.5 mi S Port Angeles
PACIFIC	Lincoln	130	Crab Cr	1650	5.4 mi N Odessa
PACKWOOD	Lewis	452	Cowlitz R	2858	5 mi E Packwood
PALISADES LKS (2)	Pierce	4-4	White R	5500	3200' N Hidden Lk
PALM	Adams	88	Palouse R	1852	7.5 mi SW Spraque
PALMER PD	Benton	5	Lk Wallula	340	15.5 mi SE Kennewick
PALMER	Okanogan	2083	Similkameen R	1145	4 mi N Loomis
PALMER LKS (2)	Pierce	4-8.5	Case Inlet	50-~70	1.8 mi W Bay Lk
PALMER	Skagit	9	Samish R	525	2600' SW Cain Lk
PAMPA PD	Whitman	3	Palouse R	1370	3.8 mi SW La Crosse
PANHANDLE	Mason	14	Oakland Bay	400	8 mi SW Shelton
PANHANDLE	Pend Orellle	10	L Spokane R	2550	8.5 mi W Newport
PANHANDLE	Skamania	15	Green R	4520	5 mi NE Spirit Lk Outlet
PANTHER	King	33	Green R	440	3.5 mi NE Kent
PANTHER	Snohomish	47	Pilchuck R	455	4.52 mi NE Snohomish
PARA	Grant	12	Crab Cr	832	8.3 mi NW Othello
PARADISE	King	18	Sammamish R	256	4.5 mi NE Woodinville
PARADISE LKS (2)	King	5-23	Nf Snoq R	4050	17 mi NE North Bend
PARK	Grant	341.5	Grand Coulee	1096	14 mi N Soap Lake City
PARKS LKS (2)	Kittitas	9-11	Kachess R	45'0	8 mi E Snoq Pass
PARKER	Pend Oreille	22	Pend Oreille R	2450	10 mi N Cusick
PASS	Skagit	99	Rosario Strait	~30	Fidalgo Island
PASS	Snohomish	2	Sf Stilly R	3700	3.8 mi NE Silverton
PATTERSON	Okanogan	143	Methow R	2380	3 mi SW Winthrop
PATTERSON (RES)	Thurston	257	Henderson Inlet	'54	8 mi SE Olympia
PAWN LKS (2)	Chelan	2.5-9	Entiat R	4625	23 mi NW Chelan
PAYNES MEADOWS	Okanogan	6	Columbia R	3120	10.2 mi NW Brewster
PEACH	Snohomish	17	Beckler R	4800	1000' S Pear Lk
PEAR	Skagit	10	Suiattle R	5200	13.4 mi NE Darrington
PEAR	Snohomish	33	Nf Rapid R	4800	10.4 mi N Stevens Pass
PEAR	Yakima	21	Rimrock Lk	5060	7.8 mi NE White Pass
PEARRYGIN (RES)	Okanogan	192	Chewack R	'975	1.4 mi NE Winthrop
PEEK-A-BOO	Snohomish	22	Sauk R	4000	10 mi SE Darrington
PEEPSIGHT	Okanogan	6	Ashnola R	7100	30 mi N Winthrop
PEGGYS PD	Kittitas	5	Waptus R	5800	11 mi N Salmon la Sac
PEMMICAN	Snohomish	1	Sauk R	400	5 mi N Barlow Pass
PENOYER	Lewis	6	Ohanapecosh R	5000	5.4 mi N White Pass
PEPOON	Stevens	11	Columbia R	2450	5.5 mi W Northport
PERCH	Grant	15	Grand Coulee	1201	Sun Lks State Park
PERCIVAL	Thurston	22	Capitol Lk		Olympia, W Capitol Lk
PERKINS	Stevens	26	Columbia R	2250	4.5 mi E Barstow
PETE	Kittitas	37	Cle Elum R	2980	23.5 mi NW Cle Elum
PETE LKS (2)	Snohomish	2-3	Rapid R	4900	6 mi N Stevens Pass
PETERSON	King	10	Cedar R	—	6 mi SE Renton
PETERSON	Jefferson	23	Pt Townsend Bay	500	8 mi W Port Ludlow
PETERSON PD	Stevens	9	Kettle R	2050	3.4 mi N Barstow
PETIT	Pend Orellle	11	Priest Lk	3975	12.5 mi NE Ruby
PFEIFFER PD	Snohomish	1	Skykomish R	230	2.8 mi E Monroe
PHANTOM	King	63	Sammamish Lk	250	3.5 mi SE Bellevue

LAKE	COUNTY	ACRES	DRAINAGE	ELEV.	LOCATION
PHANTOM	Yakima	1	Sf Tieton R	4300	7 mi S Clear Lk Dam
PHEASANT	Jefferson	4,5	Hood Canal	390	5.5 mi SW Port Ludlow
PHEBE	Skagit	15	Strawberry Bay	1000	Ctr Cypress Island
PHELAN	Stevens	1B	Colville R	2375	16 mi N Colville
PHILIPPA	King	121	Nf Snoq R	3346	11 mi NE North Bend
PHILLIPS	Lincoln	31	Crab Cr	2200	12 mi S Creston
PHILLIPS	Mason	111	Oakland Bay	188	7 mi NE Shelton
PHILLIPS	Stevens	1	Colville R	3000	9.5 mi N Chewelah
PHOEBE LKS (2)	Chelan	3_13	Wenatchee R	5450	20.5 mi W Leavenworth
PICNIC POINT	Snohomish	4	Possession Snd	10	5.8 mi N Edmonds
PICTURE	Whatcom	3	Nf Nooksack R	4100	1000' NE Mt Baker Ldg
PIERRE	Stevens	106	Kettle R	2012	4 mi NE Orient
PILLAR	Grant	9	Crab Cr	968	8.8 mi N Othello
PILLAR	Yakima	4	Tieton R	5273	1050' NE Long John Lk
PILOT	Snohomish	6	Suiattle R	5500	2200' NE Downey LkAdams
PINES	Adams		Palouse R	1870	3.5 mi S Sprague
PINE	King	88	Sammamish Lk	390	4 mi N Issaquah
PINE	Mason	8	Sf Skok R	2250	23.5 mi NW Shelton
PINE	Whatcom	7	Chuckanut Bay	1570	5 mi S Bellingham
PINE TREE	Okanogan	6		2320	750' N No end Salmon Lk
PINNACLE	Snohomish	6.5	Sf Stllly R	3820	10 mi E Granite Falls
PINUS	Whatcom	1.5	Nf Nooksack R	2450	7 mi E Glacier
PIONEER PD	Snohomish	2	Stilly R	110	1 mi SW Arlington
PIPE	King	52	Cedar R	530	4.5 mi NW Blk Diamond
PIT	Grant	40	Crab Cr	985	6 mi N Othello
PITCHER MTN	Pierce	7	Carbon R	4650	1.8 mi W Summit Lk
PITMAN	Thurston	27	Black R	198	8.8 mi S Olympia
PLACID	Skamania	19	Nf Lewis R	4000	22 mi N Carson
PLATT PD	King	14	Tolt R	560	3 mi SE Carnation
PLEASANT	Clallam	486	Soleduck R	390	12 mi S Sekiu
PLEASANT LKS (2)	Yakima	1-1	American R	3940	11 mi NE Chinook Pass
PLUMMER	Lewis	12	Chehalis R	180	W portion Centralia
POACHER	Grant	1	Crab Cr	945	8.5 mi N Othello
POCKET	Whatcom	2	Baker R	4540	12.5 mi N Concrete
PONDILLA	Island	4	Juan de Fuca	20	W side Whidbey Island
PORTAGE BAY	King	148	Puget Sound	12	In Seattle
POST OFFICE	Clark	77	Columbia R	10	9 mi NW Vancouver
POTHOLES RES	Grant	28200	Crab Cr	1046	10 mi S city Moses Lake
POTHOLE	King	3	Taylor R	3900	1800' S Dream Lk
POTHOLE	Klickitat	8.5	L Klickitat R	2300	6 mi N Goldendale
POWER	Chelan	3	Wenatchee R	6050	4 mi SW Leavenworth
POWER	Pend Oreille	55	Pend Oreille R	2421	6.4 mi SW Usk
PRAIRIE LKS (2)	Skagit	3-5,5	Suiattle R	1500	8.5 mi NE Darrington
PRATT LKS (2)	King	4 43 5	Pratt R	3385	13.5 mi SE North Bend
PRESTON MILL PDS	King	2-2	Raging R	400	At Preston
PRICE	King	2	Mf Snoq R	4500	6 mi N Snoq Pass
PRICE	Mason	62	Hood Canal	780	4.8 mi N Hoodsport
PRICE	Okanogan	6	Okanogan R	2360	700' SE Medicine Lk
PRICE	Whatcom	40	Nf Nooksack R	3895	N side Mt Shuksan
PRICKETT	Mason	68	Puget Sound	301	5.5 mi SW Belfalr
PRIEST RAPIDS DAM R	Grant	7700	Columbia R	488	29 mi E Yakima
PROCTOR	Okanogan	7	Okanogan R	1240	3.5 mi N Omak
PROFITTS PD	King	3	Tye R	1000	4 mi E Skykomish
PTARMIGAN LKS (2)	King	,3-2a	Tye R	4950-5000	I.4 mi SE Skykomish
PTARMIGAN	Okanogan	4	Lost R	6800	32 mi NW Winthrop
PUGSLEY	King	19	Ef Miller R	3650	8.8 mi S Skykomish
PURDY CR PDS	Snohomish	20	Pilchuck R	500	1 mi NE Lk Roesiger
PURDY	Lincoln	16	Crab Cr	2300	6 mi S Creston
PURVIS	King	9 5	Ef Miller R	5100	5.8 mi S Skykomish
PYRAMID	Whatcom	1	Skagit R	2400	1.4 mi S Diablo Dam

Q

QUAIL	Adams	12	Crab Cr	935	Adj NE Herman Lk
QUARRY	Walla Walla	9	Lk Wallula	340	4.8 mi SE Burbank
QUARTZ	King	1	Mf Snoq R	4800	3000' S Hi-Low Lk
QUARTZ	Okanogan	6	Pasayten R	6900	35.5 mi N Winthrop
QUEEN LUCAS	Spokane	37	Spokane R	2129	5 mi NE Cheney
QUIGLEY	Clark	38	Columbia R	10	.05 mi SW Ridpefield
QUINAULT	Grays Hbr	3729	Pacific Ocean	182	37 mi N Aberdeen
OUINCY	Grant	43	Columbia R	1196	7 mi S Quincy
QUINN	Pierce	1	Greenwater R	38~30	2000' N Lost Lk

R

RACHEL	Kittitas	27	Kachess R	4600	4 mi E Snoq Pass

LAKE	COUNTY	ACRES	DRAINAGE	ELEV.	LOCATION
RACHOR	King	5	Nf Snoq R	3500	4 mi NE North Bend
RADAR PDS (2)	Pacific	3-5	Naselle R	1000	4 mi N Naselle
RAE	Yakima	1	Naches R	5020	350' E N end Janet Lk
RAINBOW LKS (2)	Chelan	2-4	Stehekin R	5500	6.3 mi N Lk Chelan
RAINBOW	Columbia	10	Tucannon R	2207	2 mi S Game Range H.Q.
RAINBOW	Grant	9	Park Lk	1150	Sun Lks State Park
RAINBOW	King	6	Pratt R	4270	13 mi SE North Bend
RAINY	Chelan	54	Stehekin R	4790	12.5 mi N N end Lk Chelan
RAINY	King	5	Mf Snoq R	3764	12 mi E North Bend
RAMON LKS (3)	Okanogan	2-2.5	Ashnola R	7050	N side Sheep Mtn
RAMPART LKS (5)	Kittitas	0.5-7	Keechelus R	5100	3.8 mi E Snoq Pass
RAMPART	Okanogan	11	Lost R	6600	27 mi NW Winthrop
RAND	Skamania	5	Columbia R	280	2.7 mi SW Stevenson
RAPJOHN	Pierce	56	Nisqually R	632	4.5 mi NW Eatonville
RAT	Okanogan	63	Columbia R	1676	5.5 mi N Brewster
RATTLESNAKE	Douglas	3.5	Columbia R	2430	10 mi NW city Grand Coulee
RATTLESNAKE	King	112	Sf Snoq R	911	.05 mi NE Cedar Falls
RAVENSDALE	King	18	Green R	560	1.4 mi W Ravensdale
RAVENSDALE PDS	King	4	Cedar R	690	.03 mi S Ravensdale
R. B.	Skagit	3	Skagit R	3225	9 mi SE Sedro-Woolley
REBECCA	Kittitas	13	Waptus R	4750	11.7 mi NW Salmon la Sac
REFLECTION LKS (3)	Lewis	1-13	Nisqually R	4861	4 mi E Longmire
REID SLOUGH	King	3	Snoqualmie R	420	1.4 mi N North Bend
REILYS	Okanogan	4.5	Similkameen R	3650	7.4 mi W Oroville
REMMEL	Okanogan	13	Chewack R	6500	33.5 mi N Winthrop
RETREAT	King	53	Green R	731	1.8 mi E Ravensdale
REVEILLE LKS (2)	Whatcom	3-4	Chilliwack R	5000	16.5 mi N Newhalem
R. B.	Mason	13	Oakland Bay	240	3.4 mi NE Shelton
RICE	Jefferson	6	L Quilcene R	140	1.5 mi N Quilcene
RICHMOND	Yakima	1.5	Naches R	5900	E side Nelson Ridge
RIDGE	Kittitas	2	Yakima R	5220	3.5 mi NE Snoq Pass
REBECCA	Okanogan	53	Columbia R	1900	7.8 mi S Nespelem
RED	Stevens	9	Spokane R	1800	5 mi SE Ford
REED	Lincoln	20	Crab Cr	2300	8 mi S Creston
REED	Whatcom	15	Samish R	394	9 mi SE Bellingham
REFFETT PD	Grant	2	Crab Cr	1090	4.8 mi N city Moses Lake
REFLECTION	Jefferson	1	Quinault R	3500	10 mi NE Lk Quinault
RIDGE	Pend Oreille	2.5	Pend Oreille R	3100	9.1 mi SE Ione
RIDLEY	Whatcom	14	Ross Lk	3000	15 mi N Ross Dam
RIFFE	Lewis	—	Cowlitz R	—	Mossyrock
RIGLEY	Stevens	7	Columbia R	2531	2.5 mi W Echo
RILEY	Snohomish	30	Nf Stilly R	517	2 mi S Oso
RIMROCK (RES)	Yakima	2530	Tieton R	2918	12.5 mi E White Pass
RING	Clallam	2	Nf Boqachiel R	2875	2400' NW Misery Pk
RING	Spokane	23	Crab Cr	2400	1 mi SE twn Medical Lake
ROARING CREEK SL	Pacific	10	Naselle R	20	4.5 mi NW Naselle
ROBE MILL PD	Snohomish	1.5	Sf Stilly R	850	5 mi E Granite Falls
ROBIN LKS (2)	Kittitas	11-34	Cle Elum R	6150	12.6 mi N Salmon la Sac
ROCK	Chelan	3.5	Wenatchee R	5600	7 mi NE Stevens Pass
ROCK	Douglas	16	Columbia R	2400	11 mi NW city Grand Coulee
ROCK	King	23	Wf Foss R	4500	5 mi S Skykomish
ROCK LKS (2)	Okanogan	3.5-4.5	Okanogan R	3550	11.3 mi NW Okanogan
ROCK	Whitman	2147	Palouse R	1719	32 mi S Spokane
ROCK CREEK	Skamania	3	Columbia R	1680	8 mi NW Stevenson
ROCK CREEK PD	Skamania	2	Columbia R	1200	7.5 mi NW Stevenson
ROCKDALE	King	2	Sf Snoq R	3540	2.8 mi S Snoq Pass
ROCK ISLAND POOL	Chelan	3470	Columbia R	605	12 mi SE Wenatchee
ROCK QUARRY	King	1	White R	1000	3.5 mi SE Enumclaw
ROCK SLIDE	Snohomish	o.5	Snoqualmie R	1320	5.4 mi S Sultan
ROCKY	Stevens	20	Colville R	2275	3.5 mi S Colville
ROCKY SADDLE PDS 2	Kittitas	1	Naches R	5100	2.3 mi NW Bald Mtn
ROESIGER	Snohomish	352	Skykomish R	570	6.5 mi N Monroe
ROOT	Yakima	5	Bumping R	5300	8.3 mi SE Chinook Pass
ROSE	Snohomish	1	Wallace R	4300	5 mi NE Gold Bar
ROSS (RES)	Whatcom	11878	Skagit R	1599	9.4 mi NE Newhalem
ROUND	Chelan	10	Lk Chelan	3250	38 mi NW Chelan
ROUND	Clallam	3	Soleduck Lk	4250	3400' S Soleduck Lk
ROUND	Clark	16	Lake R	10	8 mi NW Vancouver
ROUND	Ferry	52	FDR Lk	2275	5.8 mi W Inchelium
ROUND	King	3	Sammamish Lk	470	1300' SW Tradition Lk
ROUND	Okanogan	20	Wf San Poil R	2583	16 mi E Tonasket
ROUND	Snohomish	12	White Chuck R	5100	16.5 mi SE Darrington
ROUND	Yakima	7	Yakima R	650	1 mi N Mabton
ROWEL	Okanogan	4	Columbia R	2075	10.5 mi N Brewster
ROWLAND	Klickitat	85	Columbia R	72CF	4 mi E Bingen
ROYAL	Adams	102	Crab Cr	780	Near Royal Slope

LAKE	COUNTY	ACRES	DRAINAGE	ELEV.	LOCATION
ROYAL	Jefferson	2	Dungeness R	5100	15.5 mi W Quilcene
RUBY	Snohomish	4	Nf Sauk R	5200	20 mi SE Darrington
RUFUS WOOD (RES)	Douglas	7800	Columbia R	946	1.5 mi SE Bridgeport
RUTH	Chelan	2.5	Wenatchee R	6000	9 mi W Leavenworth
RUTHERFORD SLOUGH	King	18	Snoqualmie R	80	.05 mi N Fall City
RYAN	Skamania	4	Green R	3307	7.5 mi NE Spirit Lk outlet

S

LAKE	COUNTY	ACRES	DRAINAGE	ELEV.	LOCATION
SACAJAWEA	Cowlitz	48	Columbia R	10	In Longview
SACAJAWEA	Franklin	8370	Snake R	440	10 mi E Pasco
SACHEEN	Pend Orelle	282	L SpokaneR	2250	34 mi N Spokane
SADDLE	Snohomish	4	Nf Stilly R	3780	6.7 mi N Verlot
SAGE LKS (2)	Grant	6	Crab Cr	972	7.4 mi N Othello
SAGO	Grant	1.5	Crab Cr	940	Adj E Hourglass Lk
SAHALEE-TYEE	Skamania	7	White Salmon R	4700	18.4 mi N Carson
SALMON	Okanogan	313	Okanogan R	2324	Adj E Conconully
SAMISH	Whatcom	814	Samish R	273	6.5 mi SE Bellingham
SAMMAMISH	King	4897	Lk Washington	28	10 mi E Seattle
SAND	Grant	28	Crab Cr	1120	Adj N Frenchman Hills
SANDSTONE	Yakima	3	Bumping R	3800	2.2 mi S mouth Bumping R
SANDY SHORE	Jefferson	38	Hood Canal	470	4.8 mi SW Port Ludlow
SARDINE	Skamania	2	Columbia R	280	1.4 mi SW Stevenson
SARVINSKI LKS (4)	Grays Hbr	9	Chehalls R	30	2 mi S Elma
SASSE RES	Okanogan	7	Okanogan R	2360	5.6 mi NE Conconully
SATSOP LK NO 1	Grays Hbr	4	Wf Satsop R	2195	6.8 mi NE Grisdale
SATSOP LK NO 2	Grays Hbr	3	Wf Satsop R	220	7 mi NE Grisdale
SATSOP LKS 3, 4 & 5	Grays Hbr	1.5-3	Wt Satsop R	1550	4700' SW Satsop No 1
SAUCER	Snohomish	14	Rapid R	4500	1000' NW Cup Lk
SAUK	Skagit	10	Skagit R	4025	7 mi E Concrete
SAWYER	King	279	Green R	512	2 mi NW Blk Diamond
SAWYER LK SWAMP	King	9	Green R	500	1000' SE S end Lk Sawyer
SCANLON	Okanogan	12	Okanogan R	2380	4.5 mi NW Riverside
SCATTER	Okanogan	7	Twisp R	6900	15.5 mi W Winthrop
SCHAEFER	Chelan	83	Chiwawa R	5050	20 mi NE Stevens Pass
SCHALLOW	Okanogan	10	Okanogan R	1675	4.4 mi NE Conconully
SCHWEDA PD	Lincoln	4	Crab Cr	2100	5.4 mi SW Wilbur
SCOOTENEY	Franklin	217	Columbia R	825	7.5 mi S Othello
SCOTCHMAN	Pend Oreille	34	Pend Oreille R	2500	8 mi SE Ione
SCOTT	Thurston	67	Black R	189	9 mi S Olympia
SCOUT	King	6	Sf Snoq R	3850	5.7 mi SW Snoq Pass
SCOUT	Kitsap	3	Tahuya R	875	2 mi SW Wildcat Lk
SCRABBLE	Snohomish	3	Rapid R	5000	3700' SW Saucer Lk
SEABURY PD	Skagit	2	Stilly R	1325	5 mi NE McMurray Lk
SEAFIELD	Clallam	22	Pacitic Ocean	150	12.4 mi S Neah Bay
SEARS	Pierce	4	American Lk	230	On Ft Lewis Mil Res
SECOND	King	2.5	White R	1100	3 mi E Enumclaw
SEGELSON	Skagit	3	Nt Stilly R	3500	8 mi NW Darrington
SEQUALLITCHEW	Pierce	81	Puget Sound	206	On Ft Lewis Mil Res
SERENE	Snohomish	53	Sf Skykomish R	2509	2.5 mi S Index
SERENE	Snohomish	42	Puget Sound	540	3.5 mi N Lynnwood
SHADOW	King	50	Green R	540	2.5 mi W Maple Valley
SHADOW	Snohomish	6	Snohomish R	8	1 mi NE Cathcart
SHADOW	Yakima	3	Klickitat R	5500	10.6 mi NW Glenwood
SHADY	King	21	Cedar R	520	3.5 mi NW Maple Valley
SHAMROCK	King	7.5	Mf Snoq R	4014	6.5 mi NW Snoq Pass
SHANNON (RES)	Skagit	2148	Skagit R	438	3500' N Concrete
SHAW	Snohomish	6	Nf Wallace R	2075	5.4 mi N Gold Bar
SHEEHAN	Thurston	4.5	Deschutes R	200	1 mi SW East Olympia
SHEEP	Okanogan	7	Ashnola R	6900	36 mi W Winthrop
SHEEP	Yakima	3	Yakima R	5700	1.7 mi N Chinook Pass
SHEEPHERDER	Yakima	3	Naches R	4931	10.6 mi NE Chinook Pass
SHELF	Skagit	3.5	Nf Stilly R	4050	9 mi NE Oso
SHELLEY	Spokane	36	Spokane R	2025	2.5 mi E Opportunity
SHELL ROCK	Yakima	11	Tieton R	4926	3.8 mi NE White Pass
SHELOKUM	Okanogan	2	Methow R	6347	16 mi W Winthrop
SHERMAN	Ferry	3	San Poil R	5900	12 mi E Republic
SHERRY	Stevens	26	L Pend Ore R	3159	250' S Gillette Lk
SHIELD	Chelan	38	Wenatchee R	6695	9 mi SW Leavenworth
SHINER	Adams	33.5	Crab Cr	701	6.2 mi NW Othello
SHINER	Skagit	5	Skagit R	250	.07 mi NE Montborne
SHOE	Mason	6	Hood Canal	380	8.5 mi W Belfair
SHOE	Yakima	18	Nf Tieton R	6112	3.4 mi S White Pass
SHOECRAFT	Snohomish	137	Tulalip Bay	324	600' SW Lk Goodwin
SHOVEL	Kittitas	27	Waptus R	4000	10.5 mi NW Salmon La Sac
SHOVEL	Skamania	21	Green R	4653	4.8 mi N Spirit Lk outlet

LAKE	COUNTY	ACRES	DRAINAGE	ELEV.	LOCATION
SHOVELER	Grant	6	Crab Cr	940	8.4 mi N Othello
SHUKSAN	Whatcom	28	Baker R	3700	18 mi NE Concrete
SIDLEY	Okanogan	109	Osoyoos Lk	3675	0.7 mi NW Molson
SIKES	King	14	Snoqualmie R	41	At Carnation Farm
SILENT LKS (2)	Chelan	3	Stehekin R	6700	SE side Mt Arriva
SILER MILL PD	Lewis	1	Cowlitz R	1280	4 mi W Morton
SILLS PDS (2)	Snohomish	2	Sf Stilly R	75	.08 mi NE Arlington
SILVER	Cowlitz	2996	Toutle R	484	4 mi E Castle Rock
SILVER	Island	15	Saratoga Pass	325	5.4 mi E Oak Harbor
SILVER LKS (2)	Jefferson	1-2	Dungeness R	5450	9 mi W Quilcene
SILVER	Okanogan	3	Twisp R	5550	16 mi SW Twisp
SILVER	Pierce	138	Nisqually R	605	4.5 mi W Eatonville
SILVER	Snohomish	102	Sammamish R	426	5.5 mi S Everett
SILVER	Spokane	559	Crab Cr	2341	1.1 mi E twn Medical Lake
SILVER	Whatcom	173	Nf Nooksack R	4400	3 mi N Maple Falls
SILVER	Whatcom	164	Ross Lk	6700	19 mi N Ross Dam
SILVER CR PDS	Lewis	7	Cowlitz R	600	3 mi NE Salkum
SILVER NAIL	Okanogan	5	Okanogan R	1000	4 mi N Oroville
SIMMONS	Thurston	25	Capitol Lk	140	2 mi W Olympia
SIMONSON PD	Whatcom	14	Birch Bay	240	3.4 mi SW Custer
SINK HOLE	King	3	Green R	650	1000' NW Beaver Lk
SINLAHEKIN IMP NO 2	Okanogan	3	Similkameen R	1557	700' W Forde Lk
LWR SINLAHEKIN IMP	Okanogan	58	Similkameen R	1500	5 mi S Loomis
SIOUXON	Skamania	2	Nt Lewis R	1480	4 mi NE Yale Dam
SIXTEEN	Skagit	42	Skagit R	427	2.5 mi E Conway
SKARO	Skagit	12	Cascade R	4450	1800' SW Found Lk
SKATING	Pacific	66	Pacific Ocean	20	1 mi SW Oysterville
SKOOKUMCHUCK	Lewis	8	Skookumchuck R	175	At Centralia
SKYLINE	King	2	Tye R	4950	1 mi N Stevens Pass
SKYMO	Whatcom	22.5	Ross Lk	4500	7.4 mi N Ross Dam
SLATE	Okanogan	6	Twisp R	6400	13.4 mi W Winthrop
SLAUGHTERHOUSE	Yakima	15	Yakima R	650	1.7 mi NW Mabton
SLIDE	Skagit	37	Skagit R	3300	8 mi SE Marblemount
SLIM	Skagit	7	Suiattle R	4700	.08 mi E Woods Lk
S.M.C.	King	41	Nf Snoq R	3702	.07 mi NE North Bend
SMELLING	Snohomish	7	Pilchuck R	860	4.3 mi SE Granite Falls
SMITH	Clallam	5	Sequim Bay	625	2.5 mi S Sequim
SMITH	Clallam	3	Freshwater Bay	140	9.5 mi W Port Angeles
SMITH	King	2	Ef Miller R	4500	2200' N Dream Lk
SMITH	Mason	11	Nf Skok R	4000	5.5 mi N hd Lk Cushman
SMITH	Okanogan	3	Similkameen R	7000	17 mi NW Loomis
SMITH	Okanogan	8	Okanogan R	2150	3.5 mi NW Malott
SMITH	Thurston	18	Deschutes R	200	4 mi SE Olympia
SMOKEY POINT PD	Snohomish	5	Possession Snd	110	6 mi N Marysville
SNAKE	Pierce	8	Puget Sound	300	At Tacoma
SNELL	Pierce	2	Carbon R	1150	1.4 mi SE Wilkeson
SNIP	Grant	4	Crab Cr	954	8.5 mi N 0thello
SNOQUALMIE	King	126	N Br Taylor R	3225	9.4 mi N Snoq Pass
SNOQUALMIE PTHLS	King	5	Taylor R	4100	2000' E S end Snoq Lk
SNOQUALMIE MILL PD	King	66	Snoqualmie R	408	At Snoqualmie
SNOW LKS (2)	Chelan	66-123	Wenatchee R	5420	8 mi SW Leavenworth
SNOW	King	159.5	Mf Snoq R	4016	3 mi NW Snoq Pass
SNOW	Lewis	8	Ohanapecosh R	4975	6 mi N White Pass
SNOW	Lewis	9	Cowlitz R	4678	5.5 mi E Longmire
SNOW	Skamania	5	Nf Toutle R	4700	4.5 mi N Spirit Lk outlet
SNOW KING	Skagit	36	Cascade R	4600	1800' SW Found Lk
SNOW PLOW	Yakima	6	Klickitat R	4500	8 mi SE Mt Adams
SNOW SLIDE	Snohomish	10	Nf Skykomish R	4300	5 mi N Index
SNOWY LKS (2)	Skagit	1-3	Ross Lk	6400	19 mi SE Ross Dam
SNYDER SLOUGH	Lincoln/Whit	60	Palouse R	1937	2.9 mi SE Sprague
SODA	Grant	155	Potholes Canal	998	9.5 mi N Othello
SOLEDUCK	Clallam	31	Soleduck R	3700	4.7 mi SE Sol Duc Hot Spr.
SONNY BOY LKS	Skagit	2.5-4	Cascade R	4400	15 mi SE Marblemount
SOURDOUGH	Whatcom	33	Ross Lk	4400	3.4 mi NW Ross Dam
SOUTH	Okanogan	3	Twisp R	6000	Hwtrs South Cr
SOUTH	Snohomish	13	Sauk R	4200	5.3 mi N Barlow Pass
SOUTH PRAIRIE	Skamania	14	White Salmon R	3140	9.5 mi N Willard
SOUTH SKOOKUM	Pend Orellle	32	Pend Oreille R	3525	6.6 mi NE Cusick
SOUTH TWIN	Ferry	973	FDR Lk	2572	8.5 mi W Inchelium
SOUTHWICK	Thurston	37	Henderson Inlet	173	5 mi SE Olympia
SPADE	Kittitas	122	Waptus R	5050	10.3 mi NW Salmon la Sac
SPANAWAY	Pierce	262	Steilacoom Lk	320	10 mi S Tacoma
SPARKPLUG	King	15	Tye R	5600	3 mi S Scenic
SPAULDING LKS (2)	Okanogan	2.5-5.5	Okanogan R	2300	4 mi W Okanosan
SPEARFISH	Klickitat	22	Lk Celilo	160	1 mi N The Dalles Dam
SPECTACLE	Kittitas	81	Cooper R	4239	6.7 mi NE Snoq Pass

LAKE	COUNTY	ACRES	DRAINAGE	ELEV.	LOCATION
SPECTACLE	Okanogan	315	Okanogan R	1363	2.5 mi E Loomis
SPIDER	King	15	Pratt R	2746	10.5 mi SE North Bend
SPIDER	King	4	Stuck R	420	1 mi NE Fivemile Lk
SPIDER	Mason	23	Sf Skok R	1290	21 mi NW Shelton
SPIRIT	Chelan	2	Wenatchee R	5603	16.7 mi NW Blewett Pass
SPIRIT	Skamania	1262	Nf Toutle R	3198	36 mi E Castle Rock
SPOOK	King	19.5	Tolt R	530	1.4 mi E Langlois Lk
SPRAGUE	Adams	1841	Palouse R	1879	2.2 mi SW Sprague
SPRING	Columbia	5	Tucannon R	2060	0.5 mi S Game Range H.Q.
SPRING LKS (2)	Grant	1	Columbia R	1150	500' W Crystal Lk
SPRING	King	68	Cedar R	500	3 mi NW Maple Valley
SPRING	Okanogan	3.5	Okanogan R	1900	800' W Wannacut Lk
SPRING	Skamania	6	Columbia R	300	1.4 mi NE No Bonneville
SPRINGER	Thurston	5.5	Deschutes R	300	2.5 mi W Offutt Lk
SPRINGSTEEN	Skagit	19	St Nooksack R	3550	7.5 mi NW Concrete
SPRITE	Chelan	5	Wenatchee R	6050	10 mi N Salmon la Sac
SPRUCE	Stevens	27	L Pend Ore R	3728	12 mi E Colville
SPUD	Lewis	3	St Newaukum R	3025	400' W Newaukum Lk
SPUR 3 PD	Kitsap	1	Tahuya R	500	3 mi S Hintzville
SQUALICUM	Whatcom	33	Bellinham Bay	477	6.5 mi NE Bellingham
SQUARE	Chelan	80	Wenatchee R	4950	4.7 mi S Scenic
SQUARE	Kitsap	8	Sinclair Inlet	400	4.5 mi SW Port Orchard
SQUAW	Chelan	2	Lk Wenatchee	1870	W end Lk Wenatchee
SQUAW	Kittitas	12	Cle Elum R	4850	9 mi N Salmon la Sac
SQUITCH	Kittitas	3	Cle Elum R	,17nn	8.8 mi N Salmon la Sac
ST CLAIR	Thurston	245	Nisqually R	73	6.5 mi NW Yelm
ST HELENS	Skamania	79	Spirit Lk	4567	2 mi N Spirit Lk outlet
ST MICHAEL	Lewis	9	Nf Cispus R	4750	10 mi S Packwood
STACY	Lewis	1	Nisqually R	4500	1.8 mi SE Longmire
STAN COFFIN	Grant	41	Columbia Basin	1170	6.5 mi SW Quincey
STANDSTILL	Mason	6	Hood Canal	735	S end L. Cushman
STANSBERRY	Pierce	19	Carr Inlet	238	3.5 mi NE Vaughn
STAR	Chelan	10	Lk Chelan	7400	33 mi NW Chelan
STAR	King	34	Green R	320	3 mi SW Kent
STARVATION	Stevens	28	L Pend Ore R	2375	9.8 mi SE Colville
STARZMAN LKS (2)	Okanogan	5.5-8	Columbia R	1645	9 mi N Brewster
STATE SOLDIERS HOME	Pierce	2	Puyallup R	220	700' S State Soldiers Home
STEAMBOAT	Skamania	9	White Salmon R	4050	13 mi NW Trout Lk
STEEL	King	46	Commencement B	430	4 mi NW Auburn
STEIGERWALD LKS (2)	Clark	57-258	Columbia R	19	.08 mi SE Washougal
STEILACOOM	Pierce	313	Puget Sound	210	3 mi E Steilacoom
STETSON	Mason	8.5	Hood Canal	500	7.5 mi NE Hoodsport
STEVENS	Mason	8.5	Nf Skok R	600	3.4 mi SW Potlatch
STEVENS	Okanogan	11	Okanogan R	1500	5 mi SE Loomis
STEVENS	Snohomish	1021	Pilchuck R	210	5.5 mi E Everett
STEWART	Okanogan	17	Okanogan R	2700	7.8 mi SE Okanogan
STICKNEY	Snohomish	14.5	Wallace R	3500	2 mi NE Wallace Lk
STIDHAM	Pierce	8	Nisqually R	850	6 mi N Eatonville
STILETTO	Chelan	9	Stehekin R	6800	1.5 mi NW Twisp Pass
STILWELL	Skagit	3	Lk Shannon	4150	8 mi NE Concrete
STINK LKS (3)	King	3	White R	2500	8.8 mi E Enumclaw
STIRRUP	Kittitas	9	Keechelus Lk	3550	3.5 mi W Stampede Pass
STITCH	Snohomish	10	Pilchuck R	215	5 mi E Everett
STONE	Snohomish	1.5	Sf Skyk R	3800	1800' S Eagle Lk
STONES THROW	Kittitas	2	Kachess Lk	4410	1800' NW Swan Lk
STONY	Pierce	7	Steilacoom Lk	380	3 mi SE S end Spanaway Lk
STORM	Snohomish	78	Pilchuck R	528	5.5 mi N Monroe
STORMO PD	Snohomish	4	Sf Skyk R	800	3.4 mi SE Index
STOUT	Skagit	24	Skagit R	5200	6 mi S Newhalem
STRANGERS	Jefferson	11	Juan de Fuca	150	1 mi SW Port Townsend
STRAWBERRY	Skamania	10	Green R	5374	3.8 mi NE Spirit Lk inlet
STRICKLAND	Pierce	5	Nisqually R	220	.08 mi W Dupont
STUART	Chelan	40	Wenatchee R	5064	12 mi SW Leavenworth
STUMP	Mason	23	Chehalis R	300	7.5 mi NE Elma
STURTEVANT	King	10	Lk Washington	140	1.4 mi NE Bellevue
SULLIVAN	Pend Oreille	1291	Pend Oreille R	2583	4.3 mi SE Metaline Falls
SULPHUR MTN	Snohomish	5	Suiattle R	5200	5000' N Sulphur Mtn summit
SUMMER	Skagit	8	Skagit R	522	2.8 mi NE McMurray Lk
SUMMIT	King	6	Tye R	4600	1.4 mi W Stevens Pass
SUMMIT	Okanogan	10	Okanogan R	3270	6.5 mi SE Disautel
SUMMIT	Pierce	25	Carbon R	5440	13.5 mi SE Enumclaw
SUMMIT	San Juan	10	East Sound	2200	In Moran State Park
SUMMIT	Snohomish	9.5	Pilchuck R	3880	9.4 mi SE Granite Falls
SUMMIT	Stevens	7	Kettle R	2600	7.4 mi NE Orient
SUMMIT	Thurston	523	Totten Inlet	500	9 mi W Olympia
SUMMMIT CHIEF	Kittitas	6.5	Waptus R	6500	10.5 mi NW Salmon la Sac

LAKE	COUNTY	ACRES	DRAINAGE	ELEV.	LOCATION
SUNDAY LKS (2)	King	2-21	Nf Snoq R	1865	13 mi NE North Bend
SUNDAY	Snohomish	39	Stilly R	211	5 mi E Stanwood
SUNDOWN	Jefferson	3	Quinault R	3900	15.5 mi E Lk Quinault
SUNRISE	Okanogan	11	Methow R	7300	16.5 mi W Methow
SUNRISE	Pierce	4	White R	5800	1 mi E Dege Peak
SUNSET	Snohomish	38	Nt Skyk R	4100	7 mi E Index
SURPRISE	Chelan	48	Lk Chelan	6100	33 mi NW Chelan
SURPRISE	King	28	Tye R	4600	2.7 mi S Scenic
SURPRISE	Pierce	10	Carbon R	4450	14 mi S Enumclaw
SURPRISE	Pierce	30	Commencement B	320	3.4 mi NE Puyallup
SURPRISE LKS (15)	Pierce	17	White Salmon R	4200	12.5 mi NW Trout Lk
SURPRISE	Yakima	14	Sf Tieton R	5300	12 mi S White Pass
SURVEYORS	King	5	Sf Snoq R	3980	2 mi S Snoq Pass
SUSAN	Grant	20	Crab Cr	1033	9 mi N Othello
SUSAN	Thurston	3.5	Deschutes R	140	700' W N end Munn Lk
SUSAN JANE	Chelan	3	Wenatchee R	4650	2 mi SE Stevens Pass
SUTHERLAND	Clallam	361	Elwha R	501	12 mi W Port Angeles
SWALLOW LKS (4)	Chelan	5-20	Wenatchee R	5100	20.5 mi W Leavenworth
SWAMP	Kittitas	45	Yakima R	2420	2 mi SE Keechelus Lk dam
SWAMP	Yakima	51	Bumping R	4797	4.5 mi SE Chinook Pass
SWAN	Ferry	52	San Poil R	3641	10.2 mi SW Republic
SWAN	Kittitas	7	Kachess Lk	4040	5.8 mi SE Snoq Pass
SWARTZ	Snohomish	17	Pilchuck R	525	1.5 mi S Granite Falls
SWEDE	Stevens	5	Colville R	2450	4.5 mi SW Valley
SWIFT RES	Skamania	4589	Nf Lewis R	1008	28.5 mi NE Woodland
SWIMMING DEER	Chelan	3	Wenatchee R	4850	E side Cascade Crest
SWITCH PD	Benton	7	Lake Wallula	340	15.7 mi SE Kennewick
SYLVAN	Lincoln	550	Crab Cr	1650	4 mi E Odesso
SYLVESTER	Chelan	20	Wenatchee R	7000	12.4 mi W Leavenworth
SYLVIA (RES)	Grays Hbr	31	Wynooche R	80	1 mi N Montesano

T

LAKE	COUNTY	ACRES	DRAINAGE	ELEV.	LOCATION
T'AHL	King	6.5	Foss R	5200	2750' S Locket Lk
TABLE	Grant	20	Grand Coulee	1500	1.5 mi W Coulee City
TACOMA SPORTSMENS	Pend Oreille		Pend Oreille R	2400	7.1 mi N Cusick
TAG EAR	Douglas	9	Columbia R	2230	14 mi E Bridgeport
TAKHLAK	Skamania	35.5	Cispus R	4350	24.5 mi SE Randle
TALARUS	King	18	Sf Snoq R	3270	4.7 mi W Snoq Pass
TANEUM	Kittitas	3	Yakima R	5266	10.5 mi SW Cle Elum
TANK LKS (2)	King	3-4	Wf Foss R	5800	2000' SE Bonnie Lk
TANWAX	Pierce	173	Nisqually R	600	5.5 mi N Eatonville
TAPE	Pacific	10	Willapa Bay	20	4 mi N Long Beach
TAPPS	Pierce	2296	Stuck R	540	3 mi NE Sumner
TAPTO LKS (4)	Whatcom	0.5-10	Chilliwack R	5750	N Whatcom Pass
TARBOO	Jefferson	22	Hood Canal	640	8 mi W Port Ludlow
TATOOSH LKS (2)	Lewis	2.5-10	Cowlitz R	5000	7.5 mi N Packwood
TAYLOR MILL PD	King	3	Sammamish Lk	483	.05 mi N Hobart
TAYLOR	Stevens	1	Kettle R	2200	4.5 mi NE Orient
TEAL LKS (2)	Grant	22-28	Crab Cr	954	6.4 mi N Othello
TEANAWAY	Kittitas	5	Nf Teanaway R	2730	8.5 mi N Cle Elum
TEANAWAY JUNCTION	Kittitas	5	Teanaway R	1820	5 mi SE Cle Elum
TEMPLE PDS (2)	Snohomish	8	Snohomish R	420	3.5 mi W Monroe
TEN	Skagit	16	Sf Skagit R	1210	3.5 mi NE Conway
TENAS	Mason	11	Hood Canal	850	3.5 mi NW Lilliwaup
TENNANT	Whatcom	43	Bellingham Bay	15	1 mi SE Ferndale
TERENCE	Kittitas	14	Waptus R	5550	4 mi N Salmon la Sac
TERRACE LKS (2)	King	2	Tye R	5200	7 mi S Scenic
TEXAS PDS (2)	Skagit	6	Sauk R	1500	8 mi N Darrinston
TEXAS	Whitman	24	Palouse R	1702	6.4 mi NW Winona
THESEUS	Chelan	31	L Wenatchee R	5150	7.8 mi NE Stevens Pass
THETIS	Kittitas	5	Kachess R	4420	2.5 mi NE Keechelus Lk dam
THIRD	King	2	Green R	1100	3.3 mi E Enumclaw
THOMAS CREEK PDS	Skagit	2	Samish R	300	3.5 mi N Sedro-Woolley
THOMAS	Skamania	10.5	Wind R	4450	19 mi N Carson
THOMAS	Snohomish	7	Sammamish R	387	7.5 mi N Bothell
THOMAS	Stevens	163	L Pend Ore R	3162	17 mi NE Colville
THOMPSON	Grant	14	Banks Lk	1550	7 mi SW Electric City
THOMPSON	King	47	Pratt R	3650	10 mi SE North Bend
THOMPSON	Stevens	7	Colville R	2430	4 mi SE Colville
THORNDYKE	Jefferson	4	Hood Canal	250	2 mi SW South Pt, Hood Canal
THORNTON	Snohomish	3	Suiattle R	5000	E side White Chuck Mtn
THORTON—LOWER	Whatcom	56	Skagit R	4450	3.4 mi NW Newhalem
THORNTON—MIDDLE	Whatcom	11	Skagit R	4680	3.7 mi W Newhalem
THORNTON—UPPER	Whatcom	31	Skagit R	5040	4 mi W Newhalem
THORP	Kittitas	10	Cle Elum R	4670	9.4 mi N Easton

LAKE	COUNTY	ACRES	DRAINAGE	ELEV.	LOCATION
THREAD	Adams	29	Crab Cr	915	3.3 mi N Othello
THREE LAKES RES	Chelan	33	Columbia R	871	5.7 mi SE Wenatchee
THREE LKS (3)	Lewis	1-4	Ohanapecosh R	4850	2.5 mi SE Sheep Lk
THREE LKS (3)	Skagit	1-4	Sf Nooksack R	4000	9 mi N Hamilton
THREE HORSE	Clallam	4	Lk Mills	4140	2.4 mi W Olympic Hot Spr
THREE QUEEN	Kittitas	1.5	Kachess R	5390	1 mi SE Three Queens Mtn
THUN FIELD PD	Pierce	10	Puyallup R	446	2.4 mi SW Orting
THUNDER	Whatcom	8	Diablo Lk	1500	6.5 mi E Newhalem
THUNDER	Yakima	2	Tieton R	3300	1.6 mi NW Tieton Dam
THUNDER MTN LKS (2)	Chelan	4-5	Wenatchee R	6250	4 mi SE Scenic
TIFFANY	Okanogan	20	Chewack R	6550	12.5 mi NW Conconully
TINKER	Pacific	11	Willapa Bay	20	NE side Long Beach
TOAD	Whatcom	30	Bellingham Bay	714	5 mi NE Bellingham
TOKETIE	Chelan	5	Wenatchee R	6500	7 mi SW Leavenworth
TOKETIE	Skagit	17	Suiattle R	5200	14.5 mi NE Darrington
TOKE-TIE	Skamania	3 5	White Salmon R	4700	2200' NE Sahalee-Tyee Lk
TOMBSTONE	Skamania	2.5	White Salmon R	4600	1 mi SE Gifford Peak
TOM, DICK & HARRY	Snohomish	3	Nf Skyk R	3500	4 mi NE Index
TOMTIT	Snohomish	30	Skykomish R	608	3 mi S Sultan
TOMYHOI	Whatcom	82	Chilliwack R	3700	4.5 mi N Shuksan
TONSETH	Okanogan	0.5	Andrews Cr	3100	21.5 mi N Winthrop
TOP	Chelan	7	L Wenatchee R	4700	10 mi N Stevens Pass
TOP	King	5	Foss R	4500	3.7 mi S Skykomish
TOUGAW OLSON	King	1	White R	860	2 mi E Enumclaw
TOWER ROCK BV PDS	Lewis	3	Cispus R	1300	.04 mi SE Twr Rk Forest Camp
TRADEDOLLAR	Skamania	12	Green R	3552	7 mi NW Spirit Lk outlet
TRADITION	King	19	Sammamish Lk	490	1.4 mi E Issaquah
TRAP	Chelan	12	Wenatchee R	5150	3 mi SE Scenic
TRAP	Mason	18	Oakland Bay	230	6.4 mi W Shelton
TRAPPER	Chelan	147	Stehekin R	4165	3 mi SE Cascade Pass
TRAVERS	Lincoln	20	Crab Cr	1740	8 mi N Odessa
TRESTLE SWAMP	Snohomish	5	Snoqualmie R	900	4.4 mi NE Duvall
TRIPLETT LKS (3)	Chelan	3-4	Lk Chelan	6100	4.7 mi SE Stehekin
TRIUMPH	Whatcom	4	Skagit R	3650	6 mi W Newhalem
TROSPER	Thurston	17	Budd Inlet	150	3.5 mi S Olympia
TROUT	Chelan	17	Wenatchee R	4850	11.7 mi W Leavenworth
TROUT	Ferry	8	FDR Lk	3000	8.5 mi W Kettle Falls
TROUT	King	18	White R	350	4 mi SW Auburn
TROUT	King	17	Wf Foss R	2012	6.7 mi S Skykomish
TROUT	Pend Orelile	95	Horseshoe Lk	2250	8 mi NW Elk
TROUT	Pierce	5,5	Nisqually R	700	2 mi W Tanwax Lk
TROUT	Skamania	100	White Salmon R	1950	19.5 mi N White Salmon
TROUT	Snohomish	19	Sfk Stillaguamish R		4.7 mi N Granite Falls
TROUT CREEK RES	Skamania	16	Wind R	1100	7.5 mi N Stevenson
TUCK	Kittitas	16	Cle Elum R	5250	8.6 mi S Scenic
TUCKWAY	Whatcom	1.5	Sf Nooksack R	3850	8.5 mi N Concrete
TUCQUALA	Kittitas	63	Cle Elum R	3325	7.5 mi N Salmon la Sac
TULE	Lincoln	127	Lake Cr	1475	4 mi NW Odessa
TULE	Pierce	31	Nisqually R	456	9 mi SE Yelm
TULE	Pierce	8	Puset Sound	290	1.5 mi N Spanaway Lk
TUMWATER	King	2.5	Ef Miller R	4500	5.7 mi SW Skykomish
TUNGSTEN	Okanogan	17	Chewack R	7100	NE side Apex Mtn
TUNNEL	Skamania	13	Columbia R	75	6.4 mi W White Salmon
TUPSO	Snohomish	3	Sf Stilly R	4000	11 mi NE Granite Falls
TURNBULL SL—EAST	Spokane	331	Palouse R	2290	4 mi S Cheney
TURNBULL SL—WEST	Spokane	361	Palouse R	2290	4.5 mi S Cheney
TURQUOISE	Chelan	22	Wenatchee R	5550	18 mi W Leavenworth
TURTLE	Okanogan	8	Okanogan R	2200	7.9 mi SW Tonasket
TURTLE LKS (2)	Stevens	2-9	Spokane R	2475	4.4 mi NW Wellpinit
TUSCOHATCHIE LKS (2)	King	32-58	Pratt R	3420	3.4 mi W Snoq Pass
TWELVE	King	43	Green R	718	1.5 mi NE Blk Diamond
TWENTY SEVEN	Pierce	21	Nisqually R	776	4 mi N Eatonville
TWENTYTW	Snohomish	44	Sf Stilly R	2460	9.5 mi E Granite Falls
TWILIGHT	Kittitas	2	Nf Cedar R	3575	6.5 mi S Snoq Pass
TWIN LKS (2)	Jefferson	2-5	Pt Ludlow Hbr	390	4.5 mi SW Port Ludlow
TWIN LKS (2)	Kittitas	2-4	Keechelus Lk	3090	4.7 mi S Snoq Pass
TWIN LKS—LOWER	Lincoln	45	Crab Cr	1950	13 mi W Harrington
TWIN LKS—UPPER	Lincoln	35	Crab Cr	1957	500' NE Lower Twin Lk
TWIN LKS (2)	Mason	5.5-15	Tahuya R	395	1.5 mi NE Wooten Lk
TWIN LKS (2)	Okanogan	24-77	Methow R	1950	2 mi S Winthrop
TWIN LKS (2)	Okanogan	13	Okanogan R	1975	3 mi W Riverside
TWIN LKS (2)	Pierce	2	Carbon R	4800	14 mi SE Enumclaw
TWIN LKS (2)	San Juan	3-8	Str of Georgia	1100	On Orcas Island
TWIN LKS—LOWER	Snohomish	24.5	Nf Skykomish R	4700	6 mi SE Barlow Pass
TWIN LKS—UPPER	Snohomish	89	Nf Skykomish R	4800	5.7 mi SE Barlow Pass
TWIN LKS—LOWER	Snohomish	32	Nf Stilly R		6.8 mi N Granite Falls

LAKE	COUNTY	ACRES	DRAINAGE	ELEV.	LOCATION
TWIN LKS—UPPER	Snohomish	34	Nf Stilly R	7;	1200' S Lower Twin Lk
TWIN LKS (2)	Snohomish	18-19	Suiattle R	5200	7.5 mi NW Glacier Peak
TWIN LKS (2)	Whatcom	17-20	Nf Nooksack R	5180	3.7 mi NE Shuksan
TWIN FALLS	Snohomish	1.5	Pilchuck R	2030	11.4 mi SE Granite Falls
TWIN SISTERS	Yakima	31-104.5	Bumping R	5152	6.7 mi N White Pass
TWISP	Okanogan	4.5	Sf Twisp R	6300	1.6 mi SW Twisp Pass
TWO LKS	King	1.5	White R	3500	9 mi E Enumclaw
TWO LKS	Yakima	97-118	Wf Klickitat R	4259	11 mi N Mt Adams summit
TWO LITTLE LKS	Chelan	3-10	Entiat R	5750	23 mi N Leavenworth
TY	Yakima	1	Tieton R	4000	.04 mi blw Lynne Lk
TYE	King	3	Tye R	4800	.07 mi NW Stevens Pass

U

LAKE	COUNTY	ACRES	DRAINAGE	ELEV.	LOCATION
UMATILLA	Klickitat	52000	Columbia R	265	9.5 mi SE Goldendale
UNDI	Clallam	15	Bogachiel R	220	I mi SE Forks
UNION	King	598	Puget Sound	14	In Seattle
UPPER CATHEDRAL	Okanogan	9	Ashnola R	6400	36 mi N Winthrop
UPPER CRATER	Okanogan	13	Methow R	6900	14 mi SW Twisp
UPPER FLORENCE	Chelan	4	Wenatchee R	6800	13 mi NW Leavenworth
UPPER RIVORD	Snohomish	13	Suiattle R	5675	1500' E Lime Mtn summit
UPPER WHEELER RES	Chelan	36	Columbia R	4290	10 mi S Wenatchee
VALHALLA	Chelan	29	Wenatchee R	5050	3 mi N Stevens Pass
VAN	Snohomish	2	Nf Sauk R	5500	5 mi SW Glacier Peak
VANCE CREEK	Grays Hbr	9	Chehalis R	20	1.5 mi SW Elma
VANCOUVER	Clark	2858	Columbia R	9	3 mi NW Vancouver
VANES	Pend Oreille	4	Pend Oreille R	3000	1 mi W No Name Lk
VANSON	Lewis	10	Green R	4150	6.7 mi S Kosmos
VAN VALKENBERG PD	Whatcom	1	Sumas R	50	1 mi W Sumas
VARDEN	Okanogan	4.5	Methow R	6194	17.5 mi NW Winthrop
VENUS LKS (2)	Skamania	6	Green R	4600	5.4 mi N Spirit Lk outlet
VICENTE	Kittitas	11.5	Waptus R	5700	9.9 mi NW Salmon la Sac
VICTORIA	Chelan	27	Wenatchee R	5500	8.6 mi W Leavenworth
VIEW	King	3.5	Wt Foss R	5370	1200' W Jewel Lk
VIRGIN	Grant	20	Crab Cr	1015	8.1 mi N Othello
VOGLER	Skagit	3.5	Skagit R	1060	2.4 mi N Concrete

W

LAKE	COUNTY	ACRES	DRAINAGE	ELEV.	LOCATION
WADDELL	Chelan	10	Stehekin R	4932	4 mi N High Bridge G.S.
WAGNER	Skagit	2.5	Stilly R	3000	10 mi SE Sedro-Woolley
WAGNER	Snohomish	19.5	Skykomish R	300	2.5 mi NE Monroe
WAGON WHEEL	Mason	3	Nf Skok R	4150	2 mi N Lk Cushman
WAITTS (RES)	Stevens	455	Colville R	1959	7 mi S Chewelah
WALKER	King	12	Green R	1140	1.5 mi SE Cumberland
WALL	Adams	15	Palouse R	1600	19 mi SE Ritzville
WALL PD	Benton	4	Lk Wallula	340	15 2 mi E McNary Dam
WALL	Lincoln	32	Crab Cr	2050	10.5 mi NW Harrington
WALL	Lincoln	4	Crab Cr	2200	10 mi SE Wilbur
WALLACE SL	Cowlltz	12	Columbia R	10	2.7 mi S Woodland
WALLULA	Benton	38800	Columbia R	340	20 mi SW Kennewick
WALTER	Lincoln	18	Crab Cr	1650	5.5 mi N Odessa
WALUPT	Lewis	384	Cispus R	3927	15.5 mi SE Packwood
WANAPUM DAM RES	Grant	14680	Columbia R	571	28 mi E Ellensburg
WANNACUT	Okanogan	412		1850	4.6 mi SW Oroville
WAPATO	Chelan	186	Lk Chelan	1229	8.2 mi NW Chelan
WAPATO LKS (2)	Pierce	22-28	Puget Sound	315	At Wapato Park, Tacoma
WAPIKI	Skamania	10	White Salmon	4700	10 mi W Mt Adams R.S.
WAPTUS	Kittitas	246	Cle Elum R	2980	23 mi NW Cle Elum
WARD	Thurston	87	Deschutes R	123	2.5 mi S Olympia
WARDEN LKS (2)	Grant	24-186	Crab Cr	1076	5.7 mi W Warden
WASHBURN	Okanogan	13	Okanogan R	3100	2.1 mi NE Loomis
WASHINGTON	King	22138	Puget Sound	14	E side Seattle
WASHOUGAL	Clark	o,5	L Washousal R	460	5 mi N Washousal
WATSON	Columbia	4	Tucannon R	2350	4 mi S Game Range H.Q.
WATSON LKS (2)	Whatcom	18-46	Baker R	4375	11.5 mi NE Concrete
WAYHUT	Snohomish	6	Beckler R	4000	9 mi N Skykomish
WEBSTER	King	10	Cedar R	540	2.5 mi N Maple Valley
WEDEN	Snohomish	5.5	Sf Sauk R	4400	3.4 mi SE Barlow Pass
WEDERSPAHN	Lincoln	14	Crab Cr	1655	5.4 mi N Odessa
WELLSIAN	Benton	10		350	S part Richland
WENAS (RES)	Yakima	61	Yakima R	1861	6 mi N Naches
WENATCHEE	Chelan	2445	Wenatchee R	1875	15 mi N Leavenworth
WENTWORTH	Clallam	54	Wf Dickey R	147	7.7 mi NW Forks
WENZEL SL	Grays Hbr	6	Chehalis R	20	2 mi SW Elma
WEST	Pierce	6	Puyallup R	4600	7 mi NE National

LAKE	COUNTY	ACRES	DRAINAGE	ELEV.	LOCATION
WEST MEDICAL	Spokane	235	Crab Cr	2423	1 mi W twn Medical Lake
WEST TRITT	Spokane	107	Palouse R	2290	3 mi S Cheney
WHALE	Skagit	50	Cascade R	4600	9 mi SE Marblemount
WHATCOM (RES)	Whatcom	5003	Bellingham Bay	307	3 mi E Bellingham
WHEELER	Mason	8	Hood Canal	350	1 mi E Tahuya
WHITE MUD	Stevens	59	L Pend Ore R	2168	4.4 mi SE Colville
WHITE RIVER MILL PD	King	23	White R	1040	3 mi E Enumclaw
WHITE ROCK LKS (3)	Chelan	1-20	Stehekin R	6175	8.7 mi S Cascade Pass
WHITESTONE (RES)	Okanogan	170	Okanogan R	1250	5.7 mi N Tonasket
WHITMAN	Pierce	30	Nisqually R	601	6.5 mi N Eatonville
WICKS	Kitsap	9	Carr Inlet	430	5.5 mi E Belfair
WIDGEON	Clark	38	Columbia R	10	1.5 mi W Ridgefield
WIDGEON	Grant	11	Crab Cr	937	8 mi N Othello
WIDOW	King	4	Mf Snoq R	3120	9 mi E North Bend
WILDBERRY	Mason	8	Hood Canal	500	1.5 mi NW Tahuya
WILDCAT	Jefferson	5	Dosewallips R	4150	12.5 mi W Brinnon
WILDCAT LKS (2)	King	19-54	Mf Snoq R	4218	5.4 mi NW Snoq Pass
WILDCAT	Kitsap	112	Dyes Inlet	377	6 mi NW Bremerton
WILDCAT	Yakima	2	Bumping R	5200	1900' N Cousar Lk outlet
WILDERNESS	King	67	Green R	470	2.5 mi S Maple Valley
WILDWOOD	Kitsap	7	Sinclair Inlet	420	.07 mi SE Wildwood
WILEY	Whatcom	6	Ross Lk	6650	12.5 mi NW Diablo Dam
WILLIAMS	Grant	12	Crab Cr	1250	8 mi SW Coulee City
WILLIAMS	King	15	Mf Snoq R	4500	11.5 mi NE Snoq Pass
WILLIAMS	Okanogan	7	Twisp R	6500	18.5 mi W Twisp
WILLIAMS	Spokane	319	Palouse R	2052	11.5 mi SW Cheney
WILLIAMS	Stevens	38	Colville R	1980	14.5 mi N Colville
WILLIAMS	Whatcom	3.5	Sf Nooksack R	350	2.5 mi SE Deming
WILLOUGHBY	Clallam	5.5	Pacific Ocean	200	5.5 mi Ozette
WILLOW LKS (2)	Grant	23-39	Crab Cr	1160	6.5 mi SE city Soap Lake
WILLOW	Lincoln	12	Crab Cr	2100	12.5 mi S Creston
WILLOW	Whatcom	27	Ross Lk	2900	15 mi N Ross Dam
WILSON PD	Kittitas	2	Yakima R	1450	3.5 mi SE Ellensburg
WINCHESTER WSTWY R	Grant	660	Crab Cr	1147	11 mi SE Quincey
WINDMILL	Grant	34	Crab Cr	986	7.1 mi N Othello
WINDMILL PD	Spokane	11	Palouse R	2245	1.4 mi SW Ea Cheney
WINDOM	Snohomish	4	Sauk R	3800	8.7 mi S Darrington
WINDY	King	6	Pratt R	4186	2000' SW Kaleetan Lk
WINDY	Okanogan	2	Similkameen R	7050	17 mi NW Loomis
WING	Skagit	15	Ross Lk	6400	2.7 mi SE Mt Arriva
WINNIE	Lewis	2	Nf Tilton R	2680	12.5 mi NE Onalaska
WINTERS PD	Clallam	4.5	Juan de Fuca	350	1.5 mi SE Mt Pleasant
WINTERS	Snohomish	11	Wallace R	663	3 mi NE Sultan
WISEMAN	Whatcom	18.5	Mf Nooksack R	4250	7.5 mi SW Mt Baker summit
WISER	Whatcom	123	Nooksack R	50	3 mi SW Lynden
WISHRAM	Klickitat	6	Lk Gelilo	160	1 mi E Wishram
WITTENMEYER	King	3	Lk Washington	125	2 mi NE Juanita
WOBBLY	Lewis	8	Nf Cispus R	3400	13 mi S Packwood
WOELFEL	Mason	6	Oakland Bay	350	14.7 mi NW Shelton
WOLVERINE	Chelan	8.5	Wenatchee R	5075	500' NE Square Lk
WOOD	Mason	10	Hood Canal	500	1.8 mi N Tahuya
WOOD	Skamania	12.5	Nt Lewis R	5000	1.5 mi W Cultus Cr G.S.
WOODS	Skagit	35	Suiattle R	5100	23 mi NE Darrington
WOODS	Spokane	32	Spokane R	2419	9.2 mi W Nine Mile Falls
WOOTEN	Mason	70	Tahuya R	407	7 mi W Belfair
WORTH	Franklin	10	Columbia R	770	4 mi NW Mesa
WRIGHT	Lewis	3.5	Cowlitz R	3100	9 mi SE Packwood
WYE	Kitsap	38	Case Inlet	300	3.5 mi SE Belfair
WYNOOCHE	Grays Hbr	1120	Wynooche R		39 mi N Montesano

Y

"Y"	Clallam	5	Lunch Lk	4600	E from Lunch Lk
YAHOO	Jefferson	8	Clearwater R	2350	3.5 mi N mouth Sams R
YAKIMA SPORTSMENS	Yakima	9	Yakima R	1010	2.5 mi E Yakima
YALE RES	Clark	3302	Nf Lewis R	490	20.5 mi E Woodland
YELLEPIT PD	Benton	38	Lk Wallula	340	15 mi SE Kennewick
YELLOW	King	10.5	Sammamish Lk	400	3 mi N Issaquah
YELLOW JACKET	Lewis	2	Cispus R		10.1 mi S Randle
YOCUM	Pend Oreille	42	Pend Oreille R	2875	6.4 mi N Ruby

Z

ZIG ZAG	Skamania	2.5	Nf Lewis R	3400	14.5 mi NW Stevenson
ZIMMERMAN PD	Chelan	4	Columbia R	2350	6 mi S Wenatchee
ZOSELS MILL PD	Okanogan	100	Okanogan R	910	At Oroville

Streams of Washington

A

STREAM	TRIBUTARY TO	COUNTY
ABE CR	Columbia R	Wahkiakum
ABERNATHY CR	Columbia R	Cowlitz
ABSHER CR	Chehalis R	Lewis
ADA CR	White R	Pierce
ADAMS CR	Cispus R	Skamania
ADDY CR	Colville R	Stevens
AENEAS CR	Curlew Cr	Ferry
AENEAS CR	Wf San Poil R	Okanogan
AENEAS CR	Okanogan R	Okanogan
AGENCY CR	Yakima R	Yakima
AGNES CR	Stehekin R	Chelan
AGNEW CR	L Chelan	Chelan
AHTUNUM CR	Nf Yakima R	Yakima
AHTANUM CR	Sf Yakima R	Yakima
AINSLIE CR	Cowlitz R	Lewis
ALCKEE CR	Sol Duc R	Clallam
ALDER CR	Chiwawa R	Chelan
ALDER CR	Toutle R	Cowlitz
ALDER CR	Millers Bay	Kitsap
ALDER CR	Columbia R	Klickitat
ALDER CR	Nisqually R	Pierce
ALDER CR	Tilton R	Lewis
ALDER CR	Skagit R	Skagit
ALDER CR	Columbia R	Stevens
ALDERBROOK CR	Hood Canal	Mason
ALGER CR	Columbia R	Wahkiakum
ALICE CR	San Poil R	Ferry
ALKALI CR	Snake R	Whitman
ALLEN CR	Peshastin Cr	Chelan
ALLEN CR	Pend Oreille R	Pend Oreille
ALLEN CR	Lewis R	Skamania
ALLEN CR	Ebey Slough	Snohomish
ALMOTA CR	Snake R	Whitman
ALPINE CR	Snake R	Asotin
ALPOWA CR	Snake R	Asotin/Garfield
ALTA CR	Duwamish R	King
AMAZON CR	Little Pend Oreille	Stevens
AMBER CR	Toutle R	Lewis
ANACONDA CR	Lewis R	Clark
AMERICAN R	Bumping R	Yakima
AMES CR	Snoqualmie R	King
ANDERSON CR	Puget Sound	Kins
ANDERSON CR	Sinclair Inlet	Kitsap
ANDERSON CR	Carpenter Cr	Whatcom
ANDERSON CR	Nooksack R	Whatcom
ANDERSON CR	Ef Anderson Cr	Whatcom
ANDREWS CR	Crocker Lake	Jefferson
ANDREWS CR	Elk R	Grays Harbor
ANDY CR	Nf Tieton R	Yakima
ANTOINE CR	ColumbiaR	Chelan/Okanogan
ANTON'S CR	Sol Duc R	Clallam
ANTWYNE CR	Okanogan R	Okanogan
ARCHER CR	North R	Grays Harbor
ARIEL CR	Lewis R	Cowlitz
ARKANSAS CR	Cowlitz R	Cowlitz
ARMENTROUT CR	Elk In	Thurston
ARMSTRONG CR	Willapa R	Pacific
ARMSTRONG CR L	Spokane R	Spokane
ARNOLD SPRINGS	Mud Bay	Thurston
ARNOLD CR	Kalama R	Cowlitz
ASH CR	Columbia R	Skamania

STREAM	TRIBUTARY TO	COUNTY
ARVID CR	Clearwater R	Jefferson
ASHNOLA CR	Similkameen R	Okanogan
ASMUS CR	Oakland Bay	Mason
ASOTIN CR	Snake R	Asotin
AURORA CR	Lake Crescent	Clallam
AYERS CR	Deschutes R	Thurston
AXFORD CR	Big Cr	Grays Harbor

B

STREAM	TRIBUTARY TO	COUNTY
BCR CR	Quillayute R	Clallam
BACHELOR CR	Yakima R	Yakima
BACKMAN CR	Skagit R	Skagit
BACKMAN CR	Sauk R	Snohomish
BACON CR	Skagit R	Skagit
BACON CR	Klickitat R	Yakima
BACON CR	Kettle R	Ferry
BAGLEY CR	Str. Juan de Fuca	Clallam
BAGLEY CR	Nooksack R	Whatcom
BAEKOS CR	Whitechuck R	Snohomish
BAKER CR	Satsop R	Mason
BAKER CR	Black R	Thurston
BAILEY CR	Wf San Poil R	Okanogan
BAILEYS(CRYSTAL) CR	Dyes Inlet	Kitsap
BAIRD CR	Nf Coweman R	Cowlitz
BAKER CR	Swauk Cr	Kittitas
BAKER CR	Willapa Bay	Pacific
BAKER R	Skagit R	Whatcom
BALDASSIN CR	Beaver Cr	Thurston
BALLOON CR	Johns R	Grays Harbor
BANGOR CR	Hood Canal	Kitsap
BARCLAY CR	Skykomish R	King
BAR KER (CASTLE) CR	Dyes Inlet	Kitsap
BARLOW CR	Elk R	Grays Harbor
BARNABY CR	Columbia R	Ferry
BARNES CR	Lake Crescent	Clallam
BARNUM CR	Hoquiam R	Grays Harbor
BARR CR	Skykomish R	Snohomish
BARRETT CR	Curlew Lake	Ferry
BARRETTOUTLET	Nooksack R	Whatcom
BARRON CR	Tilton R	Lewis
BASIN CR	Stehekin R	Chelan
BASIN CR	Sol Duc R	Clallam
BASKET CR	Ef Lewis R	Clark
BATES CR	Wenatchee R	Chelan
BATTLE CR	L Goodwin	Snohomish
BATTLEGROUND CR	Salmon C	Clark
BAYARD CR	Wenatchee R	Chelan
BEACH CR	Waits Lake	Stevens
BEACON CR	Woodward Cr	Skamania
BEAL CR	Nooksack R	Whatcom
BEAN CR	Black R	Thurston
BEAR CR	Soleduck R	Clallam
BEAR CR	Wishkah R	Grays Harbor
BEAR CR	Sammamish R	King
BEAR CR	Burley Cr	Kitsap
BEAR CR	Cle Elum Lake	Kittitas
BEAR CR	Tilton R	Lewis
BEAR CR	Union R	Mason
BEAR CR	Methow R	Okanogan
BEAR CR	Wallace R	Snohomish
BEAR CR	L Spokane R	Spokane
BEAR CR	L Pend Oreille R	Stevens

STREAM	TRIBUTARY TO	COUNTY
BEAR CR	Nf Bear Cr	Stevens
BEAR CR	Sf Bear Cr	Stevens
BEAR CANYON CR	Tieton R	Yakima
BEATTY SPRINGS	Woodland Cr	Thurston
BEARDSLEY CR	Lilliwaup R	Mason
BEASTROM CR	Colville R	Stevens
BEATY CR	Dempsey Cr	Thurston
BEAVER CR	Wenatchee R	Chelan
BEAVER CR	Soleduck R	Clallam
BEAVER CR	Ef Beaver Cr	Clallam
BEAVER CR	Joe Cr	Grays Harbor
BEAVER CR	Puget Sound	Kitsap
BEAVER CR	Cave Cr	Klickitat
BEAVER CR	Methow R	Okanogan
BEAVER CR	Toroda Cr	Okanogan
BEAVER CR	Dragoon Cr	Stevens
BEAVER CR	Black R	Thurston
BEAVER CR	Skagit R	Whatcom
BEAVER DAM CR	San Poil R	Ferry
BECK CR	Cowlitz	Cowlitz
BECKER'S CR	L Washington	King
BECKLER R	Sf Skykomish R	Snohomish
BEDDLE CR	L Washington	King
BEECHERS CR	Snohomish R	Snohomish
BEKLER CR	Snohomish R	Snohomish
BELL CR	Sequim Bay	Clallam
BELL'S CR	Nooksack R	Whatcom
BEN DAY CR	Snake R	Garfield
BENN CR	PacificOcean	GraysHarbor
BENSON CR	Methow R	Okanogan
BENSON CR	Stillaquamish R	Snohomish
BERRINGON SPRINGS	Columbia R	Klickitat
BERGE CR	Wind R	Skamania
BERNARD CR	Hoquiam R	Grays Harbor
BERNARD CR	Wenatchee R	Chelan
BERRY CR	Wishkah R	Grays Harbor
BERRY CR	Pend Oreille R	Pend Orellle
BERRY CR	Nisqually R	Pierce
BERRY (SqUAW) CR	Rock Cr	Skamania
BERRYMAN CR	Hoquiam R	Grays Harbor
BERT CR	Cedar R	Clark
BERTRAND CR	Nooksack R	Whatcom
BIG CR	Humptulips R	Grays Harbor
BIG CR	Yakima R	Kittitas
BIG CR	Nf Skokomish R.	Mason
BIG CR	Suiattle R	Skagit
BIG CR	L Chelan	Chelan
BIG CR	Wynoochee R	Grays Harbor
BIG CR	Quinault R	Grays Harbor
BIG CR	Wishkah R	Grays Harbor
BIG CR	Nisqually R	Lewis
BIG CR	Lilliwaup R	Mason
BIG CR	Skagit R	Skagit
BIG CR	Lewis R	Skamania
BIG ALKALI CR	Palouse R	
BIG BEEF CR	Hood Canal	Kitsap
BIG BEAVER CR	Skagit R	Whatcom
BIG BOULDER CR	Kettle R	Ferry
BIG GRADE CR	Lake Chelan	Chelan
BIG MEADOW CR	Chiwawa R	Chelan
BIG MISSION CR	Hood Canal	Mason
BIG MUDDY CR	Clark Fork	Pend Oreille
BIG MUDDY CR	Klickitat	Yakima
BIG QUILCENE R	Quilcene Bay	Jefferson
BIG R CR	Ozette Lake	Clallam
BIG SHEEP CR		Stevens
BIG SOOS CR	Green R	King
BIG SPRING CR	White Salmon R	Klickitat
BIG SPRING CR	Clark Fork	Pend Oreille
BIG SPRING CR	Walla Walla R	Walla Walla
BIGTREE CR	Ef Lewis R	Clark
BIRD CR	Outlet Cr	Klickitat
BITTER (BLACK) CR	Wynoochee R	Grays Harbor
BITTER CR	North R	Pacific
BJORK CR	Eagle Cr	Chelan
BLACK (BITTER) CR	Wynoochee R	Grays Harbor

STREAM	TRIBUTARY TO	COUNTY
BLACK CR	Wishkaw R	Grays Harbor
BLACK CR	Satsop R	Grays Harbor
BLACK CR	Chehalis R	Grays Harbor
BLACK CR	North R	Grays Harbor
BLACK CR	Snoqualmie	King
BLACK CR	Suiattle R	Snohomish
BLACK CANYON CR	Methow R	Okanogan
BLACKHORSE CR	Klickitat R	Klickitat
BLACKJACK CR	Sinclair Inlet	Kitsap
BLACKJACK CR	Stillaguamish R	Snohomish
BLACK R	Chehalis R	Thurston
BLACKMAN CR	Snohomish R	Snohomish
BLACKMAN'S CR	Sauk R	Snohomish
BLACK OAK CR	Whitechuck R	Snohomish
BLACK ROCK CR	Sauk R	Snohomish
BLACK SANDS CR	Lewis R	Skamania
BLACKWOOD CR	Sol Duc R	Clallam
BLAIR CR	Nisqually R	Pierce
BLANCHARD CR	Pend Oreille	Pend Oreille
BLANEY CR	Grays R	Pacific
BLIND CR	Cowlitz	Lewis
BLOCKHOUSE CR	Klickitat R	Klickitat
BLOODGOOD CR	L Klickitat R	Klickitat
BLOODY RUN CR	Skookumchuck R	Thurston
BLUE CR	Columbia R	Skamania
BLUE CR	Colville R	Stevens
BLUE CR	Mill Cr	Walla Walla
BLYN CR	Sequim Bay	Clallam
BOARDMAN CR	Stillaguamish R	Snohomish
BODIE CR	Toroda Cr	Okanogan
BOE CR	Big R	Clallam
BOGACHIEL R	Quillayute R	Clallam
BOISE CR	White R	King
BOLAN CR	Lewis R	Clark
BONAPARTE CR	Okanogan R	Okanogan
BOONE CR	Cowlitz R	Lewis
BONHAM CR	Wf Hoquiam R	Grays Harbor
BOSLEY CR	Quinault R	Grays Harbor
BOULDER CR	Quinault R	Grays Harbor
BOULDER CR	Cle Elum R	Kittitas
BOULDER CR	Stehekin R	Chelan
BOULDER CR	Lake Keechelus	Kittitas
BOULDER CR	Chewack Cr	Okanogan
BOULDER (ROCK) CR	Wf Methow R	Okanogan
BOULDER CR	Nf Stillaguamish R	Snohomish
BOULEVARO CR	Bogachiel R	Jefferson
BOU N DARY C R	L Sheep Cr	Stevens
BOUNDARY CR	Kettle R	Ferry
BOWERS CR	Chambers Cr	Pierce
BOWMAN CR	L Klickitat R	Klickitat
BOXCANYON CR	Kachess Lake	Kittitas
BOXLEY CR	Snoqualmie R	King
BOYCE CR	White R	Pierce
BOYD CR	Nooksack R	Whatcom
BOYL CR	Washougal R	Skamania
BRADEN CR	Hoh R	Jefferson
BRACKETT CR	Pend Oreille R	Pend Oreille
BRAIL CR	Nisqually R	Thurston
BRAZEE CR	Lewis R	Clark
BRECKENRIDGE CR	Sumas R	Whatcom
BREMER CR	Tilton R	Lewis
BRENNEGAN CR	Entiat R	Chelan
BRICKEY CR	Ef Lewis R	Clark
BRICKYARD GULCH CR	Latah Cr	Spokane
BRIDAL VEIL CR	Skykomish R	Snohomish
BRIDGE CR	Stehekin R	Chelan
BRIDGE CR	San Poil R	Ferry
BRIDGE CR	Twisp R	Okanogan
BRIDGE CR	Sol Duc R	Clallam
BRIGHT CR	Cowlitz R	Lewis
BRIM CR	Cowlitz R	Lewis
BRIM CR	Kalispel Lake	Pend Oreille
BRIM CR	S Br Brim Cr	Pend Oreille
BRITTAIN CR	Humptulips R	Grays Harbor
BROOKS CR	Spoilei Cr	Cowlitz
BROOKS CR	Stillaguamish R	Snohomish

STREAM	TRIBUTARY TO	COUNTY
BROWN CR	Pend Oreille R	Pend Oreille
BROWN CR	Colville R	Stevens
BROWN CR	Hood Canal	Mason
BROWN CR	Skokomish R	Mason
BROWN CR	Sauk R	Snohomish
BROWNELL CR	Toutle R	
BROWNS CR	HokoR	Clallam
BROWNS CR	Willapa R	Pacific
BROWNS CR	Lewis R	Cowlitz
BRUCE CR	Nf Bruce Cr	Stevens
BRUNDER SPRINGS	Columbia R	Klickitat
BRUNNER CR	Miii Cr	Klickitat
BRUSH (NICKIAM) CR	Cedar Cr	Kilckitat
BRUSH CR	Kiickitat R	Klickitat
BRUSH CR	Lewis R	Clark
BRUSH CR	Palouse R	Whitman
BUCHANAN CR	Chehaiis R	Lewls
BUCK CR	ChiwawaR	Chelan
BUCK CR	Yakima R	Kittitas
BUCK CR	White R	Pierce
BUCK CR	Suiattle R	Snohomish
BUCK CR	WhiteSalmon R	Klickitat
BUIL DOG CR	Colvlie R	Stevens
BUCKEYE CR	Stillaguamish R	Snohomish
BUMPING R	Naches R	Yakima
BUNCH CR	Quinauit R	Grays Harbor
BUNGE CR	L Spokane R	Pend Oreille
BUNKER CR	L White Salmon R	Skamania
BUNKER CR	Puyallup R	Pierce
BURKE CR	San Poil R	Ferry
BURLEY CR	Henderson Bay	Kitsap
BURNHAM CR	Paciflc	Pacific
BURKES CR	SilverLake	Cowlitz
BURNS CR	Entiat R	Chelan
BURNS CR	Green R	King
BURNT BRIDGE CR	Vancouver Lake	Clark
BURRIS CR	Columbia R	Cowiitz
BUSH CR	Cloquallum R	Grays Harbor
BURTON (FALL) CR	Cowlitz R	Lewis
BUTCHER CR	Mason Cr	Chelan
BUTCHER CR	Walla Walla R	WallaWalla
BUTLER CR	Klickitat R	Kiickitat
BUTTE CR	Grande Ronde R	Asotin
BUTTE CR	Cowlitz R	Lewls
BUTTER CR	Cowlitz R	Lewis
BUTTERMILK CR	Twisp R	Okanogan
BYRON CR	Lake Whatcom	Whatcom
BYRON CR	Clearwater R	Pierce

C

STREAM	TRIBUTARY TO	COUNTY
C CR	Sol Duc R	Clallam
C CR	Wishkah R	Grays Harbor
CCA CR	Pend Oreille R	Pend Oreille
CCC CR	Chehalis R	Grays Harbor
CABBAGE CR	Palouse R	Whitman
CABBAGE CR	W. Salmon R	Skamania
CABIN CR	Yakima R	Kittitas
CABIN CR	Tieton R	Yakima
CABIN CR	Stehekin R	Chelan
CABIN CR	Wenatchee R	Chelan
CABIN CR	Hamma Hamma R	Jefferson
CABIN CR	Grays R	Pacific
CABLE CR	Spokane R	Spokane
CACHE CR	Palouse R	Whitman
CACHE CR	Toroda Cr	Okanogan
CADWELL CR	Skykomish R	Snohomish
CADY CR	Nf Skykomish R	Snohomish
CALAWAH R	Bogachiel R	Clallam
CALDERVIN CR	Hood Canal	Mason
CALDWELL CR	Walla Walla R	Walla Walla
CALIFORNIA CR	Latah Cr	Spokane
CALISPEL CR	Washougal R	Clark
CALISPEL CR	Pend OreilleR	PendOreille
CALVIN CR	Lewis R	Colwitz
CALLIGAN CR	SnoqualmieR	King

STREAM	TRIBUTARY TO	COUNTY
CAMANO CR	Puget Sound	Island
CAMAS CR	Peshastin Cr	Chelan
CAMAS CR	Wenatchee R	Chelan
CAMP CR	Chehalis R	Grays Harbor
CAMERON CR	Greywolf R	Clallam
CAMERON CR	Columbia R	Cowlitz
CAMP CR	Chehalis R	Grays Harbor
CAMP CR	Cle Elum R	Kittitas
CAMP CR	LPend OreilleR	Stevens
CAMP CR	Sol Duc R	Clallam
CAMP CR	QuinaultR	GraysHarbor
CAMP CR	Queets R	Jefferson
CAMP CR	Twisp R	Okanogan
CAMP CR	Cowlitz R	Skawania
CAMP CR	Whitechuck R	Snohomish
CAMP CR	Colville R	Stevens
CAMPBELL CR	Skagit R	Skagit
CAMPBELL CR	Cowlitz R	Lewis
CAMPEN CR	Washougal R	Clark
CAMP JOY CR	Pend Oreille R	Stevens
CANADA CR	Carbon R	Pierce
CANNONBALL CR	Chehalis R	Lewis
CANOE CR	Lake Quinault	Grays Harbor
CANON R	Palix R	Pacific
CANYON CR	Dungeness R	Clallam
CANYON CR	Lewis R	Clark
CANYON CR	Methow R	Okanogan
CANYON CR	Twisp R	Okanogan
CANYON CR	Washougal R	Skamania
CANYON CR	Sf Stillaguamish R	Snohomish
CANYON CR	Dragoon Cr	Stevens
CANYON CR	Mf Nooksack R	Whatcom
CANYON R	Satsop R	Grays Harbor
CAPE LaBELLE CR	Wf San Poil R	Okanogan
CAPPS CR	Chehalis R	Lewis
CARACO CR	Dungeness R	Clallam
CARBON R	Puyallup R	Pierce
CAREY CR	L Sammamish	King
CARIBOU CR	Cherry Cr	Kittitas
CARLTON CR	Cowlitz R	Lewis
CARPENTER CR	Skagit R	Skagit
CARPENTER CR	Lake Whatcom	Whatcom
CARPENTER CR	Pilchuck R	Snohomish
CARPENTE R	Sekiu R	Clallam
CARSON CR	Columbia R	Skamania
CARSTEN CR	White Salmon R	Klickitat
CARTER CR	Wynoochee R	Grays Harbor
CARTER CR	Pend Oreille R	Pend Oreille
CASCADE R Nf	CascadeR	Skagit
CASCADE CR	Quinault L	Grays Harbor
CASCADE CR	White R	Pierce
CASCADE CR	Stiilaguamish R	Skagit
CASCADE CR	Nooksack R	Whatcom
CASH CR	Quinault L	Grays Harbor
CASSEL CR	Hoh R	Jefferson
CASTLE CR	Toutle R	Clark
CASTLE CR	Green R	King
CASTLE (BARKER) CR	Dyes Inlet	Kitsap
CATHERINE CR	Kettle R	Ferry
CAT CR	Greywolf R	Clallam
CAT CR	Cispus R	Skamania
CATARACT CR	Carbon R	Pierce
CATHERINE CR	Kettle R	Ferry
CATHERINE CR	Snohomish R	Snohomish
CATHLAMET R	Columbia R	Wahkiakum
CATHY CR	W. Salmon R	Klickitat
CATT CR	Nisqually R	Lewis
CAYADA CR	Carbon R	Pierce
CAVANAUGH CR	Nooksack R	Whatcom
CECIL CR	Sinlahekln Cr	Okanogan
CEDAR CR	Lewis R	Clark
CEDAR CR	Chehalis R	Grays Harbor
CEDAR CR	Yakima R	Kittitas
CEDAR CR	Salmon Cr	Lewis
CEDAR CR	Early Winters Cr	Okanogan
CEDAR CR	Sacheen Lake	Pend Oreille

STREAM	TRIBUTARY TO	COUNTY	STREAM	TRIBUTARY TO	COUNTY
CEDAR CR	Hamilton Cr	Skamania	COBEY CR	Wf San Poil R	Okanogan
CEDAR CR	Panther Cr	Skamania	COE CR	Toutle R	Skamania
CEDAR R	Lake Washington	King	COFFEE CR	Sf Goldsborough Cr	Mason
CHAMBERS CR	Puget Sound	Pierce	COFFEE CR	Chehalis R	Lewis
CHAMOKANE CR	Spokane R	Stevens	COGAN CR	Lake Quinault	Grays Harbor
CHAPARRAL CR	Klickitat R	Yakima	COLBURN CR	W. Salmon R	Klickitat
CHAMPION CR	Green R	King	COLBY CR	San Poil R	Okanogan
CHANGE CR	Snoqualmie R	King	COLBY CR	Dickey R	Clallam
CHAPLAIN CR	Sulton R	Snohomish	COLD CR	Columbia R	Benton
CHAPMAN CR	Columbia R	Klickitat	COLD CR	Denver Cr	Clallam
CHARLIES CR	Grays Harbor	Grays Harbor	COLD CR	Burnt Bridge Cr	Clark
CHEADLE CR	Willapa R	Pacific	COLD CR	Skykomish R	Snohomish
CHEADLE CR	Chehalis R	Thurston	COLD SPRING	Kalama R	Cowlitz
CHEHALIS CR	Chehalis R	Grays Harbor	COLDWATER CR	Toutle R	Cowlitz
CHEHALIS R	Grays Harbor	Grays Harbor	COLE CR	Nf Heller Cr	Stevens
CHELATCHIE CR	Tum Tum Cr	Clark	COLE CR	Lake R	Clark
CHENOIS CR	Grays Harbor	Grays Harbor	COLE CR	Icicle R	Chelan
CHENUIS CR	Carbon R	Pierce	COLEMAN CR	Yakima R	Kittitas
CHERRY CR	SnoqualmieR	King	COLLINS CR	Columbia R	Skamania
CHERRY CR	Wilson Cr	Kittitas	COLMAN CR	Nanum Cr	Kittitas
CHESTER CR	Humptulips R	Grays Harbor	COLOCKUM CR	Columbia R	Chelan
CHEWACK CR	Methow R	Okanogan	COLONIAL CR	Thunder Cr	Whatcom
CHEWEKA CR	Columbia R	Stevens	COLONY CR	Samish Bay	Skagit
CHEWEKA CR	NfCheweka R	Stevens	COLTER CR	Union R	Mason
CHEWEKA CR	Colville R	Stevens	COLTON CR	Skykomish R	Snohomish
CHEWILIKON CR	Okanogan R	Okanogan	COLUMBIA R	Pacific Ocean	
CHICKIMAN CR	Chiwawa R	Chelan	COLVILLE R	Columbia R	Stevens
CHICKEN CR	L Vancouver	Clark	COLVIN CR	Lewis R	Cowlitz
CHICO CR	Dyes Inlet	Kitsap	COMMONWEALTH CR	Snoqualmie R	King
CHILATCH CR	Lewis R	Clark	COMPANY CR	Stehekin R	Chelan
CHILDS CR	Skagit R	Skagit	CONNAWAC CR	Crab Cr	Grant
CHILLIWACK R	Chilliwack L	Whatcom	CONNELLY CR	Tilton R	Lewis
CHILLIWISTCR	Okanogan R	Okanogan	CONSTANCE CR	Dosewalllps R	Jefferson
CHIMACUM CR	Port Townsend B	Jefferson	COOK CR	Ef Satsop R	Grays Harbor
CHIMACUM CR	Wf Chimacum Cr	Jefferson	COOK CR	Quinault R	Grays Harbor
CHINA CR	Chehalis R	Lewis	COOK CR	Cherry Cr	Kittltas
CHIWAUKUM CR	Wenatchee R	Chelan	COOK CR	Cook's Lake	Spokane
CHIWAWA R	Wenatchee R	Chelan	COOL CR	Bogachiel R	Jefferson
CHOPAKA CR	Sinlahekin Cr	Okanogan	COOL CR	Yukon Harbor	Kitsap
CHOW CHOW CR	Quinault R	Grays Harbor	COON CR	Columbia R	Paclfic
CHRISTMAS CR	Queets R	Jefferson	COON CR	Pilchuck R	Snohomlsh
CHRISTMAS CR	Snoqualmie R	King	COON LAKE CR	Stehekin R	Chelan
CHUCKALOON CR	Chehalis R	Grays Harbor	COONEY CR	Lewis R	Cowlltz
CHUCKANUT CR	Chuckanut Bay	Whatcom	COOPER R	Cle Elum R	Kittitas
CHUMSTICK CR	Wenatchee R	Chelan	COPALIS R	Pacific Ocean	Grays Harbor
CHURCH CR	Skokomish R	Mason	COPPEI CR	Touchet R	Walla Walla
CINABAR CR	Tilton R	Lewis	COPPER CR	Wf Granite Cr	Ferry
CINDY CR	Hoh R	Jefferson	COPPER CR	Wf Granite Cr	Ferry
CIRCLE CR	Suiattle R	Snohomish	COPPER CR	Nisqually	Pierce
CISPUS R	Cowlltz R	Lewis/Skamania	COPPER CR	San Poil R	Ferry
CLALLAM R	Clallam Bay	Clallam	COPPER CR	Methow R	Okanogan
CLANCY CR	Toutle R	Cowlitz	COPPER CR	Lewis R	Lewis
CLARK CR	Chumstlck Cr	Chelan	CORNSTALK CR	Stranger Cr	Ferry
CLARK CR	Hood Canal	Mason	CORRAL CR	Klickltat R	Yakima
CLARK CR	Puyallup R	Pierce	CORRAL CR	Tieton R	Yakima
CLEAR CR	Chiwawa R	Chelan	CORTRIGHT CR	Cowlitz R	Lewis
CLEAR CR	Dyes Inlet	Kitsap	CORUS (WAUGH) CR	Columbia R	Stevens
CLEAR CR	Carbon R	Pierce	COSNER (DUNN) CR	Colville R	Stevens
CLEAR CR	Puyallup R	Pierce	COTTONWOOD CR	Kettle R	Ferry
CLEAR CR	Muddy R	Skamania	COTTONWOOD CR	L Deer Cr	Spokane
CLEARBROOK CR	Johnson Cr	Whatcom	COTTONWOOD CR	Columbia R	Stevens
CLEAR FORK	Cowlitz R	Lewis	COTTONWOOD CR	Colville R	Stevens
CLEARWATER CR	Muddy R	Skamania	COTTONWOOD CR	Yellowhawk Cr	Walla Walla
CLEARWATER CR	L Muddy Cr	Yakima	COUGAR CR	Hoh R	Jefferson
CLEARWATER R	Queets R	Jefferson	COUGAR CR	Clearwater R	Jefferson
CLE ELUM R	Yakima R	Kittitas	COUGAR CR	Cowlitz R	Lewis
CLIFF CR	Duckabush R	Jefferson	COUGAR CR	Stillaquamish R	Snohomish
CLOQUALLUM CR	Chehalis R	Grays Harb/Mason	COUGAR CR	Klickltat R	Yakima
CLOUGH CR	Snoqualmie R	King	COUGAR CR	Washougal R	Clark
CLOVER CR	Lake Steilacoom	Pierce	COUGAR CR	Lewis R	Cowlitz
CLOVER CR	Puyallup R	Pierce	COUGAR CR	Big Muddy R	Yakima
CLUGSTON CR	Mill Cr	Stevens	COULEE CR	Deep Cr	Spokane
COAL (DRAYS) CR	Columbia R	Cowlitz	COULTER CR	Nason Cr	Chelan
COAL CR	Lake Washlngton	King	COULTER CR	Case Inlet	Mason
COAL (HYAK) CR	Lake Keechelus	Kittitas	COUNTY LINE CR	Totten Inlet	Mason
COAL CR	Crab Cr	Lincoln	COURTNEY CR	Union R	Mason

STREAM	TRIBUTARY TO	COUNTY
COURTRIGHT CR	Cowlitz R	Lewis
COUSE CR	Snake R	Asotin
COVIL CR	Juan de Fuca Str	Clallam
COVINGTON CR	Big Soos Cr	King
COW CR	Palouse R	Adams
COW CR	Methow R	Okanogan
COW CR	Snake R	Whitman
COWEMAN R	Cowlitz R	Cowlitz
COWICHE CR	Naches R	Yakima
COWLITZ R	Columbia R	Lewis
CRAB CR	Columbia R	Grant/Lincoln
CRAB CR	Lewis R	Skamania
CRANBERRY CR	Oakland Bay	Mason
CRATER CR	Methow R	Okanogan
CRATER CR	Puyallup R	Pierce
CRAWFORD CR	Rainey Cr	Lewis
CRAWFORD CR	Snoqualmie R	King
CRAWFORD CR	L Muddy Cr	Yakima
CRESCENT CR	Cispus R	Skamania
CROSS CR	Lake Crescent	Clallam
CROWN CR	Columbia R	Stevens
CRUM CANYON CR	Entiat R	Chelan
CRUISER CR	Nemah R	Pacific
CRYSTAL CR	Dyes Inlet	Kitsap
CRYSTAL CR	White R	King
CRYSTAL CR	Sammamish R	King
CUB CR	Hoko R	Clallam
CUB CR	Methow R	Okanogan
CUCK CR	Elochoman R	Wahkiakum
CUITIN CR	Icicle R	Chelan
CULTUS CR	Bogachiel R	Clallam
CULVERT CR	Okanogan R	Okanogan
CUMBERLAND CR	Toroda Cr	Okanogan
CUNNINGHAM CR	Ef Lewis R	Clark
CUNNINGHAM CR	Klickitat R	Yakima
CUPPLES CR	Skagit R	Skagit
CURLEW CR	Kettle R	Ferry
CURLEY CR	Puget Sound	Kitsap
CURRANT CR	Deep Cr	Stevens
CUSHMAN LK SPILLWAY	Nf Skokomish R	Mason
CUSICK CR	Clark Fork	Pend Oreille
CUSSED HOLLOW CR	Lewis R	Skamania
CUTTHROAT CR	Juan de Fuca Str.	Clallam
CYCLONE CR	White R	King

D

STREAM	TRIBUTARY TO	COUNTY
DAIRY CR	Klickitat R	Yakima
DAKOTA CR		Whatcom
DALBY CR	Hood Canal	Mason
DALE CR	Sumas R	Whatcom
DALE CR	Sumas R	Whatcom
DALLES CR	White R	Pierce
DALTON CR	Cowlitz R	Lewis
DAM CR	Cowlitz R	Lewis
DAMON CR	Humptulips R	Grays Harbor
DAN CR	Sauk R	Skagit
DANDY CR	Yakima R	Yakima
DARK CANYON CR	Snake R	Asotin
DARNS CR	Methow R	Okanogan
DARTFORD(SHEEP)CR	L Spokane R	Spokane
DAVIS CR	Cle Elum Lake	Kittitas
DAVIS CR	Cowlitz R	Lewis
DAVIS CR	Methow R	Okanogan
DAVIS CR	Pend Oreille R	Pend Oreille
DAVIS CR	Chehalis R	Grays Harbor
DAVIS CR	Hoquiam R	Grays Harbor
DAVIS CR	Willapa R	Pacific
DAVIS CR	Naselle R	Pacific
DAVIS CR	Green R	King
DAY CR	Kettle R	Ferry
DAY CR	Bogachiel R	Clallam
DAY CR	Skagit R	Skagit
DAWDY CR	Lake Quinault	Grays Harbor
DEAD CANYON CR	Klickitat R	Klickitat
DEADMAN(SHERWOOD) CR	Kettle R	Ferry

STREAM	TRIBUTARY TO	COUNTY
DEADMAN CR	Snake R	Garfield
DEADMAN CR L	Spokane R	Spokane
DECEPTION CR	Tye R	King
DECEPTION CR	Clearwater R	Jefferson
DECKER CR	Satsop R	Grays Harbor
DEEGANS CR	Sf Goldsborough Cr	Mason
DEEP CR	Chiwawa R	Chelan
DEEP CR	Juan de Fuca Str	Clallam
DEEP CR	Spokane R	Spokane
DEEP CR	Columbia R	Stevens
DEEP CR	Kettle R	Stevens
DEEP CR	Humptulips R	Grays Harbor
DEEP CR	Raging R	King
DEEP CR	Chehalis R	Lewis
DEEP CR	White R	Pierce
DEEP R	Columbia R	Wahkiakum
DEER (CARRETT) CR	Curlew Lake	Ferry
DEER CR	Oakland Bay	Mason
DEER CR	Davis Lake	Pend Oreille
DEER CR	Nf Stillaguamish R	Snohomish
DEER CR	Spokane R	Spokane
DEER CR	Colville R	Stevens
DEER TRAIL FORK	Alder Cr	Stevens
DEER CR	Kettle R	Ferry
DEER CR	Cowlitz R	Lewis
DEER CR	Chehalis R	Lewis
DEER CR	Nisqually R	Lewis
DEER CR	Cowlitz R	Pierce
DEER CR	Puyallup R	Pierce
DEER CR	Washougal R	Skamania
DEER CR	Lewis R	Skamania
DEER CR	Skykomish R	Snohomish
DEER CR	Nooksack R	Whatcom
DEER CR	Klickitat R	Yakima
DELABARE CR	Eluha R	Clallam
DELAMETER CR	Cowlitz R	Cowlitz
DELEZENE CR	Chehalis R	Grays Harbor
DELL CR	Chehalis R	Lewis
DELL CR	Naselle R	Pacific
DEMPSEY CR	Black R	Thurston
DENNY CR	Snoqualmie R	King
DERBY CR	Wenatchee R	Chelan
DESCHUTES R	Puget Sound	Thurston
DES MOINES CR	Green R	King
DEVIL'S CANYON CR	Klickitat R	Klickitat
DEVIL'S CANYON CR	Naches R	Yakima
DEVIL'S DREAM CR	Nisqually R	Pierce
DEVORE CR	Stehekin R	Chelan
DEVILS CR	Naches R	Yakima
DEVILS CR	Skagit R	Whatcom
DEWATTO R	Hood Canal	Mason
DEWEY CR	Chinook R	Pierce
DIAMOND CR	Pend Oreille R	Pend Oreille
DIAMOND CR	Sol Duc R	Clallam
DIAMOND FORK	Klickitat R	Yakima
DIAMOND OUTLET	Lake Sacheen	Pend Oreille
DICK CR	Carbon R	Pierce
DICK CR	Pilchuck R	Snohomish
DICKERSON CR	Chico Cr	Kitsap
DICKEY R	Pacific Ocean	Clallam
DILLENBAUGH CR	Chehalis R	Lewis
DINGFORD CR	Snoqualmie R	King
DIOBSUD CR	Skagit R	Skagit
DISAPPOINTMENT CR	Toutle R	Cowlitz
DISMAL CR	Hoh R	Jefferson
DIXON CR	Cowlitz R	Lewis
DOAKS CR	Nooksack R	Whatcom
DOAN CR	Mill Cr	WallaWalla
DOBSONS CR	Nf Arkansas Cr	Cowlitz
DODGE CR	Chehalis R	Thurston
DOG CR	Columbia R	Skamania
DO-KA-DISHT CR	Skokomish R	Mason
DOMKE CR	Lake Chelan	Chelan
DONOVAN CR	Colville R	Stevens
DONOVAN CR	Quilcene R	Jefferson
DOSEWALLIPS R	Hood Canal	Jefferson

STREAM	TRIBUTARY TO	COUNTY
DOUBLE DITCH CR	Fishtrap Cr	Whatcom
DOUGAN CR	Washougal R	Skamania
DOUGLAS CR	Columbia R	Douglas
DOWCR	Nf Skokomish R	Mason
DOWANS CR	Bogachiel R	Jefferson
DOWNOY CR	Dungeness R	Clallam
DOWNS CR	Cedar R	King
DOYLE CR	Union R	Mason
DRAGOON CR	L Spokane R	Spokane
DRAYS (COAL) CR	Columbia R	Cowlitz
DRIFT CR	Lewis R	Skamania
DROP CR	Skookumchuck	Lewis
DRUMHELLER SPRINGS	Crab Cr	Grant
DRY CR	Chumstick Cr	Chelan
DRYCR	Juan de Fuca Str	Clallam
DRY CR	San Poil R	Ferry
DRY CR	CleElum R	Kittitas
DRY CR	L Spokane R	Spokane
DRY CR	Chamokano Cr	Stevens
DRY CR	Walla Walla R	Walla Walla
DRY CR	Naches R	Yakima
DRY CR	Satus Cr	Yakima
DRY CR	Sol Duc R	Clallam
DRY CR	Soap L	Grant
DRY CR	Hoh R	Jefferson
DRY CR	Snoqualmie R	King
DRY CANYON CR	Klickitat R	Klickitat
DRYWASH CR	Nisqually R	Pierce
DUBUQUE CR	Pilchuck R	Snohomish
DUCK CR	Crab C	Lincoln
DUCKABUSH R	Hood Canal	Jefferson
DUFFEY CR	Skykomish R	Snohomish
DUNCAN CR	Columbia R	Skamania
DUNGENESS R	Juan de Fuca Str	Clallam
DUNN (COSNER) CR	Colville R	Stevens
DURDLE CR	Big Quilcene R	Jefferson
DURHAM CR	Big R	Clallam
DURHAM CR	Duwamish R	King
DUWAMISH R	Elliott Bay	king
DYER CR	Lewis R	Clark

E

STREAM	TRIBUTARY TO	COUNTY
EAGLE CR	Skykomish R	Snohomish
EAGLE CR	Twisp R	Chelan
EAGLE CR	Chumstick Cr	Chelan
EAGLE CR	Lake Crescent	Clallam
EAGLE CR	Hood Canal	Mason
EARLY WINTERS CR	WfMethowR	Okanogan
EAST CR	Nisqually R	Lewis
EAST BRIDGE CR	Colville R	Stevens
EAST CEDAR CR	Cedar Cr	Stevens
EAST CHEWELAH CR	Colville R	Stevens
EAST DARTFORD CR	L Spokane R	Spokane
EAST DEER CR	Kettle R	Ferry
EAST DEER CR	Deer Cr	Pend Oreille
EAST MUD CR	Mud Cr	WallaWalla
EAST TORBEL CR	Colville R	Stevens
EAST TWIN R	Juan de Fuca Str	Clallam
EATON CR	St Clair Lake	Thurston
EATON CR	Chehalis R	Grays Harbor
EATON CR	Bogachiel R	Clallam
EDFRO CR	Nooksack R	Whatcom
EDMONDS CR	Puget Sound	Snohomish
EDWARDS CR	Covill Cr	Clallam
EDWARDS CR	San Poil R	Okanogan
EIGHT MILE CR	Columbia R	Klickitat
EIGHT MILE CR	WhiteSalmon R	Klickitat
EIGHT MILE CR	Methow R	Okanogan
EIGHT MILE CR	LQuilcene R	Clallam
EIPPER CR	Deadman Cr	Ferry
ELBOW CR	Quilcene R	Jefferson
ELDER CR	Riddle Cr	Stevens
ELHI CR	Puyallup R	Pierce
ELK (GOLDBAR) CR	Kalama R	Cowlitz
ELK CR	Chehalis R	Lewis

STREAM	TRIBUTARY TO	COUNTY
ELK CR	Calawah R	Clallam
ELK CR	Hoh R	Jefferson
ELK CR	Clearwater	Jefferson
ELK CR	Skokomish R	Mason
ELK CR	Willapa R	Pacific
ELK CR	Sultan R	Snohomish
ELKINS CR	Breckenridge Cr	Whatcom
ELLON CR	Nason Cr	Chelan
ELOCHOMAN R	Columbia R	Wahkiakum
ELWELL CR	Skykomish R	Snohomish
ELWHA R	Juan de Fuca Str	Clallam
EMANUEL CR	Kettle R	Ferry
EMPIRE CR	Curlew Cr	Ferry
EMPIRE CR	San Poil R	Ferry
ENIS CR	Port Angeles Harbor	Clallam
ENNIS CR	Samish R	Whatcom
ENTIAT R	Columbia R	Chelan
ENTIAT R, Nf	Entiat R	Chelan
ENTIAT R Sf	Entiat R	Chelan
EPPERSON CR	Dungeness R	Clallam
ESSENCY CR	Snoqualmie R	King
ETHOL CR	Myers Cr	Okanogan
EUREKA CR	Sol Duc R	Clallam
EUREKA CR	Okanogan R	Okanogan
EVANS CR	Sammamish R	King
EVANS CR	Carbon R	Pierce
EVARTS CR	Pend Oreille R	Pend Oreille
EVERETT CR	Baker R	Skagit

F

STREAM	TRIBUTARY TO	COUNTY
FAIRCHILD CR	Big Cr	Grays Harbor
FAIRCHILD CR	Willapa R	Pacific
FAIRHOLM CR	Lake Crescent	Clallam
FALES CR	Snohomish R	Snohomish
FALL (BURTON) CR	Cowlitz R	Lewis
FALLERT CR	Kalama R	Cowlitz
FALLS CR	Lake Chelan	Chelan
FALLS CR	Lake Quinault	GraysHarbor
FALLS CR	Rainey Cr	Lewis
FALLS CR	Chewack Cr	Okanogan
FALLS CR	Armstrong Cr	Pacific
FALLS CR	Wind R	Skamania
FALLS CR	Columbia R	Stevens
FALLS CR	Cloquallum C	Grays Harbor
FALLS CR	Hoh R	Jefferson
CALLS CR	Methow R	Okanogan
FALLS CR	Willapa R	Pacific
FALLS CR	Carbon R	Pierce
FALLS CR	Sauk R	Snohomish
FALLS CR	Grays R	Wahkiakum
FALLS CR	Lewis R	Skamania
FAN LAKE OUTLET	West Branch Cr	PendOreille
FARRIER CR	Cowlitz R	Lewis
FENCE CR	Pend Oreille R	Pend Oreille
FENNEL CR	Puyallup R	Pierce
FERN CR	Hood Canal	Kitsap
FIELD CR	Juan de Fuca Str	Clallam
FIFES CR	Bumping R	Yakima
FIFTEEN MILE CR	Columbia R	Stevens
FIN CR	Lewis R	Skamania
FINCH CR	Hood Canal	Mason
FINLAND CR	Puget Sound	Kitsap
FIR BROOK CR	Wynoochee R	Grays Harbor
FIRST CR	Lake Chelan	Chelan
FIRST CR	Chumstick Cr	Chelan
FIRST CR	Swauk Cr	Kittitas
FIRST (MASON) CR	Nf Teanaway R	Kittitas
FISH CR	Lake Chelan	Chelan
FISH CR	Cedar R	King
FISH LAKE OUTLET	Wenatchee R	Chelan
FISH LAKE STREAM	Wf Klickitat R	Yakima
FISHTRAP CR	Nooksack R	Whatcom
FISK CR	Puyallup R	Pierce
FIVE MILE CR	L Klickitat R	Klickitat
FIVE MILE CR	L Sheep Cr	Stevens

STREAM	TRIBUTARY TO	COUNTY
FLAT CR	Columbia R	Stevens
FLAT CR	Stehekin R	Chelan
FLETT CR	Chambers Cr	Pierce
FLIESS CR	Willapa Bay	Pacific
FLUME CR	Lake R	Clark
FLY CR	Lewis R	Clark
FOGGY DEW CR	Gold Cr	Okanogan
FORBES CR	Lake Washington	King
FORD CR	Calawha R	Clallam
FOREST CR	Kettle R	Ferry
FOREST CR	Chehalis R	Grays Harbor
FORKS CR	Willapa R	Pacific
FORKS CR	White R	Pierce
FORKS PRAIRIE CR	Willapa R	Pacific
FORTSON CR	Stillaguamish R	Snohomish
FORTUNE CR	Cle Elum R	Kittitas
FORTY MILE CR	San Poil R	Ferry
FOSS R	Tye R	King
FOSS R. Ef	Ross R	King
FOSS R, Wf	Foss R	King
FOSSIL CR	Grays R	Wahkiakum
FOSSIL CR	Hoh R	Jefferson
FOUNTAIN LAKE OUTLET	Nooksack R	Whatcom
FOURTH OF JULY CR	Kettle R	Ferry
FOURTH PLAIN CR	LaCamas Cr	Clark
FOX CR	Entiat R	Chelan
FOX CR	Hoh R	Clallam
FRASIER CR	Outlet Cr	Klickitat
FRAZER CR	Beaver Cr	Okanogan
FRAZIER(TUMWATER) CR	Port Angeles Harb	Clallam
FRAZIER CR	Klickitat R	Klickitat
FREDRICKSONS CR	Willapa Bay	Pacific
FRENCH CR	Methow R	Okanogan
FRENCH CR	Snohomish R	Snohomish
FRENCH CR	Stillaguamish R	Snohomish
FRENCH CABIN CR	Cle Elum R	Kittitas
FREUND CR	Chumstick Cr	Chelan
FRIDAY CR	Samish R	Skagit
FROSTY CR	Wf San Poil R	Okanogan
FRY CR	Grays H arbor	Grays H arbor
FULLER CR	Chehalis R	Grays Harbor
FURLOUGH CR	Humptulips R	Grays Harbor
FULTON CR	Hood Canal	Jefferson

G

GABOR CR	Kalama R	Cowlitz
GADDIS CR	Chehalis R	Grays Harbor
GALE CR	Green R	King
GALE CR	Yakima R	Kittitas
GALE (WILKESON) CR	S Prairie R	Pierce
GALENA CR	Nooksack R	Whatcom
GALLOP CR	Nooksack R	Whatcom
GALLUP CR	Tilton R	Lewis
GALTON CR	Quinault R	Grays Harbor
GAMAGE CR	Willapa R	Pacific
GAP CR	L Pend Oreille R	Stevens
GARDENA CR	Walla Walla R	Walla Walla
GARNETTS CR	Pend Oreille R	Pend Oreille
GARRARD CR	Chehalis R	Grays Harbor
GARRISON CR	Walla Walla R	Walla Walla
GARRISON CR	Green R	King
GATE CR	Chiwawa R	Chelan
GATTON CR	Lake Quinault	Grays Harbor
GEE CR	Columbia R	Clark
GEE CR	Skagit R	Skagit
GEISLER CR	Wynoochee R	Grays Harbor
GEORGE CR	Greenwater R	Pierce
GEORGE CR	Chehalis R	Lewis
GEORGE CR	Asotin Cr	Asotin
GERMANY CR	Columbia R	Cowlitz
GORMOND SPRINGS	Cowlitz R	Cowlitz
GIBBONS CR	Columbia R	Skamania
GIBSON CR	Chehalis R	Grays Harbor
GIDDINGS CR	Skykomish R	Snohomish
GILBERT CR	Sultan R	Snohomish

STREAM	TRIBUTARY TO	COUNTY
GILLAM CR	Duamish R	King
GILLAN CR	Green R	King
GILLETTE CR	Mill Cr	Stevens
GILLIGAN CR	Skagit R	Skagit
GILMER CR	White Salmon R	Klickitat
GIVEOUT CR	Toroda Cr	Okanogan
GLACIER CR	Nooksack R	Whatcom
GLACIER CR	Skagit R	Whatcom
GLADE CR	Columbia R	Yakima
GOAT CR	Wf Methow R	Okanogan
GOAT CR	Toutle R	Cowlitz
GOBLE CR	Coweman R	Cowlitz
GODDARD SPRINGS	White Salmon R	Skamania
GODKIN CR	Elwha R	Clallam
GODS CR	Columbia R	Stevens
GOLD CR	Lake Chelan	Chelan
GOLD (SCATTER) CR	San Poil R	Ferry
GOLD CR	Wf San Poil R	Ferry
GOLD CR	Lake Keechelus	Kittitas
GOLD CR	Methow R	Okanogan
GOLD CR	Myers Cr	Okanogan
GOLD CR	ColvilleR	Stevens
GOLD CR	Naches R	Yakima
GOLDBAR CR	Kalama R	Cowlitz
GOLDEN HARVEST CR	San Poil R	Ferry
GOLDSBOROUGH CR	Oakland Bay	Mason
GOODELL CR	Skagit R	Whatcom
GOODMAN CR	Pacific Ocean	Jefferson
GOODMAN CR	Sauk R	Snohomish
GOOSE CR	Chiwawa R	Chelan
GOOSE CR	Wilson Cr	Lincoln
GORST CR	Sinclairlnlet	Kitsap
GOSNOLLS CR	Lake Isabella	Mason
GOTCHEN CR	White Salmon R	Klickitat
GRAHAM CR	Chehalis R	Grays Harbor
GRANDE RONDE R	Snake R	Asotin
GRANDY CR	Skagit R	Skagit
GRANITE CR	San Poil R	Ferry/Okanogan
GRANITE FALLS CR	Lake Chelan	Chelan
GRAPHITE CR	Toroda Cr	Ferry
GRANITE CR	Snoqualmie R	King
GRANITE CR	Yakima R	Kittitas
GRAVES CR	Hood Canal	Mason
GRAYS R	ColumbiaR	Wahkiakum
GRAYS R, Wf	Grays R	Wahkiakum
GRAYWOLF R	Dungeness R	Clallam
GREEN CANYON CR	Reeser Cr	Kittitas
GREEN LAKE OUTLET	Ten Mile Cr	Whatcom
GREEN R	Toutle R	Cowlitz
GREEN R	Duwamish R	King
GREENHORN CR	Cispus R	Lewis
GREENLEAF CR	Columbia R	Skamania
GREENWATER R	White R	King
GRIFF CR	Elwha R	Clallam
GRIFFIN CR	Snoqualmie R	King
GROUSE CR	Chiwawa R	Chelan
GROUSE CR	Jump Off Joe Lake	Stevens
GULCH CR	George Cr	Asotin
GUNDERSON CR	Sol Duc R	Clallam
GUNNAR CR	Lewis R	Skamania

H

HACKETT CR	Coal Cr	Cowlitz
HABER CR	Cowlitz R	Lewis
HAGUS CR	Skokomish R	Mason
HALFMOON CR	Willapa R	Pacific
HALFWAY CR	Chehalis R	Lewis
HALL CR	Snoqualmie R	King
HALL CR	Cowlitz R	Lewis
HALL CR	Pend Oreille R	Pend Oreille
HALL CR	Cedar Cr	Clark
HALL CR	Columbia R	Ferry
HALTERMAN CR	Stillaguamish R	Snohomish
HAMILTON CR	Columbia R	Skamania
HAMILTON GULCH CR	Wishkah R	Grays Harbor

STREAM	TRIBUTARY TO	COUNTY
HAMMA HAMMA R	Hood Canal	Mason
HANAFORD CR	Skookumchuck R	Lewis
HANCOCK CR	Snoqualmie R	King
HANGMAN (LATAH) CR	Spokane R	Spokane/Whitman
HANSEL CR	Peshastin Cr	Chelan
HANSEN CR	Skagit R	Skagit
HANSON CR	Humptulips R	Grays Harbor
HANSON CR	Okanogan R	Okanogan
HANSON CR	Snoqualmie R	Snohomish
HAPPY HOLLOW CR	Hood Canal	Mason
HARDING SPRINGS	American R	Yakima
HARDISON CR	Colville R	Stevens
HARDY CR	Columbia R	Skamania
HARRIS CR	Snoqualmie R	King
HART CR	Nf Tieton R	Yakima
HART LAKE INLET	Hart Lake	Pierce
HART LAKE OUTLET	Nisqually R	Pierce
HARTZOIL CR	Queets R	Jefferson
HARVEY CR	Stillaguamish R	Snohomish
HARVEY CR	Columbia R	Stevens
HATCHERY CR	Kalama R	Cowlitz
HATCHERY CR	Duckabush R	Jefferson
HATCHERY CR	Humptulips R	Grays Harbor
HATHAWAY CR	McCalla Cr	GraysHarbor
HAWK CR	Columbia R	Lincoln
HAYDEN CR	Puyallup R	Pierce
HAYS CR	Lewis R	Clark
HAYS R	Elwha R	Jefferson
HAZARD CR	L Chelan	Chelan
HAZEL CR	Union R	Mason
HAZEL DELL CR	Cowlitz R	Cowlitz
HAZARD CR	White R	Pierce
HEE HEE CR	Queets R	Jefferson
HEITMAN CR	Ef Lewis R	Clark
HELLER (RIDDLE) CR	Colville R	Stevens
HELLROARING CR	Big Muddy R	Yakima
HENDERSON CR	Bonaparte Cr	Okanogan
HENRY CR	Kettle R	Ferry
HERRON CR	Curlew Lake	Ferry
HIERSCH CR	West Passage	King
HIGGENS CR	NaselleR	Pacific
HIGHLAND CR	Tilton R	Lewis
HIGLEY CR	Lake Quinault	Grays Harbor
HILL CR	Hood Canal	Mason
HILL CR	Green R	King
HILLEYS SPRINGS	Puyallup R	Pierce
HIMOS(WOODLAND) CR	South Bay	Thurston
HINTON CR	Johnson Cr	Whatcom
HODGSON (LIME) CR	Kettle R	Ferry
HOFFSTADT CR	Toutle R	Cowlitz
HOGARTY CR	Skykomish R	Snohomish
HOH R	Pacific Ocean	Jefferson
HOH R, Sf	Hoh R	Jefferson
HOKO R	Juan de Fuca Str	Clallam
HOLMES CR	Outlet Cr	Klickitat
HOLYOKE CR	Hood Canal	Mason
HOPKINS(PURCELL) CR	Cowlitz R	Lewis
HOQUIAM R	Grays Harbor	Grays Harbor
HOQUIAM R, Wf	Hoquiam R	Grays Harbor
HORN CR	Nisqually R	Pierce
HORSE CR	Sammamish R	King
HOUSE CR	Tieton R	Yakima
HOWARD CR	Puget Sound	Mason
HOWSON CR	CleElum R	Kittitas
HOZOMEEN CR	Ross L	Whatcom
HUCKLEBERRY CR	Colville R	Stevens
HUDSON CR	Yakima R	Kittitas
HUMPTULIPS R	Grays Harbor	Grays Harbor
HUMPTULIPS R, Ef	Humptulips R	Grays Harbor
HUMPTULIPS R, Wf	Humptulips R	Grays Harbor
HUNTERS CR	Columbia R	Stevens
HURDS (MILL) CR	Cowlitz R	Lewis
HURST CR	Clearwater R	Jefferson
HUTCHINSON CR	Sf Nooksack R	Whatcom
HYAK CR	Bogachiel R	Clallam
HYAK (COAL) CR	Lake Keechelus	Kittitas

STREAM	TRIBUTARY TO	COUNTY
HYLEBOS CR	Puget Sound	King/Pierce

I

STREAM	TRIBUTARY TO	COUNTY
ICE CR	Sekiu R	Clallam
ICICLE CR	Wenatchee R	Chelan
ICY CR	Green R	King
IGNAR CR	Quinault R	Jefferson
ILLABOT CR	Skagit R	Skagit
IMBODEN CR	Cowlitz R	Cowlitz
INDEPENDENCE CR	Chehalis R	Lewis
I I . CR	Willapa Bay	Pacific
INDIAN CR	Grays Harbor	Grays Harbor
INDIAN CR	Nf Teanaway R	Kittitas
INDIAN (Nasika) CR	Cowlitz R	Lewis
INDIAN CR	Hawk Cr	Lincoln
INDIAN CR	Pend Oreille R	Pend Oreille
INDIAN CR	Nf Tieton R	Yakima
I N DIAN CR	Kalama R	Cowl itz
INDIAN CR	Elwha R	Clallam
INDIAN DAN CANYON CR	Columbia R	Okanogan
INGALLS CR	Peshastin Cr	Chelan
INNIS CR	Samish R	Whatcom
IOLA CR	Stillaguamish R	Snohomish
IONE CR	Pend Oreille R	Pend Oreille
IPSUT CR	Carbon R	Pierce
IRELY CR	Quinault R	Jefferson
IRISH CR	Carbon R	Pierce
IRON CR	Chehalis R	Grays Harbor
IRON CR	Cispus R	Lewis
IRON CR	San Poil R	Ferry
ISSAQUAH CR	Lake Sammamish	King
ISSAQUAH CR. Ef	Issaquah Cr	King
ITALIAN CR	Kalama R	Cowlitz
ITWEAT CR	Queets R	Jefferson

J

STREAM	TRIBUTARY TO	COUNTY
JACK CR	Icicle R	Chelan
JACK CR	San Poil R	Ferry
JACK CR	If Teanaway	Kittitas
JACKEL CR	Colville R	Stevens
JACKMAN CR	Skagit R	Skagit
JACKSON CR	Dabop Bay	Jefferson
JACKSON CR	Toutle R	Cowlitz
JASTAD CR	Newaukum R	Lewis
JEFFERSON CR	Hamma Hamma R	Mason
JENKINS CR	Big Soos Cr	King
JENNIE CR	L Boulder Cr	Ferry
JENNINGS CR	Columbia R	Stevens
JENNY CR	Ef Lewis R	Clank
JEWETT CR	Columbia R	Klickitat
JIM CR	Juan de Fuca Str	Clallam
JIM CR	Cedar Cr	Pend Oreille
JIM CR	Sf Stillaguamish R	Snohomish
JIMMY COME LATELY CR	Sequim Bay	Clallam
JOE CR	Pacific Ocean	GraysHarbor
JOHN CR	Cedar Cr	Clark
JOHNS CR	Oakland Bay	Mason
JOHNS R	Grays Harbor	Grays Harbor
JOHNSON CR	Navarre Coulee	Chelan
JOHNSON CR	Sequim Bay	Clallam
JOHNSON CR	Lewis R	Cowlitz
JOHNSON CR	Hood Canal	Kitsap
JOHNSON CR	Cowlitz R	Lewis
JOHNSON CR	Okanogan R	Okanogan
JOHNSON CR	Naselle R	Pacific
JOHNSON CR	Sumas R	Whatcom
JOHN TOM CR	San Poil R	Ferry
JONES CR	L Washougal R	Clark
JONES CR	Cowlitz R	Lewis
JONES CR	L Washington	King
JONES CR	Chehalis R	Lewis
JONES CR	Cedar R	King
JONES CR	Nooksack R	Whatcom
JONES CR	Skagit R	Skagit

STREAM	TRIBUTARY TO	COUNTY
JORDAN CR	Skagit R	Skagit
JORDAN CR	Toutle R	Cowlitz
JORDAN CR	Stillaguamish R	Snohomish
JORSTED CR	Hood Canal	Mason
JUDD CR	Puget Sound	King
JULY CR	Lake Quinault	Grays Harbor
JUMP OFF JOE CR	Colville R	Stevens

K

STREAM	TRIBUTARY TO	COUNTY
"K" CR	Skykomish R	Snohomish
KACHESS R	Yakima R	Kittitas
KAHKWA CR	Bogachiel R	Clallam
KALALOCH CR	Pacific Ocean	Jefferson
KALAMA R	Columbia R	Cowlitz
KALISPEL CR	Priest Lake	Pend Oreille
KAMILCHE CR	Skookum Cr	Mason
KAMMERAD CR	Carbon R	Pierce
KANAKA CR	Columbia R	Skamania
KAPOWSIN CR	Puyallup R	Pierce
KARJALA CR	Chehalis R	Grays Harbor
KASTBERG CR	Colville R	Stevens
KATHRYN CR	Coweeman R	Cowlitz
KATULA CR	Chehalis R	Lewis
KEARNEY CR	Black R	Thurston
KENDALL CR	Nooksack R	Whatcom
KENNEDY CR	Totten Inlet	Mason/Thurston
KENT CR	Pend Oreille R	Pend Oreille
KERRY CR	Kettle R	Ferry
KETTLE R	Columbia R	Ferry
KINICK (DRY) CR	White R	Pierce
KIONA (MASE) CR	Cowlitz R	Lewis
KITSAP LAKE OUTLET	Chico Cr	Kitsap
KLAUS CR	Snoqualmie R	King
KLICKITAT R	Cowlitz R	Lewis
KLICKITAT R	Columbia R	Klickitat/Yakima
KLICKITAT R, Wf	Klickitat R	Yakima
KLOOCHMAN CR	Clearwater R	Jefferson
KLOSHE CR	Bogachiel R	Clallam
KNOCKEY CR	Mf Hoquiam R	Grays Harbor
KNOWLTON CR	Kalama R	Cowlitz
KOCH CR	Dyes Inlet	Kitsap

L

STREAM	TRIBUTARY TO	COUNTY
LABOR GULCH CR	Okanogan R	Okanogan
LaCAMAS CR	Cowlitz R	Lewis
LaCAMAS CR	Muck Cr	Pierce
LaCAMAS CR	Columbia R	Clark
LaCENTER CR	Ef Lewis R	Clark
LACKEY CR	Carrinlet	Pierce
LaCLORE CR	Pend Oreille R	Pend Oreille
LADDER CR	Skagit R	Whatcom
LaFLEUR CR	ColumbiaR	Ferry
LAKE CR	Entiat R	Chelan
LAKE CR	Wenatchee R	Chelan
LAKE CR	Soleduck R	Clallam
LAKE CR	Kettle R	Ferry
LAKE CR	Cowlitz R	Lewis
LAKE (MARSHALL) CR	Latah Cr	Spokane
LAKE CR	Columbia R	Stevens
LAKE ARMSTRONG OUTLET	Hood Canal	Mason
LAKESIDE CR	Lake Quinault	Grays Harbor
LAKEWOOD CR	Columbia R	Skamania
LAMB CR	Hoko R	Clallam
LAMBERT CR	Curlew Cr	Ferry
LANDERS CR	Cowlitz R	Lewis
LANDON CR	Kalama Cr	Cowlitz
LANE CR	Tahuya R	Mason
LANE CR	Naselle R	Pacific
LANG CR	Willapa R	Grays Harbor
LANGLOIS CR	Tolt R	King
LANKNER CR	Chehalis R	Grays Harbor
LAPAEL CR	Lake Crescent	Clallam
LAPHAM CR	L White Salmon R	Skamania

STREAM	TRIBUTARY TO	COUNTY
LARSON CR	Wynoochee R	Grays Harbor
LATAH (HANGMAN) CR	Spokane R	Spokane/Whitman
LATAH CR	Nf Latah Cr	Whitman
LATTIN CR	Colville R	Stevens
LAUBER GULCH SPRING	Okanogan R	Okanogan
LAVA CR	ClearF, Cowlitz R	Lewis
LAVA CR	L White Salmon R	Skamania
LAVIS (LOUIE) CR	San Poil R	Ferry
LAW CR	Kalama R	Cowlitz
LAWRENCE CR	Puyallup R	Pierce
LAWTON CR	Columbia R	Skamania
LEACH (BOWERS) CR	Chambers Cr	Pierce
LEAF CR	Cedar R	King
LEARY CR	Grays Harbor	Grays Harbor
LE CLERC CR	Pend Oreille R	Pend Oreille
LEES CR	Juan de Fuca Str	Clallam
LELAND CR	L Quilcene R	Jefferson
LELAND LAKE INLET	Leland Lake	Jefferson
LENA CR	Hamma Hamma R	Jefferson
LENNOX CR	Snoqualmie R	King
LEONARD CR	Snoqualmie R	King
LESTER CR	Chehalis R	Lewis
LEWIS R	Columbia R	Skamania
LEWIS R Ef	Lewis R	Clark
LEXI NGTON CR	Cowlitz R	Cowl itz
LIBBY CR	Methow R	Okanogan
LIBERTY BAY INLET	Liberty Bay	Kitsap
LIGHTNING CR	Bonaparte Cr	Okanogan
LIGHTNING CR	Skagit R	Whatcom
LILLIWAUP CR	Hood Canal	Mason
LIME (HODGSON) CR	Kettle R	Ferry
LIME CR	San Poil R	Ferry
LIME CR	Wf San Poil R	Ferry
LIME CR	Pend Oreille R	Pend Oreille
LIME CR	Deep Cr	Stevens
LINCOLN CR	Chehalis R	Lewis
LINCOLN CR	Deschutes R	Thurston
LINDCOULEE	Crab Cr	Grant
LINTON (METALINE) CR	Pend Oreille R	Pend Oreille
LION (WILLIAMS) CR	Swauk Cr	Kittitas
LITTLE CR	Yakima R	Kittitas
LITTLE (BEACON) CR	Woodward Cr	Skamania
LITTLE BOULDER CR	Kettle R	Ferry
LITTLEBUCK CR	White Salmon R	Skamania
LITTLE CALISPEL CR	Calispel R	Pend Oreille
LITTLE CHUMSTICK CR	Chumstick Cr	Chelan
LITTLE COLLINS CR	Collins Cr	Skamania
LITTLE DEER CR	Deer Cr	Spokane
LITTLE DRAGOON CR	Dragoon Cr	Spokane/Stevens
LITTLE ELK CR	Smith Cr	Pacific
LITTLE GRADE CR	Lake Chelan	Chelan
LITTLE HOQUIAM R	Mf Hoquiam R	Grays Harbor
LITTLEHUCKLEBERRY CR	White Salmon R	Skamania
LITTLE KLICKITAT R	Klickitat R	Klickitat
LITTLE LILLIWAUP CR	Hood Canal	Mason
LITTLE LOUP LOUP CR	Loup Loup Cr	Okanogan
LITTLE MASHELL CR	Mashell R	Pierce
LITTLE MISSION CR	Hood Canal	Mason
LITTLE MUD CR	Pine Cr	Walla Walla
LITTLE MUDDY CR	Big Muddy Cr	Pend Oreille
LITTLE MUDDY CR	Wf Klickitat R	Klickitat
LITTLE NESPELEM R	Nespelem R	Okanogan
LITTLE NISQUALLY R	Nisqually R	Thurston
LITTLE NORTH R	North R	Grays Harbor
LITTLE OHOP CR	Ohop Cr	Pierce
LITTLE PEND OREILLE	Colville R	Stevens
LITTLE QUILCENE R	Hood Canal	Jefferson
LITTLE R	Elwha R	Clallam
LITTLE SALMON LA SAC	Cle Elum R	Kittitas
LITTLE SHEEP CR	Sheep Cr	Stevens
LITTLE SOOS CR	Big Soos Cr	King
LITTLE SPANGLE CR	Latah Cr	Spokane
LITTLE SPOKANE R	Spokane R	P Oreille/Spokane
LITTLE TACOMA CR	Tacoma Cr	Pend Oreille
LITTLE TAHUYA CR	Tahuya Cr	Mason
LITTLE WALLA WALLA R	Walla Walla R	Walla Walla

STREAM	TRIBUTARY TO	COUNTY
LITTLE WASHOUGAL R	Washougal R	Clark
LITTLE WHITE SALMON R	Columbia R	Skamania
LITTLE WIND R	Wind R	Skamania
LITTLETON CR	Soleduck R	Clallam
LOCKWOOD CR	Ef Lewis R	Clark
LODGE CR	Columbia R	Stevens
LOHR CR	Hoquiam R	Grays Harbor
LONE RANCH CR	Kettle R	Ferry
LONG ALEX CR	Kettle R	Ferry
LORDS CR	Willapa R	Pacific
LOST CR	Wildcat Cr	Kitsap
LOST CR	Newaukum R	Lewis
LOST CR	Myers Cr	Okanogan
LOST CR	Wf San Poil R	Okanogan
LOST CR	Pend Oreille R	Pend Oreille
LOST CR	L Pend Oreille R	Stevens
LOST CR	Naches R	Yakima
LOST R	Methow R	Okanogan
LOWRY (MORAN) CR	Colville R	Stevens
LOUIE (LAVIS) CR	San Poil R	Ferry
LOUP LOUP CR	Okanogan R	Okanogan
LUNCH CR	Raft R	Grays Harbor
LYNCH CR	Little Skookum Cr	Mason
LYNCH CR	Ohop Cr	Pierce
LYNX CR	Hall Cr	Ferry
LYON CR	Lake Washington	King
LYRE R	Juan de Fuca Str	Clallam
LYTLE CR	Hoquiam R	Grays Harbor

M

STREAM	TRIBUTARY TO	COUNTY
MACKEY CR	Sammamish R	King
MAD R	Entiat R	Chelan
MADISON CR	Elwha R	Clallam
MADSON CR	CedarR	King
MAHAR CR	Wenatchee R	Chelan
MAIDEN HAIR CR	Wind R	Skamania
MAJORS CR	Columbia R	Klickitat
MALLORY CR	Washougal R	Clark
MALONE CR	Grays R	Wahkiakum
MANASTASH CR	Yakima R	Kittitas
MANILLA CR	San Poil R	Ferry
MANSOR CR	Skagit R	Skagit
MAPLE CR	Cowlitz R	Lewis
MAPLE CR	Wf Granite Cr	Okanogan
MAPLE CR	Nooksack R	Whatcom
MAPLEWOOD SPRINGS	Clark Cr	Pierce
MARATTA CR	Toutle R	Cowlitz
MARBLE CR	Cascade R	Skagit
MARCUS CR	Columbia R	Stevens
MARCY CR	Porter Cr	Grays Harbor
M ARGA R ET FALLS CR	Lake Crescent	Clallam
MARIAS CR	Toroda Cr	Okanogan
MARIETTA CR	Kalama R	Cowlitz
MARIETTA CR	Skagit R	Skagit
MARSHALL (LAKE CR	Latah Cr	Spokane
MARTIN CR	Columbia R	Ferry
MARTIN CR	Kettle R	Ferry
MARY ANN CR	Myers Cr	Okanogan
MASE (KIONA) CR	Cowlitz R	Lewis
MASHEL R	Nisqually R	Pierce
MASON CR	Ef Lewis R	Clark
MASON CR	Snoqualmie R	King
MASON (FIRST) CR	Nf Teanaway R	Kittitas
MATHENY CR	Queets R	Jefferson
MATTSON CR	Kettle R	Ferry
MAY CR	Lake Washington	King
MAY CR	Wallace R	Snohomish
MAYFIELD CR	Cowlitz R	Lewis
MAYNARD CR	Port Discovery Bay	Jefferson
McALCOR CR	Lake Washington	King
McALLISTER CR	Nisqually R	Thurston
McALLISTER SPRINGS	Puget Sound	Thurston
McCALLA CR	Boulder Cr	Grays Harbor
McCARTY CR	Sf Nooksack R	Whatcom
McCLOSKEY CR	Washougal R	Skamania

STREAM	TRIBUTARY TO	COUNTY
McCOY CR	Skykomish R	Snohomish
McCOY CR	Cowlitz R	Skamania
McCREA BRANCH CR	Entiat R	Chelan
McCREEDY CR	Klickitat R	Yakima
McCUMBAR SPRINGS	Bird Cr	Yakima
McDONALD CR	Juan de Fuca Str	Clallam
McDONALD CR	Colquallam Cr	Grays Harbor
McDONALD CR	Hood Canal	Jefferson
McEVOY SPRINGS BR	WallaWalla R	Walla Walla
McFARLAND CR	Methow R	Okanogan
McKENZIE (REYNOLDS)	Pend Oreille R	Pend Oreille
McLANES CR	Mud Bay	Thurston
McLEOD (WOLFRED) CF	Pend Oreille R	Pend Oreille
McMILLAN CR	Lake Kapowsin Outlet	Pierce
McMURRAY LAKE INLET	McMurray Lake	Skagit
McMURRAY LAKE OUTLET	Big Lake	Skagit
MEADOW CR	Lake Keechelus	Kittitas
MEADOW CR	Toroda Cr	Okanogan
MEADOW CR	Sf Deep Cr	Stevens
MORRISON CR	Quinault R	Grays Harbor
METHOW R	Columbia R	Okanogan
MICA CR	Spokane R	Spokane
MIDDLE CR	Nf Teanaway R	Kittitas
MIDDLE NEMA R	Willapa Bay	Pacific
MILOS CR	Lewis R	Cowlitz
MILL CR	Bogachiel R	Clallam
MILL CR	Columbia R	Clark
MILL CR	Salmon Cr	Clark
MILL CR	Columbia R	Cowlitz
MILL CR	Chehalis R	Grays Harbor
MILL CR	Duwamish R	King
MILL CR	L Klickitat R	Klickitat
MILL (HURDS) CR	Cowlitz R	Lewis
MILL (RANDLE) CR	Cowlitz R	Lewis
MILL (GOSNELL) CR	Hammersley Inlet	Mason
MILL CR	Willapa R	Pacific
MILL CR	Pend Oreille R	Pend Oreille R
MILL CR	White Salmon R	Skamania
MILL CR	Colville R	Stevens
MILL (BEAN) CR	Black R	Thurston
MILL CR	Walla Walla R	Walla Walla R
MILLER CR	Puget Sound	King
MILLER CR	Hood Canal	Mason
MILLS CANYON CR	Entiat R	Chelan
MIMA CR	Black R	Thurston
MINERS CR	Yakima R	Kittitas
MINNOW CR	Davis Lake	Lewis
MIROS CR	Curlew Lake	Ferry
MISSION CR	Wenatchee R	Chelan
MISSION CR	Hood Canal	Mason
MITCHELL CR	Lake Chelan	Chelan
MOCLIPS R	Pacific Ocean	Grays Harbor
MONEY CR	Skykomish R	Snohomish
MOON CR	Black R	Grays Harbor
MOORE CR	Hood Canal	Mason
MORAN CR	Colville R	Stevens
MOROY CR	Spanaway Cr	Pierce
MORGAN CR	Cle Elum R	Kittitas
MORRIS CR	Mill Cr	Pacific
MORSE CR	Juan de Fuca Str	Clallam
MOSER CR	Dyes Inlet	Kitsap
MOSQUITO CR	Drays Cr	Cowlitz
MOSQUITO CR	Pacific Ocean	Jefferson
MOSQUITO CR	Yakima R	Kittitas
MOSS CR	L White Salmon R	Skamania
MOUNT TOM CR	Hoh R	Jefferson
MOX CHEHALIS CR	Chehalis R	Grays Harbor
MUCK CR	Nisqually R	Pierce
MUD CR	Entiat R	Chelan
MUD CR	Dry Cr	WallaWalla
MUD CR	Walla Walla R	Walla Walla
MUDDY FORK	Cowlitz R	Lewis
MUDDY FORK	Cispus R	Skamania
MUDDY R	Lewis R	Skamania
MUIR CR	Palouse R	Whitman
MULHOLLAND CR	Coweman R	Cowlitz

STREAM	TRIBUTARY TO	COUNTY
MURDOCK CR	Juan de Fuca Str	Clallam
MURRAY CR	American Lake	Pierce
MYERS CR	Kettle R	Okanogan
MYRTLE CR	Carbon R	Pierce

N

STREAM	TRIBUTARY TO	COUNTY
NABIN CR	Dosewallips R	Jefferson
NACHES R	Yakima R	Yakima
NADLER CR	Columbia R	Skamania
NANCY CR	Columbia R	Ferry
NANEUM CR	Yakima R	Kittitas
NANUM CR	Wilson Cr	Kittitas
NARCISSE CR	L Pend Oreille R	Stevens
NASELLE R	Willapa Bay	Pacific
NASON CR	Wenatchee R	Chelan
NASTY CR	Ahtanum R	Yakima
NAVARRE COULEE CR	Columbia R	Chelan
NEFF CR	Colville R	Stevens
NEGRO CR	Peshastin Cr	Chelan
NEGRO CR	Rock Cr	Whitman
NELLITA CR	Hood Canal	Kitsap
NELSON CR	Lyre R	Clallam
NELSON CR	Columbia R	Skamania
NEMAHR	Willapa Bay	Pacific
NESIKA (INDIAN) CR	Cowlitz R	Lewis
NESPELEM R	Columbia R	Okanogan
NEWSWARTZ CR	Willapa Bay	Pacific
NEUSKAHL CR	Grays Harbor	Grays Harbor
NEWAUKUM CR	Green R	King
NEWAUKUM R	Chehalis R	Lewis
NEWBY CR	Twisp R	Okanogan
NEWHALEM CR	Skagit R	Whatcom
NEWMAN CR	Chehalis R	Grays Harbor
NEWMAN CR	Newman Lake	Spokane
NEWPORT CR	Cle Elum Lake	Kittitas
NEZ PERCE CR	Columbia R	Ferry
NICHLAM (BRUSH) CR	Cedar Cr	Clark
NICHOLSON CR	Toroda Cr	Ferry
NILE CR	Naches R	Yakima
NINE MILE (RABBIT)	San Poil R	Ferry
NINE MILE CR	Osoyoos Lake	Okanosan
NINE MILE CR	Kettle R	Stevens
NINETEEN CR	Tilton R	Lewis
NINETEEN MILE CR	San Poil R	Ferry
NISQUALLY R	Puget Sound	Pierce/Thurston
NOBLE CR	Yakima R	Kittitas
NOISY CR	Sullivan Lake	Pend Oreille
NOISY CR	Tolt R	King
NOLAN CR	Hoh R	Jefferson
NO NAME CR	Lewis R	Skamania
NOOKACHAMPS CR	Skagit R	Skaqit
NOOKSACK R	Bellingham Bay	Whatcom
NORTH ADDY CR	Colville R	Stevens
NORTH CR	Twisp R	Okanoqan
NORTH FERRIER CR	Oloqua R	Lewis
NORTH GRANITE CR	Okanogan R	Okanogan
NORTH LaFLEUR CR	Kettle R	Ferry
NORTH NOMA R	Willapa Bay	Pacific
NORTH PINE CR	Pine Cr	Spokane
NORTH R	Willapa Bay	Grays Harbor
NORTH STREAM	Millers Bay	Kitsap

O

STREAM	TRIBUTARY TO	COUNTY
OAK CR	Columbia R	Klickitat
OAK CR	Tieton R	Yakima
O BRIEN CR	San Poil R	Ferry
O BRIEN CR	Skagit R	Skagit
OHANAPECOSH R	Cowlitz R	Lewis
OHOP CR	Nisqually R	Pierce
OKANOGAN R	Columbia R	Okanogan
OLALLA CR	Puget Sound	Kitsap
OLD LAY CANYON CR	Columbia R	Klickitat
OLEQUA CR	Cowlitz R	Lewis
OLIVER CR	Kiona Cr	Lewis

STREAM	TRIBUTARY TO	COUNTY
OLNEY CR	Wallace R	Snohomish
OLSEN CR	Lake Whatcom	Whatcom
OLSON CR	L Pend Oreille R	Stevens
OMAK CR	Okanogan R	Okanogan
ONALASKA CR	Newaukum R	Lewis
ONION CR	Columbia R	Stevens
ORLO CR	Lake Quinault	Grays Harbor
OROPAHAN CR	Columbia R	Stevens
OSOYOOS CR	Okanogan R	Okanogan
OSTRANDER CR	CowlitzR	Cowlitz
OTTER(ARMSTRONG) CR	Spokane R	Spokane
OUTLET CR	Klickitat R	Klickitat
OUTLET CR	E Br Satsop R	Mason
OVINGTON CR	Lake Crescent	Clallam
OYSTER CR	Samish Bay	Skaqit
OXBOW CR	Willapa R	Pacific

P

STREAM	TRIBUTARY TO	COUNTY
PACKARD CR	White R	King
PACKWOOD CR	Cowlitz R	Lewis
PADDEN LAKE OUTLET	Bellingham Bay	Whatcom
PAGE CR	Alpowa Cr	Asotin
PAIWAKI CR	Alpowa Cr	Asotin
PALIX CR	Willapa Bay	Pacific
PALMER CR	Similkameen R	Okanogan
PALOUSE R	Snake R	Whitman
PANTHER CR	Wind R	Skamania
PARADISE R	Nisqually R	Pierce
PARIS CR	Cle Elum R	Kittitas
PARK CR	Stehekin R	Chelan
PARK CR	Cherry Cr	Kittitas
PASAYTEN R	Similkameen R	Okanogan
PASS LAKE OUTLET	Deception Pass	Skagit
PATAHA CR	Tucannon Cr	Garfield
PATIT CR	Touchet R	Columbla
PATTERSON CR	Snoqualmie R	King
PAYATO CR	Yakima R	Yakima
PEABODY CR	Port Angeles Harbor	Clallam
PEARL CR	Klickitat R	Yakima
PEARYGIN CR	Chewack Cr	Okanogan
PEAY CR	Chewelah Cr	Stevens
PECK CR	White Salmon R	Klickitat
PELTON CR	Queets R	Jefferson
PENAWAWA CR	Snake R	Whitman
PEND ORIELLE R	Columbia R	Pend Orielle
PENNINGTON CR	Brooks Cr	Cowlitz
PENNY CR	Big Quilcene R	Jefferson
PESHASTIN CR	Wenatchee R	Chelan
PEENE CR	Deadman R	Spokane
PEENY CR	Bonaparte Cr	Okanogan
PERCIVAL CR	Puget Sound	Thurston
PERRY CR	Mud Cr	Thurston
PETERS CR	Cowlitz R	Lewis
PETTIJOHN CR	Bonaparte Cr	Okanogan
PHELPS CR	ChiwawaR	Chelan
PIEDMONT CR	Lake Crescent	Clallam
PILCHUCK CR	Stillaguamish R	Snohomish
PILCHUCK R	Snohomish R	Snohomish
PINE CR	Columbia R	Klickitat
PINE CR	Wagonroad Coulee	Okanogan
PINE CR	Lewis R	Skamania
PINE CR	Rock Cr	Spokane Whitman
PINE CR	Walla Walla R	WallaWalla
PINE CR	Tieton R	Yakima
PINE CANYON CR	Columbia R	Douglas
PINGSTON CR	Columbia R	Stevens
PISCOE CR	Klickitat R	Yakima
PLUMMER CR	Puyallup R	Pierce
POLSON CR	Wf Hoquiam R	Grays Harbor
POORMAN CR	Twisp R	Okanogan
POPE CR	Entiat R	Chelan
PORTER CR	Chehalis R	Grays Harbor
POTATO CR	Entiat R	Chelan
POWELL CR	Skagit R	Skagit
PRAIRIE CR	Chehalis R	Thurston

STREAM	TRIBUTARY TO	COUNTY
PRAIRIE R	Quinault R	Grays Harbor
PRATT R	Snoqualmie R	King
PRESTON CR	Entiat R	Chelan
PRICE CR	Yakima R	Kittitas
PRINCE CR	L Chelan	Chelan
PROCTOR CR	Skykomish R	Snohomish
PROSPECT CR	L Pend Oreille R	Stevens
PURCELL (HOPKINS) CR	Cowlitz R	Lewis
PURDY CR	Skokomish R	Mason
PURDY CR	Carrs Inlet	Pierce
PUYALLUP R	Puget Sound	Pierce
PYRAMID CR	Skagit R	Whatcom
PYSHT R	Juan de Fuca Str	Clallam

Q

QUARTZ CR	Cispus R	Lewis
QUARTZ CR	Lewis R	Skamania
QUARTZCR	Skykomish R	Snohomish
QUARTZ CR	Naches R	Yakima
QUEETS R	Pacific Ocean	Jefferson
QUICK CR	Hamma Hamma R	Mason
QUILASASCUT CR	Columbia R	Stevens
QUILCENE R	Hood Canal	Jefferson
QUILCODA CR	Ebey Slough	Snohomish
QUILLAYUTE R	Pacific Ocean	Clallam
QUINAULT R	Pacific Ocean	Grays Harbor
QUINN R	Ozette R	Clallam

R

RABBIT (NINEMILE)	San Poi I R	Ferry
RACEHORSE CR	Nisqually R	Pierce
RACEHORSE CR	Nooksack R	Whatcom
RAFT R	Queets R	Grays Harbor
RAGING R	Snoqualmie	King
RAIL CR	Chamokane Cr	Stevens
RAILROAD CR	LakeChelan	Chelan
RAINBOW CR	Stehekin R	Chelan
RAINEY CR	Cowlitz R	Lewis
RAINY CR	Wenatchee R	Chelan
RAMONA CR	Coweman R	Cowlitz
RAMSAY CR	Chewack Cr	Okanogan
RANDLE (MILL) CR	Cowlitz R	Lewis
RAPID R	Beckler R	Snohomish
RATTLESNAKE CR	Columbia R	Ferry
RATTLESNAKE CR	San Poil R	Ferry
RATTLESNAKE CR	White Salmon R	Klickitat
RATTLESNAKE CR	Columbia R	Stevens
RATTLESNAKE R	Naches R	Yakima
REBEL FLAT CR	Palouse R	Whitman
RED CR	Moxlee Cr	Thurston
REESER CR	Wilson Cr	Kittitas
RENO CR	Lewis R	Cowlitz
REPUBLICAN CR	Nf Deep Cr	Stevens
RESER CR	Russell Cr	Walla Walla
RESORT CR	Lake Keechelus	Kittitas
REYNOLDS CR	Twisp R	Okanogan
RICHTER CR	Hood Canal	Mason
RICKEY CR	Columbia R	Stevens
RIDDER (HELLER) CR	Colville R	Stevens
RIFFLE (SULPHUR) CR	Cowlitz R	Lewis
RITTER CR	L White Salmon R	Skamania
RITZ(STONE) CR	Walla Walla R	Walla Walla
RIVERSIDE CR	Yakima R	Kittitas
ROARING CR	Entiat R	Chelan
ROARING CR	Lake Keechelus	Kittitas
ROCK CR	Chiwawa R	Chelan
ROCK CR	Ef Lewis R	Clark
ROCK CR	Kalama R	Cowlitz
ROCK CR	Lewis R	Cowlitz
ROCK CR	Chehalis R	Grays Harbor
ROCK CR	Cedar R	King
ROCK CR	Lake Sawyer	King
ROCK CR	Columbia R	Klickltat
ROCK(BOULDER) CR	Wf Methow R	Okanogan

STREAM	TRIBUTARY TO	COUNTY
ROCK CR	Columbia R	Skamania
ROCK CR	L White Salmon R	Skamania
ROCK CR	Latah Cr	Spokane
ROCK CR	Palouse R	Whitman
ROCK CR	Naches R	Yakima
ROCKY CR	Sf Deep Cr	Stevens
ROCKY BROOK CR	Dosewallips R	Jefferson
ROCKY FORD CR	Moses L	Grant
ROCKY RUN CR	Lake Keechelus	Kittitas
ROPER CR	Columbia R	Ferry
ROSLYN CR	Yakima R	Kittitas
RUBY CR	Peshastin Cr	Chelan
RUBY CR	Pend Oreille R	Pend Oreille
RUBY CR	Ross Lake	Whatcom
RUSH CR	Lewis R	Skamania
RUSSELL CR	Yellowhawk Cr	WallaWalla
RUSSELL CR	Nf Tieton R	Yakima
RYAN CR	Columbia R	Stevens

S

SACH E E N LAK E OUTLET	Trout Lake	Pend Orei I le
SADIE CR	E Twin R	Clallam
SAFETY HARBOR CR	Lake Chelan	Chelan
SALMON CR	Black R	Thurston
SALMON CR	Columbia R	Clark
SALMON CR	North R	Grays Harbor
SALMON CR	Pt Discovery Bay	Jefferson
SALMON CR	Cowlitz R	Lewis
SALMON CR	Hood Canal	Mason
SALMON CR	Okanogan R	Okanogan
SALMON LA SAC CR	Cle Elum R	Kittitas
SALMON R	Queets R	Jefferson
SALT CR	Juan de Fuca Str	Clallam
SAMISH R	Samish Bay	Skagit
SAMMAMISH R	Lake Washington	King
SAMS CR	Queets R	Jefferson
SAND CR	Mission Cr	Chelan
SAND CR	Cowlitz R	Lewis
SAND CR	Kettle R	Stevens
SAN POIL R	Columbia R	Ferry
SARSAPKIN CR	Sinlahekin Cr	Okanogan
SARVIS CR	Huckleberry Cr	Stevens
SATSOP R, Ef	Satsop R	Grays Harbor
SATSOP R MIDDLE BR	Ef, Satsop R	Mason
SATSOP R Wf	Satsop R	Grays Harbor
SATSOP R	Chehalis R	Grays Harbor
SATUS CR	Yakima R	Yakima
SAUK R	Skagit R	Snohomish
SCANDIA CR	Liberty Bay	Kitsap
SCATTER (GOLD) Ch	San Poil R	Ferry
SCATTER CR	Twisp R	Okanogan
SCATTER CR	Chehalis R	Thurston
SCHMIDT CR	Smith Cr	Stevens
SCHNEIDERS CR	Oysfer Bay	Thurston
SCHUMACHER CR	Mason Lake	Mason
SCOTTY CR	Peshastin Cr	Chelan
SEASTROM CR	Pacific Ocean	Grays Harbor
SECOND CR	Chumstick Cr	Chelan
SELAH CR	Yakima R	Yakima
SEVENTEEN MILE CR	San Poil R	Ferry
SHADOW CR	Tanoum Cr	Kittitas
SHANGHAI CR	Fourth Plain Cr	Clark
SHASER CR	Peshastin Cr	Chelan
SHEEP CR	Columbia R	Stevens
SHEEP CANYON CR	Klickitat R	Klickitat
SHELL CR	Puget Sound	Snohomish
SHERMAN CR	Columbia R	Ferry
SHERMAN CR	Tilton R	Lewis
SHERWOOD (DEADMAN)	Kettle R	Ferry
SHERWOOD CR	Cases Inlet	Mason
SHERWOOD (E BRIDGE)	Colville R	Stevens
SHUKSAN CR	Baker Cr	Whatcom
SIEBERT CR	Juan de Fuca Str	Clallam
SILVER CANYON CR	Klickitat R	Klickitat
SILVER CR	Entiat R	Chelan

STREAM	TRIBUTARY TO	COUNTY	STREAM	TRIBUTARY TO	COUNTY
SILVER CR	San Poil R	Ferry	SQUALICUM CR	Bellingham Bay	Whatcom
SILVER CR	Yakima R	Kittitas	SQUAW CR	Methow R	Okanogan
SILVER CR	Cowlitz R	Lewls	SQUAW (BERRY) CR	Rock Cr	Skamania
SILVER CR	Friday Cr	Skagit	SQUAW CR	Columbia R	Stevens
SILVER CR	Nf Deep Cr	Stevens	SQUAW CR	L Pend Oreille R	Stevens
SILVER CR	Bellingham Bay	Whatcom	SQUAW CR	Johnson Cr	Whatcom
SILVER CR	Humphries Cr	Whatcom	SQUILLCHUCK CR	Columbia R	Chelan
SILVER SPRINGS	Hammersley Inlet	Mason	SQUIRE CR	Nf Stillaguamish R	Snohomish
SIMCOE CR	Toppenish Cr	Yakima	STAFFORD CR	Grays Harbor	Grays Harbor
SIMILKAMEEN R	Okanogan R	Okanogan	STAFFORD CR	Nf Teanaway R	Kittitas
SINLAHEKIN CR	Similkameen R	Okanogan	STAHL CR	Mill Cr	Lewis
SIOUXON CR	Lewis R	Clark	ST CLOUD CR	Columbia R	Skamania
SIWASH CR	Okanogan R	Okanogan	STEELE CR	Port Orchard Bay	Kitsap
SIX PRONG CR	Alder Cr	Klickitat	STEHEKIN R	Lake Chelan	Chelan
SKAGIT R	Puget Sound	Whatcom	STEMILT CR	Columbia R	Chelan
SKAMOKAWA CR	Columbia R	Wahkiakum	STEPTOE C R	Snake R	Whitman
SKATE CR	Cowlitz R	Lewis	STEVENS CR	Humptulips R	Grays Harbor
SKINNEY CR	Chiwaukum Cr	Chelan	STEVENS CR	Latah Cr	Spokane
SKOKOMISH R	Hood Canal	Mason	STEVENS LAKE INLET	Stevens Lake	Snohomish
SKOKOMISH R, Nf	Skokomish R	Mason	STEVENS LAKE OUTLET	Pilchuck R	Snohomish
SKOKOMISH R, Sf	Skokomish R	Mason	STILL CR	Wf Satsop R	Grays Harbor
SKOOKUM CR	Totten Inlet	Mason	STILLAGUAMISH R	Puget Sound	Snohomish
SKOOKUM CR	Pend Oreille R	Pend Oreille	STILLAGUAMISH R, Nf	Stillaguamish R	Snohomish
SKOOKUM CR, Nf	Skookum Cr	Pend Orellle	STILLAGUAMISH R. Sf	Stillaguamish R	Snohomish
SKOOKU M CR, Sf	Skookum Cr	Pend Oreille	STILLWATER CR	Olequa Cr	Lewis
SKOOKUM CR	Sf Nooksack R	Whatcom	STILLWATER CR	Snoqualmie R	King
SKOOKUMCHUCK R	Chehalis R	Lewis/Thurston	STONE (RITZ) CR	Walla Walla R	Walla Walla
SKUNK CR	Cook Cr	Grays Harbor	STORMY CR	Entiat R	Chelan
SKUNK CR	Twisp R	Okanogan	ST PETERS CR	Curlew Cr	Ferry
SKUNK CABBAGE CR	San Poil R	Ferry	STRANGER CR	ColumblaR	Ferry
SKYKOMISH R	Snohomish R	Snohomish	STRANGER CR	ColvilleR	Stevens
SKYKOMISH R Sf	Snohomish R	King	STRINGER CR	Willapa R	Pacific
SKYKOMISH R Nf	Skykomish R	Snohomish	STROM BERG CANYON CR	Chumstick Cr	Chelan
SLASLOPOLIS CR	Hood Canal	Mason	STOSSEL CR	Snoqualmie R	King
SLATE CR	Twisp R	Okanogan	STUART CR	Drays Cr	Cowlitz
SLATE CR	Pend Oreille R	Pend Oreille	STUCK R (White)	Puyallup R	Pierce
SLIDE CR	Colville R	Stevens	STUMP CR	Colville R	Stevens
SMALL CR	San Poil R	Ferry	SUIATTLE R	Sauk R	Snohomish
SMALLE CR	Pend Oreille R	Pend Oreille	SULFUR CR	Suiattle R	Snohomish
SMALLE CR, Ef	Smalle Cr	PendOreille	SULLIVAN CR	Port Orchard Bay	Kitsap
SMITH CR	Lake Crescent	Clallam	SULLIVAN CR	Pend Oreille R	PendOreille
SMITH CR	Cowlitz R	Lewis	SULPHUR CR	White R	King
SMITH CR	Willapa Harbor	Pacific	SULPHUR (RIFFLE) CR	Cowlitz R	Lewis
SMITH CR	Dunn Cr	Stevens	SULTAN R	Skykomish R	Snohomish
SMITH CR	Nooksack R	Whatcom	SUMAS R	Fraser R	Whatcom
SNIDER CR	Soleduck R	Clallam	SUMMER CR	Kalama R	Cowlitz
SNOQUALMIE R	Snohomish R	King	SUMMIT CR	Ohanapecosh R	Lewis
SNOQUALMIE R, Nf	Snoqualmie R	King	SUMMIT CR	LoupLoup Cr	Okanogan
SNOQUALMIE R, Mf	Snoqualmie R	King	SUMMIT CR	Sol Duc R	Clallam
SNOQUALMIE R, Sf	Snoqualmie R	King	SUNDAY CR	Green R	King
SNOW CR	Discovery Bay	Jefferson	SUNDS CR	Hood Canal	Mason
SNOW CR	Crocker Lake	Jefferson	SUNITSCH CANYON CR	Chumstick Cr	Chelan
SNYDER CR	Cowlitz R	Lewis	SURVEYORS CR	Klickitat R	Yakima
SODA SPRINGS CR	Klickitat R	Yakima	SUSIE CR	Lyre R	Clallam
SOLEDUCK R	Quillayute R	Clallam	SWAKANE CR	ColumbiaR	Chelan
SOLEDUCK R, Nf	Soleduck R	Clallam	SWALE CR	Klickitat R	Klickitat
SOOES R	Pacific Ocean	Clallam	SWAMP CR	Coweman R	Cowlitz
SOOS CR	Green R	King	SWAMP CR	Yakima R	Kittltas
SOUTH PRAIRIE CR	Carbon R	Pierce	SWAMP CR	Cowlitz R	Lewis
SOUTH SLOUGH	Stillaguamish R	Snohomish	SWAMP CR	Sammamish R	Snohomish
SPANAWAY CR	Clover Cr	Pierce	SWAMP CR	Chamokane Cr	Stevens
SPANGLE CR	Latah Cr	Spokane	SWAMP CR	Klickitat R	Yakima
SPEARS CR	Siler Cr	Lewis	SWAMP CR	Naches R	Yakima
SPEILEI CR	Lewis R	Cowlitz	SWAMPY CR	Lewis R	Skamania
SPENCER CR	Dabop Bay	Jefferson	SWAUK CR	Yakima R	Kittitas
SPOKANE R	Columbia R	Spokane	SWEAT CR	Wf Granite Cr	Okanogan
SPRING CR	Ef Lewis R	Clark	SWEAT CR	Summit Cr	Okanogan
SPRING CR	Cle Elum Lake	Kittitas	SWEET CR	Pend Oreille R	Pend Oreille
SPRING CR	L Klickitat R	Klickitat	SWIFT CR	Lewis R	Skamania
SPRING (ARMSTRONG)	L Spokane R	Spokane	SWIFT CR	McLanes Cr	Thurston
SPRING CR	Dry Cr	Walla Walla	SYLVIA CR	Wynoochee R	Grays Harbor
SPRING CR	Simcoe Cr	Yakima	SYLVIA CR	Sol Duc R	Clallam
SPRING CR	Kalama R	Cowlitz	SYLVIA CR	Kalama R	Cowlitz
SPRINGBROOK CR	Green R	King			
SPRINGHOOL CR	Trout Cr	Pend Oreille			
SPURGEON CR	Deschutes R	Thurston			

STREAM	TRIBUTARY TO	COUNTY
T		
TACOMA CR	Queets R	Jefferson
TACOMA CR	Pend Oreille R	Pend Oreille
TAHUYA R	Hood Canal	Mason
TALLANT CR	Okanogan R	Okanogan
TANEUM CR	Yakima R	Kittitas
TANWAX CR	Nisqually R	Pierce
TARBOO CR	Hood Canal	Jefferson
TATE CR	Nf Snoqualmie R	King
TAYLOR CR	Carbon R	Pierce
TEANAWAY R	Yakima R	Kittitas
TELEPHONE CR	Yakima R	Kittitas
TENAS CR	Suiattle R	Skagit
TENAS MARY CR	Kettle R	Fenry
TEN MILE CR	Snake R	Asotin
TEN MILE CR	Nooskack R	Whatcom
TEN OCLOCK CR	Quinault R	Grays Harbor
TEXAS CR	Methow R	Okanogan
THIRTEEN MILE CR	San Poil R	Ferry
THIRTY MILE CR	San Poil R	Ferry
THOMASON CR	Colville R	Stevens
THORN CR	Pine Cr	Whitman
THORNTON CR	LakeWashington	King
THREE FORKS CR	Mill Cr	Stevens
THREE MILE CR	Pend Oreille R	Pend Oreille
THUNDER CR	Skagit R	Whatcom
TIETON R	Naches R	Yakima
TILTON R	Cowlitz R	Lewis
TOAD CR	Squalicum Cr	Whatcom
TOATS COULEE CR	Sinlahekin Cr	Okanogan
TOKUL CR	Snoqualmie R	King
TOLT R	Snoqualmie R	King
TONASKET CR	Curlew Cr	Ferry
TONASKET CR	Okanogan R	Okanogan
TONATA CR	Kettle R	Ferry
TOPPENISH CR	Yakima R	Yakima
TORBEL CR	Colville R	Stevens
TORODA CR	Kettle R	Okanogan
TOUCHET R	Walla Walla R	WallaWalla/Col
TOULOU CR	Kettle R	Stevens
TOUTLE R	Cowlitz R	Cowlitz/Skamania
TRAPPER CR	L Muddy Cr	Yakima
TRIMBLE CR	Pend Oreille R	Pend Oreille
TRONSON CR	Peshastin Cr	Chelan
TROUT CR	Curlew Lake	Ferry
TROUT CR	White Salmon R	Klickitat
TROUT (TURNER) CR	Toroda Cr	Okanogan
TROUT CR	Horseshoe Lake	Pend Oreille
TROUT CR	Wind R	Skamania
TROUT CR	Cottonwood Cr	Stevens
TROUT CR	Nf Deep Cr	Stevens
TSHLETSHY CR	Queets R	Jefferson
TUCANNON R	Snake R	Columbia
TUCK CR	Snoqualmie R	King
TUCKER CR	Yakima R	Kittitas
TUM TUM CR	Cedar Cr	Clark
TUMWATER CR	Port Angeles Harbor	Clallam
TUNK CR	Okanogan R	Okanogan
TURNER CR	Hood Canal	Jefferson
TURNER (TROUT) CR	Toroda Cr	Okanogan
TUTTLE CR	North R	Grays Harbor
TWELVE MILE CR	Colville R	Stevens
TWENTY-ONE MILE CR	San Poil R	Ferry
TWENTY-THREE MILE CR	San Poil R	Ferry
TWENTY-FIVE MILE CR	Lake Chelan	Chelan
TWENTY-FIVE MILE CR	San Poil R	Ferry
TWENTY-FIVE MILE CR	Ohop Cr	Pierce
TWIN CR	Chiwawa R	Chelan
TWISP R	Methow R	Okanogan
TYE R	Sf Skykomish R	King
U		
UDEN CR	Cowlitz R	Lewis
UMBRELLA CR	Ozette R	Clallam

STREAM	TRIBUTARY TO	COUNTY
UMTANUM CR	Yakima R	Kittitas
UNION CR	American R	Yakima
UNION CR	Palouse R	Whitman
UNION R	Hood Canal	Kitsap/Mason
UNION FLAT CR	Palouse R	Whitman
UPPER CASCAD E CR	White R	Pierce
V		
VALLEY CR	L Washington	King
VALLEY CR	Port Angeles Harbor	Clallam
VANCE CR	Sf Skokomish R	Mason
VAN HORN CR	White R	Pierce
VAN ORMAN CR	Chehalis R	Lewis
VASA PARK CR	L Washington	King
VAUGHN CR	Toroda Cr	Okanogan
VESTA CR	North R	Grays Harbor
VOGEL CR	Washougal R	Skamania
VOIGHTS CR	Carbon R	Pierce
W		
WAATCH R	Pacific Ocean	Clallam
WADDLES CR	Black R	Thurston
WADO CR	Colville R	Stevens
WAITS CR	Colville R	Stevens
WAKOTICKEH R	Hood Canal	Mason
WALKER CR	Meadow Cr	Okanogan
WALLACE R	Skykomish R	Snohomish
WALLA WALLA R	Coumbla R	Walla Walla
WAPATO CR	Commencement Bay	Pierce
WAR CR	Twisp R	Okanogan
WARBLE (WEBB) CR	Ef Lewis R	Clark
WARM SPRINGS	Caribou Cr	Kittitas
WARM SPRINGS CANYON	Wenatchee R	Chelan
WASHOUGAL R	Columbia R	Clark/Skamania
WASHOUGAL R, Nf	Washougal R	Skamanla
WASSUN CR	Rock Cr	Whitman
WAUGH (CORUS) CR	Columbia R	Stevens
WAWAWAI CR	Snake R	Whitman
WEAVER CR	Salmon Cr	Clark
WEAVER CR	Purdy Cr	Mason
WEBB (WARBLE) CR	Ef Lewis R	Clark
WISER LAKE OUTLET	Nooksack R	Whatcom
WELCH CR	Columbia R	Lincoln
WENAS CR	Yakima R	Yaklma
WENATCHEE R	ColumbiaR	Chelan
WEST DOOR CR	Kettle R	Ferry
WEST TWIN CR	White R	KIng
WHIPPLE CR	Lake R	Clark
WHISKEY CR	Juan de Fuca Str	Clallam
WHISKEY CR	Touchet R	Columbla
WHISTLING CR	Twisp R	Okanogan
WHITAKER CR	Klickitat R	Klickltat
WHITE CR	Ennis Cr	Clallam
WHITE R	LakeWenatchee	Chelan
WHITE R	Stuck&PuyallupR	King/Pierce
WHITECHUCK R	Sauk R	Snohomish
WHITEHALL CR	Samish Bay	Skagiit
WHITE HORSE CR	Harvey Cr	Stevens
WHITE SALMON R	Columbia R	Klickltat/Skamanla
WHITESTONE R	Rat Lake	Okanogan
WHITESTONE LK OUTLET	Okanogan R	Okanogan
WILDCAT CR	Cloquallum Cr	Grays Harbor
WILDCAT CR	Tieton R	Yakima
WILDCAT CR	Chico Cr	Kltsap
WILD HORSE CR	Kalama R	Cowlltz
WILD ROSE CR	Dragoon Cr	Spokane
WILDESON (GALE) CR	S Prairie Cr	Pierce
WILLABY CR	Lake Quinault	Grays Harbor
WILLAPA R	Willapa Bay	Pacific
WILLAPA R, Sf	Willapa R	Pacllic
WILLIAMS CR	Rock Cr	Grays Harbor
WILLIAMS (LION) CR	Swauk Cr	Kittltas
WILLIAMS CR	Nf Nemah R	Paclfic
WILLOW CR	Chiwawa R	Chelan

STREAM	TRIBUTARY TO	COUNTY
WILLOW CR	Newaukum R	Lewis
WILLOW CR	Mill Cr	Stevens
WILLOW CR	Palouse R	Whitman
WILSON CR	Port Orchard Bay	Kltsap
WILSON CR	Yakima R	Kittitas
WILSON CR	Fairchild Cr	Pacific
WILSON CR	L White Salmon R	Skamania
WINCHESTER CR	Kalispel Lake	Pend Orellle
WIND R	Columbia R	Skamania
WINSTON CR	Cowlitz R	Lewis
WISON CR	Soleduck R	Clallam
WISHKAH R	Grays Harbor	Grays Harbor
WOLF CR	Wf Methow R	Okanogan
WOLFE CR	Lake Keechelus	Kittitas
WOL FR ED (McLEOD) CR	Pend Oreille R	Pend Oreill e
WOOD CR	Sultan R	Snohomish
WOODARD CR	Henderson Inlet	Thurston
WOODCOCK CR	Dungeness R	Clallam
WOODLAND CR	Chehalis R	Grays Harbor
WOODLAND (HIMES) CR	South Bay	Thurston
WOODS CR	Skykomish R	Snohomlsh
WOODWARD CR	Columbia R	Skamania
WOOLFORD CR	Kalama R	Cowlitz
WORKMAN CR	Chehalis R	Grays Harbor
WRIGHT CR	Sinclair Inlet	Kitsap
WRIGHT CR	Union R	Kitsap
WRIGHTS CR	Colville R	Stevens
WYNOOCHEE R	Chehalis R	Grays Harbor

X

X CR	Van Winkle Cr	Grays Harbor

Y

YACOLT CR	Lewis R	Clark
YAKIMA R	Columbia R	Benton/Yak/ Kitt
YELLOW JACKET	Cispus R	Lewis
YELLOWHAWK CP	Walla Walla P	Walla Walla
YELM CR	Nisqually R	Thurston
YODER CR	Renshaw Cr	Pend Oreille

Z

ZIEGLER CR	Lake Quinault	Grays Harbor

Index